# Contents

# CIMA

## Paper P2

## Performance Management

## Study Text

Published by: Kaplan Publishing UK

Unit 2 The Business Centre, Molly Millars Lane, Wokingham, Berkshire RG41 2QZ

**Acknowledgements**

The CIMA Publishing trade mark is reproduced with kind permission of CIMA.

**Notice**

British Library Cataloguing in Publication Data
A catalogue record for this book is available from the British Library

ISBN 978-0-85732-976-9

Printed and bound in Great Britain

# Paper Introduction

## Acknowledgements

Every effort has been made to contact the holders of copyright material, but if any here have been inadvertently overlooked the publishers will be pleased to make the necessary arrangements at the first opportunity.

# How to Use the Materials

These Official CIMA learning materials brought to you by CIMA Publishing and Kaplan Publishing have been carefully designed to make your learning experience as easy as possible and to give you the best chances of success in your Performance Management exam.

The product range contains a number of features to help you in the study process. They include:

- a detailed explanation of all syllabus areas;

- extensive 'practical' materials, including readings from relevant journals;

- generous question practice, together with full solutions;

This Study Text has been designed with the needs of home-study and distance-learning candidates in mind. Such students require very full coverage of the syllabus topics, and also the facility to undertake extensive question practice. However, the Study Text is also ideal for fully taught courses.

The main body of the text is divided into a number of chapters, each of which is organised on the following pattern:

- *Detailed learning outcomes.* You should assimilate these before beginning detailed work on the chapter, so that you can appreciate where your studies are leading.

- *Step-by-step topic coverage.* This is the heart of each chapter, containing detailed explanatory text supported where appropriate by worked examples and exercises. You should work carefully through this section, ensuring that you understand the material being explained and can tackle the examples and exercises successfully. Remember that in many cases knowledge is cumulative; if you fail to digest earlier material thoroughly, you may struggle to understand later chapters.

- *Readings and activities.* Most chapters are illustrated by more practical elements, such as relevant journal articles or other readings, together with comments and questions designed to stimulate discussion.

- *Question practice.* The test of how well you have learned the material is your ability to tackle standard questions. Make a serious attempt at producing your own answers, but at this stage don't be too concerned about attempting the questions in exam conditions. In particular, it is more important to absorb the material thoroughly by completing a full solution than to observe the time limits that would apply in the actual exam.

- *Solutions.* Avoid the temptation merely to 'audit' the solutions provided. It is an illusion to think that this provides the same benefits as you would gain from a serious attempt of your own. However, if you are struggling to get started on a question you should read the introductory guidance provided at the beginning of the solution, and then make your own attempt before referring back to the full solution.

Having worked through the chapters you are ready to begin your final preparations for the examination. The final section of this Study Text provides you with the guidance you need. It includes the following features:

- A brief guide to revision technique.

- A note on the format of the exam. You should know what to expect when you tackle the real exam and in particular the number of questions to attempt.

- Guidance on how to tackle the exam itself.

- A table mapping revision questions to the syllabus learning outcomes allowing you to quickly identify questions by subject area.

You should plan to attempt the mock tests just before the date of the real exam. By this stage your revision should be complete and you should be able to attempt the mock exam within the time constraints of the real exam.

If you work conscientiously through this official CIMA Study Text according to the guidelines above you will be giving yourself an excellent chance of exam success. Good luck with your studies!

## Icon Explanations

**Definition** – these sections explain important areas of Knowledge which must be understood and reproduced in an exam environment.

**Key Point** – identifies topics which are key to success and are often examined.

**Supplementary reading** – indentifies a more detailed explanation of key terms, these sections will help to provide a deeper understanding of core areas. Reference to this text is vital when self studying.

**Test Your Understanding** – following key points and definitions are exercises which give the opportunity to assess the understanding of these core areas.

**Illustration** – to help develop an understanding of particular topics. The illustrative examples are useful in preparing for the Test Your Understanding exercises.

**Exclamation Mark** – this symbol signifies a topic which can be more difficult to understand, when reviewing these areas care should be taken.

## Study technique

Passing exams is partly a matter of intellectual ability, but however accomplished you are in that respect you can improve your chances significantly by the use of appropriate study and revision techniques. In this section we briefly outline some tips for effective study during the earlier stages of your approach to the exam. Later in the text we mention some techniques that you will find useful at the revision stage.

## Planning

To begin with, formal planning is essential to get the best return from the time you spend studying. Estimate how much time in total you are going to need for each subject you are studying for the Managerial level. Remember that you need to allow time for revision as well as for initial study of the material. You may find it helpful to read 'Pass First Time!' second edition by David R. Harris, ISBN 9781856177986. This book will provide you with proven study techniques. Chapter by chapter it covers the building blocks of successful learning and examination techniques. This is the ultimate guide to passing your CIMA exams, written by a past CIMA examiner and shows you how to earn all the marks you deserve, and explains how to avoid the most common pitfalls. You may also find "The E Word: Kaplan's Guide to Passing Exams" by Stuart Pedley-Smith ISBN: 9780857322050 helpful. Stuart Pedley-Smith is a senior lecturer at Kaplan Financial and a qualified accountant specialising in financial management. His natural curiosity and wider interests have led him to look beyond the technical content of financial management to the processes and journey that we call education. He has become fascinated by the whole process of learning and the exam skills and techniques that contribute towards success in the classroom. This book is for anyone who has to sit an exam and wants to give themselves a better chance of passing. It is easy to read, written in a common sense style and full of anecdotes, facts, and practical tips. It also contains synopses of interviews with people involved in the learning and examining process.

With your study material before you, decide which chapters you are going to study in each week, and which weeks you will devote to revision and final question practice.

Prepare a written schedule summarising the above and stick to it!

It is essential to know your syllabus. As your studies progress, you will become more familiar with how long it takes to cover topics in sufficient depth. Your timetable may need to be adapted to allocate enough time for the whole syllabus.

Students are advised to refer to the notice of examinable legislation published regularly in CIMA's magazine (Financial Management), the students e-newsletter (Velocity) and on the CIMA website, to ensure they are up-to-date.

## Tips for effective studying

(1) Aim to find a quiet and undisturbed location for your study, and plan as far as possible to use the same period of time each day. Getting into a routine helps to avoid wasting time. Make sure that you have all the materials you need before you begin so as to minimise interruptions.

(2) Store all your materials in one place, so that you do not waste time searching for items around the house. If you have to pack everything away after each study period, keep them in a box, or even a suitcase, which will not be disturbed until the next time.

(3) Limit distractions. To make the most effective use of your study periods you should be able to apply total concentration, so turn off the TV, set your phones to message mode, and put up your 'do not disturb' sign.

(4) Your timetable will tell you which topic to study. However, before diving in and becoming engrossed in the finer points, make sure you have an overall picture of all the areas that need to be covered by the end of that session. After an hour, allow yourself a short break and move away from your books. With experience, you will learn to assess the pace you need to work at. You should also allow enough time to read relevant articles from newspapers and journals, which will supplement your knowledge and demonstrate a wider perspective.

(5) Work carefully through a chapter, making notes as you go. When you have covered a suitable amount of material, vary the pattern by attempting a practice question. Preparing an answer plan is a good habit to get into, while you are both studying and revising, and also in the examination room. It helps to impose a structure on your solutions, and avoids rambling. When you have finished your attempt, make notes of any mistakes you made, or any areas that you failed to cover or covered more briefly.

(6) Make notes as you study, and discover the techniques that work best for you. Your notes may be in the form of lists, bullet points, diagrams, summaries, 'mind maps' or the written word, but remember that you will need to refer back to them at a later date, so they must be intelligible. If you are on a taught course, make sure you highlight any issues you would like to follow up with your lecturer.

(7) Organise your notes. Make sure that all your notes, calculations etc., can be effectively filed and easily retrieved later.

## Structure of subjects and learning outcomes

Each subject within the syllabus is divided into a number of broad syllabus topics. The topics contain one or more lead learning outcomes, related component learning outcomes and indicative knowledge content.

A learning outcome has two main purposes:

(a) To define the skill or ability that a well prepared candidate should be able to exhibit in the examination

(b) To demonstrate the approach likely to be taken in examination questions

The learning outcomes are part of a hierarchy of learning objectives. The verbs used at the beginning of each learning outcome relate to a specific learning objective e.g.

**Calculate** the break-even point, profit target, margin of safety and profit/volume ratio for a single product or service

The verb **'calculate'** indicates a level three learning objective. The following table lists the learning objectives and the verbs that appear in the syllabus learning outcomes and examination questions.

## Syllabus overview and structure

While Paper P2 continues the analytic theme of Paper P1 Performance Operations (for example, in terms of identifying relevant costs), its main focus is on the application of information in the management processes of decision-making and control, so as to optimise performance. The syllabus comprises the following topics and study weightings :

| A | Pricing and Product Decisions | 30% |
|---|---|---|
| B | Cost Planning and Analysis for Competitive Advantage | 30% |
| C | Budgeting and Management Control | 20% |
| D | Control and Performance Measurement of Responsibility Centres | 20% |

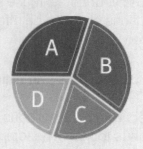

The first two sections deal respectively with the key contributors to operational performance - revenue (decisions of what to produce, and at what price) and costs (how to manage them to maximise profitability). The role of control in monitoring and improving performance then comes to the fore in the final two sections, dealing with principles and practices in the use of responsibility centres and budgeting.

# PAPER P2
# PERFORMANCE MANAGEMENT

### Syllabus overview

While Paper P2 continues the analytic theme of Paper P1 Performance Operations (for example in terms of identifying relevant costs), its main focus is on the application of information in the management processes of decision-making and control, so as to optimise performance. The first two sections deal respectively with the key contributors to operational performance – revenue (decisions of what to produce, at what price) and costs (how to manage them to maximise profitability). The role of control in monitoring and improving performance then comes to the fore in the final two sections, dealing with principles and practices in the use of responsibility centres and budgeting.

### Syllabus structure

The syllabus comprises the following topics and study weightings:

| A | Pricing and Product Decisions | 30% |
|---|---|---|
| B | Cost Planning and Analysis for Competitive Advantage | 30% |
| C | Budgeting and Management Control | 20% |
| D | Control and Performance Measurement of Responsibility Centres | 20% |

### Assessment strategy

There will be a written examination paper of three hours, plus 20 minutes of pre-examination question paper reading time. The examination paper will have the following sections:

### Section A – 50 marks
Five compulsory medium answer questions, each worth ten marks. Short scenarios may be given, to which some or all questions relate.

### Section B – 50 marks
One or two compulsory questions. Short scenarios may be given, to which questions relate.

P2 – A. PRICING AND PRODUCT DECISIONS (30%)

**Learning outcomes**
**On completion of their studies students should be able to:**

| Lead | Component | Indicative syllabus content |
|---|---|---|
| 1. discuss concepts of cost and revenue relevant to pricing and product decisions. | (a) discuss the principles of decision-making including the identification of relevant cash flows and their use alongside non-quantifiable factors in making rounded judgements; [4]<br><br>(b) discuss the possible conflicts between cost accounting for profit reporting and stock valuation and information required for decision-making; [4]<br><br>(c) discuss the particular issues that arise in pricing decisions and the conflict between 'marginal cost' principles and the need for full recovery of all costs incurred. [7] | • Relevant cash flows and their use in short-term decisions, typically concerning acceptance/rejection of contracts, pricing and cost/benefit comparisons. [4]<br>• The importance of strategic, intangible and non-financial judgements in decision-making. [4]<br>• Relevant costs and revenues in decision-making and their relation to accounting concepts. [4]<br>• Marginal and full cost recovery as bases for pricing decisions in the short and long-term. [7] |
| 2. analyse short-term pricing and product decisions. | (a) explain the usefulness of dividing costs into variable and fixed components in the context of short-term decision making; [2]<br><br>(b) interpret variable/fixed cost analysis in multiple product contexts to break-even analysis and product mix decision making, including circumstances where there are multiple constraints and linear programming methods are needed to identify 'optimal' solutions; [3], [5]<br><br>(c) discuss the meaning of 'optimal' solutions and how linear programming methods can be employed for profit maximising, revenue maximising and satisfying objectives; [5]<br><br>(d) analyse the impact of uncertainty and risk on decision models based on CVP analysis. [3] | • Simple product mix analysis in situations where there are limitations on product/service demand and one other production constraint. [4]<br>• Multi-product break-even analysis, including break-even and profit/volume charts, contribution/sales ratio, margin of safety etc. [3]<br>• Linear programming for more complex situations involving multiple constraints. Solution by graphical methods of two variable problems, together with understanding of the mechanics of simplex solution, shadow prices etc. (*Note:* questions requiring the full application of the simplex algorithm will not be set although candidates should be able to formulate an initial tableau, interpret a final simplex tableau and apply the information it contained in a final tableau). [5]<br>• Sensitivity analysis of CVP-based decision models. [3] |

| Lead | Component | Indicative syllabus content |
|---|---|---|
| 3. discuss pricing strategies and their consequences. [7] | (a) apply an approach to pricing based on profit maximisation in imperfect markets; [7] <br><br> (b) discuss the financial consequences of alternative pricing strategies; [7] <br><br> (c) explain why joint costs must be allocated to final products for financial reporting purposes, but why this is unhelpful when decisions concerning process and product viability have to be taken. [7] | • Pricing decisions for profit maximising in imperfect markets. (*Note:* tabular methods of solution are acceptable). [7] <br> • Pricing strategies and the financial consequences of market skimming, premium pricing, penetration pricing, loss leaders, product bundling/optional extras and product differentiation to appeal to different market segments. [7] <br> • The allocation of joint costs and decisions concerning process and product viability based on relevant costs and revenues. [7] |

## P2 – B. COST PLANNING AND ANALYSIS FOR COMPETITIVE ADVANTAGE (30%)

| Lead | Component | Indicative syllabus content |
|---|---|---|
| 1. evaluate techniques for analysing and managing costs for competitive advantage. [8] | (a) compare and contrast value analysis and functional cost analysis; [8] <br><br> (b) evaluate the impacts of just-in-time production, the theory of constraints and total quality management on efficiency, inventory and cost; [8] <br><br> (c) explain the concepts of continuous improvement and Kaizen costing that are central to total quality management; [8] <br><br> (d) prepare cost of quality reports; [8] <br><br> (e) apply learning curves to estimate time and cost for new products and services; [6] <br><br> (f) apply the techniques of activity-based management in identifying cost drivers/activities; [10] <br><br> (g) explain how process re-engineering can be used to eliminate non-value adding activities and reduce activity costs; [9] <br><br> (h) explain how target costs can be derived from target prices and the relationship between target costs and standard costs; [9] | • Value analysis and quality function deployment. [8] <br> • The benefits of just-in-time production, total quality management and theory of constraints and the implications of these methods for decision-making in the 'new manufacturing environment'. [8] <br> • Kaizen costing, continuous improvement and cost of quality reporting. [8] <br> • Learning curves and their use in predicting product/service costs, including derivation of the learning rate and the learning index. [6] <br> • Activity-based management in the analysis of overhead and its use in improving the efficiency of repetitive overhead activities. [9] <br> • Target costing. [9] <br> • Life cycle costing and implications for marketing strategies. [9] <br> • The value chain and supply chain management, including the trend to outsource manufacturing operations to transition and developing economies. [9] <br> • Gain sharing arrangements in situations where, because of the size of the project, a limited number of contractors or security issues (e.g. in defence work), normal competitive pressures do not apply. [9] |

**Learning outcomes**
**On completion of their studies students should be able to:**

| Lead | Component | Indicative syllabus content |
|---|---|---|
| | (i) discuss the concept of life cycle costing and how life cycle costs interact with marketing strategies at each stage of the life cycle; [9]<br><br>(j) discuss the concept of the value chain and the management of contribution/profit generated throughout the chain; [9]<br><br>(k) discuss gain sharing arrangements whereby contractors and customers benefit if contract targets for cost, delivery etc. are beaten; [9]<br><br>(l) analyse direct customer profitability and extend this analysis to distribution channel profitability through the application of activity-based costing ideas; [9]<br><br>(m) apply Pareto analysis as a convenient technique for identifying key elements of data and in presenting the results of other analyses, such as activity-based profitability calculations. [9] | • The use of direct and activity-based cost methods in tracing costs to 'cost objects', such as customers or distribution channels, and the comparison of such costs with appropriate revenues to establish 'tiered' contribution levels, as in the activity-based cost hierarchy. [9]<br><br>• Pareto analysis. [9] |

**P2 – C. BUDGETING AND MANAGEMENT CONTROL (20%)**

**Learning outcomes**
**On completion of their studies students should be able to:**

| Lead | Component | Indicative syllabus content |
|---|---|---|
| 1. explain the principles that underlie the use of budgets in control. [12] | (a) explain the concepts of feedback and feed-forward control and their application in the use of budgets for planning and control; [12]<br><br>(b) explain the concept of responsibility accounting and its importance in the construction of functional budgets that support the overall master budget; [12]<br><br>(c) identify controllable and uncontrollable costs in the context of responsibility accounting and why uncontrollable costs may or may not be allocated to responsibility centres. [12] | • Control system concepts. [12]<br>• The use of budgets in planning: 'rolling budgets' for adaptive planning. [12]<br>• Responsibility accounting and the use of budgets for control: controllable costs and; treatment of uncontrollable costs; the conceptual link between standard costing and budget flexing. [12] |
| 2. evaluate performance using budgets, recognising alternative approaches and sensitivity to variable factors. | (a) evaluate projected performance using ratio analysis; [12]<br><br>(b) evaluate the consequences of "what if" scenarios and their impact on the master budget; [13]<br><br>(c) evaluate performance using fixed and flexible budget reports. [13] | • Assessing the financial consequences of projected performance through key metrics including profitability, liquidity and asset turnover ratios. [13]<br>• What-if analysis based on alternate projections of volumes, prices and cost structures and the use of spreadsheets in facilitating these analyses. [13]<br>• The evaluation of out-turn performance using variances based on 'fixed' and 'flexed' budgets. [13] |
| 3. discuss the broader managerial issues arising from the use of budgets in control. | (a) discuss the impact of budgetary control systems and setting of standard costs on human behaviour; [12]<br><br>(b) discuss the role of non-financial performance indicators; [13]<br><br>(c) compare and contrast traditional approaches to budgeting with recommendations based on the 'balanced scorecard'; [13]<br><br>(d) discuss the criticisms of budgeting, particularly from the advocates of 'beyond budgeting' techniques. [13] | • Behavioural issues in budgeting: participation in budgeting and its possible beneficial consequences for ownership and motivation; participation in budgeting and its possible adverse consequences for 'budget padding' and manipulation; setting budget targets for motivation; implications of setting standard costs etc. [12]<br>• Non-financial performance indicators. [13]<br>• Criticisms of budgeting and the recommendations of the advocates of the balanced scorecard and 'beyond budgeting'. [13] |

**P2 – D. CONTROL AND PERFORMANCE MEASUREMENT OF RESPONSIBILITY CENTRES (20%)**

**Learning outcomes**
**On completion of their studies students should be able to:**

| Lead | Component | Indicative syllabus content |
|---|---|---|
| 1. discuss the use of responsibility centres in devising organisation structure and in management control. [14] | (a) discuss the use of cost, revenue, profit and investment centres in devising organisation structure and in management control. [14] | • Organisation structure and its implications for responsibility accounting. [14] |
| 2. discuss information suitable for management decision-making in responsibility centres. [14] | (a) discuss cost information in appropriate formats for cost centre managers, taking due account of controllable/uncontrollable costs and the importance of budget flexing; [14]<br><br>(b) discuss revenue and cost information in appropriate formats for profit and investment centre managers, taking due account of cost variability, attributable costs, controllable costs and identification of appropriate measures of profit centre 'contribution'; [14]<br><br>(c) discuss alternative measures of performance for responsibility centres. [14] | • Presentation of financial information representing performance and recognising issues of controllable/uncontrollable costs, variable/fixed costs and tracing revenues and costs to particular cost objects. [14]<br><br>• Return on investment and its deficiencies; the emergence of residual income and economic value added to address these. [14] |
| 3. discuss the broader managerial issues arising from the division of the organisation into responsibility centres. | (a) discuss the likely behavioural consequences of the use of performance metrics in managing cost, profit and investment centres; [14]<br><br>(b) discuss the typical consequences of a divisional structure for performance measurement as divisions compete or trade with each other; [15]<br><br>(c) discuss the likely consequences of different approaches to transfer pricing for divisional decision making, divisional and group profitability, the motivation of divisional management and the autonomy of individual divisions; [15]<br><br>(d) discuss in principle the potential tax and currency management consequences of internal transfer pricing policy. [15] | • The behavioural consequences of performance management and control. [14]<br><br>• The theory of transfer pricing, including perfect, imperfect and no market for the intermediate good. [15]<br><br>• Use of negotiated, market, cost-plus and variable cost based transfer prices. 'Dual' transfer prices and lump sum payments as means of addressing some of the issues that arise. [15]<br><br>• The interaction of transfer pricing and tax liabilities in international operations and implications for currency management and possible distortion of internal company operations in order to comply with Tax Authority directives. [15] |

# PRESENT VALUE TABLE

Present value of 1 unit of currency, that is $(1+r)^{-n}$ where $r$ = interest rate; $n$ = number of periods until payment or receipt.

| Periods (n) | Interest rates (r) | | | | | | | | | |
|---|---|---|---|---|---|---|---|---|---|---|
| | 1% | 2% | 3% | 4% | 5% | 6% | 7% | 8% | 9% | 10% |
| 1 | 0.990 | 0.980 | 0.971 | 0.962 | 0.952 | 0.943 | 0.935 | 0.926 | 0.917 | 0.909 |
| 2 | 0.980 | 0.961 | 0.943 | 0.925 | 0.907 | 0.890 | 0.873 | 0.857 | 0.842 | 0.826 |
| 3 | 0.971 | 0.942 | 0.915 | 0.889 | 0.864 | 0.840 | 0.816 | 0.794 | 0.772 | 0.751 |
| 4 | 0.961 | 0.924 | 0.888 | 0.855 | 0.823 | 0.792 | 0.763 | 0.735 | 0.708 | 0.683 |
| 5 | 0.951 | 0.906 | 0.863 | 0.822 | 0.784 | 0.747 | 0.713 | 0.681 | 0.650 | 0.621 |
| 6 | 0.942 | 0.888 | 0.837 | 0.790 | 0.746 | 0705 | 0.666 | 0.630 | 0.596 | 0.564 |
| 7 | 0.933 | 0.871 | 0.813 | 0.760 | 0.711 | 0.665 | 0.623 | 0.583 | 0.547 | 0.513 |
| 8 | 0.923 | 0.853 | 0.789 | 0.731 | 0.677 | 0.627 | 0.582 | 0.540 | 0.502 | 0.467 |
| 9 | 0.914 | 0.837 | 0.766 | 0.703 | 0.645 | 0.592 | 0.544 | 0.500 | 0.460 | 0.424 |
| 10 | 0.905 | 0.820 | 0.744 | 0.676 | 0.614 | 0.558 | 0.508 | 0.463 | 0.422 | 0.386 |
| 11 | 0.896 | 0.804 | 0.722 | 0.650 | 0.585 | 0.527 | 0.475 | 0.429 | 0.388 | 0.350 |
| 12 | 0.887 | 0.788 | 0.701 | 0.625 | 0.557 | 0.497 | 0.444 | 0.397 | 0.356 | 0.319 |
| 13 | 0.879 | 0.773 | 0.681 | 0.601 | 0.530 | 0.469 | 0.415 | 0.368 | 0.326 | 0.290 |
| 14 | 0.870 | 0.758 | 0.661 | 0.577 | 0.505 | 0.442 | 0.388 | 0.340 | 0.299 | 0.263 |
| 15 | 0.861 | 0.743 | 0.642 | 0.555 | 0.481 | 0.417 | 0.362 | 0.315 | 0.275 | 0.239 |
| 16 | 0.853 | 0.728 | 0.623 | 0.534 | 0.458 | 0.394 | 0.339 | 0.292 | 0.252 | 0.218 |
| 17 | 0.844 | 0.714 | 0.605 | 0.513 | 0.436 | 0.371 | 0.317 | 0.270 | 0.231 | 0.198 |
| 18 | 0.836 | 0.700 | 0.587 | 0.494 | 0.416 | 0.350 | 0.296 | 0.250 | 0.212 | 0.180 |
| 19 | 0.828 | 0.686 | 0.570 | 0.475 | 0.396 | 0.331 | 0.277 | 0.232 | 0.194 | 0.164 |
| 20 | 0.820 | 0.673 | 0.554 | 0.456 | 0.377 | 0.312 | 0.258 | 0.215 | 0.178 | 0.149 |

| Periods (n) | Interest rates (r) | | | | | | | | | |
|---|---|---|---|---|---|---|---|---|---|---|
| | 11% | 12% | 13% | 14% | 15% | 16% | 17% | 18% | 19% | 20% |
| 1 | 0.901 | 0.893 | 0.885 | 0.877 | 0.870 | 0.862 | 0.855 | 0.847 | 0.840 | 0.833 |
| 2 | 0.812 | 0.797 | 0.783 | 0.769 | 0.756 | 0.743 | 0.731 | 0.718 | 0.706 | 0.694 |
| 3 | 0.731 | 0.712 | 0.693 | 0.675 | 0.658 | 0.641 | 0.624 | 0.609 | 0.593 | 0.579 |
| 4 | 0.659 | 0.636 | 0.613 | 0.592 | 0.572 | 0.552 | 0.534 | 0.516 | 0.499 | 0.482 |
| 5 | 0.593 | 0.567 | 0.543 | 0.519 | 0.497 | 0.476 | 0.456 | 0.437 | 0.419 | 0.402 |
| 6 | 0.535 | 0.507 | 0.480 | 0.456 | 0.432 | 0.410 | 0.390 | 0.370 | 0.352 | 0.335 |
| 7 | 0.482 | 0.452 | 0.425 | 0.400 | 0.376 | 0.354 | 0.333 | 0.314 | 0.296 | 0.279 |
| 8 | 0.434 | 0.404 | 0.376 | 0.351 | 0.327 | 0.305 | 0.285 | 0.266 | 0.249 | 0.233 |
| 9 | 0.391 | 0.361 | 0.333 | 0.308 | 0.284 | 0.263 | 0.243 | 0.225 | 0.209 | 0.194 |
| 10 | 0.352 | 0.322 | 0.295 | 0.270 | 0.247 | 0.227 | 0.208 | 0.191 | 0.176 | 0.162 |
| 11 | 0.317 | 0.287 | 0.261 | 0.237 | 0.215 | 0.195 | 0.178 | 0.162 | 0.148 | 0.135 |
| 12 | 0.286 | 0.257 | 0.231 | 0.208 | 0.187 | 0.168 | 0.152 | 0.137 | 0.124 | 0.112 |
| 13 | 0.258 | 0.229 | 0.204 | 0.182 | 0.163 | 0.145 | 0.130 | 0.116 | 0.104 | 0.093 |
| 14 | 0.232 | 0.205 | 0.181 | 0.160 | 0.141 | 0.125 | 0.111 | 0.099 | 0.088 | 0.078 |
| 15 | 0.209 | 0.183 | 0.160 | 0.140 | 0.123 | 0.108 | 0.095 | 0.084 | 0.079 | 0.065 |
| 16 | 0.188 | 0.163 | 0.141 | 0.123 | 0.107 | 0.093 | 0.081 | 0.071 | 0.062 | 0.054 |
| 17 | 0.170 | 0.146 | 0.125 | 0.108 | 0.093 | 0.080 | 0.069 | 0.060 | 0.052 | 0.045 |
| 18 | 0.153 | 0.130 | 0.111 | 0.095 | 0.081 | 0.069 | 0.059 | 0.051 | 0.044 | 0.038 |
| 19 | 0.138 | 0.116 | 0.098 | 0.083 | 0.070 | 0.060 | 0.051 | 0.043 | 0.037 | 0.031 |
| 20 | 0.124 | 0.104 | 0.087 | 0.073 | 0.061 | 0.051 | 0.043 | 0.037 | 0.031 | 0.026 |

Cumulative present value of 1 unit of currency per annum, Receivable or Payable at the end of each year for $n$ years $\frac{1-(1+r)^{-n}}{r}$

| Periods (n) | Interest rates (r) | | | | | | | | | |
|---|---|---|---|---|---|---|---|---|---|---|
| | 1% | 2% | 3% | 4% | 5% | 6% | 7% | 8% | 9% | 10% |
| 1 | 0.990 | 0.980 | 0.971 | 0.962 | 0.952 | 0.943 | 0.935 | 0.926 | 0.917 | 0.909 |
| 2 | 1.970 | 1.942 | 1.913 | 1.886 | 1.859 | 1.833 | 1.808 | 1.783 | 1.759 | 1.736 |
| 3 | 2.941 | 2.884 | 2.829 | 2.775 | 2.723 | 2.673 | 2.624 | 2.577 | 2.531 | 2.487 |
| 4 | 3.902 | 3.808 | 3.717 | 3.630 | 3.546 | 3.465 | 3.387 | 3.312 | 3.240 | 3.170 |
| 5 | 4.853 | 4.713 | 4.580 | 4.452 | 4.329 | 4.212 | 4.100 | 3.993 | 3.890 | 3.791 |
| 6 | 5.795 | 5.601 | 5.417 | 5.242 | 5.076 | 4.917 | 4.767 | 4.623 | 4.486 | 4.355 |
| 7 | 6.728 | 6.472 | 6.230 | 6.002 | 5.786 | 5.582 | 5.389 | 5.206 | 5.033 | 4.868 |
| 8 | 7.652 | 7.325 | 7.020 | 6.733 | 6.463 | 6.210 | 5.971 | 5.747 | 5.535 | 5.335 |
| 9 | 8.566 | 8.162 | 7.786 | 7.435 | 7.108 | 6.802 | 6.515 | 6.247 | 5.995 | 5.759 |
| 10 | 9.471 | 8.983 | 8.530 | 8.111 | 7.722 | 7.360 | 7.024 | 6.710 | 6.418 | 6.145 |
| 11 | 10.368 | 9.787 | 9.253 | 8.760 | 8.306 | 7.887 | 7.499 | 7.139 | 6.805 | 6.495 |
| 12 | 11.255 | 10.575 | 9.954 | 9.385 | 8.863 | 8.384 | 7.943 | 7.536 | 7.161 | 6.814 |
| 13 | 12.134 | 11.348 | 10.635 | 9.986 | 9.394 | 8.853 | 8.358 | 7.904 | 7.487 | 7.103 |
| 14 | 13.004 | 12.106 | 11.296 | 10.563 | 9.899 | 9.295 | 8.745 | 8.244 | 7.786 | 7.367 |
| 15 | 13.865 | 12.849 | 11.938 | 11.118 | 10.380 | 9.712 | 9.108 | 8.559 | 8.061 | 7.606 |
| 16 | 14.718 | 13.578 | 12.561 | 11.652 | 10.838 | 10.106 | 9.447 | 8.851 | 8.313 | 7.824 |
| 17 | 15.562 | 14.292 | 13.166 | 12.166 | 11.274 | 10.477 | 9.763 | 9.122 | 8.544 | 8.022 |
| 18 | 16.398 | 14.992 | 13.754 | 12.659 | 11.690 | 10.828 | 10.059 | 9.372 | 8.756 | 8.201 |
| 19 | 17.226 | 15.679 | 14.324 | 13.134 | 12.085 | 11.158 | 10.336 | 9.604 | 8.950 | 8.365 |
| 20 | 18.046 | 16.351 | 14.878 | 13.590 | 12.462 | 11.470 | 10.594 | 9.818 | 9.129 | 8.514 |

| Periods (n) | Interest rates (r) | | | | | | | | | |
|---|---|---|---|---|---|---|---|---|---|---|
| | 11% | 12% | 13% | 14% | 15% | 16% | 17% | 18% | 19% | 20% |
| 1 | 0.901 | 0.893 | 0.885 | 0.877 | 0.870 | 0.862 | 0.855 | 0.847 | 0.840 | 0.833 |
| 2 | 1.713 | 1.690 | 1.668 | 1.647 | 1.626 | 1.605 | 1.585 | 1.566 | 1.547 | 1.528 |
| 3 | 2.444 | 2.402 | 2.361 | 2.322 | 2.283 | 2.246 | 2.210 | 2.174 | 2.140 | 2.106 |
| 4 | 3.102 | 3.037 | 2.974 | 2.914 | 2.855 | 2.798 | 2.743 | 2.690 | 2.639 | 2.589 |
| 5 | 3.696 | 3.605 | 3.517 | 3.433 | 3.352 | 3.274 | 3.199 | 3.127 | 3.058 | 2.991 |
| 6 | 4.231 | 4.111 | 3.998 | 3.889 | 3.784 | 3.685 | 3.589 | 3.498 | 3.410 | 3.326 |
| 7 | 4.712 | 4.564 | 4.423 | 4.288 | 4.160 | 4.039 | 3.922 | 3.812 | 3.706 | 3.605 |
| 8 | 5.146 | 4.968 | 4.799 | 4.639 | 4.487 | 4.344 | 4.207 | 4.078 | 3.954 | 3.837 |
| 9 | 5.537 | 5.328 | 5.132 | 4.946 | 4.772 | 4.607 | 4.451 | 4.303 | 4.163 | 4.031 |
| 10 | 5.889 | 5.650 | 5.426 | 5.216 | 5.019 | 4.833 | 4.659 | 4.494 | 4.339 | 4.192 |
| 11 | 6.207 | 5.938 | 5.687 | 5.453 | 5.234 | 5.029 | 4.836 | 4.656 | 4.486 | 4.327 |
| 12 | 6.492 | 6.194 | 5.918 | 5.660 | 5.421 | 5.197 | 4.988 | 7.793 | 4.611 | 4.439 |
| 13 | 6.750 | 6.424 | 6.122 | 5.842 | 5.583 | 5.342 | 5.118 | 4.910 | 4.715 | 4.533 |
| 14 | 6.982 | 6.628 | 6.302 | 6.002 | 5.724 | 5.468 | 5.229 | 5.008 | 4.802 | 4.611 |
| 15 | 7.191 | 6.811 | 6.462 | 6.142 | 5.847 | 5.575 | 5.324 | 5.092 | 4.876 | 4.675 |
| 16 | 7.379 | 6.974 | 6.604 | 6.265 | 5.954 | 5.668 | 5.405 | 5.162 | 4.938 | 4.730 |
| 17 | 7.549 | 7.120 | 6.729 | 6.373 | 6.047 | 5.749 | 5.475 | 5.222 | 4.990 | 4.775 |
| 18 | 7.702 | 7.250 | 6.840 | 6.467 | 6.128 | 5.818 | 5.534 | 5.273 | 5.033 | 4.812 |
| 19 | 7.839 | 7.366 | 6.938 | 6.550 | 6.198 | 5.877 | 5.584 | 5.316 | 5.070 | 4.843 |
| 20 | 7.963 | 7.469 | 7.025 | 6.623 | 6.259 | 5.929 | 5.628 | 5.353 | 5.101 | 4.870 |

# FORMULAE

## PROBABILITY

$A \cup B = \textbf{A or B}$.  $\qquad\qquad A \cap B = \textbf{A and B}$ (overlap).

$P(B \mid A)$ = probability of $B$, **given** $A$.

### Rules of Addition

| | |
|---|---|
| If $A$ and $B$ are mutually exclusive: | $P(A \cup B) = P(A) + P(B)$ |
| If $A$ and $B$ are not mutually exclusive: | $P(A \cup B) = P(A) + P(B) - P(A \cap B)$ |

### Rules of Multiplication

| | |
|---|---|
| If $A$ and $B$ are *independent*: | $P(A \cap B) = P(A) * P(B)$ |
| If $A$ and $B$ are **not** *independent*: | $P(A \cap B) = P(A) * P(B \mid A)$ |

$E(X) = \sum$ (probability * payoff)

## DESCRIPTIVE STATISTICS

Arithmetic Mean

$$\overline{x} = \frac{\sum x}{n} \qquad \overline{x} = \frac{\sum fx}{\sum f} \quad \text{(frequency distribution)}$$

Standard Deviation

$$SD = \sqrt{\frac{\sum (x - \overline{x})^2}{n}} \qquad SD = \sqrt{\frac{\sum fx^2}{\sum f} - \overline{x}^2} \quad \text{(frequency distribution)}$$

## INDEX NUMBERS

Price relative = $100 * P_1/P_0$  $\qquad$ Quantity relative = $100 * Q_1/Q_0$

Price: $\qquad \dfrac{\sum w * \left(\dfrac{P_1}{P_0}\right)}{\sum w} \times 100$

Quantity: $\qquad \dfrac{\sum w * \left(\dfrac{Q_1}{Q_0}\right)}{\sum w} \times 100$

## TIME SERIES

Additive Model

$$\text{Series} = \text{Trend} + \text{Seasonal} + \text{Random}$$

Multiplicative Model

$$\text{Series} = \text{Trend} * \text{Seasonal} * \text{Random}$$

## FINANCIAL MATHEMATICS

### Compound Interest (Values and Sums)
Future Value $S$, of a sum of $X$, invested for $n$ periods, compounded at $r\%$ interest

$$S = X[1 + r]^n$$

### Annuity
Present value of an annuity of £1 per annum receivable or payable for $n$ years, commencing in one year, discounted at $r\%$ per annum:

$$PV = \frac{1}{r}\left[1 - \frac{1}{[1+r]^n}\right]$$

### Perpetuity
Present value of £1 per annum, payable or receivable in perpetuity, commencing in one year, discounted at $r\%$ per annum:

$$PV = \frac{1}{r}$$

## LEARNING CURVE

$$Y_x = aX^b$$

where:
$Y_x$ = the cumulative average time per unit to produce $X$ units;
$a$ = the time required to produce the first unit of output;
$X$ = the cumulative number of units;
$b$ = the index of learning.

The exponent $b$ is defined as the log of the learning curve improvement rate divided by log 2.

## INVENTORY MANAGEMENT

Economic Order Quantity

$$EOQ = \sqrt{\frac{2C_oD}{C_h}}$$

where:  $C_o$ = cost of placing an order
$C_h$ = cost of holding one unit in inventory for one year
$D$ = annual demand

# CIMA Verb Hierarchy – managerial level exams

## Chapter learning objectives

### CIMA VERB HIERARCHY

CIMA place great importance on the choice of verbs in exam question requirements. It is thus critical that you answer the question according to the definition of the verb used.

## 1 Managerial level verbs

In managerial level exams you will mainly meet verbs from levels 2, 3 and 4. Very occasionally you will also see level 1 verbs but these should not account for more than 5–10% of the marks in total.

### Level 2 – COMPREHENSION

What you are expected to understand.

| VERBS USED | DEFINITION |
|---|---|
| Describe | Communicate the key features of. |
| Distinguish | Highlight the differences between. |
| Explain | Make clear or intelligible/state the meaning or purpose of. |
| Identify | Recognise, establish or select after consideration. |
| Illustrate | Use an example to describe or explain something. |

### Level 3 – APPLICATION

How you are expected to apply your knowledge.

| VERBS USED | DEFINITION |
|---|---|
| Apply | Put to practical use. |
| Calculate | Ascertain or reckon mathematically. |
| Demonstrate | Prove with certainty or exhibit by practical means. |
| Prepare | Make or get ready for use. |
| Reconcile | Make or prove consistent/compatible. |
| Solve | Find an answer to. |
| Tabulate | Arrange in a table. |

## Level 4 – ANALYSIS

How you are expected to analyse the detail of what you have learned.

| VERBS USED | DEFINITION |
|---|---|
| Analyse | Examine in detail the structure of. |
| Categorise | Place into a defined class or division. |
| Compare and contrast | Show the similarities and/or differences between. |
| Construct | Build up or compile. |
| Discuss | Examine in detail by argument. |
| Interpret | Translate into intelligible or familiar terms. |
| Prioritise | Place in order of priority or sequence for action. |
| Produce | Create or bring into existence. |

### 2 Further guidance on managerial level verbs that cause confusion

Verbs that cause students confusion at this level are as follows:

### Level 2 verbs

- **The difference between "describe" and "explain".**

    An explanation is a set of statements constructed to describe a set of facts which clarifies the **causes**, **context**, and **consequences** of those facts.

    For example, if asked to **describe** the features of activity based costing (ABC) you could talk, amongst other things, about how costs are grouped into cost pools (e.g. quality control), cost drivers identified (e.g. number of inspections) and an absorption rate calculated based on this cost driver (e.g. cost per inspection). This tells us what ABC looks like.

    However if asked to **explain** ABC, then you would have to talk about why firms were dissatisfied with previous traditional costing methods and switched to ABC (causes), what types of firms it is more suitable for (context) and the implications for firms (consequences) in terms of the usefulness of such costs per unit for pricing and costing.

    More simply, to describe something is to answer "what" type questions whereas to explain looks at "what" and "why" aspects.

- ## The verb "to illustrate"

  The key thing about illustrating something is that you may have to decide on a relevant example to use. This could involve drawing a diagram, performing supporting calculations or highlighting a feature or person in the scenario given. Most of the time the question will be structured so calculations performed in part (a) can be used to illustrate a concept in part (b).

  For example, you could be asked to explain and illustrate what is meant by an "adverse variance".

## Level 3 verbs

- ## The verb "to apply"

  Given that all level 3 verbs involve application, the verb "apply" is rare in the real exam. Instead one of the other more specific verbs is used instead.

- ## The verb "to reconcile"

  This is a numerical requirement and usually involves starting with one of the figures, adjusting it and ending up with the other.

  For example, in a bank reconciliation you start with the recorded cash at bank figure, adjust it for unpresented cheques, etc. And (hopefully!) end up with the stated balance in the cash "T account".

- ## The verb "to demonstrate"

  The verb "to demonstrate" can be used in two main ways.

  Firstly it could mean to prove that a given statement is true or consistent with circumstances given. For example, the Finance Director may have stated in the question that the company will not exceed its overdraft limit in the next six months. The requirement then asks you to demonstrate that the Director is wrong. You could do this by preparing a cash flow forecast for the next six months.

  Secondly you could be asked to demonstrate **how** a stated model, framework, technique or theory **could be used** in the particular scenario to achieve a specific result – for example, how a probability matrix could be used to make a production decision. Ensure in such questions that you do not merely describe the model but use it to generate the desired outcome.

## Level 4 verbs

- ### The verb "to analyse"

  To analyse something is to examine it in detail in order to discover its meaning or essential features. This will usually involve breaking the scenario down and looking at the fine detail, possibly with additional calculations, and then stepping back to see the bigger picture to identify any themes to support conclusions.

  For example, if asked to analyse a set of financial statements, then the end result will be a set of statements about the performance of the business with supporting evidence. This could involve the following:

  (1) You could break down your analysis into areas of profitability, liquidity, gearing and so on.

  (2) Under each heading look at key figures in the financial statements, identifying trends (e.g. sales growth) and calculating supporting ratios (e.g. margins).

  (3) Try to explain what the figures mean and why they have occurred (e.g. why has the operating margin fallen?)

  (4) Start considering the bigger picture – are the ratios presenting a consistent message or do they contradict each other? Can you identify common causes?

  (5) Finally you would then seek to pull all this information together and interpret it to make some higher level comments about overall performance.

  The main error students make is that they fail to draw out any themes and conclusions and simply present the marker with a collection of uninterrpreted, unexplained facts and figures.

- ### The verb "to discuss"

  To discuss something is very similar to analysing it, except that discussion usually involves two or more different viewpoints or arguments as the context, rather than a set of figures, say. To discuss viewpoints will involve looking at their underlying arguments, examining them critically, trying to assess whether one argument is more persuasive than the other and then seeking to reach a conclusion.

  For example, if asked to discuss whether a particular technique could be used by a company, you would examine the arguments for and against, making reference to the specific circumstances in the question, and seek to conclude.

- **The verb "to prioritise"**

To prioritise is to place objects in an order. The key issue here is to decide upon the criteria to use to perform the ordering. For example, prioritising the external threats facing a firm could be done by considering the scale of financial consequences, immediacy, implications for the underlying business model and so on.

The main mistake students make is that they fail to justify their prioritisation – why is this the most important issue? By the end of this book, you should have the answer.

- **The verb "to prioritise"**

# Basics Revisited

## Chapter learning objectives

Because of the progressive nature of the qualification, the P2 exam could include questions on topics that do not sit, strictly speaking, in the P2 syllabus. The objective of this chapter is to look at some fundamental aspects of cost and management accounting which you should recall from your earlier studies, and/or help you identify any area of priority revision in preparation for the CIMA P2 examination.

From the Examiner :

*"Due to the progressive nature of the Management Accounting Pillar candidates sitting the P2 examination are advised to closely examine the syllabi of the Certificate level subjects, particularly C01, and the P1 paper to ensure they have a thorough understanding of all the topics covered in those papers. Any identified knowledge gap must be addressed."*

## 1 Session Content Diagram

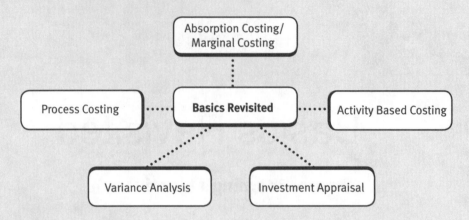

## 2 Absorption Costing

Absorption costing is a method of costing that, in addition to direct costs, assigns all, or a proportion of, production overhead costs to cost units by means of one or a number of overhead absorption rates.

Indirect costs, by their nature, cannot be economically identified with cost units. Absorption costing is a technique which is used to calculate a fair share of overheads to be attributed to each cost unit.

*[In the March 2013 PEG, the Examiner notes that a common error by candidates is to believe traditional absorption costing relates to variable costs.]*

The technique follows five steps:

- **Step 1: Establishing cost centres.**
  Cost centres are identified as production or service cost centres. Production cost centres work directly on the cost unit while service cost centres support the production activities but do not work directly on the cost unit.

- **Step 2: Allocating overhead costs to cost centres.**
  Some costs can be allocated immediately, e.g. the salary of a cost centre supervisor or indirect materials issued to a cost centre. Allocation means costing whole items of expenditure to a cost centre.

- **Step 3: Apportioning overhead costs to cost centres.**
  Some costs are shared over several cost centres, e.g. factory rent and rates or the salary of the overall factory manager. The basis for apportioning a total amount will be selected so that the charge to a specific centre will reflect, with reasonable accuracy, the benefit obtained by that centre from the cost incurred.

- **Step 4: Reapportioning service cost centre costs to production cost centres.**
  Service cost centre costs must be reapportioned to production cost centres so that all overheads can be finally attributed to the cost unit.

- **Step 5: Absorbing production cost centre costs into cost units.**
  The overhead to be absorbed by a particular cost unit will be calculated by dividing the production cost centre overhead for a period by an appropriate measure of the volume of production in the period.

If a cost centre produces dissimilar units the volume of production must be expressed in a common measurement, e.g. direct labour hours: if product X takes workers twice as long to make as product Y, it is reasonable that it should bear twice the overhead. When a cost unit passes through several centres, the overhead absorbed should be calculated separately for each centre.

*[In the March 2013 PEG, the Examiner notes the common error made by candidates who believe that the use of traditional absorption costing results in costs being spread evenly over the products.]*

**Under- and over-absorption**

A predetermined overhead absorption rate is used to smooth out seasonal fluctuations in overhead costs, and to enable unit costs to be calculated quickly throughout the year.

$$\text{Predetermined overhead absorption rate} = \frac{\text{Budgeted Overhead}}{\text{Budgeted volume}}$$

'Budgeted volume' may relate to units, direct labour hours, machine hours, etc. If either or both of the actual overhead cost or activity volume differ from budget, the use of this rate is likely to lead to what is known as **under-absorption** or **over-absorption** of overheads

**Over- and under-absorption**

**Example**

In year 9 the budget for the machine shop shows overheads $60,000 and volume of activity of 12,000 machine hours.

In January year 9, the machine shop incurred $5,400 of overhead and 1,050 machine hours were worked.

The pre-determined absorption rate and the overhead under- or over-absorbed in January can be calculated as follows :

$$\text{Absorption rate} = \frac{\text{Budgeted Overhead}}{\text{Budgeted volume}} = \frac{\$60,000}{12,000 \text{ machine hours}}$$

$$= \$5.00 \text{ per machine hour}$$

|  | $ |
|---|---|
| Actual overhead incurred | 5,400 |
| Overhead absorbed (1,050 machine hours × $5.00) | 5,250 |
|  | 150 |

The under-absorption in this example arises from a combination of two factors:

- actual overhead costs were $400 higher than the budgeted amount of ($60,000 ÷ 12) = $5,000 for the month

- actual volume was 50 hours greater than the budgeted (12,000 hours ÷ 12) = 1,000 hours for the month.

## Activity 2

A company budgeted to produce 3,000 units of a single product in a period at a budgeted cost per unit as follows:

|  | $ per unit |
|---|---|
| Direct costs | 17 |
| Fixed Overhead | 9 |
|  | 26 |

In the period covered by the budget, actual production was 3,200 units and actual fixed overhead expenditure was 5% above that budgeted – all other costs were as budgeted. What was the amount, if any, of over- or under-absorption of fixed overhead?

### Answer

Over-/(under-) absorption = Absorbed overheads − Incurred overheads
Budgeted fixed overhead = 3,000 units × $9 = $27,000

|  | $ |
|---|---|
| Fixed overhead absorbed (3,200 units × $9) | 28,800 |
| Fixed overhead incurred ($27,000 × 1.05) | 28,350 |
| Over-absorbed fixed overheads | 450 |

The unit cost of production will include overhead at the predetermined rate and, generally, overhead under- or over-absorbed will be shown as a separate item in the costing income statement.

## 3 Costing Income Statement

### Example

A company budgets to produce and sell 120 units of product at a price of $100. The direct cost of production is $30 per unit. Indirect costs are $4,800. Actual production and sales are 100 units and actual overhead cost is $5,000. Calculate the profit for the period.

### Solution

|  | $ |
|---|---|
| The full cost per unit is |  |
| Direct cost | 30 |
| Indirect cost   $4,800/120 | 40 |
|  | 70 |

|  | $ |
|---|---|
| Absorbed overhead   100 × $40 | 4,000 |
| Actual overhead cost | 5,000 |
| **Under-absorbed overhead** | **1,000** |

**Costing income statement**

|  | $000 |
|---|---|
| Sales | 10 |
| Cost of sales (units sold × unit cost including absorbed overheads) | 7 |
|  | 3 |
| (Under-)/over-absorption | (1) |
| Operating profit | 2 |

*[Tutorial note: The examination questions on this syllabus are likely to focus on comparing an absorption costing profit statement with a marginal costing profit statement. When you are producing an absorption costing profit statement remember to check for any under- or over-absorption.]*

## 4 Marginal Costing

**Marginal costing** is the accounting system in which variable costs are charged to cost units and fixed costs of the period are written off in full against the aggregate contribution. Its special value is in recognising cost behaviour, and hence assisting in decision-making.

The **marginal cost** is the extra cost arising as a result of making and selling one more unit of a product or service, or is the saving in cost as a result of making and selling one less unit.

**Contribution** is the difference between sales value and the variable cost of sales. It may be expressed per unit or in total.

Marginal costing is widely used for internal reporting and decision making within organisations. It is superior to absorption costing for decision-making purposes because of the careful separation of variable and fixed cost elements. An example will be used to illustrate.

### Marginal Costing Example

A company manufactures only one product called XY. The following information relates to the product.

|                                | $  |
|--------------------------------|----|
| Selling price per unit         | 20 |
| Direct material cost per unit  | 6  |
| Direct labour cost per unit    | 2  |
| Variable overhead cost per unit| 4  |

Fixed costs for the period are $25,000.

**Required:**

(a) Calculate the contribution per unit.

(b) In Period 1 the company manufactures and sells 4,000 units. Calculate the total contribution and profit at this level.

(c) Calculate the profit per unit at this level.

(d) Complete the following table. In each case the production level is equal to the sales level.

| Level of activity | 2,500 units | 5,000 units | 7,500 units | 10,000 units |
|---|---|---|---|---|
| Revenue | | | | |
| Variable costs | | | | |
| Total contribution | | | | |
| Fixed costs | | | | |
| Total profit/(loss) | | | | |
| Contribution per unit | | | | |
| Profit/(loss) per unit | | | | |

The table illustrates that contribution per unit remains **constant at all levels of activity.** However, profit per unit changes. Hence marginal costing is a useful method when trying to analyse and manage costs. Absorption costing does not distinguish between fixed and variable cost elements. It is not a useful method for internal reporting.

## 5 Activity-Based Costing

### Introduction and background

In traditional absorption costing, overheads are charged to products using a predetermined overhead recovery rate. This overhead absorption rate (OAR) is based upon the **volume of activity**. A full unit cost is computed in order to satisfy financial accounting requirements.

However, it is always stressed that full product costs, using financial accounting principles, are not suitable for decision-making purposes. Instead, decisions should be based on a decision-relevant approach incorporating relevant/incremental cash flows. With this approach, decisions such as introducing new products and special pricing decisions should be based on a study of only those incremental revenues and expenses that will vary with respect to the particular decision. This approach requires that special studies be undertaken when the need arises. However, studies have shown that the majority of companies base their decision making upon full product cost.

In the late 1980s Cooper and Kaplan developed a more refined approach for assigning overheads to products and computing product cost. This new approach is called **activity based costing (ABC).** It is claimed that ABC provides product-cost information that is useful for decision-making purposes.

*Activity-Based Costing* is defined in CIMA's *Official Terminology* as 'an approach to the costing and monitoring of activities which involves tracing resource consumption and costing final outputs. Resources are assigned to activities, and activities to cost objects based on consumption estimates. The latter utilise cost drivers to attach activity costs to outputs'

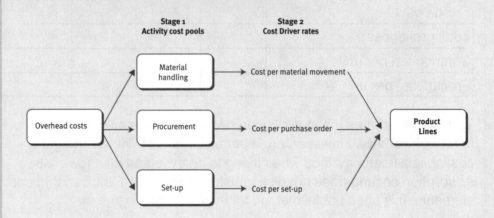

Traditional systems measure accurately volume-related resources that are consumed in proportion to the number of units produced of the individual products. Such resources include direct labour, materials, energy and machine-related costs. However, many organisational resources exist for activities that are unrelated to physical volume. Non-volume related activities consist of support activities such as materials handling, material procurement, set-ups, production scheduling and first-item inspection activities. Traditional product-cost systems, which assume that products consume all activities in proportion to their production volumes, thus report distorted product costs.

*[In the March 2013 PEG, the Examiner notes that 'most candidates were unable to describe traditional absorption costing and Activity Based Costing (ABC), and were therefore not able to explain the difference. This is worrying, as traditional absorption costing is one of the most basic and fundamental aspects of Management Accounting and is associated with many other topics within the syllabi such as establishing selling prices'.]*

### Cooper and Kaplan – The Pen Factory

The distortions arising from the use of traditional product-costing systems are most pronounced in organisations that produce a diverse range of products which differ in volume and complexity. Cooper and Kaplan (1991) use the following example to illustrate the inability of traditional systems to report accurate product costs:

'Consider two hypothetical plants turning out a simple product: Ball-point pens. The factories are the same size and have the same capital equipment. Every year plant I makes 1 million units of only one product: blue pens. Plant II, a full-line producer, also produces blue pens, but only 100,000 a year. Plant II also produces a variety of similar products: 80,000 black pens, 30,000 red pens, 5,000 green pens, 500 lavender pens, and so on. In a typical year plant II produces up to 1,000 product variations, with volumes ranging between 100 and 100,000 units. Its aggregate annual output equals the 1 million pens of plant I'.

The first plant has a simple production environment and requires limited manufacturing support facilities. With its higher diversity and complexity of operations, the second plant requires a much larger support structure. For example 1,000 different products must be scheduled through the plant, and this requires more people for scheduling the machines, performing the set-ups, inspecting items, purchasing, receiving and handling materials, and handling a large number of individual requests. Expenditure on support overheads will therefore be much higher in the second plant, even though the number of units produced and sold by both plants is identical. Furthermore, since the number of units produced is identical, both plants will have approximately the same number of direct labour hours, machine hours and material purchases. The much higher expenditure on support overheads in the second plant cannot therefore be explained in terms of direct labour, machine hours operated or the amount of materials purchased.

Traditional costing systems, however, use volume bases to allocate support overheads to products. In fact, if each pen requires approximately the same number of machine hours, direct labour hours or material cost, the reported cost per pen will be identical in plant II. Thus blue and lavender pens will have identical product costs, even though the lavender pens are ordered, manufactured, packaged and despatched in much lower volumes.

The small-volume products place a much higher relative demand on the support departments than low share of volume might suggest. Intuitively, it must cost more to produce the low-volume lavender pen than the high-volume blue pen. Traditional volume-based costing systems therefore tend to overcost high-volume products and undercost low-volume products. To remedy this discrepancy **ABC** expands the second stage assignment bases for assigning overheads to products.

### The activity-based costing procedure

Cooper and Kaplan stated that it was the support activities that were the cause of many overheads, for example, material handling, quality inspection, setting up machinery, material acquisition, etc. Thus a simple three-step philosophy was developed:

- support activities cause cost;

- the products consume these activities;

- cost should, therefore, be charged on the basis of consumption of the activities.

## Method

(1) Identify the organisation's major activities. Ideally about 30 to 50 activities should be identified. However, over time, some large firms have been known to develop hundreds of activities. A suitable rule of thumb is to apply the 80/20 rule: identify the 20% of activities that generate 80% of the overheads, and analyse these in detail.

(2) Estimate the costs associated with performing each activity – these costs are collected into **cost pools**.

(3) Identify the factors that influence the cost pools. These are known as the **cost drivers**. For example, the number of set-ups will influence the cost of setting up machinery.

(4) Calculate a cost driver rate, for example a rate per set-up, or a rate per material requisition, or a rate per inspection.

$$\text{Cost driver rate} = \frac{\text{Cost pool}}{\text{Level of cost drivers}}$$

(5) Charge the overheads to the products by applying the cost driver rates to the activity usage of the products.

To appreciate the application of this procedure it is necessary to work through an example.

## 6 Favourable Conditions For ABC

The purpose of moving from a traditional costing system to an activity-based system should be based on the premise that the new information provided will lead to action that will increase the overall profitability of the business.

This is most likely to occur when the analysis provided under the ABC system differs significantly from that which was provided under the traditional system, which is most likely to occur under the following conditions:

- when production overheads are high relative to direct costs, particularly direct labour;

- where there is great diversity in the product range;

- where there is considerable diversity of overhead resource input to products;

- when consumption of overhead resources is not driven primarily by volume.

Information from an ABC analysis may indicate opportunities to increase profitability in a variety of ways, many of which are long-term. For example, an activity-based analysis may reveal that small-batch items are relatively expensive to produce, and are therefore unprofitable at current prices.

A number of responses to this information could be adopted. The first response might be to consider stopping production of such items, and concentrate on the apparently more profitable high-volume lines. Another approach would be to investigate how the production process could be organised in such a way as to bring the cost of producing small-batch items closer to that of producing high-volume goods.

By identifying the cost of carrying out particular activities, the new approach provides opportunities for directing attention to matters of cost control. It can therefore be viewed as a much longer-term technique than the word 'costing' in the title suggests. The establishment of an ABC product cost may thus be considered to be the beginning of the process, rather than an end in itself. The recent use of the term activity-based management suggests this forward-looking orientation, which is assuming increasing importance.

## Classification of activities

Cooper (1990) has classified activities into four major categories that drive expenses at the product level. They are:

- unit-level activities;
- batch-related activities;
- product-sustaining activities;
- facility-sustaining costs.

**Unit-level activities** are performed each time a unit of product is produced. They are consumed in direct proportion to the number of units produced. Expenses in this category include direct labour, direct materials, energy costs and machine maintenance.

**Batch-related activities** are performed each time a batch is produced. The cost of batch-related activities varies with the number of batches made, but is common (or fixed) for all the units within the batch. For example, set-up resources are consumed when a machine is changed from one product to another. As more batches are produced, more set-up resources are consumed. It costs the same to set-up a machine for a run of 10 or 5,000 units. Similarly, purchasing resources are consumed each time a purchasing order is processed, but the resources consumed are independent of the number of units included in the purchase order.

**Product-sustaining activities** are performed to support different products in the product line. They are performed to enable different products to be produced and sold, but the resources consumed are independent of how many units or batches are being produced. Cooper and Kaplan (1991) identify engineering resources devoted to maintaining accurate bills of materials and routing each product as an example of product-sustaining activities. Product design costs and advertising costs of the specific product would also be counted as product-sustaining costs. The expenses of product-sustaining activities will tend to increase as the number of products manufactured increases.

**Facility-sustaining activities**. Some costs cannot be related to a particular product line, instead they are related to maintaining buildings and the facilities. Examples include maintenance of the building, plant security, business rates, etc.

## A summary of benefits and limitations

### Benefits

(1) Provides more accurate product-line costings particularly where non-volume-related overheads are significant and a diverse product line is manufactured.

(2) Is flexible enough to analyse costs by cost objects other than products such as processes, areas of managerial responsibility and customers.

(3) Provides a reliable indication of long-run variable product cost which is particularly relevant to managerial decision making at a strategic level.

(4) Provides meaningful financial (periodic cost driver rates) and non-financial (periodic cost driver volumes) measures which are relevant for cost management and performance assessment at an operational level.

(5) Aids identification and understanding of cost behaviour and thus has the potential to improve cost estimation.

(6) Provides a more logical, acceptable and comprehensible basis for costing work.

### Limitations

(1) Little evidence to date that ABC improves corporate profitability.

(2) ABC information is historic and internally orientated and therefore lacks direct relevance for future strategic decisions.

(3) Practical problems such as cost driver selection.

(4) Its novelty is questionable. It may be viewed as simply a rigorous application of conventional costing procedures.

*[In the March 2013 PEG, the Examiner notes that candidates make a mistake when they believe that the introduction of Activity Based Costing will allow the company to reduce the selling price of every product.]*

### Example 1 – Scandinavia

D has recently set up a small business, which manufactures three different types of chair to customer order. Each type is produced in a single batch per week and dispatched as individual items. The size of the batch is determined by the weekly customer orders. The three different types of chair are known as the Comfort, the Relaxer and the Scandinavia. The comfort is a fully leather-upholstered chair and is the most expensive of the range. The Relaxer is the middle-of-the range chair, and has a comfortable leather seat. The cheapest of the range, the Scandinavia, is purely a wooden chair, but D feels it has great potential and hopes it will provide at least 50% of the sales revenue.

D has employed F, an experienced but unqualified accountant, to act as the organisation's accountant. F has produced figures for the past month, July 2006, which is considered a normal month in terms of costs:

**Profit statement for July 2006**

|  | $ | $ |
| --- | ---: | ---: |
| Sales revenue |  | 79,800 |
| Material costs | 17,250 |  |
| Labour costs | 27,600 |  |
| Overheads | 34,500 |  |
|  | ——— |  |
|  |  | 79,350 |
|  |  | ——— |
| Profit |  | 450 |

|  | Comfort | Relaxer | Scandinavia |
| --- | ---: | ---: | ---: |
| Units produced and sold during July | 30 | 120 | 150 |
|  | $ | $ | $ |
| Selling price per chair | 395 | 285 | 225 |
| Less: Costs per chair |  |  |  |
| Material | 85 | 60 | 50 |
| Labour | 120 | 100 | 80 |
| Overhead absorbed on labour hours | 150 | 125 | 100 |
|  | ——— | ——— | ——— |
|  | 355 | 285 | 230 |
|  | ——— | ——— | ——— |
| Profit per chair | 40 | 0 | (5) |
|  | ——— | ——— | ——— |

D hopes to use these figures as the basis for budgets for the next three months. He is pleased to see that the organisation has made its first monthly profit, however small it might be. On the other hand, he is unhappy with F's advice about the loss-making Scandinavia, which is, either to reduce its production or to increase its price. D is concerned because this advice goes against the strategy on which he based his business idea. After much discussion F says that he has heard of a newer type of costing system, known as activity-based costing (ABC), and that he will recalculate the position on this basis. In order to do this, F extracted the following information:

|                             | Comfort | Relaxer | Scandinavia |
|-----------------------------|---------|---------|-------------|
| Wood (metres) per chair     | 10      | 9       | 9           |
| Leather (metres) per chair  | 4       | 2       | 0           |
| Labour (hours) per chair    | 24      | 20      | 16          |

The overheads included in July's profit statement comprised:

|                                          | $      |
|------------------------------------------|--------|
| Set-up costs                             | 5,600  |
| Purchasing and checking leather hides    | 4,000  |
| Purchase of wood                         | 2,400  |
| Quality inspection of leather seating    | 3,200  |
| Despatch and transport                   | 6,000  |
| Administration and personnel costs       | 13,300 |

**Required:**

(a) Use the ABC technique to prepare a revised product cost statement for July 2006 such as F might produce.

**(13 marks)**

(b) Explain whether the statement you have prepared in (a) provides an adequate basis to make decisions on the future production volume and price of the Scandinavia. What other information or approach might you seek to adopt?

**(5 marks)**

(c) It is just as important for an organisation to determine how individual customers or groups of customers differ in terms of the profitability to the organisation as it is to determine the relative profitability of products. Briefly explain how this can be done. Would you advise D to do this?

**(7 marks)**
**(Total: 25 marks)**

## 7 Using ABC In Service Industries And Activities

ABC can be used by all types of organisation, such as retail, service, nationalised, etc., and in all areas of the business.

### AT&T

AT&T, the US telephone and telecommunications company, first used ABC in the early 1990s as a pilot project in its sales invoicing department according to Hobdy et al. (1994). It used the following types of activities to collect costs:

- Monitoring billing records
- Editing checks
- Validating data
- Correcting errors
- Printing, sorting and dispatching invoices.

It then spread the activity cost pools on cost drivers that included the following:

- No. of customers tested
- Change requests
- Service orders
- Customer locations
- Printer hours
- Pages printed.

AT&T found that ABC not only helped managers to manage the costs, but it also helped them improve operating processes and supplier relationships and to raise customer satisfaction.

This shows another role for ABC, namely its use as a one-off attention-directing technique to assess an activity and its impact on the business. Whether it continues to be used as a one-off technique or becomes an integral part of the costing systems is up to management.

ABC is also used in a wide range of service industries, from hospitals to credit card companies. Research into hospital costs and activities by Huang and Kirby (1994) has identified two main cost drivers for a hospital:

- The number of days spent in hospital. Costs included in this category were routine nursing care, meals and laundry.

- The number of admissions. Costs included in this category were obtaining and using the patient's medical history, preparation for surgery, after-surgery care and invoicing insurers and collecting funds.

This particular piece of research found that Medicare (i.e. the government reimbursement scheme) had been considerably over-charged because it dealt with older patients who stayed longer in hospital than others on private insurance. As a consequence the absorption rate used prior to ABC, which was a single day rate, gave a charge which was too high for long-stay patients.

## 8 Standard Costing and Variance Analysis

**Standard costing** is a technique which establishes predetermined estimates of the costs of products and services and then compares these predetermined costs with actual costs as they are incurred. The predetermined costs are known as standard costs and the difference between the standard cost and actual cost is known as a variance.

The process by which the total difference between actual cost and standard is broken down into its different elements is known as **Variance Analysis**.

**A variance is the difference between actual results and the budget or standard.**

Taken together, cost and sales variances can be used to explain the difference between the budgeted profit for a period and the actual profit.

When actual results are *better than* expected results, a **favourable (F)** variance occurs.

When actual results are *worse than* expected results, an **adverse variance (A)** occurs.

### Variance groups

Variances can be divided into three main groups:

- sales variances
- variable cost variances
  - material variances
  - labour variances
  - variable overhead variances
- fixed overhead variances

## 9 Sales Variances

The difference between a budgeted profit and the actual profit achieved in a period is explained by both cost variances and sales variances. Cost variances explain the differences between actual costs and budgeted or standard costs. Sales variances explain the effect of differences between:

- actual and standard sales prices, and
- budgeted and actual sales volumes.

The **sales price variance** shows the effect on profit of the difference between the standard sales prices for the items sold in a period and the actual sales revenue achieved. It is calculated as follows:

(a) Standard selling price multiplied by the actual number of units sold, and

(b) Actual selling price multiplied by the actual number of units sold.

The **sales volume variance** is the difference between actual and budgeted sales volumes. This difference is valued at either standard profit, in an absorption costing system, or standard contribution in a marginal costing system. Sales volumes in turn splits into a **sales mix variance** and a **sales quantity variance**.

A **sales mix variance** indicates the effect on profit of changing the mix of actual sales from the standard mix. A **sales quantity variance** indicates the effect on profit of selling a different total quantity from the budgeted total quantity.

### Proforma

**Sales price variance**

|  |  | $ |
|---|---|---|
| Units sold should have sold for | (actual sales units × standard sales price per unit) | X |
| They did sell for | (actual sales revenue) | Y |
|  |  | ——— |
| Sales price variance |  | X–Y |
|  |  | ——— |

This variance is favourable if actual sales revenue is higher than sales at the standard selling price, and adverse if actual sales revenue is lower than standard.

**Sales volume variance**

A sales volume variance measured in units has to be calculated first. The variance is favourable if actual sales volume is higher than budgeted sales volume, and adverse if actual sales volume is lower than budget.

|  | **Units of sale** |
|---|---|
|  | *Units* |
| Actual sales volume | X |
| Budgeted sales volume | Y |
|  | ——— |
| Sales volume variance | X–Y |
|  | ——— |

The variance in units can then be valued in one of three ways:

- at the **standard gross profit per unit** – if using absorption costing;

- at the **standard contribution per unit** – if using marginal costing;

- at the **standard revenue per unit** – this is rarely used and we would only do so if it was specifically asked for in an exam question.

### Example 2

A company produces and sells two similar products, Dee and Bee. Extracts from the **budget** for the month are shown in the following table :

|  | Unit sales | Selling Price per unit | Standard cost per unit |
|---|---|---|---|
| Product Dee | 3,000 | $75 | $50 |
| Product Bee | 1,500 | $200 | $105 |

You have also obtained the following **actual** results :

|  | Unit sales | Selling Price per unit |
|---|---|---|
| Product Dee | 3,000 | $69 |
| Product Bee | 1,200 | $215 |

**Required:**

Calculate the following operational variances :

(i) The total sales mix profit margin variance;

(ii) The total sales volume profit variance.

*[In the May 2011 PEG, the Examiner notes that attempts at this [Sales Variances] question were extremely poor. Variance analysis is one of the main pillars upon which management accounting is built, and again emphasises that while variance analysis does not explicitly appear in the P2 syllabus, it can be assessed at this level due to the progressive nature of the syllabus.]*

## 10 Direct Material Cost Variances

This section has three variances. The direct material total cost variance, which shows the impact of any overall change in the amount spent on materials, and this can also be split into two further components : the materials price, and the materials usage variances.

### Direct material total variance

The difference between:

(a)  the standard direct material cost of the actual production and

(b)  the actual cost of direct material.

| Proforma |
| --- |

**Direct materials cost**

|  |  | $ |
| --- | --- | --- |
| Actual quantity of output | should cost (standard) | X |
|  | did cost | Y |
| Total cost variance |  | X–Y |

James Marshall Ltd makes a single product with the following budgeted material costs per unit:

   2 kg of material A at $10/kg

Actual details:

   Output 1,000 units
   Material purchased and used 2,200 kg
   Material cost $20,900

Calculate the total materials variance.

A total material variance actually conveys very little useful information. It needs to be analysed further. It can be analysed into two sub-variances:

(1)  a Direct Material Price variance, i.e. paying more or less than expected for materials and

(2)  a Direct Material Usage variance, i.e. using more or less material than expected.

## Direct material price variance

The difference between:

(a)  standard purchase price per kg and

(b)  actual purchase price

   multiplied by the actual quantity of material purchased or used.

**Note:** that the material price variance can be calculated either at the time of purchase or at the time of usage. Generally, the former is preferable.

| Proforma | | |
|---|---|---|
| **Direct materials price variance** | | $ |
| Actual quantity of materials | should cost (standard) | X |
| | did cost (actual) | Y |
| Direct materials price variance | | X-Y |

### Direct material usage variance

The difference between:

(a) the standard quantity of material specified for the actual production and

(b) the actual quantity used

multiplied by the standard purchase price.

> **Proforma**
>
> **Direct materials usage variance**
>
> | | | $ |
> |---|---|---|
> | Actual output produced | should use (standard quantity) | X |
> | | did use (actual quantity) | Y |
> | | | — |
> | Direct materials usage variance | (in material quantity) | X–Y |
> | | | — |
> | x standard price | (per unit of material) | $P |
> | Direct materials usage variance | | $P x (X – Y) |

> **Example 4**
>
> For example 3, calculate the price and usage variances for materials.

### 11 Material Mix and Yield Variances

In many industries, particularly process industries, input consists of more than one type of material and it is possible to vary the mix. In many cases this would then affect the quantity of output produced. To analyse this **the usage variance can be broken down into mix and yield variances**.

The **material mix variance** arises when the mix of materials used differs from the predetermined mix included in the calculation of the standard cost of an operation. If the mixture is varied so that a larger than expected proportion of a more *expensive* material is used there will be an *adverse* variance. When a larger than expected proportion of a *cheaper* material is included in the mix, then a *favourable* variance occurs.

The **material yield variance** arises when there is a difference between the standard output for a given level of input and the actual output attained. A materials yield variance is similar to a materials usage variance. However, instead of calculating a usage variance for each material separately, a single yield variance is calculated for all the materials as a whole. The yield variance is calculated first of all in terms of units of material, and is converted into a money value at the weighted average standard price per unit of material.

### Further details

#### The meaning of the mix variance

For materials and labour variances, a mix variance measures whether the actual mix that occurred was more or less expensive than the standard mix. For example, suppose that a product consists of two materials, X and Y, the standard mix of the two items is 50:50, and material X is much more expensive than material Y.

- If the actual mix used to make the product contains more than 50% of X and less than 50% of Y, the actual mix will be more expensive than the standard mix, because it includes a bigger-than-standard proportion of the expensive material. The mix variance will be adverse.

- Similarly, if the actual mix used to make the product contains less than 50% of X and more than 50% of Y, the actual mix will be less expensive than the standard mix, and the mix variance will be favourable.

#### The meaning of the yield variance

When a mix variance is calculated, it is assumed that the mix of materials or labour can be controlled.

- The material usage should therefore be assessed for all the materials combined, not for each item of material separately.

- Similarly, the labour efficiency variance should be assessed for the labour team as a whole, not for each grade of labour separately.

A yield variance is therefore an overall usage variance or efficiency variance for all the items in the mix.

## 12 Calculating Mix and Yield Variances

There are two different methods of calculating mix and yield variances mentioned in the syllabus – the individual units method and the weighted average method.

The individual units method is easier to calculate and understand (so you should use this in the exam if you have a choice).

Both methods produce exactly the same total figure for the mix variance; both methods compare the actual mix of materials with the standard mix.

- The actual mix = the actual quantities of materials used (for each material individually and in total).

- The standard mix = the actual total quantity of materials used, with the total divided between the individual materials in the standard proportions.

- The mix variance in units of material is the difference between the actual mix and the standard mix. A mix variance is calculated for each individual material in the mix.

### Mix variance - the individual method

(1) Write down the actual input. (This is the **actual mix**.)

(2) Take the actual input in total and push it down one line and then work it back in the standard proportions. (This is the **standard mix**.)

(3) Calculate the difference between the standard mix (line 2) and the actual mix (line 1). This is the mix variance in terms of physical quantities and must add up to zero in total. (If you use a higher than expected proportion of one material, you must use a lower than expected proportion of something else!)

(4) Multiply by the standard price per kg.

(5) This gives the mix variance in financial terms.

| | Material A | Material B | | Total |
|---|---|---|---|---|
| | Kg | Kg | | Kg |
| 1 Actual input | X | X | | XX |
| | | | | ⇓ |
| 2 Actual input in std proportions | X | X | ⇐ | XX |
| | — | — | | — |
| 3 Difference in quantity | X | X | | |
| 4 x Std Price | x X | x X | | |
| 5 Mix variance | X | X | | X |
| | — | — | | — |

### Mix variance - the weighted average method

The **weighted average method** is theoretically superior as it gives more meaningful variances at individual product/ingredient level compared to the individual units method. It is recommended by CIMA. The format is similar to that used for the individual units method, except that once the difference in quantity has been calculated, instead of multiplying by the individual material price, we multiply the difference between the individual price and the weighted average price.

### Example – Gin and Tonic

Company A's main product is a Gin and Tonic drink.

**Tonic** is relatively cheap and **gin** is relatively expensive. In December 2011, the company uses more tonic than the standard mix would suggest (and thus, less gin).

In the individual units method, the extra consumption of tonic would be shown as an **adverse** variance, which is incorrect, given that the use of more of the relatively cheap tonic has reduced the consumption of the relatively expensive gin within the overall mix - thus saving money overall. The weighted average method by contrast would show the extra use of tonic to be a good thing via a **favourable** variance.

### Yield variance

The yield variance only happens in total. CIMA and the examiner do not consider individual yield variances to be meaningful.

(1) Calculate the **standard yield**. This is the expected output from the actual input.

(2) Compare this to **actual yield**.

(3) The difference is the yield variance in physical terms.

(4) To express the variance in financial terms we multiply by the standard cost. One thing to be careful of however is that the yield variance considers outputs and so the standard cost is the standard cost per kg **of output.**

(5) This gives the yield variance in financial terms.

| | | Kg |
|---|---|---|
| 1 | Standard yield of actual input | X |
| 2 | Actual yield | X |
| | | — |
| 3 | | X |
| 4 | x std cost per kg of output | x X |
| | | — |
| | | X |
| | | — |

### Example 5

Company A produces a spray made by mixing three chemicals. The standard material cost details for 1 litre of this spray reads as follows:

| | $ |
|---|---|
| 0.4 litres of chemical A @ $30 per litre | 12.00 |
| 0.3 litres of chemical B @ $30 per litre | 9.00 |
| 0.5 litres of chemical C @ $15 per litre | 7.50 |
| | ——— |
| Standard material cost of 1 litre of spray | 28.50 |
| | ——— |

During the month, the company produced 1,000 litres of this spray using the following chemicals :

600 litres of chemical A
250 litres of chemical B
500 litres of chemical C

Calculate the **direct material mix** and the **direct material yield** variances.

The format of the **weighted average method** is similar to that used for the individual units method, except that once the difference in quantity has been calculated, instead of multiplying by the individual material price, we multiply by the difference between the individual price and the weighted average price.

Calculate the weighted average std cost of the materials. (This is needed for step 4). *You have to be very careful here. This weighted average is the weighted average cost per kg of input as we are just about to compare inputs.*

## Yield variance

The yield variance is calculated in the same way under both methods. Again it only happens in total.

### Using Mix and Yield Variances

Mix variances might be calculated when there is a mix of two or more items, and the mix is regarded as **controllable** by management.

- Two or more materials might be used in making a product or providing a service. If standard costing is used and the mix of the materials is seen as controllable, a materials mix variance and a materials yield variance can be calculated. These provide a further analysis of the materials usage variance.

- Two or more different types of labour might be used to make a product or provide a service. If standard costing is used and the labour mix in the team is seen as controllable, a labour mix variance and a labour yield variance can be calculated. These provide a further analysis of the labour efficiency variance.

It is also possible to calculate a sales mix variance, when a business sells more than one product or service, but these variances are not included in the syllabus, and are not described here.

If the mix cannot be controlled, it is inappropriate to calculate a mix and yield variance. Instead, a usage variance should be calculated for each individual material or an efficiency variance should be calculated for each individual type or grade of labour. *In other words, if the mix cannot be controlled, the usage or efficiency variance should not be analysed into a mix and yield variance.*

## 13 Direct labour variances

This section has four variances. The direct labour total cost variance, which shows the impact of any overall change in the amount spent on labour, and this can also be split into two further components – the labour rate and labour efficiency variances. In some scenarios we might also see a labour idle time variance.

### Direct labour total cost variance

The difference between:

(a) the standard direct labour cost of the actual production and

(b) the actual cost of direct labour.

### Proforma

**Direct labour cost**

|  |  | $ |
|---|---|---|
| Actual quantity of output | should cost (standard) | X |
|  | did cost | Y |
| Total cost variance |  | X–Y |

A total labour variance can also be analysed further. It can be analysed into two sub-variances:

(1) a Direct Labour Rate variance, i.e. paying more or less than expected per hour for labour and

(2) a Direct Labour Efficiency variance, i.e. using more or less labour per unit than expected.

## Direct labour rate variance

The difference between:

(a) standard rate per hour and the

(b) actual rate per hour

multiplied by the actual hours that were paid for.

### Proforma

**Direct labour rate variance**

|  |  | $ |
|---|---|---|
| Number of hours paid | should cost / hr (standard) | X |
|  | did cost (actual) | Y |
| Direct labour rate variance |  | X–Y |

### Direct labour efficiency variance

The difference between:

(a)  the standard hours specified for the actual production and

(b)  the actual hours worked

   multiplied by the standard hourly rate.

---

**Proforma**

*Direct labour efficiency variance:*

|  |  | Hours |
|---|---|---|
| Actual output produced | should take (standard hours) | X |
|  | did take (actual hours) | Y |
| Direct labour efficiency variance | (in hours) | X–Y |
| x standard rate per hour |  | $P |
| Direct labour efficiency variance |  | $P x (X – Y) |

---

**Example 6**

Ivan Korshunov Ltd makes a single product and has the following budgeted/standard information:

| Budgeted production | 1,000 units |
|---|---|
| Labour hours per unit | 3 |
| Labour rate per hour | $8 |

Actual results:

| Output | 1,100 units |
|---|---|
| Hours paid for and worked | 3,400 hours |
| Labour cost | $28,300 |

Calculate rate and efficiency variances for labour.

## Another method

Using the same example, calculate appropriate variances for labour using the following format:

$$
\left.
\begin{array}{l}
\text{SHSR} \\
\\
\text{AHSR} \\
\\
\text{AHAR}
\end{array}
\right\}
$$

Efficiency variance  }
Rate variance

} Total variance

| Where | SH | means Standard Hours |
|---|---|---|
| | SR | means Standard Rate |
| | AH | means Actual Hours |
| and | AR | means Actual Rate |

Standard Hours means the standard hours of the actual output.

(this assumes that there is no idle time)

|  |  |  |  |  | $ |  |
|---|---|---|---|---|---|---|
| SHSR | 3 hrs/unit x 1,100 units | x | $8/hr | = | 26,400 | Efficiency $800 A |
| AHSR | 3,400 hrs | x | $8/hr | = | 27,200 | |
| AHAR | | | | = | 28,300 | $1,100 A Rate |

## Idle time and idle time variances

The purpose of an efficiency variance should be to measure the efficiency of the work force in the time they are actively engaged in making products or delivering a service. During a period, there might be idle time, when the work force is not doing any work at all.

When idle time occurs, and if it is recorded, the efficiency variance should be separated into two parts:

• an idle time variance

• an efficiency variance during active working hours.

If there is no standard idle time set, then **the idle time variance is always adverse**, because it represents money 'wasted'. In some organisations a standard level of idle time may be set. If actual idle time is greater than standard then the variance is adverse; if it is less than standard then it would be favourable.

## Illustration 1

A product has a standard direct labour cost of $15, consisting of 1.5 hours of work for each unit at a cost of $10 per hour. During April, 100 units were produced. The direct labour workers were paid $2,000 for 160 hours of attendance, but the idle time records show that 30 hours in the month were recorded as idle time.

(a) We can record an idle time variance of 30 hours (A). This is costed at the standard rate per hour, $10, to give an idle time variance of $300(A).

(b) The efficiency variance should then be calculated using the active hours worked, not the total hours paid for.

**Direct labour efficiency variance**

|  |  | Hours |
|---|---|---|
| Actual output produced | should take (standard hours) | |
| 100 units | 1.5 hrs per unit | 150 |
| | did take (160hrs – 30hrs) | 130 |
| Direct labour efficiency variance (in hours) | | 20 F |
| x standard rate per hour | | $10/ hr |
| Direct labour efficiency variance | | $200 F |

## Example 7

Melanie Mitchell Ltd makes a single product with the following information:

**Budget/Standard**

| Output | 1,000 units |
|---|---|
| Hours | 6,000 |
| Labour cost | $42,000 |

**Actual**

| Output | 900 units |
|---|---|
| Hours paid | 5,500 |
| Hours worked | 5,200 |
| Labour cost | $39,100 |

Calculate appropriate variances for labour

## Expected idle time

Some organisations may experience idle time on a regular basis. For example, if demand is seasonal or irregular, but the organisation wishes to maintain and pay a constant number of workers, they will experience a certain level of 'expected' or 'normal' idle time during less busy periods. In this situation the standard labour rate may include an allowance for the cost of the expected idle time. Only the impact of any unexpected or abnormal idle time would be included in the idle time variance.

### Example

IT plc experiences seasonal demand for its product. During the next period the company expects that there will be an average level of idle time equivalent to 20% of hours paid. This is incorporated into the company's standard labour rate, which is $9 per hour before the adjustment for idle time payments.

The standard time to produce one unit of output is 3 active (productive) hours.

Actual results for the period were as follows:

| | |
|---|---:|
| Number of units produced | 3,263 |
| Actual hours paid for | 14,000 |
| Actual active (productive) hours | 10,304 |

### Required:

Calculate the following variances for the period:

(i)  the idle time variance;

(ii) the labour efficiency variance.

### Solution:

The basic standard rate per hour must be increased to allow for the impact of the idle time:

Standard rate per hour worked $= \dfrac{\$9.00}{0.8} = \$11.25$

The variances can now be evaluated at this increased hourly rate.

*Idle time variance*

|  | Hours |
|---|---|
| Expected idle time = 20% x 14,000 hours paid | 2,800 |
| Actual idle time = 14,000 – 10,304 hours | 3,696 |
| Variance (hours) | 896 Adverse |
| Standard rate per hour worked | $11.25 |
| Idle time variance | $10,080 Adverse |

*Labour efficiency variance*

|  | Hours |
|---|---|
| 3,263 units should have taken (x3) | 9,789 |
| But did take (productive hours) | 10,304 |
| Variance (hours) | 515 Adverse |
| Standard rate per hour worked | $11.25 |
| Labour efficiency variance | $5,794 Adverse |

## 14 Variable Overhead Variances

Variable overhead variances are similar to direct materials and direct labour cost variances.

- In standard product costing, a variable production overhead total cost variance can be calculated, and this can be analysed into an expenditure or rate variance and an efficiency variance.

- With service costing, a variable overhead total cost variance can be calculated, but this might not be analysed any further.

Since variable production overheads are assumed to vary with labour hours worked, labour hours are used in calculations. This means, for example, that the variable production overhead efficiency variance uses exactly the same hours as the direct labour efficiency variance.

## Details on the variances

### Variable production overhead total cost variance

The difference between:

(a) the standard variable overhead cost of the actual production and

(b) the actual cost of variable production overheads.

**Variable production overhead cost**

|  |  | $ |
|---|---|---|
| Actual quantity of output | should cost (standard) | X |
|  | did cost | Y |
| Total cost variance |  | X–Y |

A total variable production overhead variance can also be analysed further. It can be analysed into two sub-variances:

(1) a variable overhead expenditure variance, i.e. paying more or less than expected per hour for variable overheads and

(2) a variable overhead efficiency variance, i.e. using more or less variable overheads per unit than expected.

### Variable production overhead expenditure variance

|  |  | $ |
|---|---|---|
| Number of hours worked | should cost/hr (standard) | X |
|  | did cost (actual) | Y |
| Variable production overhead expenditure variance |  | X–Y |

### Variable production overhead efficiency variance

|  |  | Hours |
|---|---|---|
| Actual output produced | should take (standard hours) | X |
|  | did take (actual hours) | Y |
| Efficiency variance | (in hours) | X–Y |
| x standard variable overhead rate per hour |  | $P |
| Variable production overhead efficiency variance |  | $P x (X–Y) |

### Example 8

The budgeted output for Kathryn Bennett Ltd for May was 1,000 units of product A. Each unit requires 2 direct labour hours. Variable overheads are budgeted at $3/labour hour.

Actual results:

| Output | 900 units |
|---|---|
| Labour hours worked | 1,980 hours |
| Variable overheads | $5,544 |

Calculate appropriate variances for variable overheads.

### Example 9

Extracts from the standard cost of a product are as follows:

|  |  | $/unit |
|---|---|---|
| Direct labour | 2 hours x $ 15/hour | 30 |
| Variable production overhead | 2 hours x $ 4/hour | 8 |

During May, 200 units were produced. The direct labour workers were paid $6,600 for 440 hours of work, but the idle time records show that 20 hours in the month were recorded as idle time. Actual variable production overhead expenditure incurred was $1,530.

Calculate the labour and variable overhead variances.

## 15 Fixed Overhead Cost Variances

### Fixed overhead total variance

In standard absorption costing, the total cost variance for fixed production overhead variances is the amount of over-absorbed or under-absorbed overhead. Over-absorbed overhead is a favourable variance, and under-absorbed overhead is an adverse variance.

The amount of overhead absorbed for each unit of output is the standard fixed overhead cost per unit. The total cost variance is therefore calculated as follows:

The difference between:

(a)  the standard fixed overhead cost of the actual production and

(b)  the actual fixed overheads incurred

| Proforma |
|---|

**Fixed production overhead total cost variance**

|  | $ |
|---|---|
| Overheads absorbed  (Actual output x standard fixed cost per unit) | X |
| Actual fixed overhead incurred | Y |
| | |
| Fixed production overhead total cost variance | X–Y |

The total fixed overhead variance can be split as follows :

Total fixed overhead variance

Fixed overhead expenditure variance

– Did the fixed overhead cost more or less than expected?

Fixed overhead volume variance

– Did the organisation absorb more or less overhead than expected?

– Can be split further into:

Fixed overhead capacity variance

– Did employees work more or less hours than expected?

Fixed overhead efficiency variance

– Did employees work faster or slower than expected?

## Marginal Costing System

With marginal costing profit and loss, no overheads are absorbed, the amount spent is simply written off to the income statement.

So with marginal costing, the only fixed overhead variance is the difference between what was budgeted to be spent and what was actually spent, i.e. the fixed overhead expenditure variance.

## Absorption Costing System

Under absorption costing we use an overhead absorption rate to absorb overheads. Variances will occur if this absorption rate is incorrect (just as we will get over/under absorption).

So, with absorption costing, we calculate the fixed overhead expenditure variance and the fixed overhead volume variance (this can be split into a capacity and efficiency variance).

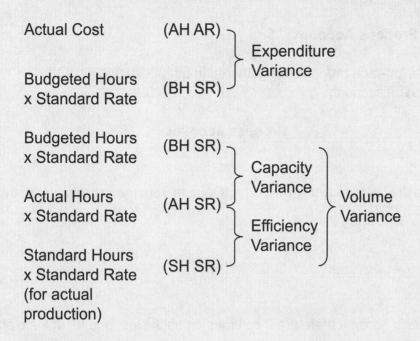

## 16 Process Costing

Process costing is used in those industries where the end products are more or less identical and where goods and services result from a sequence of **continuous or repetitive operations** or processes to which costs are charged before being averaged over the output produced during the period.

In a process costing industry production moves from one process to the next until final completion occurs. Each production department performs some part of the total operation and transfers its completed production to the next department where it becomes the input for further processing. The completed production of the last department is transferred to the finished goods inventory.

Process costing differs from **job and batch costing** in that the product is not customer specific and the range of products available is likely to be limited, but it is likely that the customer base will be large.

## 17 The Process Account

The costs for each process are gathered in a process account. This is shown as a T account:

<table>
<tr><th colspan="2" align="center">Process account</th></tr>
<tr>
<td>Inputs to the process are shown on this side (debit)</td>
<td>Outputs from the process are shown on this side (credit)</td>
</tr>
</table>

In a process account there are 2 columns on each side, one for volume and one for cost:

<table>
<tr><td></td><td align="right">kg</td><td>$</td><td></td><td align="right">kg</td><td>$</td></tr>
</table>

The purpose of the process account is to gather all of the information for the process together and calculate the cost per unit. The cost per unit can be calculated as:

$$\frac{\textbf{Total input costs}}{\textbf{Output units}}$$

Note: this basic calculation will change as we add some complications to the process account.

## Illustration 2

A company operates 2 processes, the output of process 1 is transferred to process 2 and the output of process 2 is the final product. Details for June are given:

|  | Process 1 | Process 2 |
|---|---|---|
| Direct materials | $10,000 | $9,500 |
| Direct Labour | $15,000 | $7,500 |
| Production Overheads | $12,000 | $6,000 |
|  |  |  |
| Input quantity | 1,000 kg | 500 kg |
| Output quantity | 1,000 kg | 1,500 kg |

Complete the process accounts for process 1 and 2 for June.

**Solution:**

**Step 1:** set up the process account, and input all the information available from the question:

**Process 1**

|  | Kg | $ |  | Kg | $ |
|---|---|---|---|---|---|
| Material | 1,000 | 10,000 | Output * | 1,000 |  |
| Labour |  | 15,000 |  |  |  |
| Overhead |  | 12,000 |  |  |  |

* the output of process 1 is the amount transferred to process 2

45

**Step 2:** balance the quantity column, ensure that both sides agree:

### Process 1

|          | Kg    | $      |        | Kg    | $ |
|----------|-------|--------|--------|-------|---|
| Material | 1,000 | 10,000 | Output | 1,000 |   |
| Labour   |       | 15,000 |        |       |   |
| Overhead |       | 12,000 |        |       |   |
|          | 1,000 |        |        | 1,000 |   |

**Step 3**: calculate the cost per unit and value the output:

Total input costs
───────────────
Output units

= (10,000 + 15,000 + 12,000) / 1,000 = $37

So the value of the output = $37 x 1,000 = **$37,000**

**Step 4:** finally balance the $ column.

### Process 1

|          | Kg    | $      |        | Kg    | $      |
|----------|-------|--------|--------|-------|--------|
| Material | 1,000 | 10,000 | Output | 1,000 | 37,000 |
| Labour   |       | 15,000 |        |       |        |
| Overhead |       | 12,000 |        |       |        |
|          | 1,000 | 37,000 |        | 1,000 | 37,000 |

Repeat the steps for process 2, remembering to include the transfer from process 1:

**Process 2**

|  | Kg | $ |  | Kg | $ |
|---|---|---|---|---|---|
| From Process 1 | 1,000 | 37,000 | Output | 1,500 | 60,000 |
| Material | 500 | 9,500 |  |  |  |
| Labour |  | 7,500 |  |  |  |
| Overhead |  | 6,000 |  |  |  |
|  | 1,500 | 60,000 |  | 1,500 | 60,000 |

The unit cost in process 2 is: 60,000/1,500 = **$40.**
So the value of the output = $40 x 1,500 = **$60,000**

### Test Your Understanding 1

During August a processing company incurred the following costs in its three processes:

|  | Process 1 $ | Process 2 $ | Process 3 $ |
|---|---|---|---|
| Direct materials | 6,000 | 4,000 | 9,000 |
| Direct labour | 1,000 | 2,000 | 3,000 |
| Direct expenses | 2,000 | 3,000 | 4,000 |
| Production overhead | 1,000 | 2,000 | 3,000 |

The quantities of input and output were as follows:

|  | Process 1 kg | Process 2 kg | Process 3 kg |
|---|---|---|---|
| Input | 500 | 200 | 300 |
| Output | 500 | 700 | 1,000 |

The input quantities shown above do not include the output from the previous process. The output from process 1 is transferred to process 2, which in turn transfers its output to process 3 which after further processing results in the final product.

**Required:**

Show the process accounts.

**18 Normal Loss**

Certain losses are inherent in the production process and cannot be eliminated, e.g. liquids may evaporate, part of the cloth cut to make a suit may be lost. These losses occur under efficient working conditions and are expected. They are known as normal losses and are often expressed as a percentage of the input.

Normal loss may have a small value, known as scrap value, if it can be sold. From the above examples, the offcuts of cloth from the suit manufacturer may be sold, but clearly the loss from evaporation could have no value.

Normal loss is shown on the credit side of the process account, it will have a quantity entry and may have a $ entry if it has a scrap value:

**Process 1**

|  | kg | $ |  | kg | $ |
|---|---|---|---|---|---|
| Materials |  |  | Output |  |  |
| Labour |  |  | NORMAL LOSS |  |  |
| Expenses |  |  |  |  |  |
| Overheads |  |  |  |  |  |

We have to change the unit cost formula to take account of the normal loss:

$$\text{Unit Cost} = \frac{\textbf{Total input costs} - \textbf{scrap value of normal loss}}{\textbf{Expected output}}$$

The expected output can be calculated as the input units less normal loss units

---

**Normal Loss – Illustration**

A company operates a single process. The costs of the process are as follows:

|  | Process 1 $ |
|---|---|
| Direct materials | 6,000 |
| Direct labour | 1,000 |
| Production overhead | 3,000 |

The input quantity was 500 kg and the expected or normal loss was 10 per cent of input. Actual output was 450 kg. Show the process account.

**Solution:**

**Step 1:** set up the process account, and input all the information available from the question:

|  | Process 1 | | | | | |
|---|---|---|---|---|---|---|
|  | Kg | $ |  | Kg | $ |
| Material | 500 | 6,000 | Output | 450 | |
| Labour | | 1,000 | Normal loss | 50 | 0 |
| Overhead | | 3,000 | | | |

**Step 2:** balance the quantity column, ensure that both sides agree:

|  | Process 1 | | | | | |
|---|---|---|---|---|---|---|
|  | Kg | $ |  | Kg | $ |
| Material | 500 | 6,000 | Output | 450 | |
| Labour | | 1,000 | Normal loss | 50 | 0 |
| Overhead | | 3,000 | | | |
| | 500 | | | 500 | |

**Step 3**: calculate the cost per unit and value the output:

$$\text{Unit Cost} = \frac{\text{Total input costs} - \text{scrap value of normal loss}}{\text{Expected output}}$$

= (6,000 + 1,000 + 3,000) / 450 = $22.22

So the value of the output = $22.22 x 450 = **$10,000**

**Step 4: finally balance the $ column.**

### Process 1

| | Kg | $ | | Kg | $ |
|---|---|---|---|---|---|
| Material | 500 | 6,000 | Output | 450 | 10,000 |
| Labour | | 1,000 | Normal loss | 50 | 0 |
| Overhead | | 3,000 | | | |
| | 500 | 10,000 | | 1,000 | 10,000 |

Look at the previous example again, but this time assume the scrap can be sold for $5 per kg.

The normal loss will be shown with a value of $5 x 50 = $250.

### Process 1

| | Kg | $ | | Kg | $ |
|---|---|---|---|---|---|
| Material | 500 | 6,000 | Output | 450 | |
| Labour | | 1,000 | Normal loss | 50 | 250 |
| Overhead | | 3,000 | | | |
| | 500 | | | 500 | |

When we calculate the cost per unit this time, we must remember to deduct the scrap value from the input costs.

**Unit Cost =** $\dfrac{\textbf{Total input costs – scrap value of normal loss}}{\textbf{Expected output}}$

= (10,000 – 250) / 450 = $21.67

So the value of the output = $21.67 x 450 = $9,750

### Process 1

| | Kg | $ | | Kg | $ |
|---|---|---|---|---|---|
| Material | 500 | 6,000 | Output | 450 | 9,750 |
| Labour | | 1,000 | Normal loss | 50 | 250 |
| Overhead | | 3,000 | | | |
| | 500 | 10,000 | | 1,000 | 10,000 |

The double entry for the normal loss is usually made in a scrap account. Note the scrap account is balanced off to receivables/cash.

### Scrap account

| | Kg | $ | | $ |
|---|---|---|---|---|
| Process 1 – normal loss | 50 | 250 | Receivable/cash | 250 |

### Test Your Understanding 2

NB Ltd manufactures paint in a 2-stage process. The normal loss in process 1 is 10% of input and can be sold for $2/kg. The following costs were incurred in May:

Materials 1,000 kg at $4.30/kg
Labour  500 hours @ $6/hour
Overheads are absorbed at $2/labour hour

Losses were at the normal level.

**Required:**

(a)  Show the process account

(b)  What is the cost/kg?

## 19 Abnormal Losses and Gains

We have seen that the normal loss is an estimate of the loss expected to occur in a particular process. This estimate may be incorrect and a different amount of loss may occur.

> If the actual loss is greater than the normal loss then the excess loss is referred to as an abnormal loss.

> If the actual loss is less than the normal loss then the difference is referred to as an abnormal gain.

### Example: input 10,000kg, normal loss 10%

*If the actual loss is 1,200 kg – normal loss 1,000 kg and abnormal loss 200 kg*

Abnormal losses are shown on the credit side of the process account:

Process 1

| | Kg | $ | | Kg | $ |
|---|---|---|---|---|---|
| Materials | | | Output | | |
| Labour | | | Normal loss | 1,000 | |
| Overheads | | | ABNORMAL LOSS | 200 | |

*If the actual loss is 900 kg – normal loss 1,000 kg and abnormal gain 100 kg*

Abnormal gains are shown on the debit side of the process account:

### Process 1

|  | Kg | $ |  | Kg | $ |
|---|---|---|---|---|---|
| Materials |  |  | Output |  |  |
| Labour |  |  | Normal loss | 1,000 |  |
| Overheads |  |  |  |  |  |
| ABNORMAL GAIN | 100 |  |  |  |  |

Abnormal losses and gains are treated differently from normal losses. In the process account, the normal loss is valued at scrap value, but the abnormal losses and gains are valued at the same rate as good output.

### Illustration 3

The following example illustrates the calculations and entries in the process account when an **abnormal loss** occurs.

#### Example

| | |
|---|---|
| Input 500 kg of materials costing | $6,000 |
| Labour cost | $1,000 |
| Expenses cost | $2,000 |
| Overhead cost | $1,000 |

Normal loss is estimated to be 10 per cent of input.
Losses may be sold as scrap for $5 per kg.
Actual output was 430 kg.

The process account is shown below.

Remember that, earlier in the chapter, we recommended that you should insert the units into the process account first, and then balance them off. In this example, this results in a balancing value on the credit side of 20 kg, which is the abnormal loss.

### Process account

| | Kg | $ | | Kg | $ |
|---|---|---|---|---|---|
| Materials | 500 | 6,000 | Output | 430 | 9,317 |
| Labour | | 1,000 | Normal loss | 50 | 250 |
| Expenses | | 2,000 | Abnormal loss | 20 | 433 |
| Overheads | | 1,000 | | | |
| | 500 | 10,000 | | 500 | 10,000 |

The valuation per kg is calculated as follows:

$$\frac{\text{Cost incurred} - \text{scrap value of normal loss}}{\text{Expected output}} = \frac{\$10,000 - \$250}{450} = \$21.67$$

The abnormal loss units are valued at the same rate per unit as the good output units, so the valuation are:

Output: 430 x $21.67 = $9,317

Abnormal loss: 20 x $21.67 = $433

The normal loss is valued at its scrap value only.

**Accounting for scrap**: The next step is to prepare the scrap and abnormal loss accounts. The normal loss is debited to the scrap account and the abnormal loss is debited to the abnormal loss account:

### Scrap account

| | $ | | $ |
|---|---|---|---|
| Process – normal loss | 250 | | |

### Abnormal loss account

| | $ | | $ |
|---|---|---|---|
| Process | 433 | | |
| | —— | | —— |
| | —— | | —— |

In reality the value of the abnormal loss is also scrap value, so we have to account for this. We show this by doing a double entry debiting the scrap account and crediting the abnormal loss account:

### Scrap account

| | $ | | $ |
|---|---|---|---|
| Process – normal loss | 250 | | |
| Abnormal loss transfer | 100 | | |
| | —— | | —— |
| | —— | | —— |

The scrap balance now represents the total of 70 kg scrapped, with a total scrap value of $350.

### Abnormal loss account

| | $ | | $ |
|---|---|---|---|
| Process | 433 | Scrap account: 20 × $5 | 100 |
| | —— | | —— |
| | —— | | —— |

The next step is to balance the scrap and the abnormal loss account. Note: the quantities are not required.

The scrap account is balanced to receivables/cash – this reflects the amount received from selling the scrap.

**Scrap account**

| | $ | | $ |
|---|---|---|---|
| Process – normal loss | 250 | Receivables/cash | 350 |
| Abnormal loss transfer | 100 | | |
| | 350 | | 350 |

The abnormal loss account is balanced to the income statement – this reflects the net cost of the excess loss (i.e. after deducting the scrap sales proceeds). It has now been highlighted separately for management attention, and the balance is transferred to the income statement as an expense.

**Abnormal loss account**

| | $ | | $ |
|---|---|---|---|
| Process | 433 | Scrap account: 20 × $5 | 100 |
| | | Income statement | 333 |
| | 433 | | 433 |

**Illustration 4**

If the actual loss is smaller than the amount expected, then an abnormal gain is said to have occurred. The abnormal gain is the extent to which the loss is smaller than expected. If we consider the same example again, except that the actual output achieved was 470 kg, we can see that the following process account results. Remember to balance the units column first. The normal loss is the same, because the input is the same.

**Process account**

|  | kg | $ |  | kg | $ |
|---|---|---|---|---|---|
| Materials | 500 | 6,000 | Output | 470 | 10,183 |
| Labour |  | 1,000 |  |  |  |
| Expenses |  | 2,000 | Normal loss | 50 | 250 |
| Overheads |  | 1,000 |  |  |  |
| Abnormal gain | 20 | 433 |  |  |  |
|  | 520 | 10,433 |  | 520 | 10,433 |

Note that the balancing value in the quantity column is now on the debit side. It represents the abnormal gain. The calculation of the cost per unit remains the same, but now there is an additional entry on the debit side.

**Accounting for scrap:** When we account for the scrap in this case, we need an abnormal gain account:

The normal loss is debited to the scrap account as before, but the abnormal gain has been debited to the process account, so the double entry is to credit the abnormal gain to the abnormal gain account.

As before, we do a double entry between the 2 accounts, this time we debit the abnormal gain account and credit the scrap account:

**Abnormal gain account**

|  | $ |  | $ |
|---|---|---|---|
| Scrap account: 20 × $5 | 100 | Process | 433 |

Balance the scrap and the abnormal gain account.

The scrap account is balanced to receivables/cash – this reflects the amount received from selling the scrap.

The abnormal gain account is balanced to the income statement – this reflects the net gain from the lower than expected process loss. It will be shown as an income in the income statement.

**Scrap account**

| | $ | | $ |
|---|---|---|---|
| Process – normal loss | 250 | Abnormal gain transfer | 100 |
| | | Receivables/cash | 150 |
| | 250 | | 250 |

**Abnormal gain account**

| | $ | | $ |
|---|---|---|---|
| Scrap account: 20 × $5 | 100 | Process | 433 |
| Income statement | 333 | | |
| | 433 | | 433 |

### Test Your Understanding 3

A company operates a single process, Details for November are given:

| | |
|---|---|
| Direct materials | $8,500 |
| Direct Labour | $2,500 |
| Direct Expenses | $7,000 |
| Production Overheads | $7,800 |

Input quantity 1,200 kg
Output quantity 1,000 kg

Normal loss (scrap value = $3.50/kg) 10% of input

**Required:**

Complete the process account for November and the scrap and abnormal gain or loss account.

### Test Your Understanding 4

Amy Archer Ltd makes a chemical ABC in a three stage manufacturing process. The details for process 3 are as follows:

| | |
|---|---|
| Transferred from process 2 | 200 litres at a value of $510 |
| Material | 500 litres at $3.10/litre |
| Labour | 300 hours at $6/hour |
| Overheads | absorbed at 133⅓% of direct labour cost |
| Normal loss | 5% of input |
| | lost units have a scrap value of $2/unit |
| Output | 590 litres |

Show the process account, abnormal loss or gain account and the scrap/normal loss account.

## 20 Closing Work-In-Progress: Concept of Equivalent Units

To calculate a unit cost of production, it is necessary to know how many units were produced in the period. In any given accounting period there are likely to be partially completed units, we call this **work in progress (WIP).**

We have closing WIP at the end of the accounting period. This closing WIP is carried forward to the next accounting period as opening WIP.

Opening WIP and closing WIP are the final two entries in our process account. Opening WIP is shown as a debit and closing WIP is shown as a credit. The following shows all the potential entries in a process account:

**Process 1**

| | kg | $ | | kg | $ |
|---|---|---|---|---|---|
| OPENING WIP | | | | | |
| Materials | | | Output | | |
| Labour | | | Normal loss | | |
| Overheads | | | Abnormal loss * | | |
| Abnormal gain * | | | CLOSING WIP | | |

* Remember a process account can only have either an abnormal loss OR an abnormal gain, it can never have both.

If some units were only partly processed at the end of the period, then these must be taken into account in the calculation of production output. The concept of equivalent units provides a basis for doing this. The work in progress (the partly finished units) is expressed in terms of how many equivalent complete units it represents. For example, if there are 500 units in progress which are 25 per cent complete, these units would be treated as the equivalent of 500 x 25% = 125 complete units.

A further complication arises if the work in progress has reached different degrees of completion in respect of each cost element. For example, you might stop the process of cooking a casserole just as you were about to put the dish in the oven. The casserole would probably be complete in respect of ingredients, almost complete in respect of labour, but most of the overhead cost would be still to come in terms of the cost of the power to cook the casserole.

It is common in many processes for the materials to be added in full at the start of processing and for them to be converted into the final product by the actions of labour and related overhead costs. For this reason, labour and overhead costs are often referred to as **conversion costs**.

Conversion cost is the 'cost of converting material into finished product, typically including direct labour, direct expense and production overhead'. *CIMA Terminology*

To overcome the problem of costs being incurred at different stages in the process, a separate equivalent units calculation is performed for each cost element.

## Illustration 5

| | |
|---|---|
| Input materials | 1,000 kg @ $9 per kg |
| Labour cost | $4,800 |
| Overhead cost | $5,580 |
| Outputs | Finished goods: 900 kg |
| | Closing work in progress: 100 kg |

The work in progress is completed:

100% as to material
60% as to labour
30% as to overhead

For simplicity, losses have been ignored.

Now that you are beginning to learn about more complications in process costing, this is a good point to get into the habit of producing an input/output reconciliation as the first stage in your workings. This could be done within the process account, by balancing off the quantity columns in the way that we have done so far in this chapter. However, with more complex examples it is better to have total quantity columns in your working paper and do the 'balancing off' there.

In the workings table which follows, the first stage is to balance the input and output quantities, that is, check that the total kg input is equal to the total kg output. Then, each part of the output can be analysed to show how many equivalent kg of each cost element it represents.

|  |  |  |  | Equivalent kg to absorb cost | | |
| --- | --- | --- | --- | --- | --- | --- |
| *Input* | *kg* | *Output* | *kg* | *Materials* | *Labour* | *Overhead* |
| Materials | 1,000 | Finished goods | 900 | (100%) 900 | (100%) 900 | (100%) 900 |
|  |  | Closing WIP | 100 | (100%) 100 | (60%) 60 | (30%) 30 |
|  | 1,000 |  | 1,000 | 1,000 | 960 | 930 |
|  |  | Costs |  | $9,000 | $4,800 | $5,580 |
|  |  | Cost/eq. unit |  | $9 | $5 | $6 |

For the equivalent unit calculations there is a separate column for each cost element. The number of equivalent units is found by multiplying the percentage completion by the number of kg in progress. For example, equivalent kg of labour in progress is 100 kg × 60% = 60 equivalent kg.

The number of equivalent units is then totalled for each cost element and a cost per equivalent unit is calculated.

These costs per equivalent unit are then used to value the finished output and the closing work in progress.

The process account is shown below, together with the calculation of the value of the closing work in progress. Note that this method may be used to value the finished output, but it is easier to total the equivalent unit costs ($9 + $5 + $6) and use the total cost of $20 multiplied by the finished output of 900 kg.

| *Closing WIP valuation* | | $ |
|---|---|---|
| Materials | 100 equivalent units × $9 | 900 |
| Labour | 60 equivalent units × $5 | 300 |
| Overheads | 30 equivalent units × $6 | 180 |
| | | ───── |
| | | 1,380 |
| | | ───── |

### Process account

| | kg | $ | | kg | $ |
|---|---|---|---|---|---|
| Materials | 1,000 | 9,000 | Finished goods | 900 | 18,000 |
| Labour | | 4,800 | WIP | 100 | 1,380 |
| Overheads | | 5,580 | | | |
| | ───── | ───── | | ───── | ───── |
| | 1,000 | 19,380 | | 1,000 | 19,380 |
| | ───── | ───── | | ───── | ───── |

### Supplementary reading – Previous process costs

A common problem that students experience when studying process costing is understanding how to deal with previous process costs. An important point that you should have grasped by now is that production passes through a number of sequential processes. Unless the process is the last in the series, the output of one process becomes the input of the next. A common mistake is to forget to include the previous process cost as an input cost in the subsequent process.

You should also realise that all of the costs of the previous process (materials, labour and overhead) are combined together as a single cost of 'input material' or 'previous process costs' in the subsequent process.

We assumed that the work in progress must be 100 per cent complete in respect of Process 1 costs. This is also an important point to grasp. Even if the process 2 work had only just begun on these units, there cannot now be any more cost to add in respect of process 1. Otherwise the units would not yet have been transferred out of process 1 into process 2.

## 21 Opening Work-In-Progress

Opening work in progress consists of incomplete units in process at the beginning of the period. Your syllabus requires you to know how to value work in progress using the **average cost method**. With this method, opening work in progress is treated as follows:

(1)  The opening work in progress is listed as an additional part of the input to the process for the period.

(2)  The cost of the opening WIP is added to the costs incurred in the period.

(3)  The cost per equivalent unit of each cost element is calculated as before, and this is used to value each part of the output. The output value is based on the average cost per equivalent unit, hence the name of this method.

## 22 Investment Appraisal Methods

To appraise a potential capital project:

*  Estimate the costs and benefits from the investment

*  Select an appraisal method

*  Use the appraisal method to ascertain if the investment is financially worthwhile

*  Decide to go ahead with the project

It is important to note that the costs and benefits from the investment are estimates. Many take place in the future and many assumptions are made in calculating these figures. The costs and benefits for the investment are called **cash flows**. Remember that all the rules of relevant cost apply to investment decision, only **relevant cash flows** should be used. To recap the main relevant cost rules:

*  Sunk costs should be ignored

*  Only incremental costs should be included (i.e. those which will change as a result of the decision)

*  Non cash flows are excluded. (including depreciation, provisions or allocated fixed costs)

*  Opportunity costs should be included

## Appraisal methods

There are a number of appraisal methods which are used to assess how financially worthwhile investments are. The three techniques covered in this paper are:

- Payback
- Net present value (NPV)
- Internal rate of return (IRR)

Each of the methods uses a different calculation, it is important to know how to do each of the calculations, and the decision rule used in each. The different methods can give different answers. In practice, most organisations use more than one appraisal method.

Based on the decision rule of the method used, a decision can be made as to whether the investment is financially worthwhile, although there will be other, non financial considerations which must also be taken into account.

## 23 Payback

The payback technique considers the time a project will take to pay back the money invested in it. It is based on expected cash flows. To use the payback technique a company must set a **target payback period**.

### Decision criteria

- Compare the payback period to the company's target return time and if the payback for the project is quicker the project should be accepted.
- Faced with mutually exclusive projects choose the project with the quickest payback.

### Calculation constant annual cash flows

$$\textbf{Payback period} = \frac{\textbf{Initial investment}}{\textbf{Annual cash flow}}$$

### Test Your Understanding 5

An investment of $1 million is expected to generate net cash inflows of $200,000 each year for the next 7 years.

Calculate the payback period for the project.

A payback period may not be for an exact number of years. The payback period is usually given in years and months. To calculate the payback in years and months you should multiply the decimal fraction of a year by 12 to calculate the number of months.

**Example:**

A project will cost $300,000. The annual cash flows are estimated at $90,000 per annum. Calculate the payback period.

Payback period = initial investment/annual cash flow

$$= 300,000/90,000 = 3.33 \text{ years}$$

In years and months: 3 years plus (0.33 x 12) = 3 years 4 months.

**Calculation – uneven annual cash flows**

However, if cash inflows are uneven (a more likely state of affairs), the payback has to be calculated by working out the cumulative cash flow over the life of a project.

### Illustration 6

KLJ are considering purchasing a new machine. The machine will cost $550,000. The management accountant of KLJ has estimated the following additional cash flows will be received over the next 6 years if the new machine is purchased:

Year 1: $40,000
Year 2: $65,000
Year 3: $140,000
Year 4: $175,000
Year 5: $140,000
Year 6: $70,000

KLJ have a target payback period of 4 years. Calculate the payback period for the new machine and advise KLJ whether or not to proceed with the investment.

**Solution:**

**Note the investment is shown as year 0**. We treat year 0 as today and assume that the investment is made today. Show the initial investment as a negative cash flow for year 0. Work out the cumulative cash flow for each year until the cash flow becomes positive. This will highlight when payback has been achieved.

| Year | Cash flow | Cumulative cash flow |
|---|---|---|
| | $000 | $000 |
| 0 | (550) | (550) |
| 1 | 40 | (510) |
| 2 | 65 | (445) |
| 3 | 140 | (305) |
| 4 | 175 | (130) |
| 5 | 140 | 10 |
| 6 | 70 | 80 |

You can see that payback is achieved between years 4 and 5. Again we show the payback in years and months. To calculate the months, go to the year where the cumulative cash flow becomes positive, take the cumulated cash flow from the previous year divided by the cash flow in the year. As before multiply this by 12 to get the answer in months.

Here the cumulative cash flow becomes positive in year 5, so payback is 4 years plus (130/140 x 12) months = 4 years 11 months.

KLJ have a target payback period of 4 years. The payback is after this target, so the advice to KLJ would be to **not undertake the investment.**

### Test Your Understanding 6

Abbly Machines (AM) are considering making an investment of $1.2m on launching a new product. They have undertaken some market research and have estimated that the new product could generate the following cash flows:

Year 1: $140,000
Year 2: $265,000
Year 3: $340,000
Year 4: $560,000
Year 5: $290,000

AM require payback within 4 years. Advise if they should go ahead with the investment.

### Test Your Understanding 7

Snocold Limited (SL) are considering two projects. Both cost $450,000 and only one may be undertaken. SL use the payback method for appraising investments and require payback within three years.

The details of the cash flows for the two projects are given:

| Year | Project A | Project B |
|------|----------:|----------:|
|      | $000 | $000 |
| 1 | 200 | 50 |
| 2 | 150 | 120 |
| 3 | 100 | 190 |
| 4 | 50 | 310 |
| 5 | 20 | 260 |

Advise SL which project they should undertake.

### Advantages and disadvantages of payback

| Advantages | Disadvantages |
|------------|---------------|
| • Simple to understand | • It is not a measure of absolute profitability |
| • A project with a long payback period tends to be riskier than one with a short payback period. Payback is a simple measure of risk. | • Ignores the time value of money. That is it assumes that $100 received in year 5 would be worth the same as $100 received in year 1. We will look at this in more detail later in the chapter. |
| • Uses cash flows, not subjective accounting profits | • Does not take account of cash flows beyond the payback period. |
| • Emphasises the cash flows in the earlier years | |
| • A company selecting projects on the basis of payback may avoid liquidity problems | |

## 24 Time Value of Money

One characteristic of all capital expenditure projects is that the cash flows arise over the long term (a period usually greater than 12 months). Under this situation it becomes necessary to carefully consider the time value of money.

Money received today is worth more than the same sum received in the future, i.e. it has a time value.

If you were offered $1,000 today or $1,000 in 2 years, you would select to receive the money now as you believe it is worth more.

Discounted cash flow (DCF) techniques take account of this time value of money when appraising investments.

Before looking at discounting, we have to firstly understand **compounding.**

A sum invested today will earn interest. Compounding calculates the future value of a given sum invested today for a number of years.

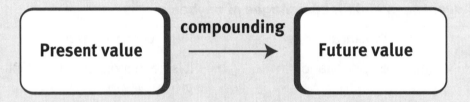

### Illustration 7

$100 is invested in an account for five years. The interest rate is 10% per annum. Find the value of the account after five years.

To compound a sum, the figure is increased by the amount of interest it would earn over the period.

If $100 is invested, by the end of the first year this will be worth:

Year 1: $100 + 10% = $110.

If the $110 is now invested for a further year, by the end of the 2nd year it will be worth:

Year 2: $110 + 10% = $121

If this is continued f or 5 years, at the end of 5 years it will be worth:

Year 3: $121 + 10% = $133.10
Year 4: $133.10 + 10% = $146.41
Year 5: $146.41 + 10% = $161.05

There is a formula to speed up this calculation:

## Formula for compounding

$$V = X(1 + r)^n$$

Where    V  =  Future value

          X  =  Initial investment (present value)

          r  =  Interest rate (expressed as a decimal)

          n  =  Number of time periods

In the above example:

$$V = X(1 + r)^n$$
$$= 100(1 + 0.1)^5$$
$$= \underline{\$161.05}$$

### Test Your Understanding 8

$5,000 is invested in an account earning 2.75% interest p.a. Calculate the fund value after 12 years.

### Test Your Understanding 9

$5,000 is invested for 10 years in an account earning 5% interest p.a. Calculate how much this will be worth at the end of the 10 years.

## 25 Discounting

Discounting performs the opposite function to compounding. Compounding finds the future value of a sum invested now, whereas discounting considers a sum receivable in the future and establishes its equivalent value today. This value in today's terms is known as the **Present Value (PV).**

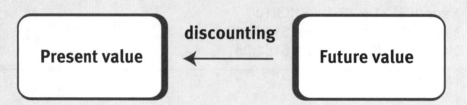

In potential investment projects, cash flows will arise at many different points in time. Calculating the present value of future cash flows will be a key technique in investment appraisal decisions.

### Formula for discounting

The formula is simply a rearrangement of the compounding formula:

$$\text{Present value} = \frac{\text{Future value}}{(1+r)^n}$$

It is also valuable to remember that:

Present value = Future value x discount factor                    **LEARN**

Where:        Discount factor $= \dfrac{1}{(1+r)^n}$   or   $(1+r)^{-n}$          **GIVEN**

where:        r is the interest rate expressed as decimal

              n is the number of time periods

---

### Illustration 8

How much should be invested now in order to have $250 in eight years' time? The account pays 12% interest per annum.

**Solution:**

present value = future value x discount factor

$= \$250 \times (1 + 0.12)^{-8}$
$= \$250 \times 0.404$
$= \$101$

$(1 + r)^{-n}$ can be looked up in discounting tables. It is known as the **discount factor.**

On the present value table, look along the top row for the interest rate (12%) and down the columns for the number of years (8), where the two intersect you can read off the discount factor (0.404).

*NOTE: at the top of the table, you are given the formula for calculating the discount factor.*

### Test Your Understanding 10

Find the present value of $2,000 receivable in six years' time, if the interest rate is 10% p.a.

### Test Your Understanding 11

How much would $40,000 receivable in 4 years time be worth in today's value, if the interest rate is 7%?

### Test Your Understanding 12

HJK Ltd can either receive $12,000 in 2 years time or $14,000 in 4 years time. The interest rate is 6%. Advise HJK which they should select.

**Interest rate**

In the above calculations we have referred to the rate of interest. There are a number of alternative terms used to refer to the rate a firm should use to take account of the time value of money:

- Cost of capital
- Discount rate
- Required return

Whatever term is used, the rate of interest used for discounting reflects the cost of the finance that will be tied up in the investment.

We can now move on to the investment appraisal methods which use discounting. Remember one of the criticisms of payback was that it did not take account of the time value of money.

The two methods which use discounted cash flow (DCF) techniques are:

- **Net Present Value (NPV)**
- **Internal Rate of Return (IRR)**

### 26 Net Present Value (NPV)

Discounting future cash flows into present value terms is extremely valuable when appraising financial investment opportunities.

Typically an investment opportunity will involve a significant capital outlay initially with cash benefits being received in the future for several years. To compare all these cash flows on an equitable basis (like with like) it is usual practice to convert all future cash flows into present values. Hence a net present value can be established.

The NPV represents the surplus funds (after funding the investment) earned on the project. This tells us the impact the project has on shareholder wealth.

### Decision criteria

- Any project with a positive NPV is viable – it will increase shareholder wealth
- Faced with mutually-exclusive projects, choose the project with the highest NPV.

**Illustration 9**

Consider the following cash flows for a project with an initial investment of $30,000.

| Year | Cash flow |
|------|-----------|
| 1 | $ 5,000 |
| 2 | $ 8,000 |
| 3 | $10,000 |
| 4 | $ 7,000 |
| 5 | $ 5,000 |

If we added up all of the cash flows, the total is $35,000. Given the initial investment of $30,000, it looks like the project has generated an additional $5,000. (total cash inflows less initial investment), but this assumes that the $5,000 received in year 5 is worth exactly the same as the $5,000 received in year 1. We know that this is not the case due to the time value of money. The technique used here – total cash inflows less initial investment is a sound one, but first we must discount all the cash flows back to the present value. Assume an interest rate of 10%.

When you have a number of cash flows to discount, it is easier to use a table to lay out your workings:

| Year | Cash flow ($) | Discount factor (10%) | Present value (future value x discount factor) |
|------|---------------|-----------------------|-----------------------------------------------|
| 0 | (30,000) | 1 | (30,000) |
| 1 | 5,000 | 0.909 | 4,545 |
| 2 | 8,000 | 0.826 | 6,608 |
| 3 | 10,000 | 0.751 | 7,510 |
| 4 | 7,000 | 0.683 | 4,781 |
| 5 | 5,000 | 0.621 | 3,105 |
| | | **NPV =** | **(3,451)** |

Note: the initial investment is shown as a negative in year zero. Year zero is today, so this figure is already in present day terms, therefore the discount factor in year zero is always 1.

We can now add the cash flows together as they are all in present value terms.

The present value of the total cash inflows less initial investment is called the Net Present Value (NPV)

In this example the NPV is negative $3,451. The decision rule is that projects with a positive NPV should be accepted and those with a negative NPV should be rejected, therefore in this case **the project should be rejected**.

### Test Your Understanding 13

A project requires an initial investment of $500,000. The following cash flows have been estimated for the life of the project:

| Year | Cash flow |
|------|-----------|
| 1 | $ 120,000 |
| 2 | $ 150,000 |
| 3 | $ 180,000 |
| 4 | $ 160,000 |

The company uses NPV to appraise projects. Using a discount rate of 7%, calculate the NPV of the project and recommend whether the project should be undertaken.

### Test Your Understanding 14

SH Company have decided to expand their manufacturing facility. The cost of this expansion will be $2.3m. Expected cash flows from the expansion are estimated as $600,000 for the first 2 years and $800,000 for the following 2 years. The company uses a discount rate of 5% when appraising investment projects. Calculate the NPV of the project and advise SH if they should go ahead with the expansion.

## Advantages and disadvantages of NPV

| Advantages | Disadvantages |
|------------|---------------|
| • Considers the time value of money | • Fairly complex |
| • It is a measure of absolute profitability | • Not well understood by non-financial managers |
| • Considers cash flows | • It may be difficult to determine the cost of capital |
| • It considers the whole life of the project | |
| • Should maximise shareholder wealth | |

## The superiority of NPV

When appraising projects or investments, NPV is considered to be superior (in theory) to most other methods. This is because it:

- Considers the time value of money – discounting cash flows to present value takes account of the impact of interest. This is ignored by the payback method.

- Is an absolute measure of return – the NPV of an investment represents the actual surplus raised by the project. This allows a business to plan more effectively.

- Is based on cash flows not profits – the subjectivity of profits makes them less reliable than cash flows and therefore less appropriate for decision making.

- Considers the whole life of the project – methods such as payback only considers the earlier cash flows associated with the project. NPV takes account of all relevant flows. Discounting the flows takes account of the fact that later flows are less reliable.

- Should lead to the maximisation of shareholder wealth. If the cost of capital reflects the shareholders' required return then the NPV reflect the theoretical increase in their wealth. For a company, this is considered to be the primary objective of business.

However there are several potential drawbacks:

- It is difficult to explain to managers. To understand the meaning of the NPV calculation requires an understanding of discounting. The method is not as intuitive as methods such as payback.

- It requires knowledge of the cost of capital. The calculation of the cost of capital is, in practice, a complex calculation.

- It is relatively complex – for the reasons explained above NPV may be rejected in favour of simpler techniques.

## 27 Internal Rate of Return (IRR)

The next investment appraisal technique, which is linked to NPV, is Internal Rate of Return (IRR). IRR calculates the rate of return at which the project has an NPV of zero. The IRR is compared to the company's cost of capital (this is the target rate).

### Decision criteria

*   If the IRR is greater than the cost of capital the project should be accepted.

*   Faced with mutually exclusive projects choose the project with the higher IRR.

### Calculating IRR

The steps are:

(1)  Calculate two NPVs for the project at two different costs of capital.

(2)  Use the following formula to find the IRR:

$$IRR \approx L + \frac{N_L}{N_L - N_H} (H - L)$$

**LEARN**

| where: | L | = | lower discount rate |
|---|---|---|---|
| | H | = | higher discount rate |
| | $N_L$ | = | NPV at the lower discount rate |
| | $N_H$ | = | NPV at the higher discount rate. |

### Illustration 10

You are given the following data on Project Z:

> At 10% the NPV was $33,310
> At 20% the NPV is $8,510
> At 30% the NPV is – $9,150

Calculate the IRR for project Z.

**Note:** it does not matter what 2 discounts rate you use, but different rates will give slightly different answers. (This method for calculating IRR is an approximation). Normal we try to use one NPV which is positive and one which is negative. The higher the discount rate – the lower the NPV will be.

In this case we will use 10% and 30%.

H = 30%

L = 10%

$N_H$ = ($9,150)

$N_L$ = $33,310

$$IRR \approx L + \frac{N_L}{N_L - N_H}(H - L)$$

$$IRR = 10 + \frac{33,310}{33,310 - (-9,150)} \times (30 - 10)$$

**= 25.7%**

Advantages and disadvantages of IRR:

| Advantages | Disadvantages |
| --- | --- |
| • Considers the time value of money | • It is not a measure of absolute profitability |
| • % measure – easy to understand | • Fairly complicated to calculate |
| • Considers cash flows | • Calculation only provides an estimate |
| • It considers the whole life of the project | |
| • Should maximise shareholder wealth | |

IRR is closely linked to the NPV method and shares most of the advantages of NPV:

- Considers the time value of money – discounting cash flows to present value takes account of the impact of interest. This is ignored by the payback method.

- Is based on cash flows not profits – the subjectivity of profits makes them less reliable than cash flows and therefore less appropriate for decision making.

- Considers the whole life of the project – methods such as payback only considers the earlier cash flows associated with the project. As IRR is based on NPV, it takes account of all relevant flows. Discounting the flows takes account of the fact that later flows are less reliable.

- Should lead to the maximisation of shareholder wealth. If all projects which generate a rate of return higher than the cost of capital are accepted, this should increase shareholder's wealth. For a company, this is considered to be the primary objective of business.

Where IRR differs from NPV is that it is a relative (%) measure rather than an absolute measure. This makes IRR easy to understand and aids comparisons between projects of different sizes.

However there are several potential drawbacks:

- It is difficult to explain to managers. To understand the meaning of IRR, users must first understand the NPV calculation and this requires an understanding of discounting. The method is not as intuitive as methods such as payback.

- The IRR calculation does not yield an exact answer, but is an approximation.

- Unlike NPV it is not an absolute measure. It does not give an indication of absolute profitability as NPV does.

Given the choice of methods, NPV is seen as the superior method.

## 28 Projects With Equal Annual Cash Flows

In the special case where a project has equal annual cash flows, the discounted cash flow can be calculated in a quicker way. There are 2 types of equal annual cash flows:

**Annuity** – a constant annual cash flow for a number of years

**Perpetuity** – a constant annual cash flow that continues indefinitely

Note: students should be aware of annuities and perpetuities, but will not be required to calculate them.

| Illustration 11 |
|---|

### Annuity

Pluto Ltd has been offered a project costing $30,000. The returns are expected to be $10,000 each year for 5 years. Cost of capital is 7%. Calculate the NPV of the project and recommend if it should be accepted.

Solution, using the normal discounting method.

| Year | Cash flow ($) | Discount factor (7%) | Present value ($) |
|---|---|---|---|
| 0 | (30,000) | 1 | (30,000) |
| 1 | 10,000 | 0.935 | 9,350 |
| 2 | 10,000 | 0.873 | 8,730 |
| 3 | 10,000 | 0.816 | 8,160 |
| 4 | 10,000 | 0.763 | 7,630 |
| 5 | 10,000 | 0.713 | 7,130 |
| | | **NPV =** | **11,000** |

You can see from this that there is a lot of repetition as we multiply each of the discount factors by the same amount. If we add up all of the discount factors from years 1 to 5 we get 4.100. This is known as the **annuity factor.**

The annuity factor can be looked up on the second present value table – the cumulative present value table. Go to 7% and look down to year 5, the annuity factor is given as 4.100. (there can be small differences due to roundings)

It would have been quicker to calculate the NPV as follows, using the annuity method:

| Year | Cash flow ($) | Annuity factor (7%) | Present value ($) |
|------|------|------|------|
| 0 | (30,000) | 1 | (30,000) |
| 1 – 5 | 10,000 | 4.100 | 41,000 |
| | | **NPV =** | **11,000** |

In this case, the NPV is positive, therefore **the project should be accepted.**

### Illustration 12

### Perpetuity

The present value of a perpetuity can be found using the formula:

$$PV = \text{cash flow} \times \frac{1}{r}$$

Where r = interest rate.

### Example:

In order to earn a perpetuity of $2,000 per annum how much would need to be invested today? The account will pay 10% interest.

### Solution:

Initial investment required = $2,000 ÷ 0.10 = **$20,000**

# Test your understanding answers

## Example 1 – Scandinavia

(a)

| | Comfort | Relaxer | Scandinavia | Total |
|---|---|---|---|---|
| Production units | 30 | 120 | 150 | 300 |
| Wood (metres) per chair | 10 | 9 | 9 | 2730 |
| Leather (metres) per chair | 4 | 2 | 0 | 360 |
| Labour (hours) per chair | 24 | 20 | 16 | 5520 |

There are three single batches made per week, hence there are three set-ups per week. Assuming four weeks in one month, this becomes 12 set-ups per month.

| | $ | Cost driver | Cost driver rate |
|---|---|---|---|
| Set-up costs | 5,600 | 12 set-ups | $466.67 per set-up |
| Purchasing and checking leather hides | 4.000 | 360 m leather | $11.11 per metre |
| Purchase of wood | 2,400 | 2,730 m wood | $0.879 per m |
| Quality inspection of leather seating | 3,200 | 360 m leather | $8.889 per metre |
| Despatch and transport | 6,000 | 300 chairs | $20 per chair |
| Administration and personnel costs | 13,300 | 5,520 hours | $2.409 per hour |

| | Comfort | Relaxer | Scandinavia |
|---|---|---|---|
| | $ | $ | $ |
| Set-up (4 set-ups each) | 1,866.67 | 1,866.67 | 1,866.67 |
| Purchasing leather | 1,333.33 | 2,666.67 | – |
| Purchasing wood | 263.74 | 949.45 | 1,186.81 |
| Quality inspection | 1,066.67 | 2,133.33 | – |
| Despatch | 600.00 | 2,400.00 | 3,000.00 |
| Administration | 1,734.78 | 5,782.61 | 5,782.61 |
| | | | |
| Total overhead | 6,865.19 | 15,798.73 | 11,836.09 |
| Number of units | ÷ 30 | ÷ 120 | ÷ 150 |

|  | $ | $ | $ |
|---|---:|---:|---:|
| Overhead per unit | 228.84 | 131.66 | 78.91 |
| Material | 85.00 | 60.00 | 50.00 |
| Labour | 120.00 | 100.00 | 80.00 |
| Total cost per unit | 433.84 | 291.66 | 208.91 |
| Selling price | 395.00 | 285.00 | 225.00 |
| Profit/Loss | (38.84) | (6.66) | 16.09 |

(b) This more detailed analysis of overheads shows a different view, i.e. that only the simple wooden chair was making a profit. The more luxurious chairs were making a loss especially the top of range Comfort model. This analysis may be of more use for long-term planning.

However for short-term decision making, marginal costing should be used. The analysis in part (a) shows that the ratios of contribution to selling price were all very similar. There the business plan to make the high-volume Scandinavia product is the correct long-term decision.

The plan for the other two leather chairs needs to be reviewed. Either the overhead costs for purchasing leather and quality control must be reduced and/or the sales prices need to be revised upwards. If these options are not viable then D may need to downsize the business and produce a single product, the Scandinavian.

Therefore the combination of marginal and ABC is required to make future decisions about volumes and prices of the products.

(c) Information has not been gathered on the costs of supplying different customers in D's company. Some customers may require high levels of service within the product-service package while other customers may only require the product itself. The price charged to each customer could be calculated to reflect these differing levels of requirement.

ABC may be used to determine the costs to D in providing different levels of service. The costs would comprise such elements as:

| Customer development costs | – Number of visits/meetings and the time spent on customised service |
| Production costs | – Batch and order sizes |
| | – Specials or extras, e.g. packaging in a different form |
| Despatch | – Order time, distance, pattern of deliveries and availability of return loads |
| After sales | – Follow-up time required, extra availability or speed of response for spares |

Based upon the existing cost analysis, D's business does not appear to incur extra customer costs for: pre-sales costs, production costs, despatch and after-sales costs. These costs are hidden from D at the moment and may be built into existing cost areas, not only production and despatch, but also administration, quality, etc.

There, D must determine for each customer their price/quality/service profile, i.e. some customers may be prepared to pay more for the extra service they are receiving. The information generated by an ABC analysis could and should be used to justify different charges for different packages of product and service.

## Example 2

(i) Total sales mix profit margin variance

**Method 1** : Difference between the actual total quantity sold in the standard mix and the actual quantities sold, valued at the standard profit per unit. The total quantity of units is 3,000 Dees and 1,200 Bees = 4,200 units.

| | Standard Mix | Actual Mix | Standard Profit | Variance |
|---|---|---|---|---|
| Dee | 4,200 x (3,000/4,500) = 2,800 | 3,000 | $25 | $25 *(3,000 – 2,800) = $5,000 F |
| Bee | 4,200 x (1,500/4,500) = 1,400 | 1,200 | $95 | $95 *(1,200 – 1,400) = $19,000 A |
| Total | **4,200 units** | 4,200 | | **$14,000 A** |

**Method 2** : Difference between the actual sales mix and the standard sales mix, valued at the standard profit per unit less the budgeted weighted average profit per unit.

$$\text{Budgeted Weighted Average profit per unit} = \frac{(3{,}000 \times \$25) + (1{,}500 \times \$95)}{4{,}500 \text{ units}}$$

Budgeted Weighted     =     **$48.33**
Average profit per unit

| | Actual Sales Mix | Standard Sales Mix | Difference | Profit per unit | Variance |
|---|---|---|---|---|---|
| Dee | 3,000 | 2,800 | +200 | $48.33 – $25 | $4,667 A |
| Bee | 1,200 | 1,400 | -200 | $48.33 – $95 | $9,334 A |
| Total | **4,200 units** | **4,200 units** | 0 | | **$14,000 A** |

(ii)   Total Sales volume profit variance relates only to Product Bee, because the actual and Budgeted volumes of Dee are the same.

Therefore, the variance is 300 units of Bee x $95 = **$28,500 A.**

**Example 3**

**Material total variance**

|  | $ |
|---|---|
| Std cost of actual output | |
| 2kg x 1,000 units x $10/kg | 20,000 |
| Actual cost | 20,900 |
| | ———— |
| | 900 A |
| | ———— |

## Example 4

| Direct materials price variance: | | | $ |
|---|---|---|---|
| Actual quantity of materials | should cost (standard) | | |
| 2,200kgs | $10 / kg | 22,000 | |
| | did cost (actual) | 20,900 | |
| | | _____ | |
| Direct materials price variance | | | 1,100 F |
| | | | _____ |

| Direct materials usage variance: | | | $ |
|---|---|---|---|
| Actual output produced | should use (standard quantity) | | |
| 1,000 units | 2 ks / unit | 2,000 | |
| | did cost (actual quantity) | 2,200 | |
| | | _____ | |
| Direct materials usage variance | (in material quantity) | 200 A | |
| | | _____ | |
| × standard price | (per unit of material) | $10 | |
| Direct materials usage variance | | 2,000 A | |
| | | _____ | |

### Material price variance – Alternative method

| | $ |
|---|---|
| Std cost of actual output | |
| $10/kg x 2,200 kg | 22,000 |
| Actual cost | 20,900 |
| | _____ |
| | 1,100 F |
| | _____ |

### Example 5

**(i) Direct materials mix variance, using the individual units method:**

|  | Chemical A | Chemical B | Chemical C | Total |
|---|---|---|---|---|
| (1) Actual input | 600 litres | 250 litres | 500 litres | 1,350 |
| (2) Actual input, in standard proportions | 1,350 * (0.4 / 1.2) = 450 l | 1,350 * (0.3 / 1.2) = 337.5 l | 1,350 * (0.5 / 1.2) = 562.5 l | 1,350 |
| (3) Difference in quantity | 150 litres A | 87.5 litres F | 62.50 F | |
| (4) x standard cost | $30 | $30 | $62.50 | |
| (5) Variance | $4,500 A | $2,625 F | $937.50 F | **$937.50 A** |

**(ii) Direct materials mix variance, using the weighted average method:**

|  | Chemical A | Chemical B | Chemical C | Total |
|---|---|---|---|---|
| (1) Actual input | 600 litres | 250 litres | 500 litres | 1,350 |
| (2) Actual input, in standard proportions | 1,350 * (0.4 / 1.2) = 450 l | 1,350 * (0.3 / 1.2) = 337.5 l | 1,350 * (0.5 / 1.2) = 562.5 l | 1,350 |
| (3) Difference in quantity | 150 litres A | 87.5 litres F | 62.50 F | |
| (4) x Difference between individual price and weighted average price (W1) | $30 - $23.75 = $6.25 A | $30 - $23.75 = $6.25F | $15-$23.75 =($8.75) | |
| (5) Variance | $937.5A | $546.875 F | $546.875 A | **$937.50 A** |

(iii) Direct materials yield variance

| | |
|---|---|
| (1) Standard yield of actual input | 1,350 litres input should yield (1,350 / 1.2 litres) = 1,125 litres |
| (2) Actual yield | 1,000 litres |
| (3) Difference in quantity | 125 litres |
| (4) x standard cost | $28.50 per litre |
| (5) Total Yield variance | **$3,562A** |

*[ In the PEG Sept 2011, the Examiner notes the following common mistakes made by candidates : the inability to calculate variances, incorrectly showing an adverse variance as a favourable variance and vice versa; and not showing a $ sign before the variance.]*

## Example 6

| *Direct labour rate variance:* | | $ |
|---|---|---|
| Number of hours worked | should cost / hr (standard) | |
| 3,400 hours | $8 / hr | 27,200 |
| | did cost (actual) | 28,300 |
| | | ――― |
| Direct labour rate variance | | 1,100  A |
| | | ――― |

| *Direct labour efficiency variance:* | | Hours |
|---|---|---|
| Actual output produced | should take (standard hours) | |
| 1,100 units | 3 hrs per unit | 3,300 |
| | did take (actual hours) | 3,400 |
| | | ――― |
| Direct labour efficiency variance | (in hours) | 100 |
| | | ――― |
| x standard rate per hour | | $8/ hr |
| Direct labour efficiency variance | | $800  A |

### Example 7

|  |  |  |  |  | $ |  |
|---|---|---|---|---|---|---|
| SHSR |  |  |  |  |  |  |
|  | 6 hrs/unit x 900 units | x | $7/hr | = | 37,800 | } Efficiency $1,400 F |
| AHSR |  |  |  |  |  |  |
|  | 5,200 hrs | x | $7/hr | = | 36,400 |  |

The efficiency variance looks at whether people **WORK** fast or slow and looks at hours **WORKED**.

|  |  |  |  |  | $ |  |
|---|---|---|---|---|---|---|
| AHSR |  |  |  |  |  |  |
|  | 5,500 hrs | x | $7/hr | = | 38,500 | } $600 A Rate |
| AHAR |  |  |  |  |  |  |
|  |  |  |  | = | 39,100 |  |

The rate variance looks at the rate of **PAY** so it looks at the hours **PAID**.

### Idle time variance

(5,500 – 5,200) x $7 per hour                              $2,100 A

Or the idle time variance is simply the difference between the $38,500 and the $36,400 above = $2,100 A.

### Example 8

| *Variable production overhead expenditure variance:* |  | $ |
|---|---|---|
| Number of hours worked | should cost / hr (standard) |  |
| 1,980 hours | $3 / hour | 5,940 |
|  | did cost (actual) | 5,544 |
| Variable production overhead expenditure variance |  | 396  F |

| *Variable production overhead efficiency variance:* |  | Hours |
|---|---|---|
| Actual output produced | should take (standard hours) |  |
| 900 units | 2 hours / unit | 1,800 |
|  | did take (actual hours) | 1,980 |
| Efficiency variance | (in hours) | 180 A |
| x standard variable overhead rate per hour |  | $3 |
| Variable production overhead efficiency variance |  | $540  A |

### Example 9

(a) The idle time variance is 20 hours × $15 = $300 (A).

(b) The efficiency variances are then calculated based on the active hours worked, not on the total hours paid for.

| *Efficiency variances:* | | *Hours* |
|---|---|---|
| Actual output produced 200 units | should take (standard hours) 2 hours / unit | 400 |
| | did take (440 – 20) | 420 |
| Efficiency variance | (in hours) | 20 A |
| × standard direct labour rate per hour | | $15 |
| Direct labour efficiency variance | | $300 A |
| × standard variable overhead rate per hour | | $4 |
| Variable production overhead efficiency variance | | $80 A |

(c) The variable production overhead expenditure variance is based on active hours only, since variable production overhead cost is not incurred during idle time.

| *Variable production overhead expenditure variance:* | | $ |
|---|---|---|
| Number of hours worked 420 hours | should cost / hr (standard) $4 / hour | 1,680 |
| | did cost (actual) | 1,530 |
| Variable production overhead expenditure variance | | 150  F |

### Process 1

| | kg | $ | | kg | $ |
|---|---|---|---|---|---|
| Materials | 500 | 6,000 | Output | 500 | 10,000 |
| Labour | | 1,000 | | | |
| Expenses | | 2,000 | | | |
| Overheads | | 1,000 | | | |
| | 500 | 10,000 | | 500 | 10,000 |

### Process 2

| | kg | $ | | kg | $ |
|---|---|---|---|---|---|
| Process 1 | 500 | 10,000 | Output | 700 | 21,000 |
| Materials | 200 | 4,000 | | | |
| Labour | | 2,000 | | | |
| Expenses | | 3,000 | | | |
| Overheads | | 2,000 | | | |
| | 700 | 21,000 | | 700 | 21,000 |

### Process 3

| | kg | $ | | kg | $ |
|---|---|---|---|---|---|
| Process 2 | 700 | 21,000 | Output | 1,000 | 40,000 |
| Materials | 300 | 9,000 | | | |
| Labour | | 3,000 | | | |
| Expenses | | 4,000 | | | |
| Overheads | | 3,000 | | | |
| | 1,000 | 40,000 | | 1,000 | 40,000 |

**Unit cost calculations:**

| Process 1 | Process 2 | Process 3 |
|---|---|---|
| 10,000 / 500 = $20 | 21,000 / 700 = $30 | 40,000 / 1,000 = $40 |

## Test Your Understanding 2

(a)

### Process 1

|  | kg | $ |  | kg | $ |
|---|---|---|---|---|---|
| Material | 1,000 | 4,300 | Output | 900 | 8,100 |
| Labour |  | 3,000 | Normal loss | 100 | 200 |
| Overhead |  | 1,000 |  |  |  |
|  | 1,000 | 8,300 |  | 1,000 | 8,300 |

Note: when balancing the quantity column, the output quantity was not given, but as losses were as expected, the output quantity must be 900.

(b) **Calculate the cost per unit**

$$\text{Unit Cost} = \frac{\text{Total input costs } - \text{ scrap value of normal loss}}{\text{Expected output}}$$

= (8,300 − 200) / 900 = **$9.00**

## Test Your Understanding 3

### Process account

|  | kg | $ |  | kg | $ |
|---|---|---|---|---|---|
| Materials | 1,200 | 8,500 | Output | 1,000 | 23,500 |
| Labour |  | 2,500 | Normal loss | 120 | 420 |
| Overheads |  | 7,000 | Abnormal loss | 80 | 1,880 |
|  |  | 7,800 |  |  |  |
|  | 1,200 | 25,800 |  | 1,200 | 25,800 |

To balance the quantity column the abnormal loss must be 80 kg.

The cost per unit and value the output and the abnormal loss:

Unit Cost = $\dfrac{\textbf{Total input costs – scrap value of normal loss}}{\textbf{Expected output}}$

Remember the abnormal loss was unexpected, so the expected output is the input less the normal loss

Unit cost = (8,500 + 2,500 + 2,000 + 7,000 + 7,800) – 420 / (1,200 – 120)
= $23.50

So  the value of the output = $23.50 x 1,000 = $23,500
And the value of the abnormal loss  = $23.50 x 80 = $1,880

### Scrap account

|  | $ |  | $ |
|---|---|---|---|
| Process – normal loss | 420 | Receivables/cash | 700 |
| Abnormal loss transfer | 280 |  |  |
|  | 700 |  | 700 |

### Abnormal loss account

|  | $ |  | $ |
|---|---|---|---|
| Process | 1,880 | Scrap account: 80 × $3.50 | 280 |
|  |  | Income statement | 1,600 |
|  | 1,880 |  | 1,880 |

### Test Your Understanding 4

#### Process 3 account

| | litres | $ | | litres | $ |
|---|---|---|---|---|---|
| Process 2 | 200 | 510 | Output | 590 | 5,492 |
| Materials added | 500 | 1,550 | Normal loss | 35 | 70 |
| Labour | | 1,800 | Abnormal loss | 75 | 698 |
| Overhead | | 2,400 | | | |
| | 700 | 6,260 | | 700 | 6,260 |

#### Abnormal loss account

| | $ | | $ |
|---|---|---|---|
| Process 3 | 698 | Scrap account (75 x $2) | 150 |
| | | Income statement | 548 |
| | 698 | | 698 |

#### Scrap account

| | $ | | $ |
|---|---|---|---|
| Process 3 | 70 | Bank/receivables | 220 |
| Abnormal loss account | 150 | | |
| | 220 | | 220 |

### Test Your Understanding 5

Payback with constant cash flows:

**Payback period =** $\dfrac{\textbf{Initial investment}}{\textbf{Annual cash flow}}$

= 1,000,000/200,000 = 5

The payback period is 5 years.

### Test Your Understanding 6

| Year | Cash flow | Cumulative cash flow |
|---|---|---|
| | $000 | $000 |
| 0 | (1,200) | (1,200) |
| 1 | 140 | (1,060) |
| 2 | 265 | (795) |
| 3 | 340 | (455) |
| 4 | 560 | 105 |
| 5 | 290 | 395 |

Payback is achieved between years 3 and 4.

Payback is 3 years plus (455/560 x 12) months = 3 years 10 months.

This is less than the target payback period of 4 years, therefore the **investment should be undertaken**.

### Test Your Understanding 7

Project A:

| Year | 0 | 1 | 2 | 3 | 4 | 5 |
|---|---|---|---|---|---|---|
| Annual cash flow ($000) | (450) | 200 | 150 | 100 | 50 | 20 |
| Cumulative cash flow | (450) | (250) | (100) | 0 | 50 | 70 |

Project B:

| Year | 0 | 1 | 2 | 3 | 4 | 5 |
|---|---|---|---|---|---|---|
| Annual cash flow ($000) | (450) | 50 | 120 | 190 | 310 | 260 |
| Cumulative cash flow | (450) | (400) | (280) | (90) | 220 | 480 |

SL require a payback of 3 years. Project A pays back in exactly 3 years, while project B pays back in 3 years plus (90/310 x 12) months = 3 years 3 months

**SL should undertake project A.**

**Note:**

This question demonstrates a problem with using payback as an investment appraisal method. You can see from the above tables that project B is in fact a more financially worthwhile that A. Over the 5 years project A has net cash flows of $70,000, while project B has $480,000, but SL would select project A as it pays back the initial investment sooner. This highlights one of the problems with payback, which is that it does not take account of the cash flows over the whole project, but only looks at the cash flows up to the target payback period.

### Test Your Understanding 8

Future Value (V) = $5,000(1.0275)^{12} = **$6,923.92**

### Test Your Understanding 9

$V = 5000(1.05)^{10}$ = **$8,144.47**

### Test Your Understanding 10

PV = $2,000 × 0.564 = **$1,128**

## Test Your Understanding 11

present value = future value x discount factor
= $40,000 x 0.763
= $30,520

## Test Your Understanding 12

Receive $12,000 in 2 years time:

present value = future value x discount factor
= $12,000 x 0.89
= $10,680

Receive $14,000 in 4 years time:

present value = future value x discount factor
= $14,000 x 0.792
= $11,088

**It would be better to receive $14,000 in 4 years time.**

## Test Your Understanding 13

| Year | Cash flow ($) | Discount factor (7%) | Present value (future value x discount factor) |
|---|---|---|---|
| 0 | (500,000) | 1 | (500,000) |
| 1 | 120,000 | 0.935 | 112,200 |
| 2 | 150,000 | 0.873 | 130,950 |
| 3 | 180,000 | 0.816 | 146,880 |
| 4 | 160,000 | 0.763 | 122,080 |
| | | **NPV =** | **12,110** |

On the basis of the positive NPV, **the project should be undertaken.**

### Test Your Understanding 14

| Year | Cash flow ($000) | Discount factor (5%) | Present value (future value x discount factor) |
|------|------------------|----------------------|-----------------------------------------------|
| 0 | (2,300) | 1 | (2,300) |
| 1 | 600 | 0.962 | 571.2 |
| 2 | 600 | 0.907 | 544.2 |
| 3 | 800 | 0.864 | 691.2 |
| 4 | 800 | 0.823 | 658.4 |
| | | **NPV =** | **165** |

On the basis of the positive NPV of $165,000, **the project should be undertaken.**

# Break-Even Analysis

## Chapter learning objectives

- **Explain** the usefulness of dividing costs into variable and fixed components in the context of short-term decision making. (Syllabus link A2a)

- **Interpret** variable/fixed cost analysis in multiple product contexts to breakeven analysis and product mix decision making, including circumstances where there are multiple constraints and linear programming methods are needed to identify 'optimal' solutions. (Syllabus link A2b)

- **Analyse** the impact of uncertainty and risk on decision models based on CVP analysis. (Syllabus link A2d)

## 1 Session Content Diagram

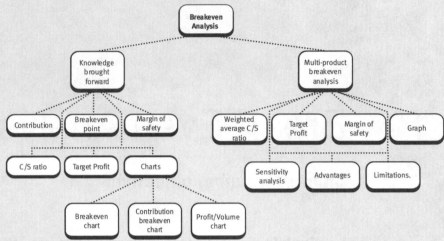

## 2 Introduction

One of the most important decisions that need' to be made before any business even starts is 'how much do we need to sell in order to break even?' By 'break-even' we mean simply covering all our costs without making a profit. This type of analysis is known as Cost-Volume-Profit Analysis (CVP Analysis).

In this chapter, we will apply the principles of Marginal costing and contribution analysis to breakeven analysis in single and multi-product contexts. We will also look into some related short-term decisions. We will also consider how uncertainty and risk may be taken into account when using breakeven analysis.

## 3 Knowledge Brought Forward

You will already have covered CVP analysis is Papers C01 and P1. We will build on this knowledge in P2 with more advanced CVP techniques, but make sure you are comfortable with the assumed knowledge, that should have been brought forward as a base, in this section.

> *Cost – Volume – Profit analysis* is defined in CIMA's *Official Terminology* as 'the study of the effects on future profit of changes in fixed cost, variable cost, sales price, quantity and mix.'

CVP analysis is a particular example of *'what if?'* analysis. A business sets a budget based upon various assumptions about revenues, costs, product mixes and overall volumes. CVP analysis considers the impact on the budgeted profit of changes in these various factors.

## The concept of contribution

Earlier you learned that variable costs are those that vary with the level of activity. If we can identify the variable costs associated with producing and selling a product or service we can highlight a very important measure: *contribution.*

**Contribution = sales value  LESS variable cost**

Variable costs are sometimes referred to as **marginal costs**. The two terms are often used interchangeably.

Contribution is so called because it literally does contribute towards fixed costs and profit. Once the contribution from a product or service has been calculated, the fixed costs associated with the product or service can be deducted to determine the profit for the period.

### Illustration 1

Consider a product with a variable cost per unit of $26 and selling price of $42. Fixed costs for the period are $12,000.

(a) What is the contribution per unit for the product?

(b) If 1,000 units are sold, what is the total contribution?

(c) What is the total profit and the profit per unit at this level of sales?

(d) Calculate the total profit for the following levels of sales:
 – 500
 – 1,000
 – 1,200

(e) Calculate the contribution per unit and profit per unit for each level of sales

**Solution:**

(a) Contribution per unit  = sales – variable cost
$42 – $26 = $16

(b) Total contribution = contribution per unit x number of units
$16 x 1,000 = $16,000

(c) Total profit = total contribution – fixed costs
$16,000 – $12,000 = $4,000

Profit per unit = total profit/number of units
$4,000/1,000 = $4

(d) It is easier to use a table for these calculations:

| Units | 500 | 1,000 | 1,200 |
|---|---|---|---|
| | $ | $ | $ |
| Sales | 21,000 | 42,000 | 50,400 |
| Variable cost | 13,000 | 26,000 | 31,200 |
| | | | |
| Total contribution | 8,000 | 16,000 | 19,200 |
| Fixed costs | 12,000 | 12,000 | 12,000 |
| | | | |
| Total Profit/(Loss) | (4,000) | 4,000 | 7,200 |
| | | | |
| (e) Contribution per unit | $16 | $16 | $16 |
| Profit per unit | ($8) | $4.00 | $6 |

You can see from this that the contribution per unit does not change, but that the profit per unit can change significantly as the volume changes.

This makes contribution much more useful than profit in many decisions.

In the above example, it would have been quicker to start with contribution when working out the profit, as shown below. This saves some unnecessary calculations:

| | $ | $ | $ |
|---|---|---|---|
| Contribution per unit | 16 | 16 | 16 |
| x units | 500 | 1,000 | 1,200 |
| Total contribution | 8,000 | 16,000 | 19,200 |
| Fixed costs | 12,000 | 12,000 | 12,000 |
| Total Profit/(Loss) | (4,000) | 4,000 | 7,200 |

## 4 Breakeven Point

As sales revenues grow from zero, the contribution also grows until it just covers the fixed costs. This is the **breakeven point** where neither profits nor losses are made.

It follows that to break even the amount of contribution must exactly match the amount of fixed costs. If we know how much contribution is earned from each unit sold, then we can calculate the number of units required to break even as follows:

$$\text{Breakeven point in units} = \frac{\text{Fixed costs}}{\text{Contribution per unit}}$$

For example, suppose that an organisation manufactures a single product, incurring variable costs of $30 per unit and fixed costs of $20,000 per month. If the product sells for $50 per unit, then the breakeven point can be calculated as follows:

$$\text{Breakeven point in units} = \frac{\$20,000}{\$50 - \$30} = 1,000 \text{ units per month}$$

## 5 The Margin of Safety

The margin of safety is the difference between the budgeted level of sales and the breakeven point. The larger the margin of safety, the more likely it is that a profit will be made, that is, if sales start to fall there is more leeway before the organisation begins to incur losses (assuming projected sales are greater than breakeven sales).

Margin of safety can be expressed in units or as a % of projected sales.

**Margin of safety = budgeted sales – breakeven sales**

**or**

$$\text{Margin of safety \%} = \frac{\text{Budgeted sales – breakeven sales}}{\text{Projected sales}}$$

Example: if a company has breakeven level of sales of 1,000 and is forecasting sales of 1,700, the margin of safety can be calculated as follows:

Margin of safety = 1,700 – 1,000 = 700 units

or

Margin of safety % = (1,700 – 1,000)/1,700 = 0.41 = 41%

Using the margin of safety % puts it in perspective. To quote a margin of safety of 700 units without relating it to the projected sales figure is not giving the full picture.

### Illustration 2

RT organisation manufactures one product. The product sells for $250, and has variable costs per unit of $120. Fixed costs for the month were $780,000. The monthly projected sales for the product were 8,000. The margin of safety can be calculated as:

First calculate the breakeven sales: 780,000/(250 -120) = 6,000

Margin of safety in units = projected sales – breakeven sales

$$= 8,000 – 6,000 = 2,000$$

Margin of safety %  = (projected sales – breakeven sales) / projected sales

$$= (8,000 – 6,000) / 8,000 = 25\%$$

The margin of safety can also be used as one route to a profit calculation. We have seen that the contribution goes towards fixed costs and profit. Once breakeven point is reached the fixed costs have been covered. After the breakeven point there are no more fixed costs to be covered and all of the contribution goes towards making profits grow.

From the above example (RT), the monthly profit from sales of 8,000 would be $260,000.

This can be calculated the normal way:

| | |
|---|---|
| Contribution | $130 |
| Total Contribution ($130 x 8,000) | $1,040,000 |
| Fixed costs | $ 780,000 |
| | ――――― |
| Profit | $ 260,000 |
| | ――――― |

Or using margin of safety:

Margin of safety = 2,000 units per month
Monthly profit     = 2,000 x contribution per unit
                            = 2,000 x $130
                            = $260,000

## Test Your Understanding 1

OT Ltd plans to produce and sell 4,000 units of product C each month, at a selling price of $18 per unit. The unit cost of product C is as follows:

| | $ per unit |
|---|---|
| Variable cost | 8 |
| Fixed cost | 4 |
| | — |
| | 12 |
| | — |

To the nearest whole number, the monthly margin of safety, as a percentage of planned sales is _____ %.

## 6 The Contribution to Sales (C/S) Ratio

The contribution to sales ratio is a useful calculation in CVP analysis. It is usually expressed as a percentage. It can be calculated as follows.

$$\text{C/S ratio} = \frac{\textbf{Contribution}}{\textbf{Sales}}$$

*It can be calculated using unit contribution and sales, or total contribution and sales.*

A higher contribution to sales ratio means that contribution grows more quickly as sales levels increase. Once the breakeven point has been passed, profits will accumulate more quickly than for a product with a lower contribution to sales ratio.

Using the RT example from illustration 2, the C/S ratio can be calculated as:

C/S ratio  = contribution/sales
= 130/250 = 52%

If we can assume that a unit's variable cost and selling price remain constant then the C/S ratio will also remain constant. It can be used to calculate the breakeven point as follows (using the data from the RT example):

$$\text{Breakeven point in sales value} \quad = \frac{\text{Fixed costs}}{\text{C/S ratio}} = \frac{\$780,000}{0.52} = \$1,500,000$$

This could have been calculated as: breakeven point x selling price

$$= 6,000 \times \$250 = \$1,500,000$$

### Sales required for a required level of profit

A further calculation which is used as part of CVP analysis is the calculation of the level of sales required to achieve a certain level of profit. As with the breakeven points, this can be calculated in sales units or in $ of sales revenue.

The calculations are as follows:

$$\textbf{Sales units required to achieve a profit of X} = \frac{\textbf{Fixed costs + X}}{\textbf{Contribution per unit}}$$

or

$$\textbf{Sales revenue required to achieve a profit of X} = \frac{\textbf{Fixed costs + X}}{\textbf{C/S ratio}}$$

## Test Your Understanding 2

A company manufactures and sells a single product which has the following cost and selling price structure

|  | $/unit | $/unit |
|---|---|---|
| Selling price | | 120 |
| Direct material | 22 | |
| Direct labour | 36 | |
| Variable overhead | 14 | |
| Fixed overhead | 12 | |
| | — | |
| | | 84 |
| | | — |
| Profit per unit | | 36 |
| | | — |

The fixed overhead absorption rate is based on the normal capacity of 2,000 units per month. Assume that the same amount is spent each month on fixed overheads.

Budgeted sales for next month are 2,200 units.

*You are required* to calculate:

(i) the breakeven point, in sales units per month;

(ii) the margin of safety for next month;

(iii) the budgeted profit for next month;

(iv) the sales required to achieve a profit of $96,000 in a month.

(v) the contribution to sales ratio

(vi) the breakeven revenue that must be generated in order to break even.

## Test Your Understanding 3

A summary of a manufacturing company's budgeted profit statement for its next financial year, when it expects to be operating at 75% capacity, is given below.

| | $ | $ |
|---|---|---|
| Sales 9,000 units at $32 | | 288,000 |
| Less: | | |
| direct materials | 54,000 | |
| direct wages | 72,000 | |
| production overhead – fixed | 42,000 | |
| – variable | 18,000 | |
| | | 186,000 |
| Gross profit | | 102,000 |
| Less: admin., selling and dist'n costs: | | |
| – fixed | 36,000 | |
| – varying with sales volume | 27,000 | |
| | | 63,000 |
| Net profit | | 39,000 |

It has been estimated that:

(i) if the selling price per unit were reduced to $28, the increased demand would utilise 90 per cent of the company's capacity without any additional advertising expenditure;

(ii) to attract sufficient demand to utilise full capacity would require a 15 per cent reduction in the current selling price and a $5,000 special advertising campaign.

*You are required to:*

(a) calculate the breakeven point in units, based on the original budget;

(b) calculate the profits and breakeven points which would result from each of the two alternatives and compare them with the original budget.

The manufacturing company decided to proceed with the original budget and has asked you to determine how many units must be sold to achieve a profit of $45,500.

## 7 Drawing a Basic Breakeven Chart

A basic breakeven chart records costs and revenues on the vertical axis (y) and the level of activity on the horizontal axis (x). Lines are drawn on the chart to represent costs and sales revenue. The breakeven point can be read off where the sales revenue line cuts the total cost line.

We will use a basic example to demonstrate how to draw a breakeven chart. The data is:

| | |
|---|---|
| Selling price | $50 per unit |
| Variable cost | $30 per unit |
| Fixed costs | $20,000 per month |
| Forecast sales | 1,700 units per month |

The completed graph is shown below:

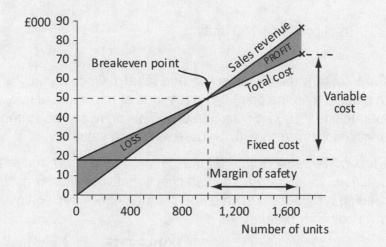

Learning to draw a chart to scale will provide a firm foundation for your understanding of breakeven charts. To give yourself some practice, it would be a good idea to follow the step-by-step guide which follows to produce your own chart on a piece of graph paper.

- *Step 1. Select appropriate scales for the axes and draw and label them.* Your graph should fill as much of the page as possible. This will make it clearer and easier to read. You can make sure that you do this by putting the extremes of the axes right at the end of the available space.

The furthest point on the vertical axis will be the monthly sales revenue, that is,

1,700 units × $50 = $ 85,000

The furthest point on the horizontal axis will be monthly sales volume of 1,700 units.

Make sure that you do not need to read data for volumes higher than 1,700 units before you set these extremes for your scales.

- *Step 2. Draw the fixed cost line and label it.* This will be a straight line parallel to the horizontal axis at the $20,000 level.

The $20,000 fixed costs are incurred in the short term even with zero activity.

- *Step 3. Draw the total cost line and label it.* The best way to do this is to calculate the total costs for the maximum sales level, which is 1,700 units in our example. Mark this point on the graph and join it to the cost incurred at zero activity, that is, $20,000.

|  | $ |
|---|---|
| Variable costs for 1,700 units (1,700 × $30) | 51,000 |
| Fixed costs | 20,000 |
| Total cost for 1,700 units | 71,000 |

- *Step 4. Draw the revenue line and label it.* Once again, the best way is to plot the extreme points. The revenue at maximum activity in our example is 1,700 × $50 = $85,000. This point can be joined to the origin, since at zero activity there will be no sales revenue.

- *Step 5. Mark any required information on the chart and read off solutions as required.* You can check that your chart is accurate by reading off the breakeven point and then check this against the calculation for breakeven:

$$\text{Breakeven point in units} = \frac{\textbf{Fixed costs}}{\textbf{Contribution per unit}}$$

$$= 20,000/(50-30) = \textbf{1,000 units.}$$

The margin of safety can be seen as the area to the right of the breakeven point up to the forecast sales level of 1,700.

**The contribution breakeven chart**

One of the problems with the conventional or basic breakeven chart is that it is not possible to read contribution directly from the chart. A contribution breakeven chart is based on the same principles but it shows the variable cost line instead of the fixed cost line. The same lines for total cost and sales revenue are shown so the breakeven point and profit can be read off in the same way as with a conventional chart. However, it is also possible also to read the contribution for any level of activity.

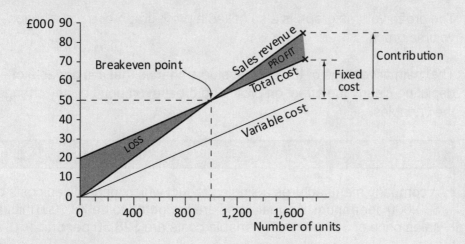

Using the same basic example as for the conventional chart, the total variable cost for an output of 1,700 units is 1,700 x $30 = $51,000. This point can be joined to the origin since the variable cost is nil at zero activity.

The contribution can be read as the difference between the sales revenue line and the variable cost line.

This form of presentation might be used when it is desirable to highlight the importance of contribution and to focus attention on the variable costs.

Ensure you are familiar with these charts and that you are able to identify all the component parts.

## 8 The Profit–Volume Chart

Another form of breakeven chart is the profit–volume chart. This chart plots a single line depicting the profit or loss at each level of activity. The breakeven point is where this line cuts the horizontal axis. A profit–volume graph for our example is shown below.

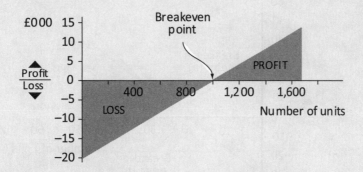

The vertical axis shows profits and losses and the horizontal axis is drawn at zero profit or loss.

At zero activity the loss is equal to $20,000, that is, the amount of fixed costs. The second point used to draw the line could be the calculated breakeven point or the calculated profit for sales of 1,700 units.

The profit–volume graph is also called a profit graph or a contribution–volume graph.

The main advantage of the profit–volume chart is that it is capable of depicting clearly the effect on profit and breakeven point of any changes in the variables.

### Illustration 3

A company manufactures a single product which incurs fixed costs of $30,000 per annum. Annual sales are budgeted to be 70,000 units at a sales price of $30 per unit. Variable costs are $28.50 per unit.

(a) Draw a profit–volume graph, and use it to determine the breakeven point.

The company is now considering improving the quality of the product and increasing the selling price to $35 per unit. Sales volume will be unaffected, but fixed costs will increase to $45,000 per annum and variable costs to $33 per unit.

(b) Draw, on the same graph as for part (a), a second profit–volume graph and comment on the results.

**Solution:**

The profit–volume chart is shown below:

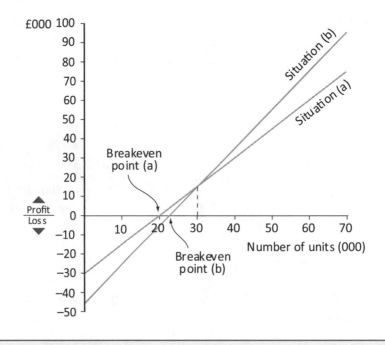

The two lines have been drawn as follows:

- *Situation (a).* The profit for sales of 70,000 units is $75,000.

|  | $000 |
|---|---|
| Contribution 70,000 × $(30 − 28.50) | 105 |
| Fixed costs | 30 |
|  | —— |
| Profit | 75 |
|  | —— |

This point is joined to the loss at zero activity, $30,000, that is, the fixed costs.

- *Situation (b).* The profit for sales of 70,000 units is $95,000.

|  | $000 |
|---|---|
| Contribution 70,000 × $(35 − 33) | 140 |
| Fixed costs | 45 |
|  | —— |
| Profit | 95 |
|  | —— |

This point is joined to the loss at zero activity, $45,000, that is, the fixed costs.

Comment on the results. The graph depicts clearly the larger profits available from option (b). It also shows that the breakeven point increases from 20,000 units to 22,500 units but that this is not a large increase when viewed in the context of the projected sales volume. It is also possible to see that for sales volumes above 30,000 units the profit achieved will be higher with option (b). For sales volumes below 30,000 units option (a) will yield higher profits (or lower losses).

The profit–volume graph is the clearest way of presenting information like this. If we attempted to draw two conventional breakeven charts on one set of axes the result would be a jumble, which is very difficult to interpret.

## 9 Multi-Product Break-Even Analysis

The basic breakeven model can be used satisfactorily for a business operation with only one product. However, most companies sell a range of different products, and the model has to be adapted when one is considering a business operation with several products.

CVP Analysis assumes that, if a range of products is sold, sales will be in accordance with a **pre-determined sales mix**.

When a pre-determined sales mix is used, it can be depicted in the CVP Analysis by assuming average revenues and average variable costs for the given sales mix.

However, the assumption has to be made that the sales mix remains **constant**. This is defined as the relative proportion of each product's sale to total sales. It could be expressed as a ratio such as 2:4:6, or as a percentage as 20%, 40%, 60%.

The calculation of breakeven point in a multi-product firm follows the same pattern as in a single product firm. While the numerator will be the same fixed costs, the denominator now will be the **weighted average contribution margin**.

In multi-product situations, a weighted average C/S ratio is calculated by using the formula:

$$\text{Weighted Average C/S ratio} = \frac{\text{Total Contribution}}{\text{Total Revenue}}$$

The Weighted Average C/S ratio is useful in its own right, as it tells us what percentage each $ of sales revenue contributes towards fixed costs; it is also invaluable in helping us to quickly calculate the breakeven point in sales revenue:

$$\text{Breakeven revenue} = \frac{\text{Fixed costs}}{\text{Weighted Average C/S ratio}}$$

## Weighted Average Contribution to Sales ratio

Company A produces Product X and Product Y. Fixed overhead costs amount to $200,000 every year. The following budgeted information is available for both products for next year:

|  | Product X | Product Y |
| --- | --- | --- |
| Sales Price | $50 | $60 |
| Variable Cost | $30 | $45 |
| Contribution per unit | $20 | $15 |
| Budgeted Sales (in units) | 20,000 | 10,000 |

In order to calculate the breakeven revenue for the next year, using the budgeted sales mix, we need the weighted Average C/S ratio as follows :

$$\text{Weighted Average C/S Ratio} = \frac{\text{Total Contribution}}{\text{Total Revenue}}$$

$$\text{Weighted Average C/S Ratio} = \frac{(20,000 \times \$20) + (10,000 \times \$15)}{(20,000 \times \$50) + (10,000 \times \$60)}$$

$$\text{Weighted Average C/S Ratio} = 34.375\%$$

This indicates that for every $1 of revenue generated, the company will earn $0.34 in contribution.

The breakeven revenue can now be calculated this way for company A:

$$\text{Breakeven revenue} = \frac{\text{Fixed costs}}{\text{Weighted Average C/S ratio}}$$

$$\text{Breakeven revenue} = \frac{\$200,000}{0.34375}$$

$$\text{Breakeven revenue} = \$581,819$$

Calculations in the illustration above provide only estimated information because they assume that products X and Y are sold in a constant mix of 2x to 1y. In reality, this constant mix is unlikely to exist and, at times, more Y may be sold than X. Such changes in the mix throughout a period, even if the overall mix for the period is 2:1, will lead to the actual breakeven point being different than anticipated.

## 10 Establishing a Target Profit For Multiple Products

The approach is the same as in single product situations, but the weighted average contribution to Sales Ratio is now used so that:

**Revenue required to generate a target profit** $=$ $\dfrac{\text{Fixed costs + required profit}}{\text{Weighted Average C/S ratio}}$

### Target Profit in Company A

To achieve a target profit of $300,000 in Company A :

Sales revenue required for profit of $300,000 $= \dfrac{\text{(Fixed costs + required profit)}}{\text{W.A. C/S ratio}}$

Sales revenue required for profit of $300,000 $= \dfrac{\$200,000 + \$300,000}{0.34375}$

Sales revenue required for profit of $300,000 $= \$1,454,545$

## Margin of safety calculations

The basic breakeven model for calculating the margin of safety can be adapted to multi-product environments. Three alternative approaches are considered in the example below.

A business operation produces three products, the X, the Y and the Z. Relevant details are:

|  | Product X | Product Y | Product Z |
|---|---|---|---|
| Normal sales mix (units) | 2 | 2 | 1 |
| Selling price per unit | $9 | $7 | $5 |
| Variable cost per unit | $6 | $5 | $1 |
| Contribution per unit | $3 | $2 | $4 |
| Forecast unit sales | 400 | 400 | 200 |

Fixed costs are $2,000 per period, not attributable to individual products. A budget for the forecast is as follows:

|  | Product X | Product Y | Product Z | Total |
|---|---|---|---|---|
| Sales Revenue | $3,600 | $2,800 | $1,000 | $7,400 |
| Variable cost | $2,400 | $2,000 | $200 | $4,600 |
| Contribution | $1,200 | $800 | $800 | $2,800 |
| Fixed Costs |  |  |  | $2,000 |
| Profit |  |  |  | $800 |

To calculate the margin of safety, three approaches are possible:

(1) Consider the products in sequence, X then Y then Z . In this case, it can be seen that breakeven occurs at 800 units of sales (400X plus 400Y) and **the margin of safety is 200 units of Z.**

(2) Consider output in terms of $ sales and assume a constant product mix (2X:2Y:1Z). Inspection of the budget (above) shows that $1 sales is associated with $0.6216 variable costs (that is, $4,600 variable costs ÷ $7,400 sales). The contribution per $1 sales is $0.3784 (i.e. $1 - $0.6216). So, if the fixed costs are $2,000 then the breakeven point is $5,285 sales and **the margin of safety is $2,115** (i.e. $7,400 forecast sales - $5,285).

(3) Consider output in terms of percentage of forecast sales and a constant product mix. Inspection of the budget shows that 1 per cent of forecast sales is associated with a contribution of $28.00 (i.e. $2,800 total contribution ÷ 100 per cent). So, if fixed costs are $2,000 it follows that the breakeven point is 71.43 per cent and **the margin of safety is 28.57 per cent.**

## 11 The Multi-Product Profit-Volume Graph – Step-By-Step

In a multi-product environment, two lines must be shown on the profit-volume graph: one straight line, where a constant mix between the products is assumed; and one bow shaped line, where it is assumed that the company sells its most profitable product first and then its next most profitable product and so on.

We will use the following example to illustrate our step-by-step approach :

| | Sales units | Selling price per unit | Variable cost per unit |
|---|---|---|---|
| Bags | 1,000 | $400 | $210 |
| Belts | 2,000 | $125 | $65 |
| Shoes | 1,500 | $150 | $95 |
| Jackets | 3,500 | $300 | $215 |

Fixed costs amount to $580,000.

**STEP 1**: Calculate the C/S ratio of each product being sold, and rank the products in order of profitability.

| | C/S ratio | Rank |
|---|---|---|
| Bags | 0.475 | 2 |
| Belts | 0.480 | 1 |
| Shoes | 0.367 | 3 |
| Jackets | 0.283 | 4 |

**STEP 2**: Draw the graph, showing cumulative sales revenue on the x-axis. For example, if we assume 3 products X, Y and Z, then the following graph could be drawn , with 'V' representing the total sales revenue. At an revenue of 0, the loss incurred will amount to the company's fixed costs, represented by point *k* on the chart.

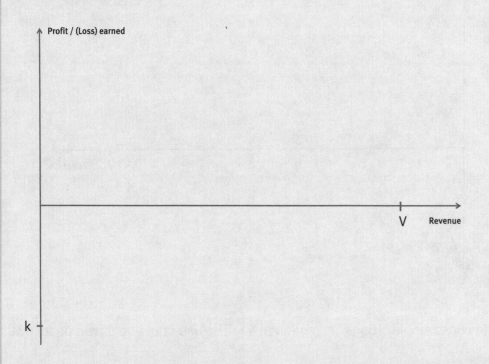

In our example, the following calculations and graphs could be drawn :

| Sales | Cumulative revenue | Individual product contribution | Cumulative profit or loss |
|---|---|---|---|
| None | $0 | $0 | $(580,000) |
| Belts | $250,000 | $120,000 | $(460,000) |
| Bags | $650,000 | $190,000 | $(270,000) |
| Shoes | $875,000 | $82,500 | $(187,500) |
| Jackets | $1,925,000 | $297,500 | $110,000 |

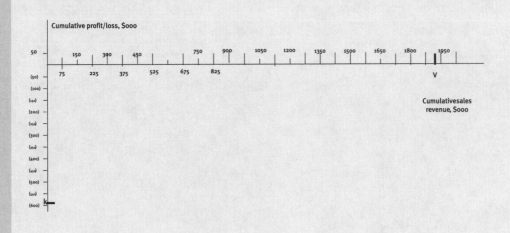

**STEP 3**: Draw the line *km*, that represents the profit earned by product X – the slope of the line is determined by the C/S ratio achieved on sales of that product.

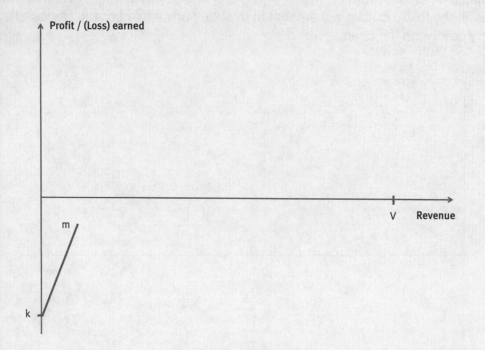

In our example, 'Belts ' is ranked at #1. The line could be drawn as follows :

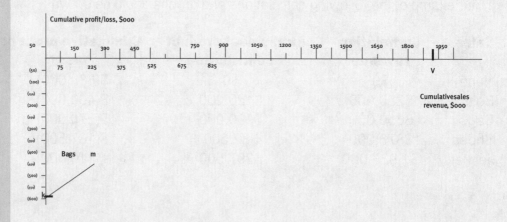

**STEP 4**: Draw the line *mn*, that represents the profit earned by product y, which has a lower C/S ratio than product X. The line *nj* is the profit earned by the least profitable product, product Z.

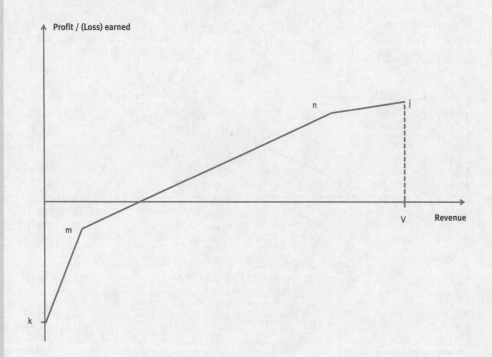

In our example, 'Bags ' is ranked at #2and 'Shoes' at #3. The lines could be drawn as follows :

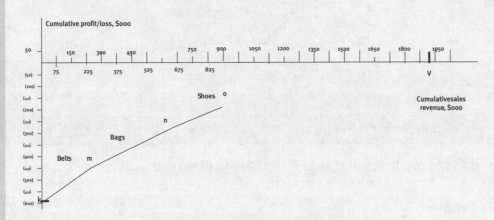

**STEP 5**: Draw the line joining points *k* and *j*: it reflects the average profitability of the three products, and each point on that line represents the profit earned for the associated output, assuming that the three products are sold in the standard product mix, i.e. the mix implied in the construction of the chart.

Accordingly, the indicated breakeven point only applies if the products are sold in the standard product mix.

It can also be seen that breakeven can also occur at lower levels of output, provided the proportions of the products are changed. For example, the point B where the line *kmnj* crosses the horizontal axis indicates a possible breakeven point.

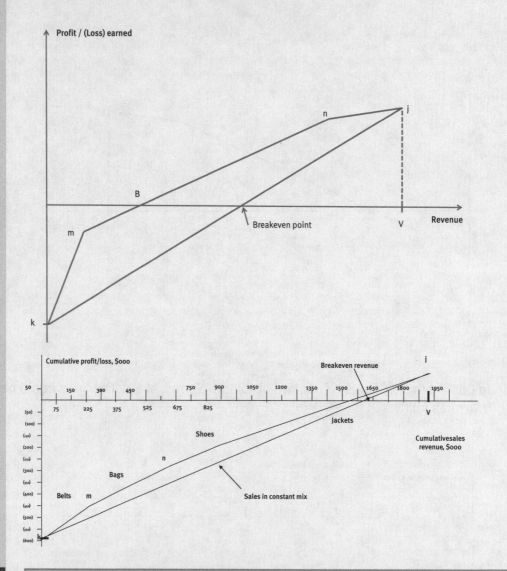

## Example 1 – Multi-Product

BJS Ltd produces and sells the following three products:

| Product | X | Y | Z |
|---|---|---|---|
| Selling price per unit | $16 | $20 | $10 |
| Variable cost per unit | $5 | $15 | $7 |
| Contribution per unit | $11 | $5 | $3 |
| Budgeted sales volume | 50,000 units | 10,000 units | 100,000 units |

The company expects the fixed costs to be $300,000 for the coming year. Assume that sales arise throughout the year in a constant mix.

**Required:**

(a) Calculate the weighted average C/S ratio for the products.

(b) Calculate the break-even sales revenue required.

(c) Calculate the amount of sales revenue required to generate a profit of $600,000.

(d) Draw a multi-product profit-volume chart assuming the budget is achieved.

**Example 2 – R, S and T**

A company makes and sells three products, R, S and T. Extracts from the weekly profit statements are as follows:

|  | R | S | T | Total |
|---|---|---|---|---|
|  | $ | $ | $ | $ |
| Sales revenue | 10,000 | 15,000 | 20,000 | 45,000 |
| Variable cost of sales | 4,000 | 9,000 | 10,000 | 23,000 |
| Fixed costs (*) | 3,000 | 3,000 | 3,000 | 9,000 |
| Profit | 3,000 | 3,000 | 7,000 | 13,000 |

(*) General fixed costs absorbed using a unit absorption rate.

If the sales revenue mix of products produced and sold were to be changed to : R 20%, S 50% and T 30%, would the new average contribution to sales ratio be higher, lower, or remain unchanged?

## 12 Sensitivity Analysis

Sensitivity or *'What-if?'* analysis involves determining the effects of various types of changes in the CVP model. These effects can be determined by simply changing the constants in the CVP model, i.e., prices, variable cost per unit, sales mix ratios etc.

Sensitivity analysis answers the following questions:

*What will be the impact on our revenue if units sold decrease by 10% from original prediction?*

*What will be the impact on our revenue if variable cost per unit increases by 30%?*

*What impact would a change of the standard sales mix have on the company's performance?*

The sensitivity of revenue to various possible outcomes broadens the perspective of management regarding what might actually occur before making cost commitments. This would be fairly easy with spreadsheets, or other software developed to handle these calculations.

## Test Your Understanding 4 – Sensitivity Analysis

MC Ltd manufactures one product only, and for the last accounting period has produced the simplified profit and loss statement below:

|  | $ | $ |
|---|---|---|
| Sales |  | 300,000 |
| Costs |  |  |
| Direct materials | 60,000 |  |
| Direct wages | 40,000 |  |
|  | ——— |  |
| Prime cost | 100,000 |  |
| Variable production overhead | 10,000 |  |
| Fixed production overhead | 40,000 |  |
| Fixed administration overhead | 60,000 |  |
| Variable selling overhead | 40,000 |  |
| Fixed selling overhead | 20,000 |  |
|  | ——— |  |
|  |  | 270,000 |
|  |  | ——— |
| **Net profit** |  | **30,000** |
|  |  | ——— |

**Required:**

(a) Construct a profit–volume graph from which you should state the breakeven point and the margin of safety.

(b) Based on the above, draw separate profit–volume graphs to indicate the effect on profit of each of the following:

   (i)   an increase in fixed cost;

   (ii)  a decrease in variable cost;

   (iii) an increase in sales price;

   (iv) a decrease in sales volume.

## Test Your Understanding 5 – Sensitivity Analysis – Sales Mix

Vivaldi Ltd manufactures and sells four types of products under the brand name Summer, Autumn , Winter and Spring. The Sales Mix in value comprises the following:

| Brand name | Percentage |
|---|---|
| Summer | 33.33% |
| Autumn | 41.67% |
| Winter | 16.67% |
| Spring | 8.33% |
| | **100%** |

Total Budgeted sales are set to reach 600,000 units per month.

Variable costs are as follows:

| Brand name | |
|---|---|
| Summer | 60% of selling price |
| Autumn | 68% of selling price |
| Winter | 80% of selling price |
| Spring | 40% of selling price |

Fixed costs amount to $159,000 per month.

**Required:**

(a)  Calculate the breakeven point for the products on an overall basis.

(b)  It has been proposed to change the Sales Mix as follows, with the Sales per month remaining at 600,000 units:

| Brand name | Percentage |
|---|---|
| Summer | 25% |
| Autumn | 40% |
| Winter | 30% |
| Spring | 5% |
| | **100%** |

Assuming that the above proposal is implemented, calculate the new breakeven point.

An economist would probably depict a breakeven chart as shown below.

The total cost line is not a straight line which climbs steadily as in the accountant's chart. Instead it begins to reduce initially as output increases because of the effect of economies of scale. Later it begins to climb upwards according to the law of diminishing returns.

The revenue line is not a straight line as in the accountant's chart. The line becomes less steep to depict the need to give discounts to achieve higher sales volumes.

However, you will see that within the middle range the economist's chart does look very similar to the accountant's breakeven chart. This area is marked as the relevant range on the chart.

For this reason, it is unreliable to assume that the cost–volume–profit relationships depicted in breakeven analysis are relevant across a wide range of activity. In particular, the economist's chart shows that the constant cost and price assumptions are likely to be unreliable at very high or very low levels of activity. Managers should therefore ensure that they work within the relevant range, that is, within the range over which the depicted cost and revenue relationships are more reliable.

> You may recall that we discussed the relevant range in the context of cost behaviour patterns.

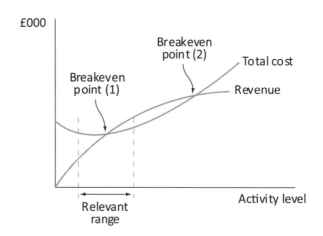

## 13 Advantages Of Break-Even Analysis

The major benefit of using breakeven analysis is that it indicates the lowest amount of activity necessary to prevent losses.

Breakeven analysis aids Decision Making as it explains the relationship between cost, production volume and returns. It can be extended to show how changes in fixed costs – variable costs relationships or in revenues will affect profit levels and breakeven points.

## 14 Limitations Of Break-Even Analysis

Cost behaviour is affected by the interplay of a number of factors. Physical volume is only one of these factors; others include unit prices of input, efficiency, changes in production technology, wars, strikes, legislation, and so forth. Any CVP analysis is based on assumptions about the behaviour of revenue, costs and volume. A change in expected behaviour will alter the break-even point; in other words, profits are affected by changes in other factors besides volume. A CVP chart must be interpreted in the light of the limitations imposed by its underlying assumptions. The real benefit of preparing CVP charts is in the enrichment of understanding of the interrelationships of all factors affecting profits, especially cost behaviour patterns over ranges of volume.

The following underlying assumptions will limit the precision and reliability of a given cost-volume-profit analysis.

(1) The behaviour of total cost and total revenue has been reliably determined and is linear over the relevant range.

(2) All costs can be divided into fixed and variable elements.

(3) Total fixed costs remain constant over the relevant volume range of the CVP analysis.

(4) Total variable costs are directly proportional to volume over the relevant range.

(5) Selling prices are to be unchanged.

(6) Prices of the factors of production are to be unchanged (for example, material, prices, wage rates).

(7) Efficiency and productivity are to be unchanged.

(8) The analysis either covers a single product or assumes that a given sales mix will be maintained as total volume changes.

(9) Revenue and costs are being compared on a single activity basis (for example, units produced and sold or sales value of production).

(10) Perhaps the most basic assumption of all is that volume is the only relevant factor affecting cost. Of course, other factors also affect costs and sales. Ordinary cost-volume-profit analysis is a crude oversimplification when these factors are unjustifiably ignored.

(11) The volume of production equals the volume of sales, or changes in beginning and ending inventory levels are insignificant in amount.

## 15 Practice Questions

### Test Your Understanding 6

A company manufactures five products in one factory. The company's budgeted fixed costs for the next year are $300,000. The table below summarises the budgeted sales and contribution details for the five products for the next year.

| Product | A | B | C | D | E |
|---|---|---|---|---|---|
| Unit Selling Price | $40 | $15 | $40 | $30 | $20 |
| Total Sales ($000) | 400 | 180 | 1,400 | 900 | 200 |
| Contribution to Sales ratio | 45% | 30% | 25% | 20% | (10%) |

The following diagram has been prepared to summarise the above budget figures:

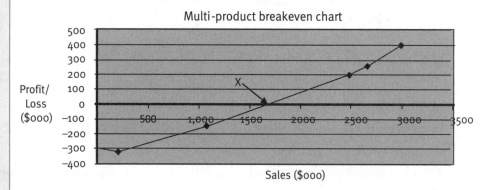

**Required:**

(a) Explain the meaning of point X on the chart.

(b) Calculate the breakeven revenue for the next year using the budgeted sales mix.

## Test Your Understanding 7

JK Ltd has prepared a budget for the next 12 months when it intends to make and sell four products, details of which are shown below:

| Product | Sales in units (thousands) | Selling price per unit $ | Variable cost per unit $ |
|---|---|---|---|
| J | 10 | 20 | 14.00 |
| K | 10 | 40 | 8.00 |
| L | 50 | 4 | 4.20 |
| M | 20 | 10 | 7.00 |

Budgeted fixed costs are $240,000 per annum and total assets employed are $570,000.

**Required:**

(a) to calculate the total contribution earned by each product and their combined total contributions;

(b) to plot the data of your answer to (a) above in the form of a profit-volume graph;

(c) to explain your graph to management, to comment on the results shown and state the break-even point;

(d) to describe briefly three ways in which the overall contribution to sales ratio could be improved.

## Mini-Quiz

(1) What is the formula for calculating the breakeven point in terms of the number of units required to break even?

(2) Give the formula which uses the C/S ratio to calculate the breakeven point.

(3) What is the margin of safety?

(4) What do the axes of a breakeven chart represent?

(5) A company provides three different levels of customer service support for one of its software products. The following data relate to these three levels of support:

| Support level | Superior $ per contract | Standard $ per contract | Basic $ per contract |
|---|---|---|---|
| Annual fee | 1,000 | 750 | 400 |
| Annual Variable costs | 450 | 250 | 180 |
| Annual fixed costs (see note below) | 200 | 100 | 50 |
| Profit | 350 | 400 | 170 |

**Note:** The total annual fixed costs are budgeted to be $1,000,000. None of these costs are specific to any type of customer service support.

Assume that the number of customer service support contracts sold are in the following proportion : Superior 20%, Standard 30%, Basic 50%.

What annual revenue that needs to be generated in order to break even?

## Test your understanding answers

### Test Your Understanding 1

Monthly fixed costs = 4,000 units × $4 = $16,000.

First calculate the breakeven sales: 16,000/(18–8) = 1,600

Margin of safety % = (projected sales – breakeven sales) / projected sales

$$= (4,000 – 1,600) / 4,000 = 60\%$$

### Test Your Understanding 2

(i) The key to calculating the breakeven point is to determine the contribution per unit.

Contribution point = $120 – ($22 + $36 + $14) = $48

$$\text{Breakeven point} = \frac{\text{Fixed overhead}}{\text{Contribution per unit}}$$

$$= \frac{\$12 \times 2,000}{\$48} = \textbf{500 units}$$

(ii) Margin of safety = budgeted sales – breakeven point
= 2,200 – 500
= **1,700 units** (or 1,700 /2,200 × 100 %)
= **77 %**

(iii) Once breakeven point has been reached, all of the contribution goes towards profits because all of the fixed costs have been covered.

Budgeted profit = 1,700 units margin of safety × $48 contribution per unit
= **$81,600**

(iv) To achieve the desired level of profit, sufficient units must be sold to earn a contribution which covers the fixed costs and leaves the desired profit for the month.

$$\text{Number of sales units required} = \frac{\text{Fixed overhead + desired profit}}{\text{Contribution per unit}}$$

$$= \frac{(\$12 \times 2{,}000) + \$96{,}000}{\$48}$$

$$= \textbf{2,500 units}$$

(v) Contribution per unit is calculated as $120 - $72 sum of variable costs = $48.

$$\text{Contribution to sales ratio} = \frac{\text{Contribution per unit}}{\text{Sales revenue per unit}}$$

$$= \frac{\$48}{\$120}$$

$$= \textbf{40\%}$$

(iv) Breakeven revenue can be calculated in two ways .

$$\text{B.E.R} = \frac{\text{Monthly fixed costs}}{\text{Contribution to sales ratio}}$$

$$= \frac{\$12 \times 2{,}000 \text{ units}}{40\%}$$

$$= \textbf{\$60,000}$$

This could also have been calculated as Breakeven Point 500 units x Selling price $120

$$= \textbf{\$60,000}$$

## Test Your Understanding 3

(a)  First calculate the current contribution per unit.

|  | $000 | $000 |
|---|---|---|
| Sales revenue | | 288 |
| Direct materials | 54 | |
| Direct wages | 72 | |
| Variable production overhead | 18 | |
| Variable administration etc. | 27 | |
| | | 171 |
| Contribution | | 117 |
| Contribution per unit ($117,000/9,000 units) | | $13 |

Now you can use the formula to calculate the breakeven point.

Breakeven point =

$$\frac{\text{Fixed costs}}{\text{Contribution per unit}} = \frac{\$42,000 + \$36,000}{\$13} = 6,000 \text{ units}$$

(b)  *Alternative (i)*

| | |
|---|---|
| Budgeted contribution per unit | $13 |
| Reduction in selling price ($32 – $28) | $4 |
| Revised contribution per unit | $9 |
| Revised breakeven point = $78,000/$9 | 8,667 units |
| Revised sales volume = 9,000 × (90/75) | 10,800 units |
| Revised contribution = 10,800 × $9 | $97,200 |
| Less fixed costs | $78,000 |
| Revised profit | $19,200 |

*Alternative (ii)*

| | |
|---|---:|
| Budgeted contribution per unit | $13.00 |
| Reduction in selling price (15% × $32) | $4.80 |
| | ––––– |
| Revised contribution per unit | $8.20 |
| | ––––– |

$$\text{Revised breakeven point} \quad = \quad \frac{\$78,000 + \$5,000}{\$8.20} \qquad 10,122 \text{ Units}$$

| | |
|---|---:|
| Revised sales volume : 9,000 units × (100/75) | 12,000 Units |
| Revised contribution : 12,000 × $8.20 | $98,400 |
| Less fixed costs | $83,000 |
| | ––––– |
| Revised profit | $15,400 |
| | ––––– |

Neither of the two alternative proposals is worthwhile. They both result in lower forecast profits. In addition, they will both increase the breakeven point and will therefore increase the risk associated with the company's operations.

This exercise has shown you how an understanding of cost behaviour patterns and the manipulation of contribution can enable the rapid evaluation of the financial effects of a proposal. We can now expand it to demonstrate another aspect of the application of CVP analysis to short-term decision-making.

Once again, the key is the required contribution. This time the contribution must be sufficient to cover both the fixed costs and the required profit. If we then divide this amount by the contribution earned from each unit, we can determine the required sales volume.

$$\text{Required sales} \quad = \quad \frac{\text{Fixed costs + required profit}}{\text{Contribution per unit}}$$

$$= \quad \frac{(\$42,000 + \$36,000 + \$45,500)}{\$13} \quad = \underline{\textbf{9,500 units}}$$

**Example 1 – Multi-Product**

(a)

| Product | Contribution $000 | Sales revenue $000 | C/S ratio |
|---|---|---|---|
| X | 550 | 800 | 0.6875 |
| Y | 50 | 200 | 0.25 |
| Z | 300 | 1,000 | 0.30 |
| Total | 900 | 2,000 | |

Weighted Average Contribution to Sales Ratio

$$= \frac{\text{Total Contribution}}{\text{Total sales}}$$

$$= \frac{\$900,000}{\$2,000,000}$$

$$= 0.45 \text{ or } 45\%$$

(b)

Breakeven Sales Revenue required

$$= \frac{\text{Fixed costs}}{\text{C/S ratio}}$$

$$= \frac{\$300,000}{45\%}$$

$$= \$666,667$$

(c)

Sales Revenue Required

$$= \frac{\text{Fixed costs + required profit}}{\text{C/S ratio}}$$

$$= \frac{\$300,000 + \$600,000}{0.45}$$

$$= \$2,000,000$$

Firstly, products must be ranked according to their C/S ratios. Then assume that the products are sold in the order of highest C/S ratio first. The table below provides the workings to enable the chart to be drawn.

| Product | Contribution $000 | Cumulative Profit / (Loss) $000 | Revenue $000 | Cumulative Revenue $000 |
|---|---|---|---|---|
| | | (300) | | 0 |
| X | 550 | 250 | 800 | 800 |
| Z | 300 | 550 | 1,000 | 1,800 |
| Y | 50 | 600 | 200 | 2,000 |

The chart is, essentially, a profit/volume chart. Cumulative profit is plotted against cumulative sales revenue. Like P/V charts for single products the line drawn starts at the fixed costs below the line.

## Multi-product break-even chart

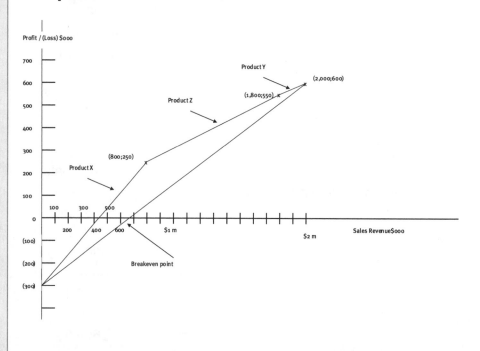

## Example 2 – R, S and T

**Answer B**

|  | R | S | T | Total |
|---|---|---|---|---|
|  | $ | $ | $ | $ |
| Sales revenue | 10,000 | 15,000 | 20,000 | 45,000 |
| Contribution | 6,000 | 6,000 | 10,000 | 22,000 |
| C/S ratio | 0.6 | 0.4 | 0.5 | 0.489 |
| New weightings | 20% | 50% | 30% | 13,000 |
| New C/S ratio | 0.12 | 0.2 | 0.15 | 0.47 |

So the new C/S ratio is lower.

## Test Your Understanding 4 – Sensitivity Analysis

Try to obtain a piece of graph paper and practise drawing your graphs to scale. Remember to use the whole of the paper – do not produce a tiny graph in the corner of the sheet. Remember that the graph in part (a) will cut the vertical axis at the point equal to the fixed costs, that is, the loss when no sales are made. Practice good exam technique: check your breakeven point arithmetically to verify that your graph is accurate.

(a)

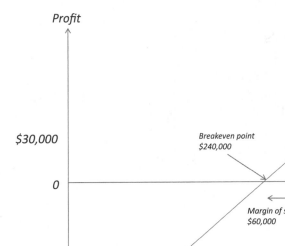
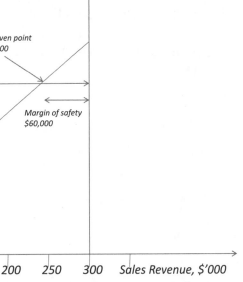

(b) These graphs show increase or decrease in profit by +x or −x.

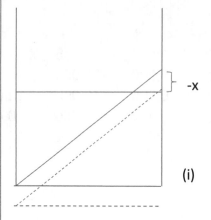

(i)

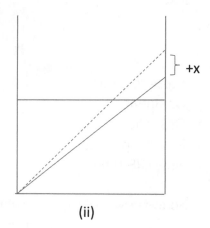

(ii)

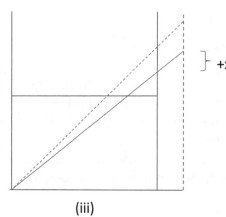

(iii)

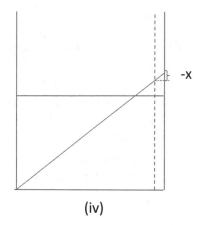

(iv)

(i) An increase in fixed costs

(ii) A decrease in variable costs

(iii) An increase in Sales Price

(iv) A decrease in Sales Volume

**Test Your Understanding 5 – Sensitivity Analysis – Sales Mix**

(a) To calculate the overall breakeven point (expressed in Sales value terms), we need to calculate a weighted average Contribution to Sales ratio. To this end, we will need a total Sales Revenue, as well as a Total Contribution in $:

|  | Summer | Autumn | Winter | Spring | **Total** |
|---|---|---|---|---|---|
| Sales Mix | 33.33% | 41.23% | 16.67% | 8.33% | 100% |
| Sales in $ | 200,000 | 250,000 | 100,000 | 50,000 | 600,000 |
| Less: Variable costs in $ | 120,000 | 170,000 | 80,000 | 20,000 | 390,000 |
| Contribution | 80,000 | 80,000 | 20,000 | 30,000 | 210,000 |

Weighted average C/S Ratio = ($210,000 / $600,000)

Weighted average C/S Ratio = $35%

$$\text{Breakeven Point (sales value)} = \frac{\text{Fixed Costs}}{\text{WA C/S ratio}}$$

Breakeven Point (sales value)                = **$454,286**

(b) After the change in Sales Mix, contribution can be calculated as follows:

|  | Summer | Autumn | Winter | Spring | Total |
|---|---|---|---|---|---|
| Sales Mix | 25% | 40% | 30% | 5% | 100% |
| Sales in $ | 150,000 | 240,000 | 180,000 | 30,000 | 600,000 |
| Less: Variable costs in $ | 90,000 | 163,200 | 144,000 | 12,000 | 409,200 |
| Contribution | 60,000 | 76,800 | 36,000 | 18,000 | 190,800 |

Weighted average C/S Ratio = ($190,800 / $600,000)

Weighted average C/S Ratio = $31.8%

$$\text{Breakeven Point (sales value)} = \frac{\text{Fixed Costs}}{\text{WA C/S ratio}}$$

Breakeven Point (sales value)                = **$500,000.**

### Test Your Understanding 6

(a) Point X on the chart shows the highest value of sales at which break-even will occur, assuming that the budgeted sales value is the maximum achievable for each of the products. It looks like that breakeven point is achieved when all of E, all of D and some of Cs are sold.

Note that it is not meaningful here, because it is unlikely that in reality, all of D and Es products will be sold whilst none of As or Bs will.

(b)

### Working 1 – Weighted Average Contribution to Sales ratio:

$$\text{Breakeven revenue} = \frac{\text{Fixed costs}}{\text{Weighted average contribution to sales ratio}}$$

$$\text{Breakeven revenue} = \frac{\$300,000}{24.16\% \text{ (working 1)}}$$

$$= \mathbf{\$1,241,935}$$

| Product | A | B | C | D | E | Total |
|---|---|---|---|---|---|---|
| Unit Selling Price | $40 | $15 | $40 | $30 | $20 | |
| Total Sales ($000) | 400 | 180 | 1,400 | 900 | 200 | 3,080 |
| Contribution to Sales ratio | 45% | 30% | 25% | 20% | (10%) | |
| Contribution ($000) | 180 | 54 | 350 | 180 | (20) | 744 |

$$\text{Weighted average C/S ratio} = \frac{\text{Total Contribution } \$744,000}{\text{Total sales } \$3,080,000}$$

$$= \mathbf{0.2416 \text{ or } 24.16\%}$$

> ### From the Post Exam Guide – September 2010:
>
> *From the answers submitted it was abundantly clear that most candidates did not fully understand that there are two acceptable approaches when constructing a multi-product breakeven chart; in particular that it can be constructed with the products with the highest C/S ratio first, or vice versa (as is the case here).*
>
> *Many answers displayed a poor grasp of maths e.g. totalling the ratios for the five products, and then dividing by five to obtain a weighted average C/S ratio.*
>
> (1) *Not understanding that when the graph is constructed starting with the product with the lower C/S ratio, the point X on the chart shows the highest value of sales at which break even will occur.*
> *Point X is not simply 'the breakeven point'.*
>
> (2) *Not reading the question correctly and attempting to show the breakeven point in units – completely meaningless.*

## Test Your Understanding 7

(a)

| Product | Revenue $000 | Variable Costs $000 | Contribution $000 | C/S ratio |
|---------|--------------|---------------------|-------------------|-----------|
| J | 200 | 140 | 60 | 0.30 |
| K | 400 | 80 | 320 | 0.80 |
| L | 200 | 210 | (10) | (0.05) |
| M | 200 | 140 | 60 | 0.30 |
| | **1,000** | **570** | **430** | |

(b)

| Product | Contribution $000 | Cumulative Profit / (Loss) | Revenue $000 | Cumulative Revenue |
|---------|-------------------|----------------------------|--------------|--------------------|
| | | (240) | | 0 |
| K | 320 | 80 | 400 | 400 |
| J | 60 | 140 | 200 | 600 |
| M | 60 | 200 | 200 | 800 |
| L | (10) | 190 | 200 | 1,000 |

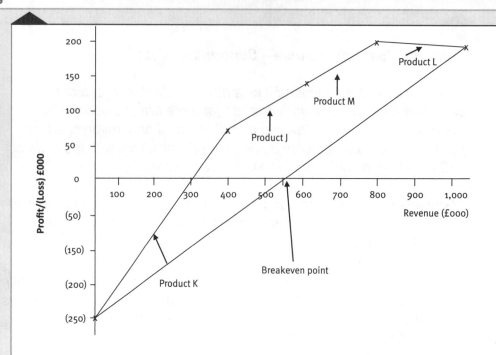

(c) The products are plotted in the order of their C/S ratios. The fixed costs of the company are $240,000. The chart reveals that if only product K is produced, the company will generate a profit of $80,000. The profit of the company is maximised at $200,000. This is achieved by producing Products K, J and M only.

If all four products are produced then JK Ltd can expect a profit of $190,000 from sales revenue of $1,000,000. If all four products are sold in the budget sales mix then the company will break even when revenue reaches $558,140. This point has been indicated on the graph. This point can also be calculated. Thus:

Average contribution/     = 430/1,000 = 43%
sales ratio

$$\text{Break-even point} = \frac{\text{Fixed costs}}{\text{Average C/S ratio}}$$

$$= \frac{\$240,000}{0.43} = \$558,140$$

(d) The overall C/S ratio could be improved by:

– Changing the product mix in favour of products with above-average C/S ratios. In this example that would mean increasing production of Product K.

– Increasing sales revenue.

– Deleting product L.

## Mini-Quiz

(1) Breakeven point (units) = Total fixed costs/Contribution per unit

(2) Sales value at breakeven point = Total Fixed Cost divide by C/S ratio, or WA C/S ratio in a multi-product environment.

(3) The margin of safety is the difference in units between the budgeted sales volume and the breakeven sales volume.

(4) The vertical axis represents money (costs and revenue) and the horizontal axis represents the level of activity (production and sales).

(5)

| Volume | Contribution per contract | Total Contribution | Selling Price | Total Revenue |
|---|---|---|---|---|
| | $ | $ | $ | $ |
| 2 | 550 | 1,100 | 1,000 | 2,000 |
| 3 | 500 | 1,500 | 750 | 2,250 |
| 5 | 220 | 1,100 | 400 | 2,000 |
| | | **3,700** | | **6,250** |

Average C/S ratio = $3,700 / $6,250 = 0.592

Breakeven point = $1,000,000 / 0.592 = $1,689,189

# Decision Making and Relevant Costs

## Chapter learning objectives

- **Discuss** the principles of decision-making including the identification of relevant cash flows and their use alongside non-quantifiable factors in making rounded judgements. (Syllabus link A1a)

- **Explain** why joint costs must be allocated to final products for financial reporting purposes, but why this is unhelpful when decisions concerning process and product viability have to be taken. (Syllabus link A3c)

- **Explain** the usefulness of dividing costs into variable and fixed components in the context of short-term decision making. (Syllabus link A2a)

## 1 Session Content Diagram

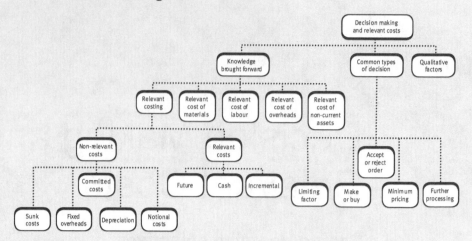

## 2 Introduction To Relevant Costs And Revenues

Decision making involves making a choice between two or more alternatives. The decision will be 'rational', i.e. profit maximising.

A distinction must be made between **relevant** and **non-relevant** costs for the purposes of management decision-making. All decisions will be made using relevant costs and revenues; many of the costs recorded by a business are crucial for the purposes of calculating accounting profits, but should be ignored when making decisions about particular future investments.

In this chapter, we will consider a number of short-term decision making scenarios, and how to solve them using relevant costs and revenues.

## 3 Knowledge Brought Forward

You will already have covered Relevant Costing and Decision Making in Papers C01 and P1. We will build on this knowledge in P2 with more complex decision-making situations, but make sure you are comfortable with the assumed knowledge, that should have been brought forward as a base, in the following sections (up to and including section 11).

> In its *Official Terminology,* CIMA defines **'relevant costs'** and 'relevant revenues' as the 'costs and revenues appropriate to a specific management decision; they are represented by future cash flows whose magnitude will vary depending upon the outcome of the management decision made(...)'.

Organisations face many decisions, and they usually must choose between two or more alternatives. Decisions will generally be based on taking the decision that maximises shareholder value, so all decisions will be taken using relevant costs and revenues. **Relevant costs and revenues are those costs and revenues that *change* as a direct result of a decision taken.**

Relevant costs and revenues have the following features:

(1) **They are future costs and revenues** – as it is not possible to change what has happened in the past, then relevant costs and revenues must be future costs and revenues.

(2) **They are incremental** or **differential** – relevant costs are incremental costs and it is the increase in costs and revenues that occurs as a direct result of a decision taken that is relevant. Common costs can be ignored for the purposes of decision making. Look out for costs detailed as *differential, specific or avoidable*.

> CIMA defines 'avoidable costs' as 'the specific costs of an activity or sector of a business which would be avoided if that activity or sector did not exist.'

For example, if a company is considering shutting down a department, then the avoidable costs are those that would be saved as a result of the shutdown. Such costs might include the labour costs of those employed in the department and the rental cost of the space occupied by the department. The latter is an example of an **attributable** or **specific** fixed cost. Costs such as apportioned head office costs that would not be saved as a result of the shutdown are unavoidable costs. They are not relevant to the decision.

(3) **They are cash flows** – in addition, future costs and revenues must be cash flows arising as a direct consequence of the decision taken. Relevant costs do not include items which do not involve cash flows (depreciation and notional costs for example).

*In an examination, unless told otherwise, assume that variable costs are relevant costs.*

## 4 Non-Relevant Costs

Costs that are not usually relevant in management decisions include the following:

(a)  **Sunk** or **past** costs, that is money already spent that cannot now be recovered. An example of a sunk cost is expenditure that has been incurred in developing a new product. The money cannot be recovered even if a decision is taken to abandon any further development of the product. The cost is therefore not relevant to future decisions concerning the product.

(b)  **Fixed overheads that will not increase or decrease** as a result of the decision being taken. If the actual amount of overhead incurred by the company will not alter, then the overhead is not a relevant cost. This is true even if the amount of overhead to be absorbed by a particular cost unit alters as a result of the company's cost accounting procedures for overheads.

(c)  Expenditure that will be incurred in the future, but as a result of decisions taken in the past that cannot now be changed. These are known as **committed costs**. They can sometimes cause confusion because they are future costs. However, a committed cost will be incurred regardless of the decision being taken and therefore it is not relevant. An example of this type of cost could be expenditure on special packaging for a new product, where the packaging has been ordered and delivered but not yet paid for. The company is obliged to pay for the packaging even if they decide not to proceed with the product; therefore it is not a relevant cost.

(d)  Historical cost **depreciation** that has been calculated in the conventional manner. Such depreciation calculations do not result in any future cash flows. They are merely the book entries that are designed to spread the original cost of an asset over its useful life.

(e)  **Notional costs** such as notional rent and notional interest. These are only relevant if they represent an identified lost opportunity to use the premises or the finance for some alternative purpose. In these circumstances, the notional costs would be opportunity costs.

## 5 Opportunity Costs

> An opportunity cost is a special type of relevant cost. It is defined in the *CIMA Terminology* as 'the value of the benefit sacrificed when one course of action is chosen, in preference to an alternative. The opportunity cost is represented by the forgone potential benefit from the best rejected course of action.'

'Opportunity cost' is an important concept in decision making. It represents **the best alternative that is forgone in taking the decision.** The opportunity cost emphasises that decision making is concerned with alternatives and that a cost of taking one decision is the profit or contribution forgone by not taking the next best alternative.

If resources to be used on projects are scarce (e.g. labour, materials, machines), then consideration must be given to profits or contribution which could have been earned from alternative uses of the resources.

For example, the skilled labour which may be needed on a new project might have to be withdrawn from normal production. This withdrawal would cause a loss in contribution which is obviously relevant to the project appraisal.

The cash flows of a single department or division cannot be looked at in isolation. It is always the effects on cash flows of the whole organisation which must be considered.

## Examples of Opportunity Costs

The best way to demonstrate opportunity costs is to consider some examples:

(a) A company has some obsolete material in inventory that it is considering using for a special contract. If the material is not used on the contract it can either be sold back to the supplier for $2 per tonne or it can be used on another contract in place of a different material that would usually cost $2.20 per tonne.

   The opportunity cost of using the material on the special contract is $2.20 per tonne. This is the value of the next best alternative use for the material, or the benefit forgone by not using it for the other contract.

(b) Chris is deciding whether or not to take a skiing holiday this year. The travel agent is quoting an all-inclusive holiday cost of $675 for a week. Chris will lose the chance to earn $200 for a part-time job during the week that the holiday would be taken. The relevant cost of taking the holiday is $875. This is made up of the out-of-pocket cost of $675, plus the $200 opportunity cost that is the part-time wages forgone.

### Example 1 – Opportunity Cost

A company which manufactures and sells one single product is currently operating at 85% of full capacity, producing 102,000 units per month. The current total monthly costs of production amount to $330,000, of which $75,000 are fixed and are expected to remain unchanged for all levels of activity up to full capacity.

A new potential customer has expressed interest in taking regular monthly delivery of 12,000 units at a price of $2.80 per unit.

All existing production is sold each month at a price of $3.25 per unit. If the new business is accepted, existing sales are expected to fall by 2 units for every 15 units sold to the new customer.

What is the overall increase in monthly profit which would result from accepting the new business?

## 6 Notional Costs and Opportunity Costs

**Notional costs** and **opportunity costs** are in fact very similar. This is particularly noticeable in the case of notional rent.

The notional rent could be the rental that the company is forgoing by occupying the premises itself, i.e. it could be an opportunity cost. However, it is only a true opportunity cost if the company can actually identify a forgone opportunity to rent the premises. If nobody is willing to pay the rent, then it is not an opportunity cost.

If an examination question on relevant costs includes information about notional costs, read the question carefully and state your assumptions concerning the relevance of the notional cost.

## 7 Incremental Revenues

Just as incremental costs are the differences in cost between alternatives, so incremental revenues are the differences in revenues between the alternatives. Matching the incremental costs against the incremental revenues will produce a figure for the incremental gain or loss between the alternatives.

## 8 The Relevant Cost Of Materials

If a particular material or component is needed for a course of action the relevant cost of that material must be considered carefully. The following decision model may be used:

The flow chart hopefully provides a useful reminder of the points that must be considered when ascertaining the relevant cost of materials.

**Do remember to apply basic logic, consider relevant cash flows, and then use a bit of common sense!**

## Example 2 – Relevant Cost Of Materials

A company is considering a short-term pricing decision for a contract that would utilise some material P that it has held in inventory for some time. The company does not foresee any other use for the material. The work would require 1,000 kgs of Material P.

There are 800 kgs of Material P in inventory, which were bought some time ago at a cost of $3 per kg. The material held in inventory could currently be sold for $3.50 per kg. The current purchase price of Material P is $4.50 per kg.

What is the relevant cost of Material P for the company to use when making its pricing decision for the contract closest to?

## Example 3 – Relevant Cost Of Material

A company is considering a short-term pricing decision to utilise some spare capacity. The item to be manufactured and sold would use 1,500 kgs of raw material Q.

Material Q is in regular use by the company. It currently has 1,000 kgs in inventory, which was purchased last month at a cost of $4 per kg. The current replacement cost of material Q is $4.80 per kg and the current inventory could be sold for $4.30 per kg.

Calculate the relevant cost of material Q for the purposes of this decision.

## Example 4 – Relevant Cost Of Material

A firm is considering undertaking a contract for a special client. The contract requires 200 kg of material D. There is a stock of 1,000 kg, which was bought for $10/kg last year. The current resale value is $5/kg, although to buy in any extra kilograms would cost $17/kg. There is no other use for material D, except as a substitute for material E, which is in constant use. Details of material E are shown below:

|  | $/kg |
| --- | --- |
| Original purchase price | 8 |
| Resale value | 3 |
| Replacement cost | 15 |

What is the relevant cost of material D?

## 9 The Relevant Cost Of Labour

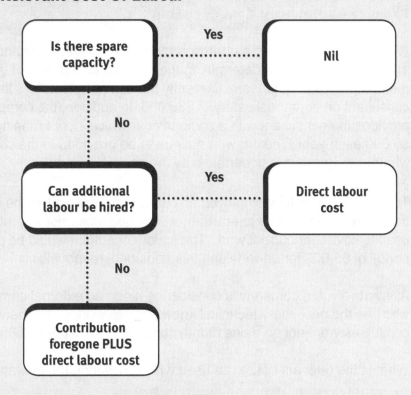

**Again, remember to apply basic logic, consider relevant cash flows, and then use a bit of common sense!**

### Example 5 – Relevant Cost Of Labour

100 hours of skilled labour are needed for a special contract. The staff are working at full capacity at the moment and the workers would have to be taken off production of a different product in order to work on the special contract. The details of the other product are shown below:

|  | $/unit |
|---|---|
| Selling price | 60 |
| Direct material | 10 |
| Direct labour 1 hour @ $10/hour | 10 |
| Variable overheads | 15 |
| Fixed overheads | 15 |

The skilled workers' pay rate would not change, regardless of which product they worked on. What would be the relevant cost?

## Example 6 – Relevant Cost Of Labour

A company is preparing a quotation for a one-month consultancy project and seeks your help in determining the relevant cost of one of the members of its project team. Currently the company employs the consultant on an annual salary of $36,000. In addition, the company provides the consultant with a company car which incurs running costs of $6,000 each year. The car will continue to be provided to the consultant whether this project is undertaken by the company or not.

This consultant is fully employed on current projects and, if she were to be transferred to this new project, then an existing junior consultant would be used to cover her current work. The junior consultant would be paid a bonus of $5,000 for undertaking this additional responsibility.

Alternatively, the company is considering hiring an external consultant who has the necessary technical knowledge to work on the new consultancy project on a one month contract at a cost of $4,500.

What is the relevant cost to be used when preparing the quotation?

## Example 7 – Relevant Cost Of Labour

Company A has been asked to quote for a special contract, that would require 100 hours of labour. However, the labourers, who are each paid $15 per hour, are working at full capacity. There is a shortage of labour in the market and therefore the labour required to undertake this special contract would have to be taken from another contract, Z, which currently utilises 500 hours of labour and generates $5,000 worth of contribution.

If the labour was taken from contract Z, then the whole of contract Z would have to be delayed, and such delay would invoke a penalty fee of $1,000.

What is the relevant cost of labour for the special contract?

## Example 8 – The CS Group

The CS group is planning its annual marketing conference for its sales executives and has approached the VBJ Holiday company (VBJ) to obtain a quotation. VBJ has been trying to win the business of the CS group for some time and is keen to provide a quotation which the CS group will find acceptable in the hope that this will lead to future contracts.

The manager of VBJ has produced the following cost estimate for the conference:

| | |
|---|---|
| Coach running costs | $2,000 |
| Driver costs | $3,000 |
| Hotel costs | $5,000 |
| General Overheads | $2,000 |
| **Sub total** | **$12,000** |
| Profit 30% | $3,600 |
| **Total** | **$15,600** |

You have considered this cost estimate but you believe that it would be more appropriate to base the quotation on relevant costs. You have therefore obtained the following further information:

Coach running costs represent the fuel costs of $1,500 plus an apportionment of the annual fixed costs of operating the coach. No specific fixed costs would be incurred if the coach is used on this contract. If the contract did not go ahead, the coach would not be in use for eight out of the ten days of the conference. For the other two days a contract has already been accepted which contains a significant financial penalty clause. This contract earns a contribution of $250 per day. A replacement coach could be hired for $180 per day.

Driver costs represent the salary and related employment costs of one driver for 10 days. If the driver is used on this contract the company will need to replace the driver so that VBJ can complete its existing work. The replacement driver would be hired from a recruitment agency that charges $400 per day for a suitably qualified driver. Hotel costs are the expected costs of hiring the hotel for the conference.

General overheads are based upon the overhead absorption rate of VBJ and are set annually when the company prepares its budgets. The only general overhead cost that can be specifically identified with the conference is the time that has been spent in considering the costs of the conference and preparing the quotation. This amounted to $250.

**Required:**

Prepare a statement showing the total relevant cost of the contract. Explain clearly the reasons for each of the values in your quotation and for excluding any of the costs (if appropriate).

### 10 Relevant Cost of Overheads

In addition to calculating the relevant cost of materials and labour, you may also be required to calculate the relevant cost of overheads.

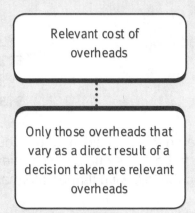

Relevant cost of overheads

Only those overheads that vary as a direct result of a decision taken are relevant overheads

### Illustration 1

JB Ltd absorbs overheads on a machine hour rate, currently $20/hour, of which $7 is for variable overheads and $13 for fixed overheads. The company is deciding whether to undertake a contract in the coming year. If the contract is undertaken, it is estimated that fixed costs will increase for the duration of the contract by $3,200.

**Required:**

Identify the relevant costs of the fixed and variable overheads for the contract.

**Solution:**

- The variable cost per hour of overhead is relevant since this cost would be avoidable if the contract were not undertaken. The relevant cost of variable overheads is therefore $7 per machine hour.

> - The fixed cost per hour is an absorption rate. Actual fixed costs would not increase by $13 per hour, but by $3,200 in total. The incremental relevant cost of fixed overheads is therefore $3,200.

## 11 Relevant Cost of Non-Current Assets

The relevant costs associated with non-current assets, such as plant and machinery, are determined in a similar way to the relevant costs of materials.

- If plant and machinery is to be replaced at the end of its useful life, then the relevant cost is the current replacement cost.

- If plant and machinery is not to be replaced, then the relevant cost is the higher of the sale proceeds (if sold) and the net cash inflows arising from the use of the asset (if not sold).

### Test your understanding 1

Equipment owned by a company has a net book value of $1,800 and has been idle for some months. It could now be used on a six months contract that is being considered. If not used on this contract, the equipment would be sold now for a net amount of $2,000. After use on the contract, the equipment would have no resale value and would be dismantled.

What is the total relevant cost of the equipment to the contract?

## 12 Common Types Of Decision

(1) Limiting factor decisions

(2) Make or buy decisions

(3) Shutdown decisions, including deleting a segment or temporary closure.

(4) Accept or reject an order decisions

(5) Minimum Pricing decisions

(6) Joint product and further processing decisions

(7) Extra shift decisions and overtime.

## Limiting factor

Also known as principal budget factor or key budget factor. It is that factor which prevents a company from achieving the output and sales that it would like. In practice the limiting factor is often sales demand, but in the exam it may be a shortage of labour in total or a shortage of one particular grade of labour or a shortage of material or machine capacity or capital or anything the Examiner fancies.

## Single limiting factor

If there is a just one limiting factor then the rule is to maximise the contribution per unit of scarce resource. The contribution per unit of each product is calculated and divided by the amount of scarce resource each product uses. The higher the contribution per unit of scarce resource the greater the priority that should be given to the product. Once the priorities have been decided the scarce resource is allocated to the products in the order of the priorities until used up.

*[In the PEG November 2012, the Examiner notes that some candidates are showing the correct ranking of the products but failing to correctly distribute the scarce resource.]*

### Example 9 – Limiting Factor Decisions – Single Limiting Factor

A company produces three products, and is reviewing the production and sales budgets for the next accounting period. The following information is available for the three products:

|  | Product P | | Product Q | | Product R | |
|---|---|---|---|---|---|---|
|  | $ | $ | $ | $ | $ | $ |
| Selling price |  | 600 |  | 300 |  | 100 |
| Labour ($20 per hour) | 300 |  | 160 |  | 40 |  |
| Other variable costs | 90 |  | 68 |  | 14 |  |
|  | —— |  | —— |  | —— |  |
|  |  | (390) |  | (228) |  | (54) |
|  |  | —— |  | —— |  | —— |
| Contribution/unit |  | 210 |  | 72 |  | 46 |
|  |  | —— |  | —— |  | —— |
| Maximum demand (units) |  | 200 |  | 600 |  | 1,000 |

Labour hours are strictly limited to 7,800 hours in total.

**Required:**

(a) Calculate the optimum product mix and the maximum contribution.

(b) A special contract requires 3,000 labour hours. What is the relevant cost of obtaining these hours?

## Make or buy decisions

Businesses may be faced with the decision whether to make components for their own products themselves or to concentrate their resources on assembling the products, obtaining the components from outside suppliers instead of making them 'in house'.

If the resources are bought in, their purchase cost is wholly marginal (i.e. direct). However, if it is decided to manufacture the components internally, the comparative costs of doing so will be the direct materials and wages costs, plus the variable factory overhead. If the total variable costs of internally manufactured components is seen to be greater than the cost of obtaining similar components elsewhere, it is obviously uneconomic to produce these items internally.

[In the PEG March 2011, the Examiner notes the following problems with answers :

(1) Not fully understanding a make or buy situation in the same context as limiting factors.

(2) Poorly presented answers.

(3) Figures appearing with no explanations.

(4) Answers not clearly identified.

(5) No workings to support figures.]

### Example 10 – Make Or Buy

A company manufactures four components (L, M, N and P) which are incorporated into different products. All the components are manufactured using the same general purpose machinery. The following production cost and machine hour data are available, together with the purchase prices from an outside supplier.

| Production cost: | L $ | M $ | N $ | P $ |
|---|---|---|---|---|
| Direct material | 12 | 18 | 15 | 8 |
| Direct labour | 25 | 15 | 10 | 8 |
| Variable overhead | 8 | 7 | 5 | 4 |
| Fixed overhead | 10 | 6 | 4 | 3 |
| **Total** | **55** | **46** | **34** | **23** |

| | L | M | N | P |
|---|---|---|---|---|
| Purchase price from outside supplier | $57 | $55 | $54 | $50 |
| | Hours | Hours | Hours | Hours |
| Machine hours per unit | 3 | 5 | 4 | 6 |

Manufacturing requirements show a need for 1,500 units of each component per week. The maximum number of general purpose machinery hours available per week is 24,000.

**What number of units should be purchased from the outside supplier?**

## Accept or reject an order decisions

In an 'accept or reject an order' decision, the selling price will already be known and if it is greater than the relevant costs the order should be accepted.

### Example 11 – Make Or Buy / Accept Or Reject An Order

A company manufactures two models of a pocket calculator: The basic model sells for $5.50, has a direct material cost of $1.25 and requires 0.25 hours of labour time to produce. The other model, the Scientist, sells for $7.50, has a direct material cost of $1.63 and takes 0.375 hours to produce.

Labour, which is paid at the rate of $6 per hour, is currently very scarce, while demand for the company's calculators is heavy. The company is currently producing 8,000 of the basic model and 4,000 of the Scientist model per month, while fixed costs are $24,000 per month.

An overseas customer has offered the company a contract, worth $35,000, for a number of calculators made to its requirements. The estimating department has ascertained the following facts in respect of the work:

- The labour time for the contract would be 1,200 hours.

- The material cost would be $9,000 plus the cost of a particular component not normally used in the company's models.

- These components could be purchased from a supplier for $2,500 or alternatively, they could be made internally for a material cost of $1,000 and an additional labour time of 150 hours.

**Required:**

Advise the management as to the action they should take.

## Shutdown decisions

This type of decision may involve deleting (or shutting down) a segment of the business, a product line, a service, etc. In the normal everyday reporting system of the business, it is likely that absorption costing will be used. It may appear under this system that one or more of the business segments appears unprofitable. Closure decisions taken on the basis of full absorption costs statements may fail to consider the fact that certain fixed costs allotted to the segment to be discontinued are fixed and may continue if the segment is dropped. The focus for shutdown decisions should be whether the costs and revenues are avoidable.

### Example 12 – Make or Buy and Limiting Factors

Company A manufactures four products in two different locations. It operates under strict Just-In-Time principles and does not hold any inventory of either finished goods or raw materials.

Company A has a long-standing agreement to supply its main customer with 100 units of each of its products Product 1, Product 2, Product 3 and Product 4. No negotiation is possible and the contract must be fulfilled.

Details of the company's additional, non-contract related production on Site 1 are as follows :

|  | Product 1 | Product 2 | Product 3 | Product 4 |
|---|---|---|---|---|
| Selling Price | $60 | $70 | $80 | $90 |
| | | | | |
| Direct labour, at $8 per hour | $16 | $8 | $12 | $16 |
| Direct Material A, at $3 per litre | $4.50 | $3.00 | $0 | $3.00 |
| Direct Material B, at $5 per kg | $5.00 | $- | $15 | $10 |
| | | | | |
| Variable overhead, labour related (*) | $1.25 | $0.63 | $0.94 | $1.25 |
| Variable overhead, machine related (*) | $1.25 | $2.00 | $0.75 | $1.00 |
| | | | | |
| Total Variable cost | $28.00 | $13.63 | $28.69 | $31.25 |
| | | | | |
| Machine hours per unit | 5 | 8 | 3 | 4 |
| Maximum demand per week | 900 units | 950 units | 950 units | 900 units |

(*) An analysis of the variable overhead shows that some of it is caused by the number of labour hours and the remainder is caused by the number of machine hours.

All the above products use the same resources (materials A and B). Currently, the company also purchases a component, Component Alpha, from an external supplier in the US for $50. A single unit of this component is used in producing Product 5, the company's only other product, on Site 2. Product 5 yields a positive contribution and does not use any materials used by the other products.

Company A could manufacture Component Alpha on Site 1, but to do so would require 2 hours of direct labour, half an hour of machine time as well as 1.5 kilograms of Material B.

The purchasing director has recently advised you that the availability of Direct Materials A and B is to be restricted to 5,000 litres and 6,000 kilograms every week. This restriction is unlikely to change in the near future, but no restrictions are expected on any other materials.

**Required :**

(a) Calculate whether Company A should continue to purchase Component Alpha or whether it should manufacture it internally.

(b) Prepare a statement to show the optimum weekly usage of Site 1's available resources.

(c) Assuming no other changes, calculate the purchase price of Component Alpha at which your advice in (a) would change.

## Example 13 – Shutdown Decision

Wye plc makes and sells four products. The profit and loss statement for April is as follows:

|  | W | X | Y | Z | Total |
|---|---|---|---|---|---|
|  | $ | $ | $ | $ | $ |
| Sales | 30,000 | 20,000 | 35,000 | 15,000 | 100,000 |
| Cost of sales | 16,000 | 8,000 | 22,000 | 10,000 | 56,000 |
| Gross Profit | 14,000 | 12,000 | 13,000 | 5,000 | 44,000 |
| Overhead Cost: |  |  |  |  |  |
| Selling | 8,000 | 7,000 | 8,500 | 6,500 | 30,000 |
| Administration | 2,000 | 2,000 | 2,000 | 2,000 | 8,000 |
| Net Profit | 4,000 | 3,000 | 2,500 | (3,500) | 6,000 |

The management team is concerned about the results, particularly those of product Z, and it has been suggested that Wye plc would be better off if it ceased production of product Z. The production manager has said that if product Z were discontinued the resources which would become available could be used to increase production of product Y by 40 per cent.

You have analysed the cost structures of each of the products and discovered the following:

|  | W | X | Y | Z | Total |
|---|---|---|---|---|---|
|  | $ | $ | $ | $ | $ |
| Variable costs | 4,800 | 1,600 | 13,200 | 5,000 | 24,600 |
| Fixed costs | 11,200 | 6,400 | 8,800 | 5,000 | 31,400 |
| Gross Profit | 16,000 | 8,000 | 22,000 | 10,000 | 56,000 |

The total fixed costs figure includes $20,000 which is not specific to any one product, and which has been apportioned to each product on the basis of sales values. If the quantity of any product increases by more than 25 per cent, then the specific fixed production costs of the product will increase by 30 per cent.

The selling overhead comprises a fixed cost of $5,000 per product plus a variable cost which varies in proportion to sales value. The fixed cost is not specific to any product but the sales director believes that it should be shared equally by the four products.

The administration cost is a central overhead cost; it is not affected by the products made.

**Required:**

(a) Prepare a statement which shows clearly the results of continuing to produce products W, X, Y and Z at the same volumes as were achieved in April. Present your statement in a format suitable for management decision-making.

(b) (i) Prepare a statement showing clearly the results if product Z is discontinued, and the number of units of Y is increased in accordance with the production manager's statement. (Assume that no change in selling price per unit is necessary to sell the additional units.)

    (ii) Reconcile the profit calculated in (a) and (b) (i) above; advise the management team as to whether product Z should be discontinued.

(c) Explain briefly any non-financial factors which should be considered before discontinuing a product.

## 13 Minimum Pricing Decisions

The minimum pricing approach is a useful method in situations where there is a lot of intense competition, surplus production capacity, clearance of old stocks, getting special orders and/or improving market share of the product.

Minimum Price is equal to incremental costs of manufacturing, plus opportunity costs (if any).

For this type of pricing, the selling price is the lowest price that a company may sell its product at – usually the price will be the Total Relevant Costs of Manufacturing.

### Illustration – Minimum Pricing

ABC Company has prepared a summary of its relevant costs for a special order:

| | | |
|---|---|---|
| (i) | Material P | $120 |
| | Material Q | $(280) |
| (ii) | Labour | – |
| (iii) | Variable overhead | $600 |
| (iv) | Rent forgone | $210 |
| | **Total relevant cost** | **$650** |

This cost of $650 represents the minimum price that the company should charge for the order if they wish to make neither a profit nor a loss. As long as the customer pays $650 for the order, the company profits will not be affected.

Obviously, this represents the absolute minimum price that could be charged. It is unlikely that ABC Ltd would actually charge this amount. They would probably wish to add a profit margin to improve the company's profits. However, this absolute minimum value does give managers a starting point for their pricing decision. They know that the company will be worse off if the price is less than $650. If perhaps ABC Ltd is tendering for the order in competition with other suppliers, they may try to obtain some information on the likely prices to be tendered by their competitors. If these prices are less than or close to $650, then ABC knows that they will not be able to offer a competitive price.

On the other hand, if competitors are likely to tender a much higher price, then the managers know that they are able to price competitively.

## Accounting for joint costs

A joint cost is the cost of a process that results in more than one main product. A common cost is a cost relating to more than one product or service.

The term 'joint cost' refers to the cost of some common process before a split-off point after which various joint products and by-products can be identified. 'Common costs' is a wider term that need not relate to a process. For example, the absorption of fixed production overheads in total absorption costing described earlier in this chapter is an example of assigning common costs to cost units.

### Joint products and by-products

The nature of process costing is that the process incurs joint costs and often produces more than one product. These additional products may be described as either joint products or by-products. Essentially joint products are all the main products, whereas by-products are incidental to the main products.

- *Joint products* are two or more products produced by the same process and separated in processing, each having a sufficiently high saleable value to merit recognition as a main product.

- A *by-product* is output of some value produced incidentally in manufacturing something else (main product).

These definitions still leave scope for subjective judgement, but they provide a basis for such judgement. The distinction is important because the accounting treatment of joint and by-products differs. Costs incurred in processing prior to the separation of the products are known as **joint costs**.

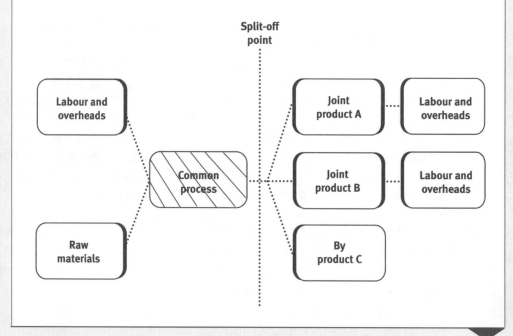

*Accounting for by-products*

Either of the following methods may be adopted: the proceeds from the sale of the by-product may be treated as pure profit, or the proceeds from the sale, less any handling and selling expenses, may be used to reduce the cost of the main products.

If a by-product needs further processing to improve its marketability, the cost will be deducted in arriving at net revenue. Note that recorded profits will be affected by the method adopted if stocks of the main product are maintained.

*Accounting for joint products*

Joint products are, by definition, subject to individual accounting procedures.

Joint costs will require apportionment between products for inventory valuation purposes. The main bases for appointment are as follows:

- *Physical measurement of joint products:* Joint costs can be apportioned to the units of output of each joint product. When the unit of measurement is different, e.g. litres and kilos, some method should be found of expressing them in a common unit. Some joint costs are not incurred equally for all joint products: such costs can be separated and apportioned by introducing weighting factors.

- *Market value:* Joint costs can be apportioned on the basis of the market value of each joint product at the point of separation. The effect is to make each product appear to be equally profitable.

- *Net realisable value:* Where certain products are processed after the point of separation, further processing costs may be deducted from the market values before joint costs are apportioned.

It is essential to realise that apportionment is, of necessity, an arbitrary calculation and product costs that include such an apportionment can be misleading if used as a basis for decision-making.

**Valuation of joint product stocks**

In the following example joint costs are apportioned on the following bases:

- physical measurement
- market value at point of separation
- net realisable value/net relative sales value
- technical estimates of relative usage.

The methods will result in different inventory valuations and, therefore, different recorded profits.

**Example**

|  | Kgs produced | Kgs sold | Selling price per kg | Joint cost |
|---|---|---|---|---|
| Product A | 100 | 80 | $5 | |
| | | | | $750 |
| Product B | 200 | 150 | $2 | |

**Solution**

- **Apportionment by physical measurement**

$$\frac{\text{Joint cost}}{\text{Kgs produced}} = \frac{\$750}{300} = \$2.50 \text{ per kg for A+B}$$

**Trading results**

|  | Product A | | Product B | | Total | |
|---|---|---|---|---|---|---|
| | | $ | | | $ | $ |
| Sales | 80 × $5.00 | 400 | 150×$2.00 | 300 | | 700 |
| Cost of Sales | 80 × $2.50 | 200 | 150×$2.50 | 375 | | 575 |
| Profit / (Loss) | | 200 | | (75) | | 125 |
| Value of closing inventory | 20 × $2.50 | 50 | 50 × $2.50 | 125 | | 125 |

The main point to emphasise about joint products is the production mix. In this case the production ratio is 100 : 200 which means that, in order to obtain 1 kg of A, it is necessary also to produce 2 kg of B. Although in the longer term it may be possible through research and development work to change the mix, in many processes this is not possible and for exam purposes you should assume that the ratio of output is fixed.

In attempting to assess the profitability of the common process it is necessary to assess the overall position as follows:

|  |  | $ |
|---|---|---|
| Sales value of product A | 100 × $5 | 500 |
| Sales value of product B | 200 × $2 | 400 |
|  |  | 900 |
| Joint cost |  | 750 |
| Profit |  | 150 |

This total profit figure should be used to evaluate the viability of the common process.

Referring back to the trading results, it is important to appreciate that the 'loss' on B has been created by the joint cost apportionment, i.e.:

|  | $ |
|---|---|
| Selling Price | 2.00 |
| Share of joint cost | 2.50 |
| Loss | 0.50 |

A decision not to produce and sell product B is not possible because, if product B were not purchased, then neither could product A be produced. A further point to note is that inventory of B could not be valued in the financial statements at $2.50 bearing in mind that inventory should be valued at the lower of cost and net realisable value.

**Apportionment by market value at point of separation**

|  | Sales value of production $ | Proportion | Joint cost apportionment $ | Per kg $ |
|---|---|---|---|---|
| A 100 × $5 | 500 | 5/9 | 417 | 4.17 |
| B 200 × $2 | 400 | 4/9 | 333 | 1.67 |
|  |  |  | 750 |  |

**Trading results:**

|  | A | B | Total |
|---|---|---|---|
| Sales | 400 | 300 | 700 |
| Cost of sales | 333.6 | 250.5 | 585.1 |
| Profit | 66.4 | 49.5 | 114.9 |
| Profit/sales | 16.6% | 16.5% | |
| Closing inventory | (20 × 4.17) | (50 × 1.67) | |
| | 83 | 83 | |

Notes:

(1) Apportionment is on the basis of proportionate sales value of production.

(2) Profit per unit is the same (with a small rounding difference).

(3) This approach provides a more realistic estimate of cost to use for valuing inventory of B, i.e. $1.67.

**Apportionment by net realisable value**

This approach should be used in situations where the sales value at the split-off point is not known – either because the product is not saleable, or if the examiner does not tell you – or if specifically asked for by the examiner.

Further information needed:

| **Further processing costs** | Selling price after further processing |
|---|---|
| $2.80 + + $2.00 per kg | $8.40 |
| $160 + $1.40 per kg | $4.50 |

**Apportionment of joint costs:**

|  | Product A | Product B |
|---|---|---|
|  | $ | $ |
| Final sales value of production | 840 | 900 |
| (100 × $8.40; 200 × $4.50) | | |
| Further processing cost | 480 | 440 |
| (280 + 100 × $2; 160 + 200 × $1.40) | | |
|  | 360 | 460 |
| Joint cost apportionment (360 : 460) | 329 | 421 |
| Joint cost per kg | $3.29 | $2.10 |

Trading Result (for common process only) :

|  | $ | $ | $ |
|---|---|---|---|
| Sales | | | 700 |
| Joint cost | | 750 | |
| Less : Closing inventory | | | |
| A   20 × $3.29 | 66 | | |
| B   50 × $2.10 | 105 | | |
| | | 171 | |
| Cost of sales | | | 579 |
| Profit | | | 121 |

**Notes:**

(1) As we know sales value of product B at the point of separation is $2, we can see that this method results in an unrealistic inventory value of $2.10. Bear in mind that this approach should only be used where the sales value at the split-off point is not known, or if instructed to use it by the examiner.

(2) The effect of further processing is considered in more detail below. Note that all the methods produce similar, but not identical results.

**Problems of common costs and joint costs**

Even if careful technical estimates are made of relative benefits, any apportionment of common costs or joint costs will inevitably be an arbitrary calculation. When providing information to assist decision-making, therefore, the cost accountant will emphasise cost and revenue differences arising from the decision.

The main decisions involving joint products are:

- To carry out the whole process or not. This decision is made by considering the total revenues and costs of the process. A decision cannot be taken to just process some of the products as all products are produced simultaneously. The basis of common cost apportionment is irrelevant but the common costs in total are relevant.

- Whether or not to further process products. This decision is based on the incremental costs and incremental revenues of further processing. Revenue and cost at the split-off point are irrelevant to the decision as they will not change.

### Joint products and further processing decisions

Joint products are two or more products which are output from the same processing operation, but which are indistinguishable from each other up to their point of separation. The point of separation is called the SPLIT-OFF point. Joint products usually have a substantial sales value and are the main reason for the processing.

Joint products may require processing after the split-off point.

With many joint products it is possible to sell the product at the split-off point or to send it through a further process which will enhance its value. There are two rules to follow when ascertaining whether the further processing is worthwhile:

(1)   Only the incremental costs and revenues of the further process are relevant.

(2)   The joint process costs are irrelevant – they are already sunk at the point of separation.

### Example 14 – Further Processing I

A processing company operates a common process from which three different products emerge. Each of the three products can then either be sold in a market that has many buyers and sellers or further processed independently of each other in three other processes. After further processing, each of the products can be sold in the same market for a higher unit selling price. Which of the following is required to determine whether or not any of the products should be further processed?

(i)     Total cost of the common process

(ii)    The basis of sharing the common process cost between the three products

(iii)   The total cost of each of the three additional processes

(iv)   The unit selling price of each product after further processing

(v)    The unit selling price of each product before further processing

(vi)   The percentage normal loss of each further process

(vii)  The actual units of output of each product from the common process

A      (iii), (iv), (vi) and (vii) only

B      (i), (ii), (iii), (iv), (vi) and (vii) only

C      (i), (ii), (v) and (vii) only

D      (iii), (iv), (v), (vi) and (vii) only

## Example 15 – Further Processing 2

Z is one of a number of companies that produce three products for an external market. The three products, R, S and T may be bought or sold in this market. The common process account of Z for March 2007 is shown below:

|  | Kg | $ |  | Kg | $ |
|---|---|---|---|---|---|
| Inputs : |  |  |  |  |  |
| Material A | 1,000 | 3,500 | Normal loss | 500 | 0 |
| Material B | 2,000 | 2,000 | Outputs : |  |  |
| Material C | 1,500 | 3,000 | Product R | 800 | 3,500 |
| Direct Labour |  | 6,000 | Product S | 2,000 | 8,750 |
| Variable Overhead |  | 2,000 | Product T | 1,200 | 5,250 |
| Fixed Cost |  | 1,000 |  |  |  |
| **Totals** | **4,500** | **17,500** |  | **4,500** | **17,500** |

Z can sell products R, S or T after this common process or they can be individually further processed and sold as RZ, SZ and TZ respectively. The market prices for the products at the intermediate stage and after further processing are (Market prices per kg):

|  | $ |
|---|---|
| R | 3.00 |
| S | 5.00 |
| T | 3.50 |
| RZ | 6.00 |
| SZ | 5.75 |
| TZ | 6.75 |

The specific costs of the three individual further processes are:

Process R to RZ – variable cost of $1.40 per kg, no fixed costs

Process S to SZ – variable cost of $0.90 per kg, no fixed costs

Process T to TZ – variable cost of $1.00 per kg, fixed cost of $600 per month

**Required:**

(a) Produce calculations to determine whether any of the intermediate products should be further processed before being sold. Clearly state your recommendations together with any relevant assumptions that you have made.

(b) Produce calculations to assess the viability of the common process:

 (i) assuming that there is an external market for products R, S and T; and

 (ii) assuming that there is not an external market for products R, S and T.

State clearly your recommendations.

## Qualitative Factors in Decision Making

In some decision-making situations, qualitative aspects are more important than immediate financial benefit from a decision. They will vary with different business circumstances and are those factors relevant to a decision that are difficult or impossible to measure in terms of money.

CIMA's *Official Terminology* defines 'Qualitative factors' as *'factors that are relevant to a decision but are not expressed numerically'*.

For an organisation faced with a decision , qualitative factors may include:

(1) The state of the economy, and its levels of inflation;

(2) The availability of cash;

(3) Effect of a decision on employee morale, schedules and other internal elements;

(4) Effect of a decision on relationships with and commitments to different stakeholders, such as:

 – Shareholders

 – Managers

 – Environment

 – Local Community

 – Suppliers

(5) Effect of a decision on long-term future profitability;

(6) Effect of a decision on a company's public image and the reaction of customers;

(7) The likely reaction of competitors.

## 14 Practice Questions

### Test Your understanding 2

P Limited is considering whether to continue making a component or buy it from an outside supplier. It uses 12,000 of the components each year.

The internal manufacturing cost comprises:

|  | $/unit |
|---|---|
| Direct materials | 3.00 |
| Direct labour | 4.00 |
| Variable overhead | 1.00 |
| Specific fixed cost | 2.50 |
| Other fixed costs | 2.00 |
|  | 12.50 |

If the direct labour were not used to manufacture the component, it would be used to increase the production of another item for which there is unlimited demand. This other item has a contribution of $10.00 per unit but requires $8.00 of labour per unit.

The maximum price per component at which buying is preferable to internal manufacture is:

A    $8.00

B    $10.50

C    $12.50

D    $15.50

## Test Your understanding 3

Budgeted data relating to a single-product firm that is working to full capacity are as follows:

| | |
|---|---|
| Production and sales for the year | 20,000 units |
| Machine capacity available and fully utilised | 40,000 hours |

| | $ |
|---|---|
| Variable cost | 8.20 |
| Fixed cost | 1.30 |
| | ——— |
| Total cost | 9.50 |
| Selling price | 12.50 |
| | ——— |
| Net profit per unit | 3.00 |
| | ——— |

An order is received for 3,000 modified units which will use 6,600 hours of machine time and cost $1.00 per unit for additional materials.

At what price should the firm be indifferent between taking on, and rejecting, the order?

A  $41,790

B  $40,500

C  $27,600

D  $17,190

## Test Your understanding 4

Lauda Ltd operates a joint process from which four products arise. The products may be sold at the separation point of the process or can be refined further and be sold at a premium. Information regarding the products and the refining process can be found below:

| Products | E | F | G | H |
|---|---|---|---|---|
| Selling prices per litre ($) | | | | |
| At separation point | 12 | 16 | 15 | 18 |
| After refining | 20 | 23 | 25 | 22 |
| Costs ($) | | | | |
| Joint process (per litre): | 8 | 8 | 8 | 8 |
| Refining process: | | | | |
| Variable (per litre) | 5 | 5 | 5 | 5 |
| Specific fixed (in total) | 1,000 | 2,000 | 3,000 | 4,000 |
| Budgeted litres | 2,000 | 500 | 5,000 | 6,000 |

The general fixed overheads in the refining process amount to $30,000.

Which products should be further processed?

A   E, F and G only

B   E and G only

C   G only

D   None of them

**(3 marks)**

## Test Your understanding 5 – Brown Ltd

Brown Ltd is a company which has in stock some materials of type XY which cost $150,000 but which are now obsolete and have a scrap value of only $42,000. Other than selling the material for scrap there are only two alternative uses for them.

### Alternative 1

Converting the obsolete materials into a specialised product which would require the following additional work and materials:

| | |
|---|---|
| Material A | 600 units |
| Material B | 1,000 units |
| Direct labour: | |
| 5,000 hours unskilled | |
| 5,000 hours semi-skilled | |
| 5,000 hours highly skilled | 15,000 hours |
| Extra selling and delivery expenses | $54,000 |
| Extra advertising | $36,000 |

The conversion would produce 900 units of saleable product and these could be sold for $600 per unit.

Material A is already in stock and is widely used within the firm. Although present stocks together with orders already planned will be sufficient to facilitate normal activity, any extra material used by adopting this alternative will necessitate such materials being replaced immediately. Material B is also in stock but it is unlikely that any additional supplies can be obtained for some considerable time because of an industrial dispute. At the present time material B is normally used in the production of product Z which sells at $780 per unit and incurs total variable cost (excluding material B) of $420 per unit. Each unit of product Z uses four units of material B.

The details of materials A and B are as follows:

| | Material A | Material B |
|---|---|---|
| | $ | $ |
| Acquisition cost at time of purchase | 200 per unit | 20 per unit |
| Net realisable value | 170 per unit | 36 per unit |
| Replacement cost | 180 per unit | |

## Alternative 2

Adapting the obsolete materials for use as a substitute for a sub-assembly which is regularly used within the firm. Details of the extra work and materials required are:

Material C 1,000 units

Direct labour:

| | |
|---|---|
| 4,000 hours unskilled | |
| 1,000 hours semi-skilled | |
| 4,000 hours highly skilled | 9,000 hours |

1,200 units of the sub-assembly are regularly used per quarter at a cost of $1,800 per unit. The adaptation of material XY would reduce the quantity of the sub-assembly purchased from outside the firm to 900 units for the next quarter only. However, as the volume purchased would be reduced some discount would be lost, and the price of those purchased from outside would increase to $2,100 per unit for that quarter.

Material C is not available externally but is manufactured by Brown Ltd. The 1,000 units required would not be available from stocks but would be produced as extra production. The standard cost per unit of material C would be as follows:

| | $ |
|---|---|
| Direct labour, 6 hours' unskilled labour | 36 |
| Raw materials | 26 |
| Variable overhead, 6 hours at $2 | 12 |
| Fixed overhead, 6 hours at $6 | 36 |
| | 110 |

The wage rates and overhead recovery rates for Brown Ltd are:

| | |
|---|---|
| Variable overhead | $2 per direct labour hour |
| Fixed overhead | $6 per direct labour hour |
| Unskilled labour | $6 per direct labour hour |
| Semi-skilled labour | $8 per direct labour hour |
| Highly skilled labour | $10 per direct labour hour |

The unskilled labour is employed on a casual basis and sufficient labour can be acquired to exactly meet the production requirements. Semi-skilled labour is part of the permanent labour force but the company has temporary excess supply of this type of labour at the present time. Highly skilled labour is in short supply and cannot be increased significantly in the short term; this labour is presently engaged in meeting the demand for product L which requires 4 hours of highly skilled labour. The contribution from the sale of one unit of product L is $48.

**Required:**

Given this information you are required to present cost information advising whether the stocks of material XY should be sold, converted into a specialised product (Alternative 1) or adapted for use as a substitute for a sub-assembly (Alternative 2).

### Test Your understanding 6 – Retail outlet

A small retail outlet sells four main groups of products: basic foods (milk, bread, etc); newspapers and magazines; frozen foods; and canned foods. A budgeted weekly profit statement is shown below:

|  | Basic foods | Newspapers & magazines | Frozen foods | Canned foods |
|---|---|---|---|---|
|  | $ | $ | $ | $ |
| Sales revenue | 800 | 1,000 | 1,500 | 2,400 |
| Cost of sales | 600 | 700 | 550 | 1,200 |
| Gross margin | 200 | 300 | 950 | 1,200 |
| Power for freezers * |  |  | 100 |  |
| Overheads ** | 100 | 100 | 200 | 400 |
| Net margin | 100 | 200 | 650 | 800 |

*The freezers would be emptied and switched off as necessary during redecoration.

**Overhead costs comprise general costs of heating and lighting, rent and rates, and other general overhead costs. These costs are attributed to products in proportion to the floor area occupied by each product group which is as follows:

|  | Basic foods | Newspapers & magazines | Frozen foods | Canned foods |
|---|---|---|---|---|
| Floor area (m2) | 50 | 50 | 100 | 200 |

For each product group, analysis has shown that the sales revenue achieved changes in direct proportion to the floor space allocated to the product.

The owner of the retail outlet has decided that the premises need to be redecorated but is undecided as to which of the following two options would be the most profitable.

**Option 1**: Close the retail outlet completely for four weeks while the redecoration takes place. The company that is to complete the redecoration would charge $2,500 under this option. It is expected that, following the re-opening of the retail outlet, there would be a loss of sales for the next 12 weeks because customers would have had to find alternative suppliers for their goods. The reduction in sales due to lost customers has been estimated to be 30% of the budgeted sales during the first four weeks of reopening; 20% during the next four weeks; and 10% during the third four weeks. In addition, in order to encourage customers to return to the retail outlet, there would be a 10% price reduction on all basic foods and canned foods for the entire 12-week period.

**Option 2**: Continue to open the retail outlet while the redecoration takes place but with a reduced amount of floor area.

The useable floor area would be reduced to 40% of that originally available. After three weeks, the retail outlet would be closed for 0.5 weeks while the goods are moved to the newly redecorated area. The retail outlet would then continue to operate using 40% of its original floor area for a further three weeks before the work was fully completed. The company that is to complete the redecoration would charge $3,500 under this option and, in addition, there would be product movement costs of $1,000. The owner has determined that, in order to avoid losing customers, there should be no reduction in the amount of floor area given to basic foods and newspapers and magazines throughout this period. The floor area to be used by frozen foods and canned foods should be determined on the basis of their profitability per unit of area. However, the frozen foods are presently kept in four freezers, and therefore any reductions in floor area must be determined by complete freezer units. It may be assumed that each freezer unit incurs equal amounts of power costs.

**Required:**

Advise the owner of the retail outlet which option to choose in order to minimise the losses that will occur as a result of the decision.

All workings must be shown.

## Mini-Quiz

(1) X plc intends to use relevant costs as the basis of the selling price for a special order: the printing of a brochure. The brochure requires a particular type of paper that is not regularly used by X plc although a limited amount is in X plc's inventory which was left over from a previous job. The cost when X plc bought this paper last year was $15 per ream and there are 100 reams in inventory. The brochure requires 250 reams. The current market price of the paper is $26 per ream, and the resale value of the paper in inventory is $10 per ream.

The relevant cost of the paper to be used in printing the brochure is:

A   $2,500

B   $4,900

C   $5,400

D   $6,500

(2) A farmer grows potatoes for sale to wholesalers and to individual customers. The farmer currently digs up the potatoes and sells them in 20 kg sacks. He is considering a decision to make a change to this current approach. He thinks that washing the potatoes and packaging them in 2 kg cartons might be more attractive to some of his individual customers. Which of the following is relevant to his decision?

(i)   the sales value of the dug potatoes

(ii)  the cost per kg of growing the potatoes

(iii) the cost of washing and packaging the potatoes

(iv)  the sales value of the washed and packaged potatoes

A   (ii), (iii) and (iv) only

B   (i), (ii) and (iii) only

C   (i), (ii) and (iv) only

D   (i), (iii) and (iv) only

(3) The following details relate to ready meals that are prepared by a food processing company:

| Ready Meal | K $/meal | L $/meal | M $/meal |
|---|---|---|---|
| Selling Price | 5.00 | 3.00 | 4.40 |
| Ingredients | 2.00 | 1.00 | 1.30 |
| Variable conversion costs | 1.60 | 0.80 | 1.85 |
| Fixed conversion costs* | 0.50 | 0.30 | 0.60 |
| Profit | 0.90 | 0.90 | 0.65 |
| Oven time (minutes per ready meal) | 10 | 4 | 8 |

Each of the meals is prepared using a series of processes, one of which involves cooking the ingredients in a large oven. The availability of cooking time in the oven is limited and, because each of the meals requires cooking at a different oven temperature, it is not possible to cook more than one of the meals in the oven at the same time.

*The fixed conversion costs are general fixed costs that are not specific to any type of ready meal.

The most and least profitable use of the oven is (Most profitable / Least profitable)

A   Meal K / Meal L

B   Meal L / Meal M

C   Meal L / Meal K

D   Meal M / Meal L

(4) The following unit cost information relates to a component currently manufactured by a firm for its own use.

| | $ |
|---|---|
| Materials | 2.50 |
| Labour | 1.25 |
| Variable overheads | 1.75 |
| Allocated fixed overheads | 3.50 |
| | 9.00 |

The costs are based on a normal monthly production of 50,000 components. The components could be bought in for $7.75 each, in which case all production capacity could be diverted to make 25,000 units per month of another product, earning a unit contribution of $4.80.

The allocated fixed overheads would be charged to this other product.

If the firm decides to buy in the component, what will be the overall effect on monthly profit?

A   A decrease of $167,500

B   An increase of $7,500

C   An increase of $63,750

D   An increase of $182,500

## Test your understanding answers

### Example 1 – Opportunity Cost

| 100% capacity | = 102,000 ÷ 0.85 | = 120,000 units |
|---|---|---|

Spare capacity amounts to 18,000 units. So there is sufficient slack to meet the new order.

| Variable costs | = $330,000 less $75,000 | = $255,000 |
|---|---|---|
| Variable cost per unit | = $255,000 ÷ 102,000 | = $2.50 |
| Contribution per unit from existing product | | = $3.25 – $2.50 = $0.75 |
| Contribution per unit from new product | | = $2.80 – $2.50 = $0.30 |

|  | $ |
|---|---|
| Increase in contribution from new product: | |
| $0.30 × 12,000 units | 3,600 |
| Fall in contribution from existing product: | |
| $0.75 × (12,000 ÷ 15) × 2 | |
| $0.75 × 1,600 | (1,200) |
| **Net Gain in contribution** | **2,400** |

### Example 2 – Relevant Cost Of Materials

1,000 kgs of P:

| Purchase 200 kgs; Current Replacement Price $4.50/Kg | = $900 |
|---|---|
| Use 800 kgs from inventory 800 × $3.50 | = $2,800 |
| Total | **= $3,700** |

### Example 3 – Relevant Cost Of Material

In regular use, so relevant cost = replacement cost

Replacement cost for Q  = 1500 kgs × $4.80
                        = $7,200

### Example 4 – Relevant Cost Of Material

If the contract were NOT undertaken what would be the best alternative use?

The 200 kg could be sold for 200 kg x $5 = $1,000

**OR**

Used as a substitute for material E. If D is used instead of E then LESS E needs to be bought. This will SAVE the company 200 kg x $15 = $3,000.

So substituting is the best of these two choices.

When the contract is undertaken the $3,000 saving will be foregone as a consequence.

### Example 5 – Relevant Cost Of Labour

Existing product earns a contribution per hour of $60 – $10 – $10 – $15 = $25

| Relevant cost | = Contribution foregone PLUS direct labour cost | |
|---|---|---|
|  | = $25 + $10 | = $35 per hour |
| Total cost | = $35 × 100 hours | = $3,500 |

### Example 6 – Relevant Cost Of Labour

**$4,500.**

It is cheaper to hire the external consultant for $4,500 rather than pay the $5,000 bonus to the existing junior consultant.

## Example 7 – Relevant Cost Of Labour

Labour is in short supply so there is an opportunity cost. The contribution from Contract Z will still be earned, but will be delayed. The relevant cost is therefore the wages earned plus the penalty fee.

($15 x 100) + ($1,000) = **$2,500**

## Example 8 – The CS Group

*[**From the PEG, May 2009**: Relevant costing questions are attempted by nearly every candidate, with most candidates attaining a high mark. The main weakness, and where most candidates lose marks, is the poor explanations provided to explain why a figure has been included or excluded. When a question says "you must clearly explain", an answer cannot be sufficient or awarded marks if it purely states "sunk cost" or "not relevant". This emphasises the need for all candidates to fully understand the verbs associated with this paper.]*

| | Note | $ |
|---|---|---|
| Relevant costs: | | |
| Fuel costs | 1 | 1,500 |
| Replacement coach | 2 | 360 |
| Replacement driver | 3 | 800 |
| Hotel costs | 4 | 5,000 |
| Total | | 7,660 |

**Notes:**

(1) The fuel cost is directly traceable to the contract and is therefore relevant. The apportionment of annual fixed costs for operating the coach are not relevant. The total fixed cost would remain the same whether the contract were accepted or not.

(2) The company should hire a replacement coach for two days @ $180 per day. This will ensure that the contribution of $250 per day continues to be earned from the other contract.

(3) The company's employed driver will be paid whether VBJ wins the contract or not. As a consequence of winning the contract, it would become necessary to hire a replacement driver for two days @ $400 per day to cover the existing work. This incremental cost is relevant.

(4) The hotel cost is directly attributable to the contract and is therefore relevant.

(5) The general overhead that has been traced to the contract ($250) should be ignored as this cost is sunk.

(6) The profit is not a relevant cost.

### Test your understanding 1

Opportunity cost now          = **$2,000**

### Example 9 – Limiting Factor Decisions – Single Limiting Factor

(a)

|  | Product | | |
|---|---|---|---|
|  | P | Q | R |
| Contribution per unit | $210 | $72 | $46 |
| Hours per unit | 15 | 8 | 2 |
| Contribution per hour | $14 | $9 | $23 |
| Rank | 2nd | 3rd | 1st |

| Product | Units | Hrs/ per unit | Total hours | Contribution per hour | Total contribution |
|---|---|---|---|---|---|
| R | 1,000 | 2 | 2,000 | $23 | $46,000 |
| P | 200 | 15 | 3,000 | $14 | $42,000 |
| Q | 350 | 8 | 2,800 | $9 | $25,200 |
|  |  |  | 7,800 |  | $113,200 |

(b) The special contract requires 3,000 SCARCE labour hours.

Relevant cost = Direct cost + Opportunity cost

| | | |
|---|---|---|
| Direct cost | 3,000 hrs × $20 | $60,000 |
| Opportunity cost | 2,800 hrs × $9 | $25,200 |
| | 200 hrs × $14 | $2,800 |
| **Relevant cost** | | **$88,000** |

### Example 10 – Make Or Buy

The following method could be adopted in this example :

(1) The saving per unit of each product is calculated. Saving = Purchases price – VC to make.

(2) Divide this by the amount of scarce resource (a.k.a. limiting factor) each product uses. This gives the saving per unit of limiting factor (LF).

(3) Rank. The higher the saving per unit of LF the greater the priority to make that should be given to the product.

(4) Once the priorities have been decided, the scarce resource is allocated to the products in the order of the priorities until it is fully used up.

(5) Any products with unsatisfied demand can be satisfied by buying from the external source.

(1) Calculate saving = Purchases price – VC to make:

| | L | M | N | P |
|---|---|---|---|---|
| External Purchase Price | $57 | $55 | $54 | $50 |
| Variable Costs to make | $45 | $40 | $30 | $20 |
| Saving | $12 | $15 | $24 | $30 |

(2) Calculate the saving per unit of limiting factor / scarce resource:

| | L | M | N | P |
|---|---|---|---|---|
| Saving | $12 | $15 | $24 | $30 |
| Scarce resource (machine hours) per unit | 3 hours | 5 hours | 4 hours | 6 hours |
| Saving per unit of the scarce resource | $4 | $3 | $6 | $5 |

(3) Rank

| | L | M | N | P |
|---|---|---|---|---|
| Saving per unit of the scarce resource | $4 | $3 | $6 | $5 |
| Ran : product to make in priority | 3 | 4 | 1 | 2 |

(4) Allocate scarce resource of 24,000 machine hours to production

Make all Ns (1,500 units). This will use up 1,500 x 4 hours = 6,000 hours.

Then, make all Ps (1,500 units). This will use up 1,500 x 6 hours = 9,000 hours. The cumulative total is 6,000 + 9,000 = 15,000 hours.

Then, make all Ls (1,500 units). This will use up 1,500 x 3 hours = 4,500 hours. The cumulative total is 15,000 + 4,500= 19,500 hours.

This leaves (24,000 – 19,500) = 4,500 hours, in which to make

$$\frac{4500}{5} = 900 \text{ units of Product M}$$

(5) Unsatisfied demand = 1,500 Ms – 900 Ms = 600 Ms. These will have to be bought externally.

|  | L | M | N | P |
|---|---|---|---|---|
| Variable production cost | $45 | $40 | $30 | $20 |
| External cost | $57 | $55 | $54 | $50 |
| **Incremental cost** | **$12** | **$15** | **$24** | **$30** |
| Hours per unit | ÷ 3 | ÷ 5 | ÷ 4 | ÷ 6 |
| **Incremental cost per hour** | **$4** | **$3** | **$6** | **$5** |
| Cheapest per hour | 2nd | 1st | 4th | 3rd |

The analysis shows that it is actually cheaper to try and make ALL the components within the factory.

Hours required to make 1,500 units of each component:

(1,500 × 3) + (1,500 × 5) + (1,500 × 4) + (1,500 × 6) = 27,000 hours

The company only has 24,000 hours available. So, 3,000 hours of work must be sub-contracted. The CHEAPEST component per hour must be bought externally. This is component M.

3,000 hours of time on M equates to 3,000 ÷ 5 = **600 units of M.**

## Example 11 – Make Or Buy / Accept Or Reject An Order

In view of its scarcity, labour is taken as the limiting factor.

The decision on whether to make or buy the component has to be made before it can be decided whether or not to accept the contract. In order to do this the contribution per labour hour for normal production must first be calculated, as the contract will replace some normal production.

| *Normal products* | | *Basic* | | *Scientist* |
|---|---|---|---|---|
| | $ | $ | $ | $ |
| Selling Price | | 5.50 | | 7.50 |
| Materials | 1.25 | | 1.63 | |
| Labour | 1.50 | | 2.25 | |
| | | 2.75 | | 3.88 |
| Contribution | | 2.75 | | 3.62 |
| Contribution per direct labour hour (@0.25 / 0.375 hours per unit) | | 11.00 | | 9.65 |

Therefore, if the company is to make the component it would be better to reduce production of the 'Scientist' model, in order to accommodate the special order.

The company should now compare the costs of making or buying the component.

An opportunity cost arises due to the lost contribution on the basic model.

| *Special Contract* | *Manufacture of component* |
|---|---|
| | $ |
| Materials | 1,000 |
| Labour ($6 x 150 hours) | 900 |
| Opportunity cost (150 hours x $9.6533) | 1,448 |
| | 3,348 |

Since this is higher than the bought-in price of $2,500 the company would be advised to buy the component from the supplier if they accept the contract.

The contract can now be evaluated:

| Normal products | | Contract contribution |
|---|---:|---:|
| | $ | $ |
| Sales Revenue | | 35,000 |
| Material cost | 9,000 | |
| Component | 2,500 | |
| Labour ($6 x 1,200) | 7,200 | |
| | ‾‾‾‾‾ | |
| | | 18,700 |
| Contribution | | 16,300 |
| | | ‾‾‾‾‾ |
| Contribution per direct labour hour (@0.25 / 0.375 hours per unit) | | $13.58 |
| | | ‾‾‾‾‾ |

Since the contribution is higher than either of the existing products, the company should accept the contract assuming this would not prejudice the market for existing products. As the customer is overseas this seems a reasonable assumption.

Because the contribution is higher for the 'Basic' model, it would be wise to reduce production of the Scientist model. However, the hours spent on producing the Scientist model per month are 4,000 units x 0.375 hours – 1,500, and so the contract would displace 80% of the production time of the scientist model. The recommendation assumes that this can be done without harming long-term sales of the scientist model.

As the customer is overseas, this seems a reasonable assumption.

## Example 12 – Make or Buy and Limiting Factors

(a) The Internal Manufacturing cost of Component Alpha is as follows :

| | Component Alpha |
|---|---|
| 2 hours of direct labour, at $8 per hour | $16.00 |
| 1.5 kg direct Material B, at $5 per kg | $7.50 |
| | |
| Variable overhead, labour related 2 hours | $1.25 |
| Variable overhead, machine related, 0.5 hours | $0.125 |
| | |
| Total Variable cost | **$24.875** |

The buying price of the component is **$50** per unit. So, if resources are readily available, the company should manufacture the component, because it is cheaper than buying it. However, due to the scarcity of resources in the near future, the contribution earned from the component needs to be compared with the contribution that can be earned from the other products.

Using Product 1 (though any product could be used) the variable overhead rates per hour can be calculated:

Labour related variable overhead per unit = $1.25

Direct labour hours per unit = $16 / $8 = 2 hours

Labour related variable overhead per hour = $1.25 / 2 hours = $0.625 per hour

Machine related variable overhead per unit = $1.25

Machine related variable overhead per hour = $1.25 / 5 hours = $0.25 per hour

Both material A and material B are limited in supply, but calculations are required to determine whether this scarcity affects our production plans. The resources required for the maximum demand must be compared with the resources available to determine whether either of the materials is a binding constraint.

| | Product 1 | Product 2 | Product 3 | Product 4 | Total |
|---|---|---|---|---|---|
| **Existing Contract** | 100 units | 100 units | 100 units | 100 units | |
| Direct Material A | 150 litres | 100 litres | 0 litres | 100 litres | **350 litres** |
| Direct Material B | 100 kgs | 0 kgs | 300 kgs | 200 kgs | **600 kgs** |

We can now determine whether Material A or Material B is a limiting factor:

| | Maximum Availability | Post-contract availability | Needed for total production |
|---|---|---|---|
| Direct Mat. A | 5,000 litres | 4,650 litres | 3,200 litres |
| Direct Mat. B | 6,000 kgs | 5,400 kgs | 5,500 kgs |

The scarcity of **material B** is a binding constraint and therefore the contributions of each product and the component per kg of material B must be compared. (At this point, Product 2 can be ignored because it does not use material B):

| | Product 1 | Product 3 | Product 4 | Component Alpha |
|---|---|---|---|---|
| Contribution | $32 | $51.325 | $58.75 | |
| Direct Material B | 1kg | 3 kgs | 2 kgs | |
| Contribution per kg of Material B | $32.00 | $17.10 | $29.38 | $16.75 **(W1)** |
| Rank | 1 | 3 | 2 | 4 |

Since Component Alpha is the lowest ranked usage of material B, **the company should continue to purchase the component** so that the available resources can be used to manufacture Product 1, Product 4 and Product 3.

**W1 – Component Alpha – Contribution per kg of B**

| | |
|---|---:|
| Buying cost of component Alpha | $50.00 |
| 2 hours of direct labour, at $8 per hour | ($16.00) |
| 1.5 kg direct Material B, at $5 per kg | ($7.50) |
| | |
| Variable overhead, labour related 2 hours | ($1.250) |
| Variable overhead, machine related, 0.5 hours | ($0.125) |
| | |
| Contribution per component | **$25.125** |

Contribution per kg of Material B = $25.125/1.5 kgs of B = **$16.75**

(b)

Direct material B at $5/ kg available :  5,400 kgs

First, we make **Product 1** : 900 units @ 1 kgs per unit = 900 kgs.

This leaves 4,500 kgs available for the next best-ranking product, **Product 4**. That is enough for (4,500 kgs/2 kgs per unit) = 2,250 units of Product 4. We only need 900 units of Product 4 though i.e. 1,800 kgs, which leaves (4,500 – 1,800 kgs = 2,700 kgs) available for the next product, **Product 3.**

Each unit of Product 3 uses 3 kgs of Material B, we can therefore make 900 units of Product 3.

**Summary**

| | Product 1 | Product 2 | Product 3 | Product 4 |
|---|---|---|---|---|
| Contractual units | 100 units | 100 units | 100 units | 100 units |
| Non-contractual units | 900 units | 950 units | 900 units | 900 units |
| Total | 1,000 units | 1,050 units | 1,000 units | 1,000 units |

(c)

The decision concerning the purchase of the component would change if the contribution from its manufacture were equal to the least best contribution from the products using material B. Apart from the minimum demand constraint the least best usage is derived from product 3 which has a contribution per kg of $17.10 which is $0.35 per kg higher than that from component Alpha.

Since each unit of Alpha requires 1.5 kgs of B then the buying price would have to be 1.5 x $0.35 = $0.525 per component higher than at present before it would have the same rank as product 3. Thus the buying price at which the decision would change = $50 + $0.525 = $50.525.

## Example 13 – Shutdown Decision

(a)  The profit statement needs to be restated in a marginal costing format if it is to be useful for decision-making.

| | W $ | X $ | Y $ | Z $ | Total $ |
|---|---|---|---|---|---|
| Sales | 30,000 | 20,000 | 35,000 | 15,000 | |
| Variable cost of sales | 4,800 | 1,600 | 13,200 | 5,000 | |
| Variable selling overhead (*) | 3,000 | 2,000 | 3,500 | 1,500 | |
| Contribution | 22,200 | 16,400 | 18,300 | 8,500 | |
| Specific fixed costs (W1) | 5,200 | 2,400 | 1,800 | 2,000 | |
| Net benefit | 17,000 | 14,000 | 16,500 | 6,500 | 54,000 |
| Non-specific fixed cost of sales | | | | | 20,000 |
| Fixed selling overhead (W2) | | | | | (20,000) |
| Administration costs | | | | | (8,000) |
| Net Profit | | | | | 6,000 |

(*) Total overhead less $5,000 fixed cost.

**Workings**

(1)

| | W $ | X $ | Y $ | Z $ | Total $ |
|---|---|---|---|---|---|
| Fixed costs | 11,200 | 6,400 | 8,800 | 5,000 | 31,400 |
| Non-specific fixed costs (*) | 6,000 | 4,000 | 7,000 | 3,000 | 20,000 |
| Specific fixed costs | 5,200 | 2,400 | 1,800 | 2,000 | 11,400 |

(*) Given as $20,000 apportioned on the basis of sales value (3:2:3.5:1.5)

(2) $5,000 per product x 4 = $20,000

(b) (i) **Z discontinued**

|  | $ |
|---|---:|
| Contribution from 40% additional sales of Y ($18,300 x 0.4) | 7,320 |
| Additional specific fixed costs | (540) |
| Loss of net benefit from Z | (6,500) |
| Net Gain | 280 |

(ii) **Profit reconciliation**

|  | $ |
|---|---:|
| Existing Profit | 6,000 |
| Discontinuation of Z | (6,500) |
| Additional contribution from Y | 7,320 |
| Additional specific fixed costs | (540) |
| Profit if Z is discontinued and sales of Y substituted | 6,280 |

(c) Non-financial factors to consider include:

(1) Possible redundancies among the workforce;

(2) Signals which it may give to competitors, who may perceive the company as being unwilling to support its products;

(3) The reaction of customers, particularly those who may recently have purchased the product.

Sometimes, even when management has made the decision to discontinue a product or activity, there is still a further decision to be made: when to discontinue it. The following exercise shows how such a decision could be made.

## Example 14 – Further Processing I

**D**

Incremental cost and revenue information is required to determine whether or not any of the products should be further processed. (i) and (ii) are related to common costs and are not relevant so options B and C are incorrect. (iv) and (v) are required to calculate incremental revenue so the answer must be D. (iii) represents incremental total cost. (vi) and (vii) will be required to calculate total output per product after further processing. The incremental cost per unit can then be calculated and compared to the incremental revenue per unit.

### Example 15 – Further Processing 2

*[Tutorial note: This an example of a question for which obtaining maximum marks depends not just on carrying out the calculations correctly but on demonstrating that you are aware of the other factors which affect the decision, such as marketing.]*

(a)  On financial grounds, further processing is worthwhile if the further processing cost is less than the incremental revenue.

Evaluation of further processing, based on March 2007 output and assuming no losses in the further process:

| Product | Incremental revenue $ | Incremental cost $ | Increase / (decrease) in profit |
|---|---|---|---|
| RZ | 800 × (6.00 – 3.00) = 2,400 | 800 × $1.40 = $1,120 | 1,280 |
| SZ | 2,000 × (5.75 – 5.00) = 1,500 | 2,000 × 0.90 = 1,800 | (300) |
| TZ | 1,200 × (6.75 – 3.50) = 3,900 | 1,200 × 1.00 + 600 = 1,800 | 2,100 |

Taking each product individually, it can be seen that products R and T should be converted as the incremental revenue exceeds the incremental cost of further processing. In the case of T, this assumes that the March 2007 output is representative of other months and that the quantity produced is sufficient to ensure that the incremental revenue covers both the fixed and variable costs. However, as TZ can be sold for a relatively high price, volumes would have to drop considerably for this to become an issue.

This is not true of S. Considered in isolation product S should not be converted. However there may be other reasons for producing all three products, in particular marketing considerations such as whether the company needs to supply all three products in order to sell the two profitable products, RZ and TZ.

(b)  (i)   If there is a market for R, S and T, and assuming that all March 2007 output can be sold at the prices given:

| Product | Selling Price per kg in $ | Output in Kgs | Sales Value in $ |
|---|---|---|---|
| R | $3.00 | 800 | $2,400 |
| S | $5.00 | 2,000 | $10,000 |
| T | $3.50 | 1,200 | $4,200 |
| | | | **$16,600** |

Total cost of common process in March 2007 = $17,500

Loss in March 2007 = $900 and therefore the common process is not financially viable.

(ii) If there is not an external market for R, S and T:

| Revenue from selling RZ, SZ, TZ : | | | $ | |
|---|---|---|---|---|
| RZ | 800 x $6.00 | | 4,800 | |
| SZ | 2000 x $5.75 | | 11,500 | |
| TZ | 1,200 x $6.75 | | 8,100 | 24,400 |
| | | | **17,500** | |

**Common Costs**

| Further costs : | | | | | |
|---|---|---|---|---|---|
| R –> RZ | 800 x $1.40 | | 1,120 | | |
| S–>SZ | 2,000 x $0.90 | | 1,800 | | |
| T–>TZ | 1,200 x $1.00 | 1,200 | | | |
| | Fixed | 600 | 1,800 | 4,720 | 22,220 |
| | | | | | **2,180** |

Based on this analysis the common process is financially viable.

**Test Your understanding 2**

**D**

The relevant cost of making the product is the variable cost of $3, $4 and $1 AND the specific fixed cost of $2.50. In addition there is another cost – an opportunity cost – every unit of the component that we make uses $4 of labour. If $8 of labour were used on the other product contribution would increase by $10. So therefore there is an extra opportunity cost of $5 per $4 of labour.

## Test Your understanding 3

**A**

The 6,600 hours of machine time for the special order would have produced 3,300 units (2 hours each).

| Existing contribution | = | 3,300 × $4.30 |
|---|---|---|
| | = | $14,190 |

The firm will be indifferent to the new order if the 3,000 modified units also give $14,190 contribution.

| Variable cost per unit of special order | = $9.20 |
|---|---|
| Total variable costs | = 3,000 × $9.20 |
| | = $27,600 |
| Therefore required selling price | = $27,600 + $14,190 |
| | = $41,790 |

## Test Your understanding 4

**D**

| | E | F | G | H |
|---|---|---|---|---|
| Incremental revenue per litre | 8 | 7 | 10 | 4 |
| Variable cost of refining | (5) | (5) | (5) | (5) |
| Additional contribution from refining | 3 | 2 | 5 | (1) |
| | | | | Sell at split-off |
| Units | 2,000 | 500 | 5,000 | |
| Additional total contribution($) | 6,000 | 1,000 | 25,000 | |
| Specific fixed costs | (1,000) | (2,000) | (3,000) | |
| Additional profit from refining | 5,000 | (1,000) | 22,000 | |
| | Refine | Sell at split-off | Refine | |

| | |
|---|---:|
| Total relevant profit from refining is | $27,000 |
| General fixed costs of refining are | 30,000 |
| | ——— |
| Total loss from refining | $–3,000 |
| | ——— |

None of the products should be further processed.

## Test Your understanding 5 – Brown Ltd

| | |
|---|---:|
| Proceeds from sale of XY | $42,000 |

**Alternative 1**

| | $000 | $000 |
|---|---:|---:|
| Material A Replacement value | | |
| 600 × $180 | 108 | |
| Material B Benefit foregone from Z | | |
| 1,000/4 × $360 | 90 | |
| | | 198 |
| Unskilled labour 5,000 × $6 | 30 | |
| Semi-skilled | Nil | |
| Skilled: Direct cost 5,000 × $10 | 50 | |
| Opportunity cost 5,000/4 × $48 | 60 | |
| | ——— | |
| | | 140 |
| Variable overhead 15,000 × $2 | | 30 |
| Selling and delivery | | 54 |
| Advertising | | 36 |
| | | ——— |
| Total cost | | 458 |
| Revenue 900 × $600 | | 540 |
| | | ——— |
| **Benefit** | | **82** |
| | | ——— |

### Alternative 2

| | $000 | $000 |
|---|---|---|
| Material C Variable cost per unit $74 × 1,000 | 74 | |
| | ——— | |
| | | 74 |
| Unskilled labour 4,000 × $6 | 24 | |
| Semi-skilled | Nil | |
| Skilled:  Direct cost 4,000 × $10 | 40 | |
| Opportunity cost 4,000/4 × $48 | 48 | |
| | | 112 |
| | ——— | |
| Variable overhead 9,000 × $2 | | 18 |
| | | ——— |
| Total cost | | 204 |
| Benefit | | |
| Amount normally paid for sub-assembly | | |
| 1,200 × $1,800 | 2,160 | |
| Less amount paid now 900 × $2100 | (1,890) | |
| | ——— | 270 |
| | | ——— |
| **Net Benefit** | | **66** |
| | | ——— |

In conclusion, Alternative 1 is preferable to both selling material XY and Alternative 2.

### Test Your understanding 6 – Retail outlet

Assuming that overheads will be incurred throughout the redecoration even if floor space is not used, the overhead cost will not be relevant to the decision.

The two options will be assessed by considering the lost contribution from closure of retail space.

#### Option 1

No sales for first 4 week period
Weeks 5 – 8: 30% of sales lost
Weeks 9 – 12: 20% of sales lost
Weeks 13 – 16: 10% of sales lost
10% reduction in price of basic and canned foods for 12 weeks

Assuming that all four freezers are kept running and stocked throughout the period:

| | Weeks 1 – 4 100% of budgeted contribution | Weeks 5 – 8 30% of budgeted contribution | Weeks 9 – 12 20% of budgeted contribution | Weeks 13 – 16 10% of budgeted contribution |
|---|---|---|---|---|
| Change in contribution per week due to lower sales ($) | | | | |
| Basic foods | (200) | (60) | (40) | (20) |
| Newspapers | (300) | (90) | (60) | (30) |
| Frozen foods | (950) | (285) | (190) | (95) |
| Canned foods | (1,200) | (360) | (240) | (120) |
| Further change in contribution due to price reduction ($) | | 10% of sales price on actual sales | | |
| Basic foods | | (56) | (64) | (72) |
| Canned foods | | (168) | (192) | (216) |
| Power costs not incurred ($) | 100 | | | |
| Loss per week ($) | (2,550) | (1,019) | (786) | (553) |

Total loss over 16 week period = 4 × 2,550 + 4 × 1,019 + 4 × 786 + 4 × 553

|  |  |
|---|---|
| | = $19,632 |
| Cost of redecoration | = $2,500 |
| **Total cost of option 1** | **= $22,132** |

## Option 2

Total floor area = 400 m2
Option 2 used 40% of floor area = 160 m2
Basic foods and newspapers and magazines use 100 m2. Remaining 60 m2 to be split between frozen and canned foods based on profitability per unit of area.

Comparing contribution per m2 of normal space:

Frozen foods: contribution per m2 = 950 / 100 = $9.5 per m2
Canned foods: contribution per m2 = 1,200 / 200 = $6.0 per m2

As frozen food space must be allocated in complete freezer units of 25 m2, contribution will be maximised by allocating as much space as possible to frozen foods, i.e. 50 m2 frozen foods, 10 m2 canned foods.

40% floor space for first 3 week period. No change in sales of basic foods and newspapers.

0.5 week closure

40% floor space for next 3 week period. No change in sales of basic foods and newspapers.

Assuming no changes to prices in this period:

| | 6 weeks at 40% | Closure period (0.5 weeks) |
|---|---|---|
| Change in contribution per week due to lower sales ($) | | |
| Basic foods | 0 | (200) |
| Newspapers | 0 | (300) |
| Frozen foods (50% of budget) | (475) | (950) |
| Canned foods (95% of budget) | (1,140) | (1,200) |
| Power costs not incurred ($) | 50 | 100 |
| Loss per week ($) | (1,565) | (2,550) |

Total loss over period = $(6 × 1,565 + 0.5 × 2,550) = $10,665

Cost of redecoration and moving products = $(3,500 + 1,000) = $4,500

**Total cost of option 2 = $15,165**

Losses will be minimised by option 2 with two freezer units running.

## Mini-Quiz

(1)  Answer: (B)

100 reams @ resale value of $10 +150 reams @ market price of $26 = $4,900

(2)  Answer: (C)

(3)

|                        | K      | L      | M      |
|------------------------|--------|--------|--------|
| Contribution per meal  | $ 1.40 | $1.20  | $1.25  |
| Minutes                | 10     | 4      | 8      |
| Contribution per minute| $0.14  | $0.30  | $0.16  |

(4)  Answer (B)

|                                                    | $         |
|----------------------------------------------------|-----------|
| If buy, increase in cost ($7.75 – $5.50) × 50,000  | (112,500) |
| Extra contribution 25,000 × $4.80                  | 120,000   |
| Net benefit                                        | 7,500     |

# Linear Programming

## Chapter learning objectives

- **Interpret** variable / fixed cost analysis in multiple product contexts to breakeven analysis and product mix decision making, including circumstances where there are multiple constraints and linear programming methods are needed to identify 'optimal ' solutions. (Syllabus link A2b)

- **Discuss** the meaning of 'optimal' solutions and how linear programming methods can be employed for profit maximising, revenue maximising and satisfying objectives. (Syllabus link A2c)

### 1 Session Content Diagram

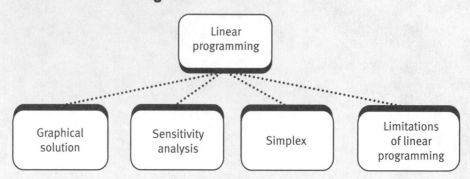

### 2 Knowledge Brought Forward

In the 'Decision Making and Relevant Costs' chapter, you saw how to use basic limiting factor analysis to determine the profit-maximising sales mix for a company with a single resource constraint. The decision rule was to allocate the resource to products according to the **contribution earned per unit of scarce resource**, subject to any other constraints such as maximum or minimum demands for the individual products.

This technique cannot be applied when there is more than one limiting factor. In this situation a **linear programming** technique is used.

Linear programming is the name given to a collection of tools that are among the most widely used in management science. It is essentially a technique that encompasses the problem of allocating scarce resources between competing activities so as to maximise or minimise some numerical quantity, such as contribution or cost. In the area of business it can be applied in areas such as planning production to maximise profit, mixing ingredients to minimise costs, selecting a portfolio of investments to maximise worth, transporting goods to minimise distance, assigning people to maximise efficiency and scheduling jobs to minimise time.

Linear programming involves the construction of a mathematical model to represent the decision problem. The model is then solved by an appropriate method or by the use of a computer package to obtain the optimal values for the activities.

In decision making when faced with one limiting factor, we calculate the contribution per unit of the limiting factor and rank the products, allocating the scarce resource to the best product and then the next best product and so on until the resource is fully utilised.

If faced with two or more limiting factors, then the situation is more complicated and linear programming techniques must be used (and the limiting factors are now called **constraints**).

There are two main methods:

- The **graphical method** which can only be used with problems involving just two products;

- The **simplex solution** (also known as the computer input and output method).

There is no knowledge brought forward from Papers C01 and P1, but you will need to be comfortable with some basic maths concepts covered in Paper C03. We will use this knowledge in P2 with more equations and graph-reading skills, so make sure you are comfortable with the assumed knowledge, that should have been brought forward as a base, in the following sections (up to and including section 2).

### Simultaneous Equations

Simultaneous equations are where you have two equations that must both be satisfied at the same time, of the type:

$$3X + 4Y = 18 \qquad \text{(i)}$$
$$5X + 2Y = 16 \qquad \text{(ii)}$$

which must both be satisfied by the solutions X and Y.

Provided you multiply both sides of an equation by the same amount, it continues to be true. In the solution of these equations, one or both of the equations are multiplied by numbers chosen so that either the $X$ or the $Y$ terms in the two equations become numerically identical.

We have labelled the equations (i) and (ii) for clarity. Suppose we were to multiply (i) by 5 and (ii) by 3. Both equations would contain a 15$X$-term that we could eliminate by subtraction, it being the case that you can add or subtract two equations and the result remains true.

In this case, however, the simplest method is to multiply equation (ii) by 2, so that both equations will contain 4$Y$ and we can subtract to eliminate $Y$. The full solution is shown below.

$$3X + 4Y = 18 \qquad \text{(i)}$$
$$5X + 2Y = 16 \qquad \text{(ii)}$$

Multiply (ii) by 2:

$$10X + 4Y = 32 \qquad \text{(iii)}$$

Subtract (iii) – (i):

$7X + 0 = 14$
$X = 14 \div 7 = 2$

Substitute X = 2 into (i)

$6 + 4Y = 18$
$4Y = 18 - 6 = 12$
$Y = 12 \div 4 = 3$

Check the results in (ii):

$5 \times 2 + 2 \times 3 = 16$

The solution is X = 2, Y = 3.

Had we chosen to substitute X = 2 into equation (ii) it would not have affected the result but we would then have checked in the other equation (i).

## Test Your Understanding 1

Solve the equations:

$2X - 3Y = 23$ (i)
$7X + 4Y = 8$ (ii)

## Simultaneous Equations using a graph

### Solving simultaneous linear equations using graphs

Each equation represents a straight line and solving simultaneous equations is the same as identifying the point at which the two lines cross.

This is the graphical interpretation of the solution of simultaneous linear equations, and a graphical method could be used instead of an algebraic method (provided that the scale was big enough to give the required accuracy).

## Test Your Understanding 2

Solve the simultaneous equations

2x + 3y = 8     (i)
5x − 2y = 1     (ii)

by first graphing the lines using the values x = 0 and x = 5 and then by solving algebraically .

## Inequalities

Inequalities are treated in almost exactly the same way as equations. In fact an inequality says much the same thing as an equation, except that one side will be

- less than the other (<)

- greater than the other, (>)

- less than or equal to the other, (≤ ), or

- greater than or equal to the other.( ≥)

Inequalities can be manipulated in the same way as equations, except that when multiplying or dividing by a negative number it is necessary to **reverse** the inequality sign.

For example,

5 − 2x < 25

−2x < 20 (deduct 5 from each side)

−x < 10 (divide each side by 2)

x > −10 (divide each side by −1, so reverse direction of inequality)

## Test Your Understanding 3

Solve for x in each of the following:

A   3x + 10 > 40

B   5x + 20 < 60

C   10 – 3x > 40

## 3 Procedure For The Graphical Solution

In order to determine the optimum production plan, it is necessary to formulate the mathematical model, first of all.

In practice, this is probably the most challenging part of linear programming and requires the translation of a decision problem into a system of variables, equations and inequalities – a process that ultimately depends upon the skill, experience, flair and intuition of the model-builder. However, for examination purposes a five-step procedure is used to construct the mathematical model. The following illustration is used to develop this procedure.

## Product X and Product Y

A company produces two products in three departments. Details are shown below regarding the time per unit required in each department, the available hours in each department and the contribution per unit of each product :

|  | Product X | Product Y | Available hours |
|---|---|---|---|
|  | Hours per unit | Hours per unit |  |
| Department A | 8 | 10 | 11,000 |
| Department B | 4 | 10 | 9,000 |
| Department C | 12 | 6 | 12,000 |
| Contribution per unit ($) | 4 | 8 |  |

**Required:**

Following the procedure for the graphical solution, define the optimum production plan.

## Step 1 - Define the variables

Linear programming is a mathematical technique that involves converting a business problem into a mathematical problem. An algebraic solution is then applied. In order to solve the problem, it is necessary to establish the unknown variables in the problem first.

### Step 1 – Product X and Product Y

Let x = number of units of Product X produced.

Let y = number of units of Product Y produced.

## Step 2 - State the objective function

The objective of the business is usually to maximise profit, and as fixed costs are fixed this would mean  the objective function is to **maximise contribution.** In some questions, however, the objective function would be to minimise costs. The objective function is stated in terms of the defined variables.

### Step 2 – Product X and Product Y

The objective function is to maximise contribution. The contribution on each unit of X is $4 and on each unit of Y, $8. The objective function 'Z' is to be maximised is as follows :

**Contribution (Z) = 4x + 8y**

*[In the March 2013 PEG, the Examiner notes that when asked to construct the objective function, many candidates wrongly used the selling price of the two products rather than the contribution.]*

## Step 3 - State the constraints

The objective must be achieved under certain conditions and limitations stated within the problem. Express these constraints (limitations) in terms of the variables. Remember the non-negativity constraints.

### Step 3 – Product X and Product Y

We know that available hours are limited in Departments A, B and C and we can state the following inequalities :

$$8x + 10y \leq 11{,}000$$
$$4x + 10y \leq 9{,}000$$
$$12x + 6y \leq 12{,}000$$
$$x,y \geq 0$$

## Step 4 - Draw the graph

Show the constraints on a graph.

*[In the March 2013 PEG, the Examiner regrets the 'presentation of a quickly drawn sketch of the graph and not drawn to scale'.]*

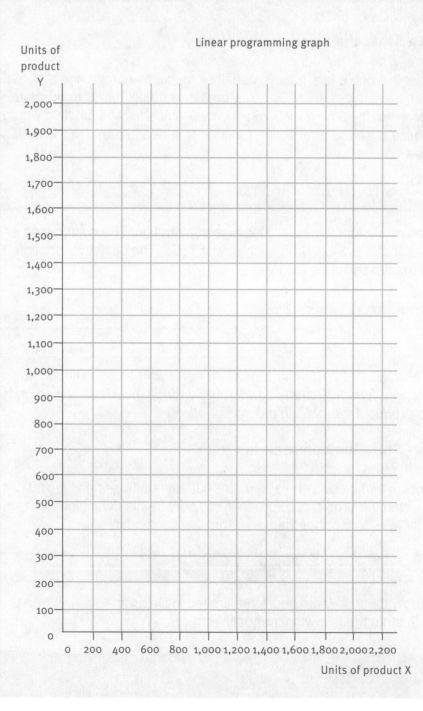

Units of product Y

Linear programming graph

Units of product X

Each constraint is drawn initially as a straight line. Then, shade the **feasible region** : this area represents all the possible production combinations that the company may undertake.

CIMA's *Official Terminology* defines a feasible area as *'an area contained within all of the constraint lines shown on a graphical depiction of a linear programming problem. All feasible combinations of output are contained within, or located on, the boundaries of the feasible region'*

If such an area does not exist, then the model has no solution.

*[In the March 2013 PEG, the Examiner notes yet again the poor quality of the graphs and emphasises that **<u>students need to practice constructing graphs.</u>** He also notes the following common errors :*

(1) *A poor choice of scale - some graphs fitted into a quarter of the sheet of graph paper, whereas others depicted lines disappearing outside the graph paper;*

(2) *Lines drawn without a ruler;*

(3) *Lines not identified;*

(4) *An incorrect feasible region marked on the graph.]*

## Step 4 – Product X and Product Y

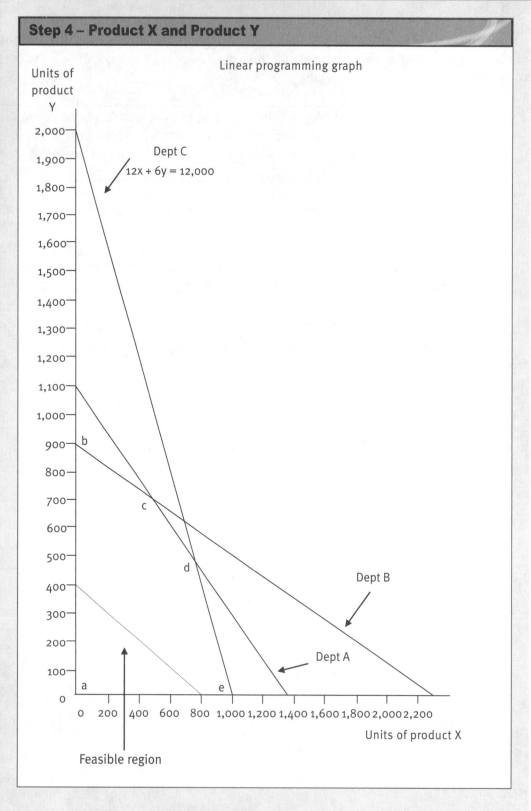

## Step 5 - Find the optimum solution

In this step, consider how the objective can be achieved. The graph is used to determine the optimum production plan. There are two methods that may be used to determine the optimum point on the graph:

(i) Method 1: Using simultaneous equations, calculate the coordinates of each vertex on the feasible region . Then calculate the contribution (objective function) at each vertex.

(ii) Method 2: We do not know the maximum value of the objective function; however, we can draw an iso-contribution (or 'profit') line   that shows all the combinations of x and y that provide the **same total value for the objective function**.

- If, for example, we need to maximise contribution $4x + $8y, we can draw a line on a graph that shows combination of values for x and y that give the same total contribution, when x has a contribution of $4 and y has a contribution of $8. Any total contribution figure can be picked, but a multiple of $4 and $8 is easiest.

- For example, assume 4x + 8y = 4,000. This contribution line could be found by joining the points on the graph x = 0, y = 500 and x= 1,000 and y = 0.

- Instead, we might select a total contribution value of 4x + 8y = $8,000.This contribution line could be found by joining the points on the graph x = 0, y = 1,000 and x= 2,000 and y = 0.

- When drawing both of these contribution lines on a graph, we find that the two lines are parallel and the line with the higher total contribution value for values x and y ($8,000) is further away from the origin of the graph (point 0).

- This can be used to identify the solution to a linear programming problem. Draw the iso-contribution line showing combinations of values for x and y that give the same total value for the objective function.

- Look at the slope of the contribution line and, using a ruler, identify which combination of values of x and y within the feasible area for the constraints is furthest away from the origin of the graph. This is the combination of values for x and y where an isocontribution line can be drawn as far to the right as possible that just touches one corner of the feasible area. This is the combination of values of x and y that provides the solution to the linear programming problem.

*[In the March 2013 PEG, the Examiner notes the common mistake candidates make of 'guessing the optimum point rather than using an iso-contribution line or solving the equations at each of the points in the feasible region'.]*

## Step 5 – Product X and Product Y

Optimum corner is at Corner C, the intersection of

$8x + 10y = 11{,}000$

and

$4x + 10y = 9{,}000$

At this corner, $x = 500$ and $y = 700$.

The optimum production plan is to produce 500 units of Product X and 700 units of Product Y.

Contribution at this point = $(500 \times \$4) + (700 \times \$8) = \$7{,}600$.

*[**From the PEG, May 2010** : Many candidates earned only half the available marks, due to a number of issues including poorly constructed graphs, presenting only an inaccurate sketch graph, and not putting forward a final answer.*

*The question asked candidates to 'show' the optimum production plan. Many candidates interpreted this request by simply drawing an arrow to indicate the maximum position, rather than setting down the figures in the answer book, or writing them on the graph paper.*

*Many of the graphs submitted were poorly constructed; the lines and the axes were not labelled, and the graphs were very untidy].*

### 4 The slack

This is the amount of a resource that is under-utilised when the optimum plan is implemented. The actual utilisation is below a maximum specification. In other terms, slack will occur when the optimum does not fall on a given resource line.

Slack is important, because unused resources can be put to another use, e.g. hired out to another manufacturer. A constraint that has a slack of zero is known as a **scarce resource**. Scarce resources are fully utilised resources.

*CIMA's Official Terminology defines slack variables as 'the amount of each resource which will be unused if a specific linear programming solution is implemented.'*

### Slack – Product X and Product Y

Slack in Department A, Department B and Department C can be calculated b ased on the optimum solution where x = 500 and y = 700, and production plan slacks are :

Department A = (500 units of Product X x 8 hours) + (700 units of Product Y x 10 hours) = 11,000 hours.

This uses all available hours in Department A. **No slack in A => Constraint is binding**.

Department B = (500 units of Product X x 4 hours) + (700 units of Product Y x 10 hours) = 9,000 hours.

This uses all available hours in Department B. **No slack in B => Constraint is binding**.

Department C = (500 units of Product X x 12 hours) + (700 units of Product Y x 6 hours) = 10,200 hours.

There are 12,000 hours available in Department C. Therefore, the slack is 12,000 - 10,200 hours = 1,800 hours.

### 5 The surplus

This is utilisation of a resource over and above a minimum. Surpluses tend to arise in minimisation of cost problems. For example, a constraint may state that it is necessary to produce a minimum of 400 widgets. If the optimum plan then recommends producing 450 widgets, the surplus in this case would be 50 widgets.

### 6 The shadow price

After finding an optimum solution to a graphical linear programming problem, it should be possible to provide further information by interpreting the graph more fully, to see what would happen if certain values in the scenario were to change.

The shadow price of a scarce resource is the extra contribution that would arise if one more unit of that scarce resource became available, or it is the drop in contribution  that would result from having one fewer unit of that scarce resource.

It is also, therefore, **the premium (over and above the normal price) it would be worth paying to obtain one more unit of the scarce resource.**

*[In the PEG November 2012, the Examiner regrets that some candidates were 'demonstrating no knowledge of shadow pricing' or were 'simply describing shadow pricing and not relating the answer to the question'.]*

CIMA's Official Terminology defines a shadow price as 'the increase in value which would be created by having available one additional unit of a limiting resource at its original cost. This represents the opportunity cost of not having the use of the one extra unit. This information is routinely produced when mathematical programming (especially linear programming) is used to model activity.'

*[The Examiner is warning students about taking this 'shadow price' definition too litterally. 'One additional unit', in the definition, does not necessarily mean one whole unit. This was the case in November 2012 when a shadow price had to be explained for 0.2 kgs of materials. Please refer to the November 2012 PEG as well as the following article on the CIMA website :*

http://www.cimaglobal.com/Documents/Student%20docs/2010%
20syllabus%20docs/P2/P2Nov12_Examiner_question6and7soloution.pdf *]*

## Shadow Prices – Product X and Product Y

### Shadow prices in Department A :

We need to calculate the impact if one extra hour of Department A time was made available, so that 11,001 hours were available. The new optimum product mix would be at the intersection of the two constraint lines :

$$\text{(i)} \quad 8x + 10y \quad = \quad 11{,}001 \text{ hours}$$
$$\text{(ii)} \quad 4x + 10y \quad = \quad 9{,}000 \text{ hours}$$

With (i) – (ii), $4x = 2{,}001$ and therefore $x = 500.25$ units.

When substituting x with '500.25' in (i) or (ii) we get $y = 699.9$ and new total contribution is calculated as follows :

| | Units | Contribution per unit | Total contribution |
|---|---|---|---|
| X | 500.25 | $4 | $2,001 |
| Y | 699.9 | $8 | $5,599.2 |
| | | | **$7,600.20** |

The original contribution was equal to (500 units of X x $4) + (700 units of Y x $8) = **$7,600.**

Therefore, the increase in contribution from one extra hour in Department A is $0.20. In other words, the shadow price of an extra hour in Department A is $0.20. The company should be prepared to pay up to $0.20 extra per hour.

**Shadow prices in Department B :**

We need to calculate the impact if one extra hour of Department B time was made available, so that 9,001 hours were available. The new optimum product mix would be at the intersection of the two constraint lines :

$$\text{(i) } 8x + 10y = 11,000 \text{ hours}$$
$$\text{(ii) } 4x + 10y = 9,001 \text{ hours}$$

With (i) - (ii), $4x = 1,999$ and therefore $x = 499.75$ units.

When substituting x with '499.75' in (i) or (ii) we get $y = 7,002$ and new total contribution is calculated as follows :

| | Units | Contribution per unit | Total contribution |
|---|---|---|---|
| X | 499.75 | $4 | $1,999 |
| Y | 7,002 | $8 | $5,601.6 |
| | | | **$7,600.60** |

The original contribution was equal to (500 units of X x $4) + (700 units of Y x $8) = **$7,600.**

Therefore, the increase in contribution from one extra hour in Department A is $0.20. In other words, the shadow price of an extra hour in Department B is $0.60. The company should be prepared to pay up to $0.60 extra per hour.

**Shadow prices in Department C :**

The shadow price of an extra hour in Department C is 0, as there is slack in Department C (1,800 hours are still available.)

## 7 Minimisation problems

Linear programming enables organisations to find optimal solutions to economic decisions. Generally, this means maximising but it could aim to minimise costs instead; so, rather than finding a contribution line touching the feasible polygon at a tangent as far away from the origin as possible, the aim is to find a total cost line touching the feasible polygon at a tangent **as close to the origin as possible**.

## Test your understanding 4

HJK Ltd is a light engineering company which produces a range of components, machine tools and electronic devices for the motor and aircraft industry. It employs about 1,000 people in 12 main divisions, one of which is the alarm systems division.

### Alarm systems division

HJK Ltd produces two types of alarm system, one for offices and homes (X) and the other for motor vehicles (Y), on the same equipment. For financial reasons, it is important to minimise the costs of production. To match the current stock and demand position, at least 100 alarm systems in total are required each week, but the quantity of one type must not exceed twice that of the other. The inputs necessary for the manufacture of one alarm system are given below, together with the availability of resources each week:

| Type | Plating | Circuitry | Assembly |
|---|---|---|---|
| X | 3 feet | 4 units | 20 mins |
| Y | 2 feet | 8 units | 8 mins |
| Totals available each week | 420 feet | 800 units | 34 hours |

The management accountant estimates that the unit costs of production are $100 for X and $80 for Y. Past experience suggests that all alarms can be sold. At present, 75 of each alarm system are produced each week.

### Required:

(a)  State the objective function and the constraints for the production of alarm systems AND use a graphical method to find the optimal product mix.

(b)  Explain briefly any points of significance for management.

## 8 The Simplex Method

This is an iterative (or repetitive) process that calculates the contribution at each vertex of the feasible region, starting with the origin. The process is normally carried out by a computer which will provide not only an optimal solution but also a sensitivity analysis for the data. The simplex method is of particular use because it is able to consider more complex problems involving **more than two output variables**.

There are three stages:

(1) Preparing the input for the computer (or a manual solution). We do this in the form of a table or tableau, known as the **initial tableau**.

(2) The computer processes the data by means of a series of matrix multiplications.

(3) The computer produces the output in the form of a **final tableau** and we have to interpret the information.

*Note that you will not have to solve a simplex problem, but you should be able to interpret the results.*

### Setting up the initial tableau

The initial tableau shows the production problem when the output of all the products is zero. It is like considering the origin of the graph. In order to produce the first tableau, read the following example and follow our step-by-step approach.

### Simplex

A company produces two products in three departments. Details are shown below regarding the time per unit required in each department, the available hours in each department and the contribution per unit of each product:

|  | Product X Hours per unit | Product Y Hours per unit | Available hours |
|---|---|---|---|
| Department A | 8 | 10 | 11,000 |
| Department B | 4 | 10 | 9,000 |
| Department C | 12 | 6 | 12,000 |
| Contribution per unit $ | 4 | 8 | |

## 9 Simplex: Step-By-Step

### Step 1 – Define the variables

Let X be the number of units of X that should be produced and sold.

Let Y be the number of units of Y that should be produced and sold.

### Step 2 – Establish the objective function

Maximise contribution $C = 4X + 8Y$, subject to the constraints below.

### Step 3 – Establish constraints

We know that available hours are limited in Departments A, B and C and we can state the following inequalities:

$8X + 10Y \leq 11{,}000$ (Department A)

$4X + 10Y \leq 9{,}000$ (Department B)

$12X + 6Y \leq 12{,}000$ (Department C)

$X, Y \geq 0$

### Step 4 – Introduce slack variables

Turn each constraint into an equation (ignore the non-negativity constraint). This is done by introducing slack variables:

| | | |
|---|---|---|
| Let $S_1$ | = | Slack in Department A |
| Let $S_2$ | = | Slack in Department B |
| Let $S_3$ | = | Slack in Department C |

### Step 5 – Values of variables – non-negatives or zero?

In our example, there are 5 variables $(x, y, S_1, S_2$ and $S_3)$ and three equations, and so in any feasible solution that is tested, three variables will have a non-negative value (since there are three equations) and two variables will have a value of 0.

The three equations will be as follows :

$8X + 10Y + S_1 = 11{,}000$ (Department A)

$4X + 10Y + S_2 = 9{,}000$ (Department B)

$12X + 6Y + S_3 = 12{,}000$ (Department C)

## Step 6 – Express objective function as an equation

It is usual to express the objective function as an equation with the right hand side equal to zero. In order to keep the problem consistent, the slack or surplus variables are inserted into the objective function equation, but as the quantities they represent should have no effect on the objective function they are given zero coefficients. In our example, the objective function will be expressed as follows:

Maximise contribution C given by $C - 4X - 8Y + 0a + 0b + 0c = 0$

## Step 7 – Produce the initial tableau

The initial tableau gathers the coefficients in our system of equations from Step 5 :

$8X + 10Y + S_1 = 11,000$ (Department A)

$4X + 10Y + S_2 = 9,000$ (Department B)

$12X + 6Y + S_3 = 12,000$ (Department C)

| Variable | X | Y | $S_1$ | $S_2$ | $S_3$ | Solution |
|---|---|---|---|---|---|---|
| $S_1$ | 8 | 10 | 1 | 0 | 0 | 11,000 |
| $S_2$ | 4 | 10 | 0 | 1 | 0 | 9,000 |
| $S_3$ | 12 | 6 | 0 | 0 | 1 | 12,000 |
| Contribution | −4 | −8 | 0 | 0 | 0 | 0 |

The contributions per unit should be entered as negative numbers. This is just a feature of the mathematics and has to be remembered as a rule.

## Interpreting the final tableau

The computer has processed the data contained in the initial tableau and it produces the following final tableau. In the examination, the final tableau will always be given. You must be able write a full interpretation of the output.

| Variable | X | Y | $S_1$ (Note 5) | $S_2$ | $S_3$ | Solution (Note 1) |
|---|---|---|---|---|---|---|
| X | 1 | 0 | 0.25 | −0.25 | 0 | 500 |
| Y | 0 | 1 | −0.1 | 0.2 | 0 | 700 |
| $S_3$ | 0 | 0 | −2.4 | 1.8 | 1 | 1,800 (Note 3) |
| Contribution | 0 | 0 | 0.2 | 0.6 | 0 | 7,600 |
| | | | (Note 4) | (Note 2) | | |

### Notes – Final Tableau:

(1) 500 units of X and 700 units of Y must be made, to earn a maximum contribution of $7,600.

(2) There is slack in Department C, as $S_3$ has a shadow price equal to 0.

(3) With the optimum production plan detailed in the 'Solution' column, 1,800 hours of Department C ($S_3$) will remain unused.

(4) $S_1$ and $S_2$ have a shadow price: all Department A and Department B hours will be used. The shadow price of one extra hour in Department A is $0.20. This represents the amount by which contribution would increase if one more hour could be made available to Department A workers, at its normal variable cost. Likewise, the shadow price of one extra hour in Department B is $0.60.

(5) Figures in the $S_1$ column tell us that, for each extra hour available in Department A:

   – Contribution would increase by $0.20

   – 0.25 units of X would be made. This would increase contribution by $0.25 \times \$4 = \$1.00$

   – 0.1 units less of Y would be made. This would lower contribution by $0.1 \times \$8 = \$0.80$

   – The net increase in contribution is therefore $1.00 – $0.80 = $0.20

   – Producing an extra 25% of X and 10% less Y would use up an extra 2.4 hours in Department C ($0.25 \times 12$ hours $- 0.1 \times 6$ hours).

The Examiner may present a different style of computer output. The following output is easier to understand, but there is less detail given.

| OBJECTIVE FUNCTION VALUE | 7,600 |
|---|---|

| Variable | Value |
|---|---|
| X | 500 |
| Y | 700 |

| Row | Slack or Surplus | Shadow prices |
|---|---|---|
| Dept A | 0 | 0.20 |
| Dept B | 0 | 0.60 |
| Dept C | 1,800 | 0.00 |

**Required:**

Interpret the above information in the context of the production problem.

**Solution:**

**Sensitivity analysis**

*Department A*

The hours are fully utilised in this department. The shadow price of one additional hour in Department A is $0.20. Each additional hour should be used to increase production of X by 0.25 of a unit and decrease production of Y by 0.10 of a unit.

*Department B*

The hours are fully utilised in this department. The shadow price of one additional hour in Department B is $0.60. Each additional hour should be used to decrease production of X by 0.25 of a unit and increase production of Y by 0.20 of a unit.

*Department C*

There is a slack of 1,800 machine hours. The shadow price is zero.

## Airlines

The airline industry uses **linear programming** to optimise profits and minimise expenses in their business. Initially, airlines charged the same price for any seat on the aircraft. In order to make money, they decided to charge different fares for different seats and promoted different prices depending on how early you bought your ticket.

This required some linear programming. Airlines needed to consider how many people would be willing to pay a higher price for a ticket if they were able to book their flight at the last minute and have substantial flexibility in their schedule and flight times. The airline also needed to know how many people would only purchase a low price ticket, without an in-flight meal. Through linear programming, airlines were able to find the optimal breakdown of how many tickets to sell at which price, including various prices in between.

Airlines also need to consider plane routes, pilot schedules, direct and in-direct flights, and layovers. There are certain standards that require pilots to sleep for so many hours and to have so many days rest before flying. Airlines want to maximise the amount of time that their pilots are in the air, as well. Pilots have certain specialisations, as not all pilots are able to fly the same planes, so this also becomes a factor. The most controllable factor an airline has is its pilot's salary, so it is important that airlines use their optimisation teams to keep this expense as low as possible. Because all of these constraints must be considered when making economic decisions about the airline, linear programming becomes a crucial job.

### 10 LP and Decision Making : minimum contractual requirements

When, in the question, information is given regarding a customer order the business has to meet, it is necessary to take this order into account **before** formulating the Linear Programming problem.

### Contractual Obligation

ND Ltd produces two products, the Alpha and the Beta. For the next quarter, the following information is relevant :

**Material A :** 1,200 kgs are available.

Per unit of Alpha : 2 kgs

Per unit of Beta : 3 kgs

**Material B :** 1,500 kgs are available.

Per unit of Alpha : 5 kgs

Per unit of Beta : 2 kgs

**Labour :** 2,000 hours are available.

Per unit of Alpha : 7 hours

Per unit of Beta : 5 hours.

Each unit of Alpha and Beta make a contribution of $8 each.

ND Ltd has already agreed a contract to supply 20 Alphas and 20 Betas with a key customer. This order, if cancelled, would incur a significant financial penalty.

**Formulate the Linear Programming problem.**

## 11 Limitations To Linear Programming

There are a number of assumptions and limitations to this technique.

- Linear relationships must exist.
- Only suitable when there is one clearly defined objective function.
- When there are a number of variables, it becomes too complex to solve manually and a computer is required.
- It is assumed that the variables are completely divisible.
- Single value estimates are used for the uncertain variables.
- It is assumed that the situation remains static in all other respects.

## 12 Practice Questions

### Test your understanding 5

**The following information is relevant to Questions 3, 4 and 5**

The following final simplex tableau was obtained in a linear programming problem involving three variables (x, y and z) and three constraints (corresponding to slack variables a, b and c).

|              | x | y    | z | a  | b | c     | Solution |
|--------------|---|------|---|----|---|-------|----------|
| x            | 1 | 0.75 | 0 | 1  | 0 | −0.25 | 62.5     |
| b            | 0 | 2.25 | 0 | −1 | 1 | 0.25  | 17.5     |
| z            | 0 | 0.25 | 1 | 0  | 0 | 0.25  | 37.5     |
| Contribution | 0 | 1.25 | 0 | 3  | 0 | 0.25  | 337.5    |

The values of x, y and z are quantities of output (in kg) per week of three different products.

Naming the constraints by their slack variables, which constraint(s) is/are critical to the optimum?

A   Constraint a only

B   Constraint b only

C   Constraint c only

D   Constraints a and c

### Test your understanding 6

How many kg in total would be produced each week at the optimum?

A   337.5

B   62.5

C   117.5

D   100

**Test your understanding 7**

If one more unit of the resource which is the subject of constraint c were to become available, which of the following would happen?

A     Output of x would fall by 0.25 kg a week and outputs of y and z would each rise by 0.25 kg a week.

B     Output of x would rise by 0.25 kg a week and outputs of y and z would each fall by 0.25 kg a week

C     Output of x would fall by 0.25 kg a week, output of z would rise by 0.25 kg a week and an extra 0.25 units a week of the resource which is the subject of constraint b would go unused

D     Output of x would fall by 0.25 kg a week, output of z would rise by 0.25 kg a week and an extra 0.25 units a week of the resource which is the subject of constraint b would be used

**Mini-quiz**

(1) A company is using linear programming to decide how many units of each of its two products to make each week. Weekly production will be x units of Product X and y units of Product Y. At least 50 units of X must be produced each week, and at least twice as many units of Y as of X must be produced each week. Each unit of X requires 30 minutes of labour, and each unit of Y requires two hours of labour. There are 5,000 hours of labour available each week.

Which of the following is the correct set of constraints?

| | | |
|---|---|---|
| A 0.5x + 2y | $\leq$ | 5,000 |
| x | $\geq$ | 50 |
| y | $\leq$ | 2x |
| B x + 4y | $\leq$ | 5,000 |
| x | $\geq$ | 50 |
| y | $\geq$ | 2x |
| C 0.5x + 2y | $\leq$ | 5,000 |
| x | $\geq$ | 50 |
| y | $\geq$ | 100 |
| D 0.5x + 2y | $\leq$ | 5,000 |
| x | $\geq$ | 50 |
| y | $\geq$ | 2x |

(2) An office manager wishes to minimise the cost of telephone calls made. 40% of calls in peak hours cost $1 each and the remainder of such calls cost $1.50 each. 30% of calls at other times cost 80c each, 50% of them cost 90c each, and 20% of them cost $1 each. These proportions cannot be varied, though the total numbers of calls made in peak hours and of calls made at other times can be. If x equals the number of calls made each day in peak hours, and y equals the number of calls made at other times, which of the following is the manager's objective?

A   Minimise 120x + 89y

B   Minimise 120x + 90y

C   Minimise 130x + 89y

D   Minimise 130x + 90y

## Test your understanding answers

### Test Your Understanding 1

Multiply (i) by 4 and (ii) by 3:

$8X - 12Y = 92$     (iii)
$21X + 12Y = 24$     (iv)

Add the equations:

$29X = 116$
$X = 116 \div 29 = 4$

Substitute $X = 4$ in (ii):

$28 + 4Y = 8$
$4Y = 8 - 28 = -20$
$Y = -20 \div 4 = -5$

Check in (i):

$2 \times 4 - 3 \times (-5) = 8 + 15 = 23$

The solution is $X = 4$, $Y = -5$

### Test Your Understanding 2

To plot the lines we simply need two points they go through:

Equation (i),

- When $x = 0$, $3y = 8$, so $y = 8 \div 3 = 2.67$.
- When $x = 5$, $3y = 8 - 10 = -2$, so $y = -2/3$.

Equation (ii),

- When $x = 0$, $-2y = 1$, so $y = -1/2$.
- When $x = 5$, $-2y = 1 - 25 = -24$, so $y = -24 \div -2 = 12$.

These values are plotted below.

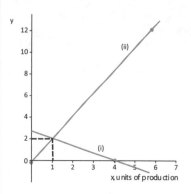

The lines meet when $x = 1$ and $y = 2$, which is the solution of the equations.

**Algebraic Solution**

$2x + 3y = 8$ (i)

$5x - 2y = 1$ (ii)

Equation (i) × 5 gives $10x + 15y = 40$ (iii)

Equation (ii) × 2 gives $10x - 4y = 2$ (iv)

(iii) − (iv) gives $19y = 38$

$y = 38/19 = 2$

Substitute $y = 2$ into (i) gives

$2x + 6 = 8$

$2x = 8 - 6 = 2$

$x = 1$

Check in (ii)

$(5 \times 1) - (2 \times 2) = 5 - 4 = 1$ OK

## Test Your Understanding 3

A   $3x > 40 - 10$
     $3x > 30$
     $x > 10$

B   $5x < 60 - 20$
     $5x < 40$
     $x < 8$

C   $-3x > 40 - 10$
     $-3x > 30$
     $x < -10$

## Test your understanding 4

(a) Let $x$ = number of alarm systems for offices and home

Let $y$ = number of alarm systems for motor vehicles

**Objective function:**

Minimise cost = $100x + 80y$

**Subject to:**

| | | | |
|---|---|---|---|
| Minimum production | $x + y$ | $\geq$ | 100 |
| | $x$ | $\leq$ | $2y$ |
| | $y$ | $\leq$ | $2x$ |
| Plating | $3x + 2y$ | $\leq$ | 420 |
| Circuitry | $4x + 8y$ | $\leq$ | 800 |
| Assembly | $20x + 8y$ | $\leq$ | 2,040 |
| Non-negativity | $x,y$ | $\geq$ | 0 |

## Workings for the graph

We are going to be drawing a number of straight lines. We need two points to define a straight line. The simplest thing to do in most cases is to make x = 0 and calculate what y must be to fit the equation and then make y = 0 and calculate what x must be.

| x + y = 100 | | x = 2y | | y = 2x | |
|---|---|---|---|---|---|
| x | y | x | y | x | y |
| 0 | 100 | 0 | 0 | 0 | 0 |
| 100 | 0 | 200 | 100 | 100 | 200 |

| 3 x + 2y = 420 | | 4x + 8y = 800 | | 20x + 8y = 2040 | |
|---|---|---|---|---|---|
| x | y | x | y | x | y |
| 0 | 210 | 0 | 100 | 0 | 255 |
| 140 | 0 | 200 | 0 | 102 | 0 |

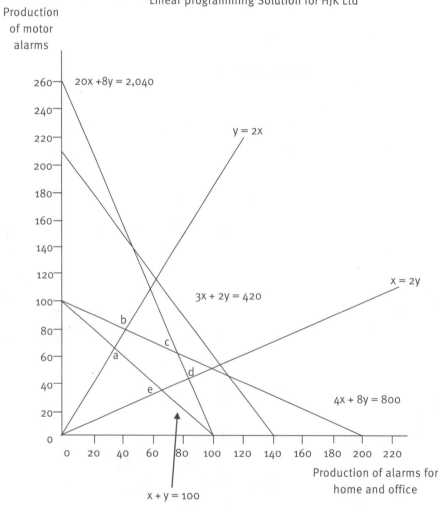

Linear programming Solution for HJK Ltd

*Solving the graph*

We are trying to minimise cost, So we want to produce as little x as possible, i.e. we want to be as far to the left as possible and we want to produce as little y as possible, i.e. we want to be as far down on the graph as possible.

We can therefore eliminate some of the possible solutions. The optimum solution has to be on a corner, i.e. has to be on an intersection of two lines, so the possible solutions are either nodes (a), (b), (c), (d) or (e) (on the graph over the page), We can see, however, that node (b) is not as good as node (a) because node (a) is both lower down the graph and to the left of node (b) and therefore represents less x and less y and less cost.

Similarly, node (c) is not as good as node (e). (Node (e) is lower down the graph and to the left of node (c) and therefore represents less x and less y and therefore less cost.) Finally node (d) is not as good as node (e) for the same reasons.

So, the optimum solution is either node (a) or (node (e).

Node (a) lies on two lines:

$$x + y = 100$$
$$y = 2x$$

This gives a solution of 33.33 units of x and 66.67 units of y.

Cost = (33.33 × $100) + (66.67 × $80) = $8,667

Node (e) lies on 2 lines:

$$x + y = 100$$
$$x = 2y$$

This gives a solution of 66.67 units of x and 33.33 units of y.

Cost = (66.67 × $100) + (33.33 × $80) = $9,333

Therefore the optimum solution is to produce 33.33 units of X and 66.67 units of Y. This minimises cost at $8,667.

(b) Management should question why HJK is trying to minimise cost. HJK Ltd is a commercial organisation and therefore its objective should be to maximise profit, not minimise cost.

The second most interesting point is that the current production plan is not feasible. It breaks the constraint for circuitry, i.e. 75 home and office alarms need 4 units each = 300 units in total and 75 motor vehicle alarms need 8 units each = 600 in total and 900 units as a grand total. This exceeds the available amount of 800.

## Contractual Obligation

|  | Available | Required for order | Remaining |
|---|---|---|---|
| Material A | 1,200 | 100 | 1,100 |
| Material B | 1,500 | 140 | 1,360 |
| Labour | 2,000 | 240 | 1,760 |

**Required for order:**

Material A : $(20*2) + (20*3) = 100$

Material B : $(20*5) + (20*2) = 140$

Labour : $(20*7) + (20*5) = 240$

(1) Define variables

Let A be the number of Alphas made **after** the customer order

Let B be the number of Betas made after the customer order.

(2) Objective function

The objective is to maximise contribution C, with C = $8A + $8B

(3) Constraints

Material A : $2A + 3B < 1,100$

Material B : $5A + 2B < 1,360$

Labour : $7A + 5B < 1,760$ and $A, B > 0$

### Test your understanding 5

Constraints a and c have positive shadow prices. Constraint b has slack. Therefore constraints a and c are binding and are critical to the optimum.

**Answer D**

### Test your understanding 6

Output of x = 62.5        Output of z = 37.5        Total output is 100 kg

**Answer D**

### Test your understanding 7

**Answer C**

### Mini-quiz

(1)  Answer D

(2)  Calculate the weighted average cost per call:

Peak hours ($1 × 0.40) + ($1.50 × 0.60) = $1.30

Other times ($0.80 × 0.30) + ($0.90 × 0.50) + ($1 × 0.20) = $0.89

Hence the objective is to minimise 130x + 89y

**Answer C**

# Learning Curves

## Chapter learning objectives

- **Apply** learning curves to estimate time and cost for new products and services. (Syllabus link B1e)

### 1 Session Content Diagram

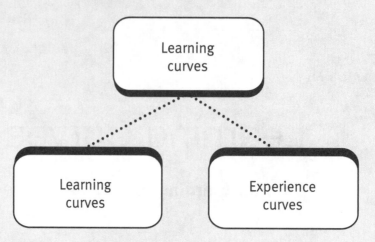

### 2 Knowledge Brought Forward

There is no knowledge brought forward from Papers C01 and P1, but you will need to be comfortable with the maths concept of logarithms, covered below.

### 3 Introduction

It has been observed in some industries that there is a tendency for labour time per unit to reduce in time: as more of the units are produced, workers become more familiar with the task.

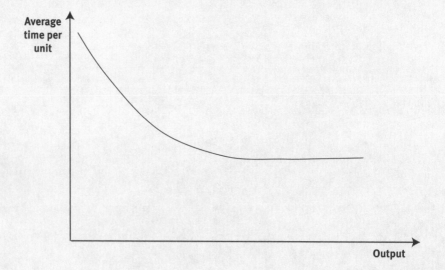

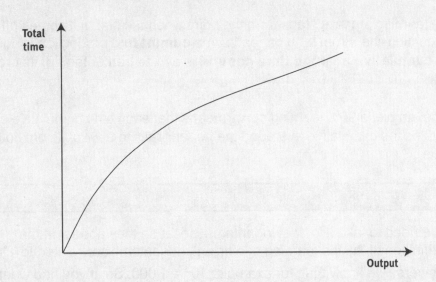

From the experience of aircraft production during World War II, aircraft manufacturers found the rate of improvement was so regular that it could be reduced to a formula, and the labour hours required could be predicted with a high degree of accuracy from a **learning curve**.

The first time a new operation is performed, both the workers and the operating procedures are untried. As the operation is repeated, the workers become more familiar with the work, labour efficiency increases and the **labour cost per unit declines.**

**Wright's Law** states that as cumulative output doubles, the cumulative average time per unit falls to a fixed percentage  (the '**learning rate**') of the previous average time.

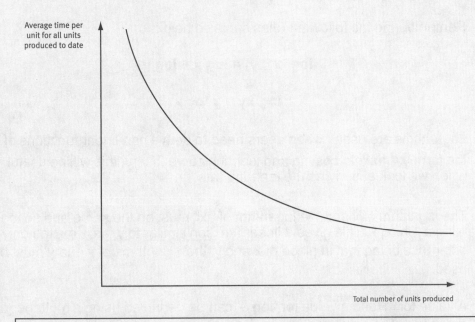

> CIMA's *Official Terminology* defines the learning curve as '*The mathematical expression of the commonly observed effect that, as complex and labour-intensive procedures are repeated, unit labour times tend to decrease.*'

The learning process starts from the point when the first unit comes off the production line. From then on, each time **cumulative** production is doubled, the **cumulative average time per unit** is a fixed percentage of its previous level.

For example, a 90% learning curve means that each time cumulative output doubles the cumulative average time per unit falls to 90% of its previous value.

## Logarithms

We need to take a look at logarithms, because they appear in the definition of **'b'**, the learning coefficient. Logarithms are related to powers : we know that, for example, $10^3 = 1,000$. So, if you had wanted to solve the equation $10^n = 1,000$, you would know that the answer is x=3.

However, what if the equation were $10^n = 2.5$?

If you want to rearrange an equation with powers, then you will have to use **log** functions:

$$10^n = 2.5 \text{ is equivalent to } n = \log_{10} 2.5 = 0.39794\ldots$$

This is read 'log 2.5 to base 10'.

Calculators will provide the logarithm of any number using the button marked 'log' or 'log 10x'. For example, the log of 72 is, using a calculator, 1.8573, which means that 10 1.8573 = 72.

Remembering the following rules can also help :

$$\log (x * y) = \log x + \log y$$

$$\log xy = y \log x$$

Logarithms are useful when users need to derive non-linear functions of the form $\mathbf{y = ax^n}$. In costing and learning curve theory, this will be useful when we look at deriving the learning rate.

The logarithm of y and the logarithm of $ax^n$ must be the same and so log y = log a + nlog x. This gives a linear function similar to y = a + nx, the only difference being that in place of x and y, the logarithms of x and y must be used.

A value for 'n' and a value for 'log a' can be deduced using simultaneous equations. The value of 'log a ' can be translated into a 'nice' number using antilogs i.e. the button 10x on your calculator.

For example, suppose the relationship between x and y can be described by the function $y = ax^n$ , and that the following applies:

**If x = 500, y = 50,250**
**If  x = 1,000, y = 42,750**

Substitute these values into log y = log a + nlog x and we find that:

Equation (1): 50,250 = a×500n gives Log 50250 = loga +nlog500, i.e. 4.7011 = loga +2.69897n

Equation (2): 42750 = a ×1000n gives Log42750 = log a + nlog1000, i.e. 4.6309 = loga + 3n

Equation (1) – Equation (2): 0.0702 = –0.30103n, so n = -0.2332

Then, replacing 'n' with '–0.2332' in Equation (1), we find that 4.7011 = loga +2.69897 x (-0.2332)

log a = 5.3305 therefore a = $10^{5.3305}$ i.e. **a = 213,796** and our function is $y = 213,796x^{-0.2332}$

*[In the PEG March 2011, the Examiner regrets that some candidates are 'unable to use logs' and in November 2012, 'unable to apply a logarithmic approach to solving the Learning Curve']*

Consider the following example of the time taken to make the first four units of a new product:

| Serial Number of Units | Time to make the unit concerned (hours) |
|---|---|
| 01 | 10 hours |
| 02 | 8 hours |
| 03 | 7.386 hours |
| 04 | 7.014 hours |

While it is clear that we are getting quicker, it is not obvious how the times to make successive units are related. However, a pattern becomes apparent if we look at the cumulative average time per unit instead:

| Serial number of unit | Time to make the unit concerned (hours) | Total cumulative time to make all units so far | Cumulative average time per unit | | |
|---|---|---|---|---|---|
| 01 | 10.000 | 10.000 | 10.000 | } | × 90% |
| 02 | 8.000 | 18.000 | 9.000 | | |
| 03 | 7.386 | 25.386 | 8.462 | } | × 90% |
| 04 | 7.014 | 32.400 | 8.100 | | |

In this example, Wright's Law is verified as the cumulative average decreases to 90% of the previous average every time we double the cumulative output, such as from 1 to 2 or from 2 to 4 units. We therefore say that the process demonstrates a **90% learning rate**.

All learning curve calculations use this idea of a cumulative average, so imagine all units having serial numbers so you can see how they fit into the cumulative picture.

For example, how long would it take to make a further 4 units, doubling the cumulative total to 8? The order of calculations is very important:

**Step 1:** Calculate the cumulative average time for the target production. Here, the cumulative average for the first 8 units = 8.100 × 90% = 7.290 hours per unit

**Step 2:** Calculate the total cumulative time. The total cumulative time for the first 8 units = 7.290 × 8 = 58.320 hours

**Step 3:** Time to make the next 4 units = the time to make 8 in total – the time to make the first 4

Time to make next 4 units = 58.320 – 32.400 = **25.920 hours**.

Or, shown as a table:

| Serial number of unit | Total cumulative time | Cumulative average time | |
|---|---|---|---|
| 04 | 32.400 | 8.100 | × 90% |
| 08 | 58.320 | 7.290 | |

*[In the PEG for the March 2013 exam, the Examiner warns against the dangers of incorrect rounding and rounding too early.]*

## Example 1

A new product will take 100 hours for the first unit. An 80% learning curve applies.

**Required:**
Complete the table.

| Cumulative | | | Incremental | | |
|---|---|---|---|---|---|
| Units | Average time per unit | Total time | Units | Total time | Average time per unit |
| | | | | | |
| | | | | | |
| | | | | | |
| | | | | | |

The problem with total doubling is that we cannot calculate averages for all levels of production. For example, to calculate how long the fifth unit should take to make, we need to use the following formula:

$$Y = a * x^b$$

The learning curve table shown above is useful if output keeps doubling, but for intermediate output levels such information could be obtained graphically or by formula.

$$Y_x = a.x^b \qquad \textbf{GIVEN}$$

where  y  =  average labour hours per unit

a  =  number of labour hours for first unit

x  =  cumulative number of units

b  =  the learning coefficient

$$b = \frac{\text{Log learning curve rate}}{\text{Log 2}}$$

For example an 80% learning curve:

$$b = \frac{\text{Log 0.8}}{\text{Log 2}} = -0.3219$$

**Note:** the value of 'b' may be given in exam questions.

*[In the PEG November 2010 exam, the Examiner notes that 'some candidates are unable to use the Learning Curve formula].*

In our first example, where

a   =   10 hours

b   =   $\dfrac{\log 0.9}{\log 2}$   =   -0.152

X   =   5

$Y_x = aX^b = 10 \times 5^{-0.152} = 7.830$ hours

The table can then be completed in the order above:

| Serial number of unit | Time to make the unit concerned | Total cumulative time | Cumulative average time |
|---|---|---|---|
| 04 | 7.014 | 32.400 | 8.100 |
| 05 | 6.750 | 39.150 | 7.830 |

### Example 2

The first unit of a new product is expected to take 100 hours. An 80% learning curve is known to apply.

**Calculate:**

(a)  the average time per unit for the first 16 units;

(b)  the average time per unit for the first 25 units;

(c)  the time it takes to make the 20th unit.

## Example 3

A firm produces 100 units and the average time per unit is 5.32 hours. A 90% learning curve applies.

**Required:**

(a)  Find the average time per unit if 500 units are produced.

(b)  Find the average time per unit for the next 250 units.

## Test your understanding 1

Average unit times for product X have been tabulated as follows :

| Unit number | Average time per unit $Y_x$ |
|:---:|:---:|
| 1 | 20 minutes |
| 2 | 17.2 minutes |
| 4 | 14.792 minutes |
| 8 | 12.72 minutes |

**Required:**

What is the Learning Curve rate?

## Test your understanding 2

Average unit times for product Alpha have been tabulated as follows :

| Unit number | Average time per unit $Y_x$ | Total time |
|:---:|:---:|:---:|
| 1 | 120 minutes | |
| 2 | | |
| 4 | | |
| 8 | | 1,375.52 minutes |

**Required:**

What is the Learning Curve rate?

## Test your understanding 3

Manufacturing the first unit of product Beta took 50 hours; and 42 hours to manufacture the second unit.

### Required:

What is the Learning Curve rate?

## 4 The Steady State

Eventually, the learning effect will cease and the time to make each successive unit stabilises at a constant time per unit. This is because there is a limit to manual dexterity and/or other limiting factors come into play such as a limit on how quickly materials can be supplied.

## 5 Learning Curves And Management Accounting

Knowledge of the learning curve for a new product can be very useful when applying management accounting techniques, such as budgeting, pricing decisions and work scheduling.

### Budgeting And Standard Setting

While the learning curve can be used for a number of purposes as it predicts time reduction, it is normally associated with budgeting : this is because budgets and standards will only provide reliable benchmarks to measure actual performance against if account is taken of the learning effect.

Therefore, it is difficult to set labour standards where a learning curve applies. Standards should not be set until the 'steady state' has been achieved.

Consequently, **cash budgets** should take into account the effect of the reduction in variable costs.

*[In the PEG May 2010, the Examiner insists on the necessity of an 'understanding of Learning curves and their interaction with budgets']*

### Pricing

The initial cost estimates for a new product may be very high, but if they fall through the learning curve, it may allow the company to sell at a lower and hence more competitive price.

For example, it is estimated that the cost of the first unit of a new product is $650, but an 80% learning curve is expected to apply. It is estimated that the company will make and sell 2,000 units during the first year. The average cost per unit for the first 2,000 units can be calculated as follows:

(80% learning/experience)

b = –0.322

$Y = \$650 \times 2000^{-0.322} = \$56.23$ per unit

This means that the selling price can be set at far below the cost of the first unit and make the company more competitive.

*[In the PEG for the March 2013 exam, the Examiner notes that, when prices are examined in a Learning Curve question, candidates 'submit answers that are not realistic' i.e. far too low or far above the limits imposed by its lifecycle phase.].*

## Work Scheduling

Understanding the learning curve allows correct scheduling of labour and enables deliveries to take place on time. Also, when a company plans to recruit new employees to help with increasing production, the learning curve or steady state assumptions will have to be reviewed.

## 6 General Conditions for a LC to apply

The Learning Curve theory will apply in practice when the following conditions are present:

(1)  The activity should be labour intensive, rather than in a highly automated or mechanised environment.

(2)  The process should be repetitive for each unit.

(3)  Labour turnover should be low, and there should be no prolonged breaks between production.

*[In the PEG for the November 2010 exam, the Examiner notes that 'Candidates are not appreciating and explaining that the Learning Curve is only prevalent in labour intensive situations'.].*

## Steady state :

In our example above, suppose we were told that the learning effect stopped after the fifth unit and we wanted to know the total time for making a further 4 units (units 6 to 9)?

The answer is simply 4 units × 6.750 hours per unit (the same time as the fifth unit) = 27 hours.

## 7 Experience Curves

Experience curves are very similar to learning curves but they cover all costs, not just labour costs. For example :

(1) **Material costs** may decrease slightly with quantity discounts, etc. but will not decrease by a large amount.

(2) **Variable overheads** often follow the pattern of direct labour and so may decrease in a similar way.

(3) **Fixed overheads** will decrease per unit as more units are made.

## 8 Practice Questions

### Test your understanding 4

Department F assembles, by hand, widgets. A new product line was commenced last week. The first widget produced took five hours. The labour hours were fully utilised making 2,000 widgets in the first week of production. No additional labour hours are available in the short term.

**Note:** the department bases its learning curve calculations on the model:

$$y = a.x^{-0.23}$$

How many units were produced in the second week?

### Test your understanding 5

*'The learning curve is a simple mathematical model but its application to management accounting problems requires careful thought.'*

**Required:**

Having regard to the above statement:

(a) **explain** the 'cumulative average-time' model commonly used to represent learning curve effects.

(b) **explain** the use of learning curve theory in budgeting and budgetary control; explain the difficulties that the management accountant may encounter in such use.

(c) **explain** the circumstances in which the use of the learning curve may be most relevant.

## Test your understanding 6

You are the management accountant of a new small company that has developed a new product using a labour-intensive production process. You have recently completed the budgets for the company for next year and, before they are approved by the Board of Directors, you have been asked to explain your calculation of the labour time required for the budgeted output. In your calculations, you anticipated that the time taken for the first unit would be 40 minutes and that a 75% learning curve would apply for the first 30 units.

**Required**:

(a) **Explain** the concept of the learning curve and why it may be relevant to the above company.

(b) **Calculate** the expected time for the 6th unit of output.

**Note:** The learning index for a 75% learning curve is −0.415.

## Mini-quiz

(1) A company has recently completed the production of the first unit of a new product. The time taken for this was 12 minutes. The company expects that there will be a 75% learning rate for this product. What was the total time (in minutes) expected to produce the first four units?

(2) A company has received an order to make 8 units of Product W. The time to produce the first unit is estimated to be 150 hours and an 80% learning curve is expected. The direct labour rate is $7 per hour.

The direct material cost for each unit is $3,000 and the fixed costs associated with the order are $10,000.

What is the average cost of each unit (to the nearest $) for this order of Product W?

(3) The first unit of a new product is expected to take 25 hours to make. A 95% learning curve is known to apply. What was the time taken to make the 18th unit?

(4) The management accountant of Shaun plc has been investigating the time taken to produce one of its products, and found that a 90% learning curve appears to be applicable. If the time taken for the first unit is 7 hours, what is the total time taken for units 5 to 8 *only*?

(5) The times taken to produce each of the first four batches of a new product were as follows:

| Batch Number | Time Taken |
|---|---|
| 1 | 100 minutes |
| 2 | 70 minutes |
| 3 | 62 minutes |
| 4 | 57 minutes |

Based upon the above data, the rate of learning was closest to

A 70%

B 72.25%

C 82%

D 85%

## Test your understanding answers

### Example 1

| Cumulative | | | Incremental | | |
|---|---|---|---|---|---|
| Units | Average time p.u. | Total time | Units | Total time | Average time p.u. |
| 1 | 100 | 100 | 1 | 100 | 100 |
| 2 | 80 | 160 | 1 | 60 | 60 |
| 4 | 64 | 256 | 2 | 96 | 48 |
| 8 | 51.2 | 409.6 | 4 | 153.6 | 38.4 |
| 16 | 40.96 | 655.36 | 8 | 245.76 | 30.72 |

### Example 2

(a) a $= 100$  $b = -0.3219$  $x = 16$

  y $= 100.16^{-0.3219}$

  $= 40.96$ hours

(b) x $= 25$

  y $= 100.25^{-0.3219}$

  $= 35.48$ hours

(c) x $= 20$

  y $= 100.20^{-0.3219}$

  $= 38.12$ hours

  Total time for
  20 units $= 38.12 \times 20$ $= 762.42$

  x $= 19$

  y $= 100.19^{-0.3219}$

  $= 38.76$ hours

  Total time for
  19 units $= 38.76 \times 19$ $= 736.35$

  $= 762.42 - 736.35$

  $= \mathbf{26.07\ hours}$

### Example 3

(a)

$$x = 100 \text{ units} \quad y = 5.32 \text{ hours} \quad b = \frac{\text{Log } 0.9}{\text{Log } 2} = -0.1520$$

$$y = a.x^b$$

$$5.32 = a.100^{-0.1520}$$

$$\therefore \ a = 10.71 \text{ hours}$$

when x = 500 units

$$y = 10.71 \times 500^{-0.1520}$$

$$y = 4.16 \text{ hours per unit}$$

**Average time per unit is 4.16 hours**

(b) Cumulative output = 750 units

Therefore

When x = 750,

$$y = 10.71 \times 750^{-0.1520}$$

$$= 3.915 \text{ hours per unit}$$

| | | |
|---|---|---|
| Total hours for 750 units | = 3.915 × 750 | = 2,936.52 hours |
| Total hours for 500 units | = 4.16 × 500 | = 2,080 hours |
| Total hours for last 250 units | = 2,936.52 − 2,080 | = 856.52 |
| Therefore, time per unit | = 856.52 ÷ 250 | **= 3.43 hours per unit** |

### Test your understanding 1

20 minutes x $r^3$ = 12.72 minutes

$r^3$ = (12.72) / 20

$r^3$ = 0.636 so r=

$\sqrt[3]{0.636}$

r = 0.86 or **86%**

### Test your understanding 2

1,352 / 16 = 85.97

120 x $r^4$ = 85.97

$r^4$ = 0.71641 so r=

$\sqrt[4]{0.7164}$

r = 0.92 or **92%**

### Test your understanding 3

$Y_1$ = 50 hours (or average time at first unit is 50 hours)

$Y_2$ = (50 hours + 42 hours) / 2

$Y_2$ = 46 (or average time after second unit is unit is 46 hours)

(46 / 50) * 100% = **92%**

r = 0.92 or **92%**

| a | = | 5 |
| x | = | 2,000 |
| b | = | −0.23 |
| y | = | $5.2000^{-0.23}$ |
|  | = | 0.8704 hours per unit |
| Total labour hours available each week | = 2,000 × 0.8704 | = 1,740.857 hours |
| Cumulative hours after two weeks | = 1,740.857 × 2 | = 3,481.71 hours |

Let 'x' be total production in two weeks

$$y = a \cdot x^b$$

$$\frac{3,481.71}{x} = 5 \cdot x^{-0.23}$$

$$\frac{3,481.71}{5} = x^1 \cdot x^{-0.23}$$

When multiplying the two x terms together, it is necessary to add the powers, i.e. 1 + − 0.23 = + 0.77

$$696.34 = x^{0.77}$$

$$\sqrt[0.77]{696.34} = x$$

$$4,920.12 = x$$

Total production after two years = 4,920 units

Therefore production in the second year = 4,920 − 2,000 = 2,920 units

## Test your understanding 5

(a) The 'cumulative average time' model commonly used to represent the learning curve effects is demonstrated below for a 70 per cent learning curve:

| Number of units produced | Cumulative average time required per unit | Total time required | Incremental time required for additional units |
|---|---|---|---|
| 1 | 100 | 100 | 0 |
| 2 | 70 | 140 | 40 |
| 4 | 49 | 196 | 56 |
| 8 | 34.3 | 274.4 | 78.4 |

In this model, the cumulative average time required to produce a unit of production is reduced by a constant proportion of the previous cumulative average time, every time the cumulative output doubles.

In the above example, unit 1 requires 100 hours, but units 1 and 2 require only 140 hours, unit 2 being produced in 40 hours due to labour having learned how to perform more efficiently. Units 3 and 4 require only a further 56 hours' work, etc.

This may be modelled mathematically by the equation

$$Y = a\,x^{\,n}$$

where Y = cumulative average hours per unit, x = cumulative demand, and *a* and *n* are constants. This is only one of the several models that may be used to predict the relationship between output and labour requirements.

(b) Budgeting, budgetary control and project evaluation all rely upon the preparation of accurate forecasts of production capacity and operating costs. Learning curve theory may be used in such forecasts.

In particular, the learning curve theory may be used when repetitive manual tasks are introduced into a production process. Under these circumstances, application of this theory may result in more accurate prediction of labour time, labour costs, variable overhead costs that are driven by labour usage, and possibly material usage savings. Furthermore, if absorption costing is used, then this theory will enable the relationship between fixed overhead recovery and production rate to be accurately included in the budgeting process.

For budgetary control to be effective, the variances calculated must be based on realistic targets. A constant standard for labour, materials and variable overhead variances is not appropriate when the learning curve effect is present. By incorporating the learning curve theory into the targets, meaningful variances may be calculated and used in budgetary control.

Problems may be experienced in obtaining data on the rate of the learning curve until significant production has taken place. High labour turnover and changes in motivation levels may have significant effects upon the learning process. If there are extensive periods of time between batches of a particular product then the learning effect may be lost. The learning curve does not model long-term behaviour when there are no further productivity gains due to the learning process.

(c) The learning curve models the speeding up of a relatively new production process that involves repetitive manual operations due to labour learning from the experience. It was first documented in the 1920s and 1930s in the aircraft industry in the United States.

It is unlikely to be noticeable in well-established organisations that operate in static markets (growth, technology, etc.) and use standardised production facilities and mainly promotional marketing strategies.

### Test your understanding 6

(a) It has been observed in some industries, particularly where skilled labour predominates such as in aircraft manufacture, that as more of the same units are produced, there is a reduction in the time taken to manufacture them until the learning process is complete.

A learning curve is the mathematical expression of the phenomenon that when complex and labour intensive procedures are repeated, unit labour times tend to decrease at a constant rate. The learning curve phenomenon states that each time the number of units produced is doubled, the cumulative average time per unit is reduced by a constant percentage. If this constant reduction is 20%, this is referred to as an 80% learning curve, and a 10% reduction as a 90% learning curve. This is an important phenomenon that has been empirically observed. The cumulative average time is the average time per unit for all units produced up to the present time, including right back to the very first unit made.

If, for instance, there is a 60% learning curve, the cumulative average time per unit of output will fall to 60% of what it was before, every time output is doubled.

### The importance of the learning effect

If the product enjoys a learning effect, but the effect is ignored, then the planned unit cost estimated will be too high, since the fact that the products will take progressively less labour will have been ignored. Budgeted costs must therefore take into account any expected learning curve when they are being formulated.

(b) From the formula sheet, the learning curve formula is given by
$$Y_x = ax_b$$

Where:

$Y_x$ = the cumulative average time per unit to produce X units

a = the time required to produce the first unit of output

X = the cumulative number of units

b = the index of learning

Here $Y_x = 40X^{-0.415}$

Expected time for 6th unit is difference between the total time to produce 6 units and the total time for 5 units.

Cumulative average time for 5 units $= 40 \times 5^{-0.415} = 20.51$ minutes

Total time for first 5 units $= 5 \times 20.51 = 102.56$ minutes

Cumulative average time for 6 units $= 40 \times 6^{-0.415} = 19.01$ minutes

Total time for first 6 units $= 6 \times 19.01 = 114.10$ minutes

Expected time to produce 6th unit $= 114.10 - 102.56 = 11.54$ minutes

Learning Curves

### Mini-quiz

(1) It took 27 minutes to produce the first four units:

| Units | Average time/ unit (minutes) | Total time (minutes) |
|---|---|---|
| 1 | 12 minutes | 12 minutes |
| 2 | 9 minutes | 18 minutes |
| 4 | 6.75 minutes | 27 minutes |

(2) The average cost per unit is $4,787.60.

Average time for 8 units = 150 hours x 80% x 80% x 80% = 76.8 hours per unit.

| | | |
|---|---|---|
| Direct Labour | 76.8 x $7 | $537.60 |
| Direct Material | | $3,000 |
| Overhead | $10,000 / 8 | $1,250 |
| **Total Cost** | | **$4,787.60** |

(3) It took 18.73 hours to make the 18th unit:

$$\text{Learning coefficient} = \frac{\text{Log } 0.95}{\text{Log } 2} = -0.074$$

| | | | |
|---|---|---|---|
| Total time to make 18 units | $= 25 \times 18^{-0.074} \times 18$ | = | 363.35 hours |
| Total time to make 17 units | $= 25 \times 17^{-0.074} \times 17$ | = | 344.62 hours |
| **Time to make the 18th unit** | = | | **18.73 hours** |

262

(4)   Total time : 18.144 hours

| | | | |
|---|---|---|---|
| Average time for first 1 unit | = 7 hours | | |
| Average time for first 2 units | = 0.9 x 7 | = | 6.3 hours |
| Average time for first 4 units | = 0 .9 x 0 .9 x 7 | = | 5.67 hours |
| Average time for first 8 units | = 0 .9 x 0 .9 x 0.9 x 7 | = | 5.103 hours |
| Total time for first 4 units | = 4 x 5.67 | = | 22.680 hours |
| Total time for first 8 units | = 8 x 5.103 | = | 40.284 hours |

**Total time for units 5 to 8**   **=**   **18.144 hours**

(5)   **Answer D**

Cumulative average time for 2 units = (100 + 70) / 2 = 85 hours

# The Pricing Decision

## Chapter learning objectives

- **Discuss** the particular issues that arise in pricing decisions and the conflict between 'marginal cost' principles and the need for full recovery of all costs incurred. (Syllabus link A1c)

- **Apply** an approach to pricing based on profit maximisation in imperfect markets. (Syllabus link A3a)

- **Discuss** the financial consequences of alternative pricing strategies.(Syllabus link A3b)

## 1 Session Content Diagram

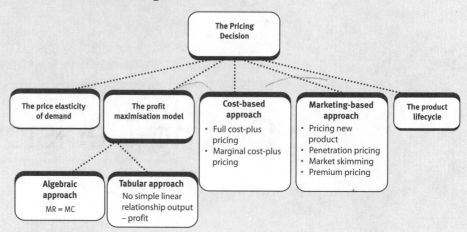

## 2 Introduction

In this chapter we will learn about the alternative strategies that an organisation may adopt in the pricing of its products or services.

The price to be charged to customers for the business's products or services is often one of the most important decisions to be made by managers. Not all businesses are free to determine their own selling prices: for example, some are unable to influence the external price and are obliged to accept the prevailing market price for their goods. For these businesses cost control is an important factor in maintaining profitability.

Other businesses are in a position to select their selling price. The objectives that they pursue in their pricing policy will affect the price to be charged for each product or service. For example, the business may be concerned with profit maximisation: in this chapter you will see how managers can use cost and demand analysis to determine the theoretical profit-maximising price.

Other objectives may also affect a company's pricing policy. For example, the company may be seeking to maximise revenue, to gain the largest share of the market, to utilise spare capacity or merely to survive. In this chapter, we will be looking at many of the different aspects which influence a company's pricing strategy, beginning with the price elasticity of demand.

## 3 Knowledge Brought Forward

There is no knowledge brought forward from Papers C01 and P1, but you may benefit from reading the Chapter on *Cost Behaviour and Pricing Decisions* from Certificate Level Paper C04.

## 4 Price Elasticity of Demand

Businesses make a profit by selling goods and services at a price that is higher than their cost. Profit is the result of the interaction between cost, volume and price:

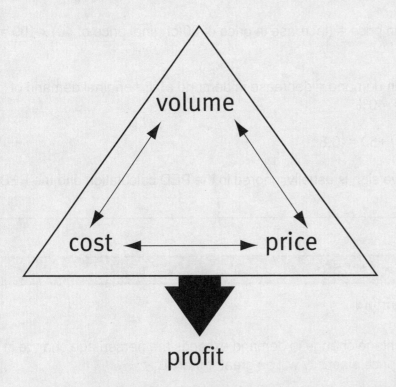

For instance, the volume of goods sold affects the cost per unit. If the volume increases, the fixed overheads are spread over more units, and so the cost per unit decreases. Lower costs give the seller the opportunity to reduce prices and so further increases volumes, or to increase profit margins. Cost is also influenced by price. This is discussed in target costing later in this text; the aim is to be able to produce at a target cost which is less than the target selling price. This chapter, however, concentrates on the link between *price* and *volume*, and its resulting effect on profit.

When a business proposes to change the price of a product or service, the key question is 'to what degree will demand be affected?'

The **price elasticity of demand** measures the change in demand as a result of a change in its price. It can be calculated as follows :

$$\text{Price elasticity of demand} = \frac{\text{Change in quantity demanded, as a percentage of demand}}{\text{Change in price, as a percentage of the price}}$$

## The price elasticity of demand

Assume that the sales of a retailer fall from 20 per day to 12 per day when the price of a chocolate bar goes up from 40c to 60c. The price elasticity can be calculated as follows :

% change in price = (increase in price of 20/original price of 40) x 100 = +50%

% change in demand = decrease in demand of -8 / original demand of 20) x 100 = -40%

PED = -40 / +50 = -0.8

The negative sign is usually ignored in the PED calculation and the PED = 0.8.

## Interpretation of PED

### Elastic Demand

If the percentage change in demand exceeds the percentage change in price, then price elasticity will be greater than 1.

Demand is 'elastic', i.e. very responsive to changes in price.

- Total revenue increases when price is reduced.
- Total revenue decreases when price is decreased.

Therefore, price increases are not recommended but price cuts are recommended.

### Inelastic Demand

If the percentage change in demand is less the percentage change in price, then price elasticity will be lower than 1.

Demand is 'inelastic', i.e. not very responsive to changes in price.

- Total revenue decreases when price is reduced.
- Total revenue increases when price is decreased.

Therefore, price increases are recommended but price cuts are not recommended.

## More on price elasticity

Pricing decisions have a major effect on volume sold and, as a consequence, on profit generated. One of the major considerations of a pricing decision is therefore the effect of a change in price will have on volume sold. If price is reduced, by how much will demand increase?

If price is increased, will a small or large decrease in demand occur? A complete answer to these questions, if such an answer does indeed exist, will involve a number of different factors in the total marketing mix, but the basic microeconomic analysis of demand is the fundamental starting point. There are two extremes of the price/demand trade off, represented graphically here :

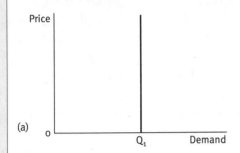

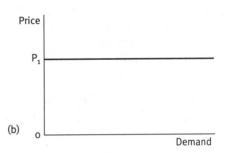

In (a), the same quantity, Q1, will be sold regardless of the selling price, as demand is completely unresponsive to changes in price. Demand is, therefore, completely inelastic, and the supplier would (theoretically) have unlimited scope, and considerable incentive, to increase price. In (b), demand is limitless at a particular price, P1, but it would vanish at prices above P1, that is demand is completely elastic. Under these circumstances there is obviously no point in reducing price below P1, as this will cause existing profits to fall. Needless to say, these two extremes are rarely seen in practice, and the more normal situation is represented by one of the following charts:

:

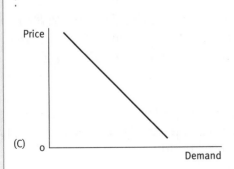

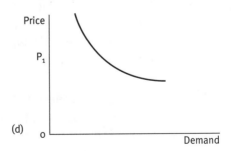

In both (c) and (d) the supplier is faced with a downward-sloping demand curve, in which reductions in price will result in increased demand and vice versa. This is a negative relationship, or negative correlation, as a decrease in price implies an increase in demand, and vice versa.

The slope of the line is the critical factor for a pricing decision, and is expressed by the following formula:

**Elasticity of Demand =** $\dfrac{\textbf{– \% change in quantity demanded}}{\textbf{\% change in price}}$

The numerator and denominator are expressed in terms of percentage change rather than in any absolute amount, in order to avoid distortions caused by the use of different units of measurement. Given the slope of the curve, the negative sign in the numerator has the effect of making the outcome positive, which is generally considered a more convenient representation. If elasticity at a point on the curve is greater than 1, demand is considered elastic. This means that a fall in price increases demand considerably, so that total revenue increases, but an increase in price decreases demand substantially, so that total revenue falls. On the other hand, if point elasticity is less than 1 (i.e. it is inelastic) a fall in price will increase demand, but not by a sufficient amount to maintain the previous revenue level, yet a rise in price will increase total revenue:

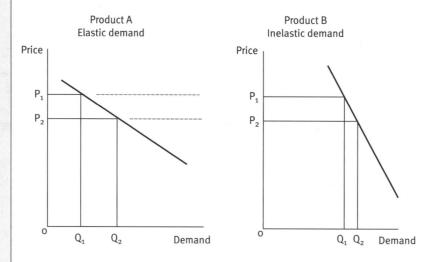

*For product A, with elastic demand, a drop in price from P1 to P2 results in a relatively greater increase in sales volume. However, the same drop in price for product B, with inelastic demand, results in a far smaller change in volume.*

Note that the formula measures movement between two discrete points on the curve, and that even though the slope itself is constant, elasticity will differ between different points on the curve:

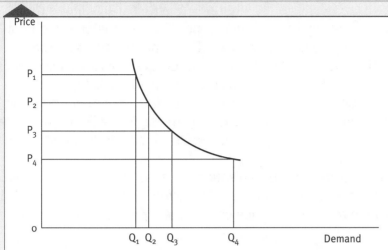

*Note that although the price drops from P1–P2 to P3–P4 are equal, the impact on the quantity sold is greater with each fall in price.*

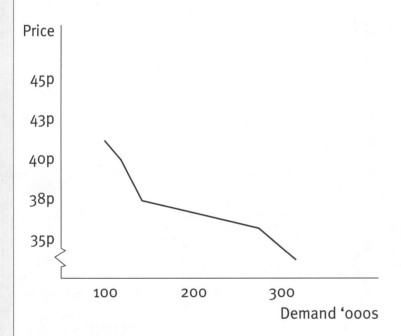

This is important information for an organisation. For example, when price elasticity is high (i.e. more than 1) the organisation will have difficulty in situations where cost inflation is higher than price inflation, because putting up prices in line with costs will cause a disproportionately large reduction in demand, and total revenues will decline. In times of inflation it is better to put up prices frequently by a small amount each time, as customers do not appear to notice the increases – or certainly do not react to them. If prices are held and then substantially increased in a single price rise, demand is likely to fall off sharply. In practice the prices of many products (e.g. consumer durable products) need to fall over time in order to increase demand. It is vital, therefore, to make costs fall by the same percentage if margins are to be maintained.

Different point elasticity can be seen in practice, as customers do not tend to react evenly to price increases. For example, $1 or $2 may be a psychological barrier and if price is increased over this level demand drops quite rapidly. If the product is sold in a supermarket the organisation needs to know how customers react to different prices in order to determine which price points are crucial. In the figure below, the rise between 38p and 40p triggers a large reduction in demand.

To complicate the issue an organisation does not decrease price with the aim of increasing volume in isolation. The effect on volume will depend on how competitors react to the price change, and on the price elasticity of the products.

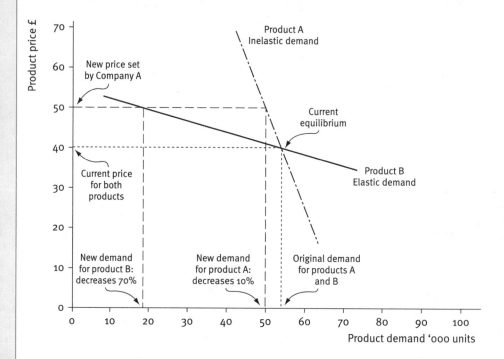

Different products in the same industry have different price elasticity because they are sold in slightly different markets due to product differentiation. This means that two or more products are sold that have different features, quality, sizes and so on. For example, a Volkswagen Golf GTI (the high-performance model) may enjoy lower price elasticity than the standard Golf 1.4E, so that the price of the former can be increased more safely than can that of the latter.

The figure above shows two companies. Company A's product A has a highly inelastic demand, while company B's product B has relatively elastic price elasticity:

In an industry in which costs of production are rising, the responsiveness of demand is an essential factor when deciding on price levels. In the above graph, the company producing product A could increase price by 25 per cent, from $40 to $50, with only a 10 per cent effect on volume (from about 54,000 down to 50,000 units). If the company that produces product B attempts to follow the price rise, its volume will fall from about 54,000 units to approximately 18,000 – the result of very elastic demand. In an industry where prices are falling, then the greater the price elasticity the greater the potential for increasing sales volume.

It is also important for an organisation to take account of expected competitors' reactions to any price increases the organisation makes.

One form of competitor reaction can be demonstrated with the kinked demand curve which shows 'price stickiness'. This occurs where competitors tend to follow price cuts with cuts of their own, but do not copy price rises. This is a pattern commonly found in the newspaper industry:

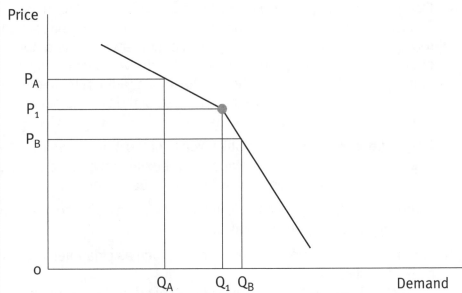

*If the price is increased beyond the current price of $P_1$ to $P_A$, since competitors do not follow suit, demand will fall away sharply to $Q_A$ (demand is elastic). If however, the price is dropped to $P_B$, competitors do follow, and little is gained in the way of extra sales (from $Q_1$ to $Q_B$) – demand is inelastic.*

*Where this occurs, firms may be reluctant to change their prices and the result is price stickiness.*

## 5 Factors Affecting Price Elasticity

When making decisions on products, markets and competitors, other factors, including the following, should be considered:

(1) **Scope of the market.** The larger the defined market, the more inelastic is the demand for the broader definition of product. For example, the total market for transport is relatively inelastic, whereas the market for 21-speed pedal cycles is comparatively elastic.

(2) **Information within the market**. Consumers may not know of the competing products in sufficient time to reassess their purchasing behaviour.

(3) **Availability of substitutes**. The less the differentiation between competing products, the greater the price elasticity of those products. Differentiated products benefit from customer awareness and preference, so their demand patterns tend to be more inelastic.

(4) **Complementary products**. The inter-dependency of products results in price inelasticity, because the volume sales of the dependent good rely on sales of the primary good. The consumer will make a purchase of the complementary product in order to achieve satisfaction from the primary good. For example, the purchase of a radio, remote control toy car or a torch, etc., all require the purchase of the complementary product – batteries.

(5) **Disposable income**. The relative wealth of the consumers over time affects the total demand in the economy. Luxury goods tend to have a high price elasticity, while necessities are usually inelastic.

(6) **Necessities**. Demand for basic items such as milk, bread, toilet rolls, etc., tend to be very price inelastic.

(7) **Habit**. Items consumers buy out of habit, such as cigarettes are usually price inelastic.
In practice few organisations attempt to set prices by calculating demand and elasticity. This is probably because it is exceptionally hard to determine demand under different circumstances with any certainty. However, most organisations will have some idea of the elasticity of their products and this will have some bearing on the way prices are set. There are a number of different techniques for setting prices that depend on the type of market and product.

## Different Types Of Market Structures

The price that a business can charge for its products or services will be determined by the market in which it operates.

In a **perfectly competitive** market, every buyer or seller is a 'price taker', and no participant influences the price of the product it buys or sells. Other characteristics of a perfectly competitive market include:

- **Zero Entry/Exit Barriers** – It is relatively easy to enter or exit as a business in a perfectly competitive market.

- **Perfect Information** – Prices and quality of products are assumed to be known to all consumers and producers.

- **Companies aim to maximise profits** – Firms aim to sell where marginal costs meet marginal revenue, where they generate the most profit.

- **Homogeneous Products** – The characteristics of any given market good or service do not vary across suppliers.

**Imperfect competition** refers to the market structure that does not meet the conditions of perfect competition. Its forms include:

(a) **Monopoly**, in which there is only one seller of a good. The seller dominates many buyers and can use its market power to set a profit-maximising price. Microsoft is usually considered a monopoly.

(b) **Oligopoly**, in which a few companies dominate the market and are inter-dependent : firms must take into account likely reactions of their rivals to any change in price, output or forms of non-price competition. For example, in the UK, four companies (Tesco, Asda, Sainsbury's and Morrisons) share 74.4% of the grocery market.

(c) **Monopolistic competition**, in which products are similar, but not identical. There are many producers ('price setters') and many consumers in a given market, but no business has total control over the market price.

For example, there are many different brands of soap on the market today. Each brand of soap is similar because it is designed to get the user clean; however, each soap product tries to differentiate itself from the competition to attract consumers. One soap might claim that it leaves you with soft skin, while another that it has a clean, fresh scent. Each participant in this market structure has some control over pricing, which means it can alter the selling price as long as consumers are still willing to buy its product at the new price.

If one product costs twice as much as similar products on the market, chances are most consumers will avoid buying the more expensive product and buy the competitors' products instead. Monopolistic products are typically found in retailing businesses. Some examples of monopolistic products and/or services are shampoo products, extermination services, oil changes, toothpaste, and fast-food restaurants.

### 6 The profit-maximisation model

A mathematical model can be used to determine an optimal selling price. The model is based on the economic theory that profit is maximised at the output level where **marginal cost is equal to marginal revenue**.

Full use of the model requires a knowledge of calculus, which is outside the scope of your syllabus. However, you are expected to understand the following basic principles:

It is worthwhile a firm producing and selling further units where the increase in revenue gained from the sale of the next unit exceeds the cost of making it (i.e. the marginal revenue exceeds the marginal cost). However, if the cost of the next unit outweighs the revenue that could be earned from it (i.e. the marginal cost exceeds the marginal revenue), production would not be worthwhile.

A firm should therefore produce units up to the point where the marginal revenue equals the marginal cost: **MR = MC**

The basic price equation is given as $p = a - bx$

where
p = price
x = quantity demanded
a and b are constants, where b is the slope of the curve and is calculated as (change in price / change in quantity)

For example,  if you are told that demand falls by 25 units for every increase in price of $1, then b = (1/25) = 0.04

The **marginal revenue** equation can be found by doubling the value of b :
**MR = a – 2bx**

The marginal cost is the variable cost of production.

## Illustration 1 – The MR= MC diagram

Marginal Revenue is the additional revenue from selling one extra unit, for example :

| Quantity | Price | Revenue | Marginal Revenue |
|----------|-------|---------|------------------|
| 1 | $70 | $70 | $70 |
| 2 | $60 | $120 | $50 |
| 3 | $50 | $150 | $30 |
| 4 | $40 | $160 | $10 |
| 5 | $30 | $150 | $(10) |

Marginal Cost is the cost from making one more unit. It is usually just the variable cost, e.g. MC = $30.

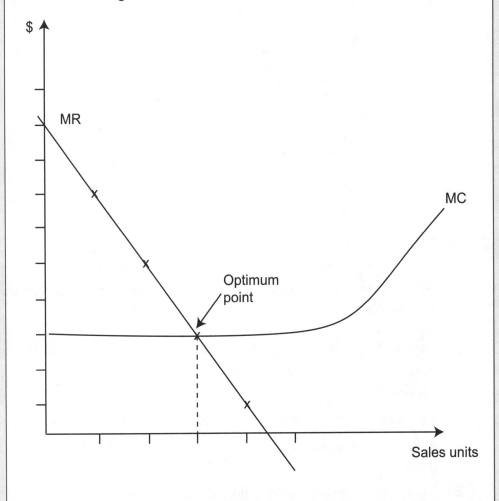

### 7 Procedure for establishing the optimum price of a product

This is a general set of rules that can be applied to most questions involving algebra and pricing.

(1)  Establish the linear relationship between price (P) and quantity demanded (Q). The equation will take the form:

$$P = a + bQ$$

where 'a' is the intercept and 'b' is the gradient of the line. As the price of a product increases, the quantity demanded will decrease. The equation of a straight line P= a + bQ can be used to show the demand for a product at a given price:

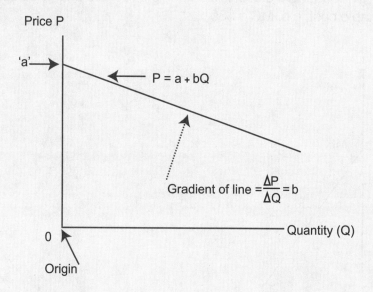

*Note: 'b' is always negative because of the inverse relationship between price and quantity.*

(2)  Double the gradient to find the marginal revenue: **MR = a + 2bQ.**

(3)  Establish the **marginal cost MC**. This will simply be the variable cost per unit.

(4)  To maximise profit, **equate MC and MR** and solve to find Q.

(5)  Substitute this value of Q into the price equation to find the optimum price.

(6)  It may be necessary to calculate the maximum profit.

## The Algebraic approach

At a price of $200, a company will be able to sell 1,000 units of its product in a month. If the selling price is increased to $220, the demand will fall to 950 units. It is also known that the product has a variable cost of $140 per unit, and fixed costs will be $36,000 per month.

**Required:**

(a)  Find an equation for the demand function (that is, price as a function of quantity demanded);

(b)  Write down the marginal revenue function;

(c)  Write down the marginal cost;

(d)  Find the quantity that maximises profit;

(e)  Calculate the optimum price;

(f)  What is the maximum profit?

## Example 1

Maximum demand for a company's product M is 100,000 units per annum. The demand will be reduced by 40 units for every increase of $1 in the selling price. The company has determined that profit is maximised at a sales volume of 42,000 units per annum.

What is the profit maximising selling price for product M?

**Solution**

In the demand equation, $p = a - bx$
where p = price
x = quantity demanded
a,b = constants

Maximum demand is achieved when the product is free, that is, when p = 0

When price = 0, demand, x = 100,000  0 = a – 100,000b (i)
When price = 1, demand, x = 99,960  1 = a – 99,960b (ii)
Subtract  1 = 40b so b = 0.025
Substitute in (i)  a = 100,000 x 0.025

so a =  2,500

The demand equation for product M is therefore p = 2,500 – 0.025b

When x = 42,000 units, p = 2,500 - (0.025 x 42,000)

so p= 1,450

Therefore, the profit-maximising selling price is $1,450 per unit.

**e.g**

## Example 2

Another product, K, incurs a total cost of $10 per unit sold, as follows.

|  | $ per unit |
|---|---|
| Variable production cost | 4 |
| Variable selling cost | 2 |
| Fixed production cost | 3 |
| Fixed selling and administration cost | 1 |
| Total cost | **10** |

The marginal revenue (MR) and demand functions for product K are:

MR = 200 – 0.4x
p = 200 – 0.2x

Where p – price, x = quantity demanded per period.

What is the profit-maximising selling price of product K, and what quantity will be sold per period at this price?

### Solution

Marginal cost per unit of product K = variable cost per unit = $6

Profit is maximised when marginal cost marginal revenue
i.e. when 6 = 200 – 0.4x

x = 485

When x = 485, p = 200 – (0.2 x 485) = 103

Therefore the profit-maximising selling price is $103 per unit, at which price 485 units will be sold per period.

## 8 The Tabular Approach

When data in the exam is given in tabular form and there is no indication about the demand function, and/or when there is no simple linear relationship between output and profit – the tabular approach is likely to be the best to define optimum profit and the associated selling price.

### Example 1 – Tabular Approach

XYZ Ltd is introducing a new product. The company intends to hire machinery to manufacture the product at a cost of $200,000 per annum. However, this will only enable 60,000 units per annum to be produced, although additional machines can be hired at $80,000 per annum. Each machine hired enables capacity to be increased by 20,000 units per annum, but it is not possible to increase production beyond 90,000 units because of shortage of space.

The minimum rental period is for one year and the variable cost is estimated to be $6 per unit produced. There are no other fixed costs that can be specifically traced to the product. Marketing management has estimated the maximum selling prices for a range of output from 50,000 units to 90,000 units. The estimates are as follows:

| Units sold | 50,000 | 60,000 | 70,000 | 80,000 | 90,000 | 90,000* |
|---|---|---|---|---|---|---|
| Selling price ($) | 22 | 20 | 19 | 18 | 17 | 15 |

* At $15 demand will be in excess of 90,000 units but production capacity will limit the sales.

### Required:

Present relevant financial information to management for the pricing and output decision.

**Answer guide**

|  | $ | $ | $ | $ | $ | $ |
|---|---|---|---|---|---|---|
| Price per unit | 22 | 20 | 19 | 18 | 17 | 15 |
| Variable cost per unit |  |  |  |  |  |  |
| Contribution per unit |  |  |  |  |  |  |
| Number of units sold | 50,000 | 60,000 | 70,000 | 80,000 | 90,000 | 90,000 |
| Total contribution ($000) |  |  |  |  |  |  |
| Less fixed costs ($000) |  |  |  |  |  |  |
| Net profit ($000) |  |  |  |  |  |  |

## 9 Limitations of the Profit-Maximisation Model

The profit-maximisation model does make some attempt to take account of the relationship between the price of a product and the resulting demand, but it is of limited practical use because of the following limitations:

(1) It is unlikely that organisations will be able to determine the demand function for their products or services with any degree of accuracy.

(2) The majority of organisations aim to achieve a target profit, rather than the theoretical maximum profit.

(3) Determining an accurate and reliable figure for marginal or variable cost poses difficulties for the management accountant.

(4) Unit marginal costs are likely to vary depending on the quantity sold. For example bulk discounts may reduce the unit materials cost for higher output volumes.

(5) Other factors, in addition to price, will affect the demand, for example, the level of advertising or changes in the income of customers.

## 10 Pricing Strategies Based on Cost: Total cost-plus pricing

Cost-plus pricing involves adding a mark-up to the total cost of the product, in order to arrive at the selling price.

Unfortunately, since fixed costs are spread over the units of production, the full cost of a product will be a function of the number of units produced, which in turn will be a response to the number of units sold. Yet, sales quantity will depend on the price charged for the product, and so the argument is circular.

Where an order is placed with a jobbing company (a company that makes products to order) for a specific quantity of a product made to the customer's specification, cost-plus may be an acceptable pricing method. But for the majority of organisations this is not the case. Other factors will influence the pricing decision, such as competition and product differentiation. Nevertheless it is reassuring to have some knowledge of cost and price at particular volumes, even if the knowledge is not perfect.

If an organisation does use cost as the basis for pricing it has to decide whether to employ a standard mark-up or whether to vary the mark-up according to the market conditions, type of customer, etc. A standard mark-up is used by some organisations, such as government contractors and some job costing companies, but the majority of companies vary the percentage to reflect differing market conditions for their products. The example below demonstrates total cost pricing, using varying cost assumptions of total cost.

**e.g**

## Total cost-plus pricing

A company is replacing product A with an updated version, B, and must calculate a base cost, to which will be added a mark-up in order to arrive at a selling price. The following variable costs have been established by reference to the company's experience with product A, although they may be subject to an error margin of + or − 10 % under production conditions for B:

|  | $ |
|---|---|
| Direct material | 4 |
| Direct labour (1/4 hr @ $16/hr) | 4 |
| Variable manufacturing overheads (1/4 hr of machine time @ $8/hr) | 2 |
| Total variable cost per unit | **10** |

As the machine time for each B would be the same as for A, the company estimates that it will be able to produce the same total quantity of B as its current production of A, which is 20,000 units. 50,000 machine hours may be regarded as the relevant capacity for the purposes of absorbing fixed manufacturing overheads. Current fixed costs are $240,000 for the production facilities, $200,000 for selling and distribution, and $180,000 for administration. For costing purposes, the 20,000 units of B can be assumed to consume 10 per cent of the total selling, distribution and administration costs.

***Alternative 1**, using conventional absorption costing principles and building in the conservative error margin*

| | $ |
|---|---:|
| Variable Production costs (as above) | 10 |
| Add: allowance for underestimate 10% | 1 |
| | |
| Add: manufacturing cost 1/4 hour of machine time @ $4.80/hour ($240,000/50,000 hours) | 1.2 |
| | |
| Base cost | **12.2** |

***Alternative 2**, as 1 but including administrative costs*

| | $ |
|---|---:|
| Base cost as under 1 above | 12.2 |
| Add: fixed administrative costs ($180,000 X 10% = $18,000 / 20,000 units) | 0.9 |
| Base cost | **13.1** |

***Alternative 3**, as 2 but including selling and distribution costs*

| | $ |
|---|---:|
| Base cost as under 2 above | 13.1 |
| Add: fixed selling and distribution costs ($200,000 X 10% = $20,000 / 20,000 units) | 1.0 |
| Base cost | **14.1** |

*Depending on the analysis adopted, the base cost varies from $12.2 to $14.1. The base cost rises with each alternative, as an increasing proportion of the total costs is recovered. The profit mark-up built into the pricing formula is therefore likely to fall with each alternative from 1 to 3.*

The profit mark-up needs to be based on some assumption. Normally it is fixed so that the company makes a specific return on capital based on a particular capacity utilisation.

A number of advantages are claimed for cost-plus pricing:

(i)   The required profit will be made if budgeted sales volumes are achieved.

(ii)  It is a particularly useful method in contract costing industries such as building, where a few large individual contracts can consume the majority of the annual fixed costs and the fixed costs are low in relation to the variable costs.

(iii) Assuming the organisation knows its cost structures, cost-plus is quick and cheap to employ. Its routine nature lends itself to delegation, thus saving management time.

(iv)  Cost-plus pricing can be useful in justifying selling prices to customers; if costs can be shown to have increased, this strengthens the case for an increase in the selling price.

However, there are a number of **problems** with cost-plus pricing:

(i)   There will always be problems associated with the selection of a 'suitable' basis on which to charge fixed costs to individual products or services. Selling prices can show great variation, depending on the apportionment basis chosen. This can lead to over-or under-pricing relative to competitors causing the firm to either lose business or make sales at an unintentional loss.

(ii)  If prices are set on the basis of normal volume, and actual volume turns out to be considerably lower, overheads will not be fully recovered from sales and predicted profits may not be attainable.

(iii) Cost-plus pricing takes no account of factors such as competitor activity.

(iv)  Cost-plus overlooks the need for flexibility in the different stages of a product's life cycle. It takes no account of the price customers are willing to pay and price elasticity of demand. The following example illustrates this point.

**Illustration**

The variable cost of product A is $10. Fixed manufacturing costs of $1m are spread over an estimated production and sales volume of 200,000 units, i.e. $5 per unit. This gives a total cost of $15 per unit. The cost-plus approach used by the manufacturer of A, based on a standard mark-up of 40 per cent on the product's total cost, dictates a selling price of $21. Assuming all costs were as anticipated, and the company managed to sell 200,000 units at the fixed price of $21, a gross profit of $1.2m ($6 x 200,000) would be earned. Suppose, however, that a market survey had indicated the price elasticity of demand for the product shown in the table below:

| Price ($) | Demand (units) |
|---|---|
| 19 | 250,000 |
| 20 | 240,000 |
| 21 | 200,000 |
| 22 | 190,000 |
| 23 | 160,000 |

A more correct analysis of the pricing problem would have concentrated on maximising total contribution, and therefore total profitability as shown in this table:

| Price ($) | Variable Cost | Contribution | Demand | Total Contribution | Profit |
|---|---|---|---|---|---|
| 19 | 10 | 9 | 250,000 | 2.25 | 1.25 |
| 20 | 10 | 10 | 240,000 | 2.40 | 1.40 |
| 21 | 10 | 11 | 200,000 | 2.20 | 1.20 |
| 22 | 10 | 12 | 190,000 | 2.28 | 1.28 |
| 23 | 10 | 13 | 160,000 | 2.08 | 1.08 |

The decision to use a full cost-plus price of $21 has an associated opportunity cost. In failing to take into consideration the market conditions the organisation has forgone an extra profit of $200,000 and its market share is lower than it could have been.

## 11 Marginal Cost-Plus Pricing

To the accountant, marginal cost is the same as variable cost. Some of the reasons for using it in preference to total cost are as follows:

(1) It is just as accurate as total cost-plus pricing. A larger mark-up percentage is added because both fixed costs and profit must be covered, but the uncertainty over the fixed costs per unit remains in both pricing methods.

(2) Knowledge of marginal cost gives management the option of pricing below total cost when times are bad, in order to fill capacity.

(3) It is particularly useful in pricing specific one-off contracts because it recognises relevant costs and opportunity costs as well as sunk costs.

(4) It also recognises the existence of scarce or limiting resources. Where these are used by competing products and services it must be reflected in the selling price if profit is to be maximised. If there is a scarce or bottleneck resource the aim must be to maximise the total contribution from the limiting factor. The contribution that each alternative product or service makes from each unit of the scarce resource must be calculated and a suitable profit margin added.

## Marginal Cost-Plus Pricing

A company has been producing A successfully for a number of years, and demand appears to be static into the foreseeable future at a market price of $15 per unit. A market has just developed in product B, which the company could produce without additional investment in plant, and without increasing or retraining the existing labour force. Unfortunately, however, B uses the same basic direct material as product A, material C – which is in short supply. The company must determine a minimum selling price for B, below which it would not be worthwhile to divert resources from A.

Costs for the two products are given in the table below:

|  | A | | B |
|---|---|---|---|
| Direct Material: 6 units of C @ $0 .60 | $3.60 | 5 units of C @ $0.60 | $3.00 |
| Direct Labour: 1/2 hour @ $6.00 | $3.00 | 1/2 hour @ $6.00 | $3.00 |
| Variable overhead | $2.40 | | $1.00 |
|  | $9.00 | | $7.00 |
| Selling Price | $15.00 | | |
| Contribution | $6.00 | | |

Contribution per unit of material C = $6 / 6 units = $1

A produces a contribution of $6 using 6 units of C, that is, a contribution per unit of C, the limiting factor, of $1. B uses five units of C. The company must therefore seek a contribution of $5 (5 units of material C x $1). So the price must cover the cost of the unit and the lost contribution from C, i.e. be at least $7 + $5 = $12.

## 12 Criticism Of Marginal Cost-Plus Pricing

Marginal costing as a basis for pricing has always had its sceptics. The main criticism is based on the following type of scenario :

There are two companies A and B competing with similar products in a market. The market is in recession and sales have decreased. Company A assesses its costs and lowers its price to below total cost, but well above marginal cost, in order to gain more market share. This tactic works; demand is elastic and so company A gains market share at the expense of company B. In order to get back its market share company B reduces its price below that of company A. Both companies now have their original market share but their margins are reduced. Company A then lowers the price again, etc. This continues, until one company is forced out of business. The remaining company now has to increase prices to the original level, which may well be difficult and can incur customer resistance.

## 13 Marketing-based Pricing Strategies

There are many different pricing strategies, and it may come as a surprise to would-be accountants that cost is only one of many methods and is certainly not universally used as the key method for pricing.

### Premium pricing

Premium pricing is pricing above competition on a permanent basis. This can only be done if the product appears 'different' and superior to competition, which normally means establishing a brand name based on one of the following:

- Quality
- Image/style
- Reliability/robustness
- Durability
- After-sales service
- Extended warranties.

### Brands and premium pricing

In order to establish a brand, heavy initial promotion is required and the name must be constantly advertised or promoted thereafter. Brand names, such as, Levi, Mars, Coca-Cola, etc., require many millions of pounds spent on them each year. The benefit is a higher selling price generating a larger profit per unit and customer loyalty, making the product relatively price inelastic. These benefits must, of course, outweigh the cost of keeping the brand name in front of the customers.

### Market skimming

Skimming is a technique where a high price is set for the product initially, so that only those who are desperately keen on the product will buy it. Then the price is lowered, making the product more accessible. When the next group of customers have had a chance to buy at that price, the price is lowered again, and so on. The aim of this strategy is usually to **maximise revenue**. But, on occasions, it is also used to prolong the life of older products.

#### Market skimming and consumer durables

Consumer durable companies tend to skim the market. This is done, to a certain extent, to recover large research and development costs quite quickly. But the products also lend themselves to this treatment as trend-setters are willing to pay a high price to own the latest gismo, and the rest of the population follow their example in later years. Books are also sold this way, with new novels published in hardback at a high price. The hard cover costs little more than a soft cover. Avid readers of that author will buy the hardback book at the high price. A year or so later the book is reissued with a soft cover at a much cheaper price in order to reach a wider audience.

Price skimming was probably first employed at the end of the eighteenth century by Josiah Wedgwood, the famous ceramics manufacturer. He made classical-shaped vases decorated with sprigs of decoration, which he sold to the rich and well-to-do. Naturally he priced his products accordingly. As the designs became old and well known he reduced the price on those lines and introduced new designs at the high price. Thus, he created different tiers of markets for his products, and people who were not so well off could afford a piece which had been in production for some years. This marketing technique helps to prolong a product's life and extracts the maximum profit from it.

If demand for a new or innovative product is relatively inelastic, the supplier has the chance of adopting a market skimming price strategy. It is usually much easier to reduce prices than increase them, so it is better to begin with a high price, and lower it if demand appears more elastic than anticipated. If profitable skimming is to be sustained beyond the introductory phase, there must be significant barriers to entry to the market, in order to deter too many potential competitors entering attracted by the high prices and returns. In the case of books only one company own the rights to publish. Wedgwood had created an image/brand among the rich and famous which others could not copy, especially if they wished to undercut his prices. Consumer durable products have high manufacturing costs that deter too many companies entering the industry.

### Penetration pricing

Penetration pricing occurs when a company sets a very low price for the new product initially. The price will usually be below total cost. The aim of the low price is to establish a large market share quickly by encouraging customers to try the product and then to repeat buy. This type of tactic is used, therefore, where barriers to entry are low. It is hoped to establish a dominant market position, which will prevent new entrants coming into the market because they could not establish a critical mass easily with prices so low.

### Penetration pricing

In the past, companies used penetration pricing when they introduced a new product, such as a new spray polish, through supermarkets. The price would be, say, between 60 per cent and 80 per cent of the ultimate price. Customers would buy the new product largely because of its price and, it was hoped, repeat buy either because they did not notice the price increase or because they did not mind paying for a good product. If customers do notice the price increase they are likely to be put off further purchases if the increase is too large. If a company succeeds with this type of pricing it wins a large market share very quickly which competitors will find hard to break into.

*[In the PEG September 2010, the Examiner highlights the necessity for candidates to be able to 'compare and contrast penetration and skimming pricing strategies'.]*

### Price differentiation

If the market can be split into different segments, each quite separate from the others and with its own individual demand function, it is possible to sell the same product to different customers at different prices. Marketing techniques can be employed to create market segmentation, if natural demarcation lines are not already in existence. Segmentation will usually be on the basis of one or more of the following:

- Time (e.g. rail travel is cheaper off-peak, hotel accommodation, telecommunications);
- Quantity (e.g. small orders at a premium, bulk orders at a discount);
- Type of customer (e.g. student and OAP rates);
- Outlet/function (e.g. different prices for wholesaler, retailer, end consumer);
- Geographical location (e.g. stalls and upper circle, urban and rural sites, wealthy and poor districts, different countries);
- Product content (e.g. sporty versions of a small car).

This type of pricing is of particular use where a service provider (theatre, leisure centre, train operator) has a high proportion of fixed costs. By attracting those willing and able to use the service at the less popular time/location will help to improve profitability.

**Loss leader pricing**

When a product range consists of one or more main products and a series of related optional 'extras', which the customer can 'add on' to the main product, the supplier can set a relatively low price for the main product and a high one for the 'extras'. Obviously, the aim is to stimulate sufficient demand for the former to ensure the target return from sales of the latter. The strategy has been used successfully by aircraft engine manufacturers, who win an order with a very competitively priced main product that can only be serviced by their own, highly priced spare parts.

### Loss leader pricing – examples

Gillette did not invent the safety razor but the market strategy Gillette adopted helped to build market share. Gillette razors were sold at 1/5 of the cost to manufacture them but only Gillette blades fitted and these were sold at a price of 5 cents. The blades cost only 1 cent to manufacture and so Gillette made large profits once it had captured the customer. One of the best known uses of this technique in recent years has been the sale of printer ink for home printers.

Investigations by Which? and by Computeractive magazine showed that whilst the price of inkjet printers can be as little as $34, the cost of running the printer over an 18-month period could be up to $1,700. The top brand names for replacement ink cartridges cost more per millilitre than vintage champagne and even where the consumer only buys two replacement cartridges a year, the cost of the ink is likely to be significantly higher than the cost of the initial printer.

**Discount pricing**

Discount pricing is the long-term pricing strategy used by firms such as Ikea and Ryanair, based on low cost, high volume and low margins.

Products are priced lower than the market norm, but are put forward as being of comparable quality. The aim is that the product will procure a larger share of the market than it might otherwise do, thereby counteracting the reduction in selling price. However, care must be taken to ensure that potential customers' perceptions of the product are not prejudiced by the lower price. The consumer will often view with suspicion a branded product that is priced at even a small discount to the prevailing market rate.

**Using discounts in pricing (short-term)**

There are a number of reasons for using discounts to adjust prices:

(1) To get cash in quickly. This is a not always a financially sound strategy as the firm may lose more in sales revenues from the discount, than they would lose in interest from a bank loan for the same amount.

(2) To differentiate between different types of customer, wholesale, retail, etc.

(3) To increase sales volume during a poor sales period without dropping the price permanently.

(4) Some industries give discounts as normal practice, for example the antique trade, and some retail shops seem to have semi-permanent sales.

(5) Perishable goods are often discounted towards the end of their life or the end of the day, or seconds are often sold off cheaply. This may not be a good strategy as it does not improve the company image, and some customers may get wise and delay their purchase until the end of the day when prices are cheaper.

## Controlled pricing

A significant proportion of the previously nationalised industries in the UK have been 'privatised' into the private sector, with a constraining influence usually called the industry 'regulator'. Examples of these regulating bodies are Oftel (telecommunications) and Ofwat (water).

Many of these companies are in a largely monopolistic situation and so regulation of these industries was perceived as desirable. Regulation largely takes the form of controlling price so that the monopolistic companies cannot exploit their unique position. The regulators use selling price as the means of controlling the volume of supply in the industry. They may also decide to specify the quality of the product or level of service that must be achieved or to prohibit the company operating in certain sectors.

When an industry is regulated on selling price, the elasticity is zero. No price change is allowed. Not only does this mean that 'small' customers pay less than they otherwise would, but large customers pay more than one might expect under more competitive positions. Over recent years all of the monopolistic industries have introduced some kind of discounted price for very large customers, which is beginning to allow genuine competition to enter the market. Gradually other billing companies have been allowed to enter the market and so price has become more flexible.

## Product bundling

Bundling is putting a package of products together to make, for example, a complete kit for customers, which can then be sold at a temptingly low price. It is a way of creating value for customers and increasing company profits. It is a strategy that is often adopted in times of recession when organisations are particularly keen to maintain sales volume. One industry where this tactic started in the recession of the early 1990s is the computer industry. A manufacturer might decide to substantially reduce the profit margin on some hardware, such as printers. If, for example, only half its PC purchasers would also buy the company's model of printer, a bundled package which includes the PC and the printer for a lower combined price may well prove very successful. On the other hand, some customers will be put off by product bundling as they do not want the complete package; they will resent the increased price, however small it is.

### Bundling

Bundling is profitable in situations in which some buyers value one of the items in a bundle relatively highly but the remainder slightly above or below cost price. Other buyers place a relatively high valuation on both or all of the items in the bundle. Four film exhibitors, A to D, are willing to pay the following prices for two films X and Y:

A values X at $16,000 and Y at $5,000
B values X at $14,000 and Y at $6,000
C values X at $11,000 and Y at $10,000
D values X at $10,000 and Y at $11,000

The distributor's marginal cost of supplying each film is $8,000.

The distributor offers X and Y separately at $14,000 and $8,000 respectively, or the pair as a package for $21,000. The result is that A, C and D hire the package and B hires film X only, as the cost of both the bundle and film Y exceed his particular valuations. The distributor's profit would be ($21,000 x 3) + ($14,000) – ($8,000 x 7) = $21,000.

However, A might also prefer to hire film X for $14,000, instead of taking the package, as the extra cost of the bundle exceeds his valuation of Y by $2,000. If A did choose this option, the distributor's profit would rise to $22,000, as he does not have to supply either A or B with film Y, which has a supply cost in excess of their valuations: ($21,000 x 2) x ($14,000 x 2) – ($8,000 x 6) = $22,000.

Bundling is a particularly efficient means of exploiting price differentiation. Buyers are offered a pricing structure in which they are charged higher prices for buying the items separately (X + Y = $22,000) than in a package (X + Y = $21,000). Bundling works as a discriminatory device by:

- Using the package to extract the most from those customers who value it most. (In our example C and D, who placed relatively high valuations on both films.)

- Charging a relatively high separate price for the item in the package that is valued very highly by some particular buyers. (In our example film X, which was valued very highly by both A and B.)

If the distributor did not bundle he would make a profit of $19,000, as A and B would purchase product X and C and D would purchase product Y.

## Bundling : Amstrad

Bundling can be extremely successful, especially when tried on mature products for the first time. For instance, Amstrad had considerable success when it entered the hi-fi market and demystified the technology by being the first company to sell a complete package of amplifier, deck and speakers. This was more than just a pricing strategy: it was a complete marketing strategy. In recent years the telecommunications industry has successfully used this technique; first with TV channel packages, and then more recently extended to TV, broadband and phone bundles.

Whether a bundling strategy will succeed depends on the predicted increase in sales volume and the changes in margin. There are likely to be other cost changes such as savings in product handling, packaging and invoicing costs. Longer-term implications and competitors' reactions must not be ignored. For example, how will customers react when products are 'unbundled'? Will this result in a marked decline in sales? Will bundling be seen as an inferior product strategy which will have long-term implications for the brand's image? Will competitors retaliate by bundling their products? If they do this, will the strategy be successful?

### Pricing With Additional Features

The decision to add extra features to a product is a similar decision to bundling products. Most people prefer to have extra features incorporated into the product but they may not be prepared to pay the extra price. Others do not require the extra features and view them as a definite disadvantage. This is likely to be the case with older customers and electrical or electronic equipment. Older people find mastering the equipment quite difficult and they do not want extra features that make operation even more difficult. The following exercise considers an extra feature, the resulting price and its effect on market share.

## 14 The Product Life Cycle

Products and services, like human beings, have a life cycle. This is represented by the generic curve shown below:

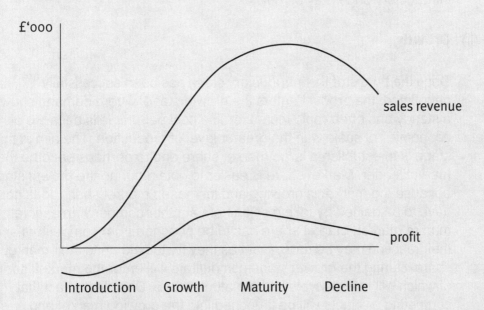

The length of the life cycle varies considerably from a year or so, for some children's toys, to hundreds of years, as in the case of binoculars, for example. The product life cycle is divided into four basic stages as shown in the figure above; each stage has different aims and expectations.

Price is a major variable over the product life cycle. Depending on market structure and demand, different pricing strategies will be appropriate for different stages in the cycle. The four stages in the life cycle and appropriate price strategies are described below:

## (i) Introductory phase

Demand will be low when a product is first launched onto the market, and heavy advertising expenditure will usually be required to bring it to consumers' attention. The aim is to establish the product in the market, which means achieving a certain critical mass within a certain period of time. The critical mass is the sales volume that must be achieved in order to make the product viable in the medium term. Depending on the nature of the product, a price penetration (low entry price) policy may be adopted in order to reach the critical mass quickly. On the other hand the market may be skimmed (exploiting those purchasers keen to have the latest product such as plasma screen TVs) and so a high introductory price may be set.

## (ii) Growth

Once the hurdle of the introductory stage has been successfully negotiated, the product enters the growth stage, where demand shows a steady and often rapid increase. The cost per unit falls because of economies of scale with the greater level of production. The aim at this stage is to establish a large market share and to perhaps become the market leader. Market share is easier to obtain during the growth stage because the market is growing and increased market share does not have to be gained by taking sales from another company. In a more mature market, market share has to be poached from competitors and their reaction may be unpleasant as they try to hold on to their market share. During the growth stage competitors will enter the market, some of which will not survive into the maturity stage. Despite the fact that competing products will be launched into the growing market and pricing is often keen in order to gain market share, it is usually the most profitable stage for the initial supplier.

## (iii) Maturity

The increase in demand slows down in this stage, as the product reaches the mass market. The sales curve flattens out and eventually begins to fall. As market maturity is reached the organisation becomes more interested in minimising elasticity. Products have to be differentiated in order to maintain their position in the market and new users for mature products need to be found to keep demand high. Generally, profits will be lower than during the growth stage.

## (iv) Decline

When the market reaches saturation point, the product's sales curve begins to decline. When the market declines price wars erupt as organisations with products which have elastic demand seek to maintain full utilisation of their production capacity.

Profits can still be made during the early part of this stage, and the products will be managed to generate cash for newer products. This will determine how prices are set. Eventually rapidly falling sales inevitably result in losses for all suppliers who stay in the market. This particular product has effectively come to the end of its life cycle, and alternative investment opportunities must be pursued.

Despite the recent general tendency to shorter life cycles, the length of any particular stage within the cycle and the total length of the life cycle itself will depend on the type of product or service being marketed. Although the curve will be characterised by a sustained rise, followed by levelling out and falling away, the precise shape of the curve can vary considerably. Life cycles are discussed further later in this text.

## 15 Other issues

### The Price/Quality Relationship

The price/quality relationship refers to the perception by most consumers that a relatively high price is a sign of good quality. The belief in this relationship is most important with complex products that are hard to test, and services, that cannot be tested until used. The greater the uncertainty surrounding a product, the more consumers depend on the price/quality hypothesis and the greater premium lights the importance of 'the relationship they are prepared to pay.

*[In the PEG September 2010, the Examiner highlights the importance of 'the relationship between price and quality, and how this affects product decisions'.]*

### Income Elasticity of Demand

In economics, the income elasticity of demand measures the responsiveness of the demand for a good to a change in the income of the people demanding the good. For example, if, in response to a 10% increase in income, the demand for a good increased by 20%, the income elasticity of demand would be 20%/10% = 2.

A negative income elasticity of demand is associated with inferior goods; an increase in income will lead to a fall in the demand and may lead to changes to more luxurious substitutes.

A positive income elasticity of demand is associated with normal goods; an increase in income will lead to a rise in demand. If income elasticity of demand of a commodity is less than 1, it is a necessity good. If the elasticity of demand is greater than 1, it is a luxury good or a superior good.

A zero income elasticity (or inelastic) demand occurs when an increase in income is not associated with a change in the demand of a good. These would be sticky goods.

### Ethical Considerations

Whether or not to exploit short-term shortages through higher prices is an ethical decision faced, for example, by companies supplying essential commodities such as gas or fuel.

### Test Your Understanding 1 – Q Organisation

(a) The Q Organisation is a large worldwide respected manufacturer of consumer electrical and electronic goods. Q constantly develops new products that are in high demand as they represent the latest technology and are 'must haves' for those consumers who want to own the latest consumer gadgets. Recently Q has developed a new handheld digital DVD recorder and seeks your advice as to the price it should charge for such a technologically advanced product.

**Required:**

Explain the relevance of the product life cycle to the consideration of alternative pricing policies that might be adopted by Q.

**(10 marks)**

(b) Market research has discovered that the price/demand relationship for the item during the initial launch phase will be as follows:

| Price ($) | Demand (units) |
|-----------|----------------|
| 100 | 10,000 |
| 80 | 20,000 |
| 69 | 30,000 |
| 62 | 40,000 |

Production of the DVD recorder would occur in batches of 10,000 units, and the production director believes that 50% of the variable manufacturing cost would be affected by a learning and experience curve. This would apply to each batch produced and continue at a constant rate of learning up to a production volume of 40,000 units when the learning would be complete. Thereafter, the unit variable manufacturing cost of the product would be equal to the unit cost of the fourth batch. The production director estimates that the unit variable manufacturing cost of the first batch would be $60 ($30 of which is subject to the effect of the learning and experience curve, and $30 of which is unaffected), whereas the average unit variable manufacturing cost of all four batches would be $52.71.

There are no non-manufacturing variable costs associated with the DVD recorder.

**Required:**

(i) Calculate the rate of learning that is expected by the production director.

**(4 marks)**

(ii) Calculate the optimum price at which Q should sell the DVD recorder in order to maximise its profits during the initial launch phase of the product.

**(8 marks)**

(iii) Q expects that after the initial launch phase the market price will be $57 per unit. Estimated product specific fixed costs during this phase of the product's life are expected to be $15,000 per month. During this phase of the product life cycle Q wishes to achieve a target monthly profit from the product of $30,000.

Calculate the number of units that need to be sold each month during this phase in order for Q to achieve this target monthly profit.

**(3 marks)**

**(Total: 25 marks)**

ML is an engineering company that specialises in providing engineering facilities to businesses that cannot justify operating their own facilities in-house. ML employs a number of engineers who are skilled in different engineering techniques that enable ML to provide a full range of engineering facilities to its customers.

Most of the work undertaken by ML is unique to each of its customers, often requiring the manufacture of spare parts for its customers' equipment, or the building of new equipment from customer drawings. As a result most of ML's work is short-term, with some jobs being completed within hours while others may take a few days.

To date, ML has adopted a cost plus approach to setting its prices. This is based upon an absorption costing system that uses machine hours as the basis of absorbing overhead costs into individual job costs. The Managing Director is concerned that, over recent months, ML has been unsuccessful when quoting for work with the consequence that there has been an increase in the level of unused capacity. It has been suggested that ML should adopt an alternative approach to its pricing based on marginal costing since 'any price that exceeds variable costs is better than no work'.

**Required:**

With reference to the above scenario:

(a) briefly explain absorption and marginal cost approaches to pricing;

(b) discuss the validity of the comment 'any price that exceeds variable costs is better than no work'.

**(10 marks)**

## Test Your Understanding 3 – AB Ltd

During the current year AB Ltd planned to produce 150,000 units of its main product, a cordless hand drill. Nearing the end of the current year, activity so far has corresponded to budget and it is anticipated that average costs for the whole year will be as shown below:

**Average cost per unit (for 150,000 activity level)**

|  | $ |
|---|---|
| Direct material | 18 |
| Direct labour | 10 |
| Variable overhead | 10 |
| Fixed overhead | 10 |
|  | — |
|  | 48 |

The budget for next year is being developed and the following cost changes have been forecast:

Direct material: price increase of 33.3%

Director labour: rate increase of 10%

Variable overhead: increase of 5%

Fixed overhead: increase of 15%

The substantial price increase for materials is causing concern and alternative sources are being considered. One source quotes a material cost per unit of $20 but tests on samples show that the cheaper materials would increase labour costs by an additional 50c per unit and would lead to a reject rate of 5%. It would also be necessary to install a test and inspection department at the end of manufacturing to identify the faulty items. This would increase fixed costs by an additional $200,000 per year.

Selling prices are also considered when the budget is being developed. Normally, selling prices are determined on a cost-plus basis, the mark-up being 50% on unit cost, but there is concern that this is too inflexible as it would lead to a substantial price rise for next year. The sales director estimates that demand varies with price thus:

|  | $ | $ | $ | $ | $ | $ | $ |
|---|---|---|---|---|---|---|---|
| Price/unit | 64 | 68 | 72 | 76 | 80 | 84 | 88 |
| Demand (000 units) | 190 | 170 | 150 | 140 | 125 | 110 | 95 |

**Required:**

(a) Calculate which type of material – regular or cheaper – would minimise cost. Explain your answer fully.

**(8 marks)**

(b) On the basis of your answer to (a), calculate what selling price would maximise profit for next year.

**(8 marks)**

It has been realised that, through better organisation, it would be possible to reduce the extra fixed costs of $200,000 originally estimated in connection with the cheaper material.

**Required:**

(c) Calculate, using the price/demand you have recommended in part (b), the level of fixed costs at which the company would be indifferent as to its choice of materials.

**(3 marks)**

(d) Comment on any other factors which should be considered before final decisions are made.

**(6 marks)**

**(Total: 25 marks)**

## Test Your Understanding 4 – Optimum Price

A company is reviewing the price of one of its products. The product has a marginal cost of $28 per unit and is currently sold for $65 per unit. At this price the demand for the product is 800 units per week. A market research study shows that for each reduction in the selling price by $5 per unit the weekly demand would increase by 40 units, and that for each increase in the selling price by $5 per unit the weekly demand would decrease by 40 units.

Calculate the optimal selling price.

## Test Your Understanding 5 – Pricing and Tabular Approach

(a) A manufacturing company is considering its pricing policy for next year. It has already carried out some market research into the expected levels of demand for one of its products at different selling prices, with the following results:

| Selling Price per unit | Annual Demand (units) |
| --- | --- |
| $100 | 50,000 |
| $120 | 45,000 |
| $130 | 40,000 |
| $150 | 25,000 |
| $160 | 10,000 |
| $170 | 5,000 |

This product is manufactured in batches of 100 units, and analysis has shown that the total production cost depends on the number of units as well as the number of batches produced each year. This analysis has produced the following formula for total cost:

$$Z = 70x + 80y + \$240,000$$

Where Z represents the total production cost; x represents the number of units produced; and y represents the number of batches of production.

**Required:**

(i)   Prepare calculations to identify which of the above six selling prices per unit will result in the highest annual profit from this product.

**(7 marks)**

(ii)  Explain why your chosen selling price might not result in the highest possible annual profit from this product.

**(3 marks)**

(b)  The company is also launching a new product to the market next year and is currently considering its pricing strategy for this new product. The product will be unlike any other product that is currently available and will considerably improve the efficiency with which garages can service motor vehicles. This unique position in the market place is expected to remain for only six months before one of the company's competitors develops a similar product.

The prototype required a substantial amount of time to develop and as a result the company is keen to recover its considerable research and development costs as soon as possible. The company has now developed its manufacturing process for this product and as a result the time taken to produce each unit is much less than was required for the first few units. This time reduction is expected to continue for a short period of time once mass production has started, but from then a constant time requirement per unit is anticipated.

**Required:**

(i)   Explain the alternative pricing strategies that may be adopted when launching a new product.

**(6 marks)**

(ii)  Recommend a pricing strategy to the company for its new product. Explain how the adoption of your chosen strategy would affect the sales revenue, costs and profits of this product over its life cycle.

**(9 marks)**

(1)  ABC plc is about to launch a new product. Facilities will allow the company to produce up to 20 units per week. The marketing department has estimated that at a price of $8,000 no units will be sold, but for each $150 reduction in price one additional unit per week will be sold.

Fixed costs associated with manufacture are expected to be $12,000 per week.

Variable costs are expected to be $4,000 per unit for each of the first 10 units; thereafter each unit will cost $400 more than the preceding one. The most profitable level of output per week for the new product is:

(A) 10 units
(B) 11 units
(C) 13 units
(D) 14 units
(E) 20 units

(2)  Market research by Company A has revealed that the maximum demand for product R is 50,000 units each year, and that demand will reduce by 50 units for every $1 that the selling price is increased. Based on this information, Company A has calculated that the profit-maximising level of sales for product R for the coming year is 35,000 units. The price at which these units will be sold is:

(A) $100
(B) $300
(C) $500
(D) $700
(E) $900

(3)  Another product manufactured by company A is product M. At a price of $700 for product M there would be zero demand, and for every $40 reduction in the selling price the demand would increase by 100 units. The variable cost of producing a unit of product M is $60.

Company A knows that if the demand equation for product M is represented by $p = a - bx$, where p is the selling price and x is the quantity demanded at price p, then the marginal revenue (MR) for product M can be represented by $MR = a - 2bx$.

The profit-maximising output of product M is:

(A) 100 units
(B) 700 units
(C) 800 units
(D) 1,600 units
(E) 1,750 units

(4) A company is considering the pricing of one of its products. It has already carried out some market research with the following results:

The quantity demanded at a price of $100 will be 1,000 units.

The quantity demanded will increase/decrease by 100 units for every $50 decrease/increase in the selling price
The marginal cost of each unit is $35

Calculate the selling price that maximises company profit.

(5) H is launching a new product which it expects to incur a variable cost of $14 per unit. The company has completed some market research to try to determine the optimum selling price with the following results. If the price charged was to be $25 per unit, then the demand would be 1,000 units each period. For every $1 increase in the selling price, demand would reduce by 100 units each period. For every $1 reduction in the selling price, the demand would increase by 100 units each period.

Calculate the optimum selling price.

**Test your understanding answers**

> ### The Algebraic approach
>
> (a)  b = (220 – 200) / (950 – 1,000) = -0.4
>
>     200 = a –0.4 x 1,000
>
>     a = 200 + 400 = 600.
>
>     So the demand function is P = 600 – 0.4Q
>
> (b)  To find MR, just double the gradient so that MR = 600 – 0.8Q
>
>     MR = 600 – 0.8Q
>
> (c)  MC = 140
>
> (d)  The optimum quantity Q is achieved when the company produces units up to the point where marginal revenue equals marginal cost, ie when MR = MC
>
> with MR = a + 2bQ
>
> i.e. MR = $600 – 0.8Q
>
> and MC = $140
>
> so q is achieved when a + 2bQ = $140
>
> i.e. when $600 – 0.8Q = $140
>
> i.e. when Q= 575 units
>
> (e)  P= 600 – 0.4 x 575 = $370
>
> (f)  Revenue = Price x Quantity = $370 x 575 = $212,750
>
>     Cost = $36,000 + $140 x 575 = $116,500
>
>     Profit = $96,250

### Example 1 – Tabular Approach

|  | $ | $ | $ | $ | $ | $ |
|---|---|---|---|---|---|---|
| Price per unit | 22 | 20 | 19 | 18 | 17 | 15 |
| Variable cost per unit | (6) | (6) | (6) | (6) | (6) | (6) |
| Contribution per unit | 16 | 14 | 13 | 12 | 11 | 9 |
| Number of units sold | 50,000 | 60,000 | 70,000 | 80,000 | 90,000 | 90,000 |
| Total contribution ($000) | 800 | 840 | 910 | 960 | 990 | 810 |
| Less fixed costs ($000) | (200) | (200) | (280) | (280) | (360) | (360) |
| Net profit ($000) | 600 | 640 | 630 | 680 | 630 | 450 |

**To maximise profit, price should be $18, output 80,000 and 1 extra machine should be hired.**

### Test Your Understanding 1 – Q Organisation

(a) **Examiner's comments:**

    (a) Common errors Describing 'life cycle costing' as opposed to the 'product life cycle'.

       –  Not relating alternative pricing policies to the stages of the product life cycle.

       –  Suggesting inappropriate pricing policies.

    (b) Common errors

       –  Not using initiative by introducing their 'own figure' from part (i) when attempting part (ii). Marks were available, as usual, for students who took this initiative.

       –  Applying the formula incorrectly, particularly when the quantity being produced falls outside the 'doubling process' (part (ii)).

       –  Applying the learning curve effect to the full $60 (part (i) and part (ii)).

       –  Not understanding what was required in part (iii).

(a) The handheld digital DVD recorder is a new hi-tech 'must have' product. It is likely to have incurred significant development and design costs. The product is also likely to have a relatively short product life cycle (of months rather than years).

The price of the product is likely to change over the four stages of the life cycle. We shall consider each stage in turn:

### Introduction stage

When a new innovative product is launched to a market there are two commonly used pricing strategies used:

– *Market skimming*

This strategy involves selling the product at a very high price during the introduction stage. This policy is likely to be successful if the product is brand new and innovative. Also, if demand is inelastic, then the product will generate a much higher return at an initial high price. Market skimming will generate a high net cash in-flow initially, which hopefully will help recover the high development costs quickly.

Q may be able to take advantage of this pricing policy as its new DVD recorder incorporates the latest technology and Q is likely to be the first on the market with this cutting-edge item.

Selling at a very high price will attract strong competition to the product.

– *Price penetration*

Q may choose to launch the product at a very low price or penetration price. Advantages of this approach include high growth is encouraged, competition is discouraged, and economies of scale may be taken advantage of. However, for this strategy to generate high profits, Q would need a high volume of sales, and be the dominant player in the market (high market share). Achieving high sales volume may be difficult with a brand new product.

– *Growth stage*

During this stage of the products life cycle, the sales of the DVD player would be expected to grow rapidly. As the product starts to become accepted and established by the mass market, competition usually significantly increases. In order to maintain market share and dominance Q will find it necessary to lower the initial market skimming launch price.

– *Maturity stage*

As product sales growth begins to slow down and level off, an established market price for the DVD recorder will become apparent. The price will often reach its lowest point during this stage. An average/going-rate price may be charged. However, Q has a good reputation and is respected worldwide, so it may be able to charge a premium price based on its reputation and a certain level of brand loyalty.

Q may try to extend the maturity phase by launching upgrades or by trying to sell in new markets.

The product must achieve its lowest unit cost during this stage. Profits are likely to be highest in the maturity stage.

– *Decline*

The decline stage is the final stage of the product's life cycle. The initial new innovative technology has now been superseded by superior products.

The DVD recorder may hold on to a small niche market. The group of loyal customers still purchasing the original DVD player may be willing to pay a price that is reasonable. Alternatively Q may use product bundling.

At the final withdrawal of the product, prices may be slashed to sell off any surplus stock.

(b) (i) Variable cost affected by the learning curve for the first batch

= \$60 – \$30 = \$30

Let 'r' be the learning curve rate.

| Output in batches | Cumulative average cost per unit |
|:---:|:---:|
| x | y |
| 1 | 30 |
| 2 | 30r |
| 4 | $30r^2 = 22.71$ |

If $30\ r^2$      = 22.71

$r^2$      = 0.757

r      = 0.87

The learning curve rate is 87%.

**Note:** This answer could be determined using the formula but this is a much more cumbersome method when doubling is possible. The approach using the formula would be:

$Y = ax^b$ so $22.71 = 30 \times 4^b$

$4^b = 22.71/30 = 0.757$

Taking logs b log 4 = log 0.757

b = log 0.757/log 4 = –0.2000

b = log learning rate/log 2

So    log learning rate = –0.200 × log2 = –0.06045

Learning rate = 0.87

(ii)

| Price ($) | Demand (000s) | LC variable cost p.u. ($) | Non-LC variable cost p.u. ($) | Total V.C. p.u. ($) | Contribution per unit ($) | **Total contribution ($000)** |
|---|---|---|---|---|---|---|
| 100 | 10 | 30.00 | 30.00 | 60.00 | 40.00 | 400.0 |
| 80 | 20 | 26.10 | 30.00 | 56.10 | 23.90 | 478.0 |
| 69 | 30 | 24.06 | 30.00 | 54.06 | 14.94 | 448.2 |
| 62 | 40 | 22.71 | 30.00 | 52.71 | 9.29 | 371.6 |

To maximise contribution the company should sell 20,000 units at $80 each.

**Learning curve workings**

| Output in batches | Average cost per unit |
|---|---|
| x | y |
| 1 | 30.00 |
| 2 | 26.10 |
| 3 | 24.06 ** |
| 4 | 22.71 |

$Y = ax^b$

$a = 30$

$b = \log 0.87 \div \log 2 = -0.2009$

$x = 3$ batches

$y = 30 \times 3^{-0.2009}$

$y = 24.06$

(iii)

$$\text{Target contribution} = \text{Fixed costs} + \text{Required profit}$$
$$= \$15,000 + \$30,000$$
$$= \$45,000 \text{ per month}$$

The initial launch phase represents the first 20,000 units (as per (b)(ii) above). However the learning effect continues until 40,000 units hence the unit cost decreases (and therefore unit contribution increases) until the 40,000 units have been completed.

The average unit cost of the batch of units from 20,001 – 30,000 is:

$$((30,000 \times \$54.06) - (20,000 \times \$56.10)) \div 10,000 = \$49.98$$

thus giving a unit contribution of $57.00 – $49.98 = $7.02 and a monthly sales target of:

$$\$45,000 \div \$7.02 = 6,411 \text{ units}$$

The average unit cost for 30,001 units and more is:

$$((40,000 \times \$52.71) - (30,000 \times \$54.06)) \div 10,000 = \$48.66$$

thus giving a unit contribution of $57 – $48.66 = $8.34

and thus the monthly sales target becomes:

$$\$45,000 \div \$8.34 = 5,396 \text{ units}$$

In the second month after the launch phase, the first 3,589 units (10,000 – 6,411) sold will generate a contribution of $7.02 per unit and the remaining units will generate a contribution of $8.34.

| | | |
|---|---|---|
| Target contribution | $45,000 | |
| Contribution from first | 3,589 × $7.02 | ($25,195) |
| Contribution still required | $19,805 | |

Number of units still to be sold $19,805 ÷ $8.34 = 2,375 units

Total unit sales in 2nd month = 3,589 + 2,375 = 5,964

## Test Your Understanding 2 – ML

*[Make sure that you focus your answer on absorption and marginal cost approaches to pricing (not costing). A main issue is therefore how the level of mark-up is determined. Your answer should take a balanced view of the comment in the short and long term. While it may be true in the short term, under certain circumstances a price which does not generate a profit in the long term could not be acceptable.]*

(a) An absorption cost approach to pricing involves adding a profit margin to the full cost of the product. The full cost is calculated by taking prime cost and adding a share of overhead which, in ML's case, is absorbed using machine hours.

A marginal cost approach to pricing takes the variable cost of the product and adds a mark-up to cover fixed cost and profit. Fixed overheads are not absorbed to product but are treated as a period cost in the accounts.

The mark-up added using a marginal costing approach would have to be greater than that under an absorption costing approach to ensure that the same profit level is achieved. Mark-ups may be varied depending on the market conditions. ML's work is unique to each of its customers and it may therefore be difficult to estimate a suitable mark-up.

(b) The comment 'any price that exceeds variable costs is better than no work' may have some validity in the short term. In the case of a company like ML, which has unused capacity, fixed costs will be incurred in the short term irrespective of workload. Any price that exceeds variable cost will provide some contribution and will reduce losses.

If resources are scarce then this statement is not true, even in the short term, as there would be an opportunity cost involved in utilising resources in addition to the variable cost.

Care must be taken that special prices based on variable cost do not become the normal expectation or upset existing customers who are paying a price which generates a profit.

In the long run fixed cost must be covered and a profit made in accordance with company objectives. An absorption costing approach may not provide an accurate total product costs and an activity-based approach may improve the accuracy of total costs and enable ML to identify those products or customers which generate most profit.

**Test Your Understanding 3 – AB Ltd**

(a)

| | Current material | Cheaper material |
|---|---|---|
| | $per unit | $ |
| Direct material | 24.00 | 20.00 |
| Direct labour | 11.00 | 11.50 |
| Variable overhead | 10.50 | 10.50 |
| | ——— | ——— |
| Total variable cost | 45.50 | 42.00 |
| | ——— | ——— |

for 0.95 of a unit

$42

$$\therefore \text{ Cost per unit} = \frac{\$42}{0.95}$$

= $44.21 per unit

Fixed costs last year: $10 × 150,000 = $1,500,000

∴ Fixed cost in coming year: $1,500,000 × 1.15 = $1,725,000

If use cheaper material fixed costs increase
by $200,000: $1,925,000

When the company switches from the current material to the cheaper material, the cost per unit will decrease but the fixed cost will increase.

At low levels of activity the cheapest material would be the current one, taking advantage of the low fixed cost.

However, as production increases the cheaper material becomes more attractive, as one wishes to take advantage of the lower unit cost. At high levels of activity the cheaper material is preferable, the lower unit cost more than compensates for the higher fixed cost.

So, in conclusion, the material choice is dependent upon the activity level.

Ascertain the level of activity where the purchaser would be **indifferent** between the two materials.

*When switch from regular to cheaper:*

Saving in variable cost is $45.50 – $44.21 = $1.29 per unit.

Increase in fixed cost is $200,000.

Therefore, the number of units where the variable cost saving is equal to the incremental fixed cost is:

$200,000 ÷ 1.29 = 155,038.8 units

## Conclusion

If production is expected to be 155,038 units or less, use the regular supplier. If production is expected to be 155,039 or more, use the cheaper material.

(b)

| Price | Demand | Variable cost per unit | Contribution per unit | Total contribution | Fixed costs | Profit |
|---|---|---|---|---|---|---|
| $ | 000s | $ | $ | $000 | $000 | $000 |
| 64 | 190 | (44.21) | 19.79 | 3,760.1 | (1,925) | 1,835.1 |
| 68 | 170 | (44.21) | 23.79 | 4,044.3 | (1,925) | 2,119.3 |
| 72 | 150 | (45.50) | 26.50 | 3,975.0 | (1,725) | 2,250.0 |
| 76 | 140 | (45.50) | 30.50 | 4,270.0 | (1,725) | 2,545.0 |
| 80 | 125 | (45.50) | 34.50 | 4,312.5 | (1,725) | 2,587.5 |
| 84 | 110 | (45.50) | 38.50 | 4,235.0 | (1,725) | 2,510.0 |
| 88 | 95 | (45.50) | 42.50 | 4,037.5 | (1,725) | 2,312.5 |

From the table above, it can be seen that profit is maximised when 125,000 units are sold for $80 each.

The maximum profit is $2,587,500.

The regular supplier should be retained.

(c)  At 125,000 units the saving in variable costs if the firm switches to the cheaper supplier is:

125,000 × $1.29 = $161,250

The company would be indifferent between the two suppliers if fixed costs increased by $161,250.

New fixed cost level         = $1,725,000 + $161,250
                             = $1,886,250

(d)  **Other factors to consider**

  (1)  It is important to recognise the inevitable reduction in standards of quality if the cheaper supplier is used. There will be a 5% reject rate. It is inevitable that not all faults will be detected and the percentage of defective finished goods sold will rise. This cannot be desirable for the firm. There may be significant, long-term repercussions as a result. For example, the company reputation may suffer and long-term sales may fall.

  (2)  Perhaps some arrangement could be reached with the cheaper supplier. For a slightly higher price, say $21 or $22, the supplier could inspect the material BEFORE delivery to AB Ltd. The supplier would be held responsible for defects.

  (3)  With defect-free deliveries, the need for the testing and inspection department would be eliminated. Thus saving money and space.

  (4)  The accuracy of the price/demand data should be considered.

  (5)  Alternative selling prices may be considered.

  (6)  The current sales level is 150,000. The recommendation for next year is to reduce this to 125,000 units. This reduction in sales level (and market share?) should be considered carefully. Is it desirable?

**Test Your Understanding 4 – Optimum Price**

If P = $65, then Q = 800 units

$$b = \frac{-\$5}{40 \text{ units}}$$

b = −0.125

P = a + bQ, so here $65 = a − (0.125 x 800 units)

a = $165

Optimum selling price is reached when MR = MC. Here, MC = $28, so optimum price is reached when

| | |
|---|---|
| a + 2bQ | = $28 |
| $165 − (2 x 0.125Q) | = $28 |
| Therefore Q | = 548 units |

| | |
|---|---|
| Optimal Selling Price P | = a + bQ |
| Optimal Selling Price P | = 165 − (0.125 x 548) |
| Optimal Selling Price P | = $96.50 |

**Test Your Understanding 5 – Pricing and Tabular Approach**

(a) (i)  Using a tabular approach:

– Total Revenue at different levels of price and demand:

| Selling Price per unit | Annual Demand (units) | Total sales revenue |
|---|---|---|
| $100 | 50,000 | $5,000,000 |
| $120 | 45,000 | $5,400,000 |
| $130 | 40,000 | $5,200,000 |
| $150 | 25,000 | $3,750,000 |
| $160 | 10,000 | $1,600,000 |
| $170 | 5,000 | $850,000 |

- Using the formula whereby $Z = 70x + 80y + \$240,000$, Total Cost may be calculated as follows:

| Annual Demand (units) x | Annual Demand (batches) y | Total Cost Z |
|---|---|---|
| 50,000 | 500 | $3,780,000 |
| 45,000 | 450 | $3,426,000 |
| 40,000 | 400 | $3,072,000 |
| 25,000 | 250 | $2,010,000 |
| 10,000 | 100 | $948,000 |
| 5,000 | 50 | $594,000 |

- Total profit can be calculated as follows:

| Annual Demand (units) | Total sales revenue | Total Cost Z | Profit |
|---|---|---|---|
| 50,000 | $5,000,000 | $3,780,000 | $1,220,000 |
| 45,000 | $5,400,000 | $3,426,000 | $1,974,000 |
| 40,000 | $5,200,000 | $3,072,000 | $2,128,000 |
| 25,000 | $3,750,000 | $2,010,000 | $1,740,000 |
| 10,000 | $1,600,000 | $948,000 | $652,000 |
| 5,000 | $850,000 | $594,000 | $256,000 |

Profit is maximised when annual demand reaches 40,000 units, i.e. when the selling price is $130.

(ii) Our chosen selling price of $130 may not result in the highest possible profit from this product if:

- The initial data provided by market research proves inaccurate or fails to incorporate the consequences of competitors' actions on our level of demand;

- The estimate of fixed costs of $240,000 is inaccurate at a level of demand of $40,000

- Total Costs are not only correlated with the level of activity but with other factors such as inflation, number of machine breakdowns, change in VAT rates, etc.

(b) (i) Alternative pricing strategies that may be adopted when launching a new product are:

**Price skimming**

Initially, it may be possible to charge a very high price if the product is new, innovative and different. This is the case for our new product. Furthermore, as we expect demand to be inelastic, price skimming is particularly appropriate so that we can exploit those sections of the market which are insensitive to price.

**Penetration pricing**

Initially, we may want to sell at a very low price to discourage competition from entering the market. This would also encourage high volumes, and we may benefit from economies of scale. Low prices would help to gain rapid acceptance of the product, and, therefore, a significant market share.

**Demand based pricing**

With this method, our company could utilise some market research information to determine the selling price and level of demand to maximise company's profits. This relies heavily on the quality of market information and the estimate of the demand curve. Also, this method assumes that price is the only factor that influences the quantity demanded and ignores other factors such as quality, packaging, advertising and promotion.

**Cost based pricing**

Cost based pricing is the simplest pricing method. We would calculate the cost of producing the product and add on a percentage (profit) to give the selling price. This method although simple has two flaws; it takes no account of demand and there is no way of determining if potential customers will purchase the product at the calculated price.

(ii) I recommend that we adopt a price skimming strategy to benefit from the lack of competition in the first six months. In such a competitive market, it is unlikely that competitors would be deterred from entry by low prices, so a penetration strategy seems unsuitable.

### Introduction stage

As our product is the first of its type, and incorporates the latest technology, we could initially set very high prices to take advantage of its novelty appeal during the introduction stage, as demand would be inelastic.

This method would help to recover the significant level of development costs quickly, and is recommended when the product life is short and competition is intense, as high initial returns and maximum profits can be gained before competitors enter the market.

### Growth stage

During this stage of the product's lifecycle, the sales of our product in garages would be expected to grow rapidly. As the product starts to become accepted and established by the mass market, competition usually increases significantly. In order to maintain market share and dominance, we may find it necessary to lower the initial market skimming launch price, thereby reducing our profits margins.

### Maturity stage

As product sales growth begins to slow down and level off, an established market price for our product will become apparent. An average price may be charged. The price will often reach its lowest point during this stage. However, if our company has a good reputation and is respected worldwide, we may be able to charge a premium price based on its reputation and a certain level of brand loyalty.

We may want to extend the maturity phase by launching upgrades, or by trying to sell in new markets. The product must achieve its lowest unit cost during this stage. Profits are likely to be highest in the maturity stage.

### Decline

The decline stage is the final stage of the product's lifecycle. The initial new innovative technology would have, by now, been superseded by superior products. Our own product may hold on to a small niche market, and the group of loyal garages still purchasing our product may be willing to pay a price that will ensure continued profitability.

### Mini-quiz

(1) The best approach is to calculate the profit for a range of outputs from 10 units upwards, then select the output with the highest profit. The answer is (B)

| Units | Total Variable Costs | Selling Price per Unit | Total Select Revenue | Total Contribution |
|-------|---------------------|------------------------|---------------------|--------------------|
| 10 | $40,000 | $6,500 | $65,000 | $25,000 |
| 11 | $44,400 | $6,350 | $69,850 | $25,540 |
| 12 | $49,200 | $6,200 | $74,400 | $25,200 |
| 13 | $54,400 | $6,050 | $78,650 | $24,250 |

(2) Answer: (B)

In the demand equation $p = a - bx$
When price = 0, demand, x = 50,000 therefore $0 = a - 50,000b$ (i)
When price = 1, demand, x = 49,950 therefore $1 = a - 49,950b$ (ii)
Subtract    1 = 50b so b = 0.02

Substitute in (i)    a = (50,000 x 0.02) so a = 1,000

The demand equation for product R is    $p = 1,000 - 0.02x$

When x = 35,000 units, $p = 1,000 - (0.02 \times 35,000) = 300$

(3) Answer: (C)

In the demand equation $p = a - bx$

When price = $700, demand = 0 therefore a = 700

When price = $660, demand = 100 therefore $660 = a - 100b$
Substitute for a 660 = 700 – 100b therefore b = 0 .4
The demand equation for product M is $p = 700 - 0.4x$
The marginal revenue equation is given by $MR = 700 - 0.8x$
Profit is maximised when marginal cost = marginal revenue, i.e. when
$60 = 700 - 0.8x$
i.e. **when x = 800.**

(4) Price at which demand equals zero = $100 + (1,000/100) x $50 = $600

P = $600 – 0.5x
MR = $600 – x
MC = $35
MC = MR
$35 = $600 2 x
x = $565
p = $600 – $(0.5 x 565)
p = $317.50

(5) Marginal cost (MC) = $14

Price (P) = $35 – 0.01q
Marginal Revenue (MR) = $35 – 0.02q
So if MC = MR, then 14 = 35 – 0.02q

Q = 1,050
Price = $35 – (0.01 x 1,050) = $24.50

# The Modern Business Environment

## Chapter learning objectives

- **Explain** the concepts of continuous improvement and Kaizen costing that are central to total quality management. (Syllabus Link B1c)

- **Prepare** cost of quality reports. (Syllabus Link B1d)

- **Compare** and contrast value analysis and functional cost analysis. (Syllabus Link B1a)

- **Discuss** the concept of the value chain and the management of contribution profit generated throughout the chain. (Syllabus Link B1j)

- **Evaluate** the impacts of just-in-time production, the theory of constraints and total quality management on efficiency, inventory and costs. (Syllabus Link B1b)

## 1 Session Content Diagram

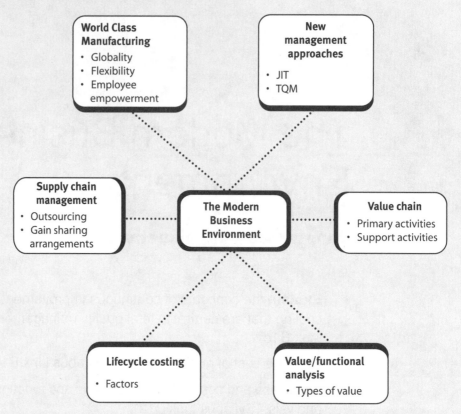

## 2 Introduction To The Modern Business Environment

*'To compete successfully in today's highly competitive global environment companies are making customer satisfaction an overriding priority, adopting new management approaches, changing their manufacturing systems and investing in new technologies. These changes are having a significant influence on management accounting systems.'*

*Colin Drury in ' Management and Cost Accounting'*

The modern manufacturing environment is very different from the traditional production environment. It means that traditional costing methods are becoming less relevant.

In this chapter we explore how the modern production system has changed, and in the following chapters we examine how costing has adapted to this and created new ways to calculate a product's production cost.

## 3 Knowledge Brought Forward

You will already have covered some key concepts in Paper P1. We will build on this knowledge in P2 with more aspects of the modern business environment, but make sure you are comfortable with the assumed knowledge, that should have been brought forward as a base, in the following sections.

## Characteristics Of The Modern Business Environment

### Global environment

- Companies operate in a world economy.
- Customers and competitors come from all over the world.
- Products are made from components from around the world.
- Firms have to be world class to compete.
- International regulations.

### Flexibility

- In a global environment, customers have far greater choice than ever before.
- There has been a huge increase in demand for new, cutting-edge innovative products.
- Customers are demanding ever-improving levels of service in cost, quality, reliability and delivery.
- Customers demand flexibility. Companies need to respond to this in order to survive.

As a consequence of this:

(1) many companies now have very diverse product ranges, with a high level of tailor-made products and services;

(2) product life cycles have dramatically reduced, often from several years to just a few months.

**The move away from standardised units of production towards individual customised units means that mass production techniques are redundant. Instead, it is of greatest importance to take an order from placement to completion in the shortest time possible. This means that production processes will be designed differently to accommodate flexibility of production rather than just throughput.**

### Employee empowerment

To ensure this flexibility, managers need to empower their employees to make decisions quickly, without reference to more senior managers. By empowering employees and giving them relevant information they will be able to respond faster to customers, increase process flexibility, reduce cycle times and improve morale.

Management accounting systems are moving from providing information to managers to monitor employees to providing information to employees to empower them to focus on continuous improvement.

### World Class Manufacturing

The World Class Manufacturing approach to quality is quite different from the traditional approach because the primary emphasis is placed on the resolution of the problems that cause poor quality, rather than merely detecting it. These systems are more proactive and try to prevent problems from occurring in the first place rather than waiting for them to occur and then fixing them.

The system might be developed formally under Total Quality Management.

### Just-In-Time

> CIMA's *Official Terminology defines* 'Just-in-Time' as *a system whose objective is to produce or procure products or components as they are required by a customer or for use, rather than for inventory. A just-in-time system is a 'pull' system, which responds to demand, in contrast to a 'push' system, in which inventory acts as a buffer between the different elements of the system, such as purchasing, production and sales.*'

JIT **production** is defined as:

*A production system which is driven by demand for finished products whereby each component on a production line is produced only when needed for the next stage.*

JIT **purchasing** as:

*A purchasing system in which material purchases are contracted so that the receipt and usage of material, to the maximum extent possible, coincide.*

*[In the PEG November 2010 Exam, the Examiner notes that some candidates failed to recognise that the system in the question was a form of JIT for production and inventory (but not for purchasing). Candidates also tend to write far too much for the marks available and often don't relate the answer to the scenario.*

*In the PEG March 2011 Exam, the Examiner regrets that some candidates do not include or mention that a JIT production system is based around the principle of zero inventories at all stages of production including finished goods. This is an important issue that specifically needs mentioning.]*

These Official Terminology definitions give JIT the appearance of being merely an alternative production management system, with similar characteristics and objectives to techniques such as MRP. However, JIT is better described as a philosophy, or approach to management, as it encompasses a commitment to continuous improvement and the pursuit of excellence in the design and operation of the production management system.

### Toyota

Organisations in the West have traditionally used a 'push' production flow system. This system has the following stages:

(1) Buy raw materials and put them into inventory.

(2) Produce a production schedule based on sales forecasts.

(3) Withdraw goods from inventory and make products according to the production schedule.

(4) Put completed units into finished goods store.

(5) Sell from finished goods store when customers request products.

Work in progress (WIP) is an unavoidable feature of such a system.

Toyota developed a different system known as JIT. This system is not a 'push' system but a 'pull' system. A product is not 'made' until the customer requests it, and components are not made until they are required by the next production stage. In a full JIT system virtually no inventory is held, that is no raw material inventory and no finished goods inventory is held, but there will be a small amount of WIP, say one-tenth of a day's production. The system works by the customer triggering the final stage of production, the assembly. As the product is assembled, components are used and this in turn triggers the component stage of production and a small amount of WIP is made ready for the next product. So the cycle goes on until the final trigger requests more raw material from the supplier.

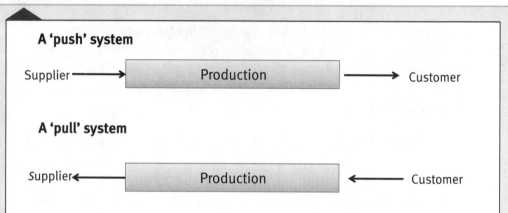

If a JIT system is to work satisfactorily, suppliers must deliver several times a day and so when the raw material arrives it may go straight into the factory and be used immediately. This means that the production lead time (i.e. the time from raw materials entering production to the finished goods emerging) should equal the processing time. In many Western organisations in the past it took several months to make a product from start to finish, despite the fact that if worked on continuously it could be made in, say, two days. The difference in time is largely due to WIP waiting to be used in the next process. It will be apparent that value is only added to the product during the actual processing stages. These have been estimated to represent as little as 10 per cent of the total manufacturing lead time in many companies, and thus up to 90 per cent of production time adds costs but no value.

JIT requires the following:

(1) The **labour force must be versatile** so that they can perform any job within reason to keep production flowing as required. Workers in a JIT cell are trained to operate all the machines within it, and perform routine preventive maintenance on them.

(2) Production processes must be **grouped by product line** rather than by function in order to eliminate inventory movements between workstations and to speed flow.

(3) A simple, **infallible information system**. Originally the Japanese used a system based on cards which were called *kanbans*. There would be a small container of components (WIP) between each workstation with a kanban resting on top. When the container was taken for use by the following workstation the card would be taken off and left behind. This would act as a trigger for the previous workstation to produce another container of that component. Nowadays computer systems are likely to be used instead of cards but the basic simplicity of the system should not change.

(4) A **'get it right first time'** approach and an aim of **'zero defects'**. Defects cause breakdowns in the value chain: they stop the flow of production, create expensive rework and lead to late deliveries to customers.

(5) **Strong supplier relationships**. Suppliers must take responsibility for the quality of their goods; the onus is on the supplier to inspect the parts or materials before delivery and guarantee their quality. The not inconsiderable savings in inspection costs go happily with the benefits of increased quality to achieve cost reduction – another facet of continuous improvement. This enhanced level of service is obtained by reducing the number of suppliers and increasing the business given to each of them. Longer-term commitments are entered into, assuring the supplier of continuity of demand, and enabling the supplier to plan to meet customers' production schedules. In essence the supplier becomes a key part of the value chain.

An important consequence of the 'pull' system, is that problems in any part of the system will immediately halt the production line, as earlier workstations will not receive the 'pull' signal and later stations will not have their own 'pull' signals answered. This has the powerful effect of concentrating all minds on finding a long-term solution to the problem. JIT exposes problems within a plant, and forces management to address problems and rectify them, rather than simply burying them by holding excess inventory.

The aims of JIT are to produce the required items, at the required quality and in the required quantities, at the precise time they are required.

## TQM (Total Quality Management)

TQM is the general name given to programmes which seek to ensure that goods are produced and services supplied of the highest quality. Its origins lie primarily in Japanese organisations and it is argued that TQM has been a significant factor in Japanese global business success.

There are two basic principles of TQM:

(1) **'Get it right, first time**.' TQM considers that the costs of prevention are less than the costs of correction. One of the main aims of TQM is to achieve zero rejects and 100% quality. One aspect of the Japanese management philosophy is a zero-defect target.

(2) **Continuous improvement**. The second basic principle of TQM is dissatisfaction with the status quo. Realistically, a zero-defect goal may not be obtainable. It does however provide a target to ensure that a company should never be satisfied with its present level of rejects. The management and staff should believe that it is always possible to improve and to be able to get more right next time!

There are two approaches to Continuous Improvement : Kaizen Costing (in this chapter) and Target Costing (in the following chapter.)

### The costs of quality

Quality costs are divided into compliance costs (or 'conformance costs') and costs of failure to comply ('non-conformance costs').

Conformance costs are further divided into prevention costs (incurred in preventing mistakes from happening) and appraisal costs (incurred in looking for mistakes before a product is manufactured).

*[In the PEG November 2012, the Examiner regrets that some candidates were 'not able to select an example of a cost for the four quality cost classifications from the question'.]*

#### Conformance Costs

**Prevention costs** are the costs of ensuring that defects do not occur in the first place. For example:

(1)  Routine preventive repairs and maintenance to equipment.

(2)  Quality training for operatives to improve skills and efficiency. Training employees works, provided the employee also understand and accept the benefits of such training. Training can occur both inside and outside the workplace. Internal training may include the ideas of team working and quality discussion groups, which are known as quality circles.

(3)  Building of quality into the design and manufacturing processes. When a product is designed, its specification should consider factors that will minimise future rectification costs. Production methods should be as simple as possible and use the skills and resources existing within the sphere of knowledge of the organisation and its employees.

(4)  Determining whether quality factors have been correctly engineered into the design of products may only be apparent when costs are reported on a 'life cycle' basis. Effective performance management involves monitoring costs and results over the whole life cycle of a product. Just considering production costs over a one-month period (in the form of traditional standard costing and variance analysis) may be of marginal relevance.

**Appraisal costs** are connected with measuring conformity with requirements and include:

(1) Cost of incoming inspections (note that if suppliers adopt a total quality approach, the cost of incoming inspections can be eliminated);

(2) Cost of set-up inspections;

(3) Cost of acquiring and operating the process control and measuring equipment.

Non-conformance costs are divided into 'internal failure' costs, that occur when the units produced fail to reach the set standard; and 'external failure' costs – These arise when the faulty product is not detected until after it reaches the customer.

### Non-Conformance Costs

**Internal failure** costs include:

(1) Costs of scrap

(2) Reworking costs

(3) Manufacturing and process engineering required to correct the failed process.

As we saw under JIT, it is the aim of total quality management (TQM) programmes to completely eliminate these internal failure costs by working towards a goal of zero defects. It is contended that, in many companies, the costs of internal failure are so great that a total quality programme can be financed entirely from the savings that are made from it – hence the expression *'quality is free'*.

There are several measurable costs of **external failure** to deliver a quality product:

(1) Marketing costs associated with failed products and loss of customer goodwill;

(2) Manufacturing or process engineering costs relating to failed products;

(3) Compensation/replacement for units returned by customers;

(4) Repair costs;

(5) Travel costs to visit sites with faulty products;

(6) Liability claims.

It is generally accepted that an increased investment in prevention and appraisal is likely to result in a significant reduction in failure costs. As a result of the trade-off, there may be an optimum operating level in which the combined costs are at a minimum. In short, an investment in "prevention" inevitably results in a saving on total quality costs.

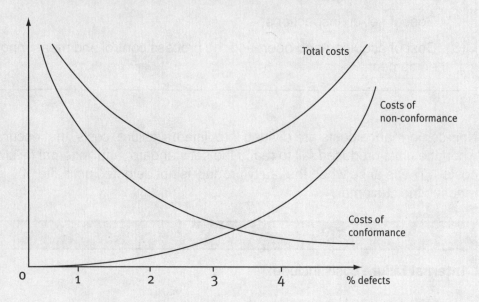

[In the PEG September 2010, the Examiner explains that candidates were required to **compare and contrast** costs of conformance and costs of non-conformance and that a good answer would have joined the two parts of the question with phrases such as 'in contrast to' or 'as opposed to'. Most candidates appeared to have a good understanding of quality costs but simply failed to put forward answers in line with the question, especially relating to the verbs.

In the November 2012 PEG, the Examiner again notes that many candidates 'were not able to describe the 'trade-off' between conformance and non-conformance costs, and were not able to discuss its importance for the company.' ]

### Recognising the importance of quality

(1)  Accept that the only thing that matters is the customer. The only way to stay in business is to relate everything to customer priorities.

(2)  Recognise the all-pervasive nature of the customer/supplier relationship. This includes internal customers. In a transfer environment, passing sub-standard material down to another division just to claim output is not satisfactory. Ultimately, the company must bear the cost of the defective product/service.

(3)  Move from relying on inspecting to a predefined level of quality, to actually preventing the cause of the defect in the first place.

(4)  Each operative or team of operatives must be personally responsible for defect-free production or service in their domain. This should not just be confined to production staff, it should be extended throughout the organisation. For example, sales, personnel, accounting and the after-sales departments should also ensure that their 'customers' are happy with their service.

(5)  In production there should be a move away from acceptable quality levels (AQL) to defect levels measured in parts per million.

(6)  Enforce zero defect programmes. These are an obsessive drive to get things right first time. Again this should be enforced throughout all departments.

(7)  Quality certification programmes such as BS5750/ISO9002 should be introduced. Although opinion is divided about these programmes, and they are often perceived to be a burden disproportionate to the benefits, the value of a third party audit of control and production procedures to ensure everything is properly controlled has both merit and, in the short term, an influence with customers.

(8)  The total cost of quality should be emphasised. Quality does generate savings. For example, better trained operators do not waste material nor do they abuse machines and equipment. Other savings can be achieved by reviewing suppliers, preventive machine maintenance and reduction of scrap and rework.

### Commitment to quality

For TQM to bring about improved business efficiency and effectiveness it must be applied throughout the whole organisation. It begins at the top with the managing director, the most senior directors and managers who must demonstrate that they are totally committed to achieving the highest quality standards. The role of middle management is also crucial. They have to understand the importance of TQM and communicate this and their own commitment to quality to the people for whom they are responsible. It is essential that TQM is adopted by all parts of the organisation. Middle management must ensure that the efforts and achievements of their subordinates receive appropriate recognition, attention and reward. This helps secure everyone's full involvement – which is crucial to the successful introduction of TQM.

## Quality chains

Throughout and beyond all organisations, whether they are manufacturing concerns, retail stores, universities or hotels, there is a series of quality chains. The ability to meet the customers' requirements is vital, not only between two separate organisations, but within the same organisation. These quality chains may be broken at any point by one person or by one piece of equipment not meeting the requirements of the customer, internal or external.

To achieve quality throughout an organisation, each person in the quality chain must be trained to ask themselves the following questions:

## Customers

- Who are my internal customers?
- What are their true requirements?
- How do I find out what the requirements are?
- How can I meet those requirements?

## Suppliers

- Who are my internal suppliers?
- What are my true requirements?
- How do I communicate my requirements?
- Do my suppliers have the capability to meet my requirements?

Each person in the organisation must also realise that they must respect their suppliers' needs and expectations if those suppliers are able to fully satisfy his requirements.

## Successful implementation of TQM

An organisation should undertake to achieve each of the following to ensure TQM is successful:

- Total commitment throughout the organisation.
- Get close to their customers to fully understand their needs and expectations.
- Plan to do all jobs right first time.
- Agree expected performance standards with each employee and customer.
- Implement a company-wide improvement process.
- Continually measure performance levels achieved.
- Measure the cost of quality mismanagement and the level of firefighting.

- Demand continuous improvement in everything you and your employees do.
- Recognise achievements.
- Make quality a way of life.

## Quality circles

A quality circle is a team of four to 12 people usually coming from the same area who voluntarily meet on a regular basis to identify, investigate, analyse and solve work-related problems. The team presents its solutions to management and is then involved in implementing and monitoring the effectiveness of the solutions. The voluntary approach and the process by which the team selects and solves its own problems are key features which give the quality circle a special character: a character which is very different to other problem-solving teams. The problems that circles tackle may not be restricted to quality of product or service topics, but may include anything associated with work or its environment. Items such as pay and conditions and other negotiated items are, however, normally excluded.

## Management accounting reports

Management accounting systems can help organisations achieve their quality goals by providing a variety of reports and measures that motivate and evaluate managerial efforts to improve quality – including financial and non-financial measures.

Traditionally, the management accounting systems focused on output, not quality.

### Examples:

- the strive to reduce the material price variance often led to the use of inferior quality material;
- the costs of normal losses were absorbed by good output.

### Non-financial measures include:

- Number of defects at inspection expressed as a percentage of the number of units completed.
- Number of reworked units expressed as a percentage of total sales value.
- Number of defective units delivered to customers as a percentage of total units delivered.
- Number of customer complaints.
- Number of defectives supplied by suppliers.
- Time taken to respond to customer requests.

### Value Analysis/Value Engineering

Value analysis/ value engineering is an activity which helps to design products which meet customer needs at a lower cost while assuming the required standard of quality and reliability. **Value Analysis** relates to existing products, whereas **Value Engineering** relates to products that have not yet been produced. CIMA's *Official Terminology* definitions read as follows:

> *Value analysis* is 'the systematic interdisciplinary examination of factors affecting the cost of a product or service, in order to devise means of achieving the specified purpose most economically at the required standard of quality and reliability'.

> *Value Engineering* is 'the redesign of an activity, product or service so that value to the customer is enhanced while costs are reduced or at least increased by less than the resulting price increase).

The **purpose** of value analysis is to identify any unnecessary cost elements within the components of goods and services. It is more comprehensive than simple cost reduction, because it examines the purposes or functions of the product and is concerned with establishing the means whereby these are achieved. Any cost data that do not add value to the product or service should be eliminated.

### Types of value

**Cost value**: this is the cost incurred by the firm producing the product.

**Exchange value**: the amount of money that consumers are willing to exchange to obtain ownership of the product, i.e. its price.

**Use value**: this is related entirely to function, i.e. the ability of a product to perform its specific intended purpose. A basic small car provides personal transport at a competitive price and is reasonably economic to run.

**Esteem value**: this relates to the status or regard associated with ownership. Products with high esteem value will often be associated with premium or even price-skimming prices.

Value is a function of both use and esteem. Value analysis aims to maintain the esteem value in a product, but at a reduced cost value. The result of value analysis is to achieve an improved value/cost relationship.

## Method of value analysis

- Determine the function of the product and each component that is used within the product.

- Determine the existing costs associated with individual components.

- Develop alternative solutions to the needs met by the components. This may involve design changes, manufacturing method, materials used, etc.

- When analysing a components a questioning attitude should be adopted. Some of these points may be considered:
    - How does this component contribute to the value of the product?
    - How much does it cost?
    - Are all its features and it specifications absolutely necessary?
    - Is there another similar part that may be used?
    - Can an alternative part be used?
    - Will an alternative design perform the same function?

- Evaluate the alternatives and their anticipated effect.

- Implement the recommendations.

Value analysis will often lead to the reduction of components used in a product, the use of alternative, cheaper components and the standardisation of parts across several product lines.

## Functional Analysis

*Functional analysis* is defined in CIMA's *Official Terminology* as an analysis of the relationships between product functions, their perceived value to the customer and their cost of provision.

Functional analysis uses the functions of a product as the cost object and is used either in initial designs or in the review of existing products. It can be extended to services, overhead expenses, and organisation structure and even to the overall strategy of the company (Innes et al, Contemporary Cost Management).

The central theme of functional analysis is, like value analysis, **customer focus**. An important aspect when gathering information is to identify the functions of the product that customers' value and identify alternative ways of achieving these functions. So, for example, a newsletter sent out by an accounting company may have the functions of advertising services, keeping clients up to date with new developments, providing details of social events and networking opportunities. There may be many ways of achieving these functions, e.g. by sending out letters, by sending emails or by posting information on a website. Analysis will be carried out to find out which alternative achieves the required function at the least cost.

Once an alternative has been chosen this must be implemented and performance measured to assess the degree to which the objective has been achieved. Lessons may be learned to help in future functional analyses.

### Functional Analysis

In functional analysis, the company will first break down the product into its many functions. For example, a mobile phone may offer an MP3 player, a voice-recording feature, a camera and an internet browser in addition to the ability to make and receive calls and texts.

Research is also carried out to identify the importance the customer attaches to each feature. This information may be obtained from a mixture of past purchasing patterns and customer interviews and questionnaires. Research will also be carried out into the amount the customer would be willing to pay for the final product – this can be used to find the overall target cost for the product by deducting an appropriate profit margin.

The company will then calculate the target cost of providing each of these functions. This is calculated as a percentage of the overall target cost based on the relative importance of each feature to the customer.

The next step will be to compare the expected cost to provide each function with the target cost. If the expected cost of the function exceeds the target (i.e. has a value ratio of less than one) then the function should be either, modified, re-evaluated and an alternative found or eliminated.

### 4 Kaizen Costing

Continuous improvement, or 'Kaizen', is an integral part of the just-in-time management philosophy. 'Kaizen' is a Japanese term meaning to improve processes via small, incremental amounts rather than through large innovations. Kaizen costing is a planning method used during the manufacturing cycle that emphasises reducing variable costs of a period below the cost level in the base period. The target reduction rate is the ratio of the target reduction amount to the cost base.

- The organisation should always seek perfection. Perfection is never achieved, so there must always be some scope for improving on current methods and procedures. Improvements should be sought all the time.

- Improvements will be small and numerous rather than occasional and far-reaching.

- Cost reduction targets are set and applied on a more frequent basis than standard costs. Typically these targets are set on a monthly basis whereas standards within a traditional standard costing system are set annually or perhaps semi-annually. The table below *(adapted from Monden and Lee)* points out the differences between the two techniques:

| Standard Costing Concepts | Kaizen Costing Concepts |
|---|---|
| Cost **Control** system concepts. | Cost **Reduction** system concepts. |
| Assume current manufacturing conditions. | Assume Continuous improvement in manufacturing. |
| Meet cost performance standards. | Achieve cost reduction targets. |
| **Standard Cost Techniques** | **Kaizen Costing Techniques** |
| Standards are set annually or semiannually. | Cost reduction targets are set and applied monthly. |
| Cost variance analysis involving standard costs and actual costs | Continuous Improvement (Kaizen) is implemented during the year to attain target profits or to reduce the gap between target profit and estimated profit. |
| Investigate and respond when standards are not met. | Cost variance analysis involving target Kaizen costs and actual costs reduction amounts. |
|  | Investigate and respond when target Kaizen amounts are not attained. |

*[In the PEG September 2010, the Examiner notes that some candidates 'failed to make it clear what Kaizen principles are'].*

The continuous improvement philosophy contrasts sharply with the concept underlying business process re-engineering (BPR). BPR is concerned with making far-reaching one-off changes to improve operations or processes.

### Business Process Re-Engineering

A business process consists of a collection of activities that are linked together in a co-ordinated manner to achieve a specific objective. Business process re-engineering involves examining business processes and radically redesigning these processes to achieve cost reduction, improved quality and customer satisfaction. BPR is all about major changes to how business processes operate.

Material handling is an example of a business process and may consist of the following separate activities; material requisitioning, purchase requisitioning, processing purchase orders, inspecting materials, storing materials and paying suppliers. This process could be re-engineered by sending the material requisitions directly to an approved supplier and entering into an agreement which entails delivering high quality material in accordance with the production requirements. This change in business process could result in cost reduction by the elimination of; the administration involved in placing orders, the need for material inspection and storage. By re-engineering the material handling business process the company will reduce costs without compromising the quality of the products delivered to customers.

## 5 The Value Chain

The value chain is a linked set of value-creating activities starting from basic raw material sources or component suppliers through to the ultimate end-use product or service delivered to the customer. Co-ordinating the individual parts of the value chain together creates conditions to improve customer satisfaction, particularly in terms of cost efficiency, quality and delivery. A firm which performs the value chain activities more efficiently, and at a lower cost, than its competitors will gain competitive advantage.

The value chain was designed by Professor Michael Porter of the Harvard Business School (1985).

## Porter's value chain

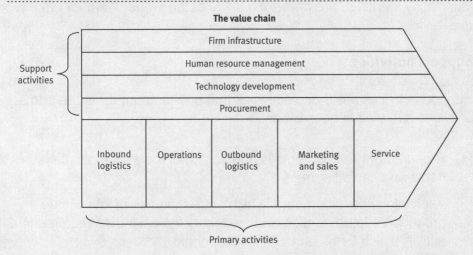

**The value chain**

Support activities: Firm infrastructure, Human resource management, Technology development, Procurement

Primary activities: Inbound logistics, Operations, Outbound logistics, Marketing and sales, Service

It is necessary to understand how value chain activities are performed and how they interact with each other. The activities are not just a collection of independent activities but a system of interdependent activities in which the performance of one activity affects the performance of other activities.

The activities which comprise the value chain are as follows:

*[In the PEG for the March 2013 exam, the Examiner notes that, although both the value chain and aspects of quality costs sit within the P2 syllabus, many candidates seem confused when the two topics are linked together.].*

## Primary activities

These are the activities which involve the physical movement of raw materials and finished products, production of goods and services, marketing sales and subsequent services to outputs of a business unit.

(1) Inbound logistics – which entail receiving, storing, materials handling, warehousing, inventory control, vehicle scheduling, returns to suppliers.

(2) Operations – which entail transferring inputs into final product form (e.g. machining, packaging, assembly, equipment maintenance, testing, printing and facility operations).

(3) Outbound logistics – which entail distributing the finished product (e.g. finished goods warehousing, material handling, operation of delivery vehicles, order processing and scheduling).

(4) Marketing and sales – which entail inducing and facilitating buyers to purchase the product, e.g. advertising, activities of sales personnel, preparation of quotations, channel selection, channel relations, pricing of goods and services.

(5) Service – which entails maintaining or enhancing the value of the product after the sale has taken place, installation, commissioning, repair, training, parts supply and product adjustment.

*[In the March 2013 PEG, the Examiner notes that some candidates incorrectly identified the primary activity of the value chain for each type of quality cost.]*

## Support activities

Support activities are those activities that provide support to the primary activities and also to each other.

(1) Procurement – which entails purchasing of raw materials, consumable items and capital items.

(2) Technology development – which entails the use of know how, procedures to be applied and the technological inputs required in every activity which forms part of the value chain.

(3) Human resource management – which entails the selection, retention and promotion of staff, the appraisal of staff and performance-rewards linkage, management development and employee relations.

(4) Firm infrastructure – which entails general management, accounting and finance, quality management and planning activities.

Each activity within the value chain provides inputs which after processing constitute added value to the output, which the customer ultimately receives in the form of a product or service or as the aggregate of values at the end of the value chain.

Each primary and support activity has the potential to contribute to the competitive advantage of the business unit by enabling it to produce, market and deliver products or services which meet or surpass the value expectations of purchasers in comparison with those resulting from other value chains.

Focusing on each of the nine activities enables management to see how each creates value that may be understood as the difference between cost and revenue.

According to Porter, an organisation can develop sustainable competitive advantage by following one of two strategies:

(1) **Low-cost strategy**. Essentially this is a strategy of cost leadership, which involves achieving a lower cost than competitors via, for example, economies of scale and tight cost control.

(2) **Differentiation strategy**. This involves creating something that customers perceive as being unique via brand loyalty, superior customer service, product design and features.

Shank and Govindarajan (1993) advocate that a company should evaluate its value chain relative to the value chains of its competitors or the industry. They suggest the following methodology:

(1)  Identify the industry's value chain and then assign costs, revenues and assets to the value activities. These activities are the building blocks with which firms in the industry created a product that buyers find valuable.

(2)  Diagnose the cost drivers regulating each value activity.

(3)  Develop sustainable cost advantage, either through controlling cost drivers better than competitors or by reconfiguring the chain value. By systematically analysing costs, revenues and assets in each activity, a firm can achieve low cost. This is achieved by comparing the firm's value chain with the value chains of a few major competitors and identifying actions needed to manage the firm's value chain better than competitors manage their value chains.

*[In the March 2013 PEG, the Examiner notes that some candidates submit impractical ideas on how to reduce cost e.g. 'cut out the number of inspections' or 'tell the warehouse staff to be more careful'.]*

## 6 Benchmarking

Benchmarking is a technique that is increasingly being adopted as a mechanism for continuous improvement. CIMA's *Official Terminology* reads as follows:

> The establishment, through data gathering, of targets and comparators, that permit relative levels of performance (and particular areas of underperformance) to be identified. The adoption of identified best practices should improve performance.

It is a continuous process of measuring a firm's products, services and activities against other best-performing organisations, either internal or external to the firm. The idea is to ascertain how the processes and activities can be improved. Ideally, benchmarking should involve an external focus on the latest developments, best practice and model examples that can be incorporated within various operations of business organisations. It therefore represents the ideal way of moving forward and achieving high competitive standards.

## 7 Supply Chain Management

Supply chain management is often explained with reference to Porter's value chain and value systems. A supply chain is the network of customers and suppliers that a business deals with.

Recent decades have seen an increasing rate of globalisation of the economy and thereby also of supply chains. The days when products were produced and consumed in the same geographical area are long past. In fact it is often the case that the different components of a product come from all over the globe. Such a trend causes longer and more complex supply chains and thus changes the requirements within supply chain management. This, in turn, affects the effectiveness of the IT systems employed within the supply chain. A longer supply chain often results in a lengthening of order-to-delivery lead times.

Supply chain management considers logistics but also relationships between members of the supply chain, identification of end-customer benefit and the organisational consequences of greater inter-firm integration to form 'network organisations'.

Supply chain management may be broken down into several areas:

### Purchasing

It is important for a company to work closely with its suppliers. A true partnership will enable a better, faster and more reliable service. Purchasing costs can be reduced by more than 10% when information systems are linked. Day-to-day purchasing, progress chasing and stock control can all be eliminated.

### Stocks

Efficient stock control relies upon accurate customer records, well-managed customer information and effective stock-control information systems. A close collaboration with suppliers and customers will enable stock levels to be kept to a minimum. Working more closely with the supply chain partners will require mutual trust and investment in technology, but it will bring benefits to all concerned.

### Customer ordering

From the customer's perspective the ordering process should be fast, flexible (meet individual customer needs) and efficient. A satisfied customer is more likely to return for repeat orders. Factors such as price, quality, availability from stock etc. are important, but a fully automated fulfilment procedure also plays a key part in overall customer satisfaction. On-line ordering is becoming a prerequisite for many customers today.

Orders should be processed smoothly within the firm. Purchasing, stock control, marketing and accounts should all be linked to the customer-ordering process.

## Delivery and logistics

Delivering to the customer is often the culmination of all the business processes. Customers will expect fast, reliable, accurate and predictable delivery schedules. Tracking systems such as radio frequency identification (RFID) enable companies to trace the physical progress of the customer order. With RFID objects are tagged. During manufacturing and delivery the whereabouts of the order can then be traced electronically and remotely (items can be detected up to 100 feet away from the sensor). In the US many large companies such as Wallmart are already requiring their suppliers to use RFID.

Some companies use third party distributors. As technology becomes more complex and sophisticated outsourcing becomes more attractive. Some companies leave distribution to professional logistics companies.

## Outsourcing

A significant trend in recent years has been for organisations and government bodies to concentrate on their core competencies. Outsourcing involves the buying in of components, sub-assemblies, finished products and services from outside suppliers rather than supplying them internally. It may be regarded as a management strategy by which an organisation delegates major non-core functions to specialised, efficient service providers.

Traditionally the insourcing/outsourcing decision was focused on a make-or-buy decision for manufacturing functions. However companies are now beginning to apply the decision analysis to nearly all functions and activities.

For example, the following functions are now coming under the outsourcing spotlight: sales; design and development, IT and distribution.

## Advantages and disadvantages of insourcing

| Advantages | Disadvantages |
|---|---|
| Higher degree of control over inputs | Requires high volumes |
| Increases visibility over the process | High investment |
| Economies of scale/scope use integration | Dedicated equipment has limited flexibility |
| | Not a core competence |

### Advantages and disadvantages of outsourcing

| Advantages | Disadvantages |
|---|---|
| Greater flexibility | Possibility of choosing wrong supplier |
| Lower investment risk | Loss of visibility and control over process |
| Improved cash flow | Possibility of increased lead times |
| Concentrates on core competence | |
| Enables more advanced technologies to be used without making investment | |

### Outsourcing manufacturing to Eastern Europe and the Far East

During recent years foreign investment has begun to pour into Eastern European countries as West European and US companies look for lower-cost manufacturing bases close to the European Union. Today, as these and other countries have joined the EU, the East and Central Europeans themselves are looking in an easterly direction for low-cost manufacturing. As rising wages force them to find ways to become more competitive, some are setting up plants or outsourcing their production to subcontractors in places such as Bosnia, Romania, Russia and the Ukraine. The investment farther east is increasing, and economists and trade experts expect it to increase substantially in the next few years as both living standards and manufacturing costs continue to rise. Taxation is also a major consideration (Russia has attractive tax rates, as low as 13%) but cheaper labour is the major factor.

The UK and other European-based organisations are aware that assembly costs in Eastern European countries are far lower than at home. This fact is leading to the transfer of production to such territories.

Some companies are already looking to China and other parts of Asia, where labour costs are even lower. An organisation which makes sports and leisure gear, now sources 70 to 80% of its production in China, India, Taiwan, Turkey and Vietnam and only uses national manufacturers for sophisticated products and small orders that would be uneconomical to produce in Asia. It is crucial that organisations maintain their ability to compete and thus as production costs in the new EU member states start to approach those in Western Europe, more and more firms could be eastward bound.

Contract manufacturing has always been about cutting costs, and today that means rapid expansion of, for example, the electronic manufacturing services (EMS) industry into China, Eastern Europe and other low-wage areas. At the same time, hand-in-hand with that expansion is contraction, as organisations cut back operations in high-wage areas such as the United States. With original equipment manufacturers (OEMs) increasingly outsourcing printed circuit boards and finished systems, a significant amount of that manufacturing is especially likely to find its way to China. Indeed, it is highly probable that a major trend over the next few years will be the migration to low-cost manufacturing centres, particularly China.

Competitive pressure forces OEMs and contract manufacturers to do all they can to take costs out of their businesses, and consequently many organisations are heading in the direction of Eastern Europe and China in an attempt to do so. As far as China is concerned, not only are costs low but also, in addition to making products there to be sold around the world, firms can entertain the possibility of sales into the Chinese market

## 8 Gain-Sharing Arrangements

In simple terms, gain-sharing is a program that returns cost savings to the employees.

While risk-sharing/gain-sharing arrangements can take different forms, companies typically guarantee their customers that they will achieve a certain amount of cost savings or top-line improvement. If targets are not met, the company commits to making up the difference in cash. If however targets are exceeded, the supplier may also receive a pre-specified percentage of the gains.

These agreements are attractive to companies because they can provide insulation from the cut-throat price competition that characterises today's technology marketplace. Suppliers that guarantee cost savings and top-line improvement can command a price premium in the marketplace. Such risk-sharing agreements are attractive to customers because they reduce the business risk and cost associated with implementing new technologies, systems, and services.

Gain-sharing is an approach to the review and adjustment of an existing contract, or series of contracts, where the adjustment provides benefits to both parties. It is a mutual activity requiring the agreement of both parties to the contract adjustment. Consideration of a gain-sharing proposal will be limited to just that area affected by the proposal.

The sharing of benefits provides an incentive to both parties to a contract to explore gain-sharing possibilities. In the UK, the **Ministry of Defence** is committed to, and industry supports, gain-sharing as one of a number of approaches to improve the efficient use of the defence procurement budget.

Gain-sharing arrangements are popular where there exists the potential to achieve mutual benefit among the parties concerned. The gain, benefit or advantage to be shared might not be financial in nature, though financial benefits are likely to feature strongly. The period of application of the sharing arrangement will need to be agreed. The sharing arrangement may apply only to the current contract; or the effects of the agreement, and the sharing arrangements, may be carried forward into future contracts.

Mutual trust and co-operation between contracting parties is essential since assessment of the financial benefit of a gain-sharing proposal will require both parties to provide each other with access to relevant cost data to provide the basis for the valuation of the benefit and to facilitate the calculation and sharing of that benefit.

Gain-sharing represents a reward for innovative thinking by the contractor; it is important that the nature of any change proposal is agreed at the outset in the light of this principle. Once a gain-sharing proposal is agreed, the concept of sharing the benefits will be fundamental to further discussion and agreement; neither party will seek to secure all the benefits.

**A gain-sharing arrangement must possess the following components:**

(1)  Mutual interdependence and trust between the parties (as opposed to a blame culture).

(2)  Identification of common goals for success.

(3)  Agreed decision-making and problem-solving procedures.

(4)  Commitment to continuous improvement.

(5)  Team working down the entire product and supply chain.

(6)  Gain-share and pain-share arrangements established in advance.

(7)  Open book accounting.

(8)  Targets that provide continuous measurable improvements on performance.

**Examples:**

| Public sector | Private sector |
|---|---|
| The Government Travel Savings Program is a gain-sharing arrangement that rewards federal government employees who save money while on official travel. In general, the cash awards equal 50% of the savings on lodging expenses and/or contract carrier airfare. For example, government employees who stay with relatives or friends and avoid lodging expenses while on official travel receive one-half of the allowed maximum lodging rate. (US) | Gain sharing involves the process by which a hospital and its medical staff identify clinical practices that increase hospital operating costs without improving quality of care, develop initiatives to reduce or eliminate such practices while maintaining quality of care, and share the resulting cost savings directly attributable to the clinical initiatives. |
| Gain-sharing in a court might depend on a court unit or program hitting performance targets such as a specific decrease in cost per case, an improvement in trial date certainty or juror utilisation, which positively impacts the bottom line of budgets and balance sheets of the court. A decrease in cost per case might be seen directly in a court's balance sheet, while an improvement in trial date certainty may be seen most significantly in decreased expenditures for witness notification by the prosecution. | A company produces rigid and steering differential axles for tractors. From its records, the company determined that every $1,000,000 of good product output required 10,000 worker hours. Under gain-sharing, the next $1,000,000 of axle output and shipment was produced with only 9,000 hours. If the average wage rate is $10 an hour, the 1,000 hours saved are worth $10,000. That is a gain to be shared equally between the workforce and company. |

## 9 Practice Questions

### Test your understanding 1 – AVN Value Chain

AVN designs and assembles electronic devices to allow transmission of audio / visual communications between the original source and various other locations within the same building. Many of these devices require a wired solution but the company is currently developing a wireless alternative. The company produces a number of different devices depending on the number of input sources and the number of output locations, but the technology used within each device is identical. AVN is constantly developing new devices which improve the quality of the audio / visual communications that are received at the output locations.

The Managing Director recently attended a conference on world-class manufacturing entitled 'The extension of the value chain to include suppliers and customers' and seeks your help.

**Required:**

(i)   Explain  the components of the extended value chain.

(ii)  Explain how each of the components may be applied by AVN.

### Test your understanding 2 – TQM

A company experiences changing levels of demand, but produces a constant number of units during each quarter. The company allows inventory levels to rise and fall to satisfy the differing quarterly demand levels for its product.

**Required:**

(a)  Identify and explain the reasons for three cost changes that would result if the company changed to a Just-In-Time production method for 2009. Assume there will be no inventory at the start and end of the year.

**(6 marks)**

(b)  Briefly discuss the importance of Total Quality Management to a company that operates a Just-In-Time production method.

**(4 marks)**

### Test your understanding 3 – Value Chain (from Specimen Paper)

You are engaged as a consultant to the DT group. At present the group source their raw materials locally, manufacture their products in a single factory, and distribute them worldwide via an international distribution company. However, their manufacturing facilities are restricting them from expanding so they are considering outsourcing some of their manufacturing operations to developing economies.

**Required:**

(a) Discuss the concept of the value chain and how the changes being considered by the DT group may impact on the management of contribution/profit generated throughout the chain.

(b) Discuss how gain sharing arrangements might be used by the DT group in the context of the changes being considered. Suggest one non-financial target that may be used as part of these gain sharing arrangements.

### Mini-Quiz

(1) The adoption of **JIT** normally requires which one of the following factors to increase?

    A    Inventory levels

    B    Work-in-progress levels

    C    Batch sizes

    D    Quality standards

(2) **Functional Analysis** is:

    A    An approach to the construction of budgets around the functions within a business

    B    An approach to the examination of the specified purpose of a product

    C    The separation of the materials mix variance into component parts

    D    A method of appraising the performance of cost centres.

(3)  In a TQM environment, **external benchmarking** is preferred to standard costing as a performance measurement technique because:

A    Standard costs quickly become obsolete

B    TQM emphasises continuous improvement and reference to a pre-determined internal standard gives no incentive to improve;

C    TQM places an emphasis on employee empowerment, and the concept of a standard cost is alien to this;

D    The use of standard costs is only possible in a traditional mass-production industry.

(4)  Match the cost to the correct cost category:

*Costs*

(a)  Reliability Studies

(b)  Returned Material processing and repair

(c)  Quality audits

(d)  Quality Control investigations of failures

*Cost categories*

–    Prevention costs

–    Appraisal costs

–    Internal failure costs

–    External failure costs

# Test your understanding answers

## Test your understanding 1 – AVN Value Chain

(i) The value chain refers to the sequence of processes through which value is added to an organisation's products and services. The components of the value chain include research and development, design, production, marketing, distribution and customer services. The extended value chain refers to the extension of this sequence outside of the organisation to include suppliers and customers.

(ii) The objective of the value chain is to focus the organisation on achieving value to the customer. Profit can then be optimised by finding the most effective processes to deliver the required product. The value chain should therefore begin with the customer. Clear requirements should be identified and communicated to departments within AVN.

The role of research and development will be to develop new products that meet customer requirements but are not necessarily constrained by currently available technology. It may be useful to carry out a functional analysis to identify what the customer requires the product to do rather than how it is to be done. In this way R and D may be able to develop new technology which will result in competitive advantage.

The role of design will be to take a new idea and produce a cost-effective design. Target costing may be useful to determine the expected market price of the product and, after deducting the required profit margin, find the target cost for which the product must be produced. The design department will try to reduce the cost of the product by using standard components and layouts. It will need to liaise with production, distribution and marketing to ensure that the design is cost effective, feasible and will deliver the product at the required quality to the customer.

At this stage supplies may be involved to help develop new sources of material and components.

The production department must then produce the product efficiently. AVN should have determined the price that customers would be prepared to pay for different levels of quality. If the strategy is for high quality/ high price products, then AVN may invest heavily in appraisal and prevention activities such as training and inspections to prevent internal and external quality failure costs.

Production must also be aware of when the customer requires the product. Customers should be able to receive the product as required. This may mean that inventories of finished goods are held and the relative costs and benefits of these inventories should be considered.

Marketing has an important role in informing potential customers of new products. This may involve identifying target markets and the most effective marketing policy to adopt. Distribution must ensure that products reach the customer as required. AVN may have to decide whether to sell directly to the customer or via retailers or wholesalers. The additional costs of a direct sales force and installation teams may have to be weighed against the benefit of remaining in control of the quality of the process and remaining in close contact with customers to be able to develop new improved products.

Customer services may be a vital link in obtaining feedback from customers which may be important in generating repeat sales. It may also be possible to assess the extent to which customers' requirements have been met.

### Test your understanding 2 – TQM

(a) The introduction of Just-In-Time production methods would output items as and when needed, and not build up stocks in period of low demand. Because of the absence of stocks, the company can expect the following changes:

   (i) A decrease in inventory-related costs such as warehousing costs and holding costs

   (ii) An increase in ordering costs; smaller orders will be placed more frequently to match production requirements exactly and avoid the build-up of inventory.

   (iii) However, because of the need to work overtime to meet fluctuating levels of demand, the company can expect an increase in labour and overhead costs.

(b) In a company operating on JIT principles, the absence of stocks deprives production of a safety net or 'buffer stock'. This exposes the business to production problems or delays and, ultimately, to lost sales and damaged customer goodwill.

In this context, the adoption of a TQM philosophy is key. In this, quality is a feature rooted in the production process and every individual is responsible for the quality of his/her output.

This will encourage good quality at all times and therefore minimise production problems that would otherwise occur due to poor quality.

**Test your understanding 3 – Value Chain (from Specimen Paper)**

(a) The Value Chain is the concept that there is a sequence of business factors by which value is added to an organisation's products and services. Modern businesses cannot survive merely by having efficient production facilities, they must also have a thorough understanding of the importance of the relationship between all of the elements in the value chain. These include: research & development, design, manufacturing, marketing, distribution and customer service.

The DT group currently has an internal manufacturing facility, this makes communications between different parts of that manufacturing process relatively straight-forward, however, if part of this process is to be outsourced this will place as added burden on the production management to ensure that all parts of the production process operate smoothly. Aside from communication difficulties, there may be different work ethics to contend with, and delays in receiving items and quality issues may disrupt the flow of goods to customers. This will lead to difficulties in identifying where profits/contributions are being earned (and lost) within the value chain.

(b) Gain sharing arrangements are based on the concept of sharing profits, however, if they are to be successful both parties must be willing to share the information necessary to determine the extent of any gain (or loss) that has arisen.

The DT group may seek to enter a gain sharing arrangement with the suppliers of the components that they have outsourced. This would require both organisations to establish some clear targets which could include quality specifications and delivery schedules. The gain from lower levels of rejects and earlier delivery of components can then be determined and shared between DT and the external supplier.

## Mini-Quiz

(1) Answer D. An increase in quality standards is one of the key factors that allows the other items listed to be reduced.

(2) Answer B. An approach to the construction of budgets around the functions within a business

(3) Answer B: **External benchmarking** is preferred to standard costing as a performance measurement technique because TQM emphasises continuous improvement and reference to a pre-determined internal standard gives no incentive to improve.

(4) (a) Prevention Failure Costs

(b) External Failure Costs

(c) Appraisal Costs

(d) Internal Failure Costs

# Costing Techniques

## Chapter learning objectives

- **Evaluate** the impacts of just-in-time production, the theory of constraints and total quality management on efficiency, inventory and costs. (Syllabus Link B1b)

- **Explain** how target costs can be derived from target prices and the relationship between target costs and standard costs. (Syllabus Link B1h)

- **Discuss** the concept of lifecycle costing and how life cycle costs interact with marketing strategies at each stage of the life cycle. (Syllabus Link B1i)

## 1 Session Content Diagram

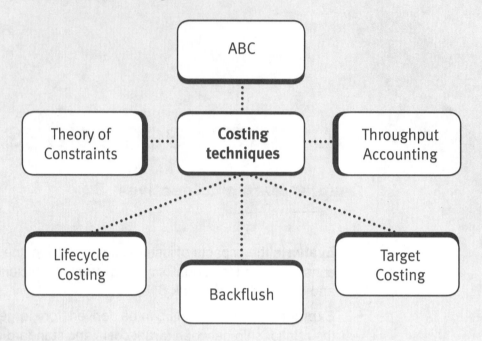

## 2 Knowledge Brought Forward

You will already have covered some of these concepts in Paper P1. We will build on this knowledge in P2 with more aspects of some key costing techniques, but make sure you are comfortable with the assumed knowledge, that should have been brought forward as a base, in the following sections.

One of these key techniques, Activity-Based Costing, is covered in the 'Basics Revisited' chapter and further applications explained in Chapter 10.

Because traditional overhead absorption was designed for production companies, it dealt with production costs only and, as a consequence, it is less suitable for service or retail organisations. Also, because inventory had to be valued at full production cost only in the published accounts, other costs such as R&D, administration, and marketing have not been related to products.

When traditional absorption costing evolved last century, overheads were only a small part, say, 10 per cent of the cost of production for the average company. Direct labour costs were much higher, say, 50 per cent of the cost of the product. This meant that the absorption method spread 10 per cent of costs on the basis of 50 per cent of costs. Because overheads were such a small part of total costs any inaccuracies in the absorption process were small and insignificant and did not distort product costs.

A few organisations may have this cost structure today, and in such cases traditional absorption costing is perfectly adequate. Most companies, however, now have those percentages reversed and it creates a considerable degree of inaccuracy if 50 per cent of the costs are spread on the behaviour of 10 per cent of the costs. Yet it is vital that an organisation's costing system spreads overheads accurately.

Traditional absorption costing was not designed to make decisions of a short-term nature, and can never be used for this purpose. Marginal costing (variable costing) should be used when short-term decisions on matters such as product/service profitability are required. But if long-term decisions need to be made, an absorption costing system is needed. The system must be accurate and for all the reasons outlined above, total absorption costing is unlikely to produce the required accuracy; alternative costing techniques are needed.

## 3 Throughput Accounting And The Theory Of Constraints

The term throughput is defined by the following equation:

**Throughput = Sales Revenues less Direct Material Cost**

The aim of throughput accounting is to maximise this measure of throughput. Goldratt and Cox advocate that managers should aim to increase throughput while simultaneously reducing inventory and operational expense.

This goal is achieved by determining what factors prevent the throughput being higher. This constraint is called a bottleneck. A bottleneck may be a machine whose capacity limits the output of the whole production process. The aim is to identify the bottlenecks and remove them or, if this is not possible, ensure that they are fully utilised at all times. Non-bottleneck resources should be scheduled and operated based on the constraints within the system, and should not be used to produce more than the bottlenecks can absorb.

Goldratt and Cox describe the process of identifying and taking steps to remove the constraints that restrict output as the **theory of constraints** (TOC). The process involves five steps:

(1) Identify the system's bottlenecks.

(2) Decide how to exploit the bottlenecks.

(3) Subordinate everything else to the decision in Step 2.

(4) Elevate the system's bottlenecks.

(5) If, in the previous steps, a bottleneck has been broken, go back to Step 1.

The bottleneck is the focus of management's attention. Decisions regarding the optimum mix of products must be undertaken. Step 3 requires that the optimum production of the bottleneck activity determines the production schedule of the non-bottleneck activities. There is no point in a non-bottleneck activity supplying more than the bottleneck activity can consume. This would result in increased work-in-progress (WIP) inventories with no increased sales volume. The TOC is a process of continuous improvement to clear the throughput chain of all the constraints. Thus, step 4 involves taking action to remove, or elevate, the constraint. This may involve replacing the bottleneck machine with a faster one, providing additional training for a slow worker or changing the design of the product to reduce the processing time required on the bottleneck activity. Once a bottleneck has been elevated it will generally be replaced by a new bottleneck elsewhere in the system. It then becomes necessary to return to Step 1.

## Constraints on throughput

The idea of constraints is central to the throughput approach. Examples of constraints may include:

- inadequately trained sales force;
- poor reputation for meeting delivery dates;
- poor physical distribution system;
- unreliability of material supplies, delivery and/or quality;
- inadequate production resources;
- inappropriate management accounting system.

### Example 1 – Theory of constraints

Demand for a product made by P Ltd is 500 units per week. The product is made in three consecutive processes – A, B, and C. Process capacities are:

| Process | A | B | C |
|---|---|---|---|
| Capacity per week | 400 | 300 | 250 |

The long-run benefit to P Ltd of increasing sales of its product is a present value of $25,000 per additional unit sold per week.

Investigations have revealed the following possibilities:

(1) Invest in a new machine for process A, which will increase its capacity to 550 units per week. This will cost $1m.

(2) Replace the machine in process B with an upgraded machine, costing $1.5m. This will double the capacity of process B.

(3) Buy an additional machine for process C, costing $2m. This will increase capacity in C by 300 units per week.

**Required:**

What is P Ltd's best course of action?

## Throughput accounting measures

### Throughput = Sales Revenues less Direct Material Cost

The only cost that is deemed to relate to volume of output is the direct material cost. All other costs (including labour costs) are deemed to be fixed. These fixed costs may be called total factory costs (TFC).

The role of the accountant in a throughput environment is to devise measures which will help production staff to achieve a greater volume of throughput. Attention should be drawn to the financial effects of bottlenecks. For example if a bottleneck resource fails to operate for one hour a whole hour's throughput is lost.

Various performance measures have been devised to help measure throughput:

$$\text{Return per factory hour} = \frac{\text{Throughput per unit}}{\text{Product time on the bottleneck resource}}$$

$$\text{Cost per factory hour} = \frac{\text{Total factory costs}}{\text{Total time on the bottleneck resource}}$$

$$\text{Throughput accounting ratio} = \frac{\text{Return per factory hour}}{\text{Cost per factory hour}}$$

The accountant may advise management on how the TA ratio may be maximised.

### Example 2 – Throughput accounting

The following data relates to three products manufactured by BJS Ltd:

|  | Product X | Product Y | Product Z |
|---|---|---|---|
| Selling price per unit | $12 | $16 | $14 |
| Direct material cost per unit | $3 | $10 | $7 |
| Maximum demand (units) | 15,000 | 40,000 | 20,000 |
| Time required on the bottleneck (hours per unit) | 3 | 1.5 | 7 |

The firm has 80,000 bottleneck hours available each period.

Total factory costs amount to $100,000 in the period.

**Required:**

(a) Calculate the throughput accounting ratio for each product.

(b) Calculate the optimum product mix and the maximum profit.

## 4 Target Costing

The target costing approach, a form of life-cycle costing, has recently received some attention. Target costing is driven by external market factors. Marketing managers first estimate the performance characteristics and market price requirements in order to achieve a desired market share for a proposed product. A standard profit margin is then subtracted from the projected selling price to arrive at the target cost for the product. The product development team must then, through its product and process design decisions, attempt to reach the product's target cost.

One of the definitions of target costing reads as follows:

Target costing is a pro-active cost control system. The target cost is calculated by deducting the target profit from a pre-determined selling price based on customers' views. Functional Analysis, value analysis and value engineering are used to change production methods and/or reduce expected costs so the target is met.

The target profit requirement should be driven by strategic profit planning rather than a standard mark-up. In Japan this is done after consideration of the medium-term profit plans which reflect management and business strategies over that period. Once it is set, the target profit is not just an expectation; it is a commitment agreed by all the people who have any part in achieving it. Therefore the procedures used to derive the target profit must be scientific, rational and agreed by all staff responsible for achieving it, otherwise no-one will accept responsibility for achieving it.

This procedure is just the opposite of that followed by many companies today in which the product is designed with little regard either to the manufacturing process or to its long-run manufacturing cost. With this traditional procedure of first designing the product and then giving the design to process engineers and costs analysts, the product cost is developed by applying standard cost factors to the materials and processes specified for the design. Frequently, this cost may be well above that which can be sustained by market prices and the product is either aborted or, if marketed, fails to achieve desired profitability levels.

### Using target cost in the concept and design stages

With the target-cost approach, the new product team, consisting of product designers, purchasing specialists, and manufacturing and process people, works together to jointly determine product and process characteristics that permit the target cost to be achieved. The target cost approach is especially powerful to apply at the design stage, since decisions made at this stage have leverage to affect long-run costs.

The great majority of manufacturing costs become locked in early in the life cycle of the product. Once the product is released into production, it becomes much harder to achieve significant cost reductions. Most of the costs become committed or locked in much earlier than the time at which the major cash expenditures are made.

The target-costing approach is a vital total cost control tool because research has shown that up to 90 per cent of costs are 'built in' at the product's design stage. Below are some examples of costs that become locked in place at the design stage:

- The design specification of the product including extra features
- The number of components incorporated in the product
- Design of components

These should be designed for reliability in use and ease of manufacture. Wherever possible standard parts should be used because they are proven to be reliable and will help reduce stock and handling costs. Where new components are required it is important that their manufacturing process is considered before the component is finally designed so that they can be manufactured as cheaply as possible consistent with quality and functionality.

- Type of packaging required

  This includes product packaging and packing per case and per pallet. The aim is to protect the product and to minimise handling costs by not breaking pallets or cases during distribution.

- The number of spare parts that need to be carried

  This ties in with the number of components used. Parts must sometimes be held for up to 15 years or so. They may be made while the product is still in production and stored for years, which is costly. The alternative is to disrupt current production to make a small batch of a past component, which is very costly.

Target costing is an iterative process that cannot be de-coupled from design. The pre-production stages can be categorised in a variety of different ways; in the detailed discussion below five different stages are used and the different activities are now listed.

(1) **Planning**

This includes fixing the product concept and the primary specifications for performance and design. A very brief product concept might be a small, town car for two people with a large amount of easily-accessible luggage space and low fuel consumption – aimed at those in their mid-twenties and so style is important. (In reality the concept would be much fuller.) Value engineering and analysis (VE) could be used to identify new and innovative, yet cost-effective, product features that would be valued by customers and meet their requirements.

Once the concept has been developed a planned sales volume and selling price, which depend on each other, will be set, as well as the required profit discussed earlier. From this the necessary target cost (or allowable cost as it is often known) can be ascertained.

**Target cost = Planned selling price – Required profit**

## (2) Concept design

The basic product is designed. The target cost in now divided into smaller parts reflecting the manufacturing process. See diagram below. First an allowance for development costs and manufacturing equipment costs are deducted from the total. The remainder is then split up into unit costs that will cover manufacturing and distribution, etc. The manufacturing target cost per unit is assigned to the functional areas of the new product. For example, a functional area for a ballpoint pen might be the flow of ink to the tip and a functional area for a car might be the steering mechanism.

### The breakdown of target cost

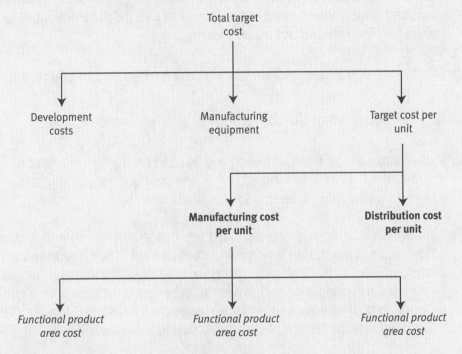

## (3) Basic design

The components are designed in detail so that they do not exceed the functional target costs. Value engineering is used to get the costs down to the target. If one function cannot meet its target, the targets for the others must be reduced or the product redesigned.

## (4) Detailed design

The detailed specifications and cost estimates are set down from the basic design stage.

### (5) Manufacturing preparation

The manufacturing process, including new machines and jigs, etc. is designed in keeping with the target cost. Standards for the materials and labour hours that should be used are set. These values are presented to the staff in the factory immediately they are set so that approval can be given.

The purchasing department negotiates prices for bought-in components.

## Target costing for existing products

Cost control is not forgotten once the product goes into production. Manufacturing performance is measured to see if the target is being achieved. The reasons for doing this are:

(1) to see who is responsible for any cost excess and to offer them help; and

(2) to judge whether the cost-planning activities were effective.

If after three months the target cost is missed by a large margin an improvement team is organised which will conduct a thorough value analysis (VA) and will stay in existence for about six months.

Although the Japanese use standard costing to some extent they do not consider it to be suitable for ongoing cost control. They see standard costing as part of budget accounting where the same value is maintained throughout the budget period, whereas they use target costing to control production cost and as a consequence revise it monthly. Monden (1989) expressed the limitations of standard costing this way:

'Since standard costing systems have constraints from a financial perspective, they are inappropriate measures for management. A typical constraint is the infrequency in which quantity standards, such as processing time per production unit or material requirements, are revised.

Normally these standards are maintained at the same level throughout the year.'

Target costing, therefore, continues to be used to control costs throughout the product's life. After the initial start-up stage target costs will be set through budgets, which in Japan tend to be set every six months rather than yearly. This type of target costing is a different technique in the eyes of the Japanese and they call this Genka Kaizen. It is widely used in Japan; about 80 per cent of assembly environments use it. If a manager cannot meet the target cost for a function, a committee will be set up to help achieve it. All costs including both variable and fixed overheads are expected to reduce on a regular basis, usually monthly.

Target costing is widely used among industries in different countries. Mercedes, Toyota, Nissan, and Daihatsu in the car industry, Matsushita, Panasonic and Sharp in the electronics industry, and Apple, Compaq and Toshiba in the personal computer market all use target pricing and target costing.

**In summary:**

| Standard costing | Target costing |
|---|---|
| A **Push** system: a standard cost per unit (onto which a mark-up is added) is the basis for calculating the selling price. | A **Pull** system that requires understanding of market demand and competition, so that the price required to achieve a target market share or sales level can be set. |
| An **Internal** tool in mass production environments that do not emphasise continual improvement. | Driven by **External** market prices and may not be attainable in the short term. |
| A **Cost control** technique. | A **Cost reduction** activity. |
| A **Reactive** technique – the selling price of a new product will be determined by estimating its standard cost and adding the required profit margin to the cost. | A **Proactive** technique that starts before the design of the product is formalised. Once this target price has been determined, a required long-term profit margin is agreed. It is only once the target cost has been agreed that the design team can begin their work. Our products must be designed with a pre-determined cost ceiling. |

### Target costs and standard costs

There are some similarities between target costs and standard costs but the significance of a target cost lies in the process of how it is developed. They both provide unit cost targets but here the similarity ends and significant differences include:

- the focus upon what a product should cost in the long term. In constructing the target cost of a new item consideration should first be given to the price at which the product should be sold in order to attract the desired market share. Once this selling price has been determined the required profit margin needs to be deducted in order to arrive at the target cost. A standard cost would tend to be based on attainable standards of efficiency whereas a target cost may incorporate a cost gap which can only be achieved over a longer term.

- A market orientated approach. The use of standard costs which have been derived from target costs ensures that external factors that are related to the marketplace are taken into account. A standard cost is usually based on production cost information only.

- Focus on continual improvement. The target cost may incorporate a series of cost targets which are continuously reduced until the target is achieved. A standard is normally set at the outset of production and may not be reviewed on a regular basis.

- Team approach. Target costing requires that all departments working on the product should be involved in the target costing exercise and should contribute to the target cost being achieved. This includes research and development, marketing and sales as well as production. This contrasts with standard costs which are normally production costs only.

- A target cost will be set before major development costs are incurred. This allows cost reductions to be designed into the product or a decision to be made to abandon the product if the required cost target cannot be achieved. In contrast, standards are set when production commences, by which time 70% to 80% of costs may already be committed.

### Kaizen Costing and Target Costing

**Kaizen** is the Japanese term for making improvements to a process through small incremental amounts, rather than through large innovations.

Target costing is aimed at reducing the costs incurred because of the way the product is designed, and occurs at the very start of the process.

Kaizen costing is applied during the manufacturing stage of the products life cycle. Kaizen costing therefore focuses on achieving cost reductions through the increased efficiency of the production process. Improvement is the aim and responsibility of every worker in every activity, at all times. Through continual efforts significant reductions in cost can be achieved over time. In order to encourage continual cost reductions an annual (or monthly) Kaizen cost goal is established. Actual results are then compared with the Kaizen goal and then the current actual cost becomes the base line for setting the new Kaizen goal the following year. It should be noted however that as the products are already at the production stage the cost savings under Kaizen costing are smaller than target costing. Because cost reductions under target costing are achieved at the design stage where 80–90% of the product costs are locked in, more significant savings can be made.

## 5 Life-Cycle Costing

Life-cycle costing is the accumulation of costs for activities that occur over the entire life cycle of a product, from inception to abandonment.

According to Berliner and Brimson (1988), companies operating in an advanced manufacturing environment are finding that about 90% of a product's life-cycle cost is determined by decisions made early in the cycle. In many industries a large fraction of the life-cycle costs consists of costs incurred on product design, prototyping, programming, process design and equipment acquisition. This has created a need to ensure that the tightest controls are at the design stage, because most costs are committed or 'locked-in' at this point in time. Management accounting systems should therefore be developed that aid the planning and control of product life-cycle costs and monitor spending and commitments at the early stages of a product's life-cycle.

### Product life-cycle costing

There are a number of factors that need to be managed in order to maximise a product's return over its life cycle. These are:

*   design costs out of the product;
*   minimise the time to market.
*   maximise the length of the life cycle itself;

These factors will be considered in turn.

### Design costs out of the product

It was stated earlier that between 80% and 90% of a product's costs were often incurred at the design and development stages of its life. That is decisions made then committed the organisation to incurring the costs at a later date, because the design of the product determines the number of components, the production method, etc. It is absolutely vital therefore that design teams do not work in isolation, but as part of a cross-functional team in order to minimise costs over the whole life cycle.

### Minimise the time to market

In a world where competitors watch each other keenly to see what new products will be launched, it is vital to get any new product into the marketplace as quickly as possible. The competitors will monitor each other closely so that they can launch rival products as soon as possible in order to maintain profitability. It is vital, therefore, for the first organisation to launch its product as quickly as possible after the concept has been developed, so that it has as long as possible to establish the product in the market and to make a profit before competition increases. Often it is not so much costs that reduce profits as time wasted.

### Maximise the length of the life cycle itself

Generally the longer the life cycle the greater the profit that will be generated, assuming that production ceases once the product goes into decline and becomes unprofitable. One way to maximise the life cycle is to get the product to market as quickly as possible because this should maximise the time in which the product generates a profit. Another way of extending a product's life is to find other uses, or markets, for the product. Other product uses may not be obvious when the product is still in its planning stage and need to be planned and managed later on. On the other hand, it may be possible to plan for a staggered entry into different markets at the planning stage.

Many organisations stagger the launch of their products in different world markets in order to reduce costs, increase revenue and prolong the overall life of the product. A current example is the way in which new films are released in the USA months before the UK launch. This is done to build up the enthusiasm for the film and to increase revenues overall. Other companies may not have the funds to launch worldwide at the same moment and may be forced to stagger it.

Skimming the market is another way to prolong life and to maximise the revenue over the product's life. This was discussed in the unit on pricing.

## Customer Life Cycle Costing

Not all investment decisions involve large initial capital outflows or the purchase of physical assets. The decision to serve and retain customers can also be a capital budgeting decision even though the initial outlay may be small. For example a credit card company or an insurance company will have to choose which customers they take on and then register them on the company's records. The company incurs initial costs due to the paperwork, checking creditworthiness, opening policies, etc. for new customers. It takes some time before these initial costs are recouped. Research has also shown that the longer a customer stays with the company the more profitable that customer becomes to the company.

Thus it becomes important to retain customers, whether by good service, discounts, other benefits, etc. A customer's 'life' can be discounted and decisions made as to the value of, say, a 'five-year-old' customer. Eventually a point arises where profit no longer continues to grow; this plateau is reached between about five years and 20 years depending on the nature of the business. Therefore by studying the increased revenue and decreased costs generated by an 'old' customer, management can find strategies to meet their needs better and to retain them.

Many manufacturing companies only supply a small number of customers, say between six and ten, and so they can cost customers relatively easily. Other companies such as banks and supermarkets have many customers and cannot easily analyse every single customer. In this case similar customers are grouped together to form category types and these can then be analysed in terms of profitability.

For example, the UK banks analyse customers in terms of fruits, such as oranges, lemons, plums, etc. Customers tend to move from one category to another as they age and as their financial habits change. Customers with large mortgages, for example, are more valuable to the bank than customers who do not have a large income and do not borrow money. Banks are not keen on keeping the latter type of customer

## The Life Cycle Cost Budget

The application of life cycle costing requires the establishment of a life cycle cost budget for a given product which in turn necessitates identification of costs with particular products. Actual costs incurred in respect of the product are then monitored against life cycle budget costs.

A company is in a weak position if all its products are at the same phase of the life cycle. If they are all in the growth phase there are problems ahead; if they are all in one of the other phases there are immediate difficulties.

Companies try to overcome this problem by introducing new products that are growing as the old products are declining and by having products with life cycles of different lengths.

In applying life cycle costing a supplier will recognise that the life of the product commences prior to its introduction to the marketplace. Indeed up to 90% of costs result from decisions made prior to its 'launch' concerning issues such as functions, materials, components and manufacturing methods to be adopted.

Life cycle costs may be classified as follows:

* development costs
* design costs
* manufacturing costs
* marketing costs, and
* distribution costs.

A pattern of costs will emerge over the life cycle of the product. Invariably the absolute level of costs will rise and this trend should 'track' the pattern of sales of the product. The supplier will always be monitoring relevant costs and revenues in an attempt to ensure that the rise in resultant sales revenues is greater than the rise in the attributable costs of the product. Moreover, the supplier will expect reductions to occur in the unit cost of a product as a consequence of economies of scale and learning and experience curves. In order to maximise the profits earned by a product over its life cycle management need give consideration to minimising the time required to get the product to the marketplace. This may enable an organisation to 'steal a march' on its competitors who will invariably attempt to launch a rival product at the earliest available opportunity. Hence 'time to market' assumes critical significance since it affords an organisation that is first to the marketplace with an opportunity to make profits prior to arrival of competitor products.

Once the product has reached the marketplace management attention should be focused upon maximising the length of the product's life cycle. In this regard 'time to market' is also critical since by definition the earlier a product reaches the marketplace the longer will be its resultant life cycle. Management should always be searching for other potential uses of the product and/or finding alternative markets for the product. Whilst it may be difficult to envisage other potential uses for product at the planning stage it may be possible for an organisation to draw up a plan which involves the staggered entry of the product into geographically separate markets with the resultant effect of increasing the overall life cycle of the product. A major benefit of this staggered approach which is often adopted by global players lies in the fact that the income streams from one market may be used to fund the launch of the product into another market.

The application of life cycle costing requires management to consider whether the anticipated cost savings that were expected to be achieved via the application of cost reduction techniques, both prior to and following the product's introduction, have actually been achieved. Its use may also assist management in allocating resources to non-production activities. For example, a product which is in the mature stage may require less marketing support than a product which is in the growth stage.

# 6 Practice Questions

**Test your understanding 1 – Standard Costing and Target**

Standard costing and target costing have little in common for the following reasons:

- the former is a costing system and the latter is not;
- target costing is proactive and standard costing is not;
- target costs are agreed by all and are rigorously adhered to whereas standard costs are usually set without wide consultation.

**Required:**

(a) Discuss the comparability of standard costing and target costing by considering the validity of the statements above

**(18 marks)**

A pharmaceutical company, which operates a standard costing system, is considering introducing target costing.

**Required:**

(b) Discuss whether the company should do this and whether the two systems would be compatible.

**(7 marks)**

**(Total: 25 marks)**

**(May 2002)**

**Test your understanding 2**

The following data relate to the single product made by Squirrel Ltd:

| | |
|---|---:|
| Selling price per unit | $16 |
| Direct material cost per unit | $10 |
| Maximum demand (units) per period | 40,000 |
| Time required (hours) in Process X, per unit | 1 |
| Time required (hours) in Process Y, per unit | 1.5 |

The capacities are 35,000 hours in Process X and 42,000 hours in Process Y.

The total factory costs are $105,000 in the period.

**Required:**

(a) Identify the process bottleneck.

(b) Calculate the throughput accounting ratio.

### Test your understanding 3 – A and B

A company produces two products, A and B, which pass through two production processes, J and K. The time taken to make each product in each process is:

|  | Product A | Product B |
| --- | --- | --- |
| Process J | 6½ mins | 9 mins |
| Process K | 22 mins | 15 mins |

The company operates a 16-hour day and the processes have an average downtime each day of:

| | |
| --- | --- |
| Process J | 2½ hours |
| Process K | 2 hours |

The costs and revenue for each unit of each product are:

|  | Product A | Product B |
| --- | --- | --- |
|  | $ | $ |
| Direct materials | 15.00 | 15.00 |
| Direct labour | 17.00 | 12.00 |
| Variable overhead | 8.00 | 6.00 |
| Fixed costs | 8.00 | 6.00 |
| | | |
| Total cost | 48.00 | 39.00 |
| | | |
| Selling price | 87.50 | 72.50 |

Sales demand restricts the output of A and B to 40 and 60 units a day respectively.

The daily production plan that would maximise the *throughput* contribution is:

A   38 units of A

B   36 units of A and 4 units of B

C   34 units of A and 5 units of B

D   56 units of B

## Mini-Quiz

(1)  Which feature distinguishes backflush accounting from other systems?

    A   Labour costs are not charged to the units produced.

    B   Costs are attached when output is completed or sold.

    C   Cost records reflect the flow of work through the production process.

    D   Entries are not made until the customer pays for goods purchased.

    E   Material entries are made when the material is received and moved.

(2)  Company X produces a single product with the following standard cost per unit:

| | |
|---|---|
| Material cost | $10 |
| Conversion cost | $12 |
| Total cost | **$22** |

The company operates a backflush costing system with a raw material inventory control account. Details for the current month are:

| | |
|---|---|
| Raw material inventory control account opening balance | $500 |
| Raw materials purchased | $4,600 |
| Conversion costs incurred | $5,200 |
| Cost of goods sold at standard cost | $8,998 |

The closing balance on the raw material inventory control account is:

A   $290

B   $502

C   $790

D   $800

E   $1,010

(3) A company produces two products, A and B, which pass through two production processes, J and K. The time taken to make each product in each process is:

|  | Product A | Product B |
|---|---|---|
| Process J | 6.5 minutes | 9 minutes |
| Process K | 22 minutes | 15 minutes |

The company operates a 16-hour day and the processes have an average downtime each day of:

| Process J | 2.5 hours |
|---|---|
| Process K | 2 hours |

The costs and revenue for each unit of each product are:

|  | Product A $ | Product B $ |
|---|---|---|
| Direct materials | 15.00 | 15.00 |
| Direct Labour | 17.00 | 12.00 |
| Variable overhead | 8.00 | 6.00 |
| Fixed costs | 8.00 | 6.00 |
| **Total cost** | **48.00** | **39.00** |
| Selling Price | 87.50 | 72.50 |

Sales demand restricts the output of A and B to 40 and 60 units a day, respectively. The daily production plan that would maximise the throughput contribution is:

A    40 units of A

B    38 units of A

C    36 units of A and 4 units of B

D    34 units of A and 5 units of B

E    56 units of B

(4)  The selling price of product Z is set at $250 for each unit and sales for the coming year are expected to be 500 units.

If the company requires a return of 15% in the coming year on its investment of $250,000 in product Z, the target cost for each unit for the coming year is:

A    $145

B    $155

C    $165

D    $175

E    $185

### Test your understanding answers

## Example 1 – Theory of constraints

|  | A | B | C | Demand |
|---|---|---|---|---|
| Current Capacity per week | 400 | 300 | 250* | 500 |
| Buy C – Capacity per week | 400 | 300* | 550 | 500 |
| Buy C & B – Capacity per week | 400* | 600 | 550 | 500 |
| Buy C, B, & A – Capacity per week | 550 | 600 | 550 | 500* |

\* = Bottleneck

**Financial viability**

**Buy C**

Additional Sales = 50

|  | $000 |
|---|---|
| Benefit = 50 × $25,000 | 1,250 |
| Cost | 2,000 |
| Net cost | 750 |

**Buy C and B**

Additional sales from current position = 150

|  | $000 |
|---|---|
| Benefit = 150 × $25,000 | 3,750 |
| Cost ($2m + $1.5m) | 3,500 |
| Net benefit | 250 |

**Buy C, B and A**

Additional sales from current position = 250

|  | $000 |
|---|---|
| Benefit = 250 × $25,000 | 6,250 |
| Cost ($2m +$1.5m +$1m) | 4,500 |
| Net benefit | 1,750 |

The company will benefit by $1,750,000 by investing in all three machines.

## Example 2 – Throughput accounting

Cost per factory hour = $100,000/80,000 = $1.25

|  | Product X | Product Y | Product Z |
|---|---|---|---|
| Selling price per unit | $12 | $16 | $14 |
| Direct material cost per unit | ($3) | ($10) | ($7) |
| Throughput p.u. | $9 | $6 | $7 |
| Time required on the bottleneck | 3 | 1.5 | 7 |
| **Return per factory hour** | **$3** | **$4** | **$1** |
| T. A. ratio | $3/$1.25 = **2.4 : 1** | $4/$1.25 = **3.2 : 1** | $1/$1.25 = **0.80** |
| **Ranking** | **2nd** | **1st** | **3rd** |

| Product | Number of units | Hours per unit | Total hours | Throughput per hour | Total throughput |
|---|---|---|---|---|---|
| Y | 40,000 | 1.5 | 60,000 | $4 | $240,000 |
| X | 6,666 | 3.0 | 20,000 | $3 | $60,000 |
|  |  |  | 80,000 |  | $300,000 |
| Less total factory costs |  |  |  |  | ($100,000) |
| Total Profit |  |  |  |  | **$200,000** |

**Test your understanding 1 – Standard Costing and Target**

(a) **Costing system or not?**

It is perhaps unclear as to what constitutes a 'costing system'. CIMA give no definition. The term 'costing' is defined as 'the process of determining the costs of products, services or activities'. Both standard and target costing do establish costs of products and services. But does this represent an ongoing system?

'Standard costing is a control technique which compares standard costs and revenues with actual results to obtain variances which are used to stimulate improved performance' (CIMA definition). It is certainly an ongoing cost monitoring system. Standard costing involves the setting of standards (expected costs and efficiency levels) and then the regular comparison of actual results to these predetermined standards. When differences arise, an investigation into the cause of the difference should be initiated followed by appropriate control action. This procedure does indeed represent a 'costing system'.

A 'target cost is a product cost estimate derived by subtracting a desired profit margin from a competitive market price' (CIMA definition). Whilst CIMA do not define 'target costing' the general understanding of target costing is that it is the system whereby a target cost is established, this forecast must be agreed by all management, who then undertake whatever action is necessary to ensure that the target cost is always met. One characteristic of target costing which does distinguish it from standard costing is that the target cost is established PRIOR to the designing of the product. The product must be designed within the confines of the target cost. Target costing then involves the ongoing comparison of actual costs against the target cost to ensure that the target is being adhered to. Target costing does represent a costing system (or procedure).

Both target costing and standard costing are costing systems.

**Proactive or not?**

Standard costing is a stable system where, once standards have been set, there is an acceptance of the targets almost without question. Actual results are compared to these standards and any significant adverse results are rectified. The response is only made to the results AFTER the events. The response is a reaction to those historical events. Hence, standard costing appears to be more reactive than proactive.

Target costing is, however, much more proactive. The target cost is gradually reduced over the life cycle of the product in question. In order to continuously achieve the reducing target, managers need to continually search for new solutions that will reduce costs and increase efficiency still further. This approach to cost monitoring necessitates a greater involvement from management and encourages continuous improvement. Target costing acts as a cost reduction technique but standard costing does not.

### Involvement and agreement

There is often a great deal of staff involvement when target costing is used. The philosophy behind the system is to allow staff to participate fully in the setting of target costs. Staff from several functions (for example, marketing, distribution and, of course, design) become involved in agreeing a target cost. All staff must agree with the targets. All staff must then take responsibility for the achievement of the targets. Management must act as a team and work together to achieve the goals. If one of the targets is broken, it is for the whole management team to develop a solution to reduce the costs still further. All actions undertaken must be governed by the overriding need to achieve the target cost. Management understand and accept this.

Standard costing tends to be much less far-reaching. Generally, the designers produce the product specifications and then the accountants produce the product costings. Other members of the management team have very little input at the standard setting stage. Once the system is running, various members of the production staff will have responsibility for achieving the standards. However, each manager will tend to have his/her own area of responsibility. The members of staff will act individually and not as a team. Additionally, adverse variances may be acceptable in certain circumstances – this is very different from the view in target costing. Planning variances may be used to explain adverse variances. Managers are often not held responsible for planning variances.

(b) Target costing is often of benefit to a company that is continuously launching new products. If the company has a significant design or research expenditure, then it may be appropriate for the company to use target costing to make staff aware of costs from the very beginning of the product life cycle, i.e. in the design stage.

A pharmaceutical company will have very large development and research expenditures. It may well be of great benefit to develop new drugs within a cost target. Against this cost incentive the company must also consider the health and safety issues of new drugs. Each new product must be researched and tested thoroughly before it is sold to world health organisations.

Once a new product is on the market, the price of the drug will be protected through its patent for perhaps many years. During this time the product will have very little or no competition and cost control may not be important to the manufacturer. However, once the patent expires, competition is likely to increase significantly. At this time market forces will drive down the selling price. Companies that have been using target costing will already be operating effectively with no wasteful activity. These lean companies will be able to compete effectively and remain profitable.

A pharmaceutical company may obtain significant benefits from target costing.

Whilst the company could continue to operate its standard costing system, there is no need for the monthly reporting system under standard costing. Indeed, whilst annual standards remain fixed each year the targets under target costing will be reducing. It is difficult to see how the company would find any benefit from its standard costing system. Managers may be confused by the two information systems.

## Test your understanding 2

(a)

$$\text{Capacity in process X} = \frac{35{,}000}{1} = 35{,}000 \text{ units per period}$$

$$\text{Capacity in process Y} = \frac{42{,}000}{1.5} = 28{,}000 \text{ units per period}$$

Therefore process Y is the bottleneck.

(b) Throughput per unit = $16 – $10 = $6

$$\text{Return per factory hour} = \frac{6}{1.5} = \$4$$

$$\text{Throughput accounting ratio} = \frac{\$4}{\$2.5} = 1.6$$

As this is above 1, this is satisfactory.

## Test your understanding 3 – A and B

Strictly speaking this problem should be solved using linear programming as there are several limiting factors – restricted time in both Process J and K and maximum demands for Products A and B.

However, both Products A and B take longer to make in Process K than in Process J, so we can deduce that the bottleneck must be in Process K.

Remember to maximise throughput.

| Product | A | B |
|---|---|---|
| Selling price | $87.50 | $72.50 |
| Less: direct material cost | (15.00) | (15.00) |
| | ——— | ——— |
| Throughput per unit | $72.50 | $57.50 |
| | ——— | ——— |

Number of minutes available in Process K

| | |
|---|---|
| = 16 hours × 60 minutes | 960 mins |
| Less: downtime | (120) |
| | ——— |
| Production time | 840 mins |
| | ——— |

| | A | B |
|---|---|---|
| Maximum production | 840/22 = 38 units | 840/15 = 56 units |
| x Throughput per unit | x $72.50 | x $57.50 |
| Throughput | $2,755.00 | $3,220.00 |

∴ Produce 56 units of B. Note: this is within the maximum of 60 units.

**Answer D**

### Mini-Quiz

(1) Answer: B. Backflush accounting is a method of costing associated with JIT. It delays the recording of costs until after the events have taken place. The recording of costs may be triggered when goods are transferred to finished goods inventory or, in a true JIT system, when goods are sold.

(2) Answer: E. Material cost of goods sold = $8,998 x$10/£22 = $4,090

### Raw materials inventory control account

| | $ | | $ |
|---|---|---|---|
| Opening Balance | 500 | Outputs from the process are shown on this side (credit) | Standard cost of goods sold |
| Materials purchased | 4,600 | Closing Balance | 1,010 |
| | 5,100 | | 5,100 |

(3) Answer: E

| | Product A | Product B |
|---|---|---|
| Throughput of J per day | 13.5 hours x 60/6.5 = 124.62 | 13.5 hours x 60/9 = 90 |
| Throughput of K per day | 14 hours x 60/22 = 38.18 | 14 hours x 60/15 = 56 |

Contribution per hour of product A = $87.50 – 15.00 = $72.50 x 60/22 = $197.73

Contribution per hour of product B = $72.50 – 15.00 = $57.50 x 60/15= 230.00

Processing product B will give the larger contribution per day = 56 units

(4) Answer: D

| | $ |
|---|---|
| Sales revenue 500 units @ $250 | 125,000 |
| Return on invst. required 15% x 250,000 | 37,500 |
| Total Cost Allowed | 87,500 |
| Target Cost per unit | 175 |

# Advanced Activity-Based Costing

## Chapter learning objectives

- **Evaluate** the impacts of just-in-time production, the theory of constraints and total quality management on efficiency inventory and cost. (Syllabus Link B1b)

- **Apply** the techniques of activity-based management in identifying cost drivers / activities. (Syllabus Link B1f)

- **Explain** how process re-engineering can be used to eliminate non-value adding activities and reduce activity costs. (Syllabus Link B 1g)

- **Analyse** direct customer profitability and extend this analysis to distribution channel profitability through the application of activity-based costing ideas. (Syllabus Link B1l)

- **Apply** Pareto analysis as a convenient technique for identifying key elements of data and in presenting the results of other analysis, such as activity-based profitability calculations.(Syllabus Link B1m)

## 1 Session Content Diagram

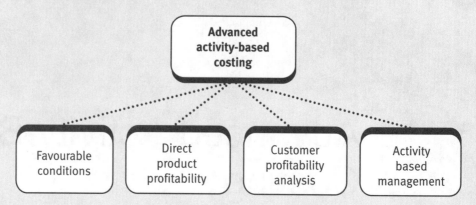

## 2 Knowledge Brought Forward

You will already have covered Activity-Based-Costing in Papers C01 and P1; It is an important technique covered in the first chapter of this book, 'Basics Revisited'. In this chapter, we will explore ABC approaches such as Direct Product Profitability, CPA and Activity-Based Management.

### ABC As The Building Block In A Costing System

Much has been written on whether an organisation should have one costing system or several. The problem is that in the past technology only really allowed one system, as it was too time-consuming to provide information in a range of different ways.

Now, however, it is possible to devise an integrated management information system (MIS) for an organisation. This is because databases have developed in size and scope so that it is now possible to store raw data rather than aggregated data. This enables a number of different systems to be used and linked, including a range of different costing systems.

In the past data were collected, aggregated according to the requirements of the particular system, stored and turned into information that was issued to management. Data once aggregated could not be dis-aggregated and used to provide information in a different way for a different system or a different need. It was rather like using bricks, cement, wood, paint, etc. to build a house: once built it could not be knocked down and the materials used to build, say, a shop.

The benefit of using a number of different systems is the different perspectives they give management; this helps better decision making.

Probably the best example of this was the introduction of ABC during the late 1980s and early 1990s. By using a new building block – activities – a completely different view of costs was provided which was used in strategic management.

When deciding what type of costing systems an organisation should use, the following factors should be considered:

(1) What is the physical flow of goods or services? The costing system must fit the physical flow and provide suitable information.

(2) What is the management philosophy and style? The costing system must reflect this.

(3) What activities are important to the organisation's success?
   – Accurate product costing.
   – Knowledge of customer costs.
   – Information to control costs.
   – Aggressive cost reduction, etc.

The activities will determine the information required, rather than the other way around.

## 3 Direct Product Profitability (DPP)

As traditional absorption costing, which normally uses labour hours as a basis for absorption, is rarely suitable for service and retail organisations other methods had to be devised. One relatively new way of spreading overheads in retail organisations, which is used in the grocery trade in particular, is direct product profitability (DPP).

> *Direct Product Profitability* is defined in CIMA's *Official Terminology* as '*used primarily within the retail sector...DPP involves the attribution of both the purchase price and other indirect costs (for example distribution, warehousing and retailing to each product line. Thus a net profit, as opposed to a gross profit, can be identified for each product. The cost attribution process utilises a variety of measures (for example warehousing space and transport time) to reflect the resource consumption of individual products').*

DPP started in the USA in the 1960s at General Electric, and was then taken up and used by Proctor and Gamble in the 1980s. In 1985 the Food Marketing Institute in the USA laid down a standard approach to the system and two years later DPP was taken up by the Institute of Grocery Distribution in the UK. The system described below was introduced in the late 1980s and has since undergone transformation as activity-based costing has developed.

Retail organisations traditionally deducted the bought-in cost of the good from the selling price to give a gross margin. The gross margin is a useless measure for controlling the costs of the organisation itself or making decisions about the profitability of the different products. This is because none of the costs generated by the retail organisation itself are included in its calculation. For example, it does not include the storage costs of the different goods and these costs vary considerably from one good to another. A method was needed which related the indirect costs to the goods according to the way the goods used or created these costs.

The table below shows the DPP for Product A. Directly-attributable costs have been grouped into three categories and are deducted from the gross margin to determine the product's DPP.

**Direct product profit for Product A**

|  | $ | $ |
|---|---|---|
| Selling price |  | 1.50 |
| Less: bought-in price |  | (0.80) |
| Gross margin |  | **0.70** |
| Less: Direct product costs: |  |  |
| Warehouse costs | 0.16 |  |
| Transport costs | 0.18 |  |
| Store costs | 0.22 |  |
|  |  | (0.56) |
| Direct product profit |  | **0.14** |

Warehouse and store costs will include items such as labour, space and insurance costs, while transport costs will include labour, fuel and vehicle maintenance costs. The usual way to spread these costs across the different goods sold is in relation to volume or area occupied, as most costs increase in direct proportion to the volume of the product or the space it occupies.

However, there are some exceptions to this; for example, insurance costs may be better spread on value or on a risk index. Risk is greater with refrigerated or perishable goods. Refrigeration costs must only be related to those products that need to be stored in the refrigerator. Handling costs can also be treated in a different manner as they tend to vary with the number of pallets handled rather than the volume of the good itself. The labour involved in shelf-stacking may also need to be spread on a different basis.

The benefits of DPP may be summarised as:

- Better cost analysis;
- Better pricing decisions;
- Better management of store and warehouse space;
- The rationalisation of product ranges;
- Better merchandising decisions.

### Example 1

Walken Supermarkets sells over 30,000 product lines. It wishes to introduce Direct Product Profitability analysis and a team of management accountants have ascertained the following information relating to the following year:

| Budgeted weekly overhead | $ |
|---|---|
| Warehouse costs | 75,000 |
| Supermarket costs | 40,000 per supermarket |
| Transportation costs | 400 per delivery |

The warehouse is expected to handle 10,000 cubic metres (m$^3$) of goods.

Each supermarket will handle 5,000 m$^3$ of goods each week.

Each transportation vehicle holds 40 m$^3$ of goods.

Three products sold by Walken are:

|  | Kitchen roll | Tinned spaghetti | Toothpaste |
|---|---|---|---|
| Retail price per item | $1.00 | $0.60 | $1.75 |
| Bought-in price per item | $0.60 | $0.30 | $1.00 |
| Number of items per case | 10 | 25 | 40 |
| Number of cases per m$^3$ | 20 | 30 | 20 |
| Time in warehouse | 1 week | 2 weeks | 3 weeks |
| Time in supermarket | 2 weeks | 4 weeks | 2 weeks |

### Required:

Calculate the profit per item using direct profitability analysis.

## More On DPP

In recent years DPP, has developed considerably in parallel with activity-based costing. DPP has become much more sophisticated and is now very similar to activity-based costing. One of the reasons for its development during the 1990s has been the development of EPOS and EFTPOS (electronic point of sale and electronic funds transfer) systems that have enabled access to the detailed data needed for direct product cost and profitability calculations.

Indirect costs may be analysed into basic cost categories as follows. These are very similar to those discussed later for activity-based costing.

- Overhead cost. This is incurred through an activity that is not directly linked to a particular product.

- Volume-related cost. Products incur this cost in relation to the space they occupy. This is the cost described previously and includes storage and transport costs.

- Product batch cost. This is often a time-based cost. If product items (i.e. a number of identical products which are handled together as a batch) are stacked on shelves, a labour time cost is incurred. If shipping documents have to be prepared for an order or batch, this again is a labour time cost.

- Inventory financing costs. This is the cost of tying up money in inventory and is the cost of the product multiplied by the company's cost of capital per day or per week.

- Each of the categories above will contain a number of individual activities, such as:

    (1) Checking incoming goods;

    (2) Repacking or packing out for storing;

    (3) Inspecting products;

    (4) Refilling store shelf.

DPP software systems can be purchased to model costs. They require a number of key variables to analyse different situations. The variables are:

(a) **Buying and selling prices**. The retailer has the option to adjust the selling price. A price increase from a supplier can always be used to increase the gross margin, but the higher the selling price relative to other retailers the slower inventory movement is likely to be.

(b) **Rate of sale**. This is critical and needs to be as fast as possible in order to minimise space costs at the warehouse and the store, and to avoid loss of interest on money tied up in inventory.

(c) **Inventory-holding size**. The aim is to hold as little inventory as possible in keeping with JIT principles without running out of inventory.

(d) **Product size**. This is the cubic area that the product occupies and is important because space costs per item will be incurred according to size.

(e) **Pallet configuration**. The larger the number of cases on the pallet the cheaper handling costs per unit will be.

(f) **Ordering costs**. Obviously fewer orders will be cheaper but fewer orders will mean holding more inventory.

(g) **Distribution routes**. Are the goods transported direct to the store or is a central warehouse used? Transporting goods direct to the store is a high cost activity for the supplier and it is usually better to use a central warehouse, even for goods with a short shelf life.

*[In the March 2013 PEG, the Examiner notes that when asked to describe Direct Product Profitability, the candidates provided 'answers that did not relate to this technique but simply described general selling price issues'.]*

## 4 Customer Profitability Analysis

In many organisations, it is just as important to cost customers as it is to cost products. Different customers or groups of customers differ in their profitability. This is a relatively new technique that ABC makes possible because it creates cost pools for activities. Customers use some activities but not all, and different groups of customers have different 'activity profiles'.

*Customer Profitability Analysis* is defined in CIMA's *Official Terminology* as *'the analysis of revenue streams and service costs associated with specific customers or customer groups')*.

Service organisations such as a bank or a hotel in particular need to cost customers. A bank's activities for a customer will include the following types of activities:

- Withdrawal of cash;
- Unauthorised overdraft;
- Request for a statement;
- Stopping a cheque;
- Returning a cheque because of insufficient funds.

Different customers or categories of customers will each use different amounts of these activities and so customer profitability profiles can be built up, and customers can be charged according to the cost to serve them. A hotel may have activities that are provided for specific types of customers, such as well-laid-out gardens, a swimming pool and a bar. Older guests may appreciate and use the garden, families the swimming pool and business guests the bar. If the activities are charged to the relevant guests a correct cost per bed occupied can be calculated for this type of category. This will show the relative profitability and lead to strategies for encouraging the more profitable guests.

Even a manufacturing organisation can benefit from costing its customers. Not all customers cost the same to serve even if they require the same products. Some customers may be located a long way from the factory and transport may cost more. Other customers may be disruptive and place rush orders that interrupt production scheduling and require immediate, special transport. Some customers need after sales service and help with technical matters, etc.

When an organisation analyses the profitability of its customers it is not unusual to find that a Pareto curve exists. That is 20 per cent of customers provide 80 per cent of the profit. This may be illustrated by a **customer profitability curve**.

## Customer profitability curve

For example:

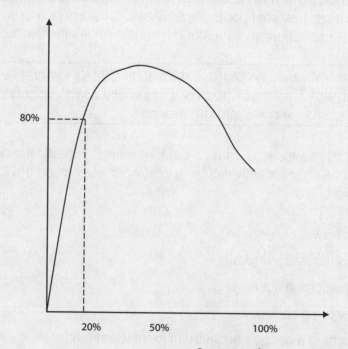

The diagram above shows that the last 80% of customers do not all generate profit. The last 50% actually reduce the total profit. There is no point in serving these customers as the situation stands but it may be foolish just to refuse to serve them. Instead it may be better to turn them into profitable customers if this is possible. A multifunctional team should be set up to find ways of making these customers profitable.

Usually it is the small volume/order customers who are unprofitable because of high production batch costs and order processing, etc. One organisation introduced a third party wholesaler into the supply chain and significantly reduced the cost of serving the small order customers. At the same time the organisation found that the product range and service to the small customers improved, and so the company saved costs and the customer received an improved service.

## Example 2

Cruise Ltd sells a single product, the TopG. The selling price to its four main customers is different because of trade discounts offered.

The data below concerns individual customer requirements:

| Customer | A | B | C | D |
|---|---|---|---|---|
| Number of units sold | 60,000 | 80,000 | 100,000 | 70,000 |
| Gross profit net of discount | 25p | 23p | 21p | 22p |
| Number of sales visits | 2 | 4 | 6 | 3 |
| Number of purchase orders | 30 | 20 | 40 | 20 |
| Number of deliveries | 10 | 15 | 25 | 14 |
| Kilometres per journey | 20 | 30 | 10 | 50 |
| Number of rush deliveries | – | – | 1 | 2 |

The management accountant has made the following activity-cost estimates:

| | |
|---|---|
| Sales visit | $210 per visit |
| Order placing | $60 per order |
| Product handling | $0.10 per item |
| Normal delivery cost | $2 per kilometre |
| Rushed delivery cost | $200 per delivery |

**Required:**

Perform a customer profitability analysis for each of the four customers.

*From November 2010 exam*

XY provides accountancy services and has three different categories of client: limited companies, self employed individuals, and employed individuals requiring taxation advice.  XY currently charges its clients a fee by adding a 20% mark-up to total costs. Currently the costs are attributed to each client based on the hours spent on preparing accounts and providing advice.

XY is considering changing to an activity based costing system.   The annual costs and the causes of these costs have been analysed as follows:

| | |
|---|---|
| Accounts preparation and advice | $580,000 |
| Requesting missing information | $30,000 |
| Issuing fee payment reminders | $15,000 |
| Holding client meetings | $60,000 |
| Travelling to clients | $40,000 |

The following details relate to three of XY's clients and to XY as a whole:

| | Client | | | XY |
|---|---|---|---|---|
| | A | B | C | |
| Hours spent on preparing accounts and providing advice | 1,000 | 250 | 340 | **18,000** |
| Requests for missing information | 4 | 10 | 6 | **250** |
| Payment reminders sent | 2 | 8 | 10 | **400** |
| Client meetings held | 4 | 1 | 2 | **250** |
| Miles travelled to clients | 150 | 600 | 0 | **10,000** |

**Required:**

Prepare calculations to show the effect on fees charged to each of these three clients of changing to the new costing system.

*[From the PEG November 2010 : Many candidates did not gain the marks available simply because they did not correctly answer the question. Candidates were asked to prepare calculations to show the effect on fees, as a result of changing to an ABC system. Therefore a* **comparison** *was needed of the fees generated from both systems. A significant number of candidates simply produced a chart showing the costs using an ABC approach. The layout of figures put forward by many candidates was extremely poor. A typical spreadsheet approach was required; simply three columns and a number of rows were required.]*

---

**Solution**

*Cost driver rates:*

| | |
|---|---|
| Accounts preparation and advice | $580,000 / 18,000 hours = $32.22 per hour |
| Requesting missing information | $30,000 / 250 times = $120 per request |
| Issuing fee payment reminders | $15,000 / 400 times = $37.50 per reminder |
| Holding client meetings | $60,000 / 250 meetings = $240 per meeting |
| Travelling to clients | $40,000 / 10,000 miles = $4 per mile |

*Client costs:*

| | Client | | |
|---|---|---|---|
| | *A* | *B* | *C* |
| Accounts preparation and advice | $32,222 | $8,055 | $10,955 |
| Requesting missing information | $480 | $1,200 | $720 |
| Issuing fee payment reminders | $75 | $300 | $375 |
| Holding client meetings | $960 | $240 | $480 |
| Travelling to clients | $600 | $2,400 | $0 |
| | | | |
| Total costs | $34,337 | $12,195 | $12,530 |
| Total costs on original basis (*) | $40,280 | $10,070 | $13,695 |
| Client fees – new basis | $41,204 | $14,634 | $15,036 |
| Client fees – original basis | $48,336 | $12,084 | $16,434 |
| Increase / (Decrease) | $(7,132) | $(2,550) | $(1,398) |

(*) $725,000 / 18,000 hours = $40.28 per hour

---

*[In the March 2013 PEG, the Examiner notes that when asked to describe Customer Profitability Analysis, the candidates provided 'answers that did not relate to this technique but simply described general selling price issues'.]*

## 5 Distribution Channel Profitability

Distribution channels are in simple terms the means of transacting with customers. The channel is the point of purchase which need not necessarily be the point of communication, payment, delivery and after sales support. Companies may transact with their customers through direct channels e.g. sales teams, telephone, shops, Internet or through indirect channels e.g. retailers, wholesalers, resellers, agents.

Regardless of whether a company's channels are direct or indirect they should always consider the ultimate needs of the customer and therefore use the channels to ensure that those needs are satisfied. Customers will look for ease of access to the supplier, reciprocal communication, products and services which satisfy their needs, prompt delivery, after sales support to name but a few.

The channel a company selects is therefore a critical driver to business profitability. A company should not only aim to satisfy the needs of the customer but must also ensure that the products and services that they are providing are profitable. The method of channel distribution chosen can account for a significant proportion of total cost and choosing the wrong channel can result in significant losses for that particular product or service. Key aspects that the company needs to consider in relation to their distribution channels include; access to the customer base, brand awareness, competitiveness, achieving sales and market targets, speed of payment, customer retention rates and most importantly of all profitability.

In companies it is just as important to cost channels as it is to cost products and customers. Different channels will differ in profitability. Activity based costing information makes this possible because it creates cost pools for activities. Channels will use some activities but not all, and different channels will have different 'activity profiles'. This makes channel profitability analysis possible and allows company's to build up distribution channel profitability profiles. It can be possible therefore for a company to identify costly distribution channels for perhaps low margin products or services which they are supplying through direct channels which may best be offered through indirect channels thus resulting in reduced channel distribution costs and a better profitability profile for the product or service.

### Activity Based Management

**CIMA definition:**

'System of management which uses activity-based cost information for a variety of purposes including cost reduction, cost modelling and customer profitability analysis.'

ABM is simply using the information derived from an ABC analysis for cost management. ABM seeks to classify each activity within a process as a value-added or non-value-added activity. Non-value-added activities are unnecessary and represent waste. The aim should be to eliminate them. For example, time spent dealing with customer complaints is wasted time, but cannot be reduced until the customers have nothing to complain about!

ABM focuses on activities within a process, decision making and planning relative to those activities and the need for continuous improvement of all organisational activity. Management and staff must determine which activities are critical to success and decide how these are to be clearly defined across all functions.

Everyone must co-operate in defining:

- cost pools;
- cost drivers;
- key performance indicators.

They must be trained and empowered to act; all must be fairly treated and success recognised.

### Outputs from the ABM information system

Organisations that are designing and implementing ABM will find there are five basic information outputs:

(1) **The cost of activities and business processes**. Since activities form the very core of what a business does, the basic output of the ABM system must be to provide relevant cost information about what a business does. Instead of reporting what money is spent for and by whom, costs are assigned to activities.

(2) **The cost of non value-added activities**. Identification of these wasteful activities is invaluable to management as it provides a crucial focal point for management.

(3) **Activity based performance measures**. Knowing the total cost of an activity is insufficient to measure activity performance. Activity measures of quality, cycle time, productivity and customer service may also be required to judge performance. Measuring the performance of activities provides a scorecard to report how well improvement efforts are working and is an integral part of continuous improvement.

(4) **Accurate product/service cost**. Products and services are provided to markets and customers through various distribution channels or contractual relationships. Because products and services consume resources at different rates and require different levels of support, costs must be accurately determined.

(5) **Cost drivers**. The final output from the ABM system is cost driver information. With this information it is possible to understand and manage these activity levels.

ABM can be used in assessing strategic decisions such as:

- whether to continue with a particular activity;
- how cost structures measure up to those of competitors;
- how changes in activities and components affect the suppliers and value chain.

Clearly ABM and employee empowerment takes a critical step forward beyond ABC by recognising the contribution that people make as the key resource in any organisation's success.

- It nurtures good communication and team work.
- It develops quality decision making.
- It leads to quality control and continuous improvement.

ABM will not reduce costs, it will only help the manager understand costs better.

Strategic activity management recognises that individual activities are part of a wider process. Activities are grouped to form a total process or service. For example, serving a particular customer involves a number of discrete activities that form the total service. Strategic activity management attempts to classify each activity within the whole as a value-added or non-value-added activity. Non-value-added activities are unnecessary and should be eliminated.

Bellis-Jones (1992) noted that typically prior to the introduction of ABM 35 per cent of staff time was spent on diversionary (non-value-added) activities. After the introduction of ABM, total staff time declined and the percentage of time spent on diversionary activities fell to 20 per cent of the reduced time.

Non-value-added activities are often caused by inadequacies within the existing processes and cannot be eliminated unless the inadequacy is addressed. For example, dealing with customer complaints is a diversionary activity, but it cannot be eliminated unless the source of the complaints is eliminated. Another example is machine set-up time. Better product design so that fewer components or more standard components are used will reduce the set-up time between component runs. So management must concentrate on eliminating non-value-added activities.

But strategic activity management is more than just eliminating non-value-added activities, important though this is.

By identifying the cost and value drivers for each activity, the firm can develop both the activities and the linkages between them, and so better differentiate the firm from its competitors. In addition, by understanding the factors which influence the costs of each activity, the firm can take action to minimize those costs in the medium term. ABC information can be used in an ABM system to assist strategic decisions, such as:

(1) Whether to continue with a particular activity.

(2) The effect on cost structure of a change in strategy, e.g. from mass production to smaller lots.

(3) How changes in activities and components affect the suppliers and the value chain.

The value chain is simply a large activity map for the organisation and its position in the industry chain. The chart below is a modified version of Porter's generic value chain. It consists of the main activities both primary (which should add value) and support (potentially non-value-adding unless they aid the primary activities to created more value-added). The organisation's value chain can be linked with other organisations' value chains to form an industry value chain.

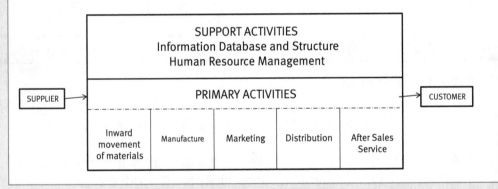

## 6 Problems With Implementing ABC / ABM

Much has been written in academic journals of the benefits of using ABC and ABM. The majority of organisations still do not use either. Why, if the majority of academics consider it to be so useful, do practitioners not employ ABC?

The obvious reason is that they do not agree on its usefulness or cost effectiveness in terms of costs and benefits. For ABC to be effective an accurate system is required with as many as 50 different activities identified and costs attributed to them. This requires considerable time and effort.

A certain amount of research has focused on the problems of implementing the system. Friedman and Lyne (1999) provide some clues as to why ABC has not been taken up with more enthusiasm from case study research they carried out. Some reasons they draw attention to are:

(1) Where it was devised for a single project that was not taken up the system got dropped as well. As communication between business units in a large organisation is often not very good, the work was not developed further by other units.

(2) Finance department opposed its implementation. Often finance staff appear less than dynamic and unable to perceive the needs of the production staff.

(3) General ledger information too poor to provide reliable ABC information. The resulting figures would have been no better than traditional absorption methods.

Of course, if organisations do not have reliable ABC information then they also forgo the cost management advantages of an ABM system. Since ABC provides the basic building blocks of activities, without ABC there can be no ABM.

### Illustration – ABC and ABM

**Tool of the trade**

*Financial Management; London; Nov 2001; Stephanie Gourdie;*

A company in New Zealand is one of the few to have implemented activity-based management successfully but it needed careful planning and a radical rethink of company culture.

Since professors Robin Cooper and Robert Kaplan codified and developed activity-based costing , many organisations have implemented it, but few are using it for cost management. The original emphasis of ABC was on developing more accurate product costs. It was based on the principle that resource-consuming activities caused costs, not volume of products, as assumed by traditional cost-allocation methods. Overhead costs were allocated and traced back to activities that consumed resources, such as purchasing, set-ups and material handling.

A cost driver was then selected for each activity centre. The choice of driver was based on two things: it had to measure the resources a product used for a particular set of activities; and it had to be linked to the changes of costs in the activity centre (cause-effect relationship).

Cost drivers can include the number of purchase orders, material movements or setup hours. The overhead rate for each activity was worked out by dividing the activity cost by the capacity of the cost driver. The costs of products were determined by multiplying the number of the cost driver of the activity used by the product, by the overhead rate for that activity, for all activities used by that product.

ABC systems could then be applied to cost management. This was labelled activity based management (ABM), defined by Don Hansen and Maryanne Mowen as "a system-wide, integrated approach that focuses management's attention on activities with the objective of improving customer value and the profit achieved by providing this value".

The progress to ABM involved a shift in focus from the original ABC system – producing information on activity-based product costs to producing information to improve management of processes. The idea is to analyse the activities that make up a company's processes and the cost drivers of those activities, then question why the activities are being carried out and how well they are being performed. ABM provides the activity information and the costs of inefficient activities, and quantifies the benefits of continuous improvements.

Companies can then improve operations by re-engineering (complete redesign of processes), redesigning plant layouts, using common parts, outsourcing or strengthening supplier and customer relationships and developing alternative product designs.

Research on the implementation of ABC in Europe, shows that adoption of ABM remains low. One organisation in New Zealand has used ABM to improve the way it manages some of its processes, to get rid of non-value added activities and to reduce costs substantially through efficiencies. It has achieved this by following certain "dos and don'ts" in implementing accounting systems.

The organisation provides information services, record-keeping, testing, research and advisory services for New Zealand's agriculture sector. Its mission is to lead the world with its research and create wealth for its stakeholders, and its profit objective is to have enough resources to fund research and development. It has been through the same changes, including restructuring, that many New Zealand public sector organisations went through in the 1980s.

The drive to implement ABM began with calls for more efficiency and accountability and a need to be seen to have efficient business practices and be more customer-orientated. The emphasis was on efficiency, total quality and effectiveness – all of which were in the firm's mission statements and business plans.

The board constantly requested more information and ABM offered the management accounting team a way of providing better quality service. But ABM was a major undertaking and the team had to proceed carefully.

ABM required a major investment in time and resources. Apart from the cost of the software, staff had to be taken away from their existing jobs and trained to set up and use the system. The activity analysis stage, for example, was long and sometimes arduous: it took three people nine months to implement.

Since ABM's introduction, the models have been reviewed annually for budgets and actuals and updated for budgets, forecasts and actuals. This process takes three people between five and 10 weeks depending on the number and complexity of process changes.

Managers had to be clear about the potential benefits of ABM and what information the organisation wanted. Members of the management accounting team attended seminars and investigated several packages. They knew they wanted more than just an ABC package. They needed to establish product profitability, improve distribution of overheads, activities and costs of processes and find out how to improve these.

The organisation's clients, who were also its shareholders, believed they had the right to query prices. So the system had to provide information about the relationship between prices and costs. It also needed an integrated decision support system that could carry out business process efficiency simulations.

There are plans to extend the system to include calculations of customer profitability, activity-based budgeting, and the balanced scorecard. The balanced scorecard "translates an organisation's mission and strategy into operational objectives and performance measures for four different perspectives: the financial perspective; the customer perspective; the internal business process perspective; and the learning and growth perspective'. In other words, activities carried out in an organisation should be linked to its strategic objectives.

The next step was to decide which model to use. Some organisations operate standalone ABM systems using either spreadsheets or third-party packaged software. Others integrate the system in their wider information systems. The maximum business advantage cannot be achieved until ABM is an integral part of an organisation's reporting system.

The New Zealand organisation chose a software package that could map the process. This approach would suit any organisation with inputs, demands, processes and constrained resources. It already had a mainframe database of activity data and a separate accounting system. The use of dataware-housing allowed summary information from its two systems to be stored and accessed for multidimensional modelling, including accounting models for budgeting ABC costs, ABM information, simulations and forecasting.

It is important to pick a model that emphasises the operational understanding of all activities in the business. Instead of going down the financial decomposition analysis route – which analyses the accounting records of the organisation – the organisation chose the process model approach. This analyses the operations, identifying the key activities and resources consumed, by asking what people do, what resources are consumed and how. From the answers, appropriate activity drivers can be established, as can the inputs and outputs to each activity and the relationship between activities.

Managers gathered data from both operational and financial sources and carried out interviews to find out about processes. Some costs were allocated on traditional cost drivers, such as area, others on transactional cost drivers, such as number of visits by truck or technician. For each cost driver, costs were divided into fixed and variable. Some were more obvious than others and work was done to find an approximate division.

A pilot project was recommended in order to achieve results in six to eight weeks, develop a team of experts and convince managers of the benefits. The pilot chosen had defined inputs and outputs and was contained with simple and clear process flows. There was also clear output from each activity.

First, the project mapped the process showing different activities outside the ABM software. This procedure was useful as it helped the "mapper" to understand the components of the process and how they interacted. The pilot study initially involved high-level mapping but, with hindsight, it would have been easier if it had been less detailed.

A key point is to involve people other than just the management accounting team. The model approach enables this because much of the original information must be obtained from people in the field. So the organisation used the management accounting team to implement the system, but seconded members from the field to use local expertise.

As part of the new system, ownership of cost management had to be transferred from the accounting department to the departments and processes where costs were incurred. Some units were not happy about this, but since there was a shift in performance criteria so divisional managers' salaries depended on results, they were motivated to make it work. Perceptions of how different departments in the company worked had not changed, so staff did not feel threatened. People were keen to contribute, perhaps because of the good relationship between management accounts and other staff.

Agreement was obtained on criteria for measuring overheads and it turned out to be pretty straightforward to put numbers to activities and capacity levels. Tests showed that figures were generally reasonable and it is unlikely that investing far more time and resources would have made them significantly more accurate. Reports and graphs were prepared for each division so they could monitor their progress.

Implementing ABM meant a change in the culture of the whole organisation. It had to change from a public-sector-style company into a commercial enterprise (there is still ambivalence about how much profit it should make). The firm also had to worry about budgets and costs for the first time – it had never before had management accounting systems for cost management and budgeting.

Transition to the ABM system had to be gradual. First, the firm developed a cash objective budget system. From this, it built a simple ABC system model. Few products were dropped and the firm still expected to make a profit or break even. Economic conditions and other external factors were taken into account since there was a high proportion of fixed costs, but the new ABM philosophy made it clear to managers that the size of the "cake" was fixed.

The information from the ABM system was used to show managers where divisions were unprofitable. It was left to them to cut costs and become more efficient. At the moment, part of the general divisional managers' salaries is performance-related, but the aim is to extend this to more layers of management. Managers and staff are more aware of their portfolios.

Reports are made to the board twice a year, so the accounting system is particularly important. The first report is for the budget, detailed forecast and product profitability, and the second for actual compared with previous. The forecasting and budgeting processes both take two months. In January, managers are asked for their capital budgeting requirements and forecasts for the year until the end of May. Departments meet the following February to finalise their budgets. Budgets are completed by mid-April and the dollars are fed into the ABM model.

Senior managers have also had to change focus. The new system gives them more information about what is going on in divisions and they have had to adjust their management practices accordingly. The systems did create some concern about how big a slice of cake people would have, and operational divisions now question expenditure on overheads.

The organisation needed to link ABM to corporate objectives in the form of increased product profitability and improved value for customers. Performance measures for divisional managers included ABM improvements. Introducing ABM was not seen as a cost-cutting exercise and the processes were seen to be important and effective at meeting the needs of customers.

Overall, ABM was used to ensure the organisation was doing the thing right. The introduction of the balanced scorecard will ensure it is also doing the right thing.

**TIPS FOR ABM**

- Get the support of senior management
- Recognise that ABM requires a major investment in time and resources
- Know what ABM can achieve and what information you want from the system
- Decide which model to use
- Choose the model approach that emphasises the operational understanding of all activities in the business
- Involve people in the field
- Transfer ownership of cost management from the accounts department to the departments and processes where costs are incurred
- Don't underestimate the need to manage the change process
- Link ABM to corporate objectives in the form of increased product profitability and added value for customers.

## 7 Pareto Analysis

Pareto analysis is based on the 80:20 rule that was a phenomenon first observed by Vilfredo Pareto, a nineteenth century Italian economist. He noticed that 80 per cent of the wealth of Milan was owned by 20 per cent of its citizens:

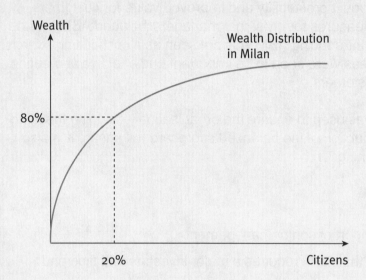

This phenomenon, or some kind of approximation of it (70:30, etc.), can be observed in many different business situations. The management accountant can use it in a number of different circumstances to help direct management's attention to the key control mechanisms or planning aspects.

The Pareto phenomenon often shows itself in relation to profitability. Often around 80 per cent of an organisation's contribution is generated by 20 per cent of the revenue. A situation similar to this can be seen in the figure below, where the contributions of five products are plotted on a cumulative basis. Twenty per cent of the sales revenue generates 80 per cent of the contribution:

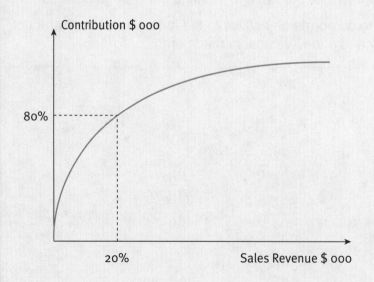

It is not always advisable to delete products from the range if they are not very profitable or their price cannot be increased, without carrying out careful analysis. The poor performers may be new products establishing themselves in the market and they may have a profitable future. However, the products that generate the largest proportion of the contribution need to be looked after. One reason for their profitability may be a high degree of branding which increases the contribution margin per unit. The company must continue to spend money promoting the brand so as to keep it in front of the public.

## Uses of Pareto analysis

Pareto analysis has a number of different uses in business; some of these are described below.

Instead of analysing products, customers can be analysed for their relative profitability to the organisation. Again, it is often found that approximately 20 per cent of customers generate 80 per cent of the profit. There will always be some customers who are less profitable than others, just as some products are less profitable than others. The key with customers is to make sure that the overall profile does not degenerate and the aim should be to improve the profile. This can be seen in the figure below, where the solid line represents the present position and the two dotted lines represent a change in performance for the better and worse. The 'better profile' dotted line shows improved performance in the sense that customers are contributing more evenly to the profit, thus stabilising the position of the organisation. With the 'worse profile', the loss of, say, two of the best customers might seriously jeopardise the organisation's future :

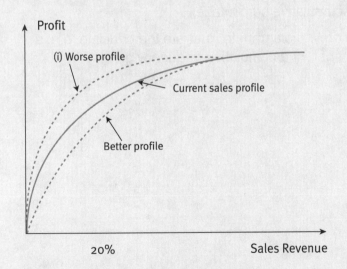

Another use for Pareto analysis is in inventory control where it may be found that only a few of the goods in inventory make up most of the value. A typical analysis of inventory may reveal the situation shown as follows:

| Product | Value | % of value | % of volume | Action |
|---------|-------|-----------|-------------|--------|
| A | High value | 70% | 10 | Control carefully |
| B | Medium value | 20% | 20 | Medium control |
| C | Little value | 10% | 70 | No control |

The outcome of this type of analysis may be to increase control and safeguards on the 10 per cent of the inventory that is of a particularly high value and to remove or reduce the controls on the inventory that is of little value. Alternatively it may be found that a few items take up most of the storage space and therefore storage costs are unduly high for these items. It may be possible to move towards a just-in-time system for these items only, thus saving money and space.

Another study might relate to activity-based costing and overheads. **It may show that 20 per cent of an organisation's cost drivers are responsible for 80 per cent of the total cost**. By analysing, monitoring and controlling those cost drivers that cause most cost, a better control and understanding of overheads will be obtained.

### Procedure

(1)  Rank the data in descending order.

(2)  Find each figure as a percentage of the total.

(3)  Turn this into a cumulative percentage.

(4)  It is possible to draw a diagram to illustrate the principle, e.g. a component bar chart or a cumulative frequency graph.

## e.g | Pareto Analysis and Charts

ABC Limited manufactures and sells seven products. The following data relates to the latest period:

| Product | Contribution in $000 |
|---------|---------------------|
| P | 96 |
| Q | 36 |
| R | 720 |
| S | 240 |
| T | 12 |
| U | 6 0 |
| V | 24 |
| | 1,188 |

To prepare a Pareto chart of product contribution and comment on the results, the first step is to rearrange the products in descending order of contribution and calculate the cumulative contribution:

| Product | Contribution in $ | Cumulative Contribution in $000 | Cumulative % |
|---------|------------------|-------------------------------|--------------|
| R | 720 | 720 | 61 |
| S | 240 | 960 | 81 |
| P | 96 | 1,056 | 89 |
| U | 60 | 1,116 | 94 |
| Q | 36 | 1,152 | 97 |
| V | 24 | 1,176 | 99 |
| T | 12 | 1,188 | 100 |
| | 1,188 | | |

The cumulative data can now be used to produce the required Pareto chart showing product contribution:

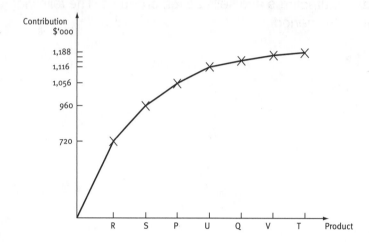

The analysis shows that more than 80 per cent of the total contribution is earned by two products: R and S. The position of these products needs protecting, perhaps through careful attention to branding and promotion. The other products require investigation to see whether their contribution can be improved through increased prices, reduced costs or increased volumes.

The term 'Pareto diagram' usually refers to a histogram or frequency chart on product quality – see figure below. In the 1950s Juran observed that a few causes of poor quality usually accounted for most of the quality problems – hence the name Pareto. The figure below shows a frequency chart for poor quality in boxed cakes, and it can easily be imagined how it could be turned into a Pareto chart.

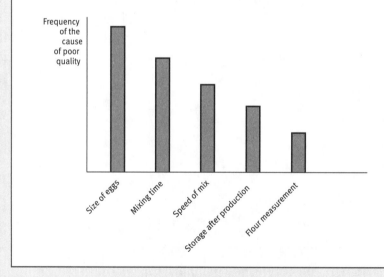

The purpose of the analysis, in this case, is to direct attention to the area where the best returns can be achieved by solving most of the quality problems, perhaps just with a single action. In this case more accurate grading of eggs by volume by the supplier may solve about 40 per cent of the total quality problem and if the mixing time is made more accurate at least 75 per cent of the problems will be removed.

## Example 3 – Pareto analysis

Green Fingers Ltd is a gardening centre.

Some financial details of broad product categories within the gardening centre for the last year are given below:

| Product | Sales $000 | Variable costs $000 | Contribution $000 |
|---|---|---|---|
| Tables and chairs | 340 | 328 | 12 |
| Sheds | 200 | 154 | 46 |
| Barbecue equipment | 140 | 120 | 20 |
| Garden seats | 120 | 103 | 17 |
| Pavilions | 70 | 41 | 29 |
| Gates | 50 | 37 | 13 |
| Lawnmowers | 30 | 22 | 8 |
| Tools, toys etc. | 15 | 14 | 1 |
| Cafe | 5 | 2 | 3 |

(a) Using the financial data, carry out a Pareto analysis (80/20 rule), including a suitable diagram, of

    (i)   sales; and

    (ii)  contribution.

(b) State your findings in a brief management report.

## 8 Practice Questions

### Test your understanding 1 – Retail organisation

RS plc is a retail organisation. It has 15 supermarkets, all of which are the same size. Goods are transported to RS plc's central warehouse by suppliers' vehicles and are stored at the warehouse until needed at the supermarkets – at which point they are transported by RS plc's lorries. RS plc's costs are:

|  | £000 |
|---|---|
| Warehouse costs, per week |  |
| Labour costs | 220 |
| Refrigeration costs | 160 |
| Other direct product costs | 340 |
|  | 720 |
|  |  |
| Head office costs, per week |  |
| Labour costs | 80 |
| Other costs | 76 |
|  | 156 |
|  |  |
| Supermarket costs, per week |  |
| Labour costs | 16 |
| Refrigeration costs | 24 |
| Other direct product costs | 28 |
|  | 68 |

|  | £ |
|---|---|
| Transport costs per trip |  |
| Standard vehicles | 3,750 |
| Refrigerated vehicles | 4,950 |

The company has always used retail sales revenue less bought-in price to calculate the relative profitability of the different products. However, the chief executive is not happy with this method and has asked for three products – baked beans, ice cream and South African white wine – to be costed on a direct product profit basis. The accountant has determined the following information for the supermarket chain.

| | Baked beans | Ice cream | White wine |
|---|---|---|---|
| No. of cases per cubic metre (m³) | 28 | 24 | 42 |
| No. of items per case | 80 | 18 | 12 |
| Sales per week – items | 15,000 | 2,000 | 500 |
| Time in warehouse – weeks | 1 | 2 | 4 |
| Time in supermarket – weeks | 1 | 2 | 2 |
| Retail selling price per item | £0.32 | £1.60 | £3.45 |
| Bought-in price per item | £0.24 | £0.95 | £2.85 |

Additional information:

| | |
|---|---|
| Total volume of all goods sold per week | 20,000 m³ |
| Total volume of refrigerated goods sold per week | 5,000 m³ |
| Carrying volume of each vehicle | 90 m³ |
| Total sales revenue per week | £5m |
| Total sales revenue of refrigerated goods per week | £650,000 |

**Required:**

(a) Calculate the profit per item using the direct product profitability method.

**(13 marks)**

(b) Discuss the differences in profitability between the company's current method and the results of your calculations in (a) and suggest ways in which profitability could be improved.

**(7 marks)**

(c) Explain how the direct product profit method differs from traditional overhead absorption.

**(5 marks)**

**(Total: 25 marks)**

### ABM and Product Life Cycle

Companies operating in an advanced manufacturing environment are finding that about 90 per cent of a product's life cycle cost is determined by decisions made early in the cycle. Management accounting systems should therefore be developed that aid the planning and control of product life cycle costs and monitor spending at the early stages of the life cycle.

*(Statement paraphrased from a well-known accounting text)*

**Required:**

Having regard to the above statement:

(a) explain the nature of the product life cycle concept and its impact on businesses operating in an advanced manufacturing environment;

(b) explain **life cycle costing** and state what distinguishes it from more traditional management accounting practices;

(c) compare and contrast **life cycle budgeting** with **activity-based management**; identify and comment on any themes that the two practices have in common.

### Test your understanding 2 – ABC and Retail

Explain how Activity-Based Costing may be used in a retail environment to improve the decision making and profitability of the business.

### Casamia

Casamia plc purchases a range of good quality gift and household products from around the world; it then sells these products through 'mail order' or retail outlets. The company receives 'mail orders' by post, telephone and Internet. Retail outlets are either department stores or Casamia plc's own small shops. The company started to set up its own shops after a recession in the early 1990s and regards them as the flagship of its business; sales revenue has gradually built up over the last 10 years. There are now 50 department stores and 10 shops.

The company has made good profits over the last few years but recently trading has been difficult. As a consequence, the management team has decided that a fundamental reappraisal of the business is now necessary if the company is to continue trading.

Meanwhile the budgeting process for the coming year is proceeding. Casamia Products plc uses an activity-based costing (ABC) system and the following estimated cost information for the coming year is available:

**Retail outlet costs:**

| | | | Per Year | |
|---|---|---|---|---|
| Activity | Cost driver | Rate per cost driver | Department store | Own shop |
| Telephone queries and request to Casamia | Calls | $15 | 40 calls | 350 calls |
| Sales visits to shops and stores by Casamia sales staff | Visits | $250 | 2 visits | 4 visits |
| Shop orders | Orders | $20 | 25 orders | 150 orders |
| Packaging | Deliveries | $100 | 28 deliveries | 150 deliveries |
| Delivery to shops | Deliveries | $150 | 28 deliveries | 150 deliveries |

Staffing, rental and service costs for each of Casamia plc's own shops cost on average $300,000 a year.

**Mail order costs:**

| | | Rate per cost driver | | |
|---|---|---|---|---|
| Activity | Cost driver | Post | Telephone | Internet |
| Processing 'mail orders' | Orders | $5 | $6 | $3 |
| Dealing with 'mail order' queries | Orders | $4 | $4 | $1 |
| | | Number of packages per order | | |
| Packaging and deliveries for 'mail orders' – cost per package $10 | Packages | 2 | 2 | 1 |

The total number of orders through the whole 'mail order' business for the coming year is expected to be 80,000. The maintenance of the Internet link is estimated to cost $80,000 for the coming year. The following additional information for the coming year has been prepared:

|  | Department Store | Own shop | Post | Telephone | Internet |
|---|---|---|---|---|---|
| Sales revenue per outlet | $50,000 | $1,000,000 |  |  |  |
| Sales revenue per order |  |  | $150 | $300 | $100 |
| Gross margin: mark-up on purchase costs | 30% | 40% | 40% | 40% | 40% |
| Number of outlets | 50 | 10 |  |  |  |
| Percentage of 'mail orders' |  |  | 30% | 60% | 10% |

## Expected Head Office and warehousing costs for the coming year:

|  | $ |
|---|---|
| Warehouse | 2,750,000 |
| IT | 550,000 |
| Administration | 750,000 |
| Personnel | 300,000 |
|  | **4,350,000** |

## Required:

(a) (i)  Prepare calculations that will show the expected profitability of the different types of sales outlet for the coming year, and comment briefly on the results of the figures you have prepared.

(b)  In relation to the company's fundamental reappraisal of its business:

    (i)  discuss how helpful the information you have prepared in (a) is for this purpose and how it might be revised or expanded so that it is of more assistance;

    (ii)  advise what other information is needed in order to make a more informed judgement.

**Mini-Quiz**

(1) Which of the following is a correct definition of activity-based management?

   A   An approach to the costing and monitoring of activities which involves tracing resource consumption and costing final outputs. Resources are assigned to activities and activities to cost objects based on consumption estimates. The latter utilise cost drivers to attach activity costs to outputs

   B   The identification and evaluation of the activity drivers used to trace the cost of activities to cost objects. It may also involve selecting activity drivers with potential to contribute to the cost management function with particular reference to cost reduction

   C   A method of budgeting based on an activity framework and utilising cost driver data in the budget-setting and variance feedback processes

   D   A system of management which uses activity-based cost information for a variety of purposes including cost reduction, cost modelling and customer profitability analysis

   E   A grouping of all cost elements associated with an activity.

(2) In an ABC system, which of the following is likely to be classified as a batch level activity?

   A   Machine set-up

   B   Product design

   C   Inspection of every item produced

   D   Production manager's work

   E   Advertising

(3) AB plc is a supermarket group which incurs the following costs:

  (i)  the bought-in price of the good;

  (ii)  inventory financing costs;

  (iii) shelf refilling costs;

  (iv) costs of repacking or 'pack out' prior to storage before sale.

AB plc's calculation of direct product profit (DPP) would include:

A   all of the above costs

B   all of the above costs except (ii)

C   all of the above costs except (iv)

D   costs (i) and (iii) only

E   cost (i) only

# Test your understanding answers

## Example 1

Warehouse cost $75,000 ÷ 10,000 = $7.50 per m$^3$

Supermarket cost $40,000 ÷ 5,000 = $8.00 per m$^3$

Transportation cost $400 ÷ 40 = $10 per m$^3$

|  | Kitchen roll $ | Tinned spaghetti $ | Tooth paste $ |
|---|---|---|---|
| Retail price | 1.00 | 0.60 | 1.75 |
| Less bought-in price | (0.60) | (0.30 | (1.00) |
| Gross margin | 0.40 | 0.30 | 0.75 |
| Less overheads: |  |  |  |
| Warehouse costs (see workings) | 0.0375 | 0.02 | 0.0281 |
| Supermarket costs (see workings) | 0.08 | 0.0427 | 0.02 |
| Transportation costs (see workings) | 0.05 | 0.0133 | 0.0125 |
| **Net profit** | **0.2325** | **0.2240** | **0.6894** |

**Workings**

| Number of items per m$^3$ | 10 × 20 = 200 | 25 × 30 = 750 | 40 × 20 = 800 |
|---|---|---|---|

*Warehouse charge:*

Kitchen roll ($7.50 ÷ 200) x 1 week = 0.0375

Tinned spaghetti ($7.50 ÷ 750) x 2 weeks = 0.02 etc

*Supermarket cost:*

Kitchen roll ($8.00 ÷ 200) x 2 weeks = 0.08

Tinned spaghetti ($8.00 ÷ 7.50) x 4 weeks = 0.0427 etc

## Example 2

| | A $ | B $ | C $ | D $ |
|---|---|---|---|---|
| Revenue net of discount | 15,000 | 18,400 | 21,000 | 15,400 |
| Costs: | | | | |
| Sales visits | 420 | 840 | 1,260 | 630 |
| Order placing | 1,800 | 1,200 | 2,400 | 1,200 |
| Product handling | 6,000 | 8,000 | 10,000 | 7,000 |
| Delivery | 400 | 900 | 500 | 1,400 |
| Rush delivery | – | – | 200 | 400 |
| | | | | |
| Total cost | 8,620 | 10,940 | 14,360 | 10,630 |
| Profit | 6,380 | 7,460 | 6,640 | 4,770 |

## Example 3 – Pareto analysis

(a) (i)   Step 1: Calculate total Sales: $970,000

Step 2: Calculate %age of sales for each item, and cumulative: we will need to get to a total of 100%

**Pareto analysis of sales**

| Product | Sales in $000 | % of total sales | Cumulative total% |
|---|---|---|---|
| Tables and chairs | 340 | 35 | 35 |
| Sheds | 200 | 21 | 56 |
| Barbecue equipment | 140 | 14 | 70 |
| Garden seats | 120 | 12 | 82 |
| Pavilions | 70 | 8 | 90 |
| Gate: | 50 | 5 | 95 |
| Lawn mowers | 30 | 3 | 98 |
| Tools, toy: etc. | 15 | 1 | 99 |
| Cafe | 5 | 1 | 100 |
| | | | |
| | 970 | | 100% |

80% of 970 = 776.  This is within the first four product groups.

## (ii) Pareto analysis of contribution

| Product | Contribution £000 | % of total | % |
|---|---|---|---|
| Sheds | 46 | 31 | 31 |
| Pavilions | 29 | 19 | 50 |
| Barbecue equipment | 20 | 14 | 64 |
| Garden seats | 17 | 11 | 75 |
| Gate: | 13 | 9 | 84 |
| Tables & chairs | 12 | 8 | 92 |
| Lawn mowers | 8 | 5 | 97 |
| Cafe | 3 | 2 | 99 |
| Tools, toy: etc. | 1 | 1 | 100 |
| | 149 | | |

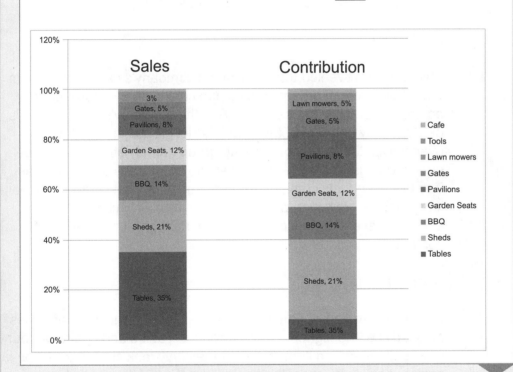

(b) **Report on the Pareto analysis of sales and contribution**

To:            All Managers

From:          Management Accountant

Date:          29/4/01

*Terms of reference:*

A report was requested by the sales and marketing director reviewing the company's product groups in terms of sales and contribution.

*Procedure:*

A Pareto analysis (80/20 rule) was carried out.

*Findings:*

The analysis revealed that 80% of the company's sales derive from four of the product groups: tables and chairs, sheds, barbecue equipment and garden seats. 80% of the company's contribution is generated by only five of the nine product groups, three of which overlap with the 'sales' generating group namely sheds, barbecue equipment, garden seats, the other two being pavilions and gates. The three products common to both groups obviously represent our key products. However, pavilions, which rank only fifth in terms of sales, represent our second most important product in terms of contribution.

*Recommendations:*

It would seem appropriate to concentrate our promotional activities on sheds i.e. the highest-margin product. Tables and chairs are our most popular selling item, however they only rank sixth in terms of contribution. A review of the pricing structure of these products may therefore be worth pursuing.

## Test your understanding 1 – Retail organisation

(a) Exclude head office costs – do not relate to products.

### Direct product profitability statement

|  |  | Baked beans | Ice cream | White wine |
|---|---|---|---|---|
| Warehouse costs per m³ |  |  |  |  |
| Labour and other costs (£) | (W1) | 28 | 56 | 112 |
| Refrigeration costs (£) | (W2) |  | 64 |  |
|  |  |  |  |  |
| Supermarket costs per m³ |  |  |  |  |
| Labour and other costs (£) | (W3) | 33 | 66 | 66 |
| Refrigeration costs (£) | (W4) |  | 144 |  |
|  |  |  |  |  |
| Transport costs per m³ |  |  |  |  |
| Standard vehicles (£) | (W5) | 41.67 |  | 41.67 |
| Refrigerated vehicles (£) | (W6) |  | 55 |  |
| Total DPP costs per m³ (£) |  | 102.67 | 385 | 219.67 |
| Items per m³ | (W7) | 2240 | 432 | 504 |
| Cost per item (£) |  | (0.046) | (0.891) | (0.436) |
| Gross profit per item (£) | (W8) | 0.08 | 0.65 | 0.60 |
| Direct product profit (£) |  | 0.034 | (0.241) | 0.164 |

**Note:** Head office costs should not be charged to products – they do not relate to products in any way.

### Workings:

(W1) Labour and other costs per m³ per week = (£220,000 + £340,000)/20,000 = £28

Ice cream is in the warehouse for two weeks, therefore cost per m³ = £56

White wine is in the warehouse for four weeks, therefore cost per m³ = £112

(W2) Refrigeration costs per $m^3$ per week =£160,000/5,000 = £32

Ice cream is in the warehouse for two weeks, therefore cost per $m^3$ = £64

(W3) Labour and other costs supermarket per week = £16,000 + £28,000 = £44,000

15 supermarkets, therefore total cost per week = 15 × £44,000 = £660,000

Cost per $m^3$ per week = £660,000/20,000 = £33

Ice cream and white wine are in the supermarket for two weeks, therefore cost per $m^3$ = £66

(W4) Refrigeration cost per supermarket per week = £24,000 x 15 supermarkets = £360,000

Cost per $m^3$ per week = £360,000/5,000 = £72

Total cost per $m^3$ for two weeks = £144

(W5) Transport costs per standard vehicle per $m^3$ = 3,750/90 = £41.67

(W6) Transport costs per refrigerated vehicle per $m^3$ = 4,950/90 = £55

(W7) Number of items per $m^3$ = cases per $m^3$ × items per case

| | | |
|---|---|---|
| Baked beans | = 28 × 80 | = 2240 |
| Ice cream | = 24 × 18 | = 432 |
| White wine | = 42 × 12 | = 504 |

(W8) Gross profit = retail selling price per item – buying in price per item

(b)

| | Baked beans | Ice cream | White wine |
|---|---|---|---|
| Current gross margin | £0.08 | £0.65 | £0.60 |
| DPP margin | £0.034 | (£0.241) | £0.164 |

Before DPP all products appear profitable. Ice cream has the biggest margin.

After DPP ice cream appears to lose money.

DPP takes into account all costs that relate to items:

- reflects refrigeration, transportation, warehouse costs;
- makes managers aware of costs previously 'hidden', e.g. refrigeration plus space taken up in warehouse;
- to reduce costs reduce turnover times – times spent in warehouse and on supermarket shelves;
- ice cream – bulky item, does not have a high profit margin or selling price per $m^3$;
- need to push products with best profit per $m^3$.

Units per $m^3$    $80 \times 28 = 2,240$     $18 \times 24 = 432$     $42 \times 12 = 504$

| | *Baked beans* | | *Ice cream* | | **White wine** | |
|---|---|---|---|---|---|---|
| | *Per unit* | *Total* | *Per unit* | *Total* | *Per unit* | *Total* |
| Revenue per $m^3$ in store | £0.32 | **£716.80** | £1.60 | **£691.20** | £3.45 | **1,738.8** |
| Cost per $m^3$ | £0.286 | **(£640.64)** | £1.841 | **(£795.31)** | £3.286 | **(£1,656.4)** |
| Profit/ (Loss) per $m^3$ | £0.034 | **£76.16** | (£0.241) | **(£104.11)** | £0.164 | **£82.66** |

This information may help managers use floor space more effectively, e.g. use space to sell wine. Helps managers decide where to place products. Better cost analysis, better pricing decisions, management of warehouses.

(c) With traditional absorption costing, all costs including administration and head office costs are charged to a product. These unrelated costs are charged using a fairly arbitrary absorption rate. Hence, the full cost per unit using traditional absorption costing will often fail to reflect the true (relevant) cost of the item. The full cost per unit will reveal very little useful information and it should not be used in any decisions concerning the product.

Direct product profitability, however, strives to only charge related costs to the products. It also aims to ascertain a fair cost of each item. The profit per unit using DPP analysis should give some idea of the actual profit earned by that product.

DPP is similar to activity-based costing in its objectives.

### ABM and Product Life Cycle

(a) When a product is first successfully introduced to the market, supported by an expensive advertising campaign, it will only achieve a relatively low sales volume. In an Advanced Manufacturing Technology (AMT) environment, a very large amount of fixed cost will already have been incurred in R&D, designing the product and building or re-equipping the production line.

In the growth stage, sales increase and unit costs fall as the high fixed costs per unit decrease. Although new entrants may start to compete at this stage, this is the most profitable stage of the PLC.

The product is said to be mature when sales demand levels off. In a static market, price competition will reduce the profitability of each firm. Firms will seek to differentiate their product at this stage.

Eventually, the product will become obsolete and falling sales will ensue. This is the decline phase of the PLC. Firms will begin to pull out of the market or focus on promotional marketing strategies and reduce selling price. Before this stage is reached, the firm must have developed a replacement product, thereby incurring further large fixed costs for R&D, design and new production facilities.

In AMT environments, the time period for the product life cycle is decreasing. For example, the longest life cycle for a mass-produced motor car has reduced from over four decades for both the VW Beetle and the Morris Minor to less than 25 years for the Renault 5, which ceased production in 1996. However, most models must be renewed in much shorter timeframes. Vauxhall is setting up new production facilities for manufacturing a revamped Corsa in the UK. The Corsa was launched only a few years ago. The PLC concept enables clear strategic planning regarding the development of new products, cash flows and marketing activities.

(b) Life cycle costing (LCC) involves collecting cost data for each product from inception, through its useful life and including any end costs. These data are compared with the life cycle budgeted costs for the product. This comparison will show if the expected savings from using new technology or production methods, etc., have been realised.

The recognition of the total support required over the life of the product should lead to a more effective allocation of resources and is therefore an improvement on traditional budgeting which focuses on financial years, rather than product life span.

There is also a change in cost focus. LCC gathers costs for each product, whereas traditional costing methods follow costs by function, for example, R&D, production, marketing and so on. Thus, for manufacturers, LCC makes explicit the relationship between design choice and production and marketing costs. The insights gained from comparing budgeted and actual life cycle costs may be used to refine future decisions.

LCC may be used by consumers as well as producers. A recent analysis has shown that the life cycle cost of purchasing a personal computer (PC) is around six times the purchase cost. Staff training and extra software will cost three times the cost of the PC and maintenance will cost twice the purchase cost over the life of the PC. It has been recognised in AMT environments that up to 90 per cent of the costs incurred throughout a product's life cycle will be determined before the product reaches the market. Thus, the early decisions regarding product design and production method are paramount and LCC attempts to recognise this situation.

The high fixed cost of introducing a new product coupled with reduced life cycle periods is a major challenge to profitability in AMT environments. LCC is a technique that may be used to improve management decision making in such conditions.

(c) Activity-based management (ABM) uses the understanding of cost drivers found from activity based costing (ABC) to make more informed decisions. In particular, this approach yields a better understanding of overhead costs in AMT environments compared to traditional absorption methods. ABM aims to improve performance by:

(1) eliminating waste;

(2) minimising cost drivers;

(3) emulating best practice; and

(4) I considering how the use of resources supports both operational and strategic decisions.

Thus, ABM seeks to consider all the activities performed by the organisation in order to serve a customer or produce a product.

Results of ABM in an AMT environment include:

(1) increased production efficiency;

(2) reduced production costs;

(3) increased throughput; and

(4) increased quality assurance.

These gains may be realised by:

(a) simplified product designs;

(b) more use of common sub-assemblies;

(c) reduced set-up times;

(d) reduced material handling; and

(e) better use of the workforce, for example, multi-skilling.

Thus, ABM is very similar to LCC in some respects. For example, both attempt to increase management understanding of overhead costs, and both consider how the use of resources supports strategic decisions, that is, both look at how resource inputs are used to obtain the required organisational outputs.

In an AMT environment, both methods focus management attention on the need to produce simplified products using common components and common sub-assemblies and to maximise the output from expensive capital investments.

LCC leads to major reviews at the end of the major stages in a product life cycle, whereas ABM is a continuous system that strives to drive down both short-term and long-term costs.

### Test your understanding 2 – ABC and Retail

ABC attempts to charge overhead costs more accurately to the products or services that, directly or indirectly, consume resources and give rise to the expenditure. It does this by charging overhead costs in a way that reflects the activities that influence those costs. The collection of overhead costs is done in the same way as with traditional overhead costing.

The next step is to allocate overhead costs to **cost pools.** There is a cost pool for each activity that consumes significant amounts of resources. Costs in each cost pool might arise in a number of different departments. (Costs are not allocated or apportioned to production and service departments, so in this respect ABC differs significantly from traditional absorption costing.) Examples of resource-consuming activities might be deliveries of goods from warehouses to stores and checking purchases through tills, or for an internet-based retailer, processing customer orders. The selection of cost pools will vary according to the exact nature of the retailer's operations and management's judgement.

For each activity pool, there should be a cost driver. A cost driver is an item or an activity that results in the consumption of resources, and so results in costs being incurred. For the costs in the cost pool, overheads are then allocated to product costs on the basis of a recovery rate per unit of cost driver.

Examples of activity pools and cost drivers in the retail industry could be:

| Activity pool | Cost driver |
|---|---|
| Checkouts | Number of customers |
| Deliveries to stores | Number of deliveries |
| Order processing (for mail order) | Number of orders |

There is no rule governing the identification of cost pools and drivers – this will depend on the nature of the business. For example, in the case of checkout costs, a store may have separate checkouts for baskets and trolleys. The time taken to check out a basket may be much shorter than the time taken for a trolley, and therefore the cost per customer will also be less. The company may decide to separate the costs of the two different types of till into cost pools, with the respective numbers of customers passing through checkouts as the cost driver.

Having established the total costs for an activity pool, and having chosen the cost driver for that pool, a cost per unit of cost driver is then calculated. This is an overhead recovery rate that will be used to allocate overhead costs to products or services, calculated as:

For each activity pool, costs are allocated to products and services, on the basis of:

Units of cost driver used up × Cost per unit of cost driver.
ABC is a form of absorption costing, and so has similarities with traditional absorption costing. However, the cost driver represents the factor that has the greatest influence on the behaviour of costs in the activity pool, and the consumption of resources. For example, if 50% of orders received and processed are for one particular product and there is a cost pool for order handling costs, the product should attract 50% of the total costs of order handling.

ABC can be used to identify activities and costs that are not contributing to the value of the products an organisation makes or the services it provides. The following questions can be asked:

- What is the purpose of this activity?

- Who benefits from the activity, and how?

- Why are so many people needed?

- What might reduce the number of staff needed?

- Why is overtime needed?

ABC can also be used as the basis for one-off exercises to identify activities that do not add value to products or services, or to identify ways in which activities might be re-organised. One-off investigations using ABC analysis are referred to as 'activity-based management'.

There are a number of disadvantages to ABC:

Setting up and operating an ABC system is costly, as the activities in each cost pool have to be monitored and measured. The system should also be reviewed periodically, to check that the selection of activity pools and cost drivers is still appropriate.

There can be a danger of taking the analysis of activities and cost pools to excessive detail. This would add to the complexity of the system, and the cost of operating it. To prevent an ABC system from becoming too complex and expensive, the number of cost pools and cost drivers should be kept to a small and manageable number.

There is a risk that ABC costs will be seen as 100% accurate economic costs of activities. This is not the case. ABC is a form of absorption costing, and although it attempts to trace overhead costs to products and services more accurately, there will inevitably be some element of shared cost apportionment. It is impossible to trace all costs objectively to specific products or services.

Activity based costing can be used as a basis for other areas of financial management:

Activity based management is a 'system of management which uses activity based cost information for a variety of purposes including cost reduction, cost modelling and customer profitability analysis'. (CIMA Official Terminology, 2000) The activity-based approach brings costs out into the open and helps management see what they get for the commitment of resources.

Activity-based budgeting is a method of budgeting based on an activity framework and utilising cost-driven data in the budget setting and variance feedback process.

### Casamia

The volume of data in this question on direct product profitability can appear a bit daunting, at first. The key is to adopt a **systematic approach** to allocating the costs to each type of outlet.

(a) (i) Calculation of net margin per type of outlet:

| | Department Store | Own shop | Post | Telephone | Internet |
|---|---|---|---|---|---|
| | | | **Mail order** | | |
| Sales revenue | 50,000 | 1,000,000 | 150.00 | 300.00 | 100.00 |
| Gross margin[1] (50,000 + 1.30, etc) | 11,538 | 285,714 | 42.86 | 85.71 | 28.57 |
| Less: Staffing etc. | | 300,000 | | | |
| Telephone queries ($15 x 40, etc) | 600 | 5,250 | | | |
| Sales visits ($250 x 2, etc) | 500 | 1,000 | | | |
| Orders ($20 x 25, etc) | 500 | 3,000 | | | |
| Packaging ($100 x 28, etc) | 2,800 | 15,000 | | | |
| Delivery ($150 x 28, etc) | 4,200 | 22,500 | | | |
| Order cost | | | 5.00 | 6.00 | 3.00 |
| Queries | | | 4.00 | 4.00 | 1.00 |
| Packing & delivery ($10 x 2, etc) | | | 20.00 | 20.00 | 10.00 |
| Internet cost[2] | | | | | 10.00 |
| | **8,600** | **346,750** | **29.00** | **30.00** | **24.00** |
| Net margin | 2,938 | (61,036) | 13.86 | 55.71 | 4.57 |
| Net margin/sales | 5.9% | | 9.2% | 18.6% | 4.6% |
| | 4th | 5th | 2nd | 1st | 3rd |

Calculation of total margin for each type of outlet:

| | Department Stores $000 | Own shops $000 | Mail order | | | Total $000 |
| --- | --- | --- | --- | --- | --- | --- |
| | | | Post $000 | Telephone $000 | Internet $000 | |
| Total Revenue | 2,500 | 10,000 | 3,600 | 14,400 | 800 | 31,300 |
| Total Net Margin | 146.90 | (610.36) | 332.64 | 2,674.08 | 36.56 | 2,579.82 |

Notes:

(1) Gross margin calculation for 30% of purchase cost:

$$100 = 0.3X + X$$
$$X = 76.92\%$$
$$0.3\,X = 23.076\%$$
$$\$50,000 \times 23.076\% = \$11.538$$

(2) Total number of mail orders = 80,000, therefore Number of Internet orders = 80,000 x 10% = 8,000

Internet link cost per order = $80,000 / 8,000 orders = $10

(3) Calculation of total revenues and net margins ($000)

| | | Total revenue | | Total net margin |
| --- | --- | --- | --- | --- |
| Department Stores 50 outlets | (x $50,000) | $2,500 | (x 2,938) | 146.9 |
| Own shops 10 outlets | (x $1,000,000) | 10,000 | (x $61,036) | (610.36) |
| Mail order – post 80,000 x 30% = 24,000 orders | (x $150) | 3,600 | (x $13.86) | 332.64 |
| Mail order – telephone 80,000 x 60% = 48,000 orders | (x $300) | 14,400 | (x $55.71) | 2,674.08 |
| Mail order – Internet 80,000 x 10% = 8,000 orders | (x $100) | 800 | (x $4.57) | $36.56 |

(ii) The calculations on the previous page show the following:

(1) Casamia's own shops will make a considerable 'loss'.

(2) The department store sales will not generate as good a profit as the 'mail order' side.

(3) The telephone mail order, that is 46% of the business, will generate 104% of the current total profit.

(4) The Internet business is not particularly profitable in the coming year, but it will presumably grow quite quickly. If this happens, the charge for maintaining the Internet, which is expressed by each order, will presumably decline as it is likely to be a semi-fixed cost.

(b) (i) The calculations show the profitability of the different types of outlet for the coming year only, which is of some use. For example, it shows that S & P's own shops make a considerable loss and it would appear, on the surface, that the company would be better off without them, perhaps transferring the business to franchises within department stores. It also indicates that the emphasis of the business should be switched to the mail order side, as it is more profitable and, in particular, to the telephone section.

However, the latter shows how dangerous this kind of assumption can be because the telephone section may have peaked and, in future, growth in the Internet section may be at the expense of the telephone section. Therefore, decisions about future strategies cannot be made on predicted short-term costs and revenues. Any attempt to do so could prove disastrous. Growth in the market, competitors' moves, customers' needs and requirements must be the basis for any decisions.

The ABC costs could, however, be used to highlight areas for cost reduction and procedural changes which could assist longer-term profitability. ABC is a method for apportioning costs and it suffers from the same defects as every absorption method. In Casamia's case, the analysis does not look very detailed/accurate and so may be little better than a traditional absorption system.

The head office and warehousing costs need to be examined in detail to determine which type of outlet incurs what part of the cost, as these costs may be caused and used more by some types of outlets than others. If this is so, what would happen to cost if one type of outlet was abandoned and others increased in size?

(ii) Other information needed to make a more informed judgement is likely to be

(1) Customers' changing purchasing habits;

(2) Same customer purchases across outlet types, that is, do customers buy from shops and order by telephone;

(3) Competitors' moves;

(4) New entrants into the market – especially in the Internet business;

(5) Future economic conditions;

(6) Exchange rate movements – as some goods are imported;

(7) Increase in disposable income;

(8) The image created by the different types of outlet, that is do their own shops create the brand or company name;

(9) Past data to establish trends.

Then specific information will need to be collected for the fundamental reappraisal of the business. For example, if the decision to close Casamia's own shops was being considered, a detailed study of the interrelationship between outlets should be carried out, as having the products on display in shops might be necessary in order to maintain the high level of telephone orders. For instance, potential customers may visit to see colours, quality, and so on. Products on display are also a form of advertising for the company and this would be lost if the shops were closed.

**Mini-Quiz**

(1) **Answer D.**

ABM uses the information provided by an ABC analysis to improve organisational profitability.

Option A defines ABC.

Option B defines activity Driver analysis

Option C defines activity-based budgeting

Option E defines an activity cost pool.

(2) **Answer A.**

Machine setup costs are likely to be driven by the number of batches produced. Therefore, this is a batch level activity.

Product design (B) is a product level activity.

The inspection of every item produced (C) is a unit level activity.

The production manager's work cannot be related to a particular product line. Therefore, this is a facility level activity.

Advertising of individual products would be a product level activity. If the advertising is concerned with promoting the company's name, then this would be a facility level activity.

(3) **Answer A**

All of the costs described can be identified with specific goods and would be deducted from the selling price to determine the direct product profit.

# Principles of Budgeting

## Chapter learning objectives

- **Explain** the principles that underlie the use of budgets in control. (Syllabus Link C1 a, b and c)

- **Discuss** the impact of budgetary control systems and setting of standard costs on human behaviour. (Syllabus Link C3a)

- **Evaluate** the consequences of 'what-if' scenarios and their impact on the master budget. (Syllabus Link C2b)

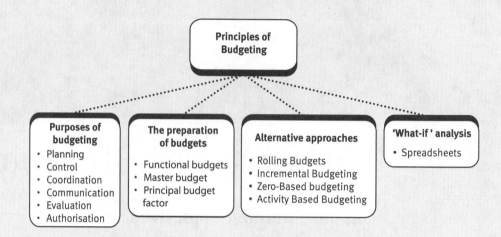

## 1 Knowledge Brought Forward

You will already have covered 'The Budgeting Framework' in Paper P1. We will build on this knowledge in P2 with more budgeting related concepts, but make sure you are comfortable with the assumed knowledge, that should have been brought forward as a base, in this section.

> *A budget* is defined in CIMA's *Official Terminology* as *'a quantitative expression of a plan for a defined period of time. It may include planned sales volumes and revenues; resource quantities, costs and expenses; assets, liabilities and cash flows'.*

## 2 Budget

A quantitative or financial plan relating to the future. It can be for the company as a whole or for departments or functions or products or for resources such as cash, materials, labour, etc. It is usually for one year or less.

## 3 Purposes of Budgeting

Budgets have several different purposes:

(1) **Planning**

Budgets **compel** planning. The budgeting process forces management to look ahead, set targets, anticipate problems and give the organisation purpose and direction. Without the annual budgeting process the pressures of day-to-day operational problems may tempt managers not to plan for future operations. The budgeting process encourages managers to anticipate problems before they arise, and hasty decisions that are made on the spur of the moment, based on expediency rather than reasoned judgements, will be minimised. Corporate planners would regard budgeting as an important technique whereby long-term strategies are converted into shorter-term action plans.

(2) **Control**

The budget provides the plan against which actual results can be compared. Those results which are out-of-line with the budget can be further investigated and corrected.

(3) **Co-ordination**

The budget serves as a vehicle through which the actions of the different parts of an organisation can be brought together and reconciled into a common plan. Without any guidance managers may each make their own decisions believing that they are working in the best interests of the organisation. A sound budgeting system helps to co-ordinate the different activities of the business and to ensure that they are in harmony with each other.

(4) **Communication**

Budgets communicate targets to managers. Through the budget, top management communicates its expectations to lower-level management so that all members of the organisation may understand these expectations and can co-ordinate their activities to attain them.

(5) **Motivation**

The budget can be a useful device for influencing managerial behaviour and motivating managers to perform in line with the organisational objectives.

(6) **Evaluation**

The performance of a manager is often evaluated by measuring his success in achieving his budgets. The budget might quite possibly be the only quantitative reference point available.

(7) **Authorisation**

A budget may act as formal authorisation to a manager for expenditure, the hiring of staff and the pursuit of the plans contained in the budget.

## 4 Functional Budgets and the Master Budget

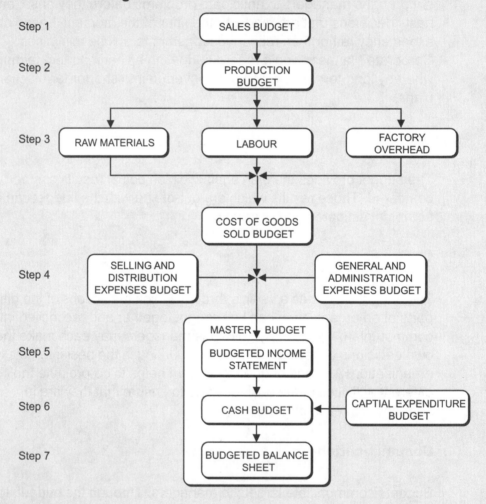

A master budget for the entire organisation brings together the departmental or activity budgets for all the departments or responsibility centres within the organisation.

The structure of a budget depends on the nature of the organisation and its operations. In a manufacturing organisation, the budgeting process will probably consist of preparing several functional budgets, beginning with a sales budget.

- **Sales budget**. Budget for future sales, expressed in revenue terms and possibly also in units of sale. The budget for the organisation as a whole might combine the sales budgets of several sales regions. Unless there is a production limiting factor, the sales budget is the starting point for preparing the master budget.

  In practice, organisations prepare their sales budget in more detail, with planned sales analysed by region and area as well as by product.

  Comparative figures for the previous year will also usually be shown, to indicate whether planned sales are higher or lower than in the previous period, and by how much.

- **Production budget**. A production budget follows on from the sales budget, since production quantities are determined by sales volume. The production volume will differ from sales volume by the amount of any planned increase or decrease in inventories of finished goods (and work-in-progress).

In order to express the production budget in financial terms (production cost), subsidiary budgets must be prepared for materials, labour and production overheads. Several departmental managers could be involved in preparing these subsidiary budgets.

- **Direct materials usage budget**. This is a budget for the quantities and cost of the materials required for the planned production quantities.

- **Materials purchasing budget**. This is a budget for the cost of the materials to be purchased in the period. The purchase cost of direct materials will differ from the material usage budget if there is a planned increase or decrease in direct materials inventory. The purchases budget should also include the purchase costs of indirect materials.

- **Direct labour budget**. This is a budget of the direct labour costs of production. If direct labour is a variable cost, it is calculated by multiplying the production quantities (in units) by the budgeted direct labour cost per unit produced. If direct labour is a fixed cost, it can be calculated by estimating the payroll cost.

- **Production overheads**. Budgets can be produced for production overhead costs. Where a system of absorption costing is used, overheads are allocated and apportioned, and budgeted absorption rates are determined.

- **Administration and sales and distribution overheads**. Other overhead costs should be budgeted.

- **The machine utilisation budget.** This is a budget for the number of machine hours required for production. A separate budget is required for each different group of machines. Once again, the starting point for preparing the budget is the production volume for each product. Since machine hours are not specifically costed, the budget is in hours only.

- **Production cost budget.** The production budget has already been prepared in units. A production cost budget can be prepared, for each product and in total.

- **Budgeted income statement, cash budget and balance sheet**. Having prepared budgets for sales and costs, the master budget can be summarised as an income statement for the period, a cash budget (or cash flow forecast) and a balance sheet as at the end of the budget period.

- **Other budgets:** A *cash budget* is a plan of cash flows during the budget period. Cash management is a critical area of financial management, and most organisations prepare a detailed budget of cash receipts and cash payments. A cash budget might cover a period of just a few months (say three or six months, divided into monthly periods), because longer-term budgeting of receipts and payments is unlikely to be accurate enough to justify detailed planning.

  A *capital expenditure budget* is a plan for spending on capital items over a planning horizon of several years, and which is reviewed and updated annually.

If the budgeted profit, cash position or balance sheet are unsatisfactory, the budgets should be revised until a satisfactory planned outcome is achieved.

### Cash budgets

Q, a new company, is being established to manufacture and sell an electronic tracking device: the Trackit. The owners are excited about the future profits that the business will generate. They have forecast that sales will grow to 2,600 Trackits per month within five months and will be at that level for the remainder of the first year.

The owners will invest a total of $250,000 in cash on the first day of operations (that is the first day of Month 1). They will also transfer non-current assets into the company. Extracts from the company's business plan are shown below.

## Sales

The forecast sales for the first five months are:

| Months | Trackit (units) |
|---|---|
| 1 | 1,000 |
| 2 | 1,500 |
| 3 | 2,000 |
| 4 | 2,400 |
| 5 | 2,600 |

The selling price has been set at $140 per Trackit.

## Sales receipts

Sales will be mainly through large retail outlets. The pattern for the receipt of payment is expected to be as follows:

| Time of payment | % of sales value |
|---|---|
| Immediately | 15* |
| One month later | 25 |
| Two months later | 40 |
| Three months later | 15 |

The balance represents anticipated bad debts. *A 4% discount will be given for immediate payment.

## Production

The budget production volumes in units are:

| Month 1 | Month 2 | Month 3 | Month 4 |
|---|---|---|---|
| 1,450 | 1,650 | 2,120 | 2,460 |

## Variable production cost

The budgeted variable production cost is $90 per unit, comprising:

| | $ |
|---|---|
| Direct materials | 60 |
| Direct wages | 10 |
| Variable production overheads | 20 |
| | |
| Total variable cost | 90 |

**Direct materials**: Payment for purchases will be made in the month following receipt. There will be no opening inventory of materials in Month 1. It will be company policy to hold inventory at the end of each month equal to 20% of the following month's production requirements. The direct materials cost includes the cost of an essential component that will be bought in from a specialist manufacturer.

**Direct wages** will be paid in the month in which the production occurs.

**Variable production overheads:** 65% will be paid in the month in which production occurs and the remainder will be paid one month later.

**Fixed overhead costs** :Fixed overheads are estimated at $840,000 per annum and are expected to be incurred in equal amounts each month. 60% of the fixed overhead costs will be paid in the month in which they are incurred and 15% in the following month. The balance represents depreciation of non-current assets.

**Required:**

Prepare a cash budget for each of the first three months and for that three-month period in total. Ignore VAT and Tax.

## 5 Principal Budget Factor

It is usually assumed in budgeting that sales demand will be the key factor setting a limit to what the organisation can expect to achieve in the budget period. Occasionally, however, there might be a shortage of a key resource, such as cash, raw material supplies, skilled labour or equipment. If a resource is in restricted supply, and the shortage cannot be overcome, the budget for the period should be determined by how to make the best use of this key budget resource, rather than be sales demand.

When a key resource is in short supply and affects the planning decisions, it is known as the **principal budget factor** or **limiting budget factor**.

### The Budget Committee

### The Budget Committee

The best way to achieve coordination of budgets is to set up a budget committee. The budget committee should comprise representatives from all the key functions of the organisation.

The committee should meet regularly to review progress and resolve any problems that arise. The meetings will ensure that a co-ordinated approach is adopted.

## Example 1

You are employed as a management accountant by SRW Ltd. The company makes two similar products, the Alpha and Beta, and operates a five-day week for both production and sales. Both products use the same material and labour, but Beta requires more labour and materials than the Alpha. The company divides its year into five-week periods for budgetary purposes. One of your responsibilities is to prepare budgets for the Alpha and the Beta.

You are given the following information to help you prepare the production and resource budgets for period 8.

| Forecast Sales Volumes (units) | Days in Period | Alpha | Beta |
|---|---|---|---|
| Period 8 | 25 | 8,460 | 9,025 |
| Period 9 | 25 | 10,575 | 12,635 |

### Finished inventories

- There will be 1,692 Alphas and 3,610 Betas in finished inventory at the beginning of Period 8

- The closing inventory of both Alphas and Betas depends on the forecast sales in period 9.

- Period 8's closing inventory of Alphas must equal 5 days sales of Alphas in period 9

- Period 8's closing inventory of Betas must equal 10 days sales of Betas in period 9.

- The first-in-first-out inventory valuation method is used to value closing inventory.

### Production and failure rates

- 10% of Alpha finished production and 5% of Beta finished production is faulty and has to be destroyed. This faulty production has no value.

- The faulty production arises from the production technology and is only discovered on completion. The cost of faulty production is part of the cost producing fault-free Alphas and Betas.

### Materials

- Each Alpha produced requires 20kg of materials and each Beta produced requires 40kg of materials

- The opening inventory of materials at the beginning of period 8 is 64,800 kg.

- The closing inventory of materials at the end of period 8 must be 52,600 kg

- The material costs 50c per kilogram.

### Labour

- Each Alpha produced requires two labour hours and each Beta produced requires three labour hours.

- SRW employs 300 production staff who work 35 hours per five-day week.

- The hourly rate per employee is $10 and if any overtime is required the overtime premium is $3 per employee per hour of overtime.

- Any overtime premium is charged to factory overheads and not to the cost of production.

### Factory overheads

- Budgeted overheads are charged to production on the basis of labour hours.

- For Alpha, the budgeted factory overheads are $62 per labour hour. For Beta, they are $58 per labour hour.

**Required:**

(a) Prepare the following information for Period 8;

    (i)   Production budgets for Alpha and Beta;

    (ii)  Material purchases budget in kilograms and $

    (iii) Budgeted labour hours to be worked, including any overtime hours

    (iv) Labour cost budget

    (v)  Total (full) cost of production budget for Alpha and Beta

    (vi) Full cost of GOOD production per unit for Alpha and Beta

The Sales Director has just informed you that the Alpha sales in period 8 will be 2,000 units more than originally forecast. You are told the following:

- SRW production employees can work up to a maximum of 5,000 overtime hours in any five-week period.

- The material used in Alpha and Beta production can only be made by one company and SRW is the only user of the material. Currently there is a shortage of the material and the maximum additional material that can be obtained is 34,000 kg.

- The demand for Beta in period 8 will remain at 9,025 units.

(b) (i)   Prepare calculations to show whether it is the material or labour hours that limits the extra production of Alpha in period 8.

    (ii)  Prepare a revised production budget in units for Alphas in period 8.

    (iii) Calculate the shortfall in the planned extra sales of Alpha caused by the limit in extra production.

    (iv) Suggest three ways how this shortfall may be overcome.

## 6 Alternative Approaches to Budgeting

### Periodic budget

A periodic budget shows the costs and revenue for one period of time, e.g. a year and is updated on a periodic basis, e.g. every 12 months.

### Rolling budgets (continuous budgets)

A rolling budget is a 'budget continuously updated by adding a further accounting period (month or quarter) when the earliest accounting period has expired'. (CIMA Official Terminology) Rolling budgets are also called 'continuous budgets'. Rolling budgets are for a fixed period, but this need not be a full financial year.

### Example

If rolling annual budgets are prepared quarterly, four rolling budgets will be prepared each year, each for a 12-month period. A new quarter is added at the end of the new budget period, to replace the current quarter just ending:

- One budget might cover the period 1 January – 31 December Year 1.

- The next rolling budget will cover 1 April Year 1 to 31 March Year 2.

- The next rolling budget will cover 1 July Year 1 to 30 June Year 2.

- The next quarterly rolling budget will cover 1 October Year 1 to 30 September Year 2, and so on.

### Reasons for rolling budgets

The reason for preparing rolling budgets is to deal with the problem of uncertainty in the budget, when greater accuracy and reliability are required. A common example is **cash budgeting.** Cash management is often a critical element of financial management in organisations, and it is essential to have reasonably reliable forecasts of cash flows, especially over the course of the next few days, weeks or months. An organisation might therefore produce rolling budgets (= revised forecasts) for cash flow. The cash budget period might be three or six months, and rolling cash budgets might be prepared monthly.

Another example is budgeting in conditions subject to rapid financial change. When a budget is prepared, the forecasts on which it is based might be uncertain due to the probability of significant financial changes during the budget period. For example:

- the forecast rate of cost inflation/price inflation might be high;

- the business might be affected by changes in an exchange rate, such as the sterling/US dollar rate and the exchange rate might be extremely volatile and subject to large movements within relatively short periods of time.

- When there is a large amount of uncertainty in the budget, it might be appropriate to prepare rolling budgets at regular intervals, in order to have plans that are reasonably realistic and achievable.

## Advantages and disadvantages of rolling budgets

| Advantages | Disadvantages |
| --- | --- |
| They reduce uncertainty in budgeting | Preparing new budgets regularly is time-consuming. |
| They can be used for cash management | It can be difficult to communicate frequent budget changes. |
| They force managers to look ahead continuously | |
| When conditions are subject to change, comparing actual results with a rolling budget is more realistic than comparing actual results with a fixed annual budget. | |

### 'Budgets on a roll'

**'Budgets on a roll: recalculating a business's outlook several times a year'**

*Randy Myers, Journal of Accountancy, December 2001. © 2001. Reprinted with permission of AICPA*

For years, senior managers at REL Consultancy Group handled budgeting and revenue forecasting much the way most other companies do. As year-end approached, they would evaluate performance, set sales targets for the upcoming year and then work to see that everyone met or exceeded the goals.

Unfortunately, the process didn't always produce the intended results.

'Invariably,' recalls Stephan Payne, president of the London-based global management consulting firm, 'one of the account directors would land a couple of good clients early in the year and make his annual budget well before the year closed. More often than not, he'd then take his foot off the gas and coast.' To make the budgeting process more timely and relevant, the firm embraced a more complex, albeit intuitive, approach to financial forecasting – the **rolling budget**. Rather than creating an annual financial forecast that remains static for the year, he and his colleagues now produce an 18-month budget and then update projections every month – in effect, recalculating the whole budget. As the firm's actual sales figures come in each month, directors plug them into their forecasting model in place of what they had projected, then roll the budget forward one more month.

### No more free rides

The result: an always-current financial forecast that reflects not only the company's most recent monthly results but also any material changes to its business outlook or the economy. In addition, it provides fewer opportunities for account directors to ride the coattails of past performance.

'Now, even the guy who booked a million dollars' worth of business in one month can't sit still because 30 days later, we're going to have an entirely new forecast,' Payne says, adding, 'It's a dynamic process that makes a lot more sense.'

Although traditional 1-year budgets are still the norm at most companies large and small, many accountants argue that rolling budgets can be a far more useful tool. Unlike static budgets, they encourage managers to react more quickly to changing economic developments or business conditions. They discourage what is too often a fruitless focus on the past ('Why didn't we meet our numbers?') in favour of a realistic focus on the future. And they produce forecasts that, over the near term, are never more than a few months old, even when companies are rolling them forward on a quarterly basis – the more common approach – rather than REL's monthly basis.

'A static budget simply doesn't reflect the pace of business today,' says Jill Langerman, CPA, president and CFO of the accounting firm Fair, Anderson & Langerman in Las Vegas. 'If at mid-year you add a new product to your line-up, you want to calculate the costs and profit margins associated with that and reflected those calculations in your budget OSC to reflect the impact that it will have on your remaining product lines. That way, you can set an accurate performance target and make informed decisions about whether you're now free to invest more in the remaining product lines or perhaps add a new line. If you're not incorporating these new analyses into your budget, it becomes a rather useless document.'

Implementing rolling budgets doesn't necessarily require any fundamental change in the way a company has been doing its budgets – except, of course, it no longer does the job just once a year. However, companies that decide to step up to rolling budgets may want to take advantage of the decision to make a change and consider what else they can do to improve the process. After all, if a company can get everyone on board to make such a fundamental change, a further nudge to make the process more effective and efficient in other ways may be possible, too.

## 7 Incremental Budgeting vs. Zero-Based Budgeting

### Incremental Budgeting

The traditional approach to budgeting is to take the previous year's budget and to add on a percentage to allow for inflation and other cost increases. In addition there may be other adjustments for specific items such as an extra worker or extra machine. In times of recession, the opposite process will take place, i.e. last year's budget minus a certain percentage.

The advantage of incremental budgeting is that it is an easy, quick and cheap method of preparing budgets for what may be many cost centres in a large organisation. However, the traditional approach has severe disadvantages.

### Disadvantages

(1)  Consideration will not be given to the justification for each activity. They will be undertaken merely because they were undertaken the previous year.

(2)  Different ways of achieving the objective will not be examined.

(3)  Past inefficiencies will be continued.

(4)  Managers know that if they fail to spend their budget, it is likely to be reduced next period. They therefore try to spend the whole budget, regardless of whether or not the expenditure is justified.

ZBB is one method which may be used to overcome these problems.

### Zero-based budgeting

In a manufacturing company it is relatively straightforward to control those costs that relate to production. However, support expenses, i.e. those costs incurred in non-production departments, do not have a clear relationship with the output level. Within these support departments, managers have a difficult task of allocating resources effectively. One technique that can be used is **Zero-based budgeting.**

ZBB may be defined as:

'A method of budgeting whereby all activities are re-evaluated each time a budget is formulated. Each functional budget starts with the assumptions that the function does not exist, and is at zero cost. Increments of costs are compared with increments of benefits, culminating in the planned maximum benefit for a given budgeted cost.'

The technique is especially useful for:

(1) service departments such as stores, maintenance, marketing, finance, etc.

(2) discretionary costs such as research and development.

(3) public sector organisations such as local authorities.

### Implementation

It is important that managers involved in ZBB examine their current practices very carefully. Questions they should ask themselves include:

(1) Is the activity essential? What would happen if it ceased?

(2) Is the provision of the activity at the correct level?

(3) Are there other alternatives for achieving the same effect?

There are four distinct stages in the implementation of ZBB:

(1) Managers should specify, for their responsibility centres, those activities that can be individually evaluated.

(2) Each of the individual activities is then described in a **decision package.** The decision package should state the costs and revenues expected from the given activity. It should be drawn up in such a way that the package can be evaluated and ranked against other packages.

(3) Each decision package is evaluated and ranked usually using cost/benefit analysis.

(4) The resources are then allocated to the various packages.

### Advantages

Inefficient or obsolete operations can be identified and discontinued.

(1) It creates an inquisitorial attitude, rather than one which assumes current practices represent value for money.

(2) Wasteful expenditure is avoided.

(3) Managers are forced to consider alternative methods of achieving their objectives.

(4) ZBB leads to increased staff involvement at all levels. This should lead to better communication and motivation.

(5) Attention is focused on outputs in relation to value for money.

(6) Knowledge and understanding of the cost behaviour patterns of the organisation will be enhanced.

(7) Resources should be allocated efficiently and economically.

**Disadvantages**

(1) The time involved and the cost of preparing the budget is much greater than for less elaborate budgeting methods. In some organisations because of the heavy paperwork involved ZBB has become known as 'Xerox-based budgeting'.

(2) It may emphasise short-term benefits to the detriment of long-term benefits.

(3) There is a need for management skills that may not be present in the organisation.

(4) Managers, staff and unions may feel threatened.

(5) The rankings of packages may be subjective where the benefits are of a qualitative nature.

(6) It is difficult to compare and rank completely different types of activity.

(7) The budgeting process may become too rigid and the company may not be able to react to unforeseen opportunities or threats.

(8) Incremental costs and benefits of alternative courses of action are difficult to quantify accurately.

In a manufacturing business, budgeting for direct costs is relatively straightforward. The costs of direct materials and direct labour are assumed to vary with production, and once production levels have been estimated, budgeting the direct costs of production is a matter of simple arithmetic.

Budgeting for overhead costs is not so simple. Traditionally, there has been a tendency to take an incremental approach in budgeting for overhead costs, and prepare next year's budget by simply adding a percentage to the current year budget, to allow for inflation. Zero-based budgeting is one method of bringing greater discipline to the process of budgeting for overhead activities and costs.

## 8 Activity – Based Budgeting

As its name should suggest, activity-based budgeting (ABB) takes a similar approach to activity-based costing.

> ABB is defined as: 'a method of budgeting based on an activity framework and utilising cost driver data in the budget-setting and variance feedback processes' (CIMA *Official Terminology*).

Whereas ZBB is based on budgets (decision packages) prepared by responsibility centre managers, ABB is based on budgeting for activities.

The basic approach of ABB is to budget the costs for each cost pool or activity.

(There will also be some general overhead costs that are not activity-related, such as factory rental costs and the salary cost of the factory manager. General overhead costs are budgeted separately.)

(1) The cost driver for each activity is identified. A forecast is made of the number of units of the cost driver that will occur in the budget period.

(2) Given the estimate of the activity level for the cost driver, the activity cost is estimated. Where appropriate, a **cost per unit of activity** is calculated.

### Advantages of ABB

The advantages of ABB are similar to those provided by activity-based costing.

- It draws attention to the costs of 'overhead activities'. This can be important where overhead costs are a large proportion of total operating costs.

- It provides information for the control of activity costs, by assuming that they are variable, at least in the longer term.

- It provides a useful basis for monitoring and controlling overhead costs, by drawing management attention to the actual costs of activities and comparing actual costs with what the activities were expected to cost.

- It also provides useful control information by emphasising that activity costs might be controllable if the activity volume can be controlled.

- ABB can provide useful information for a total quality management (TQM) programme, by relating the cost of an activity to the level of service provided (for example, stores requisitions processed) - Do the user departments feel they are getting a cost-effective service?

## Example 2 – ABB

What might be the main disadvantages of activity-based budgeting?

## Example 3 – RESEARCH DIVISION

For a number of years, the research division of Z plc has produced its annual budget (for new and continuing projects) using incremental budgeting techniques. The company is now under new management and the annual budget for 2004 is to be prepared using zero based budgeting techniques.

**Required:**

(a) Explain the differences between incremental and zero based budgeting techniques.

(b) Explain how Z plc could operate a zero based budgeting system for its research projects.

The operating divisions of Z plc have in the past always used a traditional approach to analysing costs into their fixed and variable components. A single measure of activity was used which, for simplicity, was the number of units produced. The new management does not accept that such a simplistic approach is appropriate for budgeting in the modern environment and has requested that the managers adopt an activity-based approach to their budgets for 2004.

**Required:**

(c) (i) Briefly explain activity-based budgeting (ABB).

(ii) Explain how activity-based budgeting would be implemented by the operating divisions of Z plc.

## 'What-if' analysis and the use of spreadsheets

Also known as sensitivity analysis.

Once the budget has been prepared, we can recalculate it using different assumptions. One or more variables at a time are changed and the effect on the solution recalculated. For example what would be the effect on profit:

- if sales volumes were 10% higher?
- If the selling price was $2 lower?
- If material costs increased by 10%?
- If a new machine was installed and labour efficiency increased by 20%?

The sensitivity analysis would be facilitated by the use of a spreadsheet, that should be broken down into 2 or 3 areas:

(1) Input area

(2) Processing area

(3) Output area

Often the processing area and the output area are not separated.

The relevant variables are identified and entered into the input area, with one cell for each variable. Here, they are kept separate from the rest of the spreadsheet.

This segregation enables the variables to be manipulated easily and the effects on the profit or costs or NPV, etc. to be determined. It also makes it easier to see the assumptions upon which the solution depends and if there is a mistake in the construction of the spreadsheet, it makes it easier to find

The processing area contains the formulae required to calculate the result based on the input variables.

The output area, where separate from the processing area, will show the results as calculated in the processing area in, for instance a formal report style or a table or using charts.

## Example 4 – What-if analysis

A company makes and sells two products, X and Y, for which the budgeted sales price and variable costs per unit are:

|  | *Product X* | *Product Y* |
|---|---|---|
| Variable cost | $2 | $4 |
| Sales price | $5 | $8 |

Budgeted fixed costs are $140,000. Budgeted sales are 30,000 units of Product X and 15,000 units of Product Y.

### Required

(a) Calculate the budgeted profit.

(b) Calculate how profit would be affected in each of the following separate circumstances:

   (i)   if the variable cost of Product Y were 25% higher than expected

   (ii)  if sales of Product X were 10% less than budgeted

   (iii) if sales of Product X were 5% less than budgeted and unit variable costs of X were 10% higher than budgeted

   (iv) if total sales revenue is the same as in the original budget, but the sales mix (by revenue) is 50% of Product X and 50% of Product Y.

## 9 Practice Questions

### Test your understanding 1

Hopper manufactures two products, X and Y. Budgeted information for the next financial year is as follows:

|  | Product X | Product Y |
|---|---|---|
|  | Units | Units |
| Budgeted sales | 4,000 | 6,000 |
| Budgeted closing inventory | 500 | 300 |
| Opening inventory | 200 | 400 |

|  | Product X | Product Y |
|---|---|---|
| Direct materials requirements | Kg per unit | Kg per unit |
| Material DM1 | 1.2 | 2.0 |
| Material DM2 | 0.8 | – |

|  | Material DM1 | Material DM2 |
|---|---|---|
|  | Kg | Kg |
| Budgeted Closing inventory | 1,000 | 200 |
| Opening inventory | 3,000 | 600 |
| Standard Price per kg | $0.80 | $0.50 |

**Required:**

Prepare a materials purchases budget for the year, showing the purchase quantities and cost for both materials.

## Test your understanding 2

Sales of a company's product are budgeted as follows for the next quarter:

|  | April | May | June |
|---|---|---|---|
| Sales units | 8,900 | 8,500 | 8,100 |

Two kg of material K are used to produce each unit of the company's product. The standard price of material K is $4 per kg.

The company's policy for month-end inventories is as follows:

Raw materials: 20% of the requirements for the following month's production

Finished goods: 25% of the following month's sales.

Material suppliers are paid in the month following delivery.
What value will be shown as payment to material suppliers in the cash budget for May?

## Test your understanding 3

Twenty per cent of a company's sales are made to cash customers. The records show that the credit customers settle their bills as follows:

Paid in the month following the sale 60%

Paid two months after the sale 38%

Bad debts 2%

Credit customers paying in the month following the sale receive a 3% discount.

Budgeted sales for the forthcoming period are as follows:

| January | February | March |
|---|---|---|
| $20,400 | $29,500 | $26,800 |

**Required:**

Calculate the amount to be shown as receipts from sales in the cash budget for March.

### Test your understanding 4

There is a continuing demand for three sub-assemblies – A, B and C – made and sold by MW. Sales are in the ratios of A 1, B 2, C 4 and selling prices are A $215, B $250, C $300. Each sub-assembly consists of a copper frame onto which the same components are fixed but in differing quantities as follows:

| Sub-assembly | Frame | Component D | Component E | Component F |
|---|---|---|---|---|
| A | 1 | 5 | 1 | 4 |
| B | 1 | 1 | 7 | 5 |
| C | 1 | 3 | 5 | 1 |
| Buying in costs, per unit | $20 | $8 | $5 | $3 |

Operation times by labour for each sub-assembly are:

| Sub-assembly | Skilled hours | Unskilled hours |
|---|---|---|
| A | 2 | 2 |
| B | 1½ | 2 |
| C | 1½ | 3 |

The skilled labour is paid $6 per hour and the unskilled $4.50 per hour. The skilled labour is located in a machining department and the unskilled labour in an assembly department. A five-day week of 37½ hours is worked and each accounting period is for four weeks.

Variable overhead per sub-assembly is A $5, B $4 and C $3.50. At the end of the current year, inventories are expected to be as shown below but, because interest rates have increased and the company utilises a bank overdraft for working capital purposes, it is planned to effect a 10% reduction in all finished sub-assemblies and bought-in stocks during Period 1 of the forthcoming year.

Forecast inventories at current year end:

#### Sub-assembly

| | | | |
|---|---|---|---|
| A | 300 | Copper frames | 1,000 |
| B | 700 | Component D | 4,000 |
| C | 1,600 | Component E | 10,000 |
| | | Component F | 4,000 |

Work-in-progress inventories are to be ignored.

Overhead for the forthcoming year is budgeted to be production $728,000, selling and distribution $364,000, and administration $338,000. These costs, all fixed, are expected to be incurred evenly throughout the year and are treated as period costs.

**Within Period 1 it is planned to sell one-thirteenth of the annual requirements which are to be the sales necessary to achieve the company profit target of $6.5 million before tax.**

**Required:**

(a) Prepare budgets in respect of Period 1 of the forthcoming year for:
   (i) sales, in quantities and value
   (ii) production, in quantities only
   (iii) materials usage, in quantities
   (iv) materials purchased, in quantities and value
   (v) manpower budget, i.e. number of people needed in each of the machining department and the assembly department.

(b) Discuss the factors to be considered if the bought-in stocks were to be reduced to one week's requirements – this has been proposed by the purchasing officer but resisted by the production director.

## Mini-Quiz

(1) Which ONE of the following would not be considered to be an objective of budgeting?

   A    Authorisation

   B    Expansion

   C    Performance Evaluation

   D    Resource Allocation

(2) Which ONE of the following is not one of the main purposes of a budget?

   A    To compel planning

   B    To communicate targets to the managers responsible for achieving the budget

   C    To inform shareholders of performance in meeting targets

   D    To establish a system of control by comparing budgets and actual results

(3) Which TWO of the following are characteristics of rolling budgets?

A   Each item of expenditure has to be justified in its entirety in order to be included in the next year's budget

B   A new accounting period, such as a month or a quarter, is added as each old one expires

C   The budget is more realistic and certain as there is a short period between the preparation of budgets

D   Updates to the fixed annual budget are made only when they are foreseeable.

(4) Which ONE of the following best describes 'zero-based budgeting'?

A   A budget method where an attempt is made to make expenditure under each cost heading as close to 0 as possible

B   A method of budgeting whereby all activities are re-evaluated each time a budget is formulated

C   A method of budgeting where the sum of costs and revenues for each budget centre equals 0

D   A method of budgeting that distinguishes fixed and variable cost behaviour with respect to changes in output and the budget is designed to change appropriately with such fluctuations

(5) A company that uses zero-based budgeting for its overheads has:

A   Zero as the starting point for budgeting the coming year's overhead.

B   A zero variance between budgeted and actual overhead

C   An assumed sales level of zero as the starting point for budgeting the coming year's overheads

D   An overhead budget of zero

## Test your understanding answers

### Cash budgets

|  |  | Month 1 | Month 2 | Month 3 | Total |
|---|---|---|---|---|---|
| **Receipts** |  |  |  |  |  |
| Sales | (W1) | 20,160 | 65,240 | 148,820 | 234,220 |
| Capital Investment |  | 250,000 |  |  | 250,000 |
| Total |  | 270,160 | 65,240 | 148,820 | 484,220 |
| **Payments** |  |  |  |  |  |
| Materials | (W2) |  | 106,800 | 104,640 | 211,240 |
| Wages | (W3) | 14,500 | 16,500 | 21,200 | 52,200 |
| Var. Overheads | (W4) | 18,850 | 31,600 | 39,110 | 89,560 |
| Fixed O/Hs | (W5) | 42,000 | 52,500 | 52,500 | 147,000 |
| Total |  | 75,350 | 207,400 | 217,450 | 500,200 |
| Net inflow/(outflow) |  | 194,810 | (142,160) | (68,630) | (15,980) |
| Balance b/f |  | 0 | 194,810 | 52,650 | 0 |
| Balance C/f |  | 194,810 | 52,650 | (15,980) | (15,980) |

### Working 1: Sales Receipts

|  |  | Month 1 | Month 2 | Month 3 |
|---|---|---|---|---|
| Units |  | 1,000 | 1,500 | 2,000 |
| Revenue | (@$140) | 140,000 | 210,000 | 280,000 |
| **Receipts** |  |  |  |  |
| 0 months | 15% x 96% | 20,160 | 30,240 | 40,320 |
| 1 month | 25% |  | 35,000 | 52,500 |
| 2 months | 40% |  |  | 56,000 |
| 3 months | 15% |  |  |  |
| Total |  | 20,160 | 65,240 | 148,820 |

## Working 2: Materials Cost

|  |  | Month 1 | Month 2 | Month 3 | Month 4 |
|---|---|---|---|---|---|
| Production units |  | 1,450 | 1,650 | 2,120 | 2,460 |
| + Closing Inventory |  | 330 | 424 | 492 |  |
|  |  | 1,780 | 2,074 | 2,612 |  |
| – Opening Inventory |  | 0 | (330) | (424) | (492) |
| Units purchased |  | 1,780 | 1,744 | 2,188 |  |
| Purchases | @$60 | 106,800 | 106,640 | 131,280 |  |
| Payments |  | 0 | 106,800 | 104,640 | 131,280 |

## Working 3: Labour Cost

|  |  | Month 1 | Month 2 | Month 3 | Month 4 |
|---|---|---|---|---|---|
| Production units |  | 1,450 | 1,650 | 2,120 | 2,460 |
| Wages | @$10 | 14,500 | 16,500 | 21,200 |  |

## Working 4: Variable Overhead Cost

|  |  | Month 1 | Month 2 | Month 3 | Month 4 |
|---|---|---|---|---|---|
| Production units |  | 1,450 | 1,650 | 2,120 | 2,460 |
| Cost | @$20 | 29,000 | 33,000 | 42,400 |  |
| Paid |  |  |  |  |  |
| 0 months | 65% | 18,850 | 21,450 | 27,560 |  |
| 1 month | 35% |  | 10,150 | 11,550 |  |
| Payments |  | 18,850 | 31,600 | 39,110 |  |

## Working 5: Fixed Overhead Cost

|  | Month 1 | Month 2 | Month 3 | Month 4 |
|---|---|---|---|---|
| Cost excl. depreciation | 52,500 | 52,500 | 52,500 |  |
| paid |  |  |  |  |
| 0 months | 42,000 | 42,000 | 42,000 |  |
| 1 month |  | 10,500 | 10,500 |  |
| Payments | 42,000 | 52,500 | 52,500 |  |

## Example 1

### (a) (i) Production Budget (Period 8)

|  | Alpha | Beta |
|---|---|---|
| Sales Budget | 8,460 units | 9,025 units |
| Add : Closing stock | 2,115 units (W1) | 5,054 units (W1) |
| Less : Opening stock | (1,692 units) | (3,610 units) |
| Good Production | 8,883 units | 10,469 units |
| Wastage | 987 units | 551 units |
| Total Production | 9,870 units | 11,020 units |

### Working 1 – Closing Stock

| Alpha | Beta |
|---|---|
| $\dfrac{5}{25} \times 10,575 = 2,115$ units | $\dfrac{10}{25} \times 12,635 = 5,054$ units |

### (ii) Materials Purchases

|  | Kilograms | $ |
|---|---|---|
| Alpha 9,870 x 20 kgs | 197,400 | 98,700 |
| Beta 11,020 x 40 kgs | 440,800 | 220,400 |
|  | 638,200 | 319,100 |
| Add: Closing | 52,600 |  |
| Less: Opening | (64,800) |  |
| Purchases | 626,000 | 313,000 |

### (iii) Labour hours

|  | Hours |
|---|---|
| Alpha 9,870 x 2 | 19,740 |
| Beta 11,020 x 3 | 33,060 |
|  | 52,800 |
| Normal hours 300 x 35 x 5 weeks | 52,500 |
| Overtime hours | 300 |

(iv) **Labour cost budget**

| | | |
|---|---:|---:|
| Direct Labour Cost | 52,800 x $10 = | $528,000 |
| Overtime Premium (OH) | 300 x $3 = | $900 |

(v) **Full Production Cost**

| | Alpha | Beta |
|---|---:|---:|
| Direct Material | $98,700 | $220,400 |
| Direct Labour | $197,400 | $330,600 |
| Overhead: 19,740 hours x $62 | $1,223,880 | |
| Overhead: 33,060 hours x $58 | | $1,917,480 |
| | $1,519,980 | $2,468,480 |
| ÷ Good units | ÷ 8,883 | ÷ 10,469 |
| Full Cost per unit | $171.11 | $235.79 |

(b) (i)

| | |
|---|---:|
| Increase in demand | 2,000 units |
| | ÷ 0.90 |
| Therefore, increase in Production | 2,223 units |

| | | |
|---|---|---:|
| Hours required | 2,223 units x 2 hours | 4,446 hours |
| Overtime hours available | (5,000 hours – 300 hours) | 4,700 hours |

Therefore, labour hours are not a scarce resource.

| | | |
|---|---|---:|
| Kilograms of material required | 2,223 units x 20 kgs = | 44,460 kgs |
| Available | | 34,000 ks |

Therefore, material is a scarce resource.

(ii)

$$\text{Allowable increase in production:} \quad \frac{34,000 \text{ hours}}{20} = 1,700 \text{ units}$$

New production budget:   9,870 + 1,700 = 11,570 units

(iii)  New production budget:                                         = 11,570 units

Good units produced:                     1,700 x 90%      = 1,530 units

Shortfall:                                                            = 470 units

(iv)  •    Reduce planned closing stocks levels
     •    Improve wastage rate
     •    Reduce production of Beta

## Example 2 – ABB

•    A considerable amount of time and effort might be needed to establish an ABB system, for example to identify the key activities and their cost drivers.

•    Activity-based budgeting might not be appropriate for the organisation and its activities and cost structures.

•    A budget should be prepared on the basis of responsibility centres, with identifiable budget holders made responsible for the performance of their budget centre. A problem with ABB could be to identify clear individual responsibilities for activities.

•    It could be argued that in the short term many overhead costs are not controllable and do not vary directly with changes in the volume of activity for the cost driver. The only cost variances to report would be fixed overhead expenditure variances for each activity.

### Example 3 – RESEARCH DIVISION

(a) An incremental budget starts off with last year's budget or last year's actual results and adds on a certain percentage to take account of expected inflation and/or any expected changes in the level of activity. It is a very simple, quick and cheap budget to produce, but it does not promote a questioning attitude. Activities are undertaken without thought. They are simply incorporated into the next budget because they were in the last budget and nobody has given any thought as to whether the activity is still really worthwhile.

With ZBB, each manager sets out what he or she wishes to accomplish over the forthcoming period. For each activity they want to undertake, they look at different ways of achieving the objective and they look at providing the service at different levels. They estimate the costs and benefits and the activity only takes place if the benefits exceed the costs. Also once all the activities have been evaluated, they can be ranked against each other and the company's resources directed to the best activities.

(b) The managers/researchers responsible for each project should decide which projects they wish to undertake in the forthcoming period. These projects will be a mixture of continued projects and new projects. For the projects which have already been started and which the managers want to continue in the next period, we should ignore any cash flows already incurred (they are sunk costs), and we should only look at future costs and benefits. Similarly, for the new projects we should only look at the future costs and benefits. Different ways of achieving the same research goals should also be investigated and the projects should only go ahead if the benefit exceeds the cost. Once all the potential projects have been evaluated if there are insufficient funds to undertake all the worthwhile projects, then the funds should be allocated to the best projects on the basis of a cost-benefit analysis.

ZBB is usually of a highly subjective nature. (The costs are often reasonably certain, but usually a lot of uncertainty is attached to the estimated benefits.) This will be even truer of a research division where the researchers may have their own pet projects which they are unable to view in an objective light.

(c) (i) Activity based budgeting is where the budget is based upon a number of different levels of activity, i.e. on a number of different cost drivers, rather than being based on just one level of activity such as machine hours or output in units.

The activity based budget will be based upon the number of units of the cost driver multiplied by the cost per unit of cost driver. The cost driver is that factor which actually causes the cost and therefore should lead to a more accurate budget as the budgeted cost will be based on the thing that should influence that cost. The alternative is to use absorption costing and assume that all overheads vary with output or machine hours or labour hours or that they are fixed.

(ii) Z plc may employ an outside specialist such as a management consultant who will investigate the business and determine what activities the business undertakes during the course of its operations.

The consultant will discuss matters with the staff and the process will normally be time consuming. For each activity, efforts will be made to determine the factor which is most closely related to the costs of that activity, i.e. the cost driver. The investigation may bring to light non-value-added activities which can then be eliminated. It should improve the understanding of all those involved as to the true relationship between cost and level of activity.

Managers would then estimate the expected incidence of their cost drivers and multiply by the budgeted cost driver rate to get the budget for the forthcoming period. ABB would be more complicated than a traditional budget and the overheads would be broken down into many activities such as set-up costs, materials, handling costs, etc rather than expenses such as rent, heating, depreciation, etc.

With ABB the majority of the overhead costs would be perceived as variable rather than fixed. Of course it is not necessary to employ an outside consultant. The company may feel that they have their own managers with sufficient skills and time to undertake the exercise.

### Example 4 – What-if analysis

The original budget and 'what if' budgets can be constructed quickly using a marginal costing approach.

|  | Product X | Product Y | Total |
|---|---|---|---|
|  | $ | $ | $ |
| Budgeted sales | 150,000 | 120,000 | 270,000 |
| Variable costs | 60,000 | 60,000 | 120,000 |
| Contribution | 90,000 | 60,000 | 150,000 |
| Fixed costs |  |  | 140,000 |
| Budgeted profit |  |  | 10,000 |

**(b) (i)**

|  | Product X |  | Product Y | Total |
|---|---|---|---|---|
|  | $ |  | $ | $ |
| Budgeted sales | 150,000 |  | 120,000 | 270,000 |
| Variable costs | 60,000 | (+25%) | 75,000 | 135,000 |
| Contribution | 90,000 |  | 45,000 | 135,000 |
| Fixed costs |  |  |  | 140,000 |
| Budgeted loss |  |  |  | (5,000) |

**(ii)**

|  |  | Product X | Product Y | Total |
|---|---|---|---|---|
|  |  | $ | $ | $ |
| Budgeted sales | (−10%) | 135,000 | 120,000 | 255,000 |
| Variable costs | (−10%) | 54,000 | 60,000 | 114,000 |
| Contribution |  | 81,000 | 60,000 | 141,000 |
| Fixed costs |  |  |  | 140,000 |
| Budgeted profit |  |  |  | 1,000 |

**(iii)**

|  |  | Product X | Product Y | Total |
|---|---|---|---|---|
| Sales units |  | 28,500 | 15,000 |  |
|  |  | $ | $ | $ |
| Budgeted sales | (at $5) | 142,500 | 120,000 | 262,500 |
| Variable costs | (at $2.20) | 62,700 | 60,000 | 122,700 |
| Contribution |  | 79,800 | 60,000 | 139,800 |
| Fixed costs |  |  |  | 140,000 |
| Budgeted loss |  |  |  | (200) |

(iv)

|  | | Product X | | Product Y | Total |
|---|---|---|---|---|---|
| Sales units | (135,000/5) | 27,000 | (135,000/8) | 16,875 | |
|  | | $ | | $ | $ |
| Budgeted sales | (50%) | 135,000 | (50%) | 135,000 | 270,000 |
| Variable costs | (at $2) | 54,000 | (at $4) | 67,500 | 121,500 |
| Contribution | | 81,000 | | 67,500 | 148,500 |
| Fixed costs | | | | | 140,000 |
| Budgeted profit | | | | | 8,500 |

In practice, budget models are usually much more detailed and complex, but 'what if' analysis can be carried out simply and quickly.

In the example above, the 'what if' scenarios show that profit might be less than expected if actual results are less favourable than the assumptions and forecasts in the budget. If any of these results are unacceptable, management would need to consider alternative budget strategies for improving budgeted performance or reducing the risk.

## Test your understanding 1

**Materials purchases budget**

|  | Material DM1 | Material DM2 |
|---|---|---|
|  | Kg | Kg |
| To make 4,300 units of X | 5,160 | 3,440 |
| To make 5,900 units of Y | 11,800 | 0 |
| Required for production | 16,960 | 3,440 |
| Budgeted closing inventory | 1,000 | 200 |
|  | 17,960 | 3,640 |
| Opening inventory | 3,000 | 600 |
| Budgeted purchase quantities | 14,960 | 3,040 |
| Standard price per kg | $0.80 | $0.50 |
| Budgeted cost of purchases | $11,968 | $1,520 |

## Test your understanding 2

**Production budget:**

|  |  | April Units |  | May Units |
|---|---|---|---|---|
| Sales requirement |  | 8,900 |  | 8,500 |
| Plus closing inventory | (25% x 8,500) | 2,125 | (25% x 8,100) | 2,025 |
|  |  | 11,025 |  | 10,525 |
| Less opening inventory | (25% x 8,900) | 2,225 |  | 2,125 |
| Production required |  | 8,800 |  | 8,400 |

**Material purchases budget:**

|  |  | April Kg |
|---|---|---|
| Production requirement | (8,800 units x 2 kg) | 17,600 |
| Plus closing inventory | (8,400 units x 2 kg x 20%) | 3,360 |
|  |  | 20,960 |
| Less opening inventory | (8,800 units x 2 kg x 20%) | 3,520 |
| Purchases required |  | 17,440 |

April purchases paid for in May = 17,440 kg x $4 = $69,760.

## Test your understanding 3

| | |
|---|---|
| March sales = 20% for cash ($26,800 x 0.2) | 5,360 |
| February credit sales = 80% x 60% received less 3% discount ($29,500 x 0.6 x 0.97) | 13,735.20 |
| January credit sales = 80% x 38% received ($20,400 x 0.38) | 6,201.60 |
| | 25,296.80 |

## Test your understanding 4

|  | A $ | B $ | C $ |
|---|---|---|---|
| Selling price | 215 | 250 | 300 |
| Variable costs |  |  |  |
| Frame | 20 | 20 | 20 |
| Component D | 40 | 8 | 24 |
| Component E | 5 | 35 | 25 |
| Component F | 12 | 15 | 3 |
| Skilled labour | 12 | 9 | 9 |
| Unskilled labour | 9 | 9 | 13.5 |
| Variable overhead | 5 | 4 | 3.5 |
|  | 103 | 100 | 98 |
| Contribution per unit | 112 | 150 | 202 |

Contribution per batch of sales:

|  | $ |
|---|---|
| A: 1 × $112  = | 112 |
| B: 2 × $150  = | 300 |
| C: 4 × $202  = | 808 |
| Contribution per unit | 1,220 |

|  | $ |
|---|---|
| Contribution required |  |
| Production overhead | 728,000 |
| Selling and distribution | 364,000 |
| Administration | 338,000 |
| Profit | 6,500,000 |
|  | 7,930,000 |

Sales batches required  =  $7.930,000/$1,220  =  6,500 per annum

Period 1  =  500

Sales units are therefore:

A  500 × 1  =  500

B  500 × 2  =  1,000

C  500 × 4  =  2,000

(i) **Sales budget**

**Product**

|  | A | B | C | Total |
|---|---|---|---|---|
| Sales (units) | 500 | 1,000 | 2,000 | |
| Selling price ($) | 215 | 250 | 300 | |
| | | | | |
| Sales value ($) | 107,500 | 250,000 | 600,000 | 957,500 |

(ii) **Production budget**

**Product**

|  | A | B | C |
|---|---|---|---|
| Required by sales | 500 | 1,000 | 2,000 |
| Required closing inventory | 270 | 630 | 1,440 |
| | | | |
| | 770 | 1,630 | 3,440 |
| Less opening inventory | (300) | (700) | (1,600) |
| | | | |
| Production required | 470 | 930 | 1,840 |

(iii) **Material usage budget**

|  | Product | | | |
|---|---|---|---|---|
|  | A | B | C | Total |
| Copper frames | 470 | 930 | 1,840 | 3,240 |
| Component D | 2,350 | 930 | 5,520 | 8,800 |
| Component E | 470 | 6,510 | 9,200 | 16,180 |
| Component F | 1,880 | 4,650 | 1,840 | 8,370 |

## (iv) Material purchases

| | Copper frames | Components D | E | F |
|---|---|---|---|---|
| Required by production | 3,240 | 8,800 | 16,180 | 8,370 |
| Required closing inventory | 900 | 3,600 | 9,000 | 3,600 |
| | 4,140 | 12,400 | 25,180 | 11,970 |
| Less opening inventory | (1,000) | (4,000) | (10,000) | (4,000) |
| Purchases quantity | 3,140 | 8,400 | 15,180 | 7,970 |
| Purchase price | $20 | $8 | $5 | $3 |
| Purchase value | $62,800 | $67,200 | $75,900 | $23,910 |

## (v) Manpower budget

| | | Skilled (machining) | Unskilled (assembly) |
|---|---|---|---|
| Hours required | – Product A | 940 | 940 |
| | – Product B | 1,395 | 1,860 |
| | – Product C | 2,760 | 5,520 |
| | | 5,095 | 8,320 |
| Hours per worker per period (4 37.5) | | 150 | 150 |
| Number of workers required | | 34 | 56 |

(b)  The inventory of components would be significantly reduced if this proposal were adopted, thus freeing storage space for alternative uses (or possible cost savings).  However, the holding of fewer inventories will lead to a greater number of orders being placed, albeit of lesser values, and consideration must be given to the total cost of the inventory function from ordering, handling and storage.

The risk is that inventories will not be replenished when required, leading to production being stopped or the need to make best use of the materials which are available by switching to other products. In order to reduce this risk there must be increased communication with suppliers so that they are aware of the materials required. This requires closer control of production planning.

**Mini-Quiz**

(1)  B.

(2)  C. To inform shareholders of performance in meeting targets. Budgets are prepared for **internal** use and are not usually communicated to shareholders.

(3)  B. A new accounting period, such as a  month or a quarter, is added as each old one expires

(4)  B. A method of budgeting whereby all activities are re-evaluated each time a budget is formulated.

(5)  A

# 12

# Budgetary Control

## Chapter learning objectives

- **Explain** the ideas of feedback and feedforward control and their application in the use of budgets for control. (Syllabus link C1 a)

- **Explain** the concept of responsibility accounting and its importance in the construction of functional budgets that support the overall master budget. (Syllabus link C1 b)

- **Identify** controllable and uncontrollable costs in the context of responsibility accounting and why 'uncontrollable' costs may or may not be allocated to responsibility centres. (Syllabus link C1 c)

- **Evaluate** performance using fixed and flexible budget reports. (Syllabus link C2c)

- **Discuss** the impact of budgetary control systems and the setting of standard costs on human behaviour.(Syllabus link C3 a)

## 1 Session Content Diagram

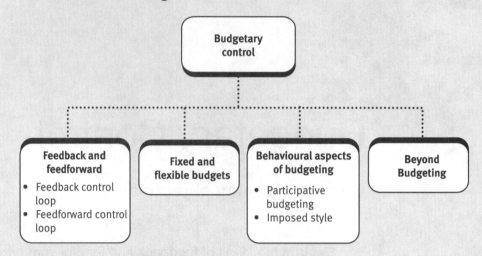

## 2 Knowledge Brought Forward

You will already have covered budgetary control with variance analysis is Papers C01 and P1. We will build on this knowledge in P2, but make sure you are comfortable with the assumed knowledge, that should have been brought forward as a base, in this section.

## 3 Planning and Operational Variances

Forecasts by their nature are unreliable, and yet most standards are set on a forecast basis, i.e. *ex ante* or before the event. A planning variance arises from an inability to make exact predictions of future costs and revenues at the budgeting stage.

If it were possible to set standards with the benefit of hindsight, i.e. *ex post* or after the event, managers would be able to see more clearly what amount of variances was genuinely attributable to operating performance (*operational variances*) and what amount to difficulties or errors in setting the original standard (*planning variances*). Such information should improve operational control and may also provide guidance for the improvement of planning procedures.

### The calculations

Planning variance       = Original standard    – Revised standard    **PRO**
Operational variance    = Revised standard     – Actual              **OAR**

The planning variance is usually regarded as uncontrollable and has arisen because the original standard was not reflective of the attainable standard. The operational variance is controllable.

*[In the PEG March 2011, the Examiner regrets that some candidates calculate cost variances based on sales volumes rather than based on production volumes].*

## Further explanation

### Operational variances

Operational variances are variances that are assumed to have occurred due to operational factors. These are materials price and usage variances, labour rate and efficiency variances, variable overhead expenditure and efficiency variances, overhead expenditure variances, and sales variances.

Operational variances are calculated with the 'realistic' ex post standard. They are calculated in exactly the same way as described in earlier chapters, the only difference being that the ex post standard is used, not the original standard.

### Planning variances

A planning variance measures the difference between the budgeted and actual profit that has been caused by errors in the original standard cost. It is the difference between the ex ante and the ex post standards.

- A planning variance is **favourable** when the ex post standard cost is lower than the original ex ante standard cost.

- A planning variance is **adverse** when the ex post standard cost is higher than the original ex ante standard cost.

## Example 1

The following data concerns Material X

| | |
|---|---|
| Original standard price $2 per kg | Revised standard price $3.50 per kg |
| Standard usage for actual output : 1,000 kg | |
| Actual price $3 per kg | Actual usage 1,200 kg |

### Required:

Calculate material price and usage variances using a planning and operational approach.

*[In the March 2013 PEG, the Examiner notes the following common errors linked to variances in the Exam :*

*(1) Only putting forward the top level variances;*

*(2) Naming the variances incorrectly;*

*(3) Not labelling the variances;*

*(4) Showing a favourable variance as adverse and vice versa;*

*(5) Submitting a written description of variances when this is not required;*

*(6) Failing to recognise planning variances;*

*(7) Extremely poor presentation of figures.]*

## 4 Causes of Planning Variances

There must be a good reason for deciding that the original standard cost is unrealistic. Deciding in retrospect that expected costs should be different from the standard should not be an arbitrary decision, aimed perhaps at shifting the blame for poor results from poor operational management to poor cost estimation.

A good reason for a change in the standard might be:

- a change in one of the main materials used to make a product or provide a service

- an unexpected increase in the price of materials due to a rapid increase in world market prices (for example, the price of oil or other commodities)

- a change in working methods and procedures that alters the expected direct labour time for a product or service

- an unexpected change in the rate of pay to the work force.

## 5 Benefits and Problems

### Benefits of Planning and Operational Variances

(1) In volatile and changing environments, standard costing and variance analysis are more useful using this approach.

(2) Operational variances provide up to date information about current levels of efficiency.

(3) Operational variances are likely to make the standard costing system more acceptable and to have a positive effect on motivation.

(4) It emphasises the importance of the planning function in the preparation of standards and helps to identify planning deficiencies.

## Problems of Planning and Operational Variances

(1) There is an element of subjectivity in determining the ex-post standards as to what is 'realistic'.

(2) There is a large amount of labour time involved in continually establishing up to date standards and calculating additional variances.

(3) There is a great temptation to put as much as possible of the total variances down to outside, uncontrollable factors, i.e. planning variances.

(4) There can then be a conflict between operating and planning staff. Each laying the blame at each other's door.

### Difference Between Budgetary Control & Variance Analysis

Budgetary control is concerned with controlling total costs, whereas standard costing and variance analysis are concerned with unit costs.

In order to use standard costing, a standard unit must be made or a standard action be performed. Budgetary control is more flexible and can be used to control costs even when a wide variety of activities are undertaken.

One disadvantage of using budgetary control is that whilst it limits expenditure it does not provide a basis for measuring the efficiency of that expenditure.

A standard costing system is integrated with the actual accounting system whereas budgetary control operates as a reporting system external to the accounting system.

Budgetary control is often used for discretionary items such as research and development, advertising and non-activity related costs such as administration.

In manufacturing organisations it is likely that the output units will be homogenous and easily measured, whereas in non-manufacturing (service organisations) there are likely to be various forms of output which may not be easy to measure.

## 6 Feedback And Feedforward

### Feedback

Feedback is the comparison of actual results against expected results and if there is a difference it is investigated and corrected.

Or more pedantically, feedback is the comparison of actual results against expected results and if there is a significant difference, then it is investigated and if possible and desirable it is corrected. The manner in which a feedback control loop might work in the context of a budgetary control system may be illustrated by the following diagram:

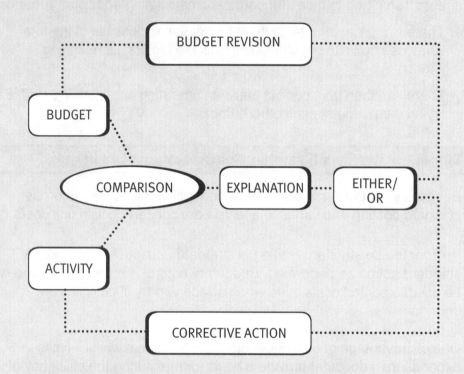

### Feedback Control

**Feedback** is a response providing useful information or guidelines for further action. Feedback can be defined in its everyday sense as a response providing useful information or guidelines for further action.

The term 'feedback' has its origins in system theory, and can be defined as 'return of part of the output of a system to the input as a means towards improved quality or self-correction of error'. (Chambers Dictionary)

Within the context of a business:

- the business is a system

- the system receives inputs (resources, such as cash, labour, materials and equipment)

- the system uses the inputs to produce outputs (products, services)

- some of the outputs of the system are measured (costs, revenues, and so on)

- this measured information is reported back to management as feedback

- management use the information, by comparing it with a plan or objective (for example, a budget) to decide whether control action is required.

**Feedback control** is the 'measurement of differences between planned outputs and actual outputs achieved, and the modification of subsequent action and/or plans to achieve future required results'.

Corrective action that brings actual performance closer to the target or plan is called *negative feedback*.

Corrective action that increases the difference between actual performance and the target or plan is called *positive feedback.*

## Feedback control in budgeting

Although the terminology of system theory might seem unusual, the application of the theory to budgeting and budgetary control might be readily apparent, in both public and private sector organisations.

- An organisation prepares a budget, and commits resources to achieving the budget targets.

- The business uses its resources to make products or provide services. Private sector organisations sell their output.

- Outputs from the system are measured. In budgetary control, output measurements will be quantities of products made or services provided, costs incurred, revenues earned, and profits and return. Some non-financial performance measurements might also be taken.

- The measurements provide feedback information to management, who compare actual results with the budget.

- Where a need for control action is identified, the manager responsible takes suitable control action.

> With negative feedback, the control action is intended to bring actual performance back into line with the budget. For example, if actual costs are higher than budget, control action might be taken to cut costs. Similarly, if actual sales volume is lower than budgeted sales, action might be taken to boost sales.
>
> **Key Point**
>
> Budgetary control systems are feedback control systems. With positive feedback, control action would be intended to increase the differences between the budget and actual results. For example, if actual sales are higher than budget, control action might be taken to make this situation continue. Similarly, when actual costs are less than budget, measures might be taken to keep costs down.
>
> Budgetary control systems are feedback control systems.

### Feedforward

Feedforward is the comparison of the results that are currently expected in the light of the latest information and the desired results. If there is a difference, then it is investigated and corrected.

Feedback happens after the event and discovers that something **has** gone wrong (or right). It is obviously too late to affect the result that has just happened, but the idea is that if we can understand what went wrong in the previous period, then we can stop the problem from recurring.

Feedforward is more proactive and aims to **anticipate** problems and prevent them from occurring. A good example of feedforward is that of a cash budget:

- Imagine that the budget at the start of the year stated that there would be a cash balance of $400,000 at the beginning of June and that a piece of capital equipment costing $320,000 was to be purchased in the month.

- Imagine further that we are now in April and we realise that the cash budget was optimistic and that we currently expect the cash balance to be only $220,000 at the start of June. Having anticipated the potential problem if we buy the machine, we can now take steps to eliminate the problem before it occurs:

  - We could simply delay the purchase of the machine for 1 or 2 months;

  - Or we could negotiate with the supplier of the equipment to see if they would be willing to accept instalments;

  - Or we could speak to the bank manager and obtain a temporary overdraft, etc.

## Feedforward Control

Feed-forward control information is an alternative approach to control. Feed-forward control is the 'forecasting of differences between actual and planned outcomes and the implementation of actions before the event, to avoid such differences' (CIMA Official Terminology).

For instance a feed-forward control model might be used to control costs. If the latest forecast shows that costs for the forthcoming period are expected to be higher than budget then control action can be taken now, before the event, to prevent or reduce the forecast overspending.

Whereas feedback is based on a comparison of historical actual results with the budget for the period to date, feed-forward looks ahead and compares:

- the target or objectives for the period, and
- what actual results are now forecast.

**Target costing** is an example of feed-forward control. When a target cost is set for a product or service it is derived by first determining a competitive market price. From this is deducted a desired profit margin in order to determine the target cost. An estimate of expected costs is made. If it is above the target cost so that the desired profit margin will not be earned, then management action is prompted to ensure that the target cost will be achieved.

### Example

A sales manager receives monthly control reports about sales values. The budgeted sales for the year to 31 December are $600,000 in total. At the end of April the manager might receive the following feedback control report.

**Sales report for April**

| Product | Month Budget $000 | Month Actual $000 | Month Variance $000 | Cumulative Budget $000 | Cumulative Actual $000 | Cumulative Variance $000 |
|---|---|---|---|---|---|---|
| P1 | 35 | 38 | 3 (F) | 90 | 94 | 4 (F) |
| P2 | 20 | 14 | 6 (A) | 50 | 39 | 11 (A) |
| P3 | 25 | 23 | 2 (A) | 50 | 45 | 5 (A) |
| Total | 80 | 75 | 5 (A) | 190 | 178 | 12 (A) |

Alternatively, the sales manager might be presented with a feed-forward control report, as follows:

**Sales report, April**

| Product | Budget $000 | Current forecast $000 | Variance $000 |
|---|---|---|---|
| P1 | 240 | 250 | 10 (F) |
| P2 | 150 | 120 | 30 (A) |
| P3 | 210 | 194 | 16 (A) |
| Total | 600 | 564 | 36 (A) |

**Advantages and problems with feed-forward control**

Feed-forward control reporting offers the key advantage that it is forward-looking. It informs management what is likely to happen unless control measures are taken. Management can compare their targets for the period with current expectations.

In contrast, feedback control is backward-looking, and historical variances or differences from plan are not necessarily a guide to what will happen over the full budget period.

A problem with feed-forward control is that control reports should be produced regularly, which means that forecasts must be updated regularly. To implement an efficient feed-forward control system, it is therefore necessary to have an efficient forecasting system. Forecasts might be prepared using computer models, with revisions to the forecast each month based on updated information about actual results to date, and where appropriate by making alterations to the basic assumptions in the model.

## 7 Fixed and Flexible Budgets

A **fixed** budget contains information on costs and revenues for one level of activity.

A **flexible** budget shows the same information, but for a number of different levels of activity. Flexible budgets are useful for both planning purposes and control purposes.

(1)  When preparing a flexible budget, managers are forced to consider the different scenarios and their responses to them. Thus for a number of different situations, managers will have calculated their costs and revenues. If an unexpected event does occur, changing the level of activity, management will be better prepared.

(2)  Budgetary control is the comparison of actual results against budget. Where the actual level of activity is different to that expected, comparisons of actual results against a fixed budget can give misleading results.

*[In the PEG November 2012, the Examiner notes that too many candidates still 'incorrectly compare the flexed budget to the original budget']*

### Example 2 – Flexible Budgets

Extracts from the budgets of B Ltd are given below:

**Sales and inventory budgets (units)**

|  | Period 1 | Period 2 | Period 3 | Period 4 | Period 5 |
|---|---|---|---|---|---|
| Opening Inventory | 4,000 | 2,500 | 3,300 | 2,500 | 3,000 |
| Sales | 15,000 | 20,000 | 16,500 | 21,000 | 18,000 |

**Cost Budgets ($000)**

|  | Period 1 | Period 2 | Period 3 |
|---|---|---|---|
| Direct materials | 108.0 | 166.4 | 125.6 |
| Direct labour | 270.0 | 444.0 | 314.0 |
| Production overheads (excluding depreciation) | 117.5 | 154.0 | 128.5 |
| Depreciation | 40.0 | 40.0 | 40.0 |
| Administration overhead | 92.0 | 106.6 | 96.4 |
| Selling overhead | 60.0 | 65.0 | 61.5 |

The following information is also available:

(i)  Production above 18,000 units incurs a bonus in addition to normal wages rates

(ii) Any variable costs contained in the selling overhead are assumed to vary with sales. All other variable costs are assumed to vary with production.

**Required:**

(a) Calculate the budgeted production for periods 1 to 4;

(b) Prepare a suitable cost budget for period 4.

In period 4 the inventory and sales budgets were achieved and the following actual costs recorded :

|  | $000 |
|---|---|
| Direct material | 176 |
| Direct labour | 458 |
| Production overhead | 181 |
| Depreciation | 40 |
| Administration overhead | 128 |
| Selling overhead | 62 |
|  | 1,045 |

**Required:**

(c) Show the budget variances from actual;

(d) Criticise the assumptions on which the cost budgets have been prepared.

## Illustration – Fixed & Flexible Budgets

A software company has the following annual budget:

|  | $ | $ |
|---|---|---|
| Sales |  | 480,000 |
| Materials | 48,000 |  |
| Labour costs | 200,000 |  |
| Other expenses | 180,000 |  |
|  |  | 428,000 |
| Budgeted profit |  | 52,000 |

Sales are expected to be a constant amount each month.

- Material costs vary with sales.

- 30% of labour costs are variable with sales, and the rest are fixed costs.

- Other expenses are part-fixed and part-variable. Variable expenses are 10% of sales.

At the end of month 6, the following report is prepared for the six months to date:

**Budgeted and actual results for the first six months**

|  | Original budget | Actual results | Difference |
|---|---|---|---|
|  | $ | $ | $ |
| Sales | 240,000 | 200,000 | 40,000 (A) |
| Materials | 24,000 | 16,000 | 8,000 (F) |
| Labour costs | 100,000 | 94,000 | 6,000 (F) |
| Other expenses | 90,000 | 89,000 | 1,000 (F) |
|  | 214,000 | 199,000 | 15,000 (F) |
| Profit | 26,000 | 1,000 | 25,000 (A) |

This comparison of actual results with a fixed budget does not provide useful control information. A more useful control report would be prepared by comparing actual results with a flexible budget.

|  | Original budget | Flexible budget | Actual results | Difference |
|---|---|---|---|---|
|  | $ | $ | $ | $ |
| Sales | 240,000 | 200,000 | 200,000 |  |
| Materials | 24,000 | 20,000 | 16,000 | 4,000 (F) |
| Labour costs (see W1) | 100,000 | 95,000 | 94,000 | 1,000 (F) |
| Other expenses (see W2) | 90,000 | 86,000 | 89,000 | 3,000 (A) |
|  | 214,000 | 201,000 | 199,000 | 2,000 (F) |
| Profit | 26,000 | (1,000) | 1,000 | 25,000 (A) |

**Workings for the flexible budget:**

**(W1) Labour costs:**

|  | $ |
|---|---|
| Budgeted labour costs, original budget | 200,000 |
| Budgeted variable costs (30%) | 60,000 |
| Budgeted fixed costs | 140,000 |

|  | $ |
|---|---|
| Fixed cost budget for the first six months (× 6/12) | 70,000 |
| Flexible budget variable costs | 25,000 |
| (60,000/480,000 × $200,000) | |
| Total labour costs in the flexed budget | 95,000 |

**(W2) Other expenses:**

|  | $ |
|---|---|
| Budgeted other expenses, original budget | 180,000 |
| Budgeted variable costs (10% of $480,000) | 48,000 |
| Budgeted fixed costs | 132,000 |

|  | $ |
|---|---|
| Fixed cost budget for the first six months (× 6/12) | 66,000 |
| Flexible budget variable costs (10% × $200,000) | 20,000 |
| Total labour costs in the flexed budget | 86,000 |

**Reconciling budgeted and actual profit: sales variance**

In order to reconcile the budgeted profit for a period with the actual profit or loss, a sales volume margin variance has to be calculated. If the flexible budget is prepared using marginal costing, the sales volume variance should be a contribution margin variance.

In the example above, the budgeted contribution margin should be calculated as a budgeted contribution/sales ratio:

|  | $ | $ |
|---|---|---|
| Sales |  | 480,000 |
| Materials (all variable) | 48,000 |  |
| Variable labour costs | 60,000 |  |
| Variable other expenses | 48,000 |  |
| Budgeted variable costs |  | 156,000 |
| Budgeted contribution |  | 324,000 |

Budgeted contribution/sales ratio = (324,000/480,000) = 0.675 or 67.5%.

The **sales volume contribution margin variance** is calculated in the same way as a sales volume margin variance in standard costing:

|  | $ |
|---|---|
| Budgeted sales for the 6 months | 240,000 |
| Actual sales for the 6 months | 200,000 |
| Sales Volume variance | 40,000 |
| Budgeted contribution/sales ratio | 67.5% |
| Sales Volume contribution variance | $27,000 |

**Note:** This variance could be calculated more quickly as the difference between the profit in the original budget ($26,000) and the 'profit' in the flexed budget (a loss of $1,000) which is $27,000 less.

There is no sales price variance, because there is no standard sales price.

## 8 Behavioural Aspects of Budgeting

### Participation in budgeting

There are basically two ways in which a budget can be set: from the top down (imposed budget) or from the bottom up (participatory budget).

### Imposed style

An imposed/top-down budget is defined in CIMA's *Official Terminology* as 'A budget allowance which is set without permitting the ultimate budget holder to have the opportunity to participate in the budgeting process'

### Advantages of imposed style

There are a number of reasons why it might be preferable for managers not to be involved in setting their own budgets:

(1) Involving managers in the setting of budgets is more time consuming than if senior managers simply imposed the budgets.

(2) Managers may not have the skills or motivation to participate usefully in the budgeting process.

(3) Senior managers have the better overall view of the company and its resources and may be better-placed to create a budget which utilises those scarce resources to best effect.

(4) Senior managers also are aware of the longer term strategic objectives of the organisation and can prepare a budget which is in line with that strategy.

(5) Managers may build budgetary slack or bias into the budget in order to make the budget easy to achieve and themselves look good.

(6) Managers cannot use budgets to play games which disadvantage other budget holders.

(7) By having the budgets imposed by senior managers, i.e. someone outside the department, a more objective, fresher perspective may be gained.

(8) If the participation is only pseudo-participation and the budgets are frequently drastically changed by senior management, then this will cause dissatisfaction and the effect will be to demotivate staff.

*[In the PEG November 2012, the Examiner notes that some candidates are 'incorrectly describing a top-down budget.']*

## Participative Budgets

Participative/bottom up budgeting is 'A budgeting system in which all budget holders are given the opportunity to participate in setting their own budgets'

(CIMA *Official Terminology*)

*[In the PEG November 2012, the Examiner regrets that some candidates are 'failing to define or describe a participative budget'.]*

### Advantages of participative budgets

(1) The morale of the management is improved. Managers feel like their opinion is listened to, that their opinion is valuable.

(2) Managers are more likely to accept the plans contained within the budget and strive to achieve the targets if they had some say in setting the budget, rather than if the budget was imposed upon them. Failure to achieve the target that they themselves set is seen as a personal failure as well as an organisational failure.

(3) The lower level managers will have a more detailed knowledge of their particular part of the business than senior managers and thus will be able to produce more realistic budgets.

### Budgetary Control – Behavioural Aspects

Another very important aspect of budgetary control systems and this is its impact on the human beings who will operate and be judged by those systems.

It is only comparatively recently that the results of years of study of personal relationships in the workplace have percolated into the field of management accounting. It is now recognised that failure to consider the effect of control systems on the people affected could result in a lowering of morale and a reduction of motivation. Further, those people may be induced to do things that are not in the best interests of the organisation.

Specific behavioural issues encountered in budgeting include the following:

#### Motivation and co-operation

To be fully effective, any system of financial control must provide for motivation and incentive. If this requirement is not satisfied, managers will approach their responsibilities in a very cautious and conservative manner. It is often found that adverse variances attract investigation and censure but there is no incentive to achieve favourable variances. Failure to distinguish controllable from uncontrollable costs in budgetary control can alienate managers from the whole process.

Personal goals and ambitions are, in theory, strongly linked to organisational goals. These personal goals may include a desire for higher income and higher social standing. To simultaneously satisfy the goals of the organisation and the goals of the individual there must be 'goal congruence'. That is, the individual manager perceives that his or her own goals are achieved by his or her acting in a manner that allows the organisation to achieve its goals. The problem is that reliance on budgetary control systems does not always result in goal congruence.

The success of a budgetary control system depends on the people who operate and are affected by it. They must work within the system in an understanding and co-operative manner. This can only be achieved by individuals who have a total involvement at all stages in the budget process. However, it is often found that

(1) A budget is used simply as a pressure device. If the budget is perceived as 'a stick with which to beat people', then it will be sabotaged in all sorts of subtle ways.

(2) The budgeting process and subsequent budgetary control exercises induce competition between individual departments and executives. Managers may be induced to do things in order to 'meet budget' that are not in the best interests of the business as a whole.

**Failure of goal congruence**

It has been seen that an essential element in budgetary control is performance evaluation. Actual results are compared with budget or standard in order to determine whether performance is good or bad. What is being evaluated is not just the business operation but the managers responsible for it. The purpose of budgetary control is to induce managers to behave in a manner that is to the best advantage of the organisation. Compliance with budget is enforced by a variety of negative and positive sanctions.

When adverse variances are reported for operations then this implies poor performance by the managers of the operations. If they are unable to correct or explain away the adverse variances, then they may suffer negative sanctions. They may have forgo salary increases, or they may be demoted to a less prestigious post. Other more subtle negative sanctions are possible that anyone who has ever worked for a large organisation will be aware of.

Positive inducements may be offered to encourage managers to avoid adverse variances. A manager who meets budget may be granted a performance-related salary bonus, promotion, a new company car or use of the executive dining room.

Consequently, the manager has a considerable incentive to ensure that the department or operation he is responsible for achieves its budgeted level of performance. However, there are a variety of ways of doing this that might not be to the advantage of the organisation as a whole.

For example, the manager of a production line can cut costs and hence improve its reported performances by reducing quality controls. This may result in long-term problems concerning failure of products in service, loss of customer goodwill and rectification costs – but these are not the concern of the production line manager. This is a clear failure of goal congruence.

The control system is capable of distorting the process it is meant to serve – or 'the tail wags the dog'. The enforcement of a budgetary control system requires sensitivity if this is not to happen.

### The budget as a pot of cash

In some environments managers may come to consider the budget as a sum of money that has to be spent. This arises particularly in service departments or public sector organisations, the performance of which is gauged mainly through comparison of actual and budget spending.

The manager of a local authority 'street cleaning' department may be given an annual budget of £120,000 to clean the streets. The manager knows that she will be punished if she spends more than £120,000 in the year. She also knows that if she spends less than £120,000 in the year then her budget will probably be reduced next year. Such a reduction will involve a personal loss of status in the organisation and will make her job more difficult in the next year.

In order to ensure that she does not overspend her annual budget in the current year the manager may spend at a rate of £9,000 per month for the first 11 months of the year. This can be achieved by reducing the frequency of street cleaning and using poor-quality materials. It allows a contingency fund to be accumulated in case of emergencies.

However, in the final month of the year the manager has to spend £21,000 if she wishes to ensure that her whole budget is fully used. She might achieve this by using extra labour and high-quality materials.

Does this behaviour make sense? Of course it does not. The whole pattern of behaviour is distorted by the control system. It means that local residents have a substandard service for 11 months of the year and money is wasted in the 12th month.

It is, however, a fact that suppliers to government departments and local councils often experience a surge in orders towards the end of the financial year. This surge is caused by managers placing orders at the last moment in order to ensure that their full budget for the year is committed.

### Budget negotiation

Budgets are normally arrived at by a process of negotiation with the managers concerned. A budget may actually be initiated by departmental managers and then corrected as a result of negotiation with the budget officer.

Clearly, a manager has an incentive to negotiate a budget that is not difficult to achieve. This produces a phenomenon known as 'padding the budget' or 'budgetary slack'. A manager will exaggerate the costs required to achieve objectives. This has the following results:

(1) If the manager succeeds in padding his budget, then the whole control exercise is damaged. Comparison of actual with budget gives no meaningful measure of performance and the manager is able to include inefficiencies in his operation if he wishes.

(2) A successful manager becomes one who is a hard negotiator. The problem with this is that the negotiations in question are between colleagues and not with customers. 'Infighting' may become entrenched in the management process.

(3) A great deal of time and energy that could be directed to the actual management of the business is distracted by what are essentially administrative procedures.

These are all examples of a control system distorting the processes they are meant to serve.

### Influence on accounting policies

Any management accountant who has been engaged in the preparation of financial control reports will be familiar with attempts by managers to influence the accounting policies that are used. For example, the apportionment of indirect costs between departments often contains subjective elements. Should security costs be apportioned on the basis of floor space or staff numbers?

The manner in which the indirect costs are apportioned can have a considerable impact on how the performance of individual departments is perceived. This position creates the scope and incentive for managers to argue over accounting policies.

If a manager perceives that her department's performance is falling below budget, then she may sift through the costs charged to her department and demand that some be reclassified and charged elsewhere. The time and energy that goes into this kind of exercise has to be diverted from that available for the regular management of the business.

### Budget constrained management styles

When the performance of a manager is assessed by his ability to meet budget, then he is likely to adopt a conservative approach to new business opportunities that appear. The immediate impact of new business ventures is likely to be a rise in capital and operating costs – with an adverse impact on current period profit. The benefits of such ventures may only be felt in the long term. Hence, when a new opportunity appears, the manager evaluating it may only perceive that its acceptance will result in below-budget performance in the current period – and turn it down on this ground alone. Another consideration is that reliance on budgetary control is an approach to management that involves sitting in an office and reading financial reports. Such an approach (in conjunction with features such as executive dining rooms) may result in an unsatisfactory corporate culture based on hierarchies and social divisions. Large organisations that rely heavily on budgetary control systems often take on an 'ossified' character.

Yet another consideration is that a reliance on budgetary planning may induce managers to favour projects and developments that are most amenable to the construction of budgets. Projects that involve little uncertainty and few unknowns are easy to incorporate in budgets and hence managers may be more inclined to adopt such projects than the alternatives. Projects that involve significant uncertainties may be attractive if they incorporate some combination of high expected returns and low cost interim exit routes – but a budget constrained manager may be disinclined to adopt such projects simply because they are difficult to incorporate in budgets. Some writers (see Section 12.8.3, 'contingency theory') suggest that the budgetary approach may be particularly inappropriate in a dynamic and turbulent business environment.

The general conclusion concerning this and previous points is that good budgetary control can offer certain benefits. However, when budgetary control is enforced in a rigid or insensitive manner it may end up doing more harm than good.

### Budgets and motivation

Much of the early academic work on budgets concerned the extent to which the 'tightness' or looseness' of a budget acted as an incentive or disincentive to management effort. This was the issue of 'budget stretch'. Seminal works in this general area included studies by A.C. Stedry (see his 1960 text 'Budget Control and Cost Behaviour') and G.H. Hofstede (see his 1968 text 'The Game of Budget Control').

The main thrust of the findings that emerged from these studies was:

(1) Loose budgets (i.e. ones easily attainable) are poor motivators;

(2) As budgets are tightened, up to a point they become more motivational;

(3) Beyond that point, a very tight budget ceases to be motivational.

The role of budget participation and the manner in which aspirations and objectives are stated was also explored in certain studies. It was suggested that the participation of managers in budget setting was a motivational factor – but see earlier discussion concerning budget padding and negotiation.

## 9 Beyond Budgeting

The whole concept of budgeting turns around the idea that the operation of an organisation can be meaningfully planned for in some detail over an extended period into the future. Further, that this plan can be used to guide, control and co-ordinate the activities of numerous departments and individuals within the organisation.

The traditional budgeting concept has its critics:

*In one division with 300 employees and $100 m in annual costs, their operating budget was more than four inches thick and involved over 100 business units. They completed the budget six months into the current fiscal year with managers and directors under great pressure to revise the budget to meet corporate goals. But each revision was just an editorial exercise in changing the numbers, not in revising operating activities. These were only changes in a lengthy and cumbersome document that few understood. Budget complexity drives out meaning and relevance.*

Bruce Neumann, *Streamlining Budgeting in the New Millennium* (Strategic Finance 12/2001)

The modern economic environment is associated with a **rapidly changing environment, flexible manufacturing, short product life-cycles and products/services which are highly customised**. The 'lean business' and the 'virtual business' are responses to this. Such businesses own limited assets of the traditional kind but assemble resources as and when needed to meet customer demand. The keys to their operation are flexibility and speed of response. They are able to move quickly to exploit opportunities as they arise and do not operate according to elaborate business plans.

*In an age of discontinuous change, unpredictable competition, and fickle customers, few companies can plan ahead with any confidence – yet most organisations remain locked into a 'plan-make-and-sell' business model that involves a protracted annual budgeting process based on negotiated targets and that assumes that customers will buy what the company decides to make. Such assumptions are no longer valid in an age when customers can switch loyalties at the click of a mouse.*

J Hope and R Fraser. *Beyond Budgeting* (Strategic Finance 10/2000)

'Beyond Budgeting' (BB) is the generic name given to a body of practices intended to replace budgeting as a management model. The core concept is the need to move from a business model based on centralised organisational hierarchies to one based on devolved networks.

> *Beyond Budgeting* is defined in CIMA's *Official Terminology* as 'the idea that companies need to move *beyond budgeting* because of the inherent flaws in budgeting especially when used to set incentive contracts. It is argued that a range of techniques , such as rolling forecasts and market-related targets, can take the place of traditional budgets.'

### Beyond Budgeting Round Table (BBRT)

BB is identified with the 'Beyond Budgeting Round Table' (BBRT). The latter is. . . *at the heart of a new movement that is searching for ways to build lean, adaptive and ethical enterprises that can sustain superior competitive performance. Its aim is to spread the idea through a vibrant community'. (*BBRT website)

BBRT is a research consortium which was set up in 1998 to promote research into and the adoption of BB. At its centre is the eight strong 'BBRT team', the best known of whom are Robin Fraser and Jeremy Hope. The full round table community consists of the team, business and academic associates and the member businesses.

Budgeting is a pervasive exercise that provides the administrative basis for organisational planning and control in many traditionally run organisations. The vision of the Chief Executive is translated into a plan which is expressed in the form of a budget. Once that budget is adopted, then the management function becomes one of securing compliance. Budgeting is a core management process which provides stability and reduces risk. This becomes a cultural phenomenon reflecting a hierarchical approach to management whereby subordinate managers are judged on how far they succeed in complying with orders. It is an approach which has been linked to some high-profile business failures. For example, managers at WorldCom claimed that working life was all about satisfying the demands of CEO Bernie Ebbers and a small group of his associates:

*'You would have a budget and he would mandate that you had to be 2 percent under budget. Nothing else was acceptable'*

BBRT advances the idea that budgeting should be abolished and an alternative business model should be substituted in its place. BB is a 'responsibility model' whereby managers are given goals which are based on benchmarks linked variously to world class performance, peers, competitors and/or earlier periods. This requires an adaptive approach whereby authority is devolved to managers. An organisation run in this manner will be more a network than a hierarchy. The whole spectrum of modern management techniques and aids should be incorporated in an implementation of the BB model. IT networks provide easy communication between different component parts of an organisation together with its customers, associates and suppliers. Quality programmes (TQM), process engineering (BPR), supply chain management (SCM), balanced scorecards and activity accounting all have a role. Advocates of BB claim that it does not provide a softer environment for management than budget compliance. Both individual and team performance should have a high visibility in a devolved management environment.

## Illustration

For example, a performance control report based on the scorecard principle might appear as follows:

**XYZ Ltd, Performance Control Report for Quarter 4**
**Scorecard**

|  | Actual | Target | Var (%) |
|---|---|---|---|
| *Financials* | | | |
| Revenue ($) | 18,360,000 | 17,500,000 | 4.91 |
| Income / Expenditure | 1.055 | 1.040 | 1.44 |
| Earnings ($) | 181,900 | 170,000 | 7.00 |
| Market capitalisation ($) | 190,800,000 | 200,000,000 | (4.60) |
| *Customers* | | | |
| Customer satisfaction (points) | 8.731 | 9.00 | (2.99) |
| Returns (%) | 2.89 | 2.00 | (44.50) |
| *Processes* | | | |
| Delivery errors (%) | 0.86 | 0.90 | 4.44 |
| Design errors (points) | 1.976 | 2.000 | 1.20 |
| Design-delivery time (days) | 94 | 90 | (4.44) |
| *Staff* | | | |
| Staff satisfaction (points) | 7.310 | 8.00 | (8.63) |
| Training hours per FTE staff member | 4.217 | 3.500 | 20.49 |

That gives a fuller impression of performance than a straight actual-budget comparison and the approach can be refined much further. Results can be reported using graphics and trends. It is possible to adopt industry averages or trend analysis based projections as the relevant benchmarks instead of fixed targets.

## 10 Beyond Budgeting – 6 principles

A BB implementation should incorporate the following six main principles:

(1) An organisation structure with **clear principles and boundaries**; a manager should have no doubts over what he/she is responsible for and what he/she has authority over; the concept of the internal market for business units may be relevant here.

(2) Managers should be given goals and targets which are based on **relative success** and linked to shareholder value; such targets may be based on key performance indicators and benchmarks following the balanced scorecard principle.

(3) Managers should be given a **high degree of freedom** to make decisions; this freedom is consistent with the total quality management and business process reengineering concepts; a BB organisation chart should be 'flat'.

(4) Responsibility for decisions that generate value should be placed with **'front line teams'**; again, this is consistent with TQM and BPR concepts.

(5) Front line teams should be made responsible for **relationships** with customers, associate businesses and suppliers; direct communication between all the parties involved should be facilitated; this is consistent with the SCM concept.

(6) Information support systems should be transparent and ethical; an activity based accounting system which reports on the activities for which managers and teams are responsible is likely to be of use in this regard.

*BB is essentially an approach that places modern management practices within a cultural framework.*

*'The process of management is not about administering fixed budgets, it is about the dynamic allocation of resources'*

Lord Browne, former CEO of BP

### 11 Benefits of Beyond Budgeting

All the cases studied are different, but the following general benefits for BB are claimed:

(1) **Faster response time** – operating within a flexible organisational network and with strategy as an 'adaptive process' allows managers to respond quickly to customer requests.

(2) **Better innovation** – managers working within an environment wherein performance is judged on the basis of team and business unit results encourages the adoption of new innovations. Relations with customers and suppliers through SCM may facilitate the adoption of new working methods and technologies.

(3) **Lower costs** – in the context of BB managers are more likely to perceive costs as scarce resources which have to be used effectively than as a budget 'entitlement' that has to be used. BB is also likely to promote an awareness of the purposes for which costs are being incurred and thereby the potential for reductions.

(4) **Improved customer and supplier loyalty** – the leading role of front line teams in dealing with customers and suppliers is likely to deepen the relevant relationships.

As with many innovations in management practice, BB was a creature of its time. It appeared in the mid-1990s at a time when globalisation and advances in IT were tending to speed up the business environment. In particular, customers had greater choice and expected faster service. The key competitive constraint in most business situations is no longer land, labour or capital. For example, if labour is locally scarce then work can be outsourced to India or manufacturing can be relocated to China. In many practical business situations the key competitive factor is likely to be intellectual and knowledge based in character.

The BB model appeared as a set of information-age best practices which was attuned to the new situation. BB is intended to be an exercise in mobilising competent managers, skilled workers and loyal customers. However, traditional budgeting still has its defenders. Such defenders claim that while budgeting may be associated with a 'command and control' management style, it is the management style that is the problem and not budgeting.

### Svenska Handelsbanken

Researchers have explored the history of BB implementations to determine whether or not these have delivered improved results. BBRT has reported several case studies, the best known of which is that of **Svenska Handelsbanken**.

This Swedish bank abandoned budgeting in 1972 and switched to delegation model (involving 600 autonomous work units) that avoids formal planning and target setting. Branch managers run their own businesses and are able to decide how many staff they need, where they obtain support services from and what products they market to which customers. Branch performance is assessed using measures such as customer profitability, customer retention and work productivity.

The Svenska Handelsbanken model might indicate a higher level of corporate risk with all that would imply for cost of money and market capitalisation. However, it is claimed that the model favours flexibility. In the absence of a fixed plan, products and projects are designed to allow easy modification and exit routes. This view suggests that the model invites a different approach to risk management rather than the acceptance of higher risk.

## 12 Practice Questions

### Test your understanding 1

A company has a sales budget of $145,000 per month for the financial year January to December. However, by the end of May, the cumulative sales variances for the year to date are:

**Sales price variance $30,000 (A);**

**Sales volume contribution variance $16,000 (A)**

The standard contribution/sales ratio is 40%. The marketing department has now estimated that sales for the next three months will be $120,000 per month, but for the rest of the year, monthly sales should rise to $148,000.

**Required:**

Prepare a statement as at the end of May that compares budgeted and forecast sales revenue and contribution for the year as a whole. Ignore variable cost variances.

### Test your understanding 2

The following fixed and flexible budgets have been prepared:

|  | Fixed budget 100% level | Flexible budget 90% level |
|---|---|---|
|  | $ | $ |
| Sales | 750,000 | 675,000 |
| Direct variable costs | 420,000 | 378,000 |
| Overheads | 230,000 | 216,800 |
| Total costs | 650,000 | 594,800 |
| Profit | 100,000 | 80,200 |

Actual sales for the period were $700,000 and there was an adverse sales price variance of $5,000 (A).

**Required:**

Prepare a flexible budget for the actual level of sales.

## Test your understanding 3

An office manager uses the high-low method to establish the expected costs for office expenses, based on the following data for monthly expenses:

|  | Costs for 6,000 labour hours | Costs for 8,000 labour hours |
| --- | --- | --- |
|  | $ | $ |
| Heating and lighting | 17,000 | 18,000 |
| Telephones | 7,200 | 8,400 |
| Sundry expenses | 29,400 | 33,400 |

Variable costs are assumed to vary with the number of labour hours worked in the office during the period.

In the most recent month, 7,700 labour hours were worked and actual costs were as follows:

|  | $ |
| --- | --- |
| Heating and lighting | 17,600 |
| Telephones | 8,750 |
| Sundry expenses | 32,600 |

**Required:**

Calculate the cost variances for the month.

## Test your understanding 4

A direct mail organisation has the following budgeted and actual results for a period:

|  | Original budget | Actual results |
| --- | --- | --- |
|  | $ | $ |
| Sales | 500,000 | 560,000 |
| Materials/stationery | 50,000 | 58,000 |
| Labour costs | 100,000 | 108,000 |
| Other expenses | 200,000 | 204,500 |
|  | 350,000 | 370,500 |
| Profit | 150,000 | 189,500 |

It is assumed that all materials and stationery costs are variable, 10% of labour costs are variable and 25% of other expenses are variable. All variable costs vary with the value of sales.

**Required:**

Prepare an operating statement that reconciles the budgeted and actual results for the period.

## Test your understanding 5

A company has prepared an activity-based budget for its stores department. The budgeted costs are:

|  | *Cost driver* | *Budgeted cost* |
|---|---|---|
| Receiving goods | Number of deliveries | $80 per delivery |
| Issuing goods from store | Number of stores requisitions | $40 per requisition |
| Ordering | Number of orders | $25 per order |
| Counting stock | Number of stock counts | $1,000 per count |

Keeping records – $24,000 each year

Supervision – $30,000 each year

Actual results for April were:

|  | *Activity* | *Actual cost* |
|---|---|---|
| Receiving goods | 45 orders delivered | 3,450 |
| Issuing goods | 100 requisitions | 4,400 |
| Ordering | 36 orders | 960 |
| Counting | 2 stock counts | 1,750 |
| Record keeping |  | 1,900 |
| Supervision | 2,700 | 15,160 |

**Required:**

Prepare a variance report for the month.

**Test your understanding 6**

Branch makes and sells two products, P and Q. The following budget has been prepared:

|  | Product P | Product Q |
|---|---|---|
| Sales price per unit | €3 | €6 |
| Variable cost per unit | €2 | €3 |

Budgeted fixed costs are €140,000. Budgeted sales are 20,000 units of Product P and 50,000 units of Product Q.

**Required:**

(a) Calculate the budgeted profit.

(b) Calculate by how much the profit would be reduced if the variable cost of Product P were 15% higher than budgeted and the variable cost of Product Q were 10% higher than budgeted.

(c) Calculate by how much the profit would be reduced or increased if total sales revenue is the same as in the original budget, but the sales mix (by revenue) is one-third Product P and two-thirds Product Q.

**Mini-Quiz**

1 Within the context of a budgetary control system:

1.1 Explain the distinction between information feedback and feedforward.

1.2 Explain the distinction between a controllable cost and an uncontrollable cost.

1.3 Explain the distinction between a fixed and a flexible budget.

1.4 Explain the term 'failure of goal congruence'.

1.5 Explain the term 'budget slack'.

## Test your understanding answers

### Example 1

#### Traditional approach

|  |  |  |  | $ |  |
|---|---|---|---|---|---|
| SQSP |  |  |  |  |  |
| 1,000 kg x | $2/kg | = | 2,000 | | Usage |
| AQSP |  |  |  | | $400 A |
| 1,200 kg x | $2/kg | = | 2,400 | | |
| AQAP |  |  |  | | $1,200 A |
| 1,200 kg x | $3/kg | = | 3,600 | | Price |

#### Planning and operational approach

| Planning variance |  |  |
|---|---|---|
| Price | ($2 - $3.50) x 1000 kg | $1,500 A |

| Operational variances |  |  |  |  |  |
|---|---|---|---|---|---|
| SQSP |  |  |  |  |  |
| 1,000 kg x | $3.50/kg | = | 3,500 | | Usage |
| AQSP |  |  |  | | $700 A |
| 1,200 kg x | $3.50/kg | = | 4,200 | | |
| AQAP |  |  |  | | $600 F |
| 1,200 kg x | $3/kg | = | 3,600 | | Price |

## Example 2 – Flexible Budgets

(a)

| | Period 1 | Period 2 | Period 3 | Period 4 | Period 5 |
|---|---|---|---|---|---|
| Sales | 15,000 | 20,000 | 16,500 | 21,000 | 18,000 |
| Add : closing stock | 2,500 | 3,300 | 2,500 | 3,000 | |
| Less : opening stock | (4,000) | (2,500) | (3,300) | (2,500) | (3,000) |
| Production | 13,500 | 20,800 | 15,700 | 21,500 | – |

(b) In Period 4, Production = 21,500 units

| | | $000 |
|---|---|---|
| Direct materials | (W1) | 172.0 |
| Direct labour | (W2) | 465.0 |
| Production Overhead | (W3) | 157.50 |
| Depreciation | | 40.0 |
| Administration Overhead | (W4) | 108.0 |
| Selling Overhead | (W5) | 66.0 |
| | | 1,008.50 |

**Working 1**

$$\frac{\$108,000 \text{ (Period 1)}}{13,500 \text{ units}} = \$8 \times 21,500 = \$172,000$$

**Working 2**

Normal wage $\dfrac{\$270,000}{13,500} = \$20$ per unit

Bonus (Period 2) = $444,000 – (20,800 x $20) = $28,000 premium

Premium rate: $\dfrac{\$28,000}{2,800 \text{ units above } 18,000} = \$10$ per unit

in Period 4, (21,500 x $20) + (3,500 x $10) = $465,000

**Working 3**

$$\text{Variable Cost per unit} = \frac{154 - 117.5}{20.8 - 13.5} = \frac{36.5}{7.3} = \$5 \text{ per unit}$$

**Working 4**

$$\text{Variable Cost per unit} = \frac{106.6 - 92.0}{20.8 - 13.5} = \frac{14.6}{7.3} = \$2 \text{ per unit}$$

**Working 5**

$$\text{Variable Cost per unit} = \frac{65.0 - 60}{20.0 \text{ sales} - 15.0} = \$1 \text{ per unit}$$

Fixed cost = $60,000 – ($1 x 15,000) = $45,000

In Period 4, $1 x 21,000 + $45,000 = $66,000

| | P4 Budget | P4 Actual | Variance | Adverse / Favourable |
|---|---|---|---|---|
| Material | 172.0 | 176.0 | 4.0 | Adverse |
| Labour | 465.0 | 458.0 | 7.0 | Favourable |
| Production Overhead | 157.5 | 181.0 | 23.5 | Adverse |
| Depreciation | 40.0 | 40.0 | 0.0 | – |
| Administration Overhead | 108.0 | 128.0 | 20.0 | Adverse |
| Selling Overhead | 66.0 | 62.0 | 4.0 | Favourable |
| | 1,008.50 | 1,045.0 | 36.5 | Adverse |

(d)

– Linear costs

– No Incremental Fixed Costs

– Variable Cost per unit is constant

– Volume the only factor to affect Total Costs

## Test your understanding 1

| | $ |
|---|---:|
| Sales volume (contribution) variance | 16,000 (A) |
| Standard contribution/sales ratio: | 40% |
| Sales volume variance in sales revenue | 40,000 (A) |
| Sales price variance | 30,000 (A) |
| Budgeted sales for the first 5 months (× 145,000) | 725,000 |
| Actual sales revenue for the first five months | 655,000 |
| Expected sales for the next 3 months (× 120,000) | 360,000 |
| Expected sales for the final 4 months (× 148,000) | 592,000 |
| **Forecast sales for the year** | **1,607,000** |

| | $ |
|---|---:|
| Forecast sales for the year (actual revenue) | 1,607,000 |
| Cumulative sales price variances | 30,000 (A) |
| Forecast sales at standard sales prices | 1,637,000 |
| Standard contribution/sales ratio | 40% |
| Forecast contribution at standard sales price | $654,800 |
| Cumulative sales price variances | $30,000(A) |
| Forecast contribution at actual sales prices | $624,800 |

Statement of budgeted and forecast annual results, as at end May

| | Budget | Forecast | Variance |
|---|---:|---:|---:|
| | $ | $ | $ |
| Sales revenue (145,000 × 12) | 1,740,000 | 1,607,000 | 133,000 (A) |
| Contribution (1,740,000 × 40%) | 696,000 | 624,800 | 71,200 (A) |

### Test your understanding 2

#### (W1) Actual sales at budgeted prices

|  | $ |
|---|---|
| Actual sales at actual prices | 700,000 |
| Sales price variance | 5,000 (A) |
| Actual sales at budgeted prices | 705,000 |

Actual sales are therefore at the (705/750) 94% activity level.

#### (W2) Fixed and variable overheads

|  | $ |
|---|---|
| Overheads at 100% activity level | 230,000 |
| Overheads at 90% activity level | 216,800 |
| Variable overheads for 10% activity | 13,200 |

|  | $ |
|---|---|
| Total overheads at 100% activity level | 230,000 |
| Variable overheads at 100% activity level | 132,000 |
| Fixed overheads | 98,000 |

#### Flexed budget 94% activity

|  | $ | $ |
|---|---|---|
| Sales |  | 705,000 |
| Direct variable costs (420,000 × 94%) |  | 394,800 |
| Variable overhead (13,200 × 94/10) |  | 124,080 |
| Fixed overhead |  | 98,000 |
| Total overheads |  | 222,080 |
| Total costs |  | 616,880 |
| Profit |  | 88,120 |

### Test your understanding 3

|  | Heating and lighting | Telephones | Sundry expenses |
|---|---|---|---|
|  | $ | $ | $ |
| Total cost for 8,000 hours | 18,000 | 8,400 | 33,400 |
| Total cost for 6,000 hours | 17,000 | 7,200 | 29,400 |
| Variable cost for 2,000 hours | 1,000 | 1,200 | 4,000 |
| Variable cost per hour | $0.50 | $0.60 | $2.00 |

|  | Heating and lighting | Telephones | Sundry expenses |
|---|---|---|---|
|  | $ | $ | $ |
| Total cost for 8,000 hours | 18,000 | 8,400 | 33,400 |
| Variable cost for 8,000 hours | 4,000 | 4,800 | 16,000 |
| Fixed costs | 14,000 | 3,600 | 17,400 |

**For 7,700 hours**

|  | Heating and lighting | Telephones | Sundry expenses |
|---|---|---|---|
|  | $ | $ | $ |
| Expected fixed costs | 14,000 | 3,600 | 17,400 |
| Expected variable cost | 3,850 | 4,620 | 15,400 |
| Expected total cost | 17,850 | 8,220 | 32,800 |
| Actual cost | 17,600 | 8,750 | 32,600 |
| **Cost variance** | **250 (F)** | **530 (A)** | **200 (F)** |

**Workings**

**Labour**

In the budget, variable labour costs are $10,000 (10% of labour costs = 2% of sales); therefore fixed labour costs are $90,000 ($100,000 – $10,000).

In the flexible budget, labour costs are $90,000 + (2% × $560,000) = $101,200.

**Other expenses**

In the budget, variable other expenses are $50,000 (25% of other expenses = 10% of sales); therefore fixed other expense costs are $150,000 ($200,000 – $50,000).

In the flexible budget, other expenses are $150,000 + (10% × $560,000) = $206,000.

|  | Original budget | Flexible budget | Actual results | Cost variance |
|---|---|---|---|---|
|  | $ | $ | $ | $ |
| Sales | 500,000 | 560,000 | 560,000 | |
|  | | | | |
| Materials | 50,000 | 56,000 | 58,000 | 2,000 (A) |
| Labour costs | 100,000 | 101,200 | 108,000 | 6,800 (A) |
| Other expenses | 200,000 | 206,000 | 204,500 | 1,500 (F) |
|  | | | | |
|  | 350,000 | 363,200 | 370,500 | 7,300 (A) |
|  | | | | |
| Profit | 150,000 | 196,800 | 189,500 | |

In the original budget, the variable costs were $(50,000 + 10,000 + 50,000) = $110,000.

Budgeted contribution was $500,000 – $110,000 = $390,000.

The budgeted contribution/sales ratio was 390,000/500,000 = 0.78 or 78%.

|  | $ |
|---|---|
| Budgeted sales | 500,000 |
| Actual sales | 560,000 |
| Sales volume variance (revenue) | 60,000 (F) |
| Budgeted contribution/sales ratio | × 0.78 |
| Sales volume contribution margin variance | $46,800 (F) |

**Note:** Alternative calculation

|  | $ |
|---|---|
| Original budgeted profit | 150,000 |
| Flexed budget profit | 196,800 |
| Sales volume contribution margin variance | 46,800 (F) |

**Operating statement**

|  | (F) $ | (A) $ | $ |
|---|---|---|---|
| Budgeted profit |  |  | 150,000 |
| **Variances** |  |  |  |
| Sales volume contribution | 46,800 |  |  |
| Materials costs |  | 2,000 |  |
| Labour costs |  | 6,800 |  |
| Other expenses costs | 1,500 |  |  |
|  | 48,300 | 8,800 | 39,500 (F) |
| Actual profit |  |  | 189,500 |

### Test your understanding 5

| Activity | Expected cost | Actual cost | Variance |
|---|---|---|---|
| | $ | $ | $ |
| Receiving goods 45 orders delivered | 3,600 | 3,450 | 150 (F) |
| Issuing goods 100 requisitions | 4,000 | 4,400 | 400 (A) |
| Ordering 36 orders | 900 | 960 | 60 (A) |
| Counting 2 stock counts | 2,000 | 1,750 | 250 (F) |
| Record keeping | 2,000 | 1,900 | 100 (F) |
| Supervision | 2,500 | 2,700 | 200 (A) |
| | | | |
| | 15,000 | 15,160 | 160 (A) |

### Test your understanding 6

The budgeted profit is €30,000

| | Product P | Product Q | Total |
|---|---|---|---|
| | € | € | € |
| Budgeted sales | 60,000 | 300,000 | 360,000 |
| Variable costs | 40,000 | 150,000 | 190,000 |
| Contribution | 20,000 | 150,000 | 170,000 |
| Fixed costs | | | 140,000 |
| Budgeted profit | | | 30,000 |

**Question 4**

The profit would fall by €21,000.

| | Product P | Product Q | Total |
|---|---|---|---|
| | € | € | € |
| Budgeted sales | 60,000 | 300,000 | 360,000 |
| Variable costs (+15%) | 46,000 (+10%) | 165,000 | 211,000 |
| Contribution | 14,000 | 135,000 | 149,000 |
| Fixed costs | | | 140,000 |
| Revised profit | | | 9,000 |
| Original budgeted profit | | | 30,000 |
| Reduction in profit | | | 21,000 |

## Question 5

The profit would fall by €10,000.

| | Product P | Product Q | Total |
|---|---|---|---|
| Sales units | 40,000 | 40,000 | |
| | € | € | € |
| Budgeted sales (at €3) | 120,000 (at €6) | 240,000 | 360,000 |
| Variable costs (at €2) | 80,000 (at €3) | 120,000 | 200,000 |
| Contribution | 40,000 | 120,000 | 160,000 |
| Fixed costs | | | 140,000 |
| Revised profit | | | 20,000 |
| Original budgeted profit | | | 30,000 |
| Reduction in profit | | | 10,000 |

## Mini-Quiz

1.1 Feedback involves obtaining information from the past operation of a process and using that information as a guide for the control of that process. Feedforward involves forecasting information in regard to the future operations of a process and using that as a guide for control. Both approaches may feature in a budgetary control report (feedback being year-to-date figures, with feedforward being forecast-to-year-end figures).

1.2 A controllable cost is one which is influenced by decision of the budget holder. An uncontrollable cost is one which is not so influenced. It is often argued that uncontrollable costs should not be brought within the remit of the budgetary control process. However, the contrary argument is that few costs really are uncontrollable if they are studied to determine the activities they relate to and who determines the level of such activities.

1.3 A fixed budget is one which is based on given levels of output and/or activity. A flexible budget is one which is based on the actual level of output/activity that takes place but at given price levels, wages rates and efficiency levels. The comparison of actual with flexed budget therefore eliminates 'volume variances' and allows a more immediate comparison of the two sets of figures.

1.4 A failure of goal congruence occurs when a manager is induced by a business control system to do something that is not in the best interests of the organisation as a whole. For example, a departmental manager may be induced to reduce quality control costs in his department in order to stay within his overall operating cost budget. Such a measure may keep the manager within his budget but it may give rise to a reduction in product quality that impacts adversely on the performance of the organisation as a whole.

1.5 Budget slack is considered to arise when a budget holder negotiates a budget that involves a lower level of performance than that which is realistically possible. For example, a departmental manager may negotiate a cost budget in excess of that which is really required to enable the department to perform its function. Such a budget will make the manager's task easier in the current period. The gap between required costs and budget costs is the budget slack.

# Budgeting and Performance Evaluation

## Chapter learning objectives

- **Evaluate** projected performance using ratio analysis (Syllabus Link C1a)
- **Discuss** the role of non-financial performance indicators. (Syllabus Link C3b)
- **Compare and contrast** traditional approaches to budgeting with recommendations based on the 'Balanced Scorecard' (Syllabus Link C3c)

## 1 Chapter summary

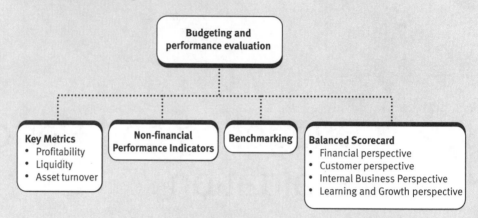

## 2 Knowledge Brought Forward

There is no knowledge brought forward from Papers C01 and P1, but you will need to be comfortable with some basic financial analysis concepts covered in Paper C02. We will use this knowledge in P2 with more advanced ratios, so make sure you are comfortable with the assumed knowledge, that should have been brought forward as a base.

An organisation should have certain targets for achievement. Targets can be expressed in terms of key metrics. The term 'metric' is now in common use within the context of measurement of performance. It is a basis for analysing performance (both budgeted and actual).

A budget should not be approved by senior management unless budgeted performance is satisfactory, as measured by the key metrics. Actual performance should then be assessed in comparison with the targets. The term 'key performance indicators' might be used.

Key areas of financial performance are:

* profitability

* liquidity

* asset turnover.

Senior management might set a target for a minimum profit/sales ratio for the budget period, and refuse to authorise a budget unless this minimum target is met in the plan.

## Profitability

A key metric for profitability might be the **profit/sales ratio** (profit margin), or the contribution/sales ratio (contribution margin).

Senior management might set a target for a minimum profit/sales ratio for the budget period, and refuse to authorise a budget unless this minimum target is met in the plan.

Three key profitability indicators recently examined are the Return on Capital Employed (ROCE, the asset turnover and the profit/sales percentage). These can be explained by the use of a diagram and a simply worked example.

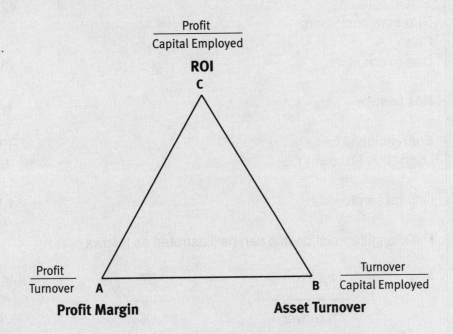

There is a direct relationship between the three figures; All figures are used twice, meaning AxB = C

$$\frac{Profit}{Turnover} \times \frac{Turnover}{Capital\ employed} = \frac{Profit}{Capital\ employed}$$

Profit margin     x     Asset turnover     =     ROCE

## Triangular relationship [DuPont model of measurement]

Extracts from the accounts of The Beta Company read as follows:

### The Beta Company

**Profit and loss extracts $000**

| | |
|---|---:|
| Sales/Revenue | 1,556 |
| **Net profit** | **67** |

**Balance sheet extracts $000**

| | |
|---|---:|
| Fixed assets | 1,380 |
| Stock | 241 |
| Due from customers | 201 |
| Cash | - |
| Due to creditors | (301) |
| **Net assets** | **1,521** |
| Shareholders' funds | 1,021 |
| Long-term borrowing | 500 |
| **Capital employed** | **1,521** |

The triangular relationship can be illustrated as follows :

**A**   $\dfrac{\text{Net Profit}}{\text{Turnover}}$ = $\dfrac{67}{1{,}556}$ = 4.306%

**B**   $\dfrac{\text{Turnover}}{\text{Capital Employed}}$ = $\dfrac{1{,}556}{1{,}521}$ = 1.023 times

**C**   $\dfrac{\text{Net Profit}}{\text{Capital Employed}}$ = $\dfrac{67}{1{,}521}$ = 4.405%

[In the PEG November 2011, the Examiner notes that 'most candidates were not aware that the three ratios/percentages being requested were interlinked and the the figures triangulated. Common errors included using different capital employed and profit figures in each ratio].

## Liquidity

Liquidity means having cash, or ready access to cash. Liquid assets are therefore cash and short-term investments that can be readily sold if the need arises. In addition, liquidity is improved by unused bank borrowing facilities.

Liquidity is improved through efficient cash management, and an important element of good cash management is control over inventory, trade receivables and trade payables.

A key metric for liquidity might therefore be the **current ratio** (which is the ratio of current assets to current liabilities), or the **quick ratio** or acid test ratio (which is the ratio of current assets excluding inventories to current liabilities).

$$\text{Current ratio} = \frac{\text{Current Assets}}{\text{Current liabilities}}$$

$$\text{Quick ratio (acid test)} = \frac{\text{Current assets} - \text{inventory}}{\text{Current liabilities}}$$

A low liquidity ratio could indicate **poor liquidity and a risk of cash flow difficulties**. The appropriate minimum value for a liquidity ratio varies from one industry to another, because the characteristics of cash flows vary between different industries. As a broad rule, however, a current ratio below 2.0 times and a quick ratio below 1.0 times might be considered low.

Within a budgeting system, senior management might set a target for liquidity, in the form of a maximum and minimum acceptable current ratio and/or quick ratio. A current ratio or quick ratio that declines from one year to the next could indicate deteriorating liquidity and greater risk.

On the other hand, a business can have **excessive liquidity, with too much capital tied up in working capital.** The current ratio and quick ratio should therefore not be expected to rise above a maximum acceptable level.

We have seen also that an important element of good cash management is control over the various parts of working capital, in particular inventory, trade receivables and trade payables. We have seen also that an important element of good cash management is control over the various parts of working capital, in particular inventory, trade receivables and trade payables.

### Example 1

A company sets a target minimum current ratio of 1.25 times as a liquidity performance metric and a minimum contribution/sales ratio target of 55% as a profitability performance metric. Compared with the previous budget period, operating costs are expected to be higher. The initial draft budget shows a current ratio of 1.10 at the end of the budget period and a contribution/sales ratio for the year of 51%.

**Required:**

Suggest the steps that the budget planners should now consider to improve the budget.

## 3 Working Capital ratios

Key metrics for working capital control might be:

$$\text{Inventory days} = \frac{\text{Closing inventory}}{\text{Cost of sales}} \times 365 \text{ days}$$

$$\text{Receivable days} = \frac{\text{Trade receivables}}{\text{Sales revenue}} \times 365 \text{ days}$$

$$\text{Payable days} = \frac{\text{Trade payables}}{\text{Cost of sales}} \times 365 \text{ days}$$

Excessive inventory ties up cash unnecessarily and therefore has an adverse effect on liquidity, as well as increasing operating costs such as storage, insurance and obsolescence.

On the other hand, a business can have too little inventory, leading to dissatisfied customers and forgone sales, or to extra costs in seeking out emergency supplies. The metric for inventory days would therefore be monitored to keep it within a minimum and a maximum level.

A high result for receivables days means that cash is tied up unnecessarily and this also has an adverse effect on liquidity.

However, if the receivables days figure is too low, customers may buy instead from competitors who offer more favourable credit terms. Therefore receivables days would also have a budgeted level which is set within an acceptable minimum and maximum level.

A high result for payables days means that good use is being made of the credit facilities offered by suppliers, thus having a favourable impact on liquidity. On the other hand, if suppliers are kept waiting too long for payment of their bills they might increases their prices for future supplies or even curtail supplies altogether. Therefore once again a minimum and a maximum level might be set for payables days.

## Asset turnover

Asset turnover is a measure of productivity in the use of assets. When asset turnover is fast, a business is making efficient use of its assets. Turnover can be measured in relation to any category of assets, such as:

$$\textbf{Non-current asset turnover} \quad = \quad \frac{\textbf{Sales revenue in the period}}{\textbf{Non-current assets}}$$

For example, a business might generate annual sales of, say, $2 for every $1 invested in non-current assets.

$$\textbf{Total asset turnover} \quad = \quad \frac{\textbf{Sales revenue in the period}}{\textbf{Net non-current assets + (Current assets – Current liabilities)}}$$

*[In the March 2013 PEG, a common mistake noted by the Examiner is that candidates 'calculate the Asset Turnover but call it ROCE - making discussions meaningless'.]*

### Example 2 – Key Business Metrics

Stately Hotels plc is considering making an offer to buy a small privately owned chain of hotels, Homely Limited. Homely Limited has 20 full-time employees. In order to carry out an initial appraisal, you have been provided with an abbreviated set of their accounts for 2010.

**Homely Limited – Profit and Loss account for the year ended 31 December 2010 (extract)**

|  | $000 |
|---|---|
| Turnover | 820 |
| Operating costs | 754 |
| Operating profit | 66 |
| Interest payable | 4 |
|  |  |
| Profit before tax | 62 |
| Taxation | 18 |

| Profit after tax | 44 |
|---|---|
| Dividends | 22 |
| Retained profits | 22 |

## Homely Ltd – Balance sheet as at 31 December 2010 (extract)

|  | $000 |
|---|---|
| Fixed assets at net book value | 230 |
| Net current assets | 70 |
| Total assets less current liabilities | 300 |
| Long-term loans | 50 |
| Shareholders funds | 250 |

| | |
|---|---|
| Number of rooms, each available for 365 nights | 18 |
| Number of room nights achieved in 2010 | 5,900 |

Stately Hotels plc uses a number of key accounting ratios to monitor the performance of the group of hotels and of individual hotels in the chain. An extract from the target ratios for 2010 is as follows:

| | | |
|---|---|---|
| (i) | Return on Capital Employed | 26% |
| (ii) | Operating Profit percentage | 13% |
| (iii) | Asset turnover | 2 times |
| (iv) | Working capital period | |

$$\frac{\text{Working Capital}}{\text{Operating costs}} \times 365 \qquad \text{20 days}$$

(v) Percentage room occupancy

$$\frac{\text{Number of room nights let}}{\text{Number of room nights available}} \times 100\% \qquad 85\%$$

(vi) Turnover per employee (full time equivalent)          $30,000

**Required:**

(1) Calculate the six target ratios above based on Homely Limited's accounts and present them in a table which enables easy comparison with Stately Hotels target ratios for 2010

(2) Prepare a memorandum for the management accountant of Stately Hotels plc, giving your initial assessment of Homely Limited based on a comparison of these ratios with Stately Hotels target ratios. Your memorandum should provide the following information for each of the six ratios:  Comments on the performance of Homely Limited and suggestions about the management action which might be necessary to correct any apparent adverse performance; and a discussion of any limitations in the use of the ratio for this performance comparison.

## 4 Shortcomings of Financial Indicators

The use of traditional financial performance metrics is widespread, but the practice has its problems. For example:

(1) They only tell what has happened over a limited period in the immediate past.

(2) They give no indication of what is going to happen in the future.

(3) They are vulnerable to manipulation and to the choice of accounting policy on matters such as depreciation and inventory valuation.

(4) They do not relate to the strategic management of the business and may induce 'short-termism', at the expense of motivation, quality and efficiency.

## 5 Non-Financial Performance Indicators

So, if we wish to obtain a fuller evaluation of performance, then we have to turn to a range of Non-financial performance indicators (NFPIs).

*Non-financial performance indicators are* defined in CIMA's *Official Terminology* as 'measures of performance based on non-financial information that may originate in, and be used by, operating departments to monitor and control their activities without any accounting input.

Non-financial performance measures may give a more timely indication of the levels of performance achieved than financial measures do, and may be less susceptible to distortion by factors such as uncontrollable variations in the effect of market forces on operations.

Certain academic writers have developed models of performance evaluation for strategic advantage. The general thrust behind these is that performance indicators should be developed that relate to the long-term strategic development of the organisation. This follows the principle advocated by management guru/writer Tom Peters: '*What gets measured gets done*'.

The performance indicators adopted for a given business or business segment should relate to its key success factors – those things that are most likely to determine its success or failure. NFPIs can be expressed in either quantitative and qualitative terms. For example, it might be reported that we have a 5 per cent market share (a quantitative measure) and we are first supplier of preference to almost all our established customers (a qualitative measure).

Let us consider a number of NFPIs, how they might be expressed and relevant information relating to them might be gathered.

**Competitiveness**

- *Sales growth by product or service;*
- *Size of customer base;*
- *Market share by product, service or customer group.*

Regular market surveys drawing on both internal and external sources of information can be used to compile reports.

**Activity level**

- *Number of Units sold;*
- *Labour and machine hours worked;*
- *Number of passengers carried;*
- *Number of overdue debts collected.*

Relevant information could be drawn mainly from internal sources, with appropriate checks to ensure accuracy.

**Productivity**

- *Manufacturing cost per unit produced;*
- *Capacity utilisation of facilities and personnel;*
- *Average number of units produced per day or per man-day;*
- *Average setting up time for new production run.*

Again, most of this information could be drawn from **internal** sources.

| | |
|---|---|
| **Quality of service** | • *Number of units rejected in manufacturing* |
| | • *Number of units failing in service;* |
| | • *Number of visits by representatives to customer premises;* |
| | • *Number of new accounts gained or lost;* |
| | • *Number of repeat customer orders received.* |

Again, most relevant information would be available from internal sources but this could be reinforced by periodic customer surveys.

| | |
|---|---|
| **Customer satisfaction** | • *Average time taken to respond to customer enquiry or order;* |
| | • *Expressed customer satisfaction with sales staff;* |
| | • *Expressed customer satisfaction with technical representatives;* |
| | • *Number of customer complaints received.* |

Relevant information would have to come mainly from customer surveys although some internal sources could be selectively used. Customer surveys can be carried out on a regular structured basis or on an occasional informal basis. If a sample of customers is being used to compile information, then care has to be taken that the sample is significant in size and representative in structure.

| | |
|---|---|
| **Quality of staff experience** | • *Days absence per week;* |
| | • *Staff turnover rate;* |
| | • *Number of new qualifications/courses completed by staff;* |
| | • *Number of new staff skills certified;* |
| | • *Expressed job satisfaction;* |
| | • *Qualification levels of newly recruited staff.* |

Some information could be taken from internal sources but much would have to come from colleges and external trainers. Exit interviews and confidential staff opinion surveys could also be used.

**Innovation**

- *Number of new products or services brought to market;*
- *Proportion of Sales relating to new products;*
- *Technical lead relative to competitors;*
- *Lead time to bring new products to market.*

This kind of information would have to be taken from a variety of internal and external sources. The slightly subjective nature of what constitutes a 'new product' is such that this may be an area where an external assessor or consultant might be used to prepare the report.

These sort of performance indicators have the advantage of being 'forward looking'. That is, they are likely to address factors that relate to how well or badly the business will perform in the future.

For example, a service business with a high staff turnover rate is at a disadvantage. If experienced and qualified staff are constantly leaving and being replaced, then this may not contribute to the quality of service being offered to customers. We have all experienced visits to a shop, travel agent or garage where we have been served by an inexperienced and obviously new member of staff – who is unfamiliar with our account history and appears to have limited knowledge of the products that he or she is trying to sell. We find it much more satisfactory to be served by an experienced member of staff who knows his or her customers and products.

Yet, a deterioration in the standard of staff being employed (as evidenced by the indicators listed above under quality of staff experience) would not impact greatly on current period ROCE. A focus on current ROCE might actually induce a business to make greater use of poorly paid, junior staff in order to minimise operating costs. The impact of this on the business might be felt only in the long term.

As with any performance indicator, an NFPI has to be viewed in some context in order to be most meaningful. A good control report will express indicators in terms of a deviation from plan, relative to an industry benchmark or as part of a trend analysis covering comparable earlier periods.

Further, it is best to consider performance indicators as part of a package giving a multi-dimensional impression of how the organisation is performing.

*[In the PEG May 2010: Candidates to "explain" two non-financial performance indicators not associated with client satisfaction (for instance, repeat business) and service quality. A significant number of candidates simply gave a bullet point as their answer e.g. "number of cases won". This type of answer does not address the requirement to "explain"].*

**BAA**

One example of the use of NFPIs frequently reported in management literature is that of BAA plc (formerly the British Airports Authority). This is the case of a service company that attempts to evaluate its own performance in terms of the quality it is able to offer to customers.

It has identified about 12 key success factors which include access, aesthetics, cleanliness, comfort, staff competence, staff courtesy, reliability, responsiveness and security. These take on board the factors that customers appreciate when using an airport–short distances to walk from point of arrival to point of departure, safety from attack or robbery, easy availability of luggage trolleys and wheel chairs and so on.

BAA carries out regular surveys involving interviews with customers, consultant reports, analysis of operational data, and monitoring customer feedback. Appropriate indicators for each factor are reported and studied through comparison between different airports and trend analysis over time. For example, if airport A persistently reports a higher level of theft from customers than other airports–then this might prompt the introduction of additional security measures at airport A. If complaints about staff courtesy at airport D have been on a persistent upward trend over time, then this might prompt enquiries into staff supervision at that site and/or additional staff training.

A customer survey might include a question as follows:

'Your impression of the service available in the cafeterias at Airport B is best described as

A   Most satisfactory

B   Satisfactory

C   Acceptable

D   Less than acceptable

E   Unsatisfactory.

Answering this involves a qualitative judgement on the part of the customer, but the survey results can be reported and evaluated in quantitative terms. For example, if 80% of customers offered A or B answers to this question, then the impression given is that the standard of service at Airport B cafeterias is not a problem–and it may even serve as a model of best practice for other airports.

This line of discussion leads us into the more modern models of performance evaluation which fall broadly under the 'Beyond Budgeting' heading encountered in the previous chapter.

In addition to monitoring performance through variance analysis, or as an alternative to variance reporting, organisations might use benchmarking to monitor their performance, and set targets for improved performance.

The basic idea of benchmarking is that performance should be assessed through a comparison of the organisation's own products or services, performance and practices with 'best practice' elsewhere.

*'Benchmarking is 'the establishment, through data gathering, of targets and comparators, through whose use relative levels of performance (and particularly areas of underperformance) can be identified. By adoption of identified best practices it is hoped that performance will improve'*

(CIMA Official Terminology).

The reasons for benchmarking may be summarised as:

- To receive an alarm call about the need for change

- Learning from others in order to improve performance

- Gaining a competitive edge (in the private sector)

- Improving services (in the public sector).

## Different types of benchmarking

It is important to remember that in order to use benchmarking, it is necessary to gather information about best practice. This leads on to the problem of how much information is available and where it can be obtained.

Benchmarking can be categorised according to what is being benchmarked and whose performance is being used for comparison (as 'best in class').

- **Internal benchmarking**. With internal benchmarking, other units or departments in the same organisation are used as the benchmark. This might be possible if the organisation is large and divided into a number of similar regional divisions. Internal benchmarking is also widely used within government. In the UK for example, there is a Public Sector Benchmarking Service that maintains a database of performance measures. Public sector organisations, such as fire stations and hospitals, can compare their own performance with the best in the country.

- **Competitive benchmarking.** With competitive benchmarking, the most successful competitors are used as the benchmark. Competitors are unlikely to provide willingly any information for comparison, but it might be possible to observe competitor performance (for example, how quickly a competitor processes customer orders). A competitor's product might be dismantled in order to learn about its internal design and its performance: this technique of benchmarking is called reverse engineering.

- **Functional benchmarking**. In functional benchmarking, comparisons are made with a similar function (for example selling, order handling, despatch) in other organisations that are not direct competitors. For example, a fast food restaurant operator might compare its buying function with buying in a supermarket chain.

- **Strategic benchmarking**. Strategic benchmarking is a form of competitive benchmarking aimed at reaching decisions for strategic action and organisational change. Companies in the same industry might agree to join a collaborative benchmarking process, managed by an independent third party such as a trade organisation. With this type of benchmarking, each company in the scheme submits data about their performance to the scheme organiser. The organiser calculates average performance figures for the industry as a whole from the data supplied. Each participant in the scheme is then supplied with the industry average data, which it can use to assess its own performance.

## 'Benchmarking', by Bob Scarlett

*CIMA Insider, October 2003*

*Benchmarking is the process of improving performance by continuously identifying, understanding (studying and analysing), and adapting outstanding practices and process found inside and outside the organisation and implementing the results'* (American Productivity and Quality Centre, 1997)

Benchmarking is an approach to performance management that starts with the premise that whatever the process (supply, production, sales or services), performance can best be measured and managed by comparing that process with an appropriate outside entity that is already achieving world-class performance. The outside entity used to provide the benchmark need not operate within the same sector as our process. Further the benchmark can be from either another organisation (an 'external' benchmark) or a different segment within the same organisation (an 'internal' benchmark).

A benchmark provides a standard of excellence against which to measure and compare. Benchmarks are performance measures – How many? (e.g. 'customers served per staff member per hour') How quickly? (e.g. 'delivery time to customer') How high? (e.g. 'proportion of sales giving rise to repeat business') How low? (e.g. 'proportion of output being defective'). To be meaningful, a benchmark should relate to a 'key performance indicator', that is something within the business process that has a major influence on results. Establishing benchmarks is a necessary part of benchmarking but of itself does not provide an understanding of best practices nor does knowledge of the benchmarks lead necessarily to improvement. Benchmarking is the learning of lessons about how best performance is achieved. Rather than merely measuring performance, benchmarking focuses on how to improve any given business process by exploiting 'best practices' by discovering the specific practices responsible for high performance, understanding how these practices work and adapting and applying them to the organisation. A benchmarking exercise may take the form of a process comparison which does not involve the use of metrics.

Some writers identify three distinct approaches to benchmarking:

(1) **Metric benchmarking**. The practice of comparing appropriate metrics to identify possible areas for improvement;

(2) **Process benchmarking**. The practice of comparing processes with a partner as part of an improvement process;

(3) **Diagnostic benchmarking**. The practice of reviewing the processes of a business to identify those which indicate a problem and offer a potential for improvement.

The Xerox corporation is often cited as the pioneer in benchmarking practice. When it wanted to improve performance in its warehousing and distribution operation it did not go down the then conventional road of process redesign. Rather, it identified the business which was acknowledged as being the very best at warehousing and distribution – the L.L. Bean catalogue merchant. L.L. Bean agreed to undertake a co-operative benchmarking project. Over a period the two exchanged data on various aspects of their inventory handling and processing of orders. As a result of this, Xerox identified those areas in its own operation which were performing at below Bean's standards and acted to implement improvements. One critical point to note is that Xerox did not adopt another office equipment business as its model – it adopted a business operating in a different sector altogether.

Benchmarking in all its varied forms is becoming increasingly widespread in industry, services and the public sector. In particular, it is perceived to offer a more sophisticated tool in performance management than more traditional approaches such as standard costing. The general thrust behind this idea is that standard costing belongs in the era when goods were produced in long continuous production runs and a high proportion of costs were 'product specific'. In the new economy, goods tend to be highly customised, contain a significant service element and are produced in short discontinuous production runs on a JIT basis. A large proportion of product costs are determined at the design stage or are 'customer specific', that is they relate to the manner in which the goods are provided to the customer. Efficiency is therefore very much a function of product engineering, the flexibility of the production operation and customer relationship management. It is argued that the traditional budgetary control report based on standard costing simply does not address these issues.

A comprehensive system of benchmarking can provide a much fuller impression of how well or badly an operation is performing. And, it is more likely to give an indication of those areas in the operation that are amenable to improvement. That said, benchmarking has its critics. For example:

*Benchmarking relies on competitive data that isn't readily available. When the data is available, it may be neither accurate nor timely. Moreover, it allows a comparison at only one point in time and does not provide a way to continually improve performance.* (John Pucket, Boston Consulting Group (quoted from 1997)).

That is fair comment, but the discussion above indicates some of the ways in which such criticism might be answered. For one thing, benchmarking need not rely on competitive data. As with most business techniques, benchmarking has to be carried out well if it is to yield results.

# 6 Kaplan And Norton – The Balanced Scorecard

## The joke

You're at the airport and there's a little while to your flight. You have a drink to pass the time and a person in uniform comes and sits next to you at the bar and after a while you get chatting and you find out that she is the pilot of the aeroplane that you are about to catch. You say that it must be very difficult flying an aeroplane with all those dials and knobs and switches and meters and things, and she says, 'No, not really. All I look at is the speedometer and I figure that if I get my speed right then things are fine.' You look at her a bit funny and you say, 'Well, what about the fuel gauge? Isn't that important?' She says, 'Yes, you're right, it is important and I used to look at it, but now I just look at the speedometer'. Then you say, 'Well what about the altimeter? Surely that's important?' She replies, 'Well, yes it is, but I try and focus on one thing at a time. Once I'm happy with my airspeed then in a few flights' time I might concentrate on altitude'

The question Kaplan and Norton now ask is would you catch that aeroplane?

The point that Kaplan and Norton are trying to make (in the unlikely event that you missed it) is that you cannot fly an aeroplane with only one instrument. Nor can you run a business by looking at one performance measure. Kaplan and Norton's Balanced Scorecard focuses on four different perspectives.

## The balanced scorecard

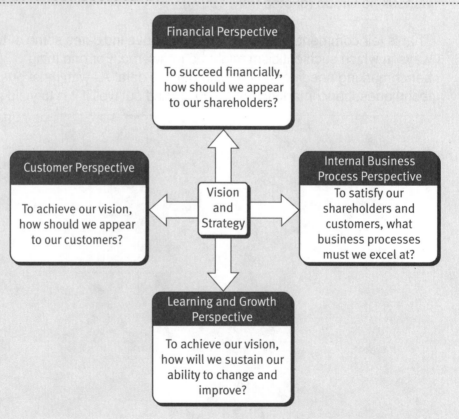

Robert Kaplan and David Norton published the original article (The Balanced Scorecard – Measures That Drive Performance) in the Harvard Business Review in January/February 1992. It has become one of the most requested HBR reprints.

The traditional performance measure for a business is of course financial, but one problem is that the financial measures relate to the past. Another is that the financial accounting model does not adequately consider the value to a company of its intangible assets such as a happy and loyal customer base, well motivated, well trained and efficient staff and good quality products or services. The Balanced Scorecard incorporates non-financial measures of the drivers of future performance as well as financial measures of past performance.

In their 1996 book Kaplan and Norton state that 'Several critics have advocated scrapping financial measures entirely to measure business unit performance. They argue that in today's technologically and customer-driven global competition, financial measures provide poor guidelines for success. They urge managers to focus on improving customer satisfaction, quality, cycle times, and employee skills and motivation. According to this theory, as companies make fundamental improvements in their operations, the financial numbers will take of themselves.' Kaplan and Norton reply that the use of financial measures still serves a purpose as it is not enough to improve quality and customer satisfaction and generate new products, etc, in the end these improvements have to be converted to financial advantage.

Kaplan and Norton also ask in their 1996 book are 4 perspectives sufficient? They answer their own question by saying that there is no rule that says that every organisation in the world should use exactly the 4 perspectives, and nothing else, but that in general across a variety of companies and industries the 4 perspectives do seem to work. They say that some companies do incorporate extra perspectives such as an environmental perspective, but they have yet to see a company use less than 4.

It can be seen from the diagram above that a vital part of the Balanced Scorecard is the company strategy and the starting point for the creation of a Balanced Scorecard is a company's mission statement or vision.

## Measures for the Balanced Scorecard

The following lists give examples of possible measures:

### Financial Perspective

Goals would be set in terms of 3 main areas and the measures would relate to those areas.

- Survival    Cash flow, gearing

- Success    Monthly or quarterly sales growth and operating income

- Prosperity    Increase in market share and ROI

### Customer Perspective

- Customer profitability
- Customer retention
- Customer satisfaction
- Customer acquisition
- Market share
- Percentage of sales from new products
- Percentage of on-time deliveries
- Preferred supplier status
- Lead time from receipt of order to delivery
- No of customer complaints

### Internal Business Process Perspective

- Percentage of sales from new products
- Percentage of sales from proprietary products
- New product introduction versus competitors also new product introduction versus plan
- Manufacturing process capabilities
- Time to develop next generation of products
- Cycle time
- Unit cost
- Efficiency

## Learning and Growth Perspective

- Employee satisfaction
- Employee retention
- Employee productivity
- Time to market
- Percentage of products giving 80% of sales

### Example 3 – Business Equipment Solutions

CM Limited was formed 10 years ago to provide business equipment solutions to local businesses. It has separate divisions for research, marketing, product design, technology and communication services, and now manufactures and supplies a wide range of business equipment (copiers, scanners, printers, fax machines and similar items).

To date it has evaluated its performance using monthly financial reports that analyse profitability by type of equipment.

The Managing Director of CM Limited has recently returned from a course on which it had been suggested that the 'Balanced Scorecard' could be a useful way of measuring performance.

**Required:**

Explain the 'Balanced Scorecard' and how it could be used by CM Limited to measure its performance.

**(13 marks)**

*[In the March 2013 PEG, the Examiner notes that 'a significant number of candidates encountered difficulties when applying the balanced scorecard to the scenario. Common errors include :*

(1) *Putting forward performance measures that do not relate to the company's objectives;*

(2) *Putting forward unrealistic objectives e.g. 'to become the best pathology laboratory in the world';*

(3) *Putting forward weak objectives for which it is difficult to establish a performance measure, e.g. 'we need to find out if customers/employees are happy' or 'we need to measure how quickly patients get better';*

(4) *Labelling the perspectives incorrectly;*

(5) *Putting forward performance measures that did not relate to the scenario'.]*

## Performance evaluation in the not-for-profit sector

An NFP organisation exists to achieve certain objectives and an evaluation of its performance in achieving those objectives must have regard to a combination of efficiency and effectiveness factors. The organisation should achieve the maximum output from the resources at its disposal (efficiency) and at the same time it should organise those resources in a manner that achieves a given result by the cheapest route (effectiveness).

Many of the performance indicators considered above can be applied to NFPs. For example, in evaluating the performance of a local authority one might consider:

(1) Cost per km of road maintained;

(2) Cost per child in school;

(3) Cost per square metre of grass verge mown;

(4) Cost per tonne of sewage disposed of.

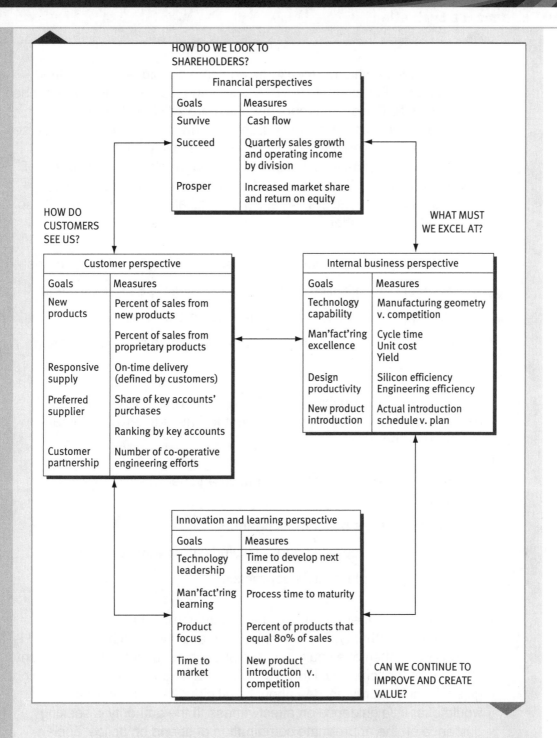

These are all quantitative measures and care should be taken in their interpretation. For example, town A's sewage disposal cost might be half that of town B. Does that mean that A is more efficient than B? Not necessarily, because A might be pumping raw sewage direct into the sea whereas B treats sewage and transports it for disposal. If A is a resort town then its 'efficiency' in disposing of sewage might have a variety of adverse knock-on effects. In considering performance one has to consider qualitative factors. A variety of qualitative indicators might also be considered in tandem with the quantitative ones listed above:

- Number of claims made by motorists arising from pot holed roads;
- Number of local children obtaining 2 A level GCEs or equivalent;
- Rating of local road system by the Automobile Association;
- Number of complaints from visitors concerning smell/taste of sea water.

Benchmarking is probably the most important recent innovation in performance evaluation in the NFP sector. The standard benchmarking practice can be used:

- Study processes in the organisation and select which are to be benchmarked;
- Secure suitable benchmark partners;
- Compare appropriate figures and indicators with partners;
- Adopt and implement 'best practices'.

A benchmark partner for one local authority need not necessarily be another local authority. For example, if the activity being benchmarked is 'office costs', then one could bench-mark against an insurance company or a mail order company. However, while such benchmark partners might give a local authority an idea about its efficiency in certain areas, they would offer little guidance on effectiveness. If the authority is seeking guidance on the appropriate combination of spend on police, social services, housing and so on in order to provide a certain level of welfare for elderly residents (a quest for effectiveness), then the appropriate benchmark partners would have to be other authorities providing a similar service.

In the United Kingdom, benchmarking and its associated concept of 'best practice' are now widely used in public sector performance evaluation. The Department of the Environment rates all local authorities on the basis of periodic reviews. The use of appropriate performance indicators are a central element in these reviews. Such indicators have regard to both quantitative and qualitative factors.

As with all performance evaluation exercises, it must be appreciated that the calculation of a particular indicator will probably mean little unless it is set in some sort of context. Calculating the value of a particular indicator means little, until it is **compared with** a budget, set in a trend or set against a best practice benchmark.

One final comment in this area should be made. You are reminded of the **Peter** principle – *'What gets measured gets done'*.

If a performance evaluation is based on an incorrect or incomplete range of metrics, then the system can induce the wrong things to get done. For example, in the late 1990s the performance of hospitals was judged on the length of their waiting lists. Specifically, the average time taken for a referred patient to have a first consultation was adopted as a key performance indicator. It is claimed that this induced hospitals to concentrate on patients with minor illnesses since they could be treated quickly and cleared off the list. The small number of patients requiring major treatments often had to wait longer than was the case before the performance indicator was adopted.

Hospital waiting lists were reduced, but not in a wholly neutral manner. Some people gained and some lost as a result of the system. That was never the intention.

## 7 Practice Questions

### Test your understanding 1

Suggest performance indicators to include in the Balanced Scorecard of a credit card company.

### Test your understanding 2

Suggest what key non-financial performance indicators might be for:

(a)  a privately-owned transport company

(b)  a hospital service

### Test your understanding 3

CM Limited was formed 10 years ago to provide business equipment solutions to local businesses. It has separate divisions for research, marketing, product design, technology and communication services, and now manufactures and supplies wide range of business equipment (copiers, scanners, printers, fax machines and similar items).

To date, it has evaluated its performance using monthly financial reports that analyse profitability by type of equipment. The Managing Director of CM Limited has recently returned from a course on which it had been suggested that the 'Balanced Scorecard' could be a useful way of measuring performance.

**Required:**

(a)  Explain the 'Balanced Scorecard' and how it could be used by CM Limited to measure its performance.

  While on the course, the Managing Director of CM Limited overhead someone mention how the performance of their company had improved after they introduced 'Benchmarking'.

(b)  Explain 'Benchmarking' and how it could be used to improve the performance of CM Limited.

## Mini-Quiz

(1) State three reasons why ROCE might be considered to be 'limited' as a performance indicator.

(2) State why compliance with budget might not be an appropriate indicator for performance evaluation in 'the new economy'.

(3) State why it might not be to the long-term advantage of a business to operate with the lowest possible inventory days.

(4) Distinguish between financial and non-financial performance indicators.

(5) Distinguish between quantitative and qualitative performance indicators.

(6) Suggest three performance indicators that might be used to measure 'responsiveness to customers'.

(7) Distinguish between efficiency and effectiveness in an NFP organisation.

(8) Explain why benchmarking is particularly appropriate for performance evaluation in local authorities.

(9) Suggest five performance indicators that might be appropriate for benchmarking at a University, having particular regard to the value of the qualifications that the University awards.

(10) Suggest three possible areas of criticism for benchmarking.

## Test your understanding answers

### Example 1

The first step by the budget planners should be to consider why liquidity and profitability are not as good in the draft budget as the minimum targets. There are several possible reasons.

- The budget allows for higher operating costs but there is no plan to increase sales prices. This will reduce profit margins and cash balances, and explain, fully or in part, the unsatisfactory performance ratios for profitability and liquidity.

- The targets of 1.25 for current ratio and 55% for the contribution/sales ratio might be unrealistic, and should therefore be re-considered.

- There could be padding (slack) in the budget estimates for expenditure.

The budget should be revised, but the way in which it should be revised will depend on the reasons why the figures in the first draft are unsatisfactory.

- If there is scope to increase sales prices, this would increase contribution and improve cash flow and liquidity.

- Any padding or slack in the budget should be removed, if it can be detected.

- If the draft budget included plans to purchase new long-term assets out of operational cash flows, this should be re-considered, as a way of improving cash flow and the current ratio.

- The planners should give some thought to improvements in cash flow management, and in the short term should ensure that if the target current ratio cannot be met, there should nevertheless be adequate liquidity. For example, the bank might be approached for an extension of committed borrowing facilities.

## Example 2 – Key Business Metrics

(a) Target ratios:

Return on capital employed $= \dfrac{66}{300} \times 100\%$ $= 22\%$

Operating profit percentage $= \dfrac{66}{820} \times 100\%$ $= 8\%$

Asset turnover $= \dfrac{820}{300}$ $= 2.7$ times

Working Capital Period $= \dfrac{70}{754} \times 365$ $= 34$ days

Percentage room occupancy $= \dfrac{5,900}{18 \times 365} \times 100\%$ $= 90\%$

Turnover per employee $= \dfrac{\$820,000}{20 \text{ employees}}$ $= \$41,000$

(b) Key ratios for 2010

|  | Stately Hotels plc, target | Homely Limited, actual |
|---|---|---|
| Return on Capital Employed | 26% | 22% |
| Operating profit percentage | 13% | 8% |
| Asset turnover | 2.0 times | 2.7 times |
| Working capital period | 20 days | 34 days |
| Percentage room occupancy | 85% | 90% |
| Turnover per employee | $30,000 | $41,000 |

**MEMORANDUM**

To: Management Accountant, Stately Hotels plc

From: Assistant to the Management Accountant

Date: 31 December 2010

Subject: Initial assessment of the performance of Homely Limited

I have carried out an initial assessment of Homely Limited, based on an extract from their accounts for 2010. I have calculated their key accounting ratios and compared them with our company's target ratios and my conclusions and recommendations are as follows:

### Return on capital employed (ROCE)

At 22% the ROCE is below the target which we set for the hotels in our chain. Management action will be necessary to improve the return on capital employed, through improved profitability of operations, increased asset turnover, or both. The main limitation in the use of this ratio is that the valuation of the capital employed can have a considerable effect on the apparent ROCE. For example, if the capital employed is undervalued, this will artificially inflate the ROCE.

### Operating profit percentage

This is considerably below the target ratio set by Stately Hotels plc and it is the cause of the depressed ROCE. Management action will be necessary to improve this, either by increasing prices or by controlling operating costs relative to sales revenue. Since the former action may depress demand in Homely Limited's market, it is likely that management will need to focus on the control of operating costs.
A limitation in the use of this ratio is that Homely's operations may not be comparable to the average hotel in the Stately group. For example, they may not have conference facilities, which would affect the profile of their costs.

### Asset turnover

At 2.7 times this is higher than the target ratio, indicating that, although Homely's operations are not as profitable, they generate more turnover per $ of capital employed. It may be that Homely has a different basis of operating, i.e. charging lower prices, and thus reducing the profitability of sales, but in the process generating a higher turnover for the level of capital employed. The main limitation of this ratio stems from the limitation of the ROCE, i.e. its accuracy relies on the correct valuation of capital employed.

### Working capital period

This is 34 days of operating costs, almost double the level which we require in our target performance ratios. Working capital levels are probably unacceptably high and need to be reduced. This will require more attention to debtor control, reduction in stocks of, for example, consumable materials and foodstuffs, and an investigation into whether full use is being made of available credit facilities. A limitation of this ratio is that it relies on the accurate valuation of working capital. For example, although stocks should not account for a high proportion of working capital in a hotel, their valuation can be very subjective.

Another major limitation is that the ratio is based on balance sheet data, which depicts the working capital level on a single day. This may not be representative of the year as a whole and therefore incorrect conclusions may be drawn from the analysis.

### Percentage room occupancy

Homely Limited is achieving a room occupancy rate which is above the level expected in our organisation's target ratios. This is a healthy sign which is encouraging.

**Turnover per employee** Homely Limited's turnover per employee is also healthy. However, we must ensure that customer service and quality are not suffering as a result of operating with a lower level of staffing.

Overall, Homely Limited seems to have some strengths which would be worth exploiting. However, their control of operating costs and of working capital needs some attention.

## Example 3 – Business Equipment Solutions

The balanced scorecard was invented by Robert Kaplan and David Norton. The first article was published in the January/February 1992 issue of the Harvard Business Review. Up to that point in time the main measure of performance was simply profit, either pure profit or a profit-related measure such as ROCE or residual income.

Kaplan and Norton related running a business to flying an aeroplane. A modern aircraft has hundreds of dials, meters, knobs and switches and to fly the aircraft the pilot has to be aware of all these devices. It is not a good idea to fly the aeroplane just by looking at the speedometer and ignoring the fuel gauge and the altimeter and the other dials and things. Similarly, they argued it is not a good idea to run a business by only looking at one measure, i.e. the financial performance. The company must also look at a number of operational measures.

After a year-long research project with 12 companies at the leading edge of performance measurement, Kaplan and Norton came up with 4 perspectives that the companies should be looking at and 4 questions that companies should be asking themselves:

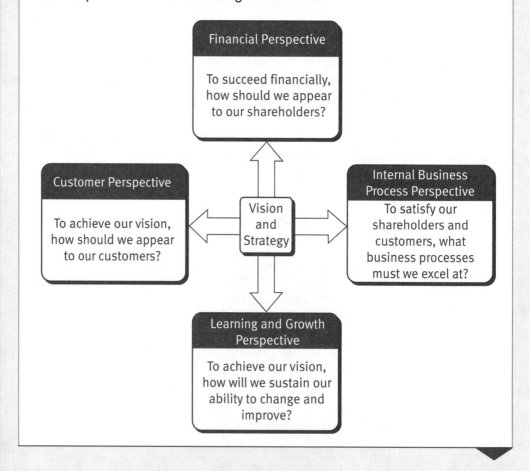

Kaplan and Norton claim that by focusing on these 4 main areas the organisation gets an overall balanced view of business performance and yet is not overwhelmed by enormous amounts of data.

As can be seen from the diagram, the balanced scorecard must be related to a company's vision and strategy.

CM Ltd can use the balanced scorecard to measure its performance in the following ways:

**The Financial Perspective**

CM Ltd can measure its success in terms of the financial perspective by using traditional ratio analysis. The ratios could be broken down into groups such as profitability, gearing, liquidity, working capital and investor ratios. In addition, CM Ltd could develop its own financial-based ratios which it would consider useful.

**The Customer Perspective**

CM Ltd should consider how it appears to its customers. Customers are interested in time, quality, performance and service, and cost. (Time could mean the time taken from an order being received to being delivered in the case of an existing product.) Appropriate targets could be set for each item for each division and then actual performance measured. Examples of possible measures would include: number of complaints, proportion of customers repeat buying, etc.

**The Internal Business Process Perspective**

The customer and financial perspectives are important, but the internal business process perspective is also vital as it focuses on what the company must do to satisfy its customers and shareholders. CM Ltd must decide what business processes have the greatest influence on achieving customer satisfaction and improving financial performance. Factors such as quality, cycle time, productivity and employee skills would be possible areas that CM Ltd could look at. Again, CM Ltd would establish targets and measure actual performance and where there was a significant difference would investigate and try to improve performance in the future.

### The Learning and Growth Perspective

Once CM Ltd has set up measures for customer satisfaction and the internal business process perspective, it is not enough to simply achieve those targets and then think that everything is OK. In today's modern business environment with rapidly changing political environments, changes in taste and fashion, technological changes and global customers and global competition, the company has to be continually thinking of the future and must be able to develop new products which will be attractive to the customer and which can be brought to the market in as short a time as possible. CM Ltd might look at its percentage of sales from new products, the number of patents from its research division, the lead time from a product being designed to being launched on the market. The learning and growth perspective also includes employee performance measures such as labour turnover, absenteeism and staff morale (perhaps measured by staff questionnaires).

### Test your understanding 1

| Financial Indicators of performance: | 'Customers' indicators of performance: |
|---|---|
| Increase market share year-on-year | Wean businesses off chequebooks |
| Increase cardholder's spending | Get banks to switch cards |
| Increase % fee | Focus on big spenders |
| Reduce debt | Issue more cards |
| | Maintain image |
| | Add reward programmes |
| **Learning and Growth indicators of performance:** | **Internal processes indicators of performance:** |
| Outsource IT jobs | Increased marketing spend |
| Acquire other companies | Offer more products |
| Improve staff training levels | Achieve economies of scale |

## Test your understanding 2

### Transport business

A privately-owned transport company should have a principal objective of maximising the owners' wealth. Non-financial performance indicators should set performance standards that will help the organisation to achieve its financial goals over the long term.

- Capacity fill. Profitability depends on passenger numbers. There should be targets for the number of passengers on each journey, or each mile of journey, as a percentage of capacity.

- Punctuality. It seems likely that the willingness of individuals to use transport services depends on the quality of service. Punctuality could therefore be a key issue. Targets could be set for the percentage of journeys that should arrive no more than X minutes late at their destination.

- Growth. There could be targets for the rate of growth in passenger numbers.

- Crime and safety performance indicators. Crime and security on journeys might be a key issue for both employees and passengers. The number of reported crimes or incidents could be monitored, with targets set for a reduction in the number of incidents.

### Hospital service

Key issues for a hospital service, should relate to the quality of service.

Non-financial performance indicators might include:

- average waiting times for treatment, for different categories of patient or condition

- recovery rates

- spare bed capacity (both minimum and maximum targets)

- average time in hospital (for different types of condition)

- response times or turn-round times (for example, time needed to obtain laboratory test reports, and if the hospital is responsible for an ambulance service, ambulance response times to emergency calls)

- percentage of jobs vacant

- staff turnover rates

- hygiene: hospital infection rates (super-bugs, etc).

### Test your understanding 3

(a) The balanced scorecard was developed and refined during the 1980s and 1990s. It has the aim of breaking the reliance of traditional performance measurement systems on financial performance measures, and widening the scope of performance measurement and therefore of managerial attention, to include both financial and non-financial information. By developing a wider focus of attention, the balanced scorecard encourages managers to look at the relationships between different aspects of performance, and highlights the links between improving operational performance and achieving improvements in financial performance.

The balanced scorecard contains three basic elements:

(1) A customer perspective, where the focus is on measuring and improving customer satisfaction. CM Limited might measure the incidence of customer complaints, or of repeat purchases, as proxies for customer satisfaction.

(2) The learning and growth perspective assesses the organisation's ability to satisfy, develop and motivate its employees. Key measures here assess employee retention, productivity and satisfaction. CM Limited would use questionnaires, surveys and/or interviews to gain information on these areas. It would seek to determine, for example, whether employees felt that they were supported in their work, and how satisfied they were with their working conditions.

(3) The internal business process perspective assesses the efficiency of the value creating process, and gathers information on areas such as innovation, operations and after-sales service. CM Limited could gather information on the percentage of sales from new products, sales growth compared with competitors and speed of response to customer service requests.

The effect of making improvements in these three areas is that profitability, cashflow and other measures in the financial perspective should improve. The balanced scorecard, however, explicitly links the operational perspectives to the financial perspective, so that a change in any of the former can be seen to have an influence on the latter. If a balanced scorecard approach were to be introduced, the focus of CM Limited's managerial attention would move from being on products to a more holistic model, in which the key performance measures, linked to the achievement of objectives, are identified and monitored. Thus, objectives are more likely to be achieved, since the key performance indicators have been identified.

(b) Benchmarking is used by many organisations as a way of achieving process improvements and cost reduction. The objective of benchmarking is to become 'best in class' in the chosen areas and to constantly compare your own performance with that of an appropriate comparator. Many business processes are not unique to businesses located in a single industry (which will be CM Limited's competitors), and therefore best in class performance might be found in a company which undertakes the same process, but in a quite different industry. By exchanging information concerning costs/times/resource requirements of the process, firms may learn from one another, and become aware of any areas of inefficiency which they may have, and thus gain an insight into where their cost reduction efforts should be targeted.

CM Limited sells business equipment, so it could investigate the possibility of benchmarking its order taking, delivery, inventory holding and similar procedures against those of a similar firm located in a different geographical area. Or, it could perhaps benchmark against a local firm selling and repairing air-conditioning units or electrical white goods.

Benchmarking improvements could impact upon the 'internal business process' of the balanced scorecard, causing efficiency improvements. Should employee training requirements be required, then 'learning and growth' changes would need to be made. In the short term, there might be a deterioration in the cash flow of CM Limited, but as the improvements begin to have an effect, the financial perspective will improve.

**Mini-Quiz**

(1) It only reports what has happened in the previous short period; It is based on subjective carrying values for assets and profit; and the concentration on current ROCE may induce 'short-termism' in managers.

(2) Compliance with budget is the classic 'command and control' approach to management and performance evaluation. It may have been appropriate in an era when the business environment was very stable and predictable. It may then have been possible to produce meaningful plans that were capable of execution. However, the modern environment is much more fluid – where the market constantly changes and success is dependent on the ability to respond quickly to new developments and customer demand.

(3) Inventory is an asset which engages capital in the business. That capital has a cost so there is a temptation to minimise inventory holding. But inventory is also a valuable business asset which is needed to provide the maximum chance of satisfying customers and even out any irregularities in the flow of deliveries and production. It may be technically possible to operate with minimal inventory but this is not always commercially advantageous.

(4) A financial performance indicator is a number drawn from money values, for example, profit margin, ROCE, receivables days and so on. Typically those money values are taken from the financial reports of an organisation which are prepared on the basis of relevant accounting standards. A non-financial performance indicator is one which is not drawn primarily from accounting data. For example, the delivery lead time in days measures the time it takes from order to delivery for a customer purchase.

(5) A quantitative indicator relates to some aspect of the operation that is amenable to being expressed as a number. For example, a 10-day delivery lead time is a quantitative indicator. 'A reputation for being a reliable supplier' is a qualitative indicator –although it may be possible to express it in quantitative terms (e.g. '75% of customers place us in the upper quartile of supplier reliability').

(6) Delivery lead time (days); Customer rating on willingness to customise products/services; Number of customer orders/enquiries leading to completed sales; Customer rating on standard of answers to technical enquiries.

(7) Efficiency relates to securing the maximum output from a given set of inputs. For example, if we say that 95 standard hours work were performed during 100 available hours labour, then we might say we were operating at 95 per cent efficiency. Effectiveness relates to finding the optimum combination of inputs to achieve a given objective. For example, we might say that the most effective means of containing youth crime is to spend £1 m on police, £1.5 m on school support services and £0.5 on sports clubs.

(8) Local authorities are engaged in a complex operation intended to secure a variety of different public objectives. One often finds that it is difficult to measure efficiency by conventional means since outputs cannot be expressed in clear and unambiguous terms. Also, effectiveness is difficult to achieve since there are often various means available to achieve given objectives and one has to 'juggle' them. Benchmarking is therefore very suitable to local authorities since it allows them to compare like aspects of their activities and outputs. If 'best practice' can be identified, then this acts as a guideline for all.

(9) Employer rating of degrees and qualifications.

    (i)   Government (UK and overseas) rating of degrees and qualifications.

    (ii)  Student/alumni rating of degrees and qualifications.

    (iii) Number of alumni in employment within 12 months of graduating.

    (iv) Average salary of alumni 5 years after graduation.

    (v)  Number of alumni in management/professional employment 5 years after graduating.

    (vi) Number of alumni judged to have achieved 'national fame' status inside 10 years after graduating.

(10)

- Organisations and businesses differ in so many detailed respects that it may be difficult to find a benchmark partner that provides a genuine like- for-like comparison.

- Potential benchmark partners may be reluctant to exchange commercially sensitive information.

- Different approaches to the provision of activities may be possible, for example, using different combinations of labour and equipment to produce the same product. There may be no such thing as 'best practice'.

- The whole culture of benchmarking is 'mimetic' – whereby organisations copy each other's practices in order to achieve some form of legitimacy. It may be better for all to adopt distinct practices in order to suit detailed differences in history and circumstances.

# Responsibility Centres

## Chapter learning objectives

- **Discuss** the use of cost, revenue, profit and investment centres in devising organisation structure and in management control. (Syllabus Link D 1a)

- **Discuss** cost information in appropriate formats for cost centre managers, taking due account of controllable / uncontrollable costs and the importance of budget flexing. (Syllabus Link D 2a)

- **Discuss** revenue and cost information in appropriate formats for profit and investment centre managers, taking due account of cost variability, attributable costs, controllable costs and identification of appropriate measures of profit centre 'contribution'. (Syllabus Link D 2b)

- **Discuss** alternative measures of performance for responsibility centres.(Syllabus Link D 2c)

- **Discuss** the likely behavioural consequences of the use of performance metrics in managing cost, profit and investment centres (Syllabus Link D 3a)

- **Discuss** the typical consequences of a divisional structure for performance measurement as divisions compete or trade with each other. (Syllabus Link D 2b)

## 1 Chapter summary

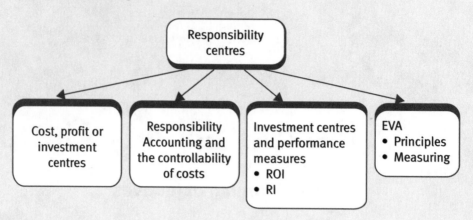

## 2 Introduction

### Decentralisation

Also known as divisionalisation.

Decentralisation seeks to overcome the problem of managing a large organisation by creating a structure based on several autonomous decision-making units.

### Objectives

(1) Ensure goal congruence

(2) Increase motivation of management

(3) Reduce head office bureaucracy

(4) Provide better training for junior and middle management.

### Problem

The major disadvantage of decentralisation is the potential for dysfunctional decision making, i.e. where divisions make decisions in their own best interests, but which are not good from the company point of view.

The problem is overcome by introducing a suitable system of performance evaluation.

## Performance evaluation

### Objectives

(1) Promote goal congruence

(2) Encourage initiative and motivation

(3) Provide feedback to management

(4) Encourage long-term rather than short term views

These objectives can only be achieved with the introduction of responsibility centres.

## 3 Cost, Profit and Investment Centres

It is usual in budgeting to apply the principles of responsibility accounting. In responsibility accounting, a specific manager is given the responsibility for a particular aspect of the budget, and within the budgetary control system, he or she is then made accountable for actual performance. Managers are therefore made accountable for their area of responsibility.

The area of operations for which a manager is responsible might be called a responsibility centre. Within an organisation, there could be a hierarchy of responsibility centres.

- If a manager is responsible for a particular aspect of operating costs, the responsibility centre is a **cost centre:** 'a production or service location, function, activity or item of equipment for which costs are accumulated.' A cost centre could be large or small, such as an entire department or the activities associated with a single item of equipment.

- If a manager is responsible for revenue as well as costs, the responsibility centre is a **profit centre**, and the manager responsible is held accountable for the profitability of the operations in his or her charge.

There could be several cost centres within a profit centre, with the cost centre managers responsible for the costs of their particular area of operations, and the profit centre manager responsible for the profitability of the entire operation.

- If a manager is responsible for investment decisions as well as for revenues and costs, the responsibility centre is an **investment centre**. The manager is held accountable not only for profits, but also for the return on investment from the operations in his or her charge. There could be several profit centres within an investment centre.

Each cost centre, profit centre and investment centre should have its own budget, and its manager should receive regular budgetary control information relating to the centre, for control and performance measurement purposes.

Divisional performance measurement

(1) Return on Capital Employed (ROCE)

(2) Residual Income (RI)

(3) Ratio Analysis

## 4 Responsibility Accounting and controllability of costs

If the principle of controllability is applied, a manager should be made responsible and accountable only for the costs (and revenues) that he or she is in a position to control. A controllable cost is a cost 'which can be influenced by its budget holder'. Controllable costs are generally assumed to be **variable** costs, and **directly attributable fixed costs**. These are fixed costs that can be allocated in full as a cost of the centre.

It is important to make managers responsible and accountable for costs they can control. Without accountability, managers do not have the incentive to control costs and manage their resources efficiently and effectively.

If the principle of controllability is applied, control reports would make managers responsible for the variable costs and directly attributable costs of the centre.

A common assumption in management accounting is that controllable costs consist of variable costs and directly attributable fixed costs. Uncontrollable costs are costs that cannot be influenced up or down by management action.

This assumption is not entirely correct, and it should be used with caution.

Some items treated as variable costs cannot be influenced or controlled in the short term. Direct labour costs are treated as a variable cost, but in reality, the direct labour work force is usually paid a fixed wage for a minimum number of working hours each week. Without making some employees redundant, and unless there is overtime working, the direct labour cost cannot be reduced in the short term because it is really a fixed cost item.

An item that is **uncontrollable** for one manager could be controllable by another. In responsibility accounting, it is important to identify areas of responsibility. In the long term, all costs are controllable. At senior management level, control should be exercised over long-term costs as well as costs in the short term.

A useful distinction can be made between **committed** fixed costs, which are costs that are uncontrollable in the short term, but are controllable over the longer term; and **discretionary** fixed costs, which are costs treated as fixed cost items that can nevertheless be controlled in the short term, because spending is subject to management discretion. Examples are advertising expenditure, and executive travel and subsistence costs.

### Controllable and uncontrollable costs

A summarised report for the profit centres of an organisation might be:

|  | Centre A | Centre B | Centre C | Total |
|---|---|---|---|---|
|  | $ | $ | $ | $ |
| Revenue | 300,000 | 260,000 | 420,000 | 980,000 |
| Variable costs | 170,000 | 100,000 | 240,000 | 510,000 |
| Directly attributable costs | 70,000 | 120,000 | 80,000 | 270,000 |
| **Controllable costs** | **240,000** | **220,000** | **320,000** | **780,000** |
| Attributable gross profit | 60,000 | 40,000 | 100,000 | 200,000 |
| Other overhead costs |  |  |  | **(180,000)** |
| Net profit |  |  |  | 20,000 |

A criticism of the controllability accounting principle is that managers are not encouraged to think about costs for which they are not responsible. In the example above, there are $180,000 of costs not attributable to any profit centre. These might be head office costs, for example, or marketing overheads.

- Within a system of responsibility accounting, there should be cost centre managers accountable for these costs.

- Even so, these overhead costs might be caused to some extent by the demands placed on head office administration or marketing services by the profit centre managers.

- When these costs are high, a further problem is that profit centre profits need to be large enough to cover the general non-allocated overhead costs.

An argument could therefore be made that profit centre managers should be made accountable for a share of overhead costs that are not under their control, and a share of these costs should be charged to each profit centre. Profit reporting would therefore be as follows:

|  | Centre A $ | Centre B $ | Centre C $ | Total $ |
|---|---|---|---|---|
| Revenue | 300,000 | 260,000 | 420,000 | 980,000 |
| Variable costs | 170,000 | 100,000 | 240,000 | 510,000 |
| Directly attributable costs | 70,000 | 120,000 | 80,000 | 270,000 |
| **Controllable costs** | **240,000** | **220,000** | **320,000** | **780,000** |
| Attributable gross profit | 60,000 | 40,000 | 100,000 | 200,000 |
| Other overhead costs | (50,000) | (50,000) | (80,000) | **(180,000)** |
| Net profit | 10,000 | (10,000) | 20,000 | 20,000 |

## Pros and Cons

The advantages of this approach to responsibility accounting are:

- profit centre managers are made aware of the significance of other overhead costs;

- profit centre managers are made aware that they need to earn a sufficient profit to cover a fair share of other overhead costs.

The disadvantages of this approach are that:

- profit centre managers are made accountable for a share of other overhead costs, but they can do nothing to control them

- the apportionment of other overhead costs between profit centres, like overhead apportionment generally, is usually a matter of judgement, lacking any economic or commercial justification.

## 5 Investment Centres and Performance Measures

### Return on Investment (ROI / ROCE)

$$\text{ROI/ ROCE} = \frac{\text{Divisional earnings before interest and tax}}{\text{Capital employed}} \times 100\%$$

## Advantages

(1)  Widely used and accepted

(2)  As a relative measure it enables comparisons to be made with divisions or companies of different sizes

(3)  It can be broken down into secondary ratios for more detailed analysis.

*[In the PEG March 2011, the Examiner regrets that some candidates do not know that 'pre-tax profit %' and 'asset turnover' are secondary ratios to the ROCE].*

## Disadvantages

(1)  May lead to dysfunctional decision making, e.g. a division with a current ROCE of 30% would not wish to accept a project offering an ROCE of 25%, as this would reduce its current figure.

(2)  Different accounting policies can confuse comparisons

(3)  ROCE increases with age of asset if NBVs are used, thus giving managers an incentive to hang on to possibly inefficient, obsolescent machines.

### Example 1

Nielsen Ltd has 2 divisions with the following information:

|  | Division A | Division B |
|---|---|---|
|  | $ | $ |
| Profit | 90,000 | 10,000 |
| Capital employed | 300,000 | 100,000 |
|  |  |  |
| ROCE | 30% | 10% |

Division A has been offered a project costing $100,000 and giving returns of $20,000. Division B has been offered a project costing $100,000 and giving returns of $12,000. The company's cost of capital is 15%. Divisional performance is judged on ROCE and the ROCE-related bonus is sufficiently high to influence the managers' behaviour.

(a)  What decisions will be made by management if they act in the best interests of their division (and in the best interest of their bonus)?

(b)  What should the managers do if they act in the best interests of the company as a whole?

*[From the PEG November 2010: Candidates were asked to calculate the ROI for the last three years and discuss the performance of the division using the data provided; A good answer would have related to the scenario, whereas a poor answer would have provided a generic explanation of performance measures.*

*It is also patently obvious that many candidates do not understand that area of the syllabus and had not included it in their revision programme. (...) The presentation of figures for parts (b) and (c) was particularly poor, with markers not being able to award marks on many occasions due to figures being set down at random, and figures appearing with no explanation and no workings to support them.]*

## 6 Residual Income

Residual income is profit less an imputed interest charge for invested capital.

### Residual Income RI = Profit - (Capital Employed x Cost of capital)

The imputed interest charge is the amount of capital employed times the cost of capital.

### Advantages

(1) It reduces ROCE's problem of rejecting projects with an ROCE in excess of the company's target, but lower than the division's current ROCE.

(2) The cost of financing a division is brought home to divisional managers

### Disadvantages

(1) Does not facilitate comparisons between divisions

(2) Does not relate the size of a division's profit to the assets employed in order to obtain that profit.

### Residual Income vs. ROI

An investment centre has net assets of $800,000, and made profits before interest of $160,000. The notional cost of capital is 12%. An opportunity has arisen to invest in a new project costing $100,000. The project would have a four-year life, and would make cash profits of $40,000 each year.

**Required:**

(a) What would be the average ROI with and without the investment? Would the investment centre manager wish to undertake the investment if performance is judged on ROI in Year 1?

(b) What would be the average annual residual income with and without the investment? Would the investment centre manager wish to undertake the investment if performance is judged on residual income in Year 1?

To calculate ROI and residual income, use the value for capital employed as at the start of Year 1.

**Solution:**

(a) It is assumed that depreciation is charged on a straight line basis at $25,000 each year, so that the increase in annual profit with the investment will be $15,000 ($40,000 – $25,000).

|  | Without the investment | With the investment |
|---|---|---|
| Profit | $160,000 | $175,000 |
| Capital Employed | $800,000 | $900,000 |
| ROI | 20% | 19.4% |

ROI would be lower; therefore the centre manager will not want to make the investment.

(b) Residual Income

|  | | Without the investment | | With the investment |
|---|---|---|---|---|
| Profit | | $160,000 | | $175,000 |
| Notional Interest | ($800,000 x 12%) | $96,000 | ($900,000 x 12%) | $108,000 |
| Residual Income | | $64,000 | | $67,000 |

The investment centre manager will want to undertake the investment because it will increase residual income. This is because the accounting return on the new investment is 15% in year 1 ($15,000/$100,000), which is higher than the notional cost of interest.

### 7 Economic Value Added (EVA®)

Economic value added (EVA) is a measure of performance similar to residual income, except the profit figure used is the ECONOMIC profit and the capital employed figure used is the ECONOMIC capital employed. It is argued that the profit and capital employed figures quoted in the financial statements do not give the true picture and that the accounting figures need to be adjusted to show the true underlying performance.

The basic concept of EVA is that the performance of a company as a whole, or of investment centres within a company, should be measured in terms of the value that has been added to the business during the period. It is a measure of performance that is directly linked to the creation of shareholder wealth.

The measurement of EVA is conceptually simple. In order to add to its economic value, a business must make an economic profit in excess of the cost of the capital that has been invested to earn that profit.

EVA Summary:

| | |
|---|---|
| (1) **PAT is adjusted to give the Net Operating Profit after tax (NOPAT)** | **X** |
| **then** | |
| (2) **Deduct the economic value of the capital employed x cost of capital** | **(X)** |
| | — |
| | **X** |
| | — |

In more detail:

| | | |
|---|---|---|
| (1) **NOPAT is calculated from PAT** | | **X** |
| **Add back items that are non cash, such as:** | | |
| Accounting depreciation | Note 1 | XX |
| Provision for doubtful debts | Note 2 | XX |
| Non cash expenses | Note 3 | XX |
| Interest paid net of tax | Note 4 | XX |
| **Add back items that add value, such as:** | | |
| Goodwill amortised | Note 5 | XX |
| Development costs | Note 6 | XX |
| Operating leases | Note 7 | XX |
| **Take off:** | | |
| Economic depreciation | Note 8 | (X) |
| Any impairment in the value of goodwill | | |
| | | — |
| = NOPAT in cash flow terms | | XX |
| | | — |

(2) Deduct the charge for the cost of capital

Capital Employed
Add adjustments to allow for the net replacement cost of
tangible non current assets
= Capital invested

(3) Multiply Capital invested by the cost of capital x%     —
   = Charge for the cost of capital                        (XX)
                                                            —
   **= EVA**                                                **X**

### Notes on EVA statement

**Note 1 – Accounting depreciation:** We add this back to PAT, because EVA is calculated after profits have been charged with economic depreciation (not accounting depreciation)

**Note 2 – Provision for doubtful debts:** Where a company had made a provision for doubtful debts, this should be reversed. Any adjustment in the income statement for an increase or decrease in the provision for doubtful debts should be reversed.

**Note 3 – Non cash expenses:** These were charged to profit, but must be added back because we want NOPAT in cash flow terms.

**Note 4 – Interest paid net of tax:** if tax is at 35%, take interest payments and multiply by 0.65

Adding this back results in earnings that would have been reported had all the companies capital requirements been financed with ordinary shares. A charge for interest and the tax effect of actual gearing are incorporated into the weighted average cost of capital (so if we leave the interest charge within the NOPAT number it will be double counted). It is the **net** interest i.e. interest after tax that is added back to reported profit because interest will already have been allowed as an expense in the computation of the taxation liability.

**Note 5 – Goodwill:** Goodwill is a measure of the price paid for a business in excess of the current cost of the net separable assets of the business. Payments in respect of goodwill may be viewed as adding value to the company. Therefore any amounts in respect of goodwill amortisation appearing in the income statement are added back to reported profit since they represent part of the intangible asset value of the business.

**Note 6 – Development costs:** Spending by the company on development costs should not be charged in full against profit in which the expenditure occurs. Instead, it should be capitalised because it has added value to the economic value of capital employed. The adjustment can be made by:

- Increasing NOPAT by the net increase in capitalised development costs, and
- Increasing the economic value of capital employed by the same amount.

### Note 7 – Leases

All leases should be capitalised. Finance leases will have already been capitalised but operating leases should be capitalised too. The economic value of the capital employed increased t o include the current value of the operating lease. The capitalised cost should then be amortised. The value of NOPAT should be increased by the operating lease charge and reduce by the amortisation charge. The net effect to increase NOPAT by the implied interest cost of the operating lease.

### Note 8 – Economic depreciation

Considered to be a measure of the economic use of assets during a year. Involves a process of valuation. It is the period by period change in the market value of the asset.

### Advantages of EVA

The advantages of EVA are as follows.

- It is a performance measure that attempts to put a figure to the increase (or decrease) that should have arisen during a period from the operations of a company or individual divisions within a company.
- Like accounting return and residual income, it can be measured for each financial reporting period.
- It is easily understood by non-accountants.
- It is based on economic profit and economic values of assets, not accounting profits and asset values.

## Measuring and using EVA

### The principle underlying EVA

The principle underlying EVA can be stated as follows.

- The objective of a company is to maximise shareholder wealth.

- The value of a company depends on the extent to which shareholders expect future economic profits to exceed the cost of the capital invested.

- A share price therefore depends on expectations of EVA.

- Current performance (EVA) is reflected in the current share price, so in order to increase the share price a company must achieve a sustained increase in EVA.

Peter Drucker has written: 'Until a business returns a profit that is greater than its cost of capital, it operates at a loss. Never mind that it pays taxes as if it had a genuine profit. The enterprise still returns less to the economy than it devours in resources…. Until then, it does not create wealth it destroys it.'

### Measuring EVA

The difficulties in applying EVA in practice arise from the problem of establishing the economic profit in a period, and the economic value of capital employed. These values are estimated by making adjustments to accounting profits and accounting capital employed.

- Accounting profits are based on the accruals concept of accounting, whereas NOPAT for EVA is based on cash flow profits. Adjustments have to be made to convert from an accruals basis to a cash flow basis.

- **Depreciation** of non-current assets is a charge in calculating EVA as well as accounting profit. Economic depreciation is the fall in the economic value of an asset during the period.

  - It might be assumed that the accounting charge for depreciation is a good approximation of the economic cost of depreciation, in which case no adjustment to accounting profit is necessary.

  - Alternatively, it might be assumed that the economic value of the assets are their net replacement cost, in which case economic depreciation will be based on replacement cost. An adjustment to accounting profit should then be made for the amount by which economic depreciation exceeds the accounting charge for depreciation.

- Similarly, an adjustment might be necessary for intangible non-current assets such as goodwill.

- Where a company had made a provision for doubtful debts, this should be reversed. Any adjustment in the income for an increase or decrease in the provision for doubtful debts should be reversed, and NOPAT increased or reduced accordingly.

- Spending by the company on development costs should not be charged in full against profit in the year the expenditure occurs. Instead, it should be capitalised because it has added to the economic value of capital employed, and it should then be amortised over an appropriate number of years. In practice, the adjustment can be made by:

  - increasing NOPAT by the net increase in capitalised development costs, and

  - increasing the economic value of capital employed by the same amount.

- All leases should be capitalised. Finance leases will have been capitalised already, but operating leases should be capitalised too, and the economic value of capital employed increased to include the current value of operating leases. Stern Stewart amortise this capitalised cost over five years. In adjusting from accounting profit to NOPAT, the value of NOPAT should be increased by the operating lease rental charge, and reduced by the amount of the amortisation charge. (The net effect is to increase NOPAT by the implied interest cost of the operating lease.)

## Using EVA

Economic value added can be used to:

- set targets for performance for investment centres (divisions) and the company as a whole

- measure actual performance

- plan and make decisions on the basis of how the decision will affect EVA.

When EVA is used to measure performance, Stern Stewart have recommended that divisional managers should be:

- given training to understand the principles of EVA. Stern Stewart have found than non-accountants find the concept of EVA fairly easy to understand, and they see the link between EVA and changes in shareholder value

- informed about the interest cost that will be applied for the capital charge

- taught how to calculate EVA for decision-making purposes

- given a pay incentive based on a bonus for achieving or exceeding a target EVA.

- EVA can also be used for control purposes, by encouraging managers to:

  - identify products and services that provide the greatest EVA, and concentrate resources on them

  - identify customers who provide the greatest EVA, and give priority to serving them

  - identify and eliminate activities that do not add to EVA

  - identify capital that is not providing a sufficient return to cover its capital cost (such as excess equipment) and seek to reduce the capital investment.

### Example 2

A division has a reported annual profit of $27m. This was after charging $6m for the development and launch costs of a new product which is expected to have a life of 3 years

The division has a risk adjusted cost of capital of 10% per annum, but it has a large bank loan, which incurs annual interest charges of 8%.

The net book value of the division's net assets is $85m. The replacement cost of the assets is estimated to be $96m.

Ignore the effects of taxation.

Calculate the division's EVA.

## Responsibility Centres and Internal Markets (extract)

*Bob Scarlett, Financial Management, April 2007*

An objective must be set for an autonomous responsibility centre. Determining how far that objective has been achieved provides a performance measure for the centre. The system must be adapted to priorities and circumstances in each case. Accordingly, responsibility centres may be grouped under three main headings:

(1) **Cost centre (CC)**

This is a responsibility centre to which costs are attributed, but not earnings or capital.

CCs can be designed in two alternative ways: either (a) the CC is given a fixed quantity of inputs and be required to maximise outputs, or (b) a required level of outputs is specified for the CC which must be achieved with minimum inputs.

An example of (a) is a public relations department, which is given a fixed budget to spend and has to use this to achieve the best possible result. An example of (b) is a cleaning department, which is given certain areas to clean and has to do this at minimum cost. In both cases, the CC manager is allowed a degree of autonomy in making decisions on how the operation is run. But the system guides the manager to act in a manner which is consistent with the interest of the organisation.

However, the CC offers one particular weakness insofar as it relies on the measurement of financial spend to assess performance. There is no direct incentive for the manager to enhance the quality of output. Costs can always be contained by reducing quality. In the case of a CC, quality reduction is not identified by the use of financial performance metrics.

Many organisations treat their IT departments as cost centres. This often has unfortunate consequences.

*The idea that IT is a cost centre and carries no profit or loss is dangerous and should be opposed wherever it is encountered, according to Simon Linsley, head of consultancy, IT and development at Philips. Will Hadfield, Computer Weekly, 30 May 2006*

This CW article describes how IT system installation projects were usually completed on time and within budget at the electronics firm Philips. However, the manner in which system projects were implemented often gave rise to serious disruption at the operational level, causing stress to the staff of client departments and degraded customer service.

## (2) Profit centres (PC)

This is a responsibility centre to which costs and revenues are attributed, but not capital.

In the case of a CC, the manager has autonomy as regards either (a) outputs or (b) inputs – but not both together. In the case of the PC, the manager has autonomy over both inputs and outputs. The objective of a PC is to maximise profit or achieve a profit target. The manager of the PC is allowed to make decisions concerning both the resources used and output (in terms of both quantity and price) achieved.

In the case of a PC, reliance on financial performance measures does not provide any incentive to lower quality. Lowering quality will impact on sales quantity and/or selling price, which will impact on profit. The PC may also induce other behaviour which is in the interests of an organisation. For example, unit costs within a CC may be minimised by use of long continuous production runs and this pattern of production may be favoured accordingly. But, it is a pattern of production which will result in high inventory holding and/or lowered response levels to individual customer requirements. These last features will adversely impact on profit and, therefore, a sub-optimum pattern of production is less likely to be induced within a PC.

An IT department within an organisation may be organised as a profit centre. Typically, this will involve invoicing client departments for its services and inviting competition from outside consultants for system installation projects.

*IT directors should push for the IT function in their organisation to be treated as a profit centre rather than a cost to the business. This was the key message from Glenn Martin, managing director and chief technology officer at financial services firm Cazenove, speaking to the City IT financial services technology forum last week. Christian Annesley, Computer Weekly, 15 November 2005*

Rather than forcing through system installations in a manner which minimises costs, IT managers are now incentivised to allow for the full operational requirements of client departments when organising projects.

The logic behind responsibility centres suggests that an organisation should be split into decoupled internal components with decision rights in each given to its own management, within certain parameters. Each component trades its services with the others on an arms length basis, giving rise to an 'internal market'.

This concept was applied widely in the British public sector in the 1990s. The BBC under Director General John Birt introduced an internal market amongst its different components – Technology, Production, News and so on. The development of an internal market has also been a feature of NHS reform, whereby different units within the NHS have the character of buyers and providers of services.

So much for the theory. Practical experience has introduced organisations to a concept known as 'failure of the internal market'. For example, the BBC Gramophone Library was rated as the greatest sound archive in the world and it was traditionally run as a cost centre. During the reforms of the 1990s, it became a profit centre and was required to charge user departments in the BBC for the issue of recordings.

*Music that was previously provided free by the Library now came with a charge and it wasn't cheap. Which is why all the music shops in Oxford Street were busy with BBC researchers buying far cheaper commercial CDs. At the prestigious Radio 4 daytime current affairs programmes The World at One and PM, staff were barred from using any material from the BBCs gramophone library because the cost was too high. Netribution, 'BBC axes Producer Choice', March 2006*

The BBC's internal market was deeply unpopular and produced unintended effects in the way that managers behaved. It has been largely abandoned in recent years. The reality was that the BBC's Gramophone Library was a vital resource that had to be seen as a cost centre and nothing other than that.

Responsibility centres and internal markets have much to offer. But insensitivity in their use or their use in inappropriate circumstances can result in them doing more harm than good.

## 8 Practice Questions

### Test your understanding 1

You have recently been appointed as a company's Assistant Management Accountant. The company is large and runs a well-developed cost centre system. The Finance Director is considering the introduction of profit centres throughout the organisation, where appropriate. She is asking for technical advice and assistance for the proposed scheme.

**Required:**

Prepare a report addressed to the Finance Director that :

(i)   describes the main characteristics and objectives of profit centres and investment centres;

(ii)   explains what conditions are necessary for the successful introduction of such centres;

(iii)   describes the main behavioural and control consequences which may arise if such centres are introduced;

(iv)   compares **two** performance appraisal measures that may be used if investment centres are introduced.

### Test your understanding 2

Zig plc has three divisions A, B and C, whose performance is assessed on Return on Investment (ROI).

Forecast data for 2010 is provided as follows:

| Division | A | B | C |
|---|---|---|---|
| ROI | 24% | 28% | 23% |

Zig operates a policy that all surplus cash balances are transferred to Head Office.

Three new proposals are being considered:

- A is considering investing £75,000 in order to increase profit by £21,000 each year.

- B is considering selling a machine, forecast to earn a profit of £2,5000 in the coming year, for its net book value of £7,000.

- C is considering giving a 2.5% discount for prompt payment. This should reduce debtors by £20,000. C's sales revenue is £500,000 each year and a 50% take up of the offer is expected.

The following division(s) will reject the proposal under consideration because of its effect on the ROI:

A    Division A

B    Divisions A and B

C    Divisions A and C

D    Divisions B and C

## Mini-Quiz

(1)  The manager of a trading division has complete autonomy regarding the purchase and use of non-current assets. The division operates its own credit control policy in respect of customers but the group operates a central purchasing function through which the division places all orders with suppliers and invoices are paid by head office.

Inventories of goods for sale are kept in central stores, from which local divisions call off requirements for local sales on a monthly basis into a local inventory.

Divisional performance is assessed on the basis of controllable Residual Income. The company requires a rate of return of 'R'.

Using the following symbols:

| | |
|---|---|
| Divisional non-current assets | N |
| Apportioned net book value of central stores | S |
| Divisional working capital | |
| Receivables | D |
| Local Inventory | I |
| Bank | B |
| Payables | (P) |
| | — |
| | W |
| | — |
| Divisional net assets | T |
| | — |
| Divisional contribution | C |
| Controllable fixed costs | (F) |
| Head Office charges | (H) |
| | — |
| Divisional net income | G |
| | — |

Which ONE of the following formulae calculates the division's **controllable residual income?**

A    [C-F] – [(N+D+B) x R]

B    [C-F] – [(N+D+I+B) x R]

C    C – [(N + D) x R]

D    G – (TxR)

*(from ICAEW)*

(2)  EF plc has 3 divisions – P, Q and R – whose performance is assessed on return on investment (ROI). The ROI for the divisions for the coming year is expected to be 24%, 28% and 23%, respectively. EF plc operates a policy that all surplus cash balances are transferred to Head Office. Three new proposals are now being considered:

(i)  P is considering investing $75,000 in order to increase profit by $21,600 each year.

(ii)  Q is considering selling a machine, forecast to earn a profit of $2,500 in the coming year, for its carrying value of $7,000.

(iii)  R is considering giving a 2.5% discount for prompt payment. This should reduce receivables by $20,000. R's sales revenue is $500,000 each year and a 50% take up of the offer is expected.

The following division(s) will REJECT the proposal under consideration because of its effect on ROI:

A  P

B  Q

C  P and Q

D  P and R

E  Q and R

(3)  Indicate which of the following statements are true:

(i)  If a company uses a balanced scorecard approach to the provision of information it will not use ROI or Residual Income as divisional performance measures.

(ii)  The Residual Income will always increase when investments earning above the cost of capital are undertaken.

(iii)  The internal business perspective of the balanced scorecard approach to the provision of information is concerned only with the determination of internal transfer price that will encourage goal congruent decisions.

(iv)  An advantage of the Residual Income performance measure is that it facilitates comparisons between investment centres.

A  (i) only

B  (ii) only

C  (iii) only

D  (i) and (iv) only.

**Test your understanding answers**

## Example 1

(a)

|  | Division A | Division B |
|---|---|---|
|  | *$000* | *$000* |
| **Old ROCE** |  |  |
| Profit | 90 | 10 |
|  | ─── | ─── |
| Capital Employed | 300 | 100 |
| Old ROCE | 30% | 10% |
| **New ROCE** | 90 + 20 | 10 + 12 |
| Profit |  |  |
|  | ─────── | ─────── |
|  | 300 + 100 | 100 + 100 |
| New ROCE | 27.5% | 11% |
| Will manager want to accept project? | No | Yes |

The manager of division A will not want to accept the project as it lowers her ROCE from 30% to 27.5%. The manager of division B will like the new project as it will increase their ROCE from 10% to 11%. Although the 11% is bad, it is better than before.

Looking at the whole situation from the group point of view, we are in the ridiculous position that the group has been offered 2 projects, both costing $100,000. One project gives a profit of $20,000 and the other $12,000. Left to their own devices then the managers would end up accepting the project giving only $12,000. This is because ROCE is a defective decision making method and does not guarantee that the correct decision will be made.

(b) There are a number of different ways of making the correct decision. The simplest way is to calculate the ROCE of the project itself.

**ROCE of Project**

| | | |
|---|---:|---:|
| Profit | 20 | 12 |
| Capital Employed | 100 | 100 |
| Old ROCE | 20% | 12% |
| Should manager accept project? | Yes | No |

Now the correct decision has been made. Division A will accept the project giving a return of 20% as it the cost of capital is only 15%, but division B will reject its project as it only gives a return of 12%.

## Example 2

**Calculation of NOPAT**

| | $m |
|---|---:|
| Accounting operating profit | 27 |
| Add back development and launch costs | 6 |
| Less one year's amortisation of development and launch costs | 2 |
| | 31 |

**Calculation of value of capital employed**

| | $m |
|---|---:|
| Replacement cost of net assets | 96 |
| Add back increase in capitalised launch and development costs | 4 |
| | 100 |

**Calculation of EVA**

The correct figure to use for calculating the capital charge is the cost of capital, i.e. the 10%. The 8% is a distracter.

| | $m |
|---|---:|
| NOPAT | 31 |
| Capital charge (10% x $100m) | 10 |
| EVA | 21 |

**Test your understanding 1**

# REPORT

**To**: Finance Director

**From**: Assistant Management Accountant

**Subject:** Responsibility centres

**Date**: XX-May 20X9

## Introduction

Please find a report that briefly explains the concepts linked with implementing profit centres and/or investment centres throughout an organisation.

(i) **Main characteristics and objectives of profit centres and investment centres**

The CIMA definition of a profit centre is 'a segment of the business entity by which both revenues are received and expenditure are caused or controlled, such revenues and expenditure being used to evaluate segmental performance. This may also be called a business centre, business unit or strategic business unit, depending upon the concept of management responsibility prevailing in the entity concerned.

An investment centre is defined as 'a profit centre in which inputs are measured in terms of expenses and outputs in terms of revenues, and in which assets are also measured, the excess of revenue over expenditure then being related to assets.'

In our case, the conversion of cost centres into profit and investment centres will have necessitated the delegation of responsibility for investment decisions. The objective of profit and investment centres will be to earn as high profits as possible either in absolute terms or, in some way, relative to the level of investment.

The objective behind setting up these centres (decentralising or divisionalising) is to improve the overall profitability of the large organisation. It is hoped that this is achieved, since divisional managers will be motivated to perform well.

*[Tutorial note: you would also have got credit for mentioning the reasons behind a decision to decentralise: size, specialisation, geographical, fiscal, etc.]*

(ii) **Conditions necessary for the successful introduction of profit centres and investment centres**

Successful introduction is likely to be achieved if those managers responsible for cost centres currently can be encouraged to propose the idea themselves rather than have it imposed on them by senior executives. Taking the process one stage further, it is likely to be a success if:

–   The activities of the cost centres are dissimilar;

–   The cost centres are more or less independent from each other;

–   It is possible to control the new profit and investment centres so that a centre cannot adversely affect the overall profit of the organisation by a decision aimed to increase its own profit.

In practice, these three conditions are unlikely to hold.

Once the new structure is introduced, policies must be adopted which achieve the three-fold aims of:

–   Motivation;

–   Independence

–   Goal congruence.

(iii) **Behavioural and control consequences**

The obvious consequence of the system proposed will be a greater need to delegate decisions and to control those making those decisions. Whereas formerly senior management made investment decisions these are now to be passed down to management committees of investment centres. Senior management may be reluctant to let loose the reins, while middle management may not be adequately prepared to make the decisions.

A major problem will be the need to achieve goal congruence. The new divisions will aim to maximise their own individual profitability; this has to be achieved without adversely affecting the overall performance of the organisation. This can only be achieved by central monitoring of divisional decisions with the consequent loss of divisional independence, and possibly a reduction in the motivation of divisional managers.

New performance measures will have to be introduced. It is important that managers feel that they can make decisions which allow them to affect the profit of their divisions. In circumstances such as this, it is often the case that one former cost centre's performance depends purely on the performance of those other divisions that they serve To this end the transfer pricing policy must be fair, and they must have a full say in investment decisions.

One potential problem is that decisions may be made that present a healthy picture of a division, although decisions are taken which adversely affect long-term profitability. Managers may try to 'fiddle the system', for example by cutting down on investment. Controls over items such as training and maintenance may have to be introduced.

Motivation is likely to be enhanced if good performance is rewarded in some way. However, such bonus schemes will exacerbate the dangers outlined above and also should not be an excuse for providing inadequate basic remuneration.

(iv) **Measures of performance**

The two main measures that are used to assess the performance of investment centres are:

$$\text{Return on Investment (ROI)} = \frac{\text{Controllable profit}}{\text{Controllable investment}} \times 100$$

$$\text{Residual Income (RI)} = \text{Controllable profit} - \text{Imputed interest cost on controllable investment}$$

**ROI** is also called Return on Capital Employed; the second requires that profit is reduced by an amount equal to the cost of capital x the capital invested. In both cases a manager's performance is best assessed by reference to those costs over which he or she has some control although allocated head office costs may be included when the investment centre is evaluated.

The obvious comparison is that ROI is a **relative** measure whereas RI is an **absolute** one.

The ROI is widely understood but has the disadvantage that it can be improved not just by increasing profit but by reducing capital employed. There may be advantages (and some dangers) of reducing working capital, but failing to carry out investment promises may affect long-term profitability.

A division may be discouraged from making an investment that reduces its current ROI, despite the fact that the organisation's overall profitability would improve. Although ROI is often used for investment centres and it does allow for comparison of operations of different sizes, it is more appropriate for profit centres where the investment decision is made centrally  and the profit centre's aim is to achieve as high a return on that investment as possible. It can however be the starting point for what some describe as pyramid analysis where secondary ratios such as asset turnover and net profit percentage are found.

RI does not suffer from the drawbacks of ROI. Its maximisation will ensure that the overall organisation's profits are maximised. It provides managers with an idea of the cost of financing their divisions. Different interest rates can be used to charge different types of asset.

## Conclusion

I hope that the above report clarifies the basic concepts linked with responsibility accounting and I look forward to providing more assistance and technical advice on the proposed scheme.

**Signed**: Assistant Management Accountant

### Test your understanding 2

**Answer D**

A's return $= \dfrac{21,600}{75,000} = 29\%$. Zig should **accept**, as this is higher than the expected 24%.

B's return $= \dfrac{\text{Decrease in profit}}{\text{Decrease in capital}} = \dfrac{(£2,500)}{(£7,000)}$

$= 36\%$. Reject, because average ROI will reduce.

$$\text{C's return} = \frac{\text{Cost of discount}}{\text{Reduction in debtors}} = \frac{(\text{£}500,000 \times 50\% \times 2.5\%)}{(\text{£}20,000)}$$

= 36%. Reject, because average ROI will reduce.

$$= \frac{\text{£}6,250}{\text{£}20,000}$$

= 31%. Reject, because average ROI will reduce.

## Mini-Quiz

(1)  Answer B

(2)  Answer E

P's return = (21,600 / 75,000) = 29% accept, because higher than expected 24%

Q's return = (Decrease in profit/Decrease in capital) = ($2,500/ $7,000) = 36% reject, because the average ROI will reduce

R's return = (Cost of discount/reduction in debtors) = ($500,000 x 50% x 2.5%)/$20,000 = ($6,250)/($20,000) = 31% reject, because average ROI will decrease.

(3)  Answer B (ii) only

# Transfer Pricing

## Chapter learning objectives

- **Discuss** the likely consequences of different approaches to transfer pricing for divisional decision making, divisional and group profitability, the motivation of divisional management and the autonomy of individual divisions. (Syllabus Link D3c)

- **Discuss** in principle the potential tax and currency management consequences of internal transfer pricing policy (Syllabus LinkD3d).

## 1 Chapter summary

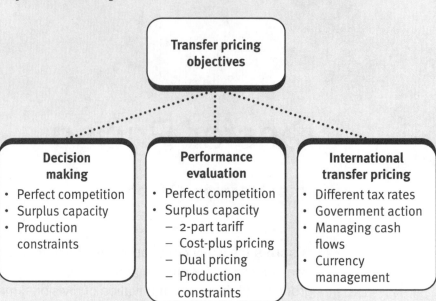

### Decentralisation and profit centres or investment centres

When an organisation is structured into profit centres or investment centres, authority is delegated to the profit centre or investment centre managers. These managers are given the authority to take decisions at a local level, without having to wait for instructions from head office. Control is applied from head office through performance measurement: centre managers are held accountable for the profits or returns that they make.

The purposes of decentralisation should be to:

(1) give autonomy to local centre managers in decision-making

(2) motivate centre managers to improve performance: with profit centres and investment centres, this includes motivating them to increase profitability

(3) through performance enhancement at a profit centre level, to achieve better results for the organisation as a whole.

Decentralisation can create tension between local centre managers and head office management.

- The performance of the managers of profit centres and investment centres will be assessed, and the managers themselves will be rewarded, on the basis of the results of their particular centre. Profit centre managers will therefore be motivated to optimise the results of their own division, regardless of other profit centres and regardless of the organisation as a whole.

When head office management believe that a profit centre manager is taking decisions that improve the profit centre performance, but are damaging for the interests of the organisation as a whole, they might want to step in and either:

(1) alter the decisions that have been made at profit centre level, or

(2) make new decisions for the profit centre.

However, if head office interferes in decision-making at profit centre level, local autonomy in decision making is lost.

## 2 Transfer Pricing

In an organisation with profit centres and investment centres, there will almost certainly be some inter-connection between different centres. Some profit centres will supply goods and services to others.

When *inter-divisional* (inter-company) trading takes place between profit centres, the centre providing the goods or services to the other will want to earn income from the transfer. Unless it receives income from the transfer, it will make a loss on the transaction.

For example, if Division A provides items to Division B that cost $10 each to make, Division A must earn at least $10 from the transfer, otherwise it will make a loss. If decision making is delegated to profit centre management, the manager of Division A would refuse to supply Division B unless it is allowed to earn income of at least $10 for each unit.

Inter-divisional transfers must therefore be priced. The price of the transfer is the **transfer price**.

- The transfer is treated as an internal sale and an internal purchase within the organisation. It provides sales income to the supplying division and is a purchase cost for the receiving division.

- The sales income of one division is offset by the purchase cost of the other division. The transfer therefore affects the profits of the two divisions individually, but has no effect on the profit of the organisation as a whole.

### Setting a transfer price: Inter-divisional trading policy

The transfer price for inter-divisional transactions is significant because:

- it determines how the total profit is shared between the two divisions, and

- in some circumstances, it could affect decisions by the divisional managers about whether they are willing to sell to or buy from the other division.

**Both divisions must benefit from the transaction if inter-divisional sales are to take place.**

- A selling division will not agree to sell items to another division unless it is profitable for the selling division to do so.

- Similarly, a buying division will not wish to purchase items from another division unless it is profitable for the division.

**Transfer prices have to be established and agreed**. They could be decided either centrally or locally.

- They could be imposed by head office.

- Alternatively, they could be decided by commercial negotiation between the profit centre managers.

- If decentralisation is to allow the power of decision making to profit centre managers, they should have the authority to agree transfer prices by discussion or negotiation between themselves.

Inter-divisional trading should take place within a broad company policy, that:

- for a 'selling division', given the choice between making a sale to an external customer or supplying goods or services to another division within the group, **the preference should be to sell internally**

- for a 'buying division', given the choice between purchasing from an external supplier or from another division within the company, the **preference should be to purchase internally**.

However, a division should be allowed to sell externally rather than transfer internally, or buy externally rather than internally, if it has a good commercial reason. Good commercial reasons would include an external customer offering a higher price, or an external supplier offering a lower price.

### Example 1 – Inter-divisional trading

A company has two profit centres, Centre A and Centre B. Centre A supplies Centre B with a part-finished product. Centre B completes the production and sells the finished units in the market at $35 per unit.

**Budgeted data for the year:**

|  | Division A | Division B |
|---|---|---|
| Number of units transferred/sold | 10,000 | 10,000 |
| Materials costs | $8 per unit | $2 per unit |
| Other variable costs | $2 per unit | $3 per unit |
| Annual Fixed Costs | $60,000 | $30,000 |

**Required:**

Calculate the budgeted annual profit of each profit centre and the organisation as a whole if the transfer price for components supplied by Division A to Division B is:

(a) $20

(b) $25

## 3 Objectives Of Transfer Pricing

### (1) Goal Congruence

Within a divisionalised company, divisional managers will have responsibility for and will be judged on their division's performance. They will act independently, autonomously and selfishly in the best interests of their own division. They neither know nor care what is happening in other divisions.

It is the task of the management accounting system in general and the transfer pricing policy in particular to ensure that what is good for an individual division is good for the company as a whole.

### (2) Performance Measurement

The transfer pricing system should result in a report of divisional profits that is a reasonable measure of the managerial performance.

### (3) Maintaining Divisional Autonomy

One of the purposes of decentralisation is to allow managers to exercise greater autonomy. There is little point in granting additional autonomy and then imposing transfer prices that will affect the profitability of the division.

### (4) Minimising the global tax liability

When a divisionalised company operates entirely within one tax regime the transfer pricing policy will have a minimal impact on the corporate tax bill. However multinational companies can and do use their transfer pricing policies to move profits around the world and thereby minimise their global tax liabilities.

### (5) Recording the movement of goods and services

In practice, an extremely important function of the transfer pricing system is simply to assist in recording the movement of goods and services.

### (6) A fair allocation of profits between divisions

Most of the advantages claimed for divisionalisation are behavioural. Insofar as transfer pricing has a material effect on divisional profit it is essential that managers perceive the allocation of corporate profit as being fair if the motivational benefits are to be retained.

Needless to say, a number of these objectives can conflict with each other, and prove difficult to achieve in practice. It is highly unlikely that any one method would meet all the firm's requirements in all circumstances the best that can be hoped for is a reasonable compromise.

### Bases for setting a transfer price

In broad terms, there are three bases for setting a transfer price:

(1)  market-based prices;

(2)  cost-based prices;

(3)  negotiated prices.

A market-based transfer price might be agreed when there is an intermediate market for the transferred item. An intermediate market is a term to describe an external market for the goods or services of the selling division. The selling division can therefore make its profits either by transferring the goods or services internally, or selling them in the external market.

A **market-based** transfer price could be:

- the price for the item in the external market ('intermediate market'), or at a discount to the external market price, to allow for a share of the savings in selling costs that the selling division enjoys by transferring internally rather than selling externally. For example, packaging, distribution and warranty costs may be saved by transferring internally.

A **cost-based** transfer price could be:

- the marginal cost to the selling division of making the product or providing the service
- the selling division's marginal cost plus a mark-up for profit
- the full cost to the selling division of making the product, or
- the selling division's full cost plus a mark-up for profit.

When a transfer price is based on cost, it could be actual cost or budgeted cost. The most suitable basis would be budgeted cost (or standard cost).

- Standard costs or budgeted costs are known in advance; therefore transfers can be priced as they occur. The selling division can invoice the buying division immediately for all items transferred.

- Actual costs are not known until after the end of the accounting period. There would consequently be a delay in pricing transfers and issuing invoices.

- If transfers are at standard or budgeted cost, the selling division's manager could be motivated to improve profits by keeping actual costs below the standard or budgeted amount.

## The intermediate market

The intermediate market for the products or services of a selling division could be:

* perfect
* imperfect, or
* non-existent.

### A perfect intermediate market

If the intermediate market is perfect, all suppliers to the market are able to sell all their output at the prevailing market price. There are no restrictions on sales demand at that price, and no individual supplier dominates market supply.

When a selling division has a perfect external market for its output, it is therefore able to:

* sell all its output on the external market at the market price, and
* provided that it can sell at a price above its marginal cost, the only limitation on profitability from external sales is the output capacity of the division.

### An imperfect intermediate market

An intermediate market is imperfect when the selling division is unable to sell all its output externally at the same market price. This can happen when the division is a dominant influence in the market, and monopoly or oligopoly conditions apply. In order to sell larger volumes of output in the intermediate market, the division is therefore required to reduce the sales price.

When there is an imperfect intermediate market, the problem of identifying a suitable transfer price for inter-divisional sales becomes fairly complex.

It might be possible to establish for the intermediate market a 'demand curve', showing the volume of sales demand at different prices. Demand curves are difficult to establish in practice, although some companies do use them. However, demand curves are common in the academic literature on transfer pricing and there could be examination questions on the topic.

### A demand curve

The rule of market prices is that the total market demand for an item varies with the sales price. If the relationship between sales price and sales demand is linear, a demand curve could be expressed by the formula:

P = a + bQ

where

P is the sales price for all items sold

Q is the quantity of items sold

Values can be established for a and b. When the price is a, Q should be zero.

### Example

Division X in Tropp Group has an imperfect intermediate market for its product B55. The demand curve for B55 is:

P = 100 – 0.005Q

This demand curve shows that:

- the maximum sales price is 100, but at this price sales demand would be zero

- for each reduction in price of 0.005, sales demand will increase by 1 unit

- at a price of 0, sales demand will be 20,000 units (= 100/0.005).

### Marginal revenue

Marginal revenue is the extra revenue that will be earned by selling one additional unit in the market. In a perfect market, the marginal revenue for a company is always the market price of the item, because all output can be sold at the prevailing market price.

When the market is imperfect, marginal revenue is always lower than the market price.

If you are familiar with differentiation, you will no doubt know how to calculate marginal revenue from a demand curve. If you are not familiar with differentiation, the following rules should be learned:

- The demand curve gives a value for P: $P = a + bQ$
- Total revenue = $P \times Q$
- Substituting, we get: Total revenue = $(a + bQ) \times Q$

Total revenue = $aQ + bQ^2$

- Marginal revenue is found by differentiating $aQ + bQ^2$

Without going into the details of the arithmetic:

Marginal revenue (MR) = $a + 2bQ$

**Example**

The demand curve for product B55 is: $P = 100 - 0.005Q$

Total revenue (TR) from selling B55 = $(100 - 0.005Q) \times Q$

TR = $100Q - 0.005 Q^2$

The marginal revenue from selling each extra unit of B55 is:

MR = $100 - (2 \times 0.005)Q$

MR = $100 - 0.010Q$

**Maximising profit**

In an imperfect market, profits are maximised by selling output up to a volume where marginal revenue = marginal cost.

The profit-maximising rule of MR = MC comes from economics and, in economics, cost includes an element for normal profit. However, the same rule can be applied in accounting, where marginal cost does not include a profit element.

This rule might have to be applied in order to determine the profit-maximising output for a company as a whole, and for a profit centre within the company.

# 4 Decision-Making

The general rule for decision-making is that all goods and services should be transferred at **opportunity cost**.

*[In the PEG 2012, the Examiner regrets that too many candidates are 'presuming that 'marginal cost' is another name for 'opportunity cost' and are 'unable to describe an opportunity cost approach to Transfer Pricing'.]*

There are 3 possible situations.

(1)  **Where there is a perfectly competitive market for an intermediate product**

A perfect market means that there is only one price in the market, there are no buying or selling costs and the market is able to absorb the entire output of the primary division and meet all of the requirements of the secondary division.

### OPTIMUM TP (DM) = MARKET PRICE + ANY SMALL ADJUSTMENTS

### TP in a perfect intermediate market

## Perfect intermediate market and no variable selling costs

Division A of the Robin Group makes a product A22, which it sells externally and to another division in the Group, Division B. Division B uses product A22 as a component in product B46, which it sells externally. There is a perfect external market for both A22 and B46.

Costs and sales prices are as follows:

|  | Division A Product A22 | Division B Product B46 |
|---|---|---|
| Variable production cost | $12 per unit |  |
| Further variable costs |  | $15 per unit |
| Fixed costs | $200,000 | $300,000 |
| Sales price | $20 per unit | $45 per unit |

Division A can either sell product A22 externally for $20, or transfer the product internally to Division B. Unless the transfer price is $20 or more, Division A will prefer to sell externally, in order to maximise its profit.

Division B can either buy product A22 from external suppliers at $20, or buy internally from Division A. If the transfer price exceeds $20, Division B will prefer to buy externally, in order to minimise its costs and so maximise its profit.

## Conclusions

- The only transfer price at which Division A and Division B will be willing to trade with each other is $20, the **external market price**;

- At a transfer price of $20, each division would produce and sell up to its capacity. Each division would maximise its profit by making and selling as much as possible, and the total company profit would be maximised. Goal congruence would be achieved.

- In both Divisions A and B, the manager should be motivated to make and sell as much as possible, and to keep costs under control, in order to maximise profit.

- This price would probably be negotiated freely between the managers of Divisions A and B, without head office interference.

- The performance of each profit centre would be measured on a fair basis.

- If company policy is to encourage inter-divisional sales unless there is a good commercial reason for selling or buying externally, the two divisions should trade internally up to the output capacity of the lower-capacity division.

Another way of stating the ideal transfer price is:

|  | $ |
|---|---|
| Marginal cost in Division A | 12 |
| Opportunity cost: contribution forgone from external sale by transferring a unit to Division B: ($20 – $12) | 8 |
|  | — |
| Ideal transfer price (= market price) | 20 |
|  | — |

It can be seen that, in these circumstances, setting the transfer price as the market price satisfies all of the objectives of a transfer pricing system.

### Perfect intermediate market, but with variable selling costs

If there are variable selling costs or buying costs in the intermediate market:

- it will cost the selling division more to sell externally than to transfer internally, or

- it will cost the buying division more to purchase from an external supplier than to buy internally.

It is therefore cheaper and more profitable to transfer internally than to sell or buy externally. The cost savings can be reflected in an adjustment to the transfer price, so that both divisions share the benefit.

### Example

The example of divisions A and B of the Robin Group will be used again, except that the costs and sales prices are as follows:

|  | Division A<br>Product A22 | Division B<br>Product B46 |
|---|---|---|
| Variable production cost | $12 per unit | |
| Variable selling cost in the external market | $3 per unit | |
| Further variable costs | | $15 per unit |
| Fixed costs | $200,000 | $300,000 |
| Sales price | $20 per unit | $45 per unit |

Division A can either sell product A22 externally for $20 to earn a contribution of $5 per unit ($20 – $15) or transfer the product internally to Division B to earn a contribution of $8. The manager of Division A would prefer to sell to Division B because it is cheaper and more profitable. The lowest transfer price that Division A would accept is $17.

|  | $ |
|---|---|
| External selling price | 20 |
| External variable selling cost | (3) |
| | --- |
| Minimum transfer price (= market price) | 17 |

Division B can either buy product A22 from external suppliers at $20, or buy internally from Division A. If the transfer price exceeds $20, Division B will prefer to buy externally, in order to minimise its costs and so maximise its profit.

### Conclusions

- There is **a range** of ideal transfer prices, between $17 and $20, at which Division A and Division B will be willing to trade with each other.

- If the transfer price is set between $17 and $20, each division would produce and sell up to its capacity. Each division would maximise its profit by making and selling as much as possible, and the total company profit would be maximised. Goal congruence would be achieved.

- In both Divisions A and B, the manager should be motivated to make and sell as much as possible, and to keep costs under control, in order to maximise profit.

- This price would probably be negotiated freely between the managers of Divisions A and B, without head office interference. However, the manager of Division B might need to be aware that Division A is saving costs by selling internally, in order to extract a price concession in negotiations on the transfer price.

- The performance of each profit centre would be measured on a fair basis.

- If company policy is to encourage inter-divisional sales unless there is a good commercial reason for selling or buying externally, the two divisions should trade internally up to the output capacity of the lower-capacity division.

It can be seen that there is a range of prices which will satisfy the general objectives of a transfer pricing system.

## (2) Where there is surplus capacity

A situation might arise where a profit centre has an intermediate market for its output, and also sells internally, but:

- there is a limit to the amount that it can sell externally, and

- it has spare capacity.

In such a situation, the opportunity cost of transferring units internally would be nil, and the ideal transfer price would be based on cost, not the external market price. The opportunity cost of transferring units internally is nil because the selling division can meet external demand in full, and still have excess capacity for making inter-divisional sales. The ideal transfer cost would therefore be marginal cost.

### OPTIMUM TP (DM) = MARGINAL COST

## (3) Where there are production constraints

The shadow price is the opportunity cost of the lost contribution from the other product or it is the extra contribution that would be earned if more of the scarce resource were available.

### OPTIMUM TP (DM) = MARGINAL COST + SHADOW PRICE

### Example 2 – Relevant costs

AB Ltd has two Divisions – A and B.  Division A manufactures a product called the aye and Division B manufactures a product called the bee. Each bee uses a single aye as a component.  A is the only manufacturer of the aye and supplies both B and outside customers. Details of A's and B's operations for the coming period are as follows:

|  | Division A | Division B |
| --- | --- | --- |
| Fixed Costs | $7,500,000 | $18,000,000 |
| Variable Costs per unit | $280 | $590 (*) |
| Capacity – Units | 30,000 | 18,000 |

*\* Note: exclude transfer costs*

Market research has indicated that demand for AB Ltd's products from outside customers will be as follows in the coming period:

- the aye: at unit price $1,000 no ayes will be demanded but demand will increase by 25 ayes with every $1 that the unit price is reduced below $1,000;

- the bee: at unit price $4,000 no bees will be demanded, but demand will increase by 10 bees with every $1 that the unit price is reduced below $4,000;

### Required:

(a) Calculate the unit selling price of the bee (accurate to the nearest $) that will maximise AB Ltd's profit in the coming period.

(b) Calculate the unit selling price of the bee (accurate to the nearest $) that is likely to emerge if the Divisional Managers of A and B both set selling prices calculated to maximise Divisional profit from sales to outside customers and the transfer price of ayes going from A to B is set at 'market selling price'.

(c) Explain why your answers to parts (a) and (b) are different, and propose changes to the system of transfer pricing in order to ensure that AB Ltd is charging its customers at optimum prices.

## 5 Performance Evaluation

The aim is to set a transfer price that will give a fair measure of performance in each division, i.e. profit.

(1) **Where there is a perfectly competitive market for an intermediate product**

When transfers are recorded at market prices, divisional performance is more likely to represent the real economic contribution of the division to total company profits.

If the supplying division did not exist, the intermediate product would have to be purchased on the outside market, at the current market price. Alternatively, if the receiving division did not exist, the intermediate product would be sold on the outside market at the current market price. Divisional profits are therefore likely to be similar to the profits that would be calculated if the divisions were separate organisations.

**OPTIMUM TP (DM) = MARKET PRICE + ANY SMALL ADJUSTMENTS**

This is fair.

(2) **Where there is surplus capacity**

**OPTIMUM TP (DM) = MARGINAL COST**

The problem is that transferring at marginal cost is unlikely to be 'fair' to the supplying division.

Possible Solutions:

(i) **2 part tariff**

The transfer price is marginal cost, but in addition a fixed sum is paid per annum or per period to the supplying division to go at least part of the way towards covering its fixed costs, and possibly even to generate a profit.

## Archer Group

Archer Group has two divisions, Division X and Division Y. Division X manufactures a component X8 which is transferred to Division Y. Division Y uses component X8 to make a finished product Y14, which it sells for $20. There is no external market for component X8.

Costs are as follows:

|  | Division X Component X8 | Division Y Product Y14 |
|---|---|---|
| Variable production cost | $5 per unit | $3 per unit* |
| Annual fixed costs | $40,000 | $80,000 |

* Excluding the cost of transferred units of X8.

Under a two-part tariff transfer pricing arrangement, Division Y would pay:

(1) a fixed fee of $40,000 each year plus possibly a negotiated mark up for profit, plus

(2) $5 for each unit of component X8 transferred.

A two-part tariff should ensure that the selling division would not make a loss, and would make a profit if its actual costs are less than the agreed transfer price fixed fee and/or a profit mark up has been allowed for in the fixed fee.

However, there is no incentive for the manager of Division X to produce more output, and a two-part tariff has a number of disadvantages:

- It may not provide motivation to the selling division manager.

- The measurement of the performance of the selling division may not be fair.

- The negotiation process may be time consuming and a fair profit may have to be imposed by head office.

### (ii) Cost-plus pricing

The transfer price is the marginal cost or full cost plus a mark-up.

### (iii) 'Dual Pricing'

Dual pricing is where one transfer price is recorded by the supplying division and a different transfer price is recorded by the buying division.

An adjustment account in the HQ books holds the differences between the divisions.

## Fern Group

Fern Group has two divisions, Domestic and Business. Business Division manufactures computer desks for business customers. Its annual capacity is 15,000 desks, but currently annual demand is only 10,000 desks.

The marginal cost of making a desk in Business Division is $600, and the desks sell for $800. Fixed costs in the Business Division are $1,500,000.

Domestic Division makes and sells furniture items for retail customers. Its manager has seen an opportunity to make some alterations and additions to the Business Division computer desk, and sell it to retail customers as an IT desk for the home.

The extra cost of amending and improving the Business Division desk would be $200 per desk. The Domestic Division manager believes he could sell 5,000 desks for the home each year at $880 each. However, he would not want to pay Business Division more than $560 for each desk.

### Required:

How might a dual transfer price arrangement help to reach an agreement between the two divisions?

### Solution:

The first step with any transfer pricing problem is to establish what is in the best interests of the company as a whole.

In this example, it is in the interests of the company for Domestic Division to make and sell the 5,000 IT desks for the home.

| | |
|---|---|
| Selling price | $880 |
| Marginal cost in Business Division | $600 |
| Marginal cost in Domestic Division | $200 |
| Total marginal cost for each unit | $800 |
| Contribution for each unit sold | $80 |
| Total increase in annual contribution (5,000 units) | $400,000 |

The company should want the Domestic Division to make and sell the IT desks, and Business Division has sufficient spare capacity to meet the demand without affecting its own external sales of computer desks.

However, Business Division will not agree to a transfer price below marginal cost. At a transfer price of $560, it would lose $40 for each unit transferred.

Head office could try to persuade the manager of Domestic Division to agree to a transfer price at marginal cost plus. A transfer price between $600 and $680 would share the marginal profits between the two divisions.

If head office suggested a price above $600, the Domestic Division manager might decide to drop the plan to make and sell the IT desks, since the hoped-for extra profit might not be sufficient to justify the risk of offering a new product to the market. To get round the problem, head office might decide on **dual transfer prices:**

(1) Domestic Division should buy desks from Business Division at $560 per unit.

(2) Business Division should be paid in excess of marginal cost for supplying desks to Domestic Division. A transfer price of $610 might be offered.

(3) The difference $50 ($610 – $560) between the two transfer prices would be a charge to head office.

(4) With this arrangement, Business Division would supply 5,000 desks to Domestic Division.

(5) Business Division would make additional annual profits of $10 per desk ($50,000 in total).

(6)  Domestic Division would make a contribution of $120 per desk sold ($880 – $200 – $560) and so increase annual profits by $600,000.

(7)  Head office would take a charge of $50 per desk or $250,000 in total.

(8)  The company as a whole would benefit by $50,000 + $600,000 – $250,000 = $400,000.

### (3)  Where there are production constraints

### OPTIMUM TP (DM) = MARGINAL COST + SHADOW PRICE

Whether the transfer price is fair for performance evaluation purposes depends on what the shadow prices reflect.

There are 2 possibilities:

(i)  Where internal demand has to be met by foregoing external sales of another product, the shadow prices reflect contribution foregone on that other product. The resulting TP (DM) is also suitable for performance evaluation.

(ii)  Where the supplying division makes only one product which is only sold internally, the shadow price must now reflect contribution from the final production. The TP (DM) builds that contribution into the supplying division's revenue.

Therefore all contribution will appear in the supplying division's books (and none in the buying division's).

The problem is that the optimum TP (DM) is unfair to the buying division.

Possible solutions:

(a)  2-part tariff
(b)  Cost-plus pricing
(c)  Dual pricing

## Example 3 – Dual Pricing: Pool Group

Pool Group has two divisions that operate as profit centres. Each centre sells similar products, but to different segments of the market:

- Division P makes product P29 which it sells to external customers for $150. Variable costs of production are $45 per unit. The maximum annual sales demand for P29 is 5,000 units, although Division P has capacity for 7,000 units. Increasing output from 5,000 to 7,000 each year would result in additional fixed cost expenditure of $8,000.

- The manager of Division L has seen an opportunity to sell an amended version of Product P29 to its own customers, and is interested in buying 2,000 units each year to re-sell externally at $90 per unit. The costs of amending Product P29, for sale as Product L77, would be $25 per unit. However, the manager of Division L will not pay more than $40 per unit of Product P29. He argues that Division P will benefit from lower fixed costs per unit by working at full capacity. The manager of Division P refuses to sell at a price that does not cover the division's incremental costs.

### Required:

Suggest a dual transfer pricing arrangement that might overcome the disagreement between the two divisional managers.

## Transfer Pricing : Behavioural considerations

Transfer prices tend to vary over the product life cycle according to Cats-Baril et al. (1988). During the introductory phase, they suggest a cost plus fixed fee or cost plus a profit share. During the growth phase, they suggest a price related to the closest substitute and during maturity a price based on identical products. This is common sense to a large extent. It is probably only during the maturity stage that identical substitutes exist and during the introductory phase there may be no basis other than cost on which to base the price.

Using any actual cost or cost plus as a transfer price does not motivate the supplying division to act in the interest of the group. Standard or predetermined costs should always be used in place of actual cost. If actual cost is used, the supplying division is not encouraged to be efficient, and control costs as inefficiencies are passed on to the receiving division by way of a higher transfer price. It is even worse if a mark-up is used because the selling division is encouraged to push up the actual cost as this will increase the mark-up, and increase the division's profit. Standard costs are at least subject to scrutiny when they are set once a year and the receiving division has a chance to challenge them. If standard cost is used, the selling division has an incentive to control actual costs below that level and so increase its own profits.

It is usual to imagine transfer pricing taking place in vertically integrated manufacturing organisations. This is not the norm today. Transfer pricing takes place in many different types of organisation and it can have a profound effect on behaviour. For example, a garage carries out a number of different activities that are linked to the activities of another section. The activities include selling new cars, selling old cars, servicing cars sold, general repairs, repairing and servicing used cars accepted in part payment, providing financing and so on. A transfer price is used to transfer a used car accepted in part-payment for a new car between the new car sales and used car sales divisions. A transfer price will also have to be established for transferring the cost of servicing and repairing these cars for sale between the servicing division and the used car sales division. These prices will have considerable implications for the profitability of the different sections and on the actions of the employees when making sales deals. If performance measurement and assessment is to be fair, transfer prices need to be set carefully.

Transfer prices can also be used to deter competitors. If a vertically integrated company concentrates profits at the stage of production where there is least competition, competitors may be attracted to enter. On the other hand, competitors operating at the other stages may be disadvantaged by the low profits the vertically integrated company is taking and they may not be able to achieve a satisfactory return if they are only operating in a limited area of the value chain. Neghandhi (1987) cites cases of US oil companies and Japanese trading and manufacturing companies doing this.

## 6 International Transfer Pricing

Transfers within an international group will often be cross-border, between divisions in different countries. With international transfers and international transfer pricing, the issues already described in this chapter still apply. In addition, other factors need to be considered.

## 7 Different tax rates

A multinational company will seek to minimise the group's total tax liability. One way of doing this might be to use transfer pricing to:

- reduce the profitability of its subsidiaries in high-tax countries, and
- increase the profitability of its subsidiaries in low-tax countries.

Changes in the transfer price can redistribute the pre-tax profit between subsidiaries, but the total pre-tax profit will be the same. However, if more pre-tax profit is earned in low-tax countries and less profit is earned in high-tax countries, the total tax bill will be reduced.

*[In the PEG September 2010, the examiner regrets that candidates are not considering the consequences of using an inflated transfer price to reduce the overall tax burden of the company.]*

### Taxation and Transfer Pricing

International and intra-group trading is a very important part of business today. One-third of the UK's exports to Europe are intra-group transactions. Foreign-owned assets in Europe and the USA increased considerably during the 1980s and 1990s. During the 1980s, foreign-owned assets in the USA tripled, but the tax paid changed very little, as more than half the companies involved reported no taxable income (Pear, 1990).

International intra-group transfer pricing has its own special considerations, and so a multinational organisation will have matters other than behavioural ones to consider when it sets its transfer prices. There is a natural inclination to set transfer prices in order to minimise tax payments.

### Taxation

If a group has subsidiaries that operate in different countries with different tax rates, the overall group corporation tax bill could be reduced by manipulating the transfer prices between the subsidiaries.

For example, if the taxation rate on profits in Country X is 25 per cent and in Country Y it is 60 per cent, the group could adjust the transfer price to increase the profit of the subsidiary in Country X and reduce the profit of the subsidiary in Country Y.

Thus, if the subsidiary in Country X provides goods or services to the subsidiary in Country Y, the use of a very high transfer price would maximise the profits in the lower-tax country, and minimise the profits in the higher-tax country.

There is also a temptation to set up marketing subsidiaries in countries with low corporation tax rates and transfer products to them at a relatively low transfer price. When the products are sold to the final customer, a low rate of tax will be paid on the difference between the two prices.

According to a survey by Ernst and Young (1995), more than 80 per cent of multinational companies viewed transfer pricing as a major international tax issue, and more than half of those companies saw it as the major issue. The taxation authorities in most countries monitor transfer prices in an attempt to control the situation and in order to collect the full amount of taxation due. Double taxation agreements between countries mean that companies pay tax on specific transactions in one country only. However, if the company sets an unrealistic transfer price in order to minimise tax, and the tax authority spots this, the company will pay taxation in both countries, that is, double taxation. This additional payment can amount to millions of pounds and, as a result, is quite an effective deterrent. On the other hand, the gains of avoiding taxation may be even greater.

There have been many cases of transfer price fixing for one reason or another over the years. One of the most notorious of UK transfer pricing cases was that of Hoffman La Roche, as it was then called. Hoffman La Roche had developed the drugs of Librium and Valium. The products were imported into the UK at prices of $437 and $979 per kilo, respectively. The UK tax authority accepted the prices; however, the Monopolies Commission sprang into life and questioned the prices on the grounds that the same chemical ingredients, which were unbranded, could be obtained from an Italian company for $9 and $28 per kilo. Hoffman La Roche argued on two grounds: (1) that the price was not set on cost but on what the market would bear, and (2) they had incurred the research and development costs and so had to recover those in the price. However, this was not accepted and they were fined $1.85 m in 1960.

More recently in the UK in 1992, Nissan was caught for unpaid tax of $237 m for falsely inflated invoices that were used to reduce profits. The freight charges were inflated by 40–60 per cent by a Norwegian company. The next year Nissan was required to pay $106 m in unpaid tax in the USA because the authorities felt that part of their USA marketing profits were being transferred to Japan as transfer prices on imports of cars and trucks were too high. Interestingly, the Japanese tax authorities took a different view and returned the double tax, which is a very rare occurrence.

Most countries now accept the Organisation for Economic Co-operation and Development's (OECD) 1995 guidelines. These guidelines were produced with the aim of standardising national approaches to transfer pricing as part of the OECD's charter to encourage the freedom of world trade. They provide guidance on the application of 'arm's length' principles. They state that where necessary transfer prices should be adjusted using an 'arm's length' price, that is, a price that would have been arrived at by two unrelated companies acting independently. There are three methods the tax authorities can use to determine an arm's length price.

The first is the comparable price method. This is the most widely used and involves setting the arm's length price by using the prices of similar products, that is, the market price or an approximation to one. The method is known as using comparable uncontrolled prices (CUPS) and is the preferred method wherever possible. This may seem a straightforward basis but as most international trade is carried out between related companies meaningful comparisons are hard to find. For example, in the UK in the 1980s, it was possible to use independent car distributorships to find a CUP but now that car manufacturers have developed their own dependent distributor networks, finding arm's length comparability is much more difficult.

Where a CUP cannot be found, or is inappropriate, one of two gross margin methods should be used. These involve a review of gross margins in comparable transactions between uncontrolled organisations. The resale price method is used for the transfer of goods to distributors and marketing operations where goods are sold on with little further processing. The price paid for a final product by an independent party is used and from this a suitable mark-up (to allow for the seller's expenses and profit) is deducted. The second gross margin method is the cost-plus method. Here an arm's length gross margin is established and applied to the seller's manufacturing cost.

These methods are of little help when attempting to establish an arm's length price for intangible property such as a patent right or trade name. Also, much of the data needed may not be in the public domain and so setting fair transfer prices is not easy. In the past, this did not matter so much but today it is often up to the taxpayer to 'prove' the price.

For example, the US section 482 regulations on transfer pricing cover 300 pages and the onus is on the taxpayer to support the transfer price with 'timely' documentation. If this is not done, a non-deductible penalty of up to 40 per cent of the arm's length price may be levied. In the past in the UK, it was up to the tax authorities to detect cases of inappropriate transfer pricing. This left the UK vulnerable to a certain amount of tax leakage. But now under the self-assessment regulations, the onus has switched to the taxpayer to provide correct information. Failure to demonstrate a reasonable attempt at an arm's length price in the tax return will give rise to a penalty of 100 per cent of any tax adjustment. Other European countries are also tightening their regulations in response to the USA and OECD's moves.

To safeguard the position, the taxpayer may enter into an Advanced Pricing Agreement (APA) with the relevant two tax authorities involved. This is a new approach and is done in advance to avoid any dispute and the costly penalty of double taxation and penalty fees. According to the Ernst and Young (1995) survey referred to earlier, more than 60 per cent of companies intend to do or are doing this.

### Example 4 – Seacross

Seacross Group has two subsidiaries, UKD in the UK and GD in Germany.

UKD makes and sells Product S99. The variable cost of manufacture in the UK is £200 per unit and annual fixed costs are £210,000. Product S99 sells for £500 per unit in the UK market and annual demand is 800 units.

GD in Germany buys 400 units of S99 from UKD each year, adapts them for the German market, and sells them for the equivalent of £700 per unit. The variable costs of adapting the product and selling it in Germany are £50 per unit. The cost of shipping the 400 units to Germany is £6,000 and these are paid by GD. Fixed costs in GD are £24,000 each year.

The rate of taxation on company profits is 30% in the UK and 50% in Germany.

**Required**:

What would be the annual after-tax profits of the group if the transfer price for S99 is:

(a) its UK market price, £500

(b) its variable cost of manufacture, £200?

## 8 Government action on transfer prices

Governments are aware of the effect of transfer pricing on profits, and in many countries, multinationals are required to justify the transfer prices that they charge. Multinationals could be required to apply 'arm's length' prices to transfer prices: in other words, they might be required under tax law to use market-based transfer prices, to remove the opportunities for tax avoidance.

It is also possible, on the other hand, that some countries wishing to attract business might have tax laws that are very favourable to business. A country with the status of a 'tax haven' might offer:

- a low rate of tax on profits
- a low withholding tax on dividends paid to foreign holding companies
- tax treaties with other countries
- no exchange controls
- a stable economy
- good communications with the rest of the world
- a well-developed legal framework, within which company rights are protected.

Multinationals might set up subsidiary companies in tax havens, trade through these companies, and hope to reduce their total tax liabilities.

## 9 Transfer Pricing to manage cash flow

Some governments might place legal restrictions on dividend payments by companies to foreign parent companies.

In this situation, it would be tempting for a multinational to sell goods or services to a subsidiary in the country concerned from other divisions in other countries, and charge very high transfer prices as a means of getting cash out of the country.

This tactic is not possible, however, when the country's tax laws require that transfer prices should be set on an arm's length basis.

## 10 International Transfer pricing and currency management

When inter-divisional transfers are between subsidiaries in different countries or currency zones, a decision has to be made about the currency to select for transfer pricing.

Exchange rates, even for strong currencies, can be very volatile and subsidiaries could make unexpected profits or losses from movements in an exchange rate.

Example: A UK subsidiary sells goods to a US subsidiary for $12.80 per unit. The exchange rate was £1 = $1.60 when the transfer price was agreed, and the cost of making each unit in the UK and shipping it to the US is £6.

When the exchange rate is $1.60, the sterling equivalent value of the $12.80 transfer price is £8, and the UK subsidiary makes a profit of £2 per unit transferred.

However, if the dollar weakened in value, and the exchange rate moved to $2.00, the sterling value of the transfer price would fall to £6.40, and the profit per unit would fall to £0.40.

The implications for an international group of currency risk in transfer prices are as follows:

(i) With inter-divisional trading between subsidiaries in different currency zones, one subsidiary or the other (or possibly both, if the transfer price is set in a third currency) will be exposed to a risk of losses from adverse movements in the exchange rate.

(ii) When one subsidiary makes a loss on an adverse exchange rate movement, the other will make a profit.

(iii) The company as a whole should manage its exposures to currency risks. This might be the responsibility of either the profit centre managers or a treasury department.

(iv) When it is fairly certain which way an exchange rate might move in the future, a multinational company might be tempted to set transfer prices in a currency such that any currency losses arise in the subsidiary in the high-tax country, and currency profits arise in the country with the lower tax rate.

### Example 5 – Multinational Computer Manufacturer

A multinational computer manufacturer has a number of autonomous subsidiaries throughout the world. Two of the group's subsidiaries are in America and Europe. The American subsidiary assembles computers using chips that it purchases from local companies. The European subsidiary manufactures exactly the same chips that are used by the American subsidiary but currently only sells them to numerous external companies throughout Europe. Details of the two subsidiaries are given below:

#### America

The American subsidiary buys the chips that it needs from a local supplier. It has negotiated a price of $90 per chip. The production budget shows that 300,000 chips will be needed next year.

## Europe

The chip production subsidiary in Europe has a capacity of 800,000 chips per year. Details of the budget for the forthcoming year are as follows:

### Sales: 600,000 chips

| | |
|---|---|
| Selling price | $105 per chip |
| Variable costs | $ 60 per chip |

The fixed costs of the subsidiary at the budgeted output of 600,000 chips are $20 million per year, but they would rise to $26 million if output exceeds 625,000 chips. The maximum external demand is 600,000 chips per year and the subsidiary has no other uses for the current spare capacity.

## Group directive

The Managing Director of the group has reviewed the budgets of the subsidiaries and has decided that, in order to improve the profitability of the group, the European subsidiary should supply chips to the American subsidiary. She is also thinking of linking the salaries of the subsidiary managers to the performance of their subsidiaries but is unsure which performance measure to use. Two measures that she is considering are 'profit' and the 'return on assets consumed' (where the annual fixed costs would be used as the 'assets consumed').

The Manager of the European subsidiary has offered to supply the chips at a price of $95 each. He has offered this price because it would earn the same contribution per chip that would be earned on external sales (this is after adjusting for increased distribution costs and reduced customer servicing costs).

## Required:

(a) Assume that the 300,000 chips are supplied by the European subsidiary at a transfer price of $95 per chip. Calculate the impact of the profits on each of the subsidiaries and the group.

**(5 marks)**

(b) Calculate the minimum unit price at which the European subsidiary would be willing to transfer the 300,000 chips to the American subsidiary if the performance and salary of the Manager of the subsidiary is to be based on:

(i) the profit of the subsidiary (currently $7 million)

(ii) the return on assets consumed by the subsidiary (currently 35%).

**(9 marks)**

(c) Write a report to the Managing Director of the group that discusses issues raised by the directive and the introduction of performance measures. (You should use your answers to parts (a) and (b), where appropriate, to illustrate points in your report.)

**(10 marks)**

(d) Briefly explain how multinational companies can use transfer pricing to reduce their overall tax charge and the steps that national tax authorities have taken to discourage the manipulation of transfer prices.

**(6 marks)**

**(Total: 30 marks)**

## 11 Practice Questions

### Test your understanding 1

A professional firm has two divisions, a computer consultancy division (CSD) and a management advisory division (MAD). Each division provides consultancy and advisory services to clients and in the year just ended, the fees earned by CSD were $500,000 and the fees earned by MAD were $700,000. Establishment costs were $400,000 for the year in CSD and $500,000 for the year in MAD.

In providing services to their clients, each division obtains supporting services from the other division. During the year, CSD provided 5,000 hours of services to MAD and MAD provided 2,000 hours of services to CSD.

It has been agreed that the transfer prices for services should be $20 per hour for work done by CSD and $30 per hour for services provided by MAD.

**Required:**

The profit for the year reported by CSD was:

A    $60,000

B    $100,000

C    $140,000

D    $200,000

### Test your understanding 2

Hock Group has two divisions, Division P and Division Q. Division P manufactures an item that is transferred to Division Q. The item has no external market, and 60,000 units produced are transferred internally each year. The costs of each division are as follows:

|  | Division P | Division Q |
|---|---|---|
| Variable cost | $10 per unit | $12 per unit |
| Fixed costs each year | $120,000 | $90,000 |

Head office management decides that a transfer price should be set that provides a profit of $30,000 to Division P. What should the transfer price per unit be?

### Test your understanding 3

An international group operates in four countries, the US, France, the UK and Malaysia. Its divisions in each country trade with each other. There are large differences between the countries in rates of taxation on corporate profits.

The company's management is reasonably confident that for the next year or so, it can predict which of its operating currencies (US dollars, euros, sterling and ringgitts) will rise in value against the others and which will fall.

**Required:**

In which currencies might the group's management wish to price inter-company sales within the group?

## Test your understanding 4

Division A of a large divisionalised organisation manufactures a single standardised product. Some of the output is sold externally whilst the remainder is transferred to Division B where it is a sub-assembly in the manufacture of that division's product. The unit costs of division A's product are as follows:

| | |
|---|---:|
| Direct material | $4 |
| Direct labour | $2 |
| Direct expense | $2 |
| Variable manufacturing overheads | $2 |
| Fixed manufacturing overheads | $4 |
| Selling and packing expenses – variable | $1 |
| | $15 |

Annually, 10,000 units of the product are sold externally at the standard price of $30.

In addition to external sales, 5,000 units are transferred annually to Division B at an internal transfer price of $29 per unit. This transfer price is obtained by deducting variable selling and packing expense from the external price since these costs are not incurred on internal transfers.

Division B incorporates the transferred in goods into a more advanced product. The unit costs of this product are as follows:

| | |
|---|---:|
| Transferred in item (from Division A) | $29 |
| Direct material and components | $23 |
| Direct labour | $3 |
| Variable overheads | $12 |
| Fixed overheads | $12 |
| Selling and packing expenses – variable | $1 |
| | $80 |

Division B's manager disagrees with the basis used to set the transfer price. She argues that the transfers should be made at variable cost plus an agreed (minimal) mark-up since she claims that her division is taking output that Division A would be unable to sell at a price of $30.

Partly because of this disagreement, a study of the relationship between selling price and demand has recently been made for each division by the company's sales director. The resulting report contains the following table:

**Customer demand at various selling prices:**

|  | Selling price | Demand |
|---|---|---|
| Division A | $20 | 15,000 |
|  | $30 | 10,000 |
|  | $40 | 5,000 |
|  |  |  |
| Division B | $80 | 7,200 |
|  | $90 | 5,000 |
|  | $100 | 2,800 |

The manager of Division B claims that this study supports her case. She suggests that a transfer price of $12 would give Division A a reasonable contribution to its fixed overheads while allowing Division B to earn a reasonable profit. She also believes that it would lead to an increase in output and an improvement in the overall level of company profits.

**Required:**

(a) Calculate the maximum contribution that can be earned by the company and the effect that the current transfer pricing system will have;

(b) Establish the likely effect on profits of adopting the manager of Division B's suggestion of a transfer price of $12.

**Mini-Quiz**

(1) Division A transfers 100,000 units of a component to Division B each year. The market price of the component is $25. Division A's variable cost is $15 per unit, and A's divisional's fixed costs are $500,000 each year.

What price would be credited to Division A for each component that it transfers to Division B under:

(i) dual pricing (based on marginal cost and market price)?

(ii) two-part tariff pricing (where the Divisions have agreed that the fixed fee will be $200,000)?

|   | Dual pricing | Two-part tariff pricing |
|---|---|---|
| A | $15 | $15 |
| B | $25 | $15 |
| C | $15 | $17 |
| D | $25 | $17 |
| E | $15 | $20 |

(2) TM plc makes components which it sells internally to its subsidiary RM Limited, as well as to its own external market. The external market price is $24.00 each unit, which yields a contribution of 40% of sales. For external sales, variable costs include $1.50 each unit for distribution costs, which are not incurred on internal sales.

TM plc has sufficient capacity to meet all of the internal and external sales. In order to maximise group profit, the component should be transferred to RM Limited at a price for each unit of:

A   $9.60

B   $12.90

C   $14.40

D   $22.50

E   $24.00

(3) Divisions A and B are part of the same group. Division A makes a component, two of which are used in each unit of a product made by Division B. There is no established market for the component. The transfer price for the component is Division A's variable cost plus 60%. Division A's variable cost is $10 per unit of component;

Division B's variable costs for the product, excluding components from Division A, are $6 per unit.

Division B

| Units produced | 1 | 2 | 3 | 4 | 5 | 6 | 7 | 8 | 9 | 10 | 11 | 12 |
|---|---|---|---|---|---|---|---|---|---|---|---|---|
| Marginal revenue, $ | 46 | 44 | 42 | 40 | 38 | 36 | 34 | 32 | 30 | 28 | 26 | 24 |

How many units of the product will the management of Division B sell if they act so as to maximise the division's profit?

A   4

B   5

C   6

D   7

E   8

*Data for Questions 4 and 5*

CF Multinational transferred 10,000 units of product Z from its manufacturing division in the USA to its selling division in the UK during the year just ended.

The manufacturing cost of each unit of product Z was $150 (60% of which was variable cost). The market price for each unit of product Z in the USA was $270. The USA division's profit after tax for its sales to the UK division for the year just ended was $900,000.

The UK division incurred marketing and distribution costs of $30 for each unit of product Z and sold the product for $200 a unit. The UK tax rate was 30%. (Exchange rate: $1 5 $1.5)

(4) If product Z had been transferred at the USA market price, the tax rate in the USA must have been

   A   15%

   B   20%

   C   25%

   D   30%

   E   33%

(5) If the transfers had been made at variable cost, the UK division's profit after tax would have been

   A   $490,000

   B   $770,000

   C   $840,000

   D   $960,000

   E   $1,100,000

### Test your understanding answers

**Example 1 – Inter-divisional trading**

(a)

If the transfer price is $20:

|  | Division A | Division B | Company as a whole |
|---|---|---|---|
|  | $000 | $000 | $000 |
| External sales | 0 | 350 | 350 |
| Inter-divisional transfers | 200 | 0 | 0 |
|  | 200 | 200 | 200 |
| Costs |  |  |  |
| Inter-divisional transfers | 0 | 200 | 0 |
| Other material costs | 80 | 20 | 100 |
| Other variable costs | 20 | 30 | 50 |
| Fixed costs | 60 | 30 | 90 |
| Total costs | 160 | 280 | 240 |
| Profit | 40 | 70 | 110 |

If the transfer price is $25:

|  | Division A | Division B | Company as a whole |
|---|---|---|---|
|  | $000 | $000 | $000 |
| External sales | 0 | 350 | 350 |
| Inter-divisional transfers | 250 | 0 | 0 |
|  | 250 | 350 | 350 |
| Costs |  |  |  |
| Inter-divisional transfers | 0 | 250 | 0 |
| Other material costs | 80 | 20 | 100 |
| Other variable costs | 20 | 30 | 50 |
| Fixed costs | 60 | 30 | 90 |
| Total costs | 160 | 330 | 240 |
| Profit | 90 | 20 | 110 |

## Conclusions from the example:

- The choice of transfer price does not affect the profit of the organisation as a whole, provided that there is agreement on the quantity of transfers.

- However, the choice of transfer price affects the profitability of the individual profit centres.

## Example 2 – Relevant costs

(a)

| Division A | Division B |
|---|---|

*Division A*

Capacity 30,000
Marginal cost = $280
Fixed cost = $7.5 million
P = 1,000 – 0.04Q
MR = 1,000 – 0.08Q

*Division B*

Capacity 18,000
Marginal cost = $590
Fixed cost = $18 million
P = 4,000 – 0.1Q
MR = 4,000 – 0.2Q

To maximise group profits from sales of bee;

| Marginal revenue from bee | = Marginal cost of bee |
|---|---|
| 4,000 – 0.2Q | = 280 + 590 |
| Q | = 15,650 |
| | |
| P | = 4,000 – 0.1 x 15,650 |
| | = $2,435 |

### Conclusion

A unit selling price of $2,435 per bee will maximise AB Ltd's profit in the coming period.

(b) Division A: Division A; for external sales of aye the division will ensure that:

| Marginal revenue from aye | = Marginal cost of aye |
|---|---|
| 1,000 – 0.04Q | = $280 |
| Q | = 9,000 |
| | |
| P | = 1,000 – 0.04 x 9,000 |
| | = $640 |

This now becomes the internal transfer price and as such forms part of Division B's divisional marginal cost.

Division B; for sales of bee they will ensure their division MR = divisional MC

| | | |
|---|---|---|
| 4,000 – 0.2Q | = | 640 + 590 |
| Q | = | 13,850 |
| | | |
| P | = | 4,000 – 0.1 x 13,850 |
| | = | $2,615 |

This now becomes the internal transfer price and as such forms part of Division B's divisional marginal cost.

(c) In part (a) of the question we establish that the group should sell 15,650 units of bee at $2,435 in order to maximise group profits. Under part (b) of the question the manager of A is not using a transfer price that will bring about this decision (goal congruency).

As the divisions are acting autonomously, it is understandable that the manager of A will aim to earn a divisional contribution from internal sales of aye. As he sells externally at a price of $640 he may consider that this seems to be a fair price for internal sales.

However, this internal transfer price then forms part of Division B's marginal costs. The divisional marginal costs at this point ($640 + $590) are NOT the same as the true marginal cost of a bee ($280 + $590). The manager of B ensures his divisional profits are maximised, however, this does not coincide with the group objective as the wrong cost data is essentially being used.

To overcome this problem, Head Office could impose a transfer price. Given the surplus capacity at A, the TP to guarantee goal congruency should be the Marginal Cost of an aye, that is $280. At this transfer price the manager of B will record a divisional marginal cost of $870 ($280 + $590) and will happily operate at the optimum level, selling 15,650 bees at $2,435.

However, at a TP of marginal cost the manager of A is likely to become demotivated as his division receives no reward or benefit for work on internal transfers. Additionally, if divisional profit is used as a performance indicator, the system will fail to measure the performance of division A adequately.

So, as an alternative to the relevant cost being used for the TP, a cost based price could be used. Three methods may be employed;

- cost plus price. Here a mark-up could be added to the marginal cost

- two part tariff. This is where the marginal cost is used as the UNIT price of an aye, but a fixed fee is paid to Division A from Div B each period

- dual pricing system could be implemented. Division A sells ayes internally recording one TP (say $640 – the external market price of an aye) and Division B records purchases of aye at a different transfer price. Div B could use a TP of $280 – the MC of an aye. Under this system Division B would operate at the optimum level for the group, and Division A would earn a contribution on internal sales. Head office would reconcile the discrepancies with a reconciliation account.

### Example 3 – Dual Pricing: Pool Group

It is in the interests of Pool Group for the additional units to be made and sold as Product L77.

The contribution per unit will be $90 – $45 – $25 = $20. The contribution from selling 2,000 units each year ($40,000) exceeds the additional fixed costs of $8,000.

To cover the incremental costs in Division P, the transfer price needs to be $45 + $(8,000/2,000 units) = $49.

Division L will not pay more than $40.

A dual transfer pricing arrangement that might win the agreement of both divisional managers is for Division P to receive $49 per unit of P29 and for Division L to pay $40. The difference of $9 per unit or $18,000 in total for the year would be a charge to head office.

### Example 4 – Seacross

[*Note: This example shows that when two profit centres are in different countries, it would be in the interests of the company as a whole to set transfer prices that keep a larger proportion of the total profit in the low-tax country.*

*In this example, the higher transfer price gives more profit to the UK division and less profit to the German division. The total pre-tax profit remains the same, but total tax charges are lower, giving a higher-total post-tax profit for the group.*]

(a) **Transfer price = £500**

|  | UKD | GD | Company as a whole |
|---|---|---|---|
|  | £ | £ | £ |
| External sales | 400,000 | 280,000 | 680,000 |
| Inter-divisional transfers | 200,000 | 0 | 0 |
|  | 600,000 | 280,000 | 680,000 |
| Costs |  |  |  |
| Inter-divisional transfers | 0 | 200,000 | 0 |
| Other variable costs | 240,000 | 20,000 | 260,000 |
| Shipping costs | 0 | 6,000 | 6,000 |
| Fixed costs | 210,000 | 24,000 | 234,000 |
| Total costs | 450,000 | 250,000 | 500,000 |
| Pre-tax profit | 150,000 | 30,000 | 180,000 |
| Tax (30%:50%) | (45,000) | (15,000) | (60,000) |
| After-tax profit | 105,000 | 15,000 | 120,000 |

**(b) Transfer price = £200**

|  | UKD | GD | Company as a whole |
|---|---|---|---|
|  | £ | £ | £ |
| External sales | 400,000 | 280,000 | 680,000 |
| Inter-divisional transfers | 80,000 | 0 | 0 |
|  | 480,000 | 280,000 | 680,000 |
| Costs |  |  |  |
| Inter-divisional transfers | 0 | 80,000 | 0 |
| Other variable costs | 240,000 | 20,000 | 260,000 |
| Shipping costs | 0 | 6,000 | 6,000 |
| Fixed costs | 210,000 | 24,000 | 234,000 |
| Total costs | 450,000 | 130,000 | 500,000 |
| Pre-tax profit | 30,000 | 150,000 | 180,000 |
| Tax (30%:50%) | (9,000) | (75,000) | (84,000) |
| After-tax profit | 21,000 | 75,000 | 96,000 |

## Example 5 – Multinational Computer Manufacturer

(a) Without the transfer the European subsidiary would make a profit of:

($105 – $60) x 600,000 – $20m = $7m

With the transfer the profit would increase to:

$45 x 800,000 – $26m = $10m

The internal transfer would lead to an increase in cost for the American subsidiary of

300,000 x $5 = $1.5m

The net impact on profit for the group would be:

| European subsidiary | American subsidiary | Group |
|---|---|---|
| Increase of $3m | Reduction of $1.5m | Increase of $1.5m |

(b) (i)   Let TP = transfer price required.

Maximum capacity is 800,000 units so to supply the American subsidiary with 300,000 units only 500,000 units can be sold externally.

Contribution per unit on external sales = $105 – $60 = $45

If contribution remains the same when the transfer price is $95 then the variable cost per unit relating to internal transfers must be $95 – $45 = $50

300,000 x (TP – 50) + 500,000  $45 – $26m = $7m

TP – 50 = $7m + $26m – $22.5m/300,000 = $35

So TP = $85

(ii)

$$\frac{300{,}000 \times (TP - 50) + 500{,}000 \times \$45 - \$26m}{\$26m} \times 100 = 35\%$$

300,000 x (TP – 50)  = 35% x $26m – 500,000 x $45 + $26m = $12.6m

TP – 50 = $12.6m/300,000 = $42

So TP = $92

(c)

## REPORT

**To**: Managing Director

**From**: Management Accountant

**Date**: XX.XX.XX

**Subject**: Group Directive

This report discusses issues raised by the directive and the introduction of performance measures.

### Internal transfer of chips

The European subsidiary has 200,000 units of spare capacity and should, in principle, be prepared to supply these at any price which exceeds incremental costs. For 200,000 units this would be $50 + $6m/200,000 = $80 per unit. (Note that the variable cost of internal transfers is lower than that of external sales – see part b). The American subsidiary would be prepared to accept any price under $90, the price at which the chips can be purchased from a local supplier. For the first 200,000 units there is a range of possible transfer prices which would be acceptable to both subsidiaries of $80 to $90.

The American subsidiary requires 300,000 units however and the additional 100,000 units could only be supplied by reducing the supply to external customers. The minimum transfer price acceptable to the European subsidiary would be $95 as this would earn the same contribution per chip as external sales. At this price the American subsidiary would be paying $5 per chip more than from the external market and so would not be motivated to buy internally.

An average price for all 300,000 units could be set using $80 for the first 200,000 units and $95 for the remaining 100,000 units.

200,000 x $80 + 100,000 x $95/300,000 = $85.

It has already been seen in part (b) that this is the minimum price the European subsidiary would consider if performance was measured on profit. The American subsidiary would be saving $5 per chip.

A better solution may be to transfer 200,000 chips internally and purchase the remaining 100,000 chips from the external supplier. Assuming the transfer price is set at $80 this would result in a profit for the European subsidiary of 600,000 x $45 + 200,000 x $30 – $26m = $7m. The American subsidiary would reduce costs by 200,000 x $15 = $3m. Group profits would increase by $3m, an increase of $1.5m compared to using a transfer price of $95 (see part a).

At $80 all of the profit increase was in the American subsidiary. Depending on where the transfer price is set in the range $80 to $90 the increase in profit can be divided more equitably between the two divisions.

### Performance measures

If performance is measured using profit then any price above $85, (for 300,000 units), but below $90 would allow both subsidiaries to increase profits. If return on assets is used however the minimum price that would be acceptable to the European subsidiary would be $92 (part b).  The American subsidiary would be unwilling to trade at that price. It would be impossible to set a transfer price that would be acceptable to both divisions.

### Conclusion

It would be beneficial for the group if 200,000 chips were transferred internally rather than the current practise of external purchase. Providing the external supplier is willing to supply only 100,000 chips at $90 per unit this is the preferred option. A performance measurement system based on profit allows a transfer price to be set which would be acceptable to both subsidiaries. This is not the case if return on assets consumed is used.

(d)  Multi-nationals may have some companies located in countries with high rates of corporate tax and others with lower rates. To reduce the overall tax charge the aim will be to keep profit as low as possible in high tax rate countries. This can be achieved by charging high transfer prices to companies in high tax countries purchasing goods and set low transfer prices for those companies in high tax countries supplying goods.

National tax authorities have taken action to discourage manipulation of profits. Internal transfers are examined closely and are expected to be at market prices, or where this is not possible, at cost. Heavy fines are imposed on companies suspected of deliberately manipulating transfer prices to avoid tax.

### Test your understanding 1

*[Tutorial note: Only the profit reported by CSD is required. Total profit is shown here for information.]*

|  | *Company* | *MAD* | *Company* |
|---|---|---|---|
| External sales | 500,000 | 700,000 | 1,200,000 |
| Internal transfers: 5,000 × $20 | 100,000 | – | – |
| Internal transfers: 2,000 × $30 | – | 60,000 | – |
|  | 600,000 | 760,000 | 1,200,000 |
| Costs |  |  |  |
| Transfers | 60,000 | 100,000 | 0 |
| Establishment costs | 400,000 | 500,000 | 900,000 |
|  | 460,000 | 600,000 | 900,000 |
| **Profit** | **140,000** | **160,000** | **300,000** |

The answer is C.

### Test your understanding 2

| | |
|---|---|
| Target profit for Division P | $30,000 |
| Fixed costs of Division P | 120,000 |
| Target contribution of Division P | $150,000 |

| | *$per unit* |
|---|---|
| Target contribution per unit (÷ 60,000) | $ 2.50 |
| Variable cost | $ 10.00 |
| **Transfer price required** | **$12.50** |

## Test your understanding 3

Provided the arrangements are permitted by the tax regulations, the group should want to increase the chances of higher profits in lower-tax countries and lower profits in the higher-tax countries. The companies might agree prices for the year and:

- sales from a division in a higher-tax country might be priced in the weaker currency

- sales from a division in a lower-tax country might be priced in a stronger currency.

If exchange rates move as expected, profits of the companies in the higher-tax countries will be reduced and the companies in the lower-tax country will obtain the matching benefit.

## Test your understanding 4

(a) A first step is to calculate the contribution that Division A could earn by selling its product on the intermediate external market.

### Division A

| | | | |
|---|---|---|---|
| Unit price ($) | $20 | $30 | $40 |
| Demand | 15,000 | 10,000 | 5,000 |
| Revenue | $300,000 | $300,000 | $200,000 |
| Variable costs (at $11 per unit) | ($165,000) | ($110,000) | ($55,000) |
| Contribution | $135,000 | $190,000 | $145,000 |

The optimal policy would be to sell 10,000 units on the intermediate market at $30.

Assuming that Division A does not have any capacity constraints, the next step is to calculate how profits would be maximised from sales to the end market. For selling to the end market, the variable cost to the company is $49 per unit (= $10 in Division A, since there is no variable selling cost with a transfer, and $39 in Division B).

## Division B

| Unit price ($) | $80 | $90 | $100 |
|---|---|---|---|
| Demand | 7,200 | 5,000 | 2,800 |
| Revenue | $576,000 | $450,000 | $280,000 |
| Variable costs (at $49 per unit) | ($352,800) | ($245,000) | ($137,200) |
| Contribution | $ 223,200 | $205,000 | $142,800 |

The optimal policy is to sell 7,200 units at a price of $80. The optimal contribution is therefore:

|  | $ |
|---|---|
| Contribution from sales in intermediate market | 190,000 |
| Contribution from sales in end market | 223,200 |
| **Total achievable contribution** | **413,200** |

At the current transfer price of $29, the maximum contribution might not be achieved. In Division B, if the transfer price is $29, the total variable cost of sale for Division B would be $68 (= variable cost $39 + transfer price $29).

The profits for Division B at each of the possible selling prices would be:

## Division B

| Unit price ($) | $80 | $90 | $100 |
|---|---|---|---|
| Demand | 7,200 | 5,000 | 2,800 |
| Revenue | $576,000 | $450,000 | $280,000 |
| Variable costs (at £68 per unit) | ($489,600) | ($340,000) | ($190,400) |
| Contribution | $86,400 | $110,000 | $89,600 |

The manager of Division B would choose to sell 5,000 units at a price of $90, in order to maximise the division's profit. This would not achieve goal congruence, and the total company profit would not be maximised.

|  | Division A | Division B | Total |
|---|---|---|---|
| Maximum contribution obtainable | $190,000 | $223,200 | $413,200 |
| Contribution if transfer price is $29 | $190,000 | $205,000 | $395,000 |

Shortfall in profit due to transfer price policy $18,200

(b) Transfer price = $12

The decision about what to sell in the intermediate market would not be affected. For Division B, the variable cost of sale, including the transfer price, would be $51 (= $39 + $12).

**Division B**

| | | | |
|---|---|---|---|
| Unit price (£) | $80 | $90 | $100 |
| Demand | 7,200 | 5,000 | 2,800 |
| Revenue | $576,000 | $450,000 | $280,000 |
| Variable costs (at £51 per unit) | ($367,200) | ($255,000) | ($142,800) |
| Contribution | $ 208,800 | $195,000 | $137,200 |

The Division B manager will now choose to sell 7,200 units at $80 each, in order to maximise profit.

The total contribution for the company, and for each division, will be:

**Division A**

| | |
|---|---|
| External market sales | $190,000 |
| Internal transfers (7,200 × (12 – 10)) | $14,400 |
| | $204,400 |
| Division B (see above) | $208,800 |
| **Company as a whole** | **$413,200** |

Goal congruence is achieved with a transfer price of $12.

## Mini-Quiz

(1) Answer B

Dual price transfer price from division A's point of view is market price $25. This ensures that the supplying division can earn a profit.

The two-part tariff transfer price per unit is marginal cost $15.

(2) Answer B

Using the general profit-maximising rule, the transfer price should be (marginal cost plus opportunity cost). There is sufficient capacity to meet all demands, therefore the opportunity cost is zero and the internal variable cost should be used: ($24 x 60%) – $1.50 = $12.90.

(3) Answer B

Variable cost of components for B's product = $10 x 2 = $20
Transfer price = variable cost plus 60% = $32
Division B's variable cost per product = $6
Total variable/marginal cost to B  = $38
B will sell till its marginal cost equals marginal revenue, that is, when marginal revenue  = $38.

(4) Answer C

|  | $ |
|---|---|
| Market Price | 270 |
| Less: Total cost | 150 |
| Pre-tax profit | 120 |
| Post-tax profit per unit: $900,000/10,000 units | 90 |
| Therefore tax is | 30 |

(5)  Answer B

| | $ |
|---|---:|
| Market Price in UK | 200 |
| Less: Transfer Price $150 x 0 .6 x 1/1.5 | 60 |
| UK costs | 30 |
| | 110 |
| Less tax 30% | 33 |
| | 77 |

$77 x 10,000 units = $770,000

# Preparing for the CIMA P2 Examination

# 1 Advice For Students Taking Professional Exams For The First Time

Many of the students who will be sitting the P2 exam will have been awarded exemptions from both the Certificate level Paper C01, and Paper P1. Most of these students will have gained their exemptions via a university degree for an approved degree course. However, a university type exam is different from a professional exam. Taking a professional exam for the first time can be difficult; the following advice is here to help you.

## Planning

To begin with, formal planning is essential to get the best return from the time you spend studying. Estimate how much time in total you are going to need for each subject you are studying for the P2 Paper. Remember that you need to allow time for revision as well as for initial study of the material. You may find it helpful to read *"Pass First Time!"* second edition by David R. Harris ISBN: 9781856177986.

This book will help you develop proven study and examination techniques. Chapter by chapter it covers the building blocks of successful learning and examination techniques. This is the ultimate guide to passing your past CIMA exams, written by a CIMA examiner and shows you how to earn all the marks you deserve, and explains how to avoid the most common pitfalls.

There is a blog that supports 'Pass First Time' by David Harris: www.cimaguru.com. You may also find *"The E Word: Kaplan's Guide to Passing Exams"* by Stuart PedleySmith (ISBN: 9780857322050) helpful. Stuart PedleySmith is a senior lecturer at Kaplan Financial and a qualified accountant specialising in financial management. His natural curiosity and wider interests have led him to look beyond the technical content of financial management to the processes and journey that we call education. He has become fascinated by the whole process of learning and the exam skills and techniques that contribute towards success in the classroom. This book is for anyone who has to sit an exam and wants to give themselves a better chance of passing. It is easy to read, written in a common sense style and full of anecdotes, facts, and practical tips. It also contains synopses of interviews with people involved in the learning and examining process. Full versions of these interviews are available online.

There is a blog that supports 'The E Word' by Stuart PedleySmith: www.pedleyssmiths.wordpress.com.

With your study material before you, decide which chapters you are going to study in each week, and which weeks you will devote to revision and final question practice.

Prepare a written schedule summarising the above and stick to it!

It is essential to know your syllabus. As your studies progress you will become more familiar with how long it takes to cover topics in sufficient depth. Your timetable may need to be adapted to allocate enough time for the whole syllabus.

Students are advised to refer to the notice of examinable legislation published regularly in CIMA's magazine (Financial Management), the students e-newsletter *(Velocity)* and on the CIMA website, to ensure they are up-to-date.

**e.g**

## Tim Thompson – Transitional Students

In this article, Tim Thompson and the P2 Examiner highlight some vital issues that students need to be aware of to give them the best chance of succeeding in the examination for paper P2 – Performance Management.

A review of the pass rates over the years for both paper P1 and paper P2 indicates that many students find difficulty in passing these 'intermediate' examinations in what is now called the performance pillar (formerly the management accounting pillar). This is a paradox; after all, CIMA is the qualification for management accountants. This article is designed to reinforce CIMA's many messages about what is expected of students in order to be successful in the paper P2 examination.

The advice in this article is based on the assumption that the student sitting P2 has already passed, or been exempted from paper P1. CIMA strongly recommends that the papers are sat in this sequence and, as you will see below, this is effectively essential.

The recent launch of CIMA's new 2010 syllabus means that each student sitting P2 in November 2010 will fit into one of two categories. Some will have achieved success in the old paper P1 under the 2005 syllabus whilst for others this will have come from the new paper P1 the new 2010 syllabus. Some of our points apply to all students, but there are some specific issues for each of the two categories to consider

A key feature of P2 (as with all management level papers) is that there is no choice of questions in the paper and all questions are compulsory. Some may have been used to having some choice in earlier studies and so now need to recognise that this flexibility does not exist in this paper. Unless they want to throw marks out of the window, students cannot disregard a question because they 'don't like the topic' or 'didn't get round to studying it'. More than ever before, students must ensure that they have a thorough understanding of the whole syllabus if they are to give themselves a meaningful chance of passing the examination.

If you have not already done so, have a look at the detailed syllabus for P2 (accessing CIMA's website www.cimaglobal.com is one way to do this). You will see from this syllabus that the paper is comprised of the following four topics:

A   Pricing and Product Decisions 30%

B   Cost Planning and Analysis for Competitive Advantage 30%

C   Budgeting and Management Control 20%

D   Control and Performance Measurement of Responsibility Centres 20%

Take a closer look at the detailed learning outcomes for syllabus topics C (Budgeting and Management Control) and D (Control and Performance Measurement of Responsibility Centres). Students who passed P1 on the former 2005 syllabus should recognise these learning outcomes; apart from some wording differences, almost all of them can be found on the syllabus for the former 2005 P1 that you have been credited with. These students will recall that these learning outcomes were in topic areas C and D on this former syllabus.

So, if you are one of the students who passed P1 under the old 2005 syllabus, being re-examined on these topics in the new 2010 P2 should present no problem to you, should it?

In this respect, the study process may have been made somewhat easier for you. But watch out; there is a sting in the tail. Take a closer look at the wording of the learning outcomes for topics C and D in the P2 syllabus. Although most of these cover the same broad ground as those that were on the former 2005 P1, can you see any differences in the wording? For example:

| Former 2005 paper P1 (outcome D6) | New 2010 paper P2 (outcome D3b) |
| --- | --- |
| 'explain the typical consequences of a divisional structure for performance measurement as divisions compete or trade with each other' | 'discuss the typical consequences of a divisional structure for performance measurement as divisions compete or trade with each other' |

These learning outcomes are very similar, but they are not identical. For the P2 examination you will be required to 'discuss' whereas on the former 2005 P1 you had to 'explain'. Is this difference significant? It certainly is, and this is why. Let's remind ourselves of CIMA's hierarchy of learning objectives. The full details of this hierarchy are available on CIMA's website, but in essence, there are five levels (level 5 being the highest and level 1 the lowest) as follows:

(5) *Evaluation* can you use your learning to evaluate, make decisions or recommendations?
(4) *Analysis* can you analyse the detail of what you have learned?
(3) *Application* can you apply your knowledge?
(2) *Comprehension* what you are expected to understand
(1) *Knowledge* what you are expected to know

Each of these levels is comprised of a number of specific verbs. If you check out the verb 'discuss', you will find this located within level 4 of the above hierarchy and defined as 'examine in detail by argument'. By comparison `explain' is to be found within the lower level 2 and is defined as 'make clear or intelligible, or state the meaning of'.

Why is this significant? It means that, in the case of this outcome, the P2 examiner will expect a higher level of response from you than would have been expected from candidates who sat the former 2005 P1. If you review the old and new syllabuses further, you will see that this upgrading of the verb relates to other learning outcomes too.

Although the above comments are directed at students who passed P1 under the former 2005 syllabus, the message is basically the same for those of you who passed under the 2010 syllabus in May 2010. Whatever your background, you will find that the P2 examiner will tend to use higher level verbs than you encountered in when you sat P1. We recommend that you make sure that your answer reflects the verb in the question; both in terms of its definition and its place in the hierarchy of learning objectives.

Now let's consider another issue. Take a look at the syllabus for P1 under the new 2010 syllabus. What are your thoughts about the following three topic areas?

C    Project Appraisal 25%

D    Dealing with Uncertainty in Analysis 15%

E    Managing Short-Term Finance 20%

Topic area E is substantially new to the performance pillar. Topic areas C and D were to be found on the syllabus for the former 2005 P2, but they are not on the new 2010 P2 syllabus. Students who passed P1 under the new 2010 syllabus in May 2010 should have a thorough understanding of these topics, but what about those who passed under the former 2005 syllabus? Having not been examined on the above syllabus topics, does this mean that you able to qualify and practice as a management accountant without mastering these topics? You will not be surprised to learn that the answer to this question is a resounding 'NO'. These topics are vital to anyone who wishes to become a Chartered Management Accountant, and this is not a sweeping generalisation about the professional knowledge and skills that you should have. You will need an in-depth understanding these topics to succeed in your management level and in your later strategic level studies.

Under the former (2005) syllabus, candidates could sit papers P1 and P2 in any order, or even simultaneously at the same diet; this was because there was no assumed knowledge taken forward from one paper to the other. Under the new syllabus, things are very different and this point applies to all students sitting P2. You are assumed to have already passed (or been exempted from) P1. Thus, in sitting the P2, you are assumed to bring to the exam a full working knowledge of the new P1 syllabus and this leads to our next sting in the tail. The examiner is very likely to require you to make use of topics from P1 in answering the P2 questions. How might this manifest itself? There are numerous possible examples; here is a speculative one.

Let's assume that the P2 examiner wishes to test you on outcome B1e ('*apply learning curves to estimate time and cost for new products and services*') and decides to set the question within a scenario. What might this scenario be? It could well be an investment appraisal scenario where the viability of the investment depends on the progressive reduction of costs through the learning curve. If this were to be the case, then to understand the question, let alone answer it, you would need to be competent in a number of the learning outcomes from the new P1 syllabus. An example of a relevant P1 learning outcome in this respect would be C2a ('evaluate project proposals using the techniques of investment appraisal'). In this case, you would need to be competent in the application of the net present value (NPV) technique to deal with the question requirement.

You also need to understand that this concept of assumed knowledge brought forward is not limited to the relationship between P1 and P2. For example, substantial elements of the strategic level papers also rely heavily on your understanding of investment appraisal. You will also find the principles of net present value used extensively at strategic level in calculations to determine the value of financial assets and corporate enterprises. If you want confirmation of this, take a look at the new 2010 strategic level syllabus, particularly that for Paper F3 (Financial Strategy).

We cannot emphasise too strongly the incremental nature of the CIMA assessment regime. If you have been exempted from a particular paper without covering every aspect of that paper's syllabus, or if you passed a paper without fully understanding all of its topics, or if you simply take the view 'learned it, passed it, forgot it', then you could be in for a nasty surprise when you sit later papers.

Here is a **summary of our advice** to help you succeed in the P2 examination.

(1) Since all questions are compulsory, ensure that you are fully conversant with all aspects of the syllabus; do not put success at risk by attempting to question spot.

(2) Reflect carefully on the precise wording of the learning outcomes in the P2 syllabus. Make sure that you are clear about the level of learning that the examiner will expect you to demonstrate and recognise that a higher level of learning will be tested compared to P1.

(3) Recognise the assumed knowledge brought forward from P1 to P2; the examiner is very likely to make use of P1 topics in formulating questions that address the requirements of P2.

(4) If you passed P1 under the former 2005 syllabus you particularly need to ensure that you are competent in the topics of Project Appraisal, Uncertainty and Short-Term Finance that you will not have covered in your P1 studies. The potential time saving that we identified earlier from the replication of certain elements of syllabus topics C and D could be helpful here.

## 2 Tips for Effective Revision

### Planning

The first thing to say about revision is that it is an addition to your initial studies, not a substitute for them. In other words, do not coast along early in your course in the hope of catching up during the revision phase. On the contrary, you should be studying and revising concurrently from the outset. At the end of each week, and at the end of each month, get into the habit of summarising the material you have covered to refresh your memory of it.

As with your initial studies, planning is important to maximise the value of your revision work. You need to balance the demands for study, professional work, family life and other commitments. To make this work, you will need to think carefully about how to make best use of your time.

Begin as before by comparing the estimated hours you will need to devote to revision with the hours available to you in the weeks leading up to the examination. Prepare a written schedule setting out the areas you intend to cover during particular weeks, and break that down further into topics for each day's revision. To help focus on the key areas try to establish:

- which areas you are weakest on, so that you can concentrate on the topics where effort is particularly needed;

- which areas are especially significant for the examination – the topics that are tested frequently.

Do not forget the need for relaxation, and for family commitments. Sustained intellectual effort is only possible for limited periods, and must be broken up at intervals by lighter activities. And don't continue your revision timetable right up to the moment when you enter the exam hall: you should aim to stop work a day or even two days before the exam. Beyond this point the most you should attempt is an occasional brief look at your notes to refresh your memory.

**Getting down to work**

By the time you begin your revision you should already have settled into a fixed work pattern: a regular time of day for doing the work, a particular location where you sit, particular equipment that you assemble before you begin and so on. If this is not already a matter of routine for you, think carefully about it now in the last vital weeks before the exam.

You should have notes summarising the main points of each topic you have covered. Begin each session by reading through the relevant notes and trying to commit the important points to memory.

Usually, this will be just your starting point. Unless the area is one where you already feel very confident, you will need to track back from your notes to the relevant chapter(s) in the Study System. This will refresh your memory on points not covered by your notes and fill in the detail that inevitably gets lost in the process of summarisation.

When you think you have understood and memorised the main principles and techniques, attempt an exam-standard question. At this stage of your studies you should normally be expecting to complete such questions in something close to the actual time allocation allowed in the exam. After completing your effort, check the solution provided and add to your notes any extra points it reveals.

**Tips for the final revision phase**

As the exam looms closer, consider the following list of techniques and make use of those that work for you:

- Summarise your notes into more concise form, perhaps on index cards that you can carry with you for revision on the way into work.

- Go through your notes with a highlighter pen, marking key concepts and definitions.

- Summarise the main points in a key area by producing a wordlist, mind map or other mnemonic device.

- On areas that you find difficult, rework questions that you have already attempted, and compare your answers in detail with those provided in the Study System.

- Rework questions you attempted earlier in your studies with a view to producing more 'polished' answers (better layout and presentation may earn marks in the exam) and to completing them within the time limits.

- Stay alert for practical examples, incidents, situations and events that illustrate the material you are studying. If you can refer in the exam to real-life topical illustrations you will impress the examiner and may earn extra marks.

## Pillar P

# P2 – Performance Management

### Specimen Examination Paper

## *Instructions to candidates*

| |
|---|
| You are allowed three hours to answer this question paper. |
| You are allowed 20 minutes reading time **before the examination begins** during which you should read the question paper and, if you wish, make annotations on the question paper. However, you will **not** be allowed, **under any circumstances**, to open the answer book and start writing or use your calculator during this reading time. |
| You are strongly advised to carefully read all the question requirements before attempting the question concerned (that is, all parts and/or sub-questions). The requirements for all questions are contained in a dotted box. |
| ALL answers must be written in the answer book. Answers or notes written on the question paper will **not** be submitted for marking. |
| Answer the FIVE compulsory questions in Section A on pages 2 to 6. |
| Answer the TWO compulsory questions in Section B on pages 7 to 11. |
| Maths Tables and Formulae are provided on pages 12 to 14. |
| The list of verbs as published in the syllabus is given for reference on page 15. |
| Write your candidate number, the paper number and examination subject title in the spaces provided on the front of the answer book. Also write your contact ID and name in the space provided in the right hand margin and seal to close. |
| Tick the appropriate boxes on the front of the answer book to indicate which questions you have answered. |

P2 – Performance Management

TURN OVER

## SECTION A – 50 MARKS

[The indicative time for answering this section is 90 minutes.]

ANSWER *ALL* FIVE QUESTIONS IN THIS SECTION - 10 MARKS EACH.

---

### Question One

You are engaged as a consultant to the DT group. At present the group source their raw materials locally, manufacture their products in a single factory, and distribute them worldwide via an international distribution company. However, their manufacturing facilities are restricting them from expanding so they are considering outsourcing some of their manufacturing operations to developing economies.

*Required:*

(a)  Discuss the concept of the value chain and how the changes being considered by the DT group may impact on the management of contribution/profit generated throughout the chain.

*(6 marks)*

(b)  Discuss how gain sharing arrangements might be used by the DT group in the context of the changes being considered. Suggest one non-financial target that may be used as part of these gain sharing arrangements.

*(4 marks)*

*(Total for Question One =10 marks)*

## Question Two

S uses a standard absorption costing system to control its production costs and monitors its performance using monthly variance reports.

S has recently launched a new product which is being manufactured in batches of 100 units. An extract from the standard cost details per unit for this new product is as follows:

5·3 hours of direct labour @ $10 per hour                              $53·00

It is now realised that the standard cost details were based on an average learning period target of 5·3 hours per unit, and that a batch related period of learning was expected. The time expected for the initial batch was 1,000 hours and 90% learning rate was anticipated.

During August production commenced on the product, and 400 units were produced in four batches of 100 units using 2500 hours of direct labour at a cost of $26,000. The direct labour variances that were reported in respect of this product were:

Direct labour rate variance                    $1,000 Adverse

Direct labour efficiency variance            $3,800 Adverse

---

*Required:*

   *(a)*    Calculate the expected length of the learning period in batches (to the nearest whole batch).

                        *(4 marks)*

   *(b)*    Calculate planning and operating variances for August.

                        *(4 marks)*

   *(c)*    Explain why the variances you have calculated in (b) above provide more meaningful information to the managers of S.

                        *(2 marks)*

             *(Total for Question Two = 10 marks)*

---

TURN OVER

## Question Three

A firm of solicitors is preparing its budgets for 2010. The structure of the firm is that it has a managing partner who is responsible for client and staff management, the firm's accounts and compliance matters and three other partners who each take responsibility for case matters depending on the branch of law that is involved in each case.

For a number of years the managing partner has prepared the budgets for the firm. These include budgets for fee income and costs analysed by each partner, and a cash budget for the firm as a whole. The firm has overdraft facilities which are renewable in June each year and sets cash balance targets for each month that reflect the seasonality of some of its work. At the end of each month there is a partners' meeting at which the managing partner presents a statement that compares the actual results of the month and the year to date with the corresponding budget. At this meeting all partners are asked to explain the reasons for the variances that have arisen.

The managing partner recently attended a course on "Budget Planning & Cost Control" at which the presenter argued that each of the partners in the firm should be involved in the budget setting process. However, the managing partner is not convinced by this argument as she believes that this could lead to budget manipulation.

---

*Required*

(a)     Explain feedback and feed-forward control systems and give an example of each in the context of the firm of solicitors.

*(5 marks)*

(b)     Discuss ONE potentially beneficial consequence and ONE potentially adverse consequence of involving the firm's other partners in the budget setting process of the firm.

*(5 marks)*

*(Total for Question Three = 10 marks)*

---

## Question Four

W is a manufacturing company that produces three products: X, Y and Z. Each uses the same resources, but in different quantities as shown in the table of budgeted data for 2010 below:

| Product | X | Y | Z |
|---|---|---|---|
| Budgeted production | 1500 | 2500 | 4000 |
| Direct labour hours per unit | 2 | 4 | 3 |
| Machine hours per unit | 3 | 2 | 3 |
| Batch size | 50 | 100 | 500 |
| Machine setups per batch | 2 | 3 | 1 |
| Purchase orders per batch | 4 | 4 | 6 |
| Material movements per batch | 10 | 5 | 4 |

W's budgeted production overhead costs for 2010 are $400,000 and current practice is to absorb these costs into product costs using an absorption rate based on direct labour hours. As a result the production overhead cost attributed to each product unit is:

Product X   $32          Product Y   $64          Product Z   $48

The management of S are considering changing to an activity based method of attributing overhead costs to products and as a result have identified the following cost drivers and related cost pools:

| Cost pool | $ | Cost driver |
|---|---|---|
| Machine maintenance | 100,000 | machine hours |
| Machine setups | 70,000 | machine setups |
| Purchasing | 90,000 | purchase orders |
| Material handling | 60,000 | material movements |

The remaining $80,000 of overhead costs are caused by a number of different factors and activities that are mainly labour related and are to be attributed to products on the basis of labour hours.

---

*Required:*

*(a)*   Calculate the production overhead cost attributed to each product unit using an activity based approach.

*(7 marks)*

*(b)*   Explain how W has applied Pareto Analysis when determining its cost drivers and how it may continue to use Pareto Analysis to control its production costs.

*(3 marks)*

*(Total for Question Four = 10 marks)*

---

## Question Five

HJ is a printing company that specialises in producing high quality cards and calendars for sale as promotional gifts. Much of the work produced by HJ uses similar techniques and for a number of years HJ has successfully used a standard costing system to control its costs.

HJ is now planning to diversify into other promotional gifts such as plastic moulded items including key fobs, card holders and similar items. There is already a well established market place for these items but HJ is confident that with its existing business contacts it can be successful if it controls its costs. Initially HJ will need to invest in machinery to mould the plastic, and it is likely that this machinery will have a life of five years. An initial appraisal of the proposed diversification based on low initial sales volumes and marginal cost based product pricing for year 1, followed by increases in both volumes and selling prices in subsequent years, shows that the investment has a payback period of four years.

---

*Required*

   *(a)*     Explain the relationship between target costs and standard costs and how HJ can derive target costs from target prices

                                      *(5 marks)*

   *(b)*     Discuss the conflict that will be faced by HJ when making pricing decisions based on marginal cost in the short term and the need for full recovery of all costs in the long term.

                                          *(5 marks)*

                    *(Total for Question Five = 10 marks)*

---

*(Total for Section A = 50 marks)*

---

## SECTION B – 50 MARKS

[The indicative time for answering this section is 90 minutes.]

ANSWER *BOTH* QUESTIONS IN THIS SECTION - 25 MARKS EACH.

**Question Six**

M is the holding company of a number of companies within the engineering sector. One of these subsidiaries is PQR which specialises in building machines for manufacturing companies. PQR uses absorption costing as the basis of its routine accounting system for profit reporting.

PQR is currently operating at 90% of its available capacity, and has been invited by an external manufacturing company, to tender for the manufacture of a bespoke machine. If PQR's tender is accepted by the manufacturing company then it is likely that another company within the M group will be able to obtain work in the future servicing the machine. As a result, the Board of Directors of M are keen to win the tender for the machine and are prepared to accept a price from the manufacturing company that is based on the relevant costs of building the machine.

An engineer from PQR has already met with the manufacturing company to determine the specification of the machine and he has worked with a non-qualified accountant from PQR to determine the following cost estimate for the machine.

|  | Note | $ |
|---|---|---|
| Engineering specification | 1 | 1,500 |
| Direct material A | 2 | 61,000 |
| Direct Material B | 3 | 2,500 |
| Components | 4 | 6,000 |
| Direct Labour | 5 | 12,500 |
| Supervision | 6 | 350 |
| Machine hire | 7 | 2,500 |
| Overhead costs | 8 | 5,500 |
| | | |
| Total | | 91,850 |

NOTES

1. The engineer that would be in charge of the project to build the machine has already met with the manufacturing company, and subsequently prepared the specification for the machine. This has taken three days of his time and his salary and related costs are $500 per day. The meeting with the manufacturing company only took place because of this potential work; no other matters were discussed at the meeting.

2. The machine would require 10,000 square metres of Material A. This material is regularly used by PQR. There is currently 15,000 square metres in inventory, 10,000 square metres were bought for $6 per square metre and the remainder were bought for $6·30 per square metre. PQR uses the weighted average basis to value its inventory. The current market price of Material A is $7 per square metre, and the inventory could be sold for $6·50 per square metre.

TURN OVER

3. The machine would also require 250 metre lengths of Material B. This is not a material that is regularly used by PQR and it would have to be purchased specifically for this work. The current market price is $10 per metre length, but the sole supplier of this material has a minimum order size of 300 metre lengths. PQR does not foresee any future use of any unused lengths of Material B, and expects that the net revenue from its sale would be negligible.

4. The machine would require 500 components. The components could be produced by HK, another company within the M group. The direct costs to HK of producing each component is $8, and normal transfer pricing policy within the M group is to add a 50% mark up to the direct cost to determine the transfer price. HK has unused capacity which would allow them to produce 350 components, but thereafter any more components could only be produced by reducing the volume of other components that are currently sold to the external market. These other components, although different, require the same machine time per unit as those required by PQR, have a direct cost of $6 per component and currently are sold for $9 each.

   Alternatively PQR can buy the components from the external market for $14 each.

5. The machine will require 1000 hours of skilled labour. The current market rate for engineers with the appropriate skills is $15 per hour. PQR currently employs engineers that have the necessary skills at a cost of $12.50 per hour, but they do not have any spare capacity. They could be transferred from their existing duties if temporary replacements were to be engaged at a cost of $14 per hour.

6. The project would be supervised by a senior engineer who currently works 150 hours per month and is paid an annual salary of $42,000. The project is expected to take a total of one month to complete, and if it goes ahead is likely to take up 10% of the supervisor's time during that month. If necessary the supervisor will work overtime which is unpaid.

7. It will be necessary to hire specialist machine for part of the project. In total the project will require the machine for 5 days but it is difficult to predict exactly which five days the machine will be required within the overall project time of one month. One option is to hire the machine for the entire month at a cost of $5,000 and then sub-hire the machine for $150 per day when it is not required by PQR. PQR expects that it would be able to sub-hire the machine for 20 days. Alternatively PQR could hire the machine on the days it requires and its availability would be guaranteed at a cost of $500 per day.

8. PQR's fixed production overhead cost budget for the year totals $200,000 and is absorbed into its project costs using a skilled direct labour hour absorption rate, based on normal operating capacity of 80%. PQR's capacity budget for the year is a total of 50,000 skilled direct labour hours. PQR's latest annual forecast is for overhead costs to total $220,000, and for capacity to be as originally budgeted.

**Required:**

(a)   You are employed as assistant Management Accountant of the M group.
For each of the resource items identified you are to:

  (i)     discuss the basis of the valuation provided for each item

  (ii)    discuss whether or not you agree with the valuation provided in the
          context of the proposed tender

  (iii)   prepare a revised schedule of relevant costs for the tender
          document on behalf of the M group.

*(15 marks)*

(b)   Assume that PQR successfully wins the bid to build the machine for a
selling price of $100,000 and that the costs incurred are as expected.
Discuss the conflict that will arise between the profit expected from the
project by the Board of M on a relevant cost basis and the project profit
that will be reported to them by PQR using its routine accounting
practices. Use at least two specific examples from the bid to explain the
conflict that you discuss.

*(5 marks)*

(c)   Discuss two non-financial matters that you consider relevant to  this
decision.

*(5 marks)*

*(Total for Question Six = 25 marks)*

## Question Seven

DEF is a trading company that is divided into three divisions: D, E and F. Each division maintains its own accounting records and prepares an annual summary of its results. These performance summaries are shown below for the year ended 30 September 2009.

| Division | D | E | F |
|---|---|---|---|
| | $000 | $000 | $000 |
| Sales (net of returns) | 150 | 200 | 400 |
| Variable production costs | 50 | 70 | 230 |
| Fixed production costs | 60 | 50 | 80 |
| Administration costs | 30 | 25 | 40 |
| Profit | 10 | 55 | 50 |
| Capital Employed | 400 | 550 | 415 |

The following additional information is available:

1. Divisions are free to trade with each other without any interference from Head Office. The managers of the respective divisions negotiate transfer prices between themselves. During the year and included in the above costs and revenues are the following transactions:

   - Division D sold goods for $20,000 to Division E. The price negotiated was agreed on a unit basis between the managers of the two divisions. The variable production cost of these items in Division D was $18,000. Division D was operating under capacity and agreed to a transfer price that was little more than its own variable cost.

   - Division F sold goods for $15,000 to Division E. The price negotiated was agreed on a unit basis between the managers of the two divisions. The variable production cost of these items in Division F was $9,000. Division F was operating under capacity and negotiated a transfer price based on its total production cost.

2. Included in the Administration costs for each division are the following management charges from Head Office:

   D:    $10,000    E:    $8,000      F:    $15,000

3. At the start of each year Head Office sets each division a target Return on Capital Employed. The target depends on their nature of the work and their industry sector. For the year ended 30 September 2009 these targets were:

   D:    6%      E:    3%      F:    15%

## Required

(a)    Discuss the shortcomings of the above performance summaries when measuring the performance of each division.

*(5 marks)*

(b)    Discuss the potential problems of negotiated transfer pricing, and how these have impacted on the performance of each of Divisions D, E, and F for the year ended 30 September 2009.

*(6 marks)*

(c)    Prepare an alternative statement that is more useful for measuring and reporting the performance of Divisions D, E, and F.

*(8 marks)*

(d)    Discuss how the use of "Dual" transfer prices could affect the measurement of divisional performance within DEF. Illustrate your answer with suggested dual prices.

*(6 marks)*

*(Total for Question Seven = 25 marks)*

*(Total for Section B = 50 marks)*

## End of Question Paper

TURN OVER

# MATHS TABLES AND FORMULAE

## Present value table

Present value of 1 unit of currency, that is $(1+r)^{-n}$ where $r$ = interest rate; $n$ = number of periods until payment or receipt.

| Periods (n) | Interest rates (r) | | | | | | | | | |
|---|---|---|---|---|---|---|---|---|---|---|
| | 1% | 2% | 3% | 4% | 5% | 6% | 7% | 8% | 9% | 10% |
| 1 | 0.990 | 0.980 | 0.971 | 0.962 | 0.952 | 0.943 | 0.935 | 0.926 | 0.917 | 0.909 |
| 2 | 0.980 | 0.961 | 0.943 | 0.925 | 0.907 | 0.890 | 0.873 | 0.857 | 0.842 | 0.826 |
| 3 | 0.971 | 0.942 | 0.915 | 0.889 | 0.864 | 0.840 | 0.816 | 0.794 | 0.772 | 0.751 |
| 4 | 0.961 | 0.924 | 0.888 | 0.855 | 0.823 | 0.792 | 0.763 | 0.735 | 0.708 | 0.683 |
| 5 | 0.951 | 0.906 | 0.863 | 0.822 | 0.784 | 0.747 | 0.713 | 0.681 | 0.650 | 0.621 |
| 6 | 0.942 | 0.888 | 0.837 | 0.790 | 0.746 | 0705 | 0.666 | 0.630 | 0.596 | 0.564 |
| 7 | 0.933 | 0.871 | 0.813 | 0.760 | 0.711 | 0.665 | 0.623 | 0.583 | 0.547 | 0.513 |
| 8 | 0.923 | 0.853 | 0.789 | 0.731 | 0.677 | 0.627 | 0.582 | 0.540 | 0.502 | 0.467 |
| 9 | 0.914 | 0.837 | 0.766 | 0.703 | 0.645 | 0.592 | 0.544 | 0.500 | 0.460 | 0.424 |
| 10 | 0.905 | 0.820 | 0.744 | 0.676 | 0.614 | 0.558 | 0.508 | 0.463 | 0.422 | 0.386 |
| 11 | 0.896 | 0.804 | 0.722 | 0.650 | 0.585 | 0.527 | 0.475 | 0.429 | 0.388 | 0.350 |
| 12 | 0.887 | 0.788 | 0.701 | 0.625 | 0.557 | 0.497 | 0.444 | 0.397 | 0.356 | 0.319 |
| 13 | 0.879 | 0.773 | 0.681 | 0.601 | 0.530 | 0.469 | 0.415 | 0.368 | 0.326 | 0.290 |
| 14 | 0.870 | 0.758 | 0.661 | 0.577 | 0.505 | 0.442 | 0.388 | 0.340 | 0.299 | 0.263 |
| 15 | 0.861 | 0.743 | 0.642 | 0.555 | 0.481 | 0.417 | 0.362 | 0.315 | 0.275 | 0.239 |
| 16 | 0.853 | 0.728 | 0.623 | 0.534 | 0.458 | 0.394 | 0.339 | 0.292 | 0.252 | 0.218 |
| 17 | 0.844 | 0.714 | 0.605 | 0.513 | 0.436 | 0.371 | 0.317 | 0.270 | 0.231 | 0.198 |
| 18 | 0.836 | 0.700 | 0.587 | 0.494 | 0.416 | 0.350 | 0.296 | 0.250 | 0.212 | 0.180 |
| 19 | 0.828 | 0.686 | 0.570 | 0.475 | 0.396 | 0.331 | 0.277 | 0.232 | 0.194 | 0.164 |
| 20 | 0.820 | 0.673 | 0.554 | 0.456 | 0.377 | 0.312 | 0.258 | 0.215 | 0.178 | 0.149 |

| Periods (n) | Interest rates (r) | | | | | | | | | |
|---|---|---|---|---|---|---|---|---|---|---|
| | 11% | 12% | 13% | 14% | 15% | 16% | 17% | 18% | 19% | 20% |
| 1 | 0.901 | 0.893 | 0.885 | 0.877 | 0.870 | 0.862 | 0.855 | 0.847 | 0.840 | 0.833 |
| 2 | 0.812 | 0.797 | 0.783 | 0.769 | 0.756 | 0.743 | 0.731 | 0.718 | 0.706 | 0.694 |
| 3 | 0.731 | 0.712 | 0.693 | 0.675 | 0.658 | 0.641 | 0.624 | 0.609 | 0.593 | 0.579 |
| 4 | 0.659 | 0.636 | 0.613 | 0.592 | 0.572 | 0.552 | 0.534 | 0.516 | 0.499 | 0.482 |
| 5 | 0.593 | 0.567 | 0.543 | 0.519 | 0.497 | 0.476 | 0.456 | 0.437 | 0.419 | 0.402 |
| 6 | 0.535 | 0.507 | 0.480 | 0.456 | 0.432 | 0.410 | 0.390 | 0.370 | 0.352 | 0.335 |
| 7 | 0.482 | 0.452 | 0.425 | 0.400 | 0.376 | 0.354 | 0.333 | 0.314 | 0.296 | 0.279 |
| 8 | 0.434 | 0.404 | 0.376 | 0.351 | 0.327 | 0.305 | 0.285 | 0.266 | 0.249 | 0.233 |
| 9 | 0.391 | 0.361 | 0.333 | 0.308 | 0.284 | 0.263 | 0.243 | 0.225 | 0.209 | 0.194 |
| 10 | 0.352 | 0.322 | 0.295 | 0.270 | 0.247 | 0.227 | 0.208 | 0.191 | 0.176 | 0.162 |
| 11 | 0.317 | 0.287 | 0.261 | 0.237 | 0.215 | 0.195 | 0.178 | 0.162 | 0.148 | 0.135 |
| 12 | 0.286 | 0.257 | 0.231 | 0.208 | 0.187 | 0.168 | 0.152 | 0.137 | 0.124 | 0.112 |
| 13 | 0.258 | 0.229 | 0.204 | 0.182 | 0.163 | 0.145 | 0.130 | 0.116 | 0.104 | 0.093 |
| 14 | 0.232 | 0.205 | 0.181 | 0.160 | 0.141 | 0.125 | 0.111 | 0.099 | 0.088 | 0.078 |
| 15 | 0.209 | 0.183 | 0.160 | 0.140 | 0.123 | 0.108 | 0.095 | 0.084 | 0.079 | 0.065 |
| 16 | 0.188 | 0.163 | 0.141 | 0.123 | 0.107 | 0.093 | 0.081 | 0.071 | 0.062 | 0.054 |
| 17 | 0.170 | 0.146 | 0.125 | 0.108 | 0.093 | 0.080 | 0.069 | 0.060 | 0.052 | 0.045 |
| 18 | 0.153 | 0.130 | 0.111 | 0.095 | 0.081 | 0.069 | 0.059 | 0.051 | 0.044 | 0.038 |
| 19 | 0.138 | 0.116 | 0.098 | 0.083 | 0.070 | 0.060 | 0.051 | 0.043 | 0.037 | 0.031 |
| 20 | 0.124 | 0.104 | 0.087 | 0.073 | 0.061 | 0.051 | 0.043 | 0.037 | 0.031 | 0.026 |

Cumulative present value of 1 unit of currency per annum, Receivable or Payable at the end of each year for $n$ years $\frac{1-(1+r)^{-n}}{r}$

| Periods | Interest rates ($r$) | | | | | | | | | |
|---|---|---|---|---|---|---|---|---|---|---|
| ($n$) | 1% | 2% | 3% | 4% | 5% | 6% | 7% | 8% | 9% | 10% |
| 1 | 0.990 | 0.980 | 0.971 | 0.962 | 0.952 | 0.943 | 0.935 | 0.926 | 0.917 | 0.909 |
| 2 | 1.970 | 1.942 | 1.913 | 1.886 | 1.859 | 1.833 | 1.808 | 1.783 | 1.759 | 1.736 |
| 3 | 2.941 | 2.884 | 2.829 | 2.775 | 2.723 | 2.673 | 2.624 | 2.577 | 2.531 | 2.487 |
| 4 | 3.902 | 3.808 | 3.717 | 3.630 | 3.546 | 3.465 | 3.387 | 3.312 | 3.240 | 3.170 |
| 5 | 4.853 | 4.713 | 4.580 | 4.452 | 4.329 | 4.212 | 4.100 | 3.993 | 3.890 | 3.791 |
| 6 | 5.795 | 5.601 | 5.417 | 5.242 | 5.076 | 4.917 | 4.767 | 4.623 | 4.486 | 4.355 |
| 7 | 6.728 | 6.472 | 6.230 | 6.002 | 5.786 | 5.582 | 5.389 | 5.206 | 5.033 | 4.868 |
| 8 | 7.652 | 7.325 | 7.020 | 6.733 | 6.463 | 6.210 | 5.971 | 5.747 | 5.535 | 5.335 |
| 9 | 8.566 | 8.162 | 7.786 | 7.435 | 7.108 | 6.802 | 6.515 | 6.247 | 5.995 | 5.759 |
| 10 | 9.471 | 8.983 | 8.530 | 8.111 | 7.722 | 7.360 | 7.024 | 6.710 | 6.418 | 6.145 |
| 11 | 10.368 | 9.787 | 9.253 | 8.760 | 8.306 | 7.887 | 7.499 | 7.139 | 6.805 | 6.495 |
| 12 | 11.255 | 10.575 | 9.954 | 9.385 | 8.863 | 8.384 | 7.943 | 7.536 | 7.161 | 6.814 |
| 13 | 12.134 | 11.348 | 10.635 | 9.986 | 9.394 | 8.853 | 8.358 | 7.904 | 7.487 | 7.103 |
| 14 | 13.004 | 12.106 | 11.296 | 10.563 | 9.899 | 9.295 | 8.745 | 8.244 | 7.786 | 7.367 |
| 15 | 13.865 | 12.849 | 11.938 | 11.118 | 10.380 | 9.712 | 9.108 | 8.559 | 8.061 | 7.606 |
| 16 | 14.718 | 13.578 | 12.561 | 11.652 | 10.838 | 10.106 | 9.447 | 8.851 | 8.313 | 7.824 |
| 17 | 15.562 | 14.292 | 13.166 | 12.166 | 11.274 | 10.477 | 9.763 | 9.122 | 8.544 | 8.022 |
| 18 | 16.398 | 14.992 | 13.754 | 12.659 | 11.690 | 10.828 | 10.059 | 9.372 | 8.756 | 8.201 |
| 19 | 17.226 | 15.679 | 14.324 | 13.134 | 12.085 | 11.158 | 10.336 | 9.604 | 8.950 | 8.365 |
| 20 | 18.046 | 16.351 | 14.878 | 13.590 | 12.462 | 11.470 | 10.594 | 9.818 | 9.129 | 8.514 |

| Periods | Interest rates ($r$) | | | | | | | | | |
|---|---|---|---|---|---|---|---|---|---|---|
| ($n$) | 11% | 12% | 13% | 14% | 15% | 16% | 17% | 18% | 19% | 20% |
| 1 | 0.901 | 0.893 | 0.885 | 0.877 | 0.870 | 0.862 | 0.855 | 0.847 | 0.840 | 0.833 |
| 2 | 1.713 | 1.690 | 1.668 | 1.647 | 1.626 | 1.605 | 1.585 | 1.566 | 1.547 | 1.528 |
| 3 | 2.444 | 2.402 | 2.361 | 2.322 | 2.283 | 2.246 | 2.210 | 2.174 | 2.140 | 2.106 |
| 4 | 3.102 | 3.037 | 2.974 | 2.914 | 2.855 | 2.798 | 2.743 | 2.690 | 2.639 | 2.589 |
| 5 | 3.696 | 3.605 | 3.517 | 3.433 | 3.352 | 3.274 | 3.199 | 3.127 | 3.058 | 2.991 |
| 6 | 4.231 | 4.111 | 3.998 | 3.889 | 3.784 | 3.685 | 3.589 | 3.498 | 3.410 | 3.326 |
| 7 | 4.712 | 4.564 | 4.423 | 4.288 | 4.160 | 4.039 | 3.922 | 3.812 | 3.706 | 3.605 |
| 8 | 5.146 | 4.968 | 4.799 | 4.639 | 4.487 | 4.344 | 4.207 | 4.078 | 3.954 | 3.837 |
| 9 | 5.537 | 5.328 | 5.132 | 4.946 | 4.772 | 4.607 | 4.451 | 4.303 | 4.163 | 4.031 |
| 10 | 5.889 | 5.650 | 5.426 | 5.216 | 5.019 | 4.833 | 4.659 | 4.494 | 4.339 | 4.192 |
| 11 | 6.207 | 5.938 | 5.687 | 5.453 | 5.234 | 5.029 | 4.836 | 4.656 | 4.486 | 4.327 |
| 12 | 6.492 | 6.194 | 5.918 | 5.660 | 5.421 | 5.197 | 4.988 | 7.793 | 4.611 | 4.439 |
| 13 | 6.750 | 6.424 | 6.122 | 5.842 | 5.583 | 5.342 | 5.118 | 4.910 | 4.715 | 4.533 |
| 14 | 6.982 | 6.628 | 6.302 | 6.002 | 5.724 | 5.468 | 5.229 | 5.008 | 4.802 | 4.611 |
| 15 | 7.191 | 6.811 | 6.462 | 6.142 | 5.847 | 5.575 | 5.324 | 5.092 | 4.876 | 4.675 |
| 16 | 7.379 | 6.974 | 6.604 | 6.265 | 5.954 | 5.668 | 5.405 | 5.162 | 4.938 | 4.730 |
| 17 | 7.549 | 7.120 | 6.729 | 6.373 | 6.047 | 5.749 | 5.475 | 5.222 | 4.990 | 4.775 |
| 18 | 7.702 | 7.250 | 6.840 | 6.467 | 6.128 | 5.818 | 5.534 | 5.273 | 5.033 | 4.812 |
| 19 | 7.839 | 7.366 | 6.938 | 6.550 | 6.198 | 5.877 | 5.584 | 5.316 | 5.070 | 4.843 |
| 20 | 7.963 | 7.469 | 7.025 | 6.623 | 6.259 | 5.929 | 5.628 | 5.353 | 5.101 | 4.870 |

TURN OVER

### *Formulae*

## TIME SERIES

Additive model:

$$\text{Series} = \text{Trend} + \text{Seasonal} + \text{Random}$$

Multiplicative model:

$$\text{Series} = \text{Trend} * \text{Seasonal} * \text{Random}$$

## REGRESSION ANALYSIS

The linear regression equation of $Y$ on $X$ is given by:

$$Y = a + bX \quad \text{or} \quad Y - \overline{Y} = b(X - \overline{X}),$$

where:

$$b = \frac{\text{Covariance}\,(XY)}{\text{Variance}\,(X)} = \frac{n\sum XY - (\sum X)(\sum Y)}{n\sum X^2 - (\sum X)^2}$$

and $\quad a = \overline{Y} - b\overline{X}$

or solve

$$\sum Y = na + b\sum X$$

$$\sum XY = a\sum X + b\sum X^2$$

Exponential $\quad Y = ab^x$

Geometric $\quad Y = aX^b$

## LEARNING CURVE

$$Y_x = aX^b$$

where:

$Y_x$ = the cumulative average time per unit to produce $X$ units;

$a$ = the time required to produce the first unit of output;

$X$ = the cumulative number of units;

$b$ = the index of learning.

The exponent $b$ is defined as the log of the learning curve improvement rate divided by log 2.

## LIST OF VERBS USED IN THE QUESTION REQUIREMENTS

A list of the learning objectives and verbs that appear in the syllabus and in the question requirements for each question in this paper.

It is important that you answer the question according to the definition of the verb.

| LEARNING OBJECTIVE | VERBS USED | DEFINITION |
|---|---|---|
| **Level 1 - Knowledge** | | |
| What you are expected to know. | List | Make a list of |
| | State | Express, fully or clearly, the details of/facts of |
| | Define | Give the exact meaning of |
| **Level 2 - Comprehension** | | |
| What you are expected to understand. | Describe | Communicate the key features |
| | Distinguish | Highlight the differences between |
| | Explain | Make clear or intelligible/state the meaning or purpose of |
| | Identify | Recognise, establish or select after consideration |
| | Illustrate | Use an example to describe or explain something |
| **Level 3 - Application** | | |
| How you are expected to apply your knowledge. | Apply | Put to practical use |
| | Calculate | Ascertain or reckon mathematically |
| | Demonstrate | Prove with certainty or to exhibit by practical means |
| | Prepare | Make or get ready for use |
| | Reconcile | Make or prove consistent/compatible |
| | Solve | Find an answer to |
| | Tabulate | Arrange in a table |
| **Level 4 - Analysis** | | |
| How you are expected to analyse the detail of what you have learned. | Analyse | Examine in detail the structure of |
| | Categorise | Place into a defined class or division |
| | Compare and contrast | Show the similarities and/or differences between |
| | Construct | Build up or compile |
| | Discuss | Examine in detail by argument |
| | Interpret | Translate into intelligible or familiar terms |
| | Prioritise | Place in order of priority or sequence for action |
| | Produce | Create or bring into existence |
| **Level 5 - Application** | | |
| How you are expected to use your learning to evaluate, make decisions or recommendations. | Advise | Counsel, inform or notify |
| | Evaluate | Appraise or assess the value of |
| | Recommend | Propose a course of action |

# *Performance Pillar*

# *Management Level Paper*

# *P2 – Performance Management*

# *Specimen Paper*

# *Wednesday Afternoon Session*

# The Examiner's Answers – Specimen Paper
# P2 - Performance Management

## SECTION A

### Answer to Question One

*Requirement (a)*

The Value Chain is the concept that there is a sequence of business factors by which value is added to an organisation's products and services. Modern businesses cannot survive merely by having efficient production facilities, they must also have a thorough understanding of the importance of the relationship between all of the elements in the value chain. These include: research & development, design, manufacturing, marketing, distribution and customer service.

The DT group currently has an internal manufacturing facility, this makes communications between different parts of that manufacturing process relatively straight-forward, however, if part of this process is to be outsourced this will place as added burden on the production management to ensure that all parts of the production process operate smoothly. Aside from communication difficulties, there may be different work ethics to contend with, and delays in receiving items and quality issues may disrupt the flow of goods to customers. This will lead to difficulties in identifying where profits / contributions are being earned (and lost) within the value chain.

*Requirement (b)*

Gain sharing arrangements are based on the concept of sharing profits, however, if they are to be successful both parties must be willing to share the information necessary to determine the extent of any gain (or loss) that has arisen.

The DT group may seek to enter a gain sharing arrangement with the suppliers of the components that they have outsourced. This would require both organisations to establish some clear targets which could include quality specifications and delivery schedules. The gain from lower levels of rejects and earlier delivery of components can then be determined and shared between DT and the external supplier.

**Answer to Question Two**

*Requirement (a)*

| Number of batches completed | Average time per batch |
|---|---|
| 1 | 1,000 hours |
| 2 | 900 hours |
| 4 | 810 hours |
| 8 | 729 hours |
| 16 | 656 hours |
| 32 | 590 hours |
| 64 | 531 hours |

It seems that the average time equals 5·3 hours per unit (i.e. 530 hours per batch after 64 batches had been completed.

*Requirement (b)*

4 batches were produced so the average time per batch should have been 810 hours (as shown in the answer to (a) above.

| | |
|---|---|
| Therefore the total time should have been 4 x 810 hours = | 3,240 hours. |
| Actual hours taken were | 2,500 hours |
| Operating efficiency difference | 740 hours Favourable |

By comparing the standard with the revised target time, the planning variance can be identified:

| | |
|---|---|
| Original standard (5·3 hours x 400 units) | 2,120 hours |
| Time allowed per learning curve | 3,240 hours |
| Planning efficiency difference | 1,120 hours Adverse |

Each of these differences in hours is valued using the standard hourly rate of $10 per hour, so the revised efficiency variances are:

| | |
|---|---|
| Planning variance | $11,200 Adverse |
| Operating variance | $7,400 Favourable |

The rate variance remains unchanged at $ 1,000 Adverse

*Requirement (c)*

The analysis of the efficiency variance into planning and operational effects provides more meaningful information because it shows the true efficiency of the operations as opposed to an invalid application of the original target. As production has only reached four batches by the end of August and the learning period seems to continue to around 64 batches it is clear that the learning has not yet been completed and therefore it is unfair to measure performance against the post learning standard. These revised calculations show that the actual learning is better than was expected whereas the original variance calculation showed that the time taken was more than it should have been. Rather than acusing the workforce of being inefficient they should be congratulated on their efficiency.

## Answer to Question Three

*Requirement (a)*

Feedback control is the comparison of actual performance with an agreed target such as the budget set by the Managing partner. An example would be a comparison of the fees earned by each partner compared to those budgeted to be earned.

Feed-forward control is the comparison of a draft version of a target with a rule or objective. An example would be the comparison of the draft cash budget with the target cash balances and the overdraft facility. As a result of this comparison it may be necessary to defer some expenditure until a later period or reduce it so as to stay within the firm's existing cash balances / overdraft facility. This will lead to a second draft of the cash budget being prepared.

*Requirement (b)*

One beneficial consequence of involving the other partners in the preparation of the firm's budgets is that they will accept ownership of their budget and accept responsibility for achieving their target. However, one adverse consequence is that since they will effectively be setting their own targets they may be tempted to set a target that is more easily achieved than that which would have been set by the Managing partner. This is known as the inclusion of budgetary slack.

## Answer to Question Four

*Requirement (a)*

Calculation of cost driver rates:

Machine maintenance
$100,000 / ((1,500 \times 3) + (2,500 \times 2) + (4,000 \times 3)) = \$4 \cdot 65$ per machine hour

Machine setups
$70,000 / [\{(1,500/50) \times 2\} + \{(2,500/100) \times 3\} + \{(4,000/500) \times 1\}] = \$489 \cdot 51$ per setup

Purchasing
$90,000 / [\{(1,500/50) \times 4\} + \{(2,500/100) \times 4\} + \{(4,000/500) \times 6\}] = \$335 \cdot 82$ per order

Material Handling
$60,000 / [\{(1,500/50) \times 10\} + \{(2,500/100) \times 5\} + \{(4,000/500) \times 4\}] = \$131 \cdot 29$ per movement

Other Costs
$80,000 / ((1,500 \times 2) + (2,500 \times 4) + (4,000 \times 3)) = \$3 \cdot 20$ per labour hour

| Product | X | Y | Z |
|---|---|---|---|
| Batch costs: | | | |
| Machine setup | 979 | 1,468·5 | 489·5 |
| Purchasing | 1,343 | 1,343 | 2,015 |
| Material handling | 1,313 | 656·5 | 525 |
| | 3,635 | 3,468 | 3,029·5 |
| Batch size | 50 | 100 | 500 |
| Unitised batch costs | 72·70 | 34·68 | 6·06 |
| Machine maintenance Other costs | 13·95 | 9·30 | 6·06 |
| Product overhead costs | 93·05 | 56·78 | 29·61 |

*Requirement (b)*

Pareto Analysis is also known as the 80:20 rule. In this context it means that 80% of the production overhead costs are caused by 20% of the total number of causes. W has identified the causes of 80% of its overhead costs (i.e. $320,000 out of the total of $400,000) and linked these with just four cost drivers. The remaining $80,000 is said to be caused by a number of factors.

By focusing attention on controlling these four cost causes in the future, and minimising the costs of cost control, W will be controlling 80% of its production overhead costs.

---

## Answer to Question Five

*Requirement (a)*

Standard costs are the estimated costs of providing one unit of goods or service. They are determined by identifying the resources expected to be required for the completion of the unit and the price expected to be paid for each unit of those resources.

Target costs are determined by taking the market price of a product or service and deducting the required profit margin to determine the cost at which the product or service must be provided in order to meet the required profit margin.

HJ is diversifying into a well established market place where it is likely to be a price taker rather than a price maker. HJ will therefore be able to determine the selling price of its range of plastic moulded items. HJ must then determine the profit that it wishes to achieve to make a reasonable return on its investment in the new machinery. By deducting the profit required from the selling price HJ will determine the target cost for its plastic moulded products. HJ will then have to consider its production methods and the impact of any learning and experience efficiencies that may arise to determine whether it is capable of producing the items for their target cost.

*Requirement (b)*

Short term marginal cost based pricing is often necessary to enter into a new market that is already well established and mature. However, this form of pricing is unlikely to be financially viable in the longer term because of the need to recover the fixed costs of the business and deliver a suitable return for the business owners.

The difficulty lies in making the switch from one pricing model to the other without losing the customer base that has been built up using the marginal cost based prices. It will therefore be necessary for HJ to develop new items which have the perception of adding value to the original product range so that they can be sufficiently differentiated to allow the new prices to be introduced.

---

## SECTION B

### Answer to Question Six

*Requirement (a)*

1. The cost of the engineering specification is based on the time spent (i.e. 3 days) multiplied by the salary and related employment costs of $500 per day. However, this is not a relevant value because the time has already been spent and is therefore a sunk cost. The relevant value is $NIL.

2. The cost of Direct Material A is based on 10,000 square metres valued using the weighted average basis. This can be shown to be calculated by:

   10,000 square metres x $6 = $60,000
   5,000 square metres x $630 = $31,500

   15,000 square metres total = $91,500 = an average of $6·10 per square metre

   This is not the correct valuation because the material is in regular use by PQR. Consequently its relevant cost is its cost of replacement which is $7 per square metre which is therefore $70,000 in total.

3. The cost of Direct Material B is based on 250 metre lengths being bought at a price of $10 per metre length. This is not the correct valuation because the sole supplier has a minimum order size of 300 metre lengths and the remainder has no foreseeable use or net sales revenue. Therefore the relevant cost is the cost of the minimum order of 300 lengths, i.e. 300 x $10 = $3,000

4. The cost of the components is based on the normal transfer pricing policy of $8 plus a 50% mark-up = $12 per component. 500 components x $12 = $6,000. However, this is not the relevant cost to the M group. The relevant cost to the M group is the variable cost of manufacturing the components plus any lost contribution from the reduction in external sales by HK. Thus:

   350 components x variable cost only = 350 x $8 = $2,800
   150 components x variable cost + lost contribution = 150 x ($8 + $3) = $1,650
   Total relevant cost of the components = $2,800 + $1,650 = $4,450
   The external market price of $14 is not relevant because it is cheaper to manufacture them internally, even if there is lost contribution caused by reduced external sales.

5. The cost of direct labour is the cost of the existing employees; 1000 hours x $12·50 per hour. This is not the relevant cost. The relevant cost is the lower of:

   a) Recruiting engineers to do the work at $15 per hour; and
   b) Transferring the existing employees and recruiting replacements to do their work at $14 per hour.

   The second of these is the lower cost option so the relevant cost is 1000 hours x $14 per hour = $14,000.

6. The cost of the supervisor is based on a monthly salary of $3,500 (annual salary of $42,000 / 12 months) multiplied by 10% as the the project time estimate = $350. This is not the relevant cost. The supervisor is already employed and will continue to be employed whether the project goes ahead or not. If the supervisor cannot complete this

work within his normal hours he will work overtime but he is not paid for this so there is no incremental cash flow. The relevant cost is $NIL.

7.  The machine hire cost is based on 5 days multiplied by a hire charge of $500 per day. However, this is not the relevant cost because there is a lower cost option available. If the machine is hired for an entire month at a cost of $5,000 and then sub hired for $150 per day for 20 days (total $3,000) the net cost of this option is $2,000. Therefore the relevant cost is $2,000.

8.  The overhead cost value is based on the latest annual forecast of overhead costs and capacity levels as follows:

    $220,000 / 80% of 50,000 hours = $5.50 per hour
    1,000 hours of skilled labour x $5.50 per hour = $5,500.

    However, this is not a relevant cost. There is no indication that these overhead costs are incurred as a result of undertaking the project, indeed being based on an absorption rate implies that they are not project specific and will be incurred whether the project goes ahead or not. The relevant cost is therefore $NIL.

| | Note | $ |
|---|---|---|
| Engineering specification | 1 | NIL |
| Direct material a | 2 | 70,000 |
| Direct material B | 3 | 3,000 |
| Components | 4 | 4,450 |
| Direct Labour | 5 | 14,000 |
| Supervision | 6 | NIL |
| Machine hire | 7 | 2,000 |
| Overhead costs | 8 | NIL |
| | | |
| Total | | 93,450 |

## Requirement (b)

The difference between the reported profit and that which would be expected based on the relevant cost schedule is caused by the differing nature of the accounting techniques used for decision making compared to those used for profit reporting and inventory valuation. For example:

(i)  The usage of material A on the project will be valued using its average cost of $6.10 per square metre rather than the replacement cost of $7 per square metre.

(ii)  The accounting system will attribute overhead costs to the project using an absorption rate that would normally be based on the budgeted costs and activity levels. This is relevant for profit reporting and is required by external reporting rules, but is not appropriate for short term decision making as these costs are not affected by the decision.

## Requirement (c)

There are a number of non-financial factors that need to be considered, these include:

(i)  Will there be any long term impact on the external market of HK as a result of them choosing to make an internal supply in preference to their external customers. Does this mean that their external customers will find a permanent alternative supplier?

(ii)  Will there be any conflicts between the temporary replacement workers being paid $14 per hour to do the work of employees who are currently being paid $12.50 per hour?

## Answer to Question Seven

*Requirement (a)*

The performance statement does not show the actual return on capital employed achieved by
each division which is:

    D:    2.5%          E:        10%              F: 12%

It can thus be seen that only Division E achieved the target that had been set for it by Head
Office. However, there are a number of other factors that need to be considered in relation to
the performance report.

1. The management charges from Head Office are presumed to be non-controllable at
divisional level, it is therefore inappropriate to include them in any measure of divisional
performance.

2. The basis of valuing the Capital Employed by each division is not stated. It is assumed to
be based on the original cost of the assets less accumulated depreciation. As a consequence
older assets will have lower original costs (due to price inflation) and lower book values (due
to more years depreciation charges). As a result comparisons between divisions may not be a
fair comparison. This may also explain the different cost structure that seems to exist in
Division F where fixed production costs are approximately 25% of total production costs
whereas in divisions D and E the fixed production costs are around 50% of total production
costs. This may imply that the equipment used in Divisions D and E is newer and more
automated.

*Requirement (b)*

The problem with negotiated transfer prices is that the results of the negotiations is as much
affected by the personalities of the managers of each division as it is by the circumstances
surrounding the transaction. If one manager has a stronger personality than another, or is a
better negotiator then this will act to the detriment of the weaker division and may not be in
the best interests of the company as a whole.

The inter-divisional trading affects the performance of all of the divisions. Assuming that the
goods sold between the divisions were similar to those that the supplying division sold into the
external market, then the following analysis can be made.

1. Goods sold by Division D.
The external sales of Division D were $130,000 during the year for which the variable cost
was $32,000, a mark-up of just over 300%. If the same mark – up were applied to the internal
sale then Division D's profits would have increased by $52,000 to $62,000 and the profits of
Division E would reduce by $52,000.

2. Goods sold by Division F
The external sales of Division F were $385,000 during the year for which the variable cost
was $221,000, a mark-up of 75%. The mark-up added to the internal sale was 67% so there
is not a significant impact on the profit reported by the divisions as a result of these internal
transactions.

## Requirement (c)

| Division | D | E | F |
|---|---|---|---|
| | $000 | $000 | $000 |
| Net sales - External | 130 | 200 | 385 |
| Sales - Internal | 72 | 0 | 15 |
| Total sales | 202 | 200 | 400 |
| | | | |
| Variable production costs | | | |
| - External | 50 | 35 | 230 |
| - Internal ** | | 27 | |
| - Internal mark-up** | | 60 | |
| | | | |
| Fixed production costs | 60 | 50 | 80 |
| | | | |
| Divisional administration costs | 20 | 17 | 25 |
| | | | |
| Divisional profit | 72 | 11 | 65 |
| | | | |
| Non-controllable Head Office management charge | 10 | 8 | 15 |
| | | | |
| Profit | 62 | 3 | 50 |
| | | | |
| Capital employed | 400 | 550 | 415 |
| | | | |
| Return on Capital Employed (based on profit) | 15·5% | 0·5% | 12·0% |
| | | | |
| Return on Capital Employed (based on divisional profit) | 18% | 2% | 15·7% |

* Internal sales have been valued at their equivalent external prices by applying the mark-up calculated earlier.

** These values show the variable cost to the company of these internal transactions and the mark-up that would normally apply to these transactions.

## Requirement (d)

A system of dual prices would mean that the selling price recorded by the selling division would not be the same as the buying price recorded by the buying division. Typically, the buyer would include the company variable cost as their cost and the seller would include a value closer to market value as their sales.

If this were done here, then the "Internal mark-up shown under Variable Production cost" would not appear and as a result the divisional profit of division E would have increased by $60,000 to $71,000 which would give the division a Return on Capital.

---

© The Chartered Institute of Management Accountants 2009

# Index

# Index

# Index

# Index